MODERN DRAMATISTS

CASEBOOKS ON MODERN DRAMATISTS

KIMBALL KING, *General Editor*

CHRISTOPHER HAMPTON
A Casebook
edited by Robert Gross

HOWARD BRENTON
A Casebook
edited by Ann Wilson

DAVID STOREY
A Casebook
edited by William Hutchings

PETER SHAFFER
A Casebook
edited by C. J. Gianakaras

SIMON GRAY
A Casebook
edited by Katherine H. Burkman

JOHN ARDEN AND
MARGARETTA D'ARCY
A Casebook
edited by Jonathan Wike

AUGUST WILSON
A Casebook
edited by Marilyn Elkins

JOHN OSBORNE
A Casebook
edited by Patricia D. Denison

ARNOLD WESKER
A Casebook
edited by Reade W. Dornan

DAVID HARE
A Casebook
edited by Hersh Zeifman

MARSHA NORMAN
A Casebook
edited by Linda Ginter Brown

BRIAN FRIEL
A Casebook
edited by William Kerwin

NEIL SIMON
A Casebook
edited by Gary Konas

TERRENCE MCNALLY
A Casebook
edited by Toby Silverman Zinman

STEPHEN SONDHEIM
A Casebook
edited by Joanne Gordon

HORTON FOOTE
A Casebook
edited by Gerald C. Wood

SAMUEL BECKETT
A Casebook
edited by Jennifer M. Jeffers

WENDY WASSERSTEIN
A Casebook
edited by Claudia Barnett

TENNESSEE WILLIAMS
A Casebook
edited by Robert F. Gross

MODERN DRAMATISTS

A CASEBOOK OF MAJOR BRITISH, IRISH, AND AMERICAN PLAYWRIGHTS

EDITED BY
KIMBALL KING

ROUTLEDGE
NEW YORK AND LONDON

Published in 2001 by
Routledge
29 West 35th Street
New York, NY 10001

Published in Great Britain by
Routledge
11 New Fetter Lane
London EC4P 4EE

Routledge is an imprint of the Taylor & Francis Group

Printed in the United States of America on acid-free paper.

10   9   8   7   6   5   4   3   2   1

Library of Congress Cataloging-in-Publication Data

Modern dramatists : a casebook of major British, Irish, and American playwrights / edited by Kimball King.
   p. cm. — (Routledge reference library of the humanities ; v. 1985. Casebooks on modern dramatists ; v. 28)
   Includes bibliographical references and index.
   ISBN 0-8153-2349-2 (hc.) — ISBN 0-8153-3926-7 (pbk.)
   1. English drama—20th century—History and criticism. 2. American drama—20th century—History and criticism.   I. King, Kimball. II. Routledge reference library of the humanities ; vol. 1985. III. Routledge reference library of the humanities. Casebooks on modern dramatists ; vol. 28.

PR736.M56 2001
822´.9109–dc21   00-065297

Contents

General Editor's Note ix

Introduction xi

List of Articles xix

Who Wrote "John Arden's" Plays? 1
 Tish Dace

Ayckbourn's Theatricality 19
 Bernard F. Dukore

Empire of Light: Luminosity and Space in Beckett's Theater 33
 William E. Gruber

The Romans in Britain: Aspirations and Anxieties
 of a Radical Playwright 49
 Robert F. Gross

Monsters and Heroines: Caryl Churchill's Women 61
 Lisa Merrill

More Real than Realism: Horton Foote's Impressionism 75
 Tim Wright

Negotiating History, Negotiating Myth: Friel among
 His Contemporaries 93
 Claire Gleitman

Hedda's Children: Simon Gray's Anti-heroes 107
 Katherine H. Burkman

Romanticism and Reaction: Hampton's Transformation
 of *Les Liaisons Dangereuses* 117
 Stephanie Barbé Hammer

Playing with Place: Some Filmic Techniques
in the Plays of David Hare 133
John Russell Brown

Master Class and the Paradox of the Diva 153
Cary M. Mazer

Phallus in Wonderland: Machismo and Business in
David Mamet's *American Buffalo* and *Glengarry Glen Ross* 167
Hersh Zeifman

A Place at the Table: Hunger as Metaphor in Lillian Hellman's
Days to Come and Marsha Norman's *'night, Mother* 177
Linda Ginter Brown

The Personal, the Political, and the Postmodern in
Osborne's *Look Back in Anger* and *Déjàvu* 197
Austin E. Quigley

The Dumb Waiter, The Collection, The Lover,
and *The Homecoming:* A Revisionist Approach 219
George E. Wellwarth

What's Wrong with this Picture? David Rabe's Comic-Strip Plays 229
Toby Silverman Zinman

The Artistic Trajectory of Peter Shaffer 241
C. J. Gianakaris

Great Expectations: Language and the Problem
of Presence in Sam Shepard's Writing 257
Ann Wilson

Funny Money in New York and London:
Neil Simon and Alan Ayckbourn 273
Ruby Cohn

Broadway Babies: Images of Women in the
Musicals of Stephen Sondheim 293
Laura Hanson

From Zurich to Brazil with Tom Stoppard 311
Felicia Hardison Londré

David Storey's Aesthetic of "Invisible Events" 325
William Hutchings

Female Laughter and Comic Possibilities:
    Uncommon Women and Others   339
    Miriam M. Chirico

Vision and Reality: *Their Very Own and Golden City* and Centre 42   361
    Clive Barker

August Wilson's Folk Traditions   369
    Trudier Harris

The Artist in the Garden: Theatre Space and Place in Lanford Wilson   383
    Thomas P. Adler

General Editor's Note

The *Casebooks on Modern Dramatists* series has attempted to provide useful collection of articles on contemporary playwrights for scholars and general readers of drama during the past twenty years. These books have offered interpretations of the works of major writers, hoping to clarify the central issues of their plays, as well as to offer original responses to what, in some cases, have become acknowledged masterpieces. For some time now, readers have requested that we assemble a single volume that contains the most notable essays the publisher has printed on recent drama. As General Editor for the series, I believed that compiling a volume with a single essay from each playwright in our distinguished group would created a valuable critical tool for an informed reader of dramatic literature. The present volume will present an effective overview of recent theatre by choosing a single essay from each of the twenty-six volumes of *Casebooks on Modern Dramatists,* a continuing series which promises new collections on authors for years to come. It is intended that the variety and richness of theatre in the late twentieth-century will be represented here and that a single volume is a useful compendium of criticism on an important literary genre.

Kimball King,
General Editor

Introduction
Kimball King

The twenty-six essays in this volume have been selected to represent insightful literary overviews of major playwrights and plays of the late twentieth-century. All have been previously published in individual casebooks. The articles have been arranged alphabetically by the playwrights' names. There has been no attempt to "rank" the achievements of the writers discussed here because only time and unforeseen circumstances will determine which of the works discussed in detail will become recognized as canonical or which may be marginalized as minor voices.

British, Irish, and American drama since World War II has produced major literary topics and techniques. Clearly, English playwrights, beginning with John Osborne's *Look Back in Anger* at the Royal Court Theatre in 1956, made the greatest initial impact on the contemporary stage. Great Britain also became a "training ground" for Irish voices as well because Brendan Behan's works were embraced by the Royal Court Theatre and Tom Kilroy was chosen to adapt a version of Chekhov's *The Seagull* for the Royal Court's twenty-fifth anniversary celebration. Furthermore, Irish playwrights like Hugh Leonard learned much of their craft in adapting classic European novels for Masterpiece Theatre presentations when they worked for England's B.B.C.

American Sam Shepard's exposure to English theatre in the period when he was living there with his wife and son in the late 1970's may have added some structure and knowledge of dramatic techniques to his first literarily important works, including *Buried Child,* a Pulitzer Prize-winning play in 1979 which bears some resemblance to Pinter's earlier *The Homecoming* (1967). David Mamet's debt to Pinter has clearly been noted and Mamet's preeminence in American theatre is now taken for granted. African-American dramatists, like August Wilson, and women playwrights like Wendy Wasserstein, Beth Henley, and Marsha Norman are also American writers who presently enjoy international audiences.

The first article in the present collection appeared in Jonathan Wike's *John Arden and Margaretta D'Arcy: A Casebook* (1994). Wike insisted that the title of his collection include the names of both John Arden and his wife, Margaretta D'Arcy, as he became thoroughly convinced by Tish Dace's article, "Who Wrote John Arden's Plays," that Arden's work, from its beginning was a combined effort with D'Arcy. Dace attributes D'Arcy's lack of proper recognition primarily to plain sexism. Her article is meticulously researched, a fine supplement to her earlier scholarly writings on the subject. Wike himself, formerly an English professor in North Carolina, is now a practicing attorney-at-law.

Classic Casebook Articles second essay is a perceptive evaluation of Alan Ayckboun's achievement by Professor-Emeritus Bernard Dukore, recognized for his extensive publications on George Bernard Shaw and more recently for *Barnestorm: The Plays of Peter Barnes* (1995) and *Alan Ayckbourn: A Casebook* (1994), both for Garland Publishing, Inc. Exploring the theatricality of Ayckbourn's many plays reveals that the most popular dramatist in Britain uses unique stage sets and sometimes jarring juxtapositions of characters and situations to satirize contemporary culture.

Ayckbourn's preeminence in English theatre may be acknowledged by theatre critics everywhere, but Samuel Beckett, born in Ireland yet writing and living out his life in France, changed the dramatic landscape of the twentieth-century. His works have been discussed by Anne-Marie Drew, *Past Crimson, Past Woe: The Shakespeare-Beckett Connection* in Garland's Studies in the Drama series and by Jennifer Jeffers as editor in the *Casebooks* Series. Currently an English professor at the University of South Dakota, Jeffers who has delivered papers on Beckett at the University of Victorian Festival and who has published in *Mosaic* and *The Journal of Narrative Techniques* has provided a wide spectrum of new critical voices to Beckett criticism in *Samuel Beckett: A Casebook* (1998). One of those voices belongs to William E. Gruber who describes Beckett's unique aesthetics for the stage. What one might call simply the "'lighted conditions' both of being and knowing." Gruber entitled his article "Empire of Light: Luminosity and Space in Beckett's Theatre." Gruber has written *Missing Persons: Characters and Characterization in Modern Drama* and *Comic Theaters.*

Although Howard Brenton may not be as well known in modern drama as Samuel Beckett, his own plays and his collaborations with David Hare have made him a staple of British theatre, particularly his large-scale Brechtian plays like *The Romans in Britain,* discussed here by Robert F. Gross in Ann Wilson's *Howard Brenton: A Casebook.* Gross, who is a Professor of Theatre and Comparative Literature at Hobart William Smith College is well known for his *Christopher Hampton: A Casebook* as well as for his *Research and Production Sourcebook* for S. N. Behrman and his book comparing Osborne, Bernard, and Bond. Wilson, a professor at the University of Guelph, is fast becoming an authority on contemporary theatre and contributed an essay on Sam Shepard to my own *Casebook*. Gross considers the paradox of Brenton's use of progressive socialist ideals and regressive personal issues in plays.

Reconciling paradoxes is also the work of Lisa Merrill in her "Monsters and Heroines" article in *Caryl Churchill: A Casebook*. Merrill, known for her book on Charlotte Cushman and Cushman's circle of friends, investigates conflicting images of women in the English playwright's long career. Phyllis Randall, who edited the Casebook is Professor Emeritus of North Carolina Central University and has contributed articles to several books in the same series.

Even as Churchill's and Brenton's plays seem quintessentially English, Horton Foote's canon is unmistakably American. Undervalued critically, Foote is a favorite playwright of actors who complete fiercely to depict his psychologically complex characters. From Gerald C. Woods' *Horton Foote: A Casebook* (1998) Tim Wright's essay, "More Real than Realism: Horton Foote's Impressionism" one learns Foote's method of recognizing and integrating objective and subjective truths in the playwright's canon, believing that the realistic surfaces of Foote's plays give way to the author's personal impressionism. Wright is an associate professor at Regent University and earned his Ph.D. in Communication Studies.

Unlike Foote, who is almost better known to actors than audiences, Ireland's Brian Friel has gained international recognition in the theatre. Professor William Kerwin of the University of Missouri has maintained a longtime interest in the plays of Brian Friel although Kerwin himself is essentially a scholar of the English Renaissance. Claire Gleitman's essay, "Negotiating History, Negotiating Myth: Friel among His Contemporaries" locates Friel in the context of recent Irish successes in Irish drama since World War II.

The next writer discussed is Simon Gray, a protégé of sorts of Harold Pinter, who was once as celebrated in the theatre as Brian Friel. But though brilliant and witty, his reputation is presently more low-key. Katherine H. Burkman, known for *The Dramatic World of Harold Pinter: Its Basis in Ritual* and other studies of ritual in books and articles on Modern Drama has contributed "Hedda's Children: Simon Gray's Anti-heroes," which explores Gray's male protagonists, frequently academics, in a range of amusing and intellectually challenging plays. Both Simon Gray and his compatriot Christopher Hampton are learned men and have placed some of their major works in academic settings. [For example, Gray's *Butley* and Hampton's *The Philanthropist* are prime examples of plays using professional protagonists.]

Stephanie Barbé Hammer has scrutinized Christopher Hampton's dazzling and erudite playwrighting techniques in "Romanticism and Reaction: Hampton's Tranformation of *Liaisons Dangereuses*. Robert Gross, mentioned earlier in this introduction, edited *Christopher Hampton: A Casebook* (1990); essayist Hammer has also contributed to several Casebooks and has written *The Sublime Crime: Fascination, Failure and Form in the Literature of the Enlightenment*.

Hampton is near in age to David Hare, a close friend and former school-mate. Both are well known to John Russell Brown, professor of theatre at the University of Michigan and former associate director of the Royal National Theatre in Great Britain who is, perhaps, best known for his many published volumes on the modern theatre and, in particular, for *Anger and After* and *The Second Wave*. In "Playing with Place: Some Filmic Techniques in the Plays of David Hare," he reveals what Hare's efforts as a filmmaker have contributed to his stage plays and celebrates the playwright's return to that medium. Brown's editor in *David Hare: A Casebook,* Hersh Zeifman, is also a major scholar of the theatre. Teaching at York University, he contributed an essay on David Mamet, published elsewhere in this book.

On the other side of the Atlantic, Toby Zinman, professor of English at the University of the Arts in Philadelphia, assembled *Terence McNally: A Casebook* in 1997. McNally is a writer about the same age as Hare and Hampton. Here Cary Mazer's article on "Master Class and the Paradox of the Diva" captures not only the essence of a major McNally play but uncovers the artistic techniques and recurrent themes of a prolific and creative dramatist. Although he is popular with audiences, McNally is less of an icon to academic and theatre critics than David Mamet.

In Leslie Kane's *David Mamet: A Casebook* (1992), Professor Hersh Zeifman of York University, Toronto, Canada, a co-editor of *Modern Drama* who also edited *David Hare: A Casebook* (1994) for Garland, has written a trenchant overview of Mamet's ethical and psychological preoccupations in "Phallus in Wonderland: Machismo and Business in David Mamet's *American Buffalo* and *Glengarry Glen Ross,* two of Mamet's most provocative theatre pieces. Resolutely masculine, Mamet is in that way, at least, opposite from the feminist Marsha Norman. To honor Norman, Linda Ginter Brown, a professor in the Humanities Department at the University of Cincinnati, assembled a collection of essays on the playwright—*Marsha Norman: A Casebook* (1996). Brown presents her own evaluation of the twentieth-century American female playwright in "A Place at the Table: Hunger as Metaphor in Lillian Hellman's *Days to Come* and Marsha Norman's *'night, Mother,*" linking Norman to a tradition of important American women writers.

Marsha Norman: A Casebook is evidence of the growing power of American women dramatists. However, the strength of the Casebooks was derived from its concentration on already recognized masters like Churchill, Shepard, Pinter, and Osborne when the series began. None was more important than the collection of essays on John Osborne.

Patricia D. Denison published *John Osborne: A Casebook* in 1997, just three years after John Osborne's death. It includes therefore playwright David Hare's eulogy at Osborne's funeral and a fine essay, published here, on the beginnings and end of the late playwright's important career by Austin F. Quigley, called "The Personal, the Political, and the Postmodern in Osborne's *Look Back in*

Anger and *Déjàvu.*" Quigley is well known for his writings which include *The Pinter Problem* (1975) and *The Modern Stage and other Worlds* (1985). He is presently Dean of the Graduate School at Columbia University.

While Harold Pinter's breakthrough in the theatre may have been *The Birthday Party* in 1958, two years after John Osborne's mythically important *Look Back in Anger,* his reputation soon eclipsed his predecessor's. Along with Beckett, Pinter is seen as one of the giants of contemporary theatre. George Wellwarth, who discusses here the earlier plays that brought fame to Pinter, stirred the critical world with his own *The Theatre of Protest and Paradox* as early as 1964. Interestingly, Wellwarth's article appeared in Lois Gordon's *Harold Pinter: A Casebook* in 1990, but Gordon's analysis of Pinter, *Stratagems Uncover Nakedness: The Drama of Harold Pinter* appeared in 1969 and provided materials for many later assessments of the English writer's works. Gordon, a Professor at Farleigh Dickinson University, is also the author of *American Chronicle* and books on Bartheleme and Coover.

Like Professor Gordon, Toby Silverman Zinman is also a devoted scholar and teacher. Zinman's *David Rabe: A Casebook* in 1991 contained her own article on the postmodern comic-strip quality of David Rabe's plays. In "What's Wrong with this Picture? David Rabe's Comic-Strip Plays," Zinman draws parallels between certain effects in Roy Lichtenstein's paintings and the dramatic impact of scenes in Rabe's plays, including his own plays like *Pavlo Hummel* and in more detail in *The Boom Boom Room* and *Hurlyburly.* Although Professor Zinman's accomplishments were noted in the introductory remarks concerning *Terrence McNally: A Casebook,* the Rabe collection actually preceded the McNally book by six years.

Following Zinman's essay on Rabe is C. J. Gianakaris's essay called "The Artistic Trajectory of Peter Shaffer," which summarizes the design and triumphs of the English playwright's career. Having written a book-length study, *Peter Shaffer,* published by Macmillan in the United Kingdom, Gianakaris, who is Professor English at Western Michigan University and a co-founder of *Comparative Drama,* summarized the esthetic and moral purposes of the playwright in his *Casebook.* Similarly, Ann Wilson, who edited the Brenton Casebook plumbs the unique linguistic flourishes and bold theatrical devices of Shepard's works in her essay for my own Casebook, *Sam Shepard: A Casebook* (1988). Shepard, of course, is known for his work as a screenwriter and film star as well as a playwright. Wilson's article makes his ideas and themes accessible to an educated reader.

Even though Sam Shepard was for many years a favorite of theatre scholars, American audiences have long considered Neil Simon one of their most admired playwrights. Appearing in Gary Konas's *Neil Simon: A Casebook* (1997), one of America's most distinguished drama critics, Professor Emeritus Ruby Cohn of the University of California at Davis, known internationally for her scholarship on Samuel Beckett has contributed an article, "Neil

Simon and Alan Ayckbourn," in which she compares two masters of comedy who dissect the material dreams of the newly affluent middle classes in American and Britain.

While Neil Simon has presented an optimistic dramatic spectrum for the most part, Stephen Sondheim's work mixes humor with disturbing insights into personal and public behavior. Joanne Gordon's *Stephen Sondheim: A Casebook* (1997) presents a series of articles which ponder the subtleties of a range of his most famous musical plays. Gordon, who is a professor of Theatre Arts at California State University, Long Beach, is also the author of *Art Isn't Easy: The Theatre of Stephen Sondheim.* In Gordon's Casebook collection, Laura Hanson, who works in the design department of New York University's Tisch School of the Arts, compares the complex, often jaded, women in Sondheim's works to the typical ingenue of more traditional American musicals.

If Sondheim's audiences demonstrate a fanatical devotion to the author, admirers of Tom Stoppard believe him to be one of the most brilliant playwrights of modern times. In John Harty's *Tom Stoppard: A Casebook,* which was the first book in the Casebook series in 1988, Felicia Hardison Londré contributed a superbly perceptive article, called "From Zurich to Brazil with Tom Stoppard," in which she discusses plays like *Travesties* and films like *Brazil.* Casebook Editor Harty has also done a collection of essays on novelist James Joyce for Garland.

Apart from their interest in sports, Stoppard and Dave Storey seem dissimilar. Stoppard is a cricketeer whereas Storey was once a professional rugby player. The latter concentrates more on physical actions in his plays and frequently explore the lives of working-class characters. William Hutchings, whose *The Plays of David Storey: A Romantic Study* sets a high standard for all critics of Storey to follow, edited Garland's *David Storey: A Casebook* in 1992. His own "David Storey's Aesthetic of Invisible Events" plumbs the origins of off-stage, unseen activities that frequently define the lives of the playwright's major characters.

Storey was a noted English athlete before he became a playwright. However, American Wendy Wasserstein has been a playwright since graduation from Mount Holyoke when she took additional writing courses with Israel Horovitz and Joseph Heller at City University in New York. Claudia Barnett who published *Wendy Wasserstein: A Casebook* in 1999 believes that Miriam Chirico's analysis of Wasserstein's career, her analysis of the playwrights themes and techniques and her balanced assessment of Wasserstein criticism, provides one of the most inclusive overviews of the writers achievement to date. Dr. Chirico, also, like Wasserstein, a graduate of Mount Holyoke College, received her PhD in English from Emory University.

Despite differences of gender and nationality, the American Wasserstein and English Wesker share a Jewish background that they often use as a point of reference in their work. Reade W. Dornan has discussed Wesker's Jewishness in *Arnold Wesker Revisited* (1992) and the introduction to her *Casebook*. She is currently a professor of English at Michigan State University. From Dornan's *Arnold Wesker: A Casebook* (1998) Englishman Clive Barker, a joint editor of the *New Theatre Quarterly* discusses productions of several of Wesker's best known plays in "Vision and Reality: *Their Very Own and Golden City* and Center 42."

Just as Wesker's plays have been frequently performed at England's Royal National Theatre, so too, was August Wilson's important play about 1920's America, called *Ma Rainey's Black Bottom*. If Wesker's plays are required reading for university or "A level" admissions exams, Wilson is recognized internationally for indispensable commentaries on the quality of America life in the twentieth-century. Wilson is possibly the best known African-American playwright in the world. Appropriately, Trudier Harris, Professor English at the University of North Carolina, author of countless books and articles on African-American literature including the *Power of the Porch* (1996) and *Exorcising Blackness* (1992), has authoritatively explored the folkloristic roots of Wilson's major works.

Another Wilson, also an American, completes the roster of new playwrights discussed in this volume. Lanford Wilson, whose heavily psychological subject matter reminds many of Tennessee Williams's plays concludes our book. Jackson R. Bryer, noted bibliographer, Hemingway scholar and Professor of English at the University of Maryland edited *Lanford Wilson: A Casebook* in 1994. In that collection Thomas Adler, Professor of English at Purdue University and author of a book-length study on playwright Robert Anderson, as well as *The Pulitzer Plays As An Approach to American Drama* and many other works, explores the connection of Lanford Wilson's settings to his themes in "The Artist in the Garden: Theatre Space and Place in Lanford Wilson."

Taken together the essays in this volume reveal the tremendous range and vitality of modern theatre in England, Ireland, and the United States.

List of Articles

John Arden and Margaretta D'Arcy: A Casebook (1994) by Jonathan Wike. Article: pp. 199–221, Tish Dace: "Who Wrote 'John Arden's' Plays?"

Alan Ayckbourn: A Casebook (1994) by Bernard F. Dukore. Article: pp. 71–86, "Ayckbourn's Theatricality," by Bernard F. Dukore.

Samuel Beckett: A Casebook (1998) by Jennifer Jeffers. Essay: pp. 65–83, "Empire of Light: Luminosity and Space in Beckett's Theatre," by William E. Gruber.

Howard Brenton: A Casebook (1992) by Ann Wilson. Article: pp. 71–84, "*The Romans in Britain:* Aspirations and Anxieties of a Radical Playwright," by Robert F. Gross.

Caryl Churchill: A Casebook (1969) by Phyllis R. Randall. Article: pp. 71–90, "Monsters and Heroines: Caryl Churchill's Women," by Lisa Merrill.

Horton Foote: A Casebook (1998) by Gerald C. Wood. Article: pp. 67–87, "More Real than Realism: Horton Foote's Impressionism," by Tim Wright.

Brian Friel: A Casebook (1997) by William Kerwin. Essay: pp. 227–241, "Negotiating History, Negotiating Myth: Friel among His Contemporaries," by Claire Gleitman.

Simon Gray: A Casebook (1992) by Katherine H. Burkman. "Hedda's Children: Simon Gray's Anti-heroes," pp. 155–164, by Katherine Burkman.

Christopher Hampton: A Casebook (1990) by Robert Gross. "Romanticism and Reaction: Hampton's Transformation of *Les Liaisons Dangereuses*," pp. 108–118, by Stephanie Barbé Hammer.

David Hare: A Casebook (1994) by Hersh Zeifman. Essay: pp. 45–69, "Playing with Place: Some Filmic Techniques in the Plays of David Hare," by John Russell Brown.

Terrence McNally: A Casebook (1997) by Toby Silverman Zinman. Article: pp. 165–179, "*Master Class* and the Paradox of the Diva," by Cary M. Mazer.

David Mamet: A Casebook (1992) by Leslie Kane. Article: pp. 123–135, "Phallus in Wonderland: Machismo and Business in David Mamet's *American Buffalo* and *Glengarry Glen Ross*," by Hersh Zeifman.

Marsha Norman: A Casebook (1996) by Linda Ginter Brown. Article: pp. 63–86, "A Place at the Table: Hunger as Metaphor in Lillian Hellman's *Days to Come* and Marsha Norman's *'night, Mother,* by Linda Ginter Brown.

John Osborne: A Casebook (1997) by Patricia Denison. Article: pp. 35–59, "The Personal, the Political, and the Postmodern in Osborne's *Look Back in Anger* and *Déjàvu,*" by Austin E. Quigley.

Harold Pinter: A Casebook (1990) by Lois Gordon. Essay: pp. 95–108, "*The Dumb Waiter, The Collection, The Lover* and *The Homecoming:* A Revisionist Approach," by George E. Wellwarth.

David Rabe: A Casebook (1991) by Toby Silverman Zinman. "What's Wrong with this Picture? David Rabe's Comic-Strip Plays," by Toby Silverman Zinman.

Peter Shaffer: A Casebook (1991) by C. J. Gianakaris. "The Artistic Trajectory of Peter Shaffer," pp. 3–24, by C. J. Gianakaris.

Sam Shepard: A Casebook (1988) by Kimball King. Article: pp. 135–153, "Great Expectations: Language and the Problems of Presence in Sam Shepard's Writing," by Ann Wilson.

Neil Simon: A Casebook (1997) by Gary Konas. Article: pp. 14037, "Funny Money in New York and London: Neil Simon and Alan Ayckbourn," by Ruby Cohn.

Stephen Sondheim: A Casebook (1997) by Joanne Gordon. Essay: pp. 13–34, "Broadway Babies: Images of Women in the Musicals of Stephen Sondheim," by Laura Hanson.

Tom Stoppard: A Casebook (1988) by John Harty. Article: pp. 343–363, "From Zurich to Brazil with Tom Stoppard," by Felicia Hardison Londré.

David Storey: A Casebook (1992) by William Hutchings. Article: pp. 105–122, "David Storey's Aesthetic of 'Invisible Events'," by William Hutchings.

Wendy Wasserstein: A Casebook (1999) by Claudia Barnett. Article: pp. 81–106, "Female Laughter and Comic Possibilities: *Uncommon Women and Others,*" by Miriam M. Chirico.

Arnold Wesker: A Casebook (1998) by Reade Dornan. Article: pp. 89–96, "Vision and Reality: *Their Very Own and Golden City* and Centre 42, by Clive Barker.

August Wilson: A Casebook (1994) by Marilyn Elkins. Essay: pp. 49–67, "August Wilson's Folk Traditions," by Trudier Harris.

Lanford Wilson: A Casebook (1994) by Jackson R. Bryer. Article: pp. 3–20, "The Artist in the Garden: Theatre Space and Place in Lanford Wilson," by Thomas P. Adler.

Who Wrote "John Arden's" Plays?
Tish Dace

Ordinarily, critics respect the authorship designated on a play's title page or production program. Although occasionally authors who also direct their own plays may employ a pseudonym to avoid the suggestion of a vanity production, usually we take our playwrights at their word. Yet an extraordinary anomaly has persisted in the case of the 34-year collaboration of John Arden and Margaretta D'Arcy: most scholars discuss their plays as though Arden alone had written them.

The books, of course, all bear the title, with or without subtitle, *John Arden* or merely *Arden*. Ronald Hayman, who wrote the first such volume, may be forgiven for mentioning D'Arcy only twice in his 1968 *John Arden* (vii, 73) for three reasons. The two had collaborated for less than a decade at that point. Arden alone had written his better known plays. And they seem to have only belatedly agreed to acknowledge their work as jointly created.

That's right: Some of the pair's plays originally appeared as solely Arden's. When William Gaskill directed the premiere of *The Happy Haven* in Bristol in April 1960, the program credited only Arden. Yet when Gaskill again mounted the play in September of the same year at London's Royal Court, the program termed it "by John Arden in collaboration with Margaretta D'Arcy." It was published with the same joint attribution (*New English Dramatists, 4; Three Plays by John Arden*). Because Arden wrote *The Happy Haven* while a Visiting Fellow in the Bristol University Drama Department, we might speculate that he initially felt reluctant to acknowledge—in 1960, mind you—that his wife had co-authored a script which Bristol University had commissioned solely from the author of *Serjeant Musgrave's Dance*.

On the other hand, since Arden persisted in receiving sole credit for plays which later they attributed to their joint efforts, he, or they, may merely have been slow to evolve a contemporary consciousness that the labor of a man and a woman should not transmute into the man's property alone.

When the first edition of *The Business of Good Government* appeared from Methuen on May 23, 1963, Arden received the credit. When Grove Press

1

finally put out an American edition on February 24, 1967, Arden's name still graced the title page. Yet two months later Arden asked his English publisher to add his wife's name as co-author to the reprint issued later that year. (I am indebted here and elsewhere to Nick Hern, who, while still an editor at Methuen, opened the editorial files to my perusal.)

To add to the confusion, *Ars Longa, Vita Brevis* appeared in *Encore* in March 1964 as Arden's work but was published by Cassell in February 1965 as the work of both Arden and D'Arcy. Evidently working out their own ground rules took the two playwrights a few years. Or perhaps publishers and producers tended to ignore their wishes. In any event, by the time the world learned (in 1967) of D'Arcy's part in writing *The Business of Good Government*, the pair had published four other plays with both names on the title page. Many others have followed.

The two playwrights' bibliographies of plays look like this:

Arden:
All Fall Down, 1955
The Life of Man 1956, radio

The Waters of Babylon, 1957
When Is a Door Not a Door, 1958
Live Like Pigs, 1958
Serjeant Musgrave's Dance, 1959

Soldier, Soldier, 1960, TV
Wet Fish, 1961, TV
Top Deck, 1961, film

The Dying Cowboy, 1961, radio
The Workhouse Donkey, 1963

Ironhand, 1963

Armstrong's Last Goodnight, 1964
Left-Handed Liberty, 1965
The True History of Squire Jonathan and His Unfortunate Treasure, 1968 (written 1963)
The Bagman, 1970, radio
Pearl, 1978, radio
To Put It Frankly, 1979, radio

Arden/D'Arcy:
The Happy Haven, 1960 (written 1959)
The Business of Good Government, 1960
Ars Longa, Vita Brevis, 1964 (D/A)
Friday's Hiding, 1966 (D/A)
The Royal Pardon, 1966
Vietnam Carnival, 1967 (D/A) New York University
Harold Muggins Is a Martyr, 1968 (D/A)
The Hero Rises Up, 1968
The Ballygombeen Bequest, 1972 (a.k.a. *The Little Gray Home in the West*, 1978) (D/A)
The Island of the Mighty, 1972
Keep Those People Moving!, 1972, radio
The Devil & the Parish Pump, 1974 (D/A)
The Non-Stop Connolly Show, 1975 (D/A)
Sean O'Scrudu, March 1976 (D/A)
The Hunting of the Mongrel Fox, Oct. 1976 (D/A)

No Room at the Inn, Dec. 1976 (D/A)
Mary's Name, 1977 (D/A)
Vandaleur's Folly, 1978 (D/A)

The Adventures of the Ingenious Gentleman, Don Quixote, 1980, radio

Garland for a Hoar Head, 1982, radio

The Old Man Sleeps Alone, 1982, radio

The Manchester Enthusiasts, 1984, radio

Whose Is the Kingdom?, 1988, nine-part radio series

A Suburban Suicide, submitted to BBC radio, December 1992.

You will note from this list that the last time Arden wrote a stage play alone was in 1965.

Although these are the plays which the more comprehensive survey of their work might include, additional dramatic work which ought to be taken into account includes these two titles by Arden:

1) Beethoven's *Fidelio,* adaptation for the 16 September 1965 performance at Saddler's Wells.
2) Stravinsky's *The Soldier's Tale,* adaptation for the Bath Festival, 1968.

Some of the less well-known collaborations between D'Arcy and Arden include

1) The *Kirkbymoorside*[1] *Entertainment,* a month-long festival in their home in 1963, which grew out of a 16-millimeter film which D'Arcy made there.
2) *The Unfulfilled Dream,* Super-8 film, 1969, which concerns a village land dispute; made for the Land League, a political organization of small farmers.
3) Film: *The Galway Rent and Rate Strike,* Super-8, 1971.
4) Twenty-minute play based on *The Emperor's New Clothes* as part of Roger Smith's *Two Hundred Years of Labor History* during the winter of 1971 for a rally of about 3,000 people sponsored by the Socialist Labor League at Alexandra Palace.
5) Two agit-prop plays presented in Muswell Hill in early spring 1971. These attacks on Heath's Tory government, based upon *Little Red Riding Hood,* were performed by a cast of Albert Hunt's students from Bradford College of Art in Theatre of Cardboard style with masks and placards.
6) *Oughterard 1972,* a Super 8 film, 1972, adapted from *The Unfulfilled Dream.*
7) *Portrait of a Rebel,* a television documentary about Sean O'Casey, spring 1973, RTE.
8) An eight-hour stage show which employs the character of Henry Dub to consider the History of the American labor movement, presented at the University of California, Davis, in 1973. Not to be confused with the *Non-Stop Connolly Show* although the two works are related.

9) A film about the AFSCME union on that campus, 1973.

10) *The Corrandulla Film* surveys life in a small village, Super-8, 1974.

11) *The Crown Strike Play,* with University College, Galway, presented in Fall 1975 in the city square. This agit-prop piece should not be confused with *Sean O'Scrudu,* which was inspired by the same on-going union/management struggle.

12) *The Menace of Ireland?,* a 1979 compilation of previous D'Arcy/ Arden scenes plus debate stimulated by them; designed and played for British audiences.

13) Since 1987 they jointly have offered the theatre workshop now termed *Duchas na Saoirse,* usually in Belfast.

In addition, D'Arcy alone devised the play *A Pinprick of History* (1977). In 1973 in a supermarket in California she shot a film in which she employs the Henry Dub character to advocate boycotting lettuce, and, while sitting outside the Arts Council Offices in 1986, she filmed "Circus Expose of the New Cultural Church," which was shown at the 1987 Celtic Film Festival in Inverness and at the Derry Film Festival in 1988. She has also filmed dozens of hours of videos with Galway Women in Media and Entertainment. She founded Women's Sceal Radio, and she is completing an opera, *Opera ag Obair,* to form part of *Utopia* for presentation in Algeria in late summer 1993. Sections of *Opera ag Obair* already have been performed at the London Irish Women's Festival, 1987; the Huddersfield Women's Festival, 1987; and in Galway, 1988.) Of course, like Arden, D'Arcy also publishes reviews, essays, non-fiction (e.g., *Tell Them Everything.* London: Pluto Press, 1981) and fiction ("The Budgeen," published in two collections of feminist fairy tales, *Sweeping Beauties* (1989) and *Ride on Rapunzel* (1992), both Dublin, Attic Press). (I am indebted to D'Arcy and Arden for most of these additions to their usual cannon.)

Given the increasing quantity of joint authorship (to date, during thirty-four years of collaboration, at least thirty-four co-authored works), one would think that the studies which followed Hayman's 1968 book would consider the two writers as a team. Not so. The books, scholarly articles, and production reviews alike tend to pay little, if any, attention to Margaretta D'Arcy's credits on playbills and title pages. It is as though English-speaking spectators and critics had forgotten how to read whenever their eyes fell on her name.

The content of Simon Trussler's 1973 study, *John Arden,* reflects its title. Trussler accurately attributes the third of the plays in the bibliography of published primary works which resulted from collaboration, yet he titles this list "Works of John Arden." In his text, he likewise correctly notes the joint authorship of the unpublished *Harold Muggins Is a Martyr,* yet he discusses this play and *The Business of Good Government* as though Arden alone had written them. Where he refers to D'Arcy, he does so as part of his disparagement of the collaborative work Trussler thus justifies his pattern of ignoring D'Arcy: "the extent and nature of the Ardens' collaboration remains conjectural" (33).

Trussler has a short memory. In his 1966 interview with John Arden in *Tulane Drama Review,* Trussler learned first-hand about D'Arcy's part in the plays. As he has in other interviews, Arden persistently discusses D'Arcy's contributions even though Trussler never asks Arden about this or refers to her at all. The result is a series of exchanges in which Trussler single-mindedly inquires about Arden and Arden frequently couches his replies in terms of D'Arcy's creative input. Of *Left-Handed Liberty* (not one of the jointly attributed plays), for example, Arden recalls, "I did get a bit tangled in a confusion of baronial and episcopal minutiae, until Margaretta D'Arcy [Arden's wife] suggested that I use the Papal Legate—until then a very minor character—to pull the whole play together and set it in a framework of medieval theology and cosmology" (50).

Then Trussler asks how Arden came to write *Ars Longa, Vita Brevis* and receives this response (which he appears to have forgotten before asserting in 1973 that we have no way of knowing who contributed what to the collaboratively created plays):

> Having accepted, rather casually, a commission to write a piece for school-children, I was at a complete loss until Margaretta D'Arcy reminded me of a curious inquest, reported in *The Times,* held on an art master shot in a wood while taking part in a Territorial Army exercise. Peter Brook then asked me for a little piece for his *Theatre of Cruelty* program, and we thought we would kill two birds with one stone. Miss D'Arcy had been doing some improvised plays with children in Kirbymoorside and also in Dublin, and she suggested that the peculiar directness and the spontaneous development of "classical" conventions which we saw in their work would be a useful starting-off point. *Ars Longa* is really more her play than mine—she decided what was to happen in each scene, and I then wrote down a sort of stream-of-consciousness dialogue to illustrate it. In order not to make the play too rigid for its potential juvenile cast—we weren't so worried about Peter Brook's adults—I did not attempt to polish or even revise this dialogue. When we later directed the play ourselves with the Kirbymoorside Girl Guides we threw out all the dialogue, except two bits of verse, and let them improvise their own words throughout. The result was, we thought, much more successful than any of the productions we have seen where my dialogue was used. (50-1)

Arden continues by describing D'Arcy's part in *The Business of Good Government, Friday's Hiding, The Royal Pardon,* and what became *The Hero Rises Up* and concludes, 'Oddly enough, *The Business of Good Government* and *Ars Longa* are the two most popular plays I have written . . . or rather, partly written" (51).

Trussler paid so little mind to this and other acknowledgement of D'Arcy's importance to the plays that he published with his interview a chronology of "John Arden's" plays which never mentions that Arden and D'Arcy wrote several of them.

The next book on "Arden," Glenda Leeming's 1974 *John Arden,* likewise mentions D'Arcy infrequently (4–5, 6–7, 26, 31, 32). Albert Hunt in 1974 refers to her somewhat more extensively—but note his title: *Arden: A Study of His Plays* ([11]-12, 32, 34, 63, 65–70, [108], 109, 110–142, 152–164, 171–2). Frances Gray in the 1982 *John Arden* devotes more attention to D'Arcy than her title suggests. Early on she notes "D'Arcy rather than Arden was the moving force behind the Carnival" (24), and throughout she proves more alert to the collaboration and quicker to acknowledge it and its importance than the authors of other books on "Arden." Surprisingly, however, Gray's insistence on considering the playwriting partnership has produced little impact on the ensuing ten years of scholarship.

By the time Malcolm Page's *John Arden* appeared in 1984, the stage had been set for appropriate credit to what should be a famous partnership. Yet the index to his 175-page book refers to D'Arcy only sporadically (4, 10–12, 22, 59, 66, 94, 95–6, 100, 109–10, 118, 130, 138, 144), and most of those citations involve convoluted excuses for avoiding discussing her. Although his bibliography acknowledges (unlike that in his more error-prone compilation *Arden on File,* issued by Methuen the following year) all the major collaborations through 1978, his text does not correctly attribute them. Beginning with the first two pages of his introduction, he refers to Arden as sole author of *The Happy Haven, The Hero Rises Up, The Island of the Mighty,* and the *Non-Stop Connolly Show* (xi–xii).

In his effort "to account for the decline of interest in John Arden's work" (xii), Page blames (1) fashion. (2) "Arden's" rejection of "careerism," for which he cites *The Royal Pardon, War Carnival, Muggins,* and *Connolly.* He neglects to mention that all four were collaborations. (3) quarrels over *The Hero Rises Up* and *The Island of the Mighty,* "giving him a reputation for being 'difficult.'" Again, no mention of his collaboration on these. Only in his fifth and sixth explanations does Page begin to refer to D'Arcy. Here and for much of the rest of his brief introduction, Page seems intent upon remedying what is wrong with the body of his volume: He actually considers the pair's creative partnership. Yet he concludes with a lame justification for ignoring her and/or dismissing her thereafter: "This book is called *John Arden.* More correctly, it might be entitled 'John Arden and Margaretta D'Arcy,' as so many of the plays are collaborative. As it is not possible to isolate D'Arcy's contribution, in general I have merely stated when a work is jointly written, then commented in terms of Arden's styles and themes. Also, D'Arcy is proudly Irish and would object to appearing in an English Authors Series" (xiii). Yet how can we conclude that the plays' themes and styles typify Arden rather than

Arden and D'Arcy when both wrote them? Would we make such an absurd supposition about the works of Beaumont and Fletcher? Kaufman and Hart? Lawrence and Lee? Or other male collaborations?

Unwary readers thereafter, should they skip the preface, can easily conclude from the rest of the book that D'Arcy is merely Arden's wife, her sole issue her children. Page mentions that Arden reviews in the *New Statesman* but neglects to add that D'Arcy does, too. When, sporadically, he does remember playwright D'Arcy, it is as part of something called "the Ardens," an appellation which neither partner would approve. Towards the end, Page defends his methodology by reiterating "the reader can only speculate about her role" (138), but then, without proof, blames her for "broad effects and unsubtle characterizations" and immediately returns to referring to the scripts as Arden's alone. He tries to have it both ways, declining to credit her for the scripts' strengths because he presumes we can't tell what she wrote, but then blaming her for those features he doesn't care for.

Through the years, the doctoral dissertations have repeated the books' patterns of generally ignoring D'Arcy, the reference books have discussed only Arden, and nearly all the interviewers have spoken solely to him. Force of habit—along, we must infer, with sexism—has perpetuated the mistaken notion that Arden alone creates "his" plays. Throughout 34 years of this creative partnership, critics and journalists publishing essays, articles, and reviews also, almost to a "man," just haven't gotten it.

In an early instance of this blindness or bias, John Russell Taylor's introduction to *Three Plays* ignores the joint attribution on the play's title page and never mentions her name. Yet he deems this "one of his [sic] richest and most satisfying plays: a lot of it is very funny, and some of it is very beautiful. . . . Technically it is probably Arden's boldest play yet. . . . Of that sort of writing, with that sort of hardwon strength and sinew, only John Arden has the secret in the modern English theatre . . ." (14–15). Carol Rosen in *Plays of Impasse: Contemporary Drama Set in Confining Institutions* also analyzes "John Arden's *The Happy Haven*" without mentioning D'Arcy's name (54–72).

A survey of other scholars' contributions to books and journals turns up similar treatment—or often lack of treatment—of one half of this playwriting team. Although Katharine J. Worth in *Revolutions in Modern English Drama* considers *The Happy Haven* and *The Royal Pardon* (108, 132–3), she fails to discuss the collaboration and barely acknowledges D'Arcy's existence, not even when she praises "the best English writing" as the product of authors (Arden, among others, but not D'Arcy) who also direct and act (descriptions which fit D'Arcy better than Arden).

Craig Clinton begins his "John Arden: The Promise Unfulfilled" by discussing *The island of the Mighty* as though D'Arcy had nothing to do with it, referring to "the author and his wife" (48). But he switches gears in a few pages and blasts D'Arcy (especially 53–6) as an "outspoken proselyte of the leftist ideals both she and her husband hold in common" (55). Although the article appeared in 1978, Clinton's footnotes all cite sources no more recent than 1971, and he bases his attack on the 1968 *The Hero Rises Up.*

When Ronald Hayman returns to "Arden" in his 1979 *British Theatre Since 1955: A Reassessment,* he mentions D'Arcy five times, each time in a derogatory context, linking the collaboration to work which Hayman judges inferior to the product of Arden's pen (16, 82–5, 108, 126). The index also refers us to 92, where Hayman mentions "the Ardens," even though D'Arcy has always used her maiden name. Many critics have chosen to ignore her wishes in this matter. Hayman praises "his early plays, which are unquestionably works of art, whereas the priority in his later work is propagandistic." Hayman gets his facts wrong, however, dating the onset of Arden's "working partnership with his wife" to 1967 and claiming that Arden had always previously started "with a story that appealed to him" instead of a message he wishes to communicate (82). For refutation of this viewpoint, we need only turn to 13, where Hayman concludes about *Musgrave* "it is obvious that message preceded character," a view which he reiterates on 23.

Redmond O'Hanlon's "The Theatrical Values of John Arden" takes as his point of departure the 1977 publication of *To Present the Pretense.* Because Arden wrote most of those essays, we may appreciate why O'Hanlon's discussion of the plays refers to Arden's work, yet he engages in a sort of double-think in which Arden and D'Arcy (or, lamentably, the Ardens) picket their production at the Royal Shakespeare company, but Arden writes the plays. Javed Malick also practices an inconsistent approach: his "The Polarized Universe of *The Island of the Mighty:* Arden and D'Arcy's Dramaturgy," as the title suggests, tends to speak of playwrights, plural, although sometimes departing from that approach even though discussing collaborative work. Yet his "Society and History in Arden's Dramaturgy," although it occasionally refers to D'Arcy in passing, discusses the collaboratively created plays *The Royal Pardon, The Island of the Mighty,* and *The Non-Stop Connolly Show* as Arden's. He demonstrates enrichment in that author's plays from their increasingly political content, yet he ignores what many people would regard as her influence (and contribution) in that regard. Could the different editors for these two journals account for the shift in Malick's approach? Or did Malick write the second article first? Whatever the cause, the second approach represents a regression.

Journalists likewise frequently ignore D'Arcy's part in creating "Arden's" plays. Mel Gussow writes in this tradition in a *New York Times* review of *The Happy Haven.* Although he acknowledges the collaboration at the outset, thereafter he refers to there "author" as male, as in "One of the problems with 'The Happy Haven' is that the author is not quite clear about his own allegiances." We may find particularly puzzling Robert Brustein's "Picketing His Own Play," also in the *New York Times,* because whatever writers say, or fail to say about the plays' authorship, most are quick to blame D'Arcy for condemning the Royal Shakespeare Company production of *The Island of the Mighty*. But Brustein, after telling us that the pair wrote this play, falls into using the third person singular male pronoun which his headline reflects. In all fairness, these reviewers shouldn't be singled out for special rebuke; reviews which ignore D'Arcy are ubiquitous.

A good index of the lack of interest in D'Arcy can be found in the clippings files of the Billy Rose research collection at the Lincoln Center division of the New York Public Library. The files marked "Arden" bulge with reviews and other journalism; the files on their jointly-written plays contain clippings which generally focus on him. The "D'Arcy" folder, however, contains a mere nine items—five of them carrying my own byline. Of course, not everyone ignores or belittles or denounces D'Anrcy's role in writing the plays. In addition to Frances Gray, Catherine Itzin's *Stages in the Revolution* maintains that Arden and D'Arcy both regard themselves as Irish and therefore feel they should not have been included in a book on British playwrights. (Arden does not, in fact, regard himself as Irish, but they do want their plays about Ireland to be seen as Irish.) Although she does not honor their wishes, Itzin at least considers them together, both in her discussion of *Harold Muggins Is a Martyr* (20–23) and her general discussion of the pair ([24]–38).

Similarly, Arthur Sainer discusses both writers in the *Village Voice* during the run of *The Ballygombeen Bequest*. James Leverett likewise departs from the established critical practice in his *Soho News* review of *The Non-Stop Connolly Show*. Robert Leach also appreciates their collaboration on that play. Though not the only examples, these number among the few publications which do not deny or castigate the partnership.

Why this prejudice against D'Arcy?

1) Ignorance. Lazy critics who know primarily *Serjeant Musgrave's Dance* and perhaps a few other of the early plays simply don't realize that most of "Arden's" work for the stage for the past 34 years has been co-authored with D'Arcy. Sloppy scholarship, however, should be no excuse for critical neglect of any writer.

2) Personal dislike. Such people reason she's a bitch, so it's her fault if critics ignore her. D'Arcy is not, as it happens, the harridan her detractors make her out. But even if she were, that's no excuse for punitive inaccuracies. I have never, incidentally, heard a woman denounce D'Arcy based on personal animosity—perhaps because so often she selects patriarchy as her primary antagonist. For the record, in my experience D'Arcy has proven joyous, spirited, assertive but not in the least self-pitying or abrasive—in short, a thoroughly easy person with whom to interact. Her reputation as a troublemaker stems from the passion of her convictions and not the genial manner in which she usually delivers them. What irritates some folks must be her persistence in trying to persuade them to march, demonstrate, write letters, and otherwise commit themselves visibly to the causes which they

claim to espouse. For this sin, she arouses a startling venom, as in the case of the well-known English writer who recently snarled in my presence, "That woman is a monster."

3) The fact D'Arcy used her maiden name years before that became common probably has contributed to the antipathy towards her of those who prefer patriarchy to partnership. (Note how many of those who notice her at all refer to her as part of something called "the Ardens.")

4) The equally sexist assumption that a female collaborator contributes only secretarial services. As it happens, I've watched the two at work on a script. In that instance, she dictated, while he typed. A variation on this involves believing that a woman in a romantic relationship with her partner could not truly collaborate with him professionally. (Hillary Rodham Clinton receives similar challenges.)

5) Fury because she's ruined his career—a dubious assumption considering the critical and financial failure of the first production of *Serjeant Musgrave's Dance* (which played a mere 28 performances to 20% capacity) and the popularity of such jointly written community dramas as *Ars Longa, Vita Brevis.* And their collaborations of the last twenty years will surely be appreciated by future writers not burdened by the political biases against Irish republicanism and feminism harbored by some late twentieth-century appraisers. *Whose Is the Kingdom?,* for example, will prove an extraordinary accomplishment once anger over its indictment of Christian misogyny has abated. In any event, Arden's own wishes about his career must count for something, and he has willingly chosen to link his personal and professional destinies to hers in what a close observer (as I was when I rented a room at the top of their Muswell Hill home in the winter of 1978) must judge an unusually happy partnership. Moreover, Arden and D'Arcy have chosen to try to change the world, and if commercial managements decide not to produce their plays, we can hardly blame the victims for that. Personally, I am elated that people of such good will make the attempt to improve life for us all.

6) Censorship of their subject matter—which critics often regard as really her subject matter—for its indictment of what Britain has done to the Irish. When censors target sexual material, critics usually jump to the artists' defense. Do they not likewise champion these playwrights' freedom of speech because they object to the message?

7) Some folks find it hard to like—or even acknowledge the contributions of—a female hero. They find it hard to warm to the woman who, while she was incarcerated in Armagh, smuggled out to me, written in tiny letters on *one* square of toilet paper, the following letter concerning her plight and that of others in her wing of the prison:

> Dear Tish: . . . Thanks for your articles. Everyone here is in fighting form,
> but the conditions are horrifying. Some of the girls look like Auschwitz

victims, old women—the doctor won't allow any outside medicos in. Death and decay like medieval gargoyles lurk in the open sewers which run past our cell doors. Flies, fleas and filth, darkness and excrement; we are the strange animals in the midden. Male guards dressed in green helmets with visors and female guards with gauze round their faces hang outside to jeer and sneer. Cold greasy food black with flies. We are locked up twenty-three hours a day: only two of us allowed out at a time, so we never see each other. I think when all this is over people are going to find it as difficult to believe as Hitler's concentration camps. Girls tortured before coming in and now being tortured with this cruel lying neglect all because they want justice, the right to some human dignity until the war is over. The women are amazing. I have never seen so much courage and self discipline. No self-pitying, always cheerful and keeping up the morale. How long they can go on, God knows. The Brits must be forced to have some humanity towards their prisoners. Otherwise hunger strike on a mass scale will be the next move. How many more must die until reason prevails? Love to you, Margaretta. (For a more detailed account, see her *Tell Them Everything.*)

Clearly D'Arcy possesses the qualities of character which, if evinced by a man of her generation, might have won her high political office, a position as a general in the armed forces, or eventually the sort of holiday which we've awarded to the equally persevering Martin Luther King, Jr.

Arden and D'Arcy themselves have reacted implicitly and explicitly to D'Arcy's negative reception—or the absence of any reception. We needn't read far between the lines to find pertinent this exchange from *Vandaleur's Folly:*

> THOMPSON: You are about to say I am a hypocrite. We shared our bed, we shared
>   our book-writing, page between page, we shared everything all these years—
> ANNA: With men, it is a common condition.
> THOMPSON: As we have abundantly proven within the argument of our joint works.
>   Our joint works with *my* name on them. (64)

In the preface to *John Arden Plays: One,* Arden laments "I am continually informed in all manner of print by all manner of critics that my later work (. . . since I started regularly working as the older half of the Arden/D'Arcy writing-production partnership) shows a distinct falling-off in dramatic tension and inspiration: I am accused of having turned my back upon the professional theatre—whereas the professional theatre, at least in certain large and influential areas, has let it be known that Arden's work is only acceptable if D'Arcy is not impertinently attached to it" (7). Yet, Arden explains, he rates his work with her as more important than his work alone because their collaborations involve the audience (7–8). As D'Arcy recently remarked to me, they have become less interested in performing in front of an audience than in participatory theatre in which the audience plays an integral role.

Arden also has commented on his work with D'Arcy in interviews (for instance with Raymond Gardner in 1972) and essays. In his introduction to the section titled "The Matter of Vietnam" in *To Present the Pretence,* Arden discusses the Vietnam Carnival at NYU: "The overall concept of the show was due largely to Margaretta D'Arcy. . . . [When asked by New York University] to conduct a group of students in whatever project suggested itself, I agreed, on condition that D'Arcy would be formally associated with me on all *practical* work, this being rather outside my own professional experience, whereas she was already well-seasoned as a performer and experimental director" (47). Later in the same volume (for those who still claim to have no notion of what part D'Arcy plays in creating the plays) Arden writes of their *Connolly* play that "D'Arcy divined a basic image for his character on which we could build the play" (106) and "it had been D'Arcy who originally conceived the Connolly idea" (110).

On the distaste of theatres for staging the collaborative work, he complains of this as censorship: "The great difficulty is that dramatists will rarely be told: 'Your play is *subversive:* we are imposing a political restriction upon its performance.' . . . In my case it has been incontrovertibly passed on to me (though never put down on paper in so many words) that any work of mine done in collaboration with D'Arcy (which in effect means all my Irish material) is altogether out of line with the requirements of more than one subsidised theatre" (157). He offers this plausible explanation of the genesis of the Royal Shakespeare Company's mythology vis-a-vis D'Arcy as termagant:

> She had, they hinted, come over for rehearsals only to sabotage the dignity of the RSC. Of course they were in a dilemma; it was necessary to attack the authors, for the authors were attacking them. But if they accused Arden of being a low-class troublemaker they would make people wonder why they chose to present the play in the first place. But the fact that there were two authors made it possible for the RSC handouts to attack one at the expense of the other, and they naturally chose the more vulnerable of the pair. D'Arcy was: (a) female, and (b) Irish. (166)

In his 1986 statement for the *Contemporary Authors Autobiography Series,* Arden describes the importance of his meeting D'Arcy in 1955:

> She was the first professional theatre-person I ever got to know: and through her I met many people without whom my career as a playwright could never have got off the ground. Two years later we were married. She was closely involved with the most progressive aspects of the theatre of that time, aspects which I knew nothing of, with my limited Shakespearean provincial

orientation and my academic (and indeed pompous) attitude towards the stage. She gave me a copy of Brecht—a writer I had only heard of: she introduced me to the works of Beckett, Strindberg, Toller, Behan. . . . Her name now appears sometimes first, sometimes second, together with mine, upon a great deal of published work which nonetheless the male critics, managements, publishers, and broadcasters, will insist upon referring to as "Arden's." Or, worse, as "the Ardens.'" . . . It would have been different if I had collaborated with a man called Hiram Hinks, or even with a woman called Evadne Pershore (assuming that she was known already as a professional author and *not* known to be married to, or living with, me). (29)

In addition to sexism, Arden identifies censorship as a cause of their troubles:

What did matter was the nature of the collaborative work, after 1968 anyway. Before then the problem had been but slight: because our plays were fairly conventional in form and content. After 1968 their political dimensions became less and less acceptable to the British cultural establishment, which has its own very decided notions of what liberties may be taken with the Imperial traditions. (30)

In a sense all D'Arcy's portion of *Awkward Corners* suggests her response to the discrimination she encounters or to the reasons why the patriarchy repudiates or ignores her or why she perseveres anyhow. Her remarks reflect her uncompromising and principled moral fibre. (See, for example, her descriptions of her imprisonment after her arrest at Greenham, 226–8.) She communicates a powerful image of the bond between her and Arden in "To John Who Complains I Never Write Nice Poems to Him": "If you died / I / Would have / No / Past / Or / Future / Only / Now: / No dreams / No time. / Conscious for only each second that passes / As the earth spins / With / Me / On it / With out / You" (217). She likewise describes jocularly their working relationship: "When I want a clear story / Arden always complicates it / By putting in too much. Like yesterday—/ A simple joke in a short scene: / One philosopher has taken five years to / Develop an argument, / The other has / Five hours / Before they are both eaten by lions. / But Arden / Has to put in how / Long they've lived, / Who they are. / I say I say / Old boy, / A shouting match—/All to show that / Arden can write" (215–6).

Her opening essay endeavors to reply to the query from Nick Hern "Why do certain people find you so obnoxious, Margaretta?" ([121]). She considers the ways her candid dissent threatens and frightens people who label her a terrorist (of all things). In Communist countries, she reasons, we call such people dissidents "and praise them: but here in the West . . .?" (123). Here, her experience demonstrates, it lands them in prison. In the essay "Breaking Chains" she traces their collaboration and the cost on their careers of the censorship of their work on English stages, which she dates from her outspoken writing beginning in the 60's when the British army occupied the Six Counties in Northern Ireland. The repression included coercion of the theatres which wished to stage their plays, loss of grants to such theatres, and the libel suit which prevented for several years further staging of *The Ballygombeen Bequest* and eventually forced its revision (133–4). "Theatre in an Age of Reform" contains similar analysis of government and press efforts to equate their exercise of freedom of expression (with respect to *Vandaleur's Folly*) with terrorism ([176]–191). And "Statement for the National Council of Civil Liberties Concerning the Prevention of Terrorism Act" recounts several further instances of government pressure in the form of withdrawal of funding which have prevented the production of their work on grounds of her "terrorism," a code word for her impertinence in presuming to criticize British policies ([204]–9).

Lest anyone continue to refuse to credit the collaboration, *Arden/D'Arcy: D'Arcy/Arden's* title page carries their notation as to which author took the leading part in writing each play (two for Arden, ten for D'Arcy). D'Arcy details in her introduction her contributions to some of their work([ix]–xiii).

Biases must not be allowed to disqualify D'Arcy's contributions from critical consideration. Critics and scholars can, of course, dislike her kind of dramaturgy and analyze what they perceive as its faults. But the ad hominem attacks on her and the pretense that only John Arden writes the Arden/D'Arcy and D'Arcy/Arden plays must no longer be tolerated. Any less will perpetuate an injustice.

Moreover, benefits will accrue from considering these two as a team. They have proven quite cooperative and forthcoming with scholars who do so, whereas those who try to deal with Arden alone have been known to meet with a less cordial reception. Entree to research assistance, interviews, and so on should prove easier to anyone who corresponds with—and respects—them both.

Those concerned with a handful of Arden-only plays will find attention to D'Arcy provides them with insights into some of the most significant influences on his drama. D'Arcy worked as a professional actor from the age of fifteen (after she left school in 1949); she, not Arden, had acquired considerable professional theatre experience by the time they met. D'Arcy had found her first acting work after her arrival in England with director Stuart Burge in a company at Hornchurch. In 1958 George Devine asked D'Arcy to join the new Royal Court Theatre company. By then D'Arcy had already met, through mutual Irish friends, the young architect Arden, unknown as a playwright. As a professional actor with a wide acquaintanceship among theatre people, D'Arcy was able to offer him introductions.

Thereafter, she originated the roles of Rosie in *Live Like Pigs,* Teresa in *The Waters of Babylon,* the King of France (disguised by a male stage name) in *The Royal Pardon,* and numerous parts in subsequent plays. She has directed or codirected many of the plays, beginning with *The Business of Good Government,* and she discussed plays with Arden as he was conceiving and writing them. Her father Joseph D'Arcy's personality even "inspired much of" *The Workhouse Donkey* (5). Arden dedicated *Musgrave* to her and acknowledged her help in his preface to *The Workhouse Donkey* (*John Arden Plays: One* 112). And would Arden have written *Pearl* had he not known D'Arcy? Certainly the Irish actor/playwright/social activist Pearl, betrayed and cast out to die, could serve as a metaphor for D'Arcy's treatment. As Jon Wike has observed, the root of Margaretta (<Latin *margarita,* <Greek *margaron*) means "pearl." And we cannot ignore the obvious autobiographical stimulus for Arden's short story "The Fork in the Head," in which the artist husband's political activist, artist wife urges him "You ought to be in there, Jackson, doing your utmost" (107), while he prefers to watch lewd films or enjoy pleasant weather (*Corners* [103]–15). Of course, he has deliberately trivialized the "Arden" character to emphasize a self-preoccupation and avoidance of political responsibility not really typical of him.

Only the short-sighted critic would assume all the Arden plays would have been written had D'Arcy not played such a crucial role in his life. Whether we like it or not, D'Arcy has profoundly affected Arden's sense of theatre, his choices of material—especially the Irish subjects—and his socialist stands. Ignoring her diminishes our understanding of the genesis and details of all that we regard as quintessentially "Arden": his view of theatre as a vehicle for social change; his celebration of Celtic, curvilinear qualifies; the conflict between the forces of order and disorder (which develop into the opposition of oppression and rebellion); and the very vigor and theatricality of "his" style. Arden told me in 1976 that his plays focus more on the psychopathology of society than on individual aberrance; Musgrave's disturbance, he said, reflects society's. Perhaps his work does not differ so profoundly from hers and theirs; if so, analysis of his plays would benefit from that insight.

And what riches await critics who turn their attention to the collaborative plays. D'Arcy has imbued these plays with a contemporary relevance and power which those who have not read or seen them should anticipate experiencing with pleasure. The kind of indomitable spirit which animates this woman who does not shrink from repeated imprisonment (while still objecting to repeated strip searches), the sort of integrity which commits her to the cause of humanity no matter what the cost to herself animates their courageous characters. My own students prefer *The Little Gray Home in the West* to other twentieth-century plays which they read in my English and Irish drama course. A full-scale, multi-evening mounting of *The Island of the Mighty* which does not reverse its sympathies (as did the truncated RSC version) would doubtless prompt further professional production of this, *The Little Gray Home,* and *Vandaleur's Folly,* but in the meantime the latter two and the radio plays should keep analysts occupied for some months. *Whose Is the Kingdom?,* for instance, will repay critical attention to its intense, theatrical, and original dramatization of the suppression of differences and dissent, as patriarchy evolves into a Christian principle, displacing the several women among Christian and pagan leaders, and the Church imposes both conformity and acceptance of its approved versions of truth and history. This nine-part series for BBC radio speaks clearly to Americans reeling from the revelations of Irangate, Iraqgate, and GOP campaigns against departure from certain sanctioned norms. For those not familiar with this and other recent collaborative plays, what riches await your critical appraisal!

NOTE

[1] This, not "Kirbymoorside," is the correct spelling.

Works Cited

Arden, John. Interview with Raymond Gardner. "Exit, Stage Left." *Guardian* November 28, 1972: 10.

―――. Interview with Simon Trussler. "Who's for a Revolution?" *Tulane Drama Review* 11.2 (Winter 1966): [49]–53.

―――. "John Arden." *Contemporary Authors Autobiography Series.* Vol. 4. Detroit: Gale Research, 1986. 29–47.

―――. *John Arden Plays: One.* London: Eyre Methuen Ltd., 1977.

―――. *The Workhouse Donkey.* New York: Grove Press, 1964.

Arden, John, and Margaretta D'Arcy. *Arden/D'Arcy: D'Arcy/Arden Plays: One.* London: Methuen Drama, 1991.

―――. "Ars Longa, Vita Brevis." *Encore* 11.2 (March–April 1964): 13–20.

―――. *Ars Longa, Vita Brevis.* Eight Plays. Ed. Malcolm Stuart Fellows. London: Cassell, 1965.

―――. *Awkward Corners.* London: Methuen London Ltd., 1988.

―――. *The Business of Good Government.* London: Methuen, 1967 reprint.

―――. "The Happy Haven." *New English Dramatists,* 4. Ed. Tom Maschler. Harmondsworth: Penguin, 1962. [85]–[167].

―――. "The Happy Haven." *Three Plays by John Arden.* Harmondsworth: Penguin, 1964. [191]–[272].

Brustein, Robert. "Picketing His Own Play." *New York Times 7* January 1973: [D1], D5.

Clinton, Craig. "John Arden: The Promise Unfulfilled." *Modern Drama* 21 (1978): 47–57.

Dace, Tish. "Stung." *Soho Weekly News* 22 November 1979: 47–8.

―――. "A Small Number." *Other Stages* 20 March 1980: 3.

―――. "Outrages in Ireland." *Other Stages* 12 June 1980: 2.

―――. "The Cells of Armagh." *Soho Weekly News* 2 July 1980: 8.

―――. "Incredible Chaos." *Other Stages* 25 September 1980: 2.

D'Arcy, Margaretta. *Tell Them Everything: A Sojourn in the Prison of Her Majesty Queen Elizabeth II at Ard Macha (Armagh).* London: Pluto Press, 1981.

D'Arcy, Margaretta, and John Arden. *Vandaleur's Folly.* London: Eyre Methuen, 1981.

Gray, Frances. *John Arden,* New York: Grove Press, 1982.

Gussow, Mel. "Theater: 'Happy Haven,' Spoof of Welfare State." *New York Times,* April 5, 1977: 38.

Hayman, Ronald. *British Theatre Since 1955: A Reassessment.* Oxford: Oxford University Press, 1979.

———. *John Arden.* London: Heinemann Educational Books, 1968.

Hunt, Albert. *Arden: A Study of His Plays.* London: Eyre Methuen, 1974.

Itzin, Catherine. *Stages in the Revolution: Political Theatre in Britain Since 1968,* London: Eyre Methuen, 1980.

Leach, Robert. "*The Non-Stop Connolly Show:* Into the Future." *Theatre Ireland 28* (Summer 1992): 39–42.

Leeming, Glenda. *John Arden.* Harlow: For the British Council by Longman Group, 1974.

Leverett, James. "Present Past." *Soho Weekly News,* April 9, 1980: 29, 56, 59.

O'Hanlon, Redmond. "The Theatrical Values of John Arden." *Theatre Research International* 5 (Autumn 1980): 218–36.

Malick, Javed. "The Polarized Universe of *The Island of the Mighty:* Arden and D'Arcy's Dramaturgy." *New Theatre Quarterly* 2 (February 1986): 38–53.

———. "Society and History in Arden's Dramaturgy." *Theatre Journal* 42 (May 1990): 208–24.

Page, Malcolm. *Arden on File.* London: Methuen, 1985.

———. *John Arden.* Boston: Twayne, 1984.

Rosen, Carol. *Plays of Impasse: Contemporary Drama Set in Confining Institutions.* Princeton: Princeton University Press, 1983.

Sainer, Arthur. "Agitprop Strikes Back." *Village Voice* 6 December 1976: 99, 101.

Taylor, John Russell. "Introduction." *Three Plays by John Arden.* Harmondsworth: Penguin, 1964. 7–[15].

Trussler, Simon. *John Arden.* New York: Columbia University Press, 1973.

Worth, Katharine J. *Revolutions in Modern English Drama.* London: G. Bell & Sons, 1972.

Ayckbourn's Theatricality

Bernard F. Dukore

As Alan Ayckbourn says, he is "basically a visual writer" who feels that the theatre has overly emphasized the verbal at the expense of the visual. Recognizing that a good play combines both verbal and visual, he believes that a play fails when someone can attend to it "with his eyes closed, listening with a serene smile on his face." Rather, he prefers that person to think, "I'd better watch this, because I may miss something" (Watson 81, 125–126). The visual is a major aspect of a play's theatrical, nonliterary qualifies. In Ayckbourn's comedies, theatricality buttresses and in many cases is inextricably combined with their literary elements.

His works contain much comedy that is entirely visual. For instance, when Sidney Hopcroft of *Absurd Person Singular* enters the kitchen expecting to find his wife Jane, all the dumbfounded man sees is a pair of empty shoes a few steps away from an open door to the rear garden, where it is raining. Shortly afterwards, when no one is in the kitchen, the helpless Jane appears on the other side of the window of the kitchen door, now locked, where she stands soaking wet in her hat, coat, and boots, unable to open the door. In *Taking Steps,* Mark and Tristram try to prop the sleeping Roland in an armchair, but he slides down the chair, fast asleep, forcing them to catch him before he hits the floor. In *Henceforward . . .,* Jerome sticks his hand up a female robot's skirt, fumbles, and removes circuitry. As the gardener of *Man of the Moment,* carrying a hose, stands beside a swimming pool and intently watches the filming of a television interview, oblivious to the fact that he is within camera range, the hose receives a fierce tug, which makes him fall backwards into the pool. *The Revengers' Comedies* has a woman, after having been thrown from the back of a horse, crawl onto the stage; she wears full riding gear and is covered with mud on just one side of her, from head to foot.

Ayckbourn uses the visual to comment on the verbal. While a wealthy businessman's wife delivers a speech on the virtues of the Conservative Party in "Gosforth's Fête," one of the plays that makes up *Confusions,* the Vicar turns the tap of a tea urn to pour himself a cup but is unable to turn the tap off;

19

noticing his dilemma, another character hurriedly passes him an empty cup to catch the flow while taking the full one from him, in a chain of filling cups as they unsuccessfully try to stem the flow of tea from the urn during the speech, "*each flow unstoppable*" (52). The spatial triangle of the setting of *Season's Greetings,* emphasized by a large Christmas tree, mirrors a sexual triangle. On the ground floor, past one end of the tree, Belinda enters, carrying a scarf and boots, so that Clive, who is at the other end of the tree, can go outside. Rachel appears at the top of the stairway, just above the top of the tree, with boots she has got for the same purpose. When she sees and overhears what is happening below, she drops the boots over the bannister.

By visual means, Ayckbourn conveys character in situation. At the start of *Relatively Speaking,* Greg, beneath bedclothes, is in the dark when Ginny's former lover telephones her—a condition in which he remains during the play. When he pulls open the jammed top drawer of her dresser, half a dozen expensive boxes of chocolate fall out, leftovers from his predecessor who thereby visually intrudes upon them. In *Absent Friends,* Paul throws a cigar to John as an afterthought; he catches it as a dog catches a bone—a demonstration of their business relationship. In *Joking Apart,* three couples and a bachelor age twelve years; but a different unmarried woman is younger in each successive scene (from late twenties to eighteen). The very sight of these women, played by the same actress, who are paired with the bachelor, his hair dyed in the last scene, suggests the type of man he is, the different ways they relate to him (extreme emotional dependence, self-sufficiency, indifference, revulsion), and the changing times. Since the same actor plays the five Rivetti brothers in *A Small Family Business,* they become virtually interchangeable both as Anita's lovers and as representatives of their business firm. Following the offstage accidental decapitation of two women in *Body Language*—one with a fat body, the other with a body whose buttocks, thighs, and calves have been firmly molded through exercise and whose breasts silicone has enlarged and shaped—a surgeon joins bodies and heads together. However, he attaches the wrong bodies to the heads. In a wordless scene, each woman, with a neck brace to prevent her from moving her head so as not to undo the stitches, slowly realizes, as her hands explore her figure, that she has the other's body. Later, when the erstwhile fat woman, a feminist, walks away from a man, she is startled to find that her body moves in its own manner, for its language is that of the other woman, an underwear model whose gait is what she considers sexually enticing.

Related to the depiction of character in situation is Ayckbourn's visual linkage of character and theme (while this category obviously overlaps the previous one, it warrants separate treatment for purposes of discussion). In *Absent Friends,* John masks his hostility toward his wife by treating it as play: as if in jest, though really in earnest, he shadowboxes near her face. In *Bedroom Farce,* Trevor's inadvertent destruction of Malcolm's assemble-it-yourself dressing table while trying to fix it shows the unintentional mess he makes of people's lives. As he surveys the wreckage, it becomes an emblem of his own marriage. Although he and his wife try to patch things up, the ruined table lies on the floor, a visual reminder. The climax of Act I of *Just Between Ourselves* shows the relationship between husband and wife: as she reaches for a water jug, she overturns the sugar, and as she pours hot tea into a cup, she begins hiccuping until the cup vibrates uncontrollably, spilling tea on the table—to his visible amusement. When Sylvie agrees to marry Lionel in "A Garden Fête," a scene in *Intimate Exchanges,* she is in a pillory so that, for a price, visitors may throw wet sponges at her. Emblematic of their relationship, Lionel hurls sponges *"with devastating and somewhat malicious accuracy"* (I, 142).

Visual irony abounds in Ayckbourn's work. In *Table Manners,* one of the plays in the trilogy *The Norman Conquests,* Sarah, though emotionally frazzled, artfully and with machinelike precision comically incongruous with her nervousness, folds six napkins into conical shapes.[1] In "Between Mouthfuls," in *Confusions,* the audience picks up the conversation of each of two couples only when the Waiter is within earshot. As it hears them yell at each other, it sees the Waiter imperturbably dole food onto their plates, and when he placidly walks away, the couples silently engage in heated argument. While audiences of *Bedroom Farce* hear Trevor's wife talk of improving their marriage, they see him fall asleep as she does so. Similarly, spectators of *Season's Greetings* see, as a husband concentrates on fixing a toy while his wife discusses their marital problems, what is wrong with their marriage. In "Events on a Hotel Terrace," in *Intimate Exchanges,* spectators see half a dozen tables with empty chairs while Toby sarcastically talks of the activity and vivacity in the hotel his wife has chosen for their holiday. During a lighting rehearsal in *A Chorus of Disapproval,* Daffyd literally brings his wife Hannah and Guy together by demanding that they stand facing each other, and he adjusts their heights until she is on tiptoe while he crouches (in Mel Shapiro's production at Arena Stage, their mouths were on kissing level). After Daffyd leaves for the lighting booth, tiptoeing Hannah and crouching Guy declare their love for each other. One of the surgeons of *Body Language* advises two convalescent women in wheelchairs not to rush about.

Ayckbourn's use of the theatre as a visual medium includes the shape and size of the entire performance space. Usually he writes his plays for the Stephen Joseph Theatre in the Round in Scarborough from which they easily transfer, with few changes other than more scenery, to proscenium arch stages and end stages elsewhere. However, when he composes a play for a first production in a different theatre he imagines it in a visually different way, appropriate to that theatre. For instance, Peter Hall's request for a play for the National Theatre's Lyttelton Theatre, whose proscenium arch is wider than usual in London or America, prompted him to conceive a work for this specific stage: *Bedroom Farce,* which used the proscenium opening as a peephole for peeping Toms to peer at three bedrooms, placed end to end.

He wrote *A Chorus of Disapproval* for the National's Olivier Theatre, which has a huge thrust stage that requires filling, so that the auditorium does not dwarf it. He filled the performance space with all the company's understudies, who appeared as members of the Pendon Amateur Light Opera Society, which in the play produces John Gay's *The Beggar's Opera.* On smaller stages, such as Scarborough's, few or no understudies are on stage. Also written for the Olivier Theatre, *A Small Family Business* effectively loads its space with a two-story house; a stairway connects the floors, each with two visible rooms and a hallway. Characters move between rooms or are in different rooms at the same time; and these rooms may be in houses of different family members. The device is more than a gimmick, for the house, traditional symbol of a family, encompasses and overwhelms its individual members. Whereas the simultaneous employment of various parts of the house suggests expansiveness, the huddling together of characters into a downstairs room produces an effect of pressure; and the gathering of all but one of the family downstairs, with that individual isolated in a bathroom upstairs, visualizes that person's emotional withdrawal.

As the last paragraph indicates, Ayckbourn's settings, his plays' visual environment, reveal the characters who inhabit them. The center of social activity in *Just Between Ourselves* is Dennis's garage, his true home; this setting graphically depicts his abandonment of the usual center of social activity, the parlor, thus his abandonment of his wife, with whom he is at cross purposes. In *Bedroom Farce,* Ayckbourn is explicit about the importance of his settings:

> DELIA: You can tell a great deal from people's bedrooms.
> ERNEST: Can you? Good heavens. (*He looks about.*)
> DELIA: If you know what to look for. (164)

The bedroom of this elderly couple is late Victorian, its furniture sturdy but unremarkable. Since the upwardly mobile Malcolm and Kate are still convening their bedroom, it is sparsely furnished, with one wall repapered, the others stripped. The bedroom of Nick and Jan, the play's most sophisticated character, is decorated "*in a more trendy style with a brass bedstead and some interesting antique stuff*" (161). Similarly, the kitchens in *Absurd Person Singular* reflect those who own them. The modern conveniences in the spotless kitchen of the hustler Sidney Hopcroft and his meticulous wife Jane, with an automatic dishwashing machine and formica working surfaces, show his desire to impress as well as her compulsive tidiness. The Jacksons' messy kitchen, with equipment that has seen better days, discloses an unkempt couple whose marriage, like the husband's career, has also seen better days. Resonating the marriage of the oldest couple, the Brewster-Wrights, the kitchen of their archaic house, with heating that no longer works, has fallen apart through disuse or ill usage.

Each play in *The Norman Conquests* trilogy has a single set and action appropriate to it. While characters try to behave well at dinner in *Table Manners,* they argue, a woman spills wine on a man's trousers, and he hits her husband. In *Living Together,* characters play a board game and a husband and wife "live together," that is, have sex with each other (the only couple who does so, albeit between scenes, during the trilogy). In *Round and Round the Garden,* Norman's arrival at Annie's house begins the play and, circularly, his return to the house ends it; in addition, the assignation he makes with Annie, which heralds the action, he makes again near the conclusion.

The scenery of *How the Other Half Loves,* which simultaneously shows the homes of two families, exemplifies Ayckbourn's theatrical dexterity. Visualizing character and theme, one part of the set reflects the well-to-do life of an affluent, childless couple; the other, the unkempt, disorganized life of a lower-middle-class couple with a baby. While each part contrasts how the other half lives (different furnishings indicate different classes) and how it manages its love affairs, the two homes are not simply side-by-side mirrors. Each overlaps the other to a different degree in each scene: in one scene a three-seater settee has two cushions belonging to one home, in another scene two belonging to the other, in still another all three belonging to the same home. Since the two homes share the same space, characters from one pass through the other—as the adulterous spouse of one makes incursions into the other's territory.

The setting of *Taking Steps* is three stories of a large Victorian manor house, but all three are on the same stage floor. Characters mime walking upstairs and down, but though they are apparently on different floors, they are really on one level. The mere placement of characters in such a set creates comedy similar to that in *How the Other Half Loves.* In *Taking Steps,* when a woman supposedly on a story above the ground floor dances, she makes a man on the ground floor look up at the source of the noise. Later, when she leaps onto the floor, several people on the ground floor look up as a cloud of plaster descends from where the ceiling would be. However, the compressed three-story setting is more than a comic gimmick, for in this play, which is largely about marriage, it visualizes confinement. As the play's two women are in danger of being crushed by marriage, so is the house that traps them crushed into one floor. For this reason, the departure of one woman from the house (and marriage) displays freedom, while the hesitation of the other on the threshold of the door reflects frustration.

Ayckbourn associates different areas of the set with different characters— in *How the Other Half Loves,* not only pieces of furniture but also parts of the same furniture. In *Time and Time Again,* the set divides into three parts—

conservatory, back garden, and part of the recreation field—each connected to, thereby the domain of, one character. The conservatory is Graham's enclosed fortress, from which he spies on people in the garden. The local recreation ground, whose edge spills onto the garden, is the sportsman Peter's province, where his athletic skills make him master. When he persuades Leonard to play cricket, he distinguishes himself and Leonard proves inept. The garden, with a murky pond containing a stone gnome, is the area of the gnomelike Leonard, who dominates anyone entering it. Although Joan begins as Peter's girlfriend, her decision to stay in the garden hints that she will transfer her affections to Leonard, which she does. Leonard tempts her to remove her sandals and join him in the polluted pond, where they dance, then kiss, then kneel, observed by the voyeuristic Graham from the conservatory. A scene in *Body Language* has a radio reporter tape an interview with a frail, old surgeon in one area of the stage while in another area a photographer takes pictures of a gorgeous model who strikes a series of sexy poses. Tying both areas together, the old surgeon watches the model during his interview.

So important are Ayckbourn's settings that when a play transfers to a different type of stage, be may rethink the function of its scenery. The Scarborough set of *Woman in Mind* did not provide separate playing areas for Susan's real family and her fantasy family, though lighting and costumes differed for each. The result was so subtle a demonstration of her ideal world impinging on the actual world that until well into the first act one was uncertain whether her imaginary family were actually real. When the production, as in Scarborough directed by the author, transferred to a proscenium arch theatre in London, the scenery in the downstate area, a cramped garden, was drearily realistic, thus associated with Susan's actual family, whereas the upstage area, behind a scrim (theatrical gauze, opaque when lighted from the front, transparent when lighted from behind), was an enchanting garden with tall trees and statues, a fantasy world where, when the scrim rose, she retreated from the real world. Each set had virtues—the one, a clear visualization of the mixture of hallucination and reality; the other, a clear separation of the different parts of Susan's mind—and each was appropriate to the type of stage that employed it.

Costumes too convey visual information about character, most obviously Neville the dog, played by an actor in a dog suit, in *Mr A's Amazing Maze Plays,* a comedy for children. The first scene of *Relatively Speaking* has Greg find under Ginny's bed a pair of size ten slippers which, too large for his feet, have clearly been left by her former lover (literally and metaphorically, Greg is in another man's shoes). The next scene has him sit in one area of the stage while Philip, the former lover, enters in another, wearing a pair of gardening boots. Since this footwear differs markedly from anyone else's, it is prominent, as is its size, which is larger—size ten, one infers—than Greg's. In *Time and Time Again,* Leonard's ill-fitting cricket flannels and unsuitable sports coat, shirt, and cravat, incongruously matched with his cricket cap, proclaim his ineptitude at the sport. The morning after Norman and Ruth make love on the rug in *Living Together,* they rise and adjust their clothing. In performance, his apron is on backwards, requiring him to twist it around to cover the front of his trousers.² Sylvie Bell's costume at the end of "The Self-Improving Woman," in *Intimate Exchanges,* shows that while her self-esteem has grown she has not yet come into her own: *"She is dressed practically but her taste somewhat reflects Celia's influence"* (I, 128). After Guy Jones pockets a large bribe in *A Chorus of Disapproval,* he changes into the costume of the high-wayman Macheath. Before anyone in *A Small Family Business* accuses Yvonne of stealing the late grandmother's jewelry, spectators see her wearing more of it each time she reappears. Geain's rejection of her mother in *Henceforward . . .* is announced by her male costume and make-up: heavy boots, cord work pants padded at the crotch, an undershirt knotted with simulated chest hair, a blue chin for beard stubble.

Theatrically, Ayckbourn uses nonverbal sound as well as sight. In "Gosforth's Fête," when Milly interrupts Gosforth's examination of the sound system at the fête to confide that he has impregnated her, she so startles him that he drops the microphone. *"The jolt causes the mike to become live. We hear, distantly, their voices echoing away on a series of loudspeakers. They alone, in their concern, remain unaware of this"* (44–45). In *Season's Greetings,* as two characters begin to make love beneath a Christmas tree at night while others sleep, the man accidentally moves a parcel with an alarm clock that rings like a firebell, which wakes the household, then inadvertently pushes a button that prompts a toy drummer to play. *Mr A's Amazing Maze Plays* makes extensive use of nonverbal sounds. Since the title character, Mr Accousticus, cannot tolerate noise, he steals sounds and hides them in his house. Until he does so, birds sing, owls hoot, cats yowl, and thunder claps. Ayckbourn demonstrates Mr A in action. "Woof! Woof! Woof! Woof! Woof! Woof!" barks the dog, at which point "MR ACCOUSTICUS *stretches out his hand and points a finger at* NEVILLE. NEVILLE *continues to bark but slowly all the sound is drained away, until he is barking silently"* (30). When Suzy, the girl who owns the dog, sneaks into Mr A's house to retrieve Neville's bark, comedy derives chiefly from incongruous nonverbal sound effects. As she opens a trap door, for example, it moos like a cow; as a rat runs away it makes a noise like a racing car; as she plays notes on a piano it makes a gargling sound. When she finally locates Mr A's Cabinet of Sounds, she opens little drawers, from which emerge such noises as a burst of applause, a clucking chicken, a toilet flush, and Neville's bark. Upon Mr A's discovery of her in his house, she and Neville open as many drawers as they can, thereby creating a cacophony of sounds.

A striking example of theatricality developing dramatic action is the conclusion of *Woman in Mind,* which visually and audibly evokes Susan's mental breakdown. After a clap of thunder, her imaginary brother appears with an unopened umbrella, unaffected by the rain. When he opens it, it looks like a sunshade or parasol, and as he holds it over her head the weather changes to sunshine and birds sing. *"Everything from here on is in a slightly heightened colour and design, suggesting* SUSAN's *own extreme mental state"* (82). Her imaginary husband Andy calls up a brass band that strikes up a cheerful tune. Her real sister-in-law, suddenly pregnant, serves champagne in glasses with small frogs, miniatures of the stone frog in Susan's pond. Her real son, unskilled and about to leave for Asia, is dressed like a rickshaw driver. Despite a thunderclap (from the real world), the weather remains sunny (her hallucinatory world). Giving a speech that becomes unintelligible to the audience as well as to the characters on stage, she becomes illuminated by the reflection of an ambulance's flashing blue light. The others, frozen in the shadows, give no evidence that they see or hear her.

Henceforward . . . elaborately treats visual and nonverbal auditory theatrical elements to lure spectators into sympathizing with the protagonist, Jerome, a solipsistic composer. The way he uses people to create art, and the art that results from such manipulation, are so ingenious that they seduce audiences who might otherwise find him repugnant. The walls of his flat are filled with custom-built video and audio apparatus, including television screens that show telephone messages and visitors at the outside door, as well as a highly sophisticated recording and playback system. When a desperate friend leaves a message appealing for help, Jerome silently ignores him or fastforwards the videotape. Jerome's thoughtless treatment of a woman as if she were a robot is an extension of his treatment of a womanlike robot as a robot, which audiences accept partly because the latter is funny, partly because a robot is not a person. Although the woman objects to his having recorded their lovemaking for use in his art, a musical expression of love, his slowing down and speeding up of the sounds of love are so fascinating, even to her (at least initially), that one forgets his manipulation of human beings. At the play's conclusion, he receives an ultimatum: either return to his estranged wife and daughter or else remain with his machinery. Although he verbally chooses them, he actually opts for the machinery. While they wait outside, attacked by local thugs, he returns to the console where, rewinding the tape and replaying it in different speeds and tones, he samples, synthesizes, and creates choruses of the word "love." Oblivious to the destruction of his wife and child, interested only in his art, he creates, *"like a man possessed,"* a dazzling musical composition of love, which though a denial of human love is theatrically overwhelming. The play's final moment, after the music ends, is visually ironic: *"He sits all alone. And realizes how alone he is"* (98).

Despite the fact that Ayckbourn's plays require realistic acting and either realistic or suggestively realistic scenery, their realization on stage is not entirely illusionistic. He relies on both the sense of actuality (people behave as they would in real life) and the acknowledgment that such behavior occurs on a stage. In *How the Other Half Loves,* when two dinner parties in two homes on two evenings occur at the same time, one's enjoyment derives from the author's deft theatricality. With the different dining tables joined, the guests, William and Mary Featherstone, sit on swivel chairs that swing ninety degrees to take in both Frank and Fiona's section and Bob and Teresa's. The swift alternations between dinner parties is theatrical, though the actors perform realistically, and the alternations require from the Featherstones a "transformational" type of acting in which changes are not motivated realistically.[3] As they discuss Bob in the Philips' home, William picks up a glass from Fiona's drinks cabinet; instantly, they switch their conversation to the Fosters. Fiona serves avocado, but Teresa's entrance with a soup tureen impels the guests to swivel toward her. In a moment, Frank enters with a bottle of wine, prompting them to swivel toward him. The climax of the scene is a dizzying whirl of transformations and swivelings as the guests, with increasing rapidity, turn from one set of hosts to the other—the Philips argumentative, the Fosters poised—and William gets drenched from two different sources at once. Throwing soup at her husband, Teresa accidentally hits William, whereupon at the other party he gets wet because of a dripping toilet from the room directly above his chair.

Ayckbourn also employs transformational techniques in *Suburban Strains,* in which Caroline alternates between different people in two time periods. While she politely speaks to Miss Dent, lights change to a previous evening when Kevin sits on a sofa, his feet up. The moment Miss Dent stops talking, Caroline angrily tells Kevin to remove his feet from the sofa. As they argue, Miss Dent speaks, prompting Caroline, in a quick transformation, to respond politely to her.

The very set of *Way Upstream,* a boat on a river, is theatrical. Ayckbourn shrewdly prevents spectators from seeing the boat for ten pages: the play begins at night, and the sound of water lapping against the boat, with beams of flashlights and lights from portholes, suggestively evokes the craft. Whether or not the set has water, there is a theatrical tension between realistic performance, including pantomime that involves a character retreating from the dock area to convey the boat leaving shore, and the audience's knowledge that the boat it sees is in a theatre.

Mr A's Amazing Maze Plays possesses abundant theatricality. Before Neville becomes a man-size dog, Ayckbourn visualizes his growth as a puppy: increasingly large heads of glove puppets emerge from holes in increasingly large boxes. Furthermore, on numerous occasions after Suzy and her dog enter Mr A's house, the audience decides what Suzy and her dog should do. For instance, when she is unsure whether to go through a door or walk further along a hall, one of the play's two Narrators declare, "I think they should go that way." The other Narrator believes they should go the other way. "All those who think they should go along the hall," the First Narrator commands the spectators, "Hands up!" After members of the audience vote, the Narrators announce the winning decision, and Suzy and Neville go where directed.

Unexpectedly turning the theatre audience into an audience at a television studio, the final minutes of *Man of the Moment* are vividly and Pirandellianly theatrical. After one character is drowned in a swimming pool, part of which is onstage, the others begin to devise an explanation. Suddenly a TV floor manager enters, the lights contract to a small area on him, he tells the theatre spectators to stand by for a few seconds, and then he announces that the scene must be reshot. When the full stage lights go up again, different, more attractive actors play the characters, and the spectators see them perform a TV reenactment of—or rather a TV enactment that falsifies—the circumstances of the drowning. At the end of the TV version, the floor manager signals the play's spectators to applaud while music plays during the closing credits of the TV show. As they applaud, the stage actors take a curtain call. After they leave, the credits music stops, the floor manager thanks the audience, and at his signal *"The stage lights snap off to be replaced with the house lights"* (89).

Regardless of how few parts of the stage are used at a given time one is aware of the entire stage. Although cinema can, using a split screen, show the three bedrooms of *Bedroom Farce* at once, their deployment on singe is different. Cross-fades on the stage areas emphasize theatricality, thereby working against total illusion. However dim the lights on one or two bedrooms may be at any moment, they are still, as they are not in movies, visually present— therefore part of one's awareness. When characters in *A Small Family Business* appear in rooms of different houses or leave one house to enter another, one of the emphases is on theatre, since the house itself, in whoever's home a room of it may be, is physically the same.

As Ayckbourn remarks in his Preface to *Absurd Person Singular,* the dramatic possibilities of offstage action fascinate him. In *Relatively Speaking* and "Gosforth's Fête," he uses variants of the offstage hamper filled with broken glass to suggest a crash. In the former play, when Philip's wife calls to him that Miss Whittaker has arrived to see him, audiences hear *"A far away crash of falling garden tools"* (50). In the latter, a loud offstage crash reveals that the scaffolding, which Gosforth previously warned the children was unsafe, has collapsed. One scene of *The Revengers' Comedies* has an offstage motorcyclist drive around an onstage character, the sound of the engine circling him through speakers in different parts of the offstage and rear-of-auditorium areas. In *Time and Time Again,* an offstage cricket match occasionally spills onto the stage; in *Joking Apart,* offstage tennis games spill onstage; in *Sisterly Feelings,* onstage characters fly offstage kites. Though *Absurd Person Singular* makes more use of offstage action, Ayckbourn does so to focus on onstage response. Braying laughter of offstage party guests reveals bow entering characters respond to them. The ferocious dog who attacks anyone venturing outside the Jackson kitchen emphasizes how those in the kitchen cope with the threat.

The three plays of *The Norman Conquests* represent Ayckbourn's most elaborate use of offstage action, since what happens in one play intrudes upon the others, whose action may occur simultaneously. Near the end of the first scene of *Living Together,* for example, a drunken Norman, reacting to Annie's offstage rejection of him at Sarah's instigation, places a gramophone on a table, winds it up, starts the record, and sings with the vocal part: "Girls were made to Love and Kiss." He opens the door to the dining room, where everyone else has gone, and *"sings out"* to the people there, returning drunkenly to sing louder as the curtain falls (Acting Edition 14). At the end of the first scene of *Table Manners, "Norman is heard singing briefly from the sitting room— 'Girls were made to Love and Kiss.' Reg and Tom register."* At the end of the scene, they and Annie *"become helpless with stifled laughter"* as Norman sings, while an angry Sarah gazes witheringly at them (Acting Edition 17, 19).[4]

Because two actors play the ten characters of *Intimate Exchanges,* part of one's enjoyment of the work in the theatre is the skill with which they execute fast costume and wig changes offstage. Ayckbourn enhances the pleasure by having an offstage actor, while changing costume, talk to an onstage character before he or she reappears as a different person; enhances it further by having two offstage characters, played by the same actor, argue with each other; enhances it still further by having each of their heads pop out at intervals; enhances it further yet by having an onstage character listen to an offstage character played by the same actor (one's recognition that the offstage voice is recorded adds to the fun). Going beyond such stage devices, Ayckbourn seems to have two characters played by the same actress appear on stage at the same time. In "Affairs in a Tent," a berserk Celia bites Miles's leg. He topples over, they roll about, and he overpowers her. In the struggle, he pulls part of a long tablecloth off the serving table and, stifling her, wraps her in it, mummylike. When he calls for help, a woman, played by the actress who plays Celia, arrives and prods the wrapping which, with comic unexpectedness, squirms. Whether or not, or how soon, one realizes that someone has replaced Celia, comedy derives from adroit use of the stage, where one person cannot be in two places simultaneously.

Clearly, Alan Ayckbourn is a distinctively theatrical writer who designs his comedies for the stage, to be performed before people who are both audiences, receiving his plays through their ears, and spectators, whose comprehension derives from what they see. What they hear includes nonverbal sounds as well as language; what they see includes scenery, costumes, action, stage pictures, and visual emblems, sometimes ironic, but usually expressive of character, story, and theme. Ayckbourn extensively employs virtually all aspects of the theatrical medium as organic parts of his plays, in which the nonliterary elements merge with the literary. In Coleridge's terms, audiences do not believe in the illusion that what happens before their eyes is reality; rather, as he perceptively points out, they suspend their disbelief that they are in a theatre, thereby experiencing what he calls a negative illusion. Ayckbourn takes advantage of the negative illusion created by this suspension of disbelief to play upon the theatricality of the stage even as he induces spectators to accept what they see and hear as real. The tension between realism and theatricality characterizes the plays of Alan Ayckbourn, whose custom does not stale the seemingly infinitely variety with which he utilizes the medium of theatre.

NOTES

[1] So Penelope Keith performed the business in the first London production and the Thames TV production, which is now available on videocassette. The Acting Edition simply states, *"She folds the napkins into a 'shape'"* (33). The edition for the general public does not mention this business.

[2] This business, in the London and TV productions, is reflected in the Acting Edition of *Living Together,* p. 41.

[3] This type of acting characterized Joseph Chaikin's Open Theatre, in New York, which was well known in America and Europe partly through writings about it, partly through the international impact of its production of Jean Claude van Itallie's *America Hurrah!* in 1966, three years before Ayckbourn wrote *How the Other Half Loves.* Whether or not Ayckbourn consciously adapted transformational techniques, he could hardly have been unaware of them, and he remembers that he was familiar with *America Hurrah!* (see "An Interview with Alan Ayckbourn" in this volume).

[4] The Acting Edition is clearer than the edition for the general public, which states only that Norman *"starts to sing softly, then louder"* at the end of the scene in *Living Together* (111). At the end of the scene in *Table Manners,* the equivalent of the first stage direction is: "NORMAN *is heard singing briefly from the sitting room.* REG *and* TOM *register"* (38); the final direction is the same.

Works Cited

Ayckbourn, Alan. "Body Language." Rehearsal Script.

———. *A Chorus of Disapproval.* London: Samuel French, 1985.

———. *Confusions: Five Interlinked One-Act Plays.* London: Samuel French, 1977.

———. *Henceforward . . .* London: Faber & Faber, 1988.

———. *How the Other Half Loves.* London: Evans Plays, 1978.

———. *Intimate Exchanges.* 2 vols. London: Samuel French, 1985.

———. *Joking Apart, Ten Times Table, Just Between Ourselves.* London: Chatto & Windus, 1979.

———. *Man of the Moment.* London: Faber & Faber, 1990.

———. *Mr A's Amazing Maze Plays.* London: Faber & Faber, 1989.

———. *The Norman Conquests.* New York: Grove Press, 1979.

———. *The Norman Conquests* (Acting Edition). London: Samuel French, 1975.

———. *Relatively Speaking.* London: Evans Plays, 1978.

———. "The Revengers' Comedies." Rehearsal Script.

———. *Season's Greetings.* London: Samuel French, 1982.

———. *Sisterly Feelings & Taking Steps.* London: Chatto & Windus, 1981.

———. *A Small Family Business.* London: Faber & Faber, 1987.

———. *Suburban Strains.* London: Samuel French, 1982.

———. *Three Plays: Absurd Person Singular, Absent Friends, Bedroom Farce.* New York Grove Press, 1979.

———. *Time and Time Again.* New York: Samuel French, 1973.

———. *Way Upstream.* London: Samuel French, 1983.

———. *Woman in Mind.* London: Faber & Faber, 1986.

Watson, Ian. *Conversations with Ayckbourn.* London: Faber & Faber, 1988.

Empire of Light: Luminosity and Space in Beckett's Theater

William E. Gruber

The following essay attempts to clarify the ways Beckett used light and shadow to control space in his dramatic works. In it I discuss the connections between theatrical space and pictorial space as well as their relationship with Beckett's scenic light. The approach is more practical and formal than theoretical. I take Beckett at his word when he said he turned to theater because it was the most regular of all literary forms: "In the theater, one enters into a game, with its rules, and one cannot not submit oneself to them" (Abbott 124). But Beckett's turn to drama for the security of its "rules" has always been something of a paradox, mainly because from the outset he seems impatient with almost all of them. *Godot* begins with a negation of the genre itself, drama (from *dran,* a "doing"): "Nothing to be done." And much of the rest of his work with the form is a history of formal renunciations: along the way from *Godot* to *Not I, Breath,* and *Quad,* Beckett demonstrated that plays could be written without plot, characters, language, or referential content.

The result is a body of drama that seems abstract, essentialist, or minimalist. S. E. Gontarski has described Beckett's plays as the products of meticulous "lessenings" or "undoings"—a striving, in Gontarski's words, "toward simplicity, toward the essential, toward the universal" (Gontarski 3). And in fact one could describe Beckett's experimental "lessenings" of literary form as a kind of phenomenological reduction, a desire on the part of the writer to rid drama of everything but the thing itself. His "undoings" led Beckett to develop drama which is in effect more visual than verbal art. The only thing that could not be omitted from drama, it seems, is spectacle.

I am not saying merely that Beckett's plays are like pictures; that is by now a familiar comparison. But it is remarkable to see how many writers want to define Beckett's plays more as painting than literature.[1] And indeed, there seems good reason to do so. Apart from the more general claim that both arts, painting and theater, possess strong visual appeal, there is the specific sense that on Beckett's stage spectacle dominates language. But it is not clear what might motivate Beckett to want to make his plays into paintings in the first place. Furthermore, once we make the comparison, it is not certain what we've proved; even for a playwright with as deep a love as Beckett's for painting, it is an odd direction to want to take.

Think of the oversights inherent in the supposition that plays can resemble paintings. In the first place, there is a crucial problem with the idea that the two arts are in fundamental ways compatible. Much as one's instincts might support the claim that drama and painting are sister arts, it is not at all easy—as a history of vain attempts to do so shows—to make drama mainly a visual art. The common belief is that theater and painting can be brought easily into accord; both arts, after all, are things seen. But Lessing long ago challenged the analogy when he distinguished between the temporal arts, on the one hand, and spatial arts, on the other. Plays, like narratives, move in time; paintings stand outside it.[2] Among recent theorists, Seymour Chatman insists that "temporal" and "pictorial" are incompatible terms (Chatman, "What Novels Can Do" 122). Likewise Wendy Steiner: "The pictorial medium is temporally static," writes Steiner, "and thus painting has long stood as a symbol of the transcendent object—beautiful, outside of time's depredations, complete in itself" (Steiner, *Pictures* 1).

Despite their obvious spectacular component, then, in certain respects plays seem anti-pictorial almost by definition. The impulse to make the stage a picture is as old as Vitruvius but probably vain. It is not easy to achieve motion in painting, nor to arrest it in drama. As a matter of fact, a deeper relationship exists between drama and narrative than between drama and painting. For plays share with narrative some important features, among which are sequence, repeated subjects—characters—and temporality. The best one can do to make plays attain the status of paintings is to suspend temporarily all language, movement, and sequence, a kind of theatrical equivalent of poetic ekphrasis. But the medium of drama is ill-suited to stopped-action techniques; if nothing else, the long history on stage of "realizations," "tableaus," and "freezes" clarifies that pictorial form is at best a momentary ideal for the theater, not its fundamental condition. The analogy between drama and painting has a venerable tradition, to be sure, but its logic is simply not sound.

Beckett's concern with the visual element of drama is of course more than an interest in costuming or special effects; but neither is it, phrased more broadly, proof of Horace's famous simile, *ut pictura* poesis. Or at least it is not simply that. Beckett's plays are increasingly defined as charts for light and space. His texts define a unique aesthetics for the stage, what one might call simply the "lighted conditions" both of being and knowing. In *Play,* for example, light can be considered a material reality (it illuminates whoever happens to be speaking) or a representational metaphor for spiritual or transcendent values. But the hypnotic power of *Play* derives from the interaction of these two qualities of light. Light in *Play* is both the thing seen and the means of our seeing: as the medium by which we see, on stage as in real life, light makes things visible; it opens the staged world to view, highlights faces, casts shadows over objects, connects bodies and objects across space. As the object of our vision, however—to the extent that we are conscious of the moving light itself as one of the things seen—light becomes transformed into an element of the represented fictional world.

A search through Beckett's plays as well as narratives yields abundant references to light. In this and other of Beckett's works light seems to have an epistemological status—it is neither simply a material reality nor a metaphysical emissary. To perceive reality, which lies behind the incidental and changing elements of the material world, requires the gift of insight, a "looking into" which depends, it turns out, on an unreliable medium. By following Beckett's work with light and darkness over the range of his works for theater, therefore, we can gain a better sense of his concern with drama as spectacle.

I.

"One must understand [Beckett's theatre] as a deliberate and intense effort to make the body come to light" (Chabert 24). Pierre Chabert's words are instructive: in contrast to Beckett, most dramatists take light for granted as the sine qua non of theatrical performance. Playwrights record their texts on paper or on video screens, and, although they surely imagine their work as it might look on stage, in the act of creating their plays they pay little attention to light as the universal condition of spectators' experience. When light is mentioned in the text at all, either by way of dialogue or in the stage directions, it is normally independent of the light by which the action is viewed. In Shakespeare, for example, references to light or to darkness sometimes appear in order to create with words a generalized idea of time and place. King Claudius, unnerved by seeing Hamlet's players enact "The Murder of Gonzago," cries out for lights, even though he and Shakespeare's spectators are already fully exposed to daylight. Likewise Friar Laurence, as he gathers medicinal plants (*Romeo and Juliet* 3.3), comments at length how the sky above him grows bright with the dawn. It does not matter that both events take place—if we imagine performances in Shakespeare's time—under the ambient lighting of a London afternoon. In scenes such as these, to apply naturalist principles of dramaturgy, in which characters' comments about their environment must accord with the *mise-en-scene,* would be an error. Shakespeare's dramas are conceived to be free of the vagaries of ambient natural light. The morning light that illuminates Friar Laurence is fixed for all eternity by the words of the text, and it shines regardless of whether spectators sit in a darkened auditorium or in the haze of a British afternoon.

Incandescent lighting makes possible much more elaborate optics, but for the most part modern dramatists still imagine light to be a component of the narrative progression. In Ibsen's *Ghosts,* for example, Mrs. Alving's parlor light provides spectators an ongoing metaphor for her intellect, and in Brecht's *Galileo* the general dimming and brightening of the house lights stand for twilight and dawn in Renaissance Italy. It would be wrong to say that Brecht and Ibsen are not interested in incandescent light and lighting and their potential thematic or spectacular effects. But even dramatists who assume their works can make use of modern forms of illumination seldom make us conscious of viewed light or that we are viewing by means of light. Most playwrights still treat light and lighting effects as an occasional embellishment of the theatrical representation. The medium itself and the consciousness of its effects—the startling brilliance of a surface, the diffusion of luminosity through space, the sheer felt presence of light, its clarity or purity or its absence—are not normally part of playwrights' concepts of their work.

Beckett takes a position with regard to light which is at once more ambitious and more ambiguous. Certainly he seems enthralled by luminosity in general. Beckett's interest in light and luminosity is a fascination comparable to that of medieval aesthetic theorists. Light everywhere in Beckett is felt to be pure and simple; it is experienced as something immediate and meaningful, like the breathtaking account in *Company* of the consciousness of light:

> You lie in the dark and are back in that light. Straining out from your nest in the gorse with your eyes across the water till they ache. You close them while you count a hundred. Then open and strain again. Again and again. Till in the end it is there. Palest blue against the pale sky. You lie in the dark and are back in that light. Fall asleep in the sunless cloudless light. Sleep till morning light. (*Company* 25)

Over the thirty years in which Beckett wrote plays, his texts show an increasing preoccupation with the medium of perception, with light. References to light and darkness, to white and black and gray—but also to color—are almost obsessive features of all his writings. It is true that much of Beckett's work looks like a form of grisaille, but this does not negate the powerful element of genuine chromatic boldness one finds in many of the plays. In fact the colorless norms in Beckett may well represent a reciprocal coupling with bold—if severely limited—displays of light and color: the "superb surge of white" in Murphy's garret, the brilliant red of the Mouth in *Not I.* Even the subdued pastels of the womens' robes in *Come and Go,* in contrast with the surrounding deep shadow, give to those colors a luminous and sensuous beauty which is pure, simple, decisive.

Yet Beckett's esteem for glittering essences of light and color is not wholly reconcilable—neither aesthetically nor philosophically—with his fondness for dimness, shadows, and the dark. Darkness in Beckett is not merely a region where light does not extend, but a distinct zone with its own separate characteristics. Darkness provides relief; it consoles, it soothes, it heals. It seems to be a kind of sanctuary, whereas where there is light, there is often suffering, torture, even terror. A common experience of Beckett's characters is to suffer from exposure to intense beams of light. Beckett's characters dwell in realms where light is more often than not a source of annoyance, where darkness and shadow alone provide relief, and where visual information is ipso facto unbearable or unreliable. The difficulties imposed on characters and spectators alike by the varying and insubstantial illumination—"one sees little in this light," says Flo in *Come and Go* (*Shorter Plays* 195)—are telling illustrations of humans' proneness to error.

This skepticism with which Beckett regards light shows how far he is from any conception of light as simply a necessary medium for the staged action. But neither does he employ light only as a symbol or sign. Properly speaking, Beckett does not arrange light and dark according to a familiar language of polarities; much as the drama tends toward symbolism, Beckett's chiaroscuro does not simply represent good and evil, life and death, spirit and flesh, or heaven and hell. This is one of the several instances in which Beckett's work looks like allegory but isn't. To put it another way, the apparent polarities of light and dark in the texts are instances of Beckett's compositional simplicities, which upon inspection turn out to be not so simplistic.[3]

Beckett's fascination with light and luminosity, like his fondness for mathematics, proportion, and symmetries, connects his drama to the concepts of intelligible beauty and aesthetics articulated by ancient theorists. His own particular version of that body of theory, however, is unique and complex. Like a neo-Platonist Beckett accepts the fundamental nature of light. Time and again he makes it the central image for being and consciousness: in *Godot,* "They give birth astride of a grave, the light gleams an instant, than it's night once more" (*Godot* 57); in *Breath,* between the initial and terminal cries (birth and death?), the light waxes and then slowly wanes.

But Beckett's concept of light is allied also to Manichaeism as well as to Plato and medieval philosophers. Light is not necessarily "being" or "insight" or "understanding"—or it is not only being or insight or understanding—and as a result light has quite a different meaning in Beckett from what it means, for instance, to the neo-Platonists. He stops well short of the clarity associated with light by Plato, Augustine, or Bacon.

In short, Beckett often makes us aware of light both as object of our seeing and as agent of it. Paul Klee once said that art does not show the visible but instead (and much more important) "renders visible," so that art makes us able to see things not seen otherwise. In other words, art is given the structure of thought. In much the same way, Beckett's theater becomes a sustained meditation on the phenomenology of seeing and knowing. This is the reason that light in Beckett's theater is at once agent of vision and object of vision, at once visible and the source of its own visibility. It expresses a duality which has no parallels in language, for it is governed both by philosophical as well as physiological principles. Especially in the television plays, where Beckett's control over the medium of light reaches its extreme, the coupled rhythms of light and shadow create the structural equivalents of an epistemology.

II.

Many of Beckett's plays seem to originate as experiments with light and luminosity rather than as propositions of narrative or character. As the control of light is the foundation in painting of the depiction of space, so in Beckett's late theater light modulation increasingly gives rise to "pictorial" effects. To see this shift from narrativity toward pictorialism we might briefly compare Beckett's lighting notes from some early plays with the notes from several later works. For example, the relatively early *Act Without Words I* (1956) specifies that the entire work be performed under a uniform "dazzling light" (*Shorter Plays* 43). Here the playwright has little use for subtlety or gradations; the absolute clarity of extreme and unvarying luminosity better suited his purpose. In this play, the stage and the objects on it have the same properties as they have in the real world. Their distances from one another and from the viewer, their relative sizes, and the space they inhabit all appear continuous with the rest of the world. Under such lighting conditions, the "dramatic illusion" appears to have both depth and physical reality. The player is seen within the confines of a coherent three-dimensional space where all the participating elements combine.

On the other hand, in the notes for lighting in some of the later plays, there seems to be an attempt to reconfigure three-dimensional space by means of light. A great many of Beckett's works for the stage (for example, *Krapp's Last Tape* or *Rockaby*) depend on narrow streams of artificial light that shine through space. In *Krapp's Last Tape,* Krapp works at his table under a "strong white light" while the rest of the stage is dark (*Shorter Plays* 55). It is clear from Beckett's production notes that this is no mere spotlight emanating from an overhead light board; the light itself is part of the play, and its luminosity is written into the text. Krapp himself refers to it; the thirty-nine-year-old Krapp calls a "new light" above his table "a great improvement" (*Shorter Plays* 57). Moreover, the light seems to express elemental states of Krapp's being. He takes pleasure in moving to and fro from light to dark to light again, and these movements are correlated with movements of his spirit. Being in the light seems to represent self-consciousness (or, perhaps, the "agony of perceivedness," such as experienced by O in *Film* or by the actors in the mime, *Act Without Words*). Darkness, on the other hand, brings Krapp relief. The dark is a region to which Krapp escapes; "I love to get up and move about in it," he says, "then back here to . . . [hesitates] . . . me" (*Shorter Plays* 57).

But the light which illuminates Krapp—because it illuminates a space for an actor's performance—can never be exclusively pictorial. Given the obvious symbolic significance of the light which shines on Krapp, the mundane significance of that same light on stage is easy to overlook. Nevertheless, light and shadow on this stage—as on any other stage—are perceived first (and mainly) as natural phenomena. Light reveals objects, and objects, in turn, are defined by their interruption of light. Whatever happens to come into view on stage, as in the real world, we view necessarily by means of light. Its presence is assumed as part of the unspoken structure of this play world or of any play world. On occasion—Claudius shouting for lights at the end of the dumb show in Hamlet is one such example—we can respond powerfully to light as part of the virtual world of the drama. But when light is not consciously invoked— even though sophisticated lighting has long been considered essential to most performances—it normally acts on stage as it acts offstage, revealing everything without yet revealing itself.

Thus Krapp's "new light"—because it shines on a real man on a real stage—cannot function purely within a world of signs. Although it modifies the stage space, it can never completely eliminate it. On the page, the light clearly stands in for the various movements of the protagonist's mind and spirit. On stage, however, our perception of it shifts considerably. There its luminosity is mainly actual, not part of the language of art. Directed simultaneously downward and outward, the light above Krapp's table creates zones of illumination and shadow that define man and table and floor as a single spatial continuum. Objects interrupt the light, shadows flee it. This play of strong light and distinct shadows establishes distinct relationships and connects figures and objects across space. Like linear perspective in painting, therefore, this unidirectional stream of light heightens our sense of the represented world's solidity; Krapp's space is real to a degree that cannot be paralleled in any purely linguistic or painterly medium. The light acts on us unconsciously as a means of orientation, and it guarantees the reality of the stage space. Unlike the space depicted in a picture, this space can be walked.

Beckett seems to he fully aware of the gross material reality of Krapp's space, and there are indications that he wishes to make use of it, as if to test its rules and limits. He calls for his protagonist to pace at the edge of the stage, to eat bananas, to slip clumsily on a banana peel, to toss one of the skins into the pit. Beckett is sometimes praised for his keen appreciation of the theater's concreteness; writing about *En attendant Godot,* Alain Robbe-Grillet "likened the effect to Heidegger's description of life on earth as a kind of raw thereness" (Abbott 46). But the pratfalls in *Krapp's Last Tape* point to a potential source of friction between the actor's "thereness" and the playwright's pictorial aesthetic. The text here constantly reminds us that the art we are watching is not pictorial but theatrical, one which includes movements, gestures, bodies moving in time and moving through space.

If we compare the lighting and the spatial arrangements in the early and late plays, then, some of the familiar differences between them take on new interest. It is common to note that one of the main differences between the early plays and Beckett's later dramas is that the latter abandon even minimal attempts to depict scenic space. A second commonplace is that the strong lighting effects of the early plays tend to give way toward a middle range of illumination, a "subdued light," according to Garner, "that only imperfectly illuminates the objects as inhabitants of the mise-en-scene" (Garner 355).

These developments are often taken to signify Beckett's growing impatience with mimesis, but the shift may be more formal than philosophical. Dim light makes it hard for viewers to orient bodies and objects in space; the more difficult it is to perceive gradations of light and shadow, the harder it is to derive visual information that tells us we are viewing objects with the same spatial properties they have in the real world. Although it seems hostile, the space we see in *Act Without Words I* looks walkable. Watching it, we recognize the stage space as a continuation of our world, and we know that we could enter it easily. On the other hand, the interior depicted in *Nacht und Traüme* lacks materiality; it has depth but not physical reality. A, the dreamer, is positioned in the left foreground, "faintly lit," while B (the dreamt self) appears to sit at a table resting "on an invisible podium about four feet above floor level, middle ground, well right of centre" (*Shorter Plays* 305). Light for the scene ("evening light" in an empty room) comes from a single window "set high in the back wall" (*Shorter Plays* 305). At first glance the framed image looks like the common Cartesian grid that brings together viewer and pictorial space; we glimpse what appears to be the interior space of a closed room. The viewer sees the represented shapes as having the same spatial relations and properties as in the real world, and the position of figures in relation to the ground follows pictorial convention. According to these conventions, the frontal plane—television's equivalent of the invisible "fourth wall," stands for the vertical dimension, while the apparent surface of the screen renders the third dimension. Position up or down on this screen, then, as in a perspective painting, serves mainly to identify whether an object is relatively nearer or further from the frontal plane and the viewer.

But subsequent images in this drama are not at all consistent with the coherent spaces of conventional televised interiors. One of the most striking features of *Nacht und Traüme* is that the play involves no continuous illusion of depth. After the evening light fades and a soft male voice hums the final bars of Schubert's "Lied, Nacht und Traüme," the screen fades down on A so that he is "minimally lit" (*Shorter Plays* 305) as he sleeps and dreams. The light then fades up on B, the dreamt sell positioned "on an invisible podium about 4 feet above floor level, middle ground, well right of centre. He is seated at a table in the same posture as A dreaming, bowed head resting on hands, but left profile, faintly lit by kinder light than A's" (*Shorter Plays* 305). It is another of Beckett's familiar mirror images, but there are significant differences between this image and the twinned old men in, say, *Ohio Impromptu*.

In the first place, the image is structured so as to contain some important ambiguities. B is actually meant to be the prominent figure, which means that his central position on the screen (further up and nearer the center, in contrast to the minimally lighted figure at lower left) is intended to convey the impression of his importance. He appears to float suspended above the dreamer (and the invisible podium on which he rests is crucial for this effect), although his position, "middle ground," would tend to locate him closer to the back wall. It is an archaic depiction of space, and functions—in a way that would not be possible on a stage—as if B and A exist in depthless projection. The same flattened effect exists in the interchange between B and the hands, L and R. The hands appear from the dark "beyond and above" B's bowed head, and occasionally he lifts his head and gazes at them, but he can do this only if the image is read in straight, depthless projection. By the logic of the room as it should appear if its depth were depicted on the screen, the apparitions are behind the dreamt self's line of sight.

Beckett seems over the course of his career increasingly impatient not only with the material presence of the actor but also with the amplitude of the represented space. It is worth stressing at this point the simple difference between the representations of space on stage and inside a picture. The former is real and invitatory, the latter illusory and exclusive. In theory any stage "picture" can legitimately be imagined from a position within it, whereas (as Rudolph Arnheim observes) "any attempt at interpreting pictorial space the way it would be seen by a hypothetical viewer inside the picture would intolerably contradict the perspective demanded of the actual viewer standing in physical space outside the picture" (Arnheim 51).

The intractable depth of stage space bears on another feature of Beckett's work, his well-known tendency to suppress actors' bodies. The problem of how to mingle real bodies with artificial spaces is one of the recurring conceptual problems of the modern stage, and its solution often results in a wholesale rejection of realistic acting styles. Early modernist solutions to the problem of the theater's real bodies and real spaces were twofold: on the one hand, mechanical figures substituted for human bodies so as to make the figure more consistent with an artificial ground; on the other, playwrights and theorists such as Gordon Craig and Adolphe Appia insisted vigorously that the stage was actual and not a site for mimesis.

In Beckett's endeavors to bring the actor and the actor's space into pictorial harmony, lighting becomes crucial. Where we cannot find familiar coordinations of light and space, the basis for normal perception will be lacking. The stage, by a process of adaptation, becomes increasingly a pictorial field, an image of two dimensions in a three-dimensional world.

Beckett's interest in limiting the degree to which light creates space appears to be a point of departure between the early plays, which tend to emphasize actors' real physical plights, and most of the later works, which focus typically on characters' inner worlds. For example, in the later *Come and Go* (1965), the figures are illuminated by a soft light concentrated only on the playing area; shining from above, it engenders on their bodies marked areas of penumbra and darker shade. Thanks to the shadows they cast, the three figures, like three pieces of sculpture, clearly dominate a region of real space; their grouping is conditioned by a kind of instinct for ideal sculptural form.

In marked contrast, however, the unlit area beside and behind the women allows each briefly to depart from illumination. Here the movement from light to dark is different from in *Krapp's Last Tape.* Krapp disappears from time to time to fetch himself more tapes or more drink, and so his comings and goings enhance one's sense of his body's material reality. When he is not visible, spectators understand that he is somewhere else. He walks to another portion of his habitat, he makes noises, and he returns to view, like a character in a conventional naturalist play, with evidence of his having been gone. But the women's disappearances in *Come and Go* do not signify the body's movements in space. No sounds emanate from the darkness to give reality to the space they visit; when they return, unlike Krapp, they bring back no traces of their presence elsewhere.

The women's successive disappearances are conceived according to a different visual schematics. Deep darkness surrounds the lighted playing area, a darkness which is neither offstage nor yet part of the scene. It is not a negative "ground" for what is situated in front of it is but a depthless surface, and as such it serves to deny the heavy materiality of their figures when they are seated in the light. This is surely the reason that Beckett suggests the women may disappear behind screens or drapes only if the light cannot be sufficiently contained on a small region of the stage. If the performance is to be effective there can be no spillage whatsoever of light onto the "black beyond"; even house exit lights normally provide too much illumination. The figures when they vanish must vanish as if by a sudden failing of our perception. Where there is no light there is no shadow, hence no location in space. The woman who steps "without sound of feet" out of the light is neither offstage, therefore, nor—like Krapp—in another part of the house; she is simply gone, absent, not there. The success of *Come and Go,* in other words, depends to a great extent on whether the stage space can "depict" spacelessness, and that effect, in turn, depends mainly on whether or not parts of the stage can be made completely dark. Much the same is true of *Not I,* which requires that all that we see on stage is Mouth, appearing to float in a depthless void, as if the stage were a uniform frontal display.

III.

When Beckett composes for television, he seems particularly interested to take advantage of its inherent two-dimensionality. In the works for television Beckett typically specifies with even greater detail the source and quality of light by which objects are seen. In *Quad, Nacht und Traüme,* and . . . *but the clouds* . . . the light appears from a single source high above; it is "dim" in *Quad,* "evening light" from a high back window in *Nacht und Traüme,* and in . . . *but the clouds* . . . it ranges from "deep shadow" at the periphery of the set to a maximum of brightness at the center. The issue is not only one of the artist's control of his medium. Beckett must have been attracted especially to the television image because of its flatness. Unlike images on film, which are illuminated by means of a strong light which penetrates the negative and so lends to the image the illusion of great depth of field, the television image is backlighted and fluoresces. The most striking quality of the television image is its inherent depthlessness. In contrast to stage plays, where the character is inevitably seen within a perfect depth of field, and where that figure therefore inevitably must appear bound together with its ground, on television the relationship between figure and ground can appear to disintegrate.

The luminosity peculiar to the television screen permits Beckett to shift his work to a drama more dependent on image. In *Ghost Trio* the narrative voice prescribes in great detail the quality and intensity of the light within which objects and events are to be seen: "The light: faint, omnipresent. No visible source. As if all luminous. Faintly luminous. No shadow. [Pause.] No shadow. Colour: None. All grey. Shades of grey. [Pause.] The colour grey if you wish, shades of the colour grey" (*Shorter Plays* 248). This is not simply a general dimming-down of ambient light; by denying shadows and making "all luminous" Beckett denies represented space to an extent that is unprecedented for a dramatist. It is as if the playwright turns from theater toward a medium of pure surface where all the elements of the image—even the light by which it is seen—are made to display the radiance of light.

Illumination from above renders objects more as surfaces than volumes, and it tends to make them seem to float freely in space, detached from their immediate environment. But the most striking aspect is the division of space into multiple planar units which can be repeated and combined in new relations. Plot and space are no longer primary in this theater; patterned repetition and a shadowless gray light deny them. Beckett is telling us instead to think of drama as having the same power as a photograph or a painting to suspend time and narrativity.

Instead of depicting a character who inhabits a portion of a fluent and continuous space, Beckett presents his figure as if in hieratic isolation. He makes little attempt to depict a coherent environment on stage, and the few common elements of the set—door, window, mirror, pallet, floor—are viewed with such extreme scrutiny that they seem alien. Walls, doors, floors, and windows—the basic compositional elements of the realist set—lose their volume, color, and familiar pictorial values. At the same time against this neutral ground there is a corresponding intensification of the human figure that reminds one in certain respects of early Christian aesthetics. Motion becomes arrested; gestures are at once stiffened and yet made more clearly expressive; and light and shadow begin to function as sources of artistic meaning. Perhaps most important, the abundance of repetitions substitute for narrative an expressly pictorial aesthetic. The old naturalist scene for drama, the room which we view by means of an invisible fourth wall, is denatured, made archaic, so that it looks less and less like the prototype from which it ultimately derives and more and more like part of a compositional motif. It is as if the life of F—did ever any protagonist have less to do?—were organized according to a visual pattern in which gestural repetition and not novelty were the motivating force.

The five works composed expressly for television seem to offer Beckett even greater freedom to control and perfect the visual image. On a small television screen, these five works are (in Jonathan Kalb's description) "jewels of astonishing precision" (*Beckett in Performance* 95). Such perfection of image does not seem possible on the stage, which is perhaps why, toward the end of his career, Beckett seemed to move decisively toward television as his preferred medium. This point is worth making because some commentators have tried to explain Beckett's preferences for television mainly as a result of his desire to eliminate the inevitable differences or errors that creep into live performances. Of course this distinction between stage and screen is valid. It matters a great deal who plays the woman in *Not I* or *Rockaby,*[4] and even an actor supremely dedicated to Beckett's texts—and Billie Whitelaw is surely that actor—cannot repeat a performance night after night. But Beckett's preference for television over theater seems to me to have more to do with the quality of his imaginings of his work. The plays for television have been so completely "visualized" as pictures that it is all but impossible for them to survive transplantation to a dimensional world. Indeed virtuality is the primary quality of the medium of television, a quality which distinguishes it even from film or photography. When we watch television, says David Cook, "neither movement nor screen are materially 'there' before us" (*Narrative Film* 2).

Thus it is important to stress that much of Beckett's success in this medium depends on formal differences between stage and film and television. One of the best ways to see the difference between stage and screen is to compare the different versions of works Beckett adapted to television, especially *Not I* and *What Where.* In the switch from stage to television screen, the stage "picture" typically contracts. *Not I* (1972; television version, 1977) provides an excellent example. Written originally for two players, Mouth and an Auditor who stands downstage audience left, *Not I* was filmed by the BBC with Beckett's supervision. In the stage version, the audience witnesses a dialectic between

Mouth and Auditor. Mouth seems tiny, forlorn, suspended in darkness eight feet high, stage right; the full body of Auditor, meanwhile, visually completes the stage picture. The Auditor—a tall, robed figure, "sex indeterminate"— stands on a four-foot podium and stares intently at Mouth during the whole of her outburst. Four times during the monologue—at moments timed precisely to match Mouth's crises—the figure gestures in "helpless compassion." In the theater, therefore, Auditor forms an important part of the stage picture. The tall standing figure both complements and anchors the image of the free-floating Mouth. It is an ironically elemental drama: protagonist and antagonist meet in an undefined public place, yet seem unable to interact.

All this changes in the version for television. The most obvious difference is the disappearance of the Auditor: the figure simply vanishes. His presence, writes Tom Bishop, would have been a "visual intrusion" on the television screen ("Beckett Transposing" 169). Vanishing with the Auditor is any sense of space or location; despite Beckett's deliberate ambiguities of time and place, the staged version of *Not I*—precisely because it is staged—has the illusion of dimensional reality that appears to surround all natural objects. When the play is transferred to the television screen, however, because of the disappearance of the Auditor, space is denied. The vanishing Auditor takes with him (or her) any grounds for believing that events occur in a world with light and space. At the same time the Auditor vanishes, the camera moves in to focus exclusively on Mouth in grotesque close-up. The difference between the stage image and the televised image is extreme; spectators' most common reaction to it is amazement, even shock. "Here the mouth in close-up became a truly horrifying, menacing organ," writes Martin Esslin; "with the tongue moving between the teeth, it was downright obscene, a kind of 'vulva dentata'" ("Beckett and the Mass Media" 214).

The works composed for television, on the other hand, fare poorly whenever they have been performed as live theater. "One occasionally comes across a stage adaptation of *Eh Joe* or *Quad*," writes Kalb, "but such productions do not provide the same experience as the works in their intended medium" (*Beckett in Performance* 95). The figures of *Quad* and *What Where* are conceived to dwell on a flat surface, backlighted and fluorescent, quite separate from the dimensional world of the viewer. On the screen, they project a ghostly depthlessness; they move in a kind of spaceless no man's land. In contrast, once those figures are placed on a stage in front of an audience, their material reality cannot help but be disappointing.

At the end of his book *Beckett/Beckett,* Vivian Mercier speculated that "the brevity of the latter works is due not to any philosophical aspiration towards silence but to . . . perfectionism: the only perfectly finished piece of workmanship is the miniature" (237). This seems to me accurate but less than complete. The brevity of the later works is connected also with Beckett's growing dissatisfaction with the medium of drama. It seems clear that his plays for television in some ways comprise a break from his work for the stage, just as his work for the stage, once, offered him relief from his dissatisfactions with narrative. There is nothing particularly surprising, after all, about artists who are skeptical of their habitual medium. In the case of the theater, at least, a measured amount of loathing for the stage may well be an important ongoing source of theater art. Like Jonson, Beckett seems philosophically hostile toward actors, mistrustful of histrionics, skeptical of the theatrical principles of movement and metamorphosis. Like Jonson, too, Beckett seems in many respects a dramatist in spite of himself. His turn from narrative to drama during the writing of *The Unnamable* has been said to result from his deep doubts about the worth of language and linguistic forms; his turn late in his life from drama to television seems to suggest similar dissatisfactions of an artist with his medium, as if theater, like narrative, provided him no lastingly satisfactory formal ground.

NOTES

[1] See, for example, Martin Esslin, "A Poetry of Moving Images," in Beekett *Translating/Translating Beckett,* eds. Alan Warren Friedman, Charles Rossman and Dana Scherzer (University Park: Penn State UP, 1987); and Stanton B. Garner, Jr., "Visual Field in Beckett's Late Plays," *Comparative Drama* 21 (1987–88): 349–75. In *Just Play: Beckett's Theater* (Princeton: Princeton UP, 1980), Ruby Cohn cites Billie Whitelaw's statement that Beckett "writes paintings" (p. 31).

[2] The distinction between spatial and temporal arts is perhaps not as clear-cut as Lessing imagined it. Nevertheless, as Wendy Steiner argues in *The Colors of Rhetoric* (Chicago: U of Chicago P, 1982), "Despite the modification of Lessing's position made by phenomenology, physiological psychology, and critics such as [Joseph] Frank, modern theory has not been able to overcome certain spatial-temporal barriers between painting and literature" (39).

[3] See, for example, James Knowlson, *Light and Darkness in the Theatre of Samuel Beckett* (London: Turret Books, 1972). Knowlson identifies light and dark (along with the intermediary gray) as "figurative modes of expressing different strata of inner mental experience" (p. 18).

[4] Even the highly mechanized *Rockaby* varies from night to night; in the documentary film made for the play's premier, its director, Alan Schneider, concedes that some rhythms and cadences differ slightly from one performance to another. And there are major differences between two of Whitelaw's taped performances, one filmed in Buffalo, New York, in 1981, and the other in 1984 at the Samuel Beckett Theater in New York City. See Kalb, *Beckett in Performance,* pp. 14–15.

Works Cited

Abbott, H. Porter. *Beckett Writing Beckett.* Ithaca: Cornell UP, 1996.

Amheim, Rudolph. *The Power of the Center.* Berkeley: U of California P, 1982.

Beckett, Samuel. *The Collected Shorter Plays.* New York: Grove Press, 1984.

———. *Company.* New York: Grove Press, 1980.

———. *Waiting for Godot.* New York: Grove Press, 1954.

Bishop, Tom. "Beckett Transposing, Beckett Transposed: Plays on Television." *Beckett Translating/Translating Beckett.* Eds. Alan Warren Friedman, Charles Rossman, and Dina Sherzer. University Park: Penn State UP, 1987. 167–73.

Chabert, Pierre. "The Body in Beckett's Theatre." *Journal of Beckett Studies* 8 (1982): 23–28.

Chatman, Seymour. "What Novels Can Do That Films Can't (and Vice Versa)." *Critical Inquiry* 7, 1 (1980): 121–40.

Cook, David A. *A History of Narrative Film.* New York: Norton, 1981.

Esslin, Martin. "A Poetry of Moving Images." *Beckett Translating/Translating Beckett.* Eds. Alan Warren Friedman, Charles Rossman, and Dina Sherzer. University Park: Penn State UP, 1987. 65–76.

———. "Telling It How It Is: Beckett and the Mass Media." *The World of Samuel Beckett.* Ed. Joseph H. Smith. Baltimore: Johns Hopkins UP, 1991. 204–16.

Garner, Stanton B., Jr. "Visual Field in Beckett's Late Plays." *Comparative Drama* 21 (1987–88): 349–73.

Gontarski, S. E. *The Intent of Undoing in Samuel Beckett's Dramatic Texts.* Bloomington: Indiana UP, 1985.

Kalb, Jonathan. *Beckett in Performance.* Cambridge: Cambridge UP, 1989.

Mercier, Vivian. *Beckett/Beckett.* New York: Oxford UP, 1977.

Steiner, Wendy. *The Colors of Rhetoric.* Chicago: U of Chicago P, 1982.

———. *Pictures of Romance.* Chicago: U of Chicago P, 1988.

The Romans in Britain: Aspirations and Anxieties of a Radical Playwright

Robert F. Gross

I

> [D]rama in England has always at its best had a certain looseness of structure;
> one might almost say that the English drama did not outlive the double plot.
> The matter is not only of theoretical interest; it seems likely that the double
> plot needs to be revived and must first be understood.
>
> (Empson 27–28)

In 1935, Empson's suggestion that a revival of the double plot might help revive English drama fell on deaf ears. The playwrights of that decade, such as Noël Coward, Terence Rattigan, J. B. Priestley and Emlyn Williams, still relied heavily on the tight, well-made structures handed down to them by Pinero, Henry Arthur Jones and Somerset Maugham. It was not until over twenty years later, during the innovative early years of the English Stage Company and the "Angry Young Men," that the English stage began to rediscover the theatrical possibilities of the double, or even multiple, plot. During these years, the influence of Bertolt Brecht's epic dramaturgy began to make its presence felt, not only by an interest in the German playwright's own work but also in the work of earlier English dramatists that could be seen as precursors of epic drama, most notably Shakespeare and Ben Jonson. John Arden's 1956 *The Waters of Babylon,* a modern citizen comedy of almost Jonsonian complexity, was perhaps the first indication of this new strain of experimentation, and his later works—including *The Workhouse Donkey, Armstrong's Last Goodnight,* and the ambitious *Island of the Mighty* trilogy (written in collaboration with Margaretta D'Arcy)—helped blaze a trail away from well-made dramaturgy toward more open and episodic forms. David Rudkin's *The Sons of Light,* Peter Barnes's *The Disenchanted,* Barrie Keefe's *A Mad World, My Masters,* and Edward Bond's *Early Morning, Lear,* and *The Sea* all weave multiple lines of action together, and thus achieve a complexity of plot structure seen only on the London stage of 1935 in classical revivals.

Howard Brenton's *The Romans in Britain* is a particularly bold experiment in multiple plots, because it weaves together stories from three different historical periods, separated by centuries: the Roman invasion of Britain in 54 BC; the Saxon invasion, in AD 515; and an incident in English-occupied Northern Ireland, in AD 1980. Apart from a single incident at the end of the first act, these three plots have no causal effect on each other. Each plot unfolds independently, with cuts from one to the other determined by thematic considerations, rather than plot.

Brenton's use of time, however, differs fundamentally from the kind of temporal disjunction found in cleverly plotted theatrical entertainments such as Peter Shaffer's *Equus* or Tom Stoppard's *Artist Descending a Staircase,* in which the audience is led to abstract a *fabula* (a chronologically ordered, causally linked, chain of events) from the temporally disjointed plot (Elam 119–126). These plays derive their form from the ratiocinative tale, in which the reader is held in suspense, waiting for the privileged piece of information that will complete the causal chain. In *The Romans in Britain,* on the other hand, the audience is not held in suspense by carefully withheld information; cuts are not made from one scene to another in order to keep the audience mystified. Each one of the play's three historical segments unfolds in strictly chronological order, with no important causal links obfuscated by Brenton to create suspense. Each is coordinated with the others within a single, overarching narrative that begins with the depiction of a society's inability to resist imperialist oppression, through increasingly powerful acts of revolt, to the tentative formation of an alternative society, articulating for the first time the myth of its golden age.

Part One of *The Romans in Britain* tells the story of the Roman invasion of Britain, and unsuccessful acts of resistance to it. It begins with two criminals in flight, Conlag and Daui. They come upon the fields of the Celtic tribe, where Daui is slain by youths and his blood used as a sacrifice. Conlag continues his flight in the company of a slave.

Envoys from a neighbouring bring news to the matriarch: the Roman armies are on their way. She insults them and ridicules their repeated assertions, but later reveals in private that they are correct. She has already reached a secret agreement with another tribe that has been forced to cooperate with the Romans; because of kinship ties, she has decided to go along with them and not oppose the invading army.

Three young Celtic brothers swim and frolic naked on the river bank, completely ignorant of the Roman threat. Three Roman soldiers enter, kill two of them, and stun, lacerate and sexually molest the third, a young Druid named Marban. When Marban returns to consciousness, he suddenly speaks in Latin, a fact that so surprises the soldiers that they take him to Caesar's camp. In the camp, we learn that the local tribe, despite its secret pact, has been massacred by the Romans. Caesar ties a figure of Venus around Marban's neck, explaining that "there are new Gods now. Do you understand? The old Gods are dead" (49), and releases him. Marban returns to his fellow Celts, explains the impossibility of resisting the Romans, and commits suicide.

Meanwhile, Conlag, still in flight with the Slave, believes he has come to the borders of a mythical land of plenty. The Slave, whom he has raped, kills him with a stone. "Now home is where I have a stone in my hand," she exults (56). Suddenly, Caesar and his soldiers reappear, this time in British army uniforms of the late 1970s. She is told to drop the stone, refuses, and is shot. The act ends, transforming a successful, though minor, act of revolt in 54 BC to a senseless loss of life in contemporary Britain.

While Part One dramatizes the hopelessness of life for those oppressed people who have no sustained and unified vision that will allow them to successfully resist their oppressors, Part Two dramatizes the hope and personal growth that come with resistance. This part alternates between scenes from the Saxon invasion in 515 and an incident on the Irish border in 1980. The Saxon scenes follow two groups of characters: a Celtic peasant, named Cai, and his daughters, Morgana and Corda; and a Roman aristocrat, dying of yellow plague, attended by her paramour/steward and two cooks. Cai, as oblivious to the import of the Saxon invasion as his ancestors were to the Roman one, insists that human sacrifices and idol worship will keep them safe. Desperate to save her own life, Corda kills him, and takes his hidden store of gold to support her and her sister in their flight from the invading troops. The Steward, out of similar motives, robs and kills his mistress. The two cooks and the two daughters meet up, and form a group that will evade the Saxons. The contemporary plot tells the story of Thomas Chichester, a British intelligence agent assigned to assassinate a leader of the IRA. Racked with guilt, he reveals his true identity to the local IRA leaders, and shares his vision of peace with them. Untouched by the liberal sentimentality of the oppressor, they kill him.

The First Part reiterates the defeat of the less powerful at the hands of those more powerful than they: the fugitive Irishman killed by the Celts, the Celts killed by the Romans, the female slave raped by the male criminal, the Irish girl shot by the British soldier. The slave's killing of her rapist, Conlag, is the only successful action of revolt. The Second Part shows the defeat of authority figures by those beneath them in the social hierarchy. The power of these characters has become largely illusory. Adona, the Roman aristocrat, has been dispossessed of her land, has fallen victim to plague and has only her memories of power. Her physical death merely confirms her political obsolescence. "We are ghosts," she admits. "Roman standards lie rotting on the ground. We stoop to pick them up. Our hands pass through them, like smoke" (87). Cai, the sexually abusive father, has only conventional wisdom and superstition to protect him, and cannot even physically defend himself against his daughter's attack; patriarchal power is revealed as a sham.

Chichester, a more complex character than either Cai or Adona, is destroyed by his own sense of guilt at the role England has played in Ireland. For him, the English appropriation of the Celtic myth of Arthur as a myth of its owns imperialism has become a symbol of modern England's blindness to its own history: "If King Arthur walked out of those fucking trees, now—know what he'd look like to us? One more fucking mick" (67). Unable to cope, he has taken to drink, and indulges in soliloquies in which he plays several figures, illustrating the psychic divisions within himself (72–73). Haunted by nightmares of the dead, he dreams of restoring the dead to life, "like King Arthur" (90). In his anguish and longing for peace, he is by far the most sympathetic of the oppressors, but this "assassin, humanised by his trade" (90), does not want justice for the Irish, but only his own peace of mind.

The Irish woman punctures Chichester's sentimental rhetoric with more specific, political insights:

> What right does he have to stand in a field in Ireland and talk of the horrors of war? What nation ever learnt from the sufferings it inflicted on others? What did the Roman Empire give to the people it enslaved? Concrete. What did the British Empire give to its colonies? Tribal wars. I don't want to hear of this British soldier's humanity. And how he comes to be howling in the middle of my country. And how he thinks Ireland is a tragedy. Ireland's troubles are not a tragedy. They are the crimes his country has done mine. That he does to me, by standing there. (90)

The very situation in which Chichester so eloquently pleads for peace in Ireland—as an assassin in the employ of an occupying army in the occupied land—reveals the extent of his bad faith. And his vilification of his executioners, "You murdering bastards" (90), comes oddly from the lips of a man who has himself made his living from murder. Peace, Brenton implies, is a luxury so long as people are oppressed, and, like all luxuries, an object for the privileged classes alone. Brenton repudiates the overwhelming tendency of British historical drama since the eighteenth century to constitute itself through an empathy with the sufferings of those who wield power, and demands that we consider history from the point of view of the oppressed.[1]

The structure of *The Romans in Britain* works to establish and maintain an essential ethical difference between the use of violence as a means of oppression and its utilization as a means of self-empowerment in the hands of the oppressed. The slave's revolt against her rapist, a brief triumph, leading to only a momentary declaration of triumph before her murder by the British soldiers at the end of Part One, opens the way in the dramatic structure for the larger and more lasting revolts in Part Two. Rather than making "little distinction between the brutality of the conquered and the brutality of the conquering, merely a difference of scale and degree of power," as Micheline Wandor has inexplicably claimed (117), Brenton uses scenes from three widely separated historical periods to tell one story of the genesis of revolutionary consciousness, and the necessary role of violence in the development of that consciousness.

II

> The history of the theater is in a certain sense a history of sensational effects whereby an audience is stunned, titillated, or drawn together in some sort of communal experience; it is only at the rarest of intervals that writers have been able to use theatrical effect as a means of stimulating serious thinking.
>
> (Lindenberger 106)

The controversy occasioned by the National Theatre's première production of *The Romans in Britain* has so eclipsed every other aspect of the play that the very title still carries an aura of notoriety among those who have neither seen nor read it.[2] Although Bernard Weiner is correct when he notes that the play primarily offered "the means for various groups and individuals to argue points, most of which had little to do with the play" (68), the ostensible occasion of the controversy, the homosexual rape of Marban, nevertheless demands analysis because it stands apart from the rest of the play in its presentation of violence. All of the other violent acts in *The Romans in Britain* either take place offstage (the molestation of Corda and Morgana, the rape of the Slave, the murder and posthumous beheading of the matriarch), or take place quickly (the murders of Adona, Chichester, Cai, Daui and Conlag). The violence against Marban, on the other hand, is sadistic, protracted, and presented in detail. Why, in a play that generally avoids sensationalism, is there one scene that stands so strongly apart? When the rape of Marban is compared with the other instances of sexual violence in the play, it differs from them in three important respects. First, it is presented onstage, rather than simply reported. Second, it is a homosexual, rather than heterosexual, act. Third, it leads its victim, not to an act of violence aimed at the aggressor, but to suicide. Since the story of Marban is the major line of action in Part One, the rape, which is the peripety in that story, is important because it transforms him from an independent character to a defeated one. The scene is pivotal in Brenton's Part One story of the inability to revolt against oppressive violence. Sexual violence against men and women is configured differently, and the concomitant gender asymmetry informs the entire action of the play.

Unlike the Slave and Cai's daughters, Marban is presented first as a perpetrator of violence and later as a victim. It is he who slits Daui's throat, and uses his blood as an offering. Knives are explicitly associated with erections in *The Romans in Britain;* indeed, one of the soldiers describes his sword as "a real hard-on" (32). Later, Julius Caesar sends Marban's knife as a gift to his mistress in Rome with the epigram, "Tell her—(*He toys with the knife.*) to guard with this knife, what I would enter as a knife" (48). Marban's knife is used against him in the rape scene, as the Second Soldier cuts him on the shoulder and buttocks. Throughout the play, men kill with human artifacts: knives (the deaths of Daui, Marban, and Adona), shields (Marban's two brothers), and rifles (the Slave and Chichester), while the women kill with stones (Conlag and Corda). The men kill with objects they have crafted as instruments of death, while the women kill with natural objects that are at hand. Marban is not the innocent that the Slave and Corda are. Just as the knife he has used against Daui and the Romans is turned against him, he becomes the victim of the very phallic power that he, as a male, embodies.

Sexual activity, which always involves men, is exclusively identified with violence and oppression; lesbianism is non-existent. The Celtic band which is formed in the last scene of the play is made up of two men and two women, but there are no suggestions whatsoever of heterosexual pairings among them. In fact, the gender roles in the band are carefully reversed. It is Corda, who murders her father, who wields a sword and declares that she is a killer and the potential mother of killers, while the male cooks (in themselves a reversal of sexist assumptions that the kitchen is a "woman's place") have vomited at the sight of a corpse and fled at the first suggestion of violence. Gender roles are revised and potential sexual aggression neutralized in Brenton's final vision of a utopian society. But with the neutralization of aggressiveness, the presentation of sexuality disappears, since there seems to be no way for this play to present heterosexuality without phallic violence.

Homosexual violence is, then, the act of male dominance *par excellence,* because it is an act of conquest and domination, in which, both literally and figuratively, Marban's knife proves to be inferior to the Roman short sword. Unlike the women, whose anger at their violation leads to heightened insight and acts of revolt, Marban sufficiently identifies with his oppressors that he can never achieve an emancipatory knowledge of his situation. His sexual violation finds a homology in his later, "spiritual" violation by Caesar, who ties a figure of Venus around his neck. Venus, as a goddess of love and fecundity, represents the female principle to which Marban has been symbolically "degraded" through his rape. Caesar takes Marban's knife, and replaces it with the figure of Venus. Twice feminized, Marban can only see himself as ". . . filthy! Filthy! Defiled!" (53), and sees Roman ways as "filthy water" (54). The equating of the phallus and weaponry as well as the imagery of his rape echo in his proclamation: "But you'll never dig out the fear they've struck in you. With their strange, foreign weapons" (60). Completely powerless, he must now beg for a knife, and, when he is given one, he turns it against himself.

There is a pronounced asymmetry in how Brenton presents the crossing of traditional gender lines for men and women. For women to become warriors (as in the case of Corda and the Slave) is seen as admirable, but for men to become "feminized" is either comic (the cowardly cooks), or pathetic (Marban). There is a lurking fear in *The Romans in Britain* that men cannot cross traditional gender lines without a loss of physical integrity.

The rape of Marban, then, is distinguished from the other acts of violence in the play by its dramatization of a phallic consciousness turned against itself in violent annihilation. But the scene, although beginning and ending in sexual violence (first, the anal penetration of Marban by the Third Soldier; later, his being forced to fellate the Second Soldier), contains a contrasting middle section of homoerotic tenderness. The Second Soldier, left alone with the unconscious Marban, tells him how his uncle, a slave, sustained a similar blow to the head. His master treated him well, his ability to speak returned, he was given his freedom, and he became a priest. He saves Marban's life by removing some bloody mucus from his throat. He tells Marban how he is a slave, but will receive his citizenship upon his discharge. He then kisses Marban, and Marban revives, miraculously speaking in Latin.[3]

This sequence is immediately striking for two reasons. First, the tenderness and solicitude of the Second Soldier stand out in sharp relief from his cruelty immediately before and after this. The difference is indeed so great and so weakly motivated that it strains the sense of psychological verisimilitude otherwise adhered to in the play. But if the Soldier's response strains verisimilitude, Marban's Latin response snaps it. This second, striking characteristic briefly moves the play into a fantastic, surreal realm. This "French" scene violates both consistency of character and consistency of plot development.

More importantly, it presents a dynamic of character interaction which is completely different from any other in the play. Whereas elsewhere, characters are defined through relationships of power that are fundamentally hostile (Irish fugitive vs. Celt; Roman soldier vs. Colt; Mistress vs. Steward; Father vs. Daughter, etc.), here is the single example where we are allowed to see a commonality of experience behind two opposed individuals. Although the Second Soldier and Marban are opposed as Roman and Celt, we find that they share a similar, subjugated, political status. The Soldier's story of his uncle draws a hopeful parallel to Marban's situation: perhaps the young Druid will regain his ability to speak; perhaps he will be free again; perhaps he will speak oracular words. The figure of the uncle, who survives enslavement and brutality to become free and empowered through his language, foreshadows the emancipatory knowledge of the oppressed characters in Part Two. The telling of the story introduces a sequence of actions much more tender than anything we have seen in the play up to this point; the Soldier removes the mucus from Marban's throat, brings him back to consciousness, and kisses him. These actions climax in the revival of Marban, now empowered to speak in the language of his oppressors, and able to communicate his defiance of them in their own language.

At this point, Marban seems an almost preternaturally empowered figure of revolt who has been initiated into that order by a commonality of experience with a figure who has hitherto been defined exclusively as an oppressor, and through a gentle physical intimacy with another man. Both phallic violence and class struggle are momentarily obliterated, and suggest a set of social and psychological dynamics that are never again acknowledged in *The Romans in Britain*. This scene collapses the differences of class and sexual roles (oppressor and oppressed; perpetrator and victim of phallic violence) on which the entire play is predicated.

Therefore, it is not surprising that this scene is abruptly curtailed by the entrance of the First and Third Soldiers, Marban's relapse into muteness, and the Second Soldier re-initiating the sexual abuse of the young Druid. "Fucking Latin talking nig nog! Suck me off!" (38). The tenderness of the preceding scene is obliterated by the renewed aggression; Marban's seemingly miraculous empowerment comes to naught; homoerotic tenderness is re-configured as rape. The play continues as if the scene between Marban and the Second Soldier never occurred. We return to brutality: Brenton's himself again. The ambivalence concerning homosexuality in this scene is related to Brenton's uneasiness about the loss of phallic power. He sees, the loss as necessary to his political program, especially as it relates to me empowerment of women, but it also brings to the surface an anxiety about the loss of traditional male identity as a form of castration. Alternating between extremes of sadism and solicitude, abuse and tenderness, antagonism and commonality, the scene is disconcerting because it comes close to removing itself completely from the context that the play has established for itself, collapsing the distinctions on which the play otherwise operates, and heading off in another direction altogether. I am tempted to speculate that part of the problem with this scene (and the strong response which it elicits) is that it dramatizes, in a very rough and abrupt manner, a set of panicked and conflicted responses to male homosexuality—horror alternating with attraction. The fact that a male homosexuality that is not violent might exist is one that the play can only briefly entertain and then ruthlessly repress. Brenton's political program here runs up against a powerful set of feelings that makes the play lurch dangerously out of control.

III

Not pity and fear, but defiance and hope.

(Bloch 215. Trans. mine.)

After the death of Chichester, the moon shines, and the last scene of the play takes place in "brilliant moonlight" (91). Here, Corda, Morgana and the Cooks come together, their immediate oppressors (Cai and Adona) defeated, and make plans for their survival. The First Cook suddenly decides to discard his current occupation to become a poet. He tells the story of "a King who never was":

> His Government was the people of Britain. His peace was as common as rain or sun. His law was as natural as grass, growing in a meadow.
>
> And there never was a Government, or a peace, or a law like that.
>
> His sister murdered his father. His wife was unfaithful. He died by the treachery of his best friend.
>
> And when he was dead, the King who never was and the Government that never was—were mourn. And remembered. Bitterly.
>
> And thought of as a golden age, lost end yet to come. (94)

The play ends with the Second Cook responding to the First Cook's question about the name of this king from the Golden Age: "Right. Er—any old name. Arthur? Arthur?" (95). This tentative naming of the king is the birth of Arthurian legend.

As a myth of the Golden Age, the Cook's tale echoes Conlag's folk vision of a natural world of plenty in Part One:

> There is a land. The stories say it's there so it's got to be. Over the sea. The forests are thick. The deer are free. The pigs are there for the taking. Put your hand in the river there, the fish come to kiss your fingers. (39)

But Conlag believes his story out of naive dependence on lore, while the Cook creates his own. Conlag takes legend for fact, while the Cook constructs his tale to stress its status as poetry: the King never was, and even the impossible story of his utopia is a story of betrayal and disaster. The poet for the free society, Brenton suggests, is the poet who creates self-deconstructing fictions that will resist being turned into fact and used as ideological weapons. Although Marban himself showed some scepticism about the Druids and their means of manipulating people, he believes enough in the objective reality of his mythic structure that he can be devastated when Caesar explains how the Roman gods will replace the Celtic ones. Chichester believes sentimentally in the historical status of the very self-deconstructing legend that the Cook created. Liberty depends on the ability to take one's sustaining fictions as fictions. The Arthurian myth, as the Cook articulates it, is one that both incarnates an ideal, and insists on its ideality, that is, the fact that it cannot be perfectly realized in this world; it keeps hope alive, even while it cautions that hope always finds its direction beyond the present moment.

Like the Cook's legend, *The Romans in Britain* is a legend meant to keep hope alive while not avoiding the excruciating realities of human existence.

Those who have attacked it for its historical inaccuracies, like Richard Beacham, and those who have defended it for its accuracy, like Philip Roberts, have mistaken a parable for a history play. It is far more useful to situate *The Romans in Britain* within the tradition that Walter Hinck, following the aesthetics of philosopher Ernst Bloch, has labelled "the Theatre of Hope," a tradition he has traced in German dramatic literature from Lessing and the playwrights of the Enlightenment through to its major twentieth-century manifestation in the works of Bertolt Brecht (Hinck 156–194). For Hinck, as for Bloch, the happy ending, which is both impossible and ardently applauded, is a manifestation of hope in dramatic form, and Hinck argues that the great examples of the Theatre of Hope both give form to that hope while ironically recognizing its unrealizability.

The Arthurian legend provides a poetic paradigm for Brenton's vision of the political playwright, but it is fair to ask whether *The Romans in Britain* fulfils that paradigm, for within the play, there are very few moments where the play reveals itself to us as a construction. Beacham's and Roberts's misidentification of the play as an historical drama itself indicates that the play is not clear about what it is trying to do. The use of anachronism and the free play with time suggest that the play is not aspiring to documentary form, but there is a difference between a play saying that it is a parable and saying that parables are to be deconstructed so as not to be mistaken for history. *The Romans in Britain* asks that its oppositions of class and gender be taken as irreducible, fundamental oppositions. The one scene that questions those oppositions, the scene between Marban and the Second Soldier, is obliterate with such a fury that little of it remains in the audience's mind as a measure of later actions. If the First Cook's poem is a statement of Brenton's dramaturgy, *The Romans in Britain,* despite its ambition and moments of theatrical brilliance, falls lamentably short of its aim.

In Part One, Brenton momentarily dramatizes nurturing physical intimacy between two men, blurring lines of gender and political identification, and then backs off from that insight. In Part Two, he postulates a deconstructive poetic that he does not apply to the rest of his drama. Both of these moments show Brenton flirting with a collapse of socially encoded differences on which his political dramas are based. Both deconstruction, and a positive image of male homosexuality, threaten to obliterate differences that Brenton is anxious to preserve. Because of these anxieties, the play fails to live up to the program it sets for itself.

NOTES

[1] For insightful studies of this development in twentieth-century drama, see Rabey and also Wikander.

² For the history of the controversy surrounding this play, see Philip Roberts, "The Trials of *The Romans in Britain*," in this volume.

³ For a different interpretation of this scene, see Roberts, "Howard Brenton's *Romans*," 17. Roberts's argument proceeds on the strange assumption that Marban already knows Latin.

Works Cited

Beacham, Richard. "Brenton Invades Britain: *The Romans in Britain.*" *Theater (Yale)* 12:2 (1981): 34–37.

Bloch, Ernst. *Ästhetik des vor-Scheins* 2. Ed. Gert Ueding. Frankfurt am Main: Suhrkamp, 1974.

Brenton, Howard. *The Romans in Britain.* 1980. Rev. ed. 1982. *Plays: Two.* London: Methuen, 1989: 1–95.

Bull, John. *New British Political Dramatists: Howard Brenton, David Hare, Trevor Griffiths and David Edgar.* London: Macmillan, 1984.

Cameron, Ben. "Howard Brenton: The Privilege of Revolt." *Theater (Yale)* 12:2 (1981): 28–33.

Elam, Keir. *The Semiotics of Theatre and Drama.* London: Methuen, 1980.

Empson, William. *Some Versions of Pastoral.* New York: New Directions, 1974.

Gaskill, William. *A Sense of Direction: Life at the Royal Court.* London: Faber, 1986.

Hinck, Walter. *Theater der Hoffnung. Von der Aufldärung bis zur Gegenwart.* Frankfurt am main: Suhrkamp, 1986.

Lindenberger, Herbert. *Historical Drama: The Relation of Literature and Reality.* Chicago: U of Chicago P, 1975.

Rabey, David Ian. *British and Irish Political Drama in the Twentieth Century: Implicating the Audience.* London: Macmillan, 1986.

Roberts, Philip. "Howard Brenton's *Romans.*" *Critical Quarterly* 23:3 (1981): 5–23.

Sedgwick, Eve Kosofsky. *Between Men: English Literature and Male Homosocial Desire.* New York: Columbia UP, 1985.

Sennett, Richard. *Authority.* New York: Vintage, 1981.

Van Dijk, Teun A. *Text and Context: Explorations in the Semantics and Pragmatics of Discourse.* London: Longmans, 1977.

Wandor, Micheline. *Look Back in Gender: Sexuality and the Family in Post-War British Drama.* London: Methuen, 1987.

Weiner, Bernard. "*The Romans in Britain* Controversy." *The Drama Review* 25:1 (1981): 57–68.

Wikander, Matthew. *The Play of Truth and the State of Historical Drama from Shakespeare to Brecht.* Baltimore: Johns Hopkins UP, 1986.

Wright, Elizabeth. *Postmodern Brecht: A Re-Presentation.* London: Routledge, 1989.

Monsters and Heroines:
Caryl Churchill's Women
Lisa Merrill

Simone de Beauvoir wrote, "Woman's awareness of herself is not defined exclusively by her sexuality; it reflects a situation that depends upon the economic organization of society" (47). Playwright Caryl Churchill defines herself as both a socialist and a feminist. In fact, in an interview published in Kathleen Betsko's and Rachel Koenig's anthology, *Interviews with Contemporary Women Playwrights,* Churchill states that "socialism and feminism aren't synonomous, but I feel strongly about both, and wouldn't be interested in a form of one that didn't include the other" (78).

To examine the intersection of gender and socioeconomic class in Churchill's work in light of current socialist feminist theory, I will consider three representative plays: *Owners* (1972), Churchill's first full-length play; *Vinegar Tom* (1976), written for and with the feminist theater company, Monstrous Regiment; and *Top Girls* (1982). Using these three plays, I will explore the socialist impetus informing Churchill's formal and stylistic conventions as well as offer a literary analysis of recurring themes in each.

Owners

Theater critic Alisa Solomon has written that Churchill's characters' "psychic emotional and ethical experience are the inexorable result of their socio-political organization; their social being determines their thought" (50). Nowhere is this more clear than in *Owners.* In this early play, Marion is the embodiment of an upwardly mobile capitalist. A financially successful real estate entrepreneur, she is an "owner." She makes her money by buying homes, evicting poor tenants, and reselling the properties for more than they are worth. Her drive to own and possess extends to people as well as property. During the course of the play, Marion buys the house in which her former lover, Alec, lives with his wife and children, thus attempting to regain control over Alec's affection. So as to have a further tie to him, Marion also manages to gain possession of Alec's infant son by tricking his wife into agreeing to the baby's adoption.

Similarly grotesque and predatory is Marion's husband, Clegg, a butcher. A virulent misogynist, Clegg is infuriated equally by Marion's financial autonomy and by her callous disregard for him. As he matter-of-factly plots to kill her, Clegg explains to Worsely, his wife's young male assistant, that Marion "can stand on her own two feet, which is something I abominate in a woman" (8). Clegg describes his own failed ambition in sexual terms. "I was thrusting" (9), he tells Worsely, reminiscing about his earlier years. Yet, despite his "thrusts," Clegg is in financial ruin, a predicament further exacerbated by his wife's achievements.

Contrasted with Marion's value system is that of her former lover, Alec. Alec's complete passivity is the embodiment of a Zen mind state of tacit acceptance and complete indifference. Incapable of work, play, anger, ambition, or love, Alec resorts to "sitting quietly doing nothing." It makes no difference to him whether or not he and his family are evicted, whether or not he and Marion resume their sexual relationship, or whether Marion or his wife, Lisa, raises and "possesses" his baby.

The complete dichotomy between Marion's orientation and Alec's is clearly presented in the first act, where Marion explains, "Everything I was taught—be clean, be quick, be top, best, you may not succeed. . . . I work like a dog. Most women are fleas, but I'm the dog . . ." (30). Marion, obviously, is not a stereotypical passive, dependent women, feeding off others; nor is Alec a prototypical aggressive, power-hungry male. By unmasking Marion's acquisitive notions of success as mercenary and malevolent, Churchill shows that success by patriarchal, capitalist standards is exploitative, whether the owners and strivers are male or female. Yet Alec's refusal to take any action is equally undesirable passive-aggressive behavior. Neither value system is presented as desirable.

Clegg and Marion both reduce human beings to property. Clegg is representative of males who view women as objects, possessions of the men who own them. In an attempt to get back at Alec for having an affair with Marion, Clegg has sex with Alec's wife, Lisa, and then insults Alec by boasting, "I wouldn't want to waste myself on something as second-rate as your wife. She was quite useful. A handy receptacle. But quite disposable after" (56). Referring to Marion, Clegg warns, "She's not like other women in just one important respect. She is mine. I have invested in Marion and don't intend to lose any part of my profit. She is my flesh" (56).

As despicable as Clegg's attitude obviously is, the most pervasive evil in *Owners* lies in the desire to possess. Both male and female characters are equally corrupted by this desire. By subscribing to the same bourgeois values of acquisitiveness as men do in their most base sexist incarnations, Marion does not liberate herself from exploitation; she merely becomes one of the exploiters. In fact, Marion equates herself with a male-identified notion of power in her words as well as her actions: she uses the male generic to refer to herself when she exclaims, "We men of destiny get what we're after, even if we're destroyed by it" (31). Marion's character is illustrative of feminist theorist Andrea Dworkin's contention that

> There is no freedom or justice or even common sense in developing a male sexual sensibility . . . which is aggressive, competitive, objectifying. . . . To believe that freedom or justice for women or for any individual woman can be found in mimicry of male sexuality is to delude oneself, and to contribute to the oppression of one's sisters. (12)

In Churchill's work, the drive to acquire dehumanizes the bourgeoisie. The tone of *Owners* is grotesque in its matter-of-factness about the behavior and attitudes of its characters. This black comedy achieves much of its macabre effect by dividing the action between all five of the characters, thus discouraging a psychological identification with any of them, with the result that, rather than indicting isolated malevolent individuals, Churchill indicts the system. As Churchill has Worsely proclaim, "The legal system was made by owners. A man can do what he likes with his own" (36).

In fact, the notion that belonging to another through relationship (familial or romantic) can potentially reduce human beings to consumable objects is made manifest in the women's conflict over Alec's and Lisa's baby. In a fit of frustration, after finding that her husband and Marion have resumed their affair, Lisa proclaims, "I'm not bringing a baby home to this. I am not. I'd sooner kill it." And, since she regards the baby as hers to keep or dispose of, Lisa tells Marion, "You can have it. If you think it's so easy. . . . You can have the baby" (33).

By the time of the adoption, however, Lisa has had second thoughts and expresses her right to her child in material terms, claiming, "I may not earn so much as you. But I'm not worth nothing" (42). While manipulating Lisa into accepting the adoption, Marion responds with an extra negative, to confuse Lisa. "Nobody said you were not worth nothing." Lisa misses the "not" in the sentence. Marion's position is a reaffirmation of her estimation of her own worth, and, therefore, her value as a parent. As Marion explains to Worsely, "She's not fit, you see. And I need it more. I'll make far better use" (43).

This reduction of children to utilitarian objects for the benefit of their owner-parents is mentioned several times throughout the play. In the first scene Clegg acknowledges to Worsely, "I envisaged a chain. Clegg and Son. I was still the son at the time. I would have liked a son myself once I was the Clegg. But now I've no business I don't need a son. Having no son I don't need a business" (9). Clegg's interest in paternity as a relationship to facilitate the inheritance of property is a modern manifestation of Karl Marx's and Friedrich Engels' contention that capitalism originated historically when men paired their new-found knowledge of paternity with the acquisition of private property. Clegg only becomes "the Clegg" when and if he has material property to pass along to his son.

Churchill's class analysis and socialist orientation are manifest at the conclusion of *Owners,* when the audience learns that Alec has died in the fire set
by Worsely at Clegg's urging. Moreover, Alec died when he returned to the
burning building to save a neighbor's child, not his "own." This act of heroism
is incomprehensible to Clegg and Marion, not part of their value system.
Instead, what is most remarkable to them is their realization that they "might
be capable of anything" (67), even the taking of a life. It is, in fact, the amorality of their capitalistic standards which unites Clegg and Marion.

Vinegar Tom

Marx and Engels believed that social changes in production have immediate
effects on the family as an institution (29). *Vinegar Tom,* set in seventeenth-
century England, a period of tumultuous religious and socioeconomic change,
gave Churchill an opportunity to explore those effects.

In *Vinegar Tom,* created in 1976 for and with the feminist acting troupe,
Monstrous Regiment, the material conditions of characters' lives are constantly
in the foreground functioning as an active antagonist with which all facets of
the society struggle. Although written by Churchill, *Vinegar Tom* was
researched and composed collaboratively, growing out of workshops with the
Monstrous Regiment troupe. This marked the first time Churchill actively participated in the rehearsal process, and the input of working in the collaborative
mode may account for some of the formal and stylistic changes which can be
observed in Churchill's work from this point on.

Set during the period of the last major English witch hunt, *Vinegar Tom*
reflects Churchill's conviction that "witchcraft existed in the minds of its per-
secutors, that 'witches' were a scapegoat in times of stress like Jews and
Blacks" (Preface 129). While researching *Vinegar Tom,* Churchill claims she
"discovered for the first time the extent of Christian teaching against women
and saw the connections between medieval attitudes to witches and continuing
attitudes to women in general" (129).

In this play, the women who are accused of witchcraft are women who are
socially powerless. Each of the four women attempts to act in an autonomous
manner (either sexually or economically), but because of the marginal social
status of each, her behavior is regarded as aberrant and unnatural.

Alice, for example, is an unmarried mother whose deviance is that she
enjoys sex. From the first scene of the play, Alice challenges her society's rigid
religious and sexual double standard. After a sexual encounter which she
refuses to regard as sinful, Alice acknowledges to her casual sexual partner,
"Any time I'm happy, someone says it's a sin" (136).

Her refusal to accept conventional judgments angers the man, who equates
her social status with her sexual conduct. As he says, "You're not a wife or a
widow. You're not a virgin. Tell me a name for what you are" (137). Since their

society has no acceptable category for an independent, sexual woman, the man (identified only as "man") brands her a whore.

A short time later, as the scapegoating escalates, another character, Jack, charges Alice with witchcraft, blaming her both for the sexual feelings he has for her and for his impotence with his wife, Margery. In turn, Margery accuses Alice's old mother, Joan, of witchcraft rather than acknowledge the poor old woman's requests for food and other essential handouts.

Repeatedly throughout the play, social outcasts are blamed for their marginal status. Alice's friend Swan upholds society's values but defies convention by attempting control over her own reproductive powers. Susan, a young married woman, pregnant for the seventh time after giving birth to three babies and suffering three more miscarriages, believes as she has been taught by the church, that "pain is what's sent to a woman for her sins" (146). Nevertheless, she goes with Alice on a visit to Ellen, whose skills with herbal medicine, healing, and abortion are also regarded as witchcraft.

Even Betty, the daughter of a wealthy landowner, risks being considered a witch because she would rather "be left alone" than marry. However, Betty's father's wealth and the rising male medical establishment (as opposed to female "cunning women" like Ellen) protect Betty from the charge by bleeding her to cure her of the desire to be independent.

In *Vinegar Tom,* Churchill appears to be illustrating Simone de Beauvoir's observation that "in epochs of social disintegration woman is [or may be] set free, but in ceasing to be man's vassal, she loses her fief, she has only a negative liberty" (120). As Ellen warns when Betty reaffirms her desires to be left alone:

> Left alone for what? To be like me? There's no doctor going to save me from being called a witch. Your best chance of being left alone is marry a rich man, because it's part of his honour to have a wife who does nothing." (169)

In fact, it is due, in part, to the paucity of options in most seventeenth-century women's lives that Goody, the female assistant witchhunter, justifies her work of humiliating and abusing those accused of witchcraft. After bemoaning the inefficient modes of torture available to her, Goody affirms:

> Yes, it's interesting work being a searcher and nice to do good at the same time as earning a living. Better than staying home a widow. I'd end up like the old women you see, soft in the head and full of spite, with their muttering and spells. (168)

Thus, although on one level Goody can acknowledge her potential similarities to the powerless women she abuses, she no more identifies with them than do the characters of Marion and Marlene (in *Owners* and *Top Girls* respectively) with those women over whom they have power. Instead, Goody takes pride in her identification with her employer, witchhunter Henry Packer. She claims, "It's an honour to work with a great professional" (168). Socialist feminist Sheila Rowbotham has written that "A dominant group is secure when it can convince the oppressed that they enjoy their actual powerlessness and give them instead a fantasy of power" (39). Clearly, this is the case with the character of Goody.

Starting with *Vinegar Tom,* Churchill's work increasingly incorporates techniques such as Brecht introduced in his epic theater, including short episodic scenes, unusual multiple or cross-sex casting, and the use of songs. In *Vinegar Tom* the seven songs punctuate, comment upon, and distance the audience from the action of the twenty-one scenes which make up the play. In her prefatory note to *Vinegar Tom,* Churchill indicates that although the play takes place in the seventeenth century, the songs are to be performed in modern dress and to take place in the present.

The first song, "Nobody Sings," occurs immediately following a scene in which Alice and her mother Joan frankly discuss sex and the absence of men in their lives (141–42). The song, which bemoans the fact that nobody sings about the physical conditions of women's maturing sexuality, includes references to menstruation, menopause, and aging. Churchill's language in the song is raw and immediate, as in the verse,

> Do you want your skin to wrinkle
> and your cunt get sore and dry?
> And they say it's just your hormones
> If you cry and cry and cry? (142)

Besides the contemporary medical references and the blunt language, the "you" in the song clearly is directed to an assumed female spectator.

The second song, "Oh, Doctor," occurs after scene six, in which Betty is bled by her doctor (150–51). Here, Churchill's lyrics foster an immediate parallel between contemporary women's enforced passivity at the hands of the medical establishment and the seventeenth-century practices which we now know to be dangerous and abusive. In both eras, it is male doctors who assume what is best for women, not the singer who wants only "to see inside myself." Again Churchill includes graphic references to rarely discussed aspects of women's sexual experience, including a reference to the speculum used in vaginal examinations: "stop looking up me with your metal eye."

However, the third song, "Something to Burn," most clearly presents the play's dominant metaphor of witches as scapegoats. As Churchill tells us,

> What can we do, there's nothing to do,
> about sickness and hunger and dying.
> ....
> Find something to burn.
> ....

> Sometimes it's witches, or what will you choose?
> Sometimes it's lunatics, shut them away.
> It's blacks and it's women and often it's Jews. (154)

By placing witch-burnings in the context of holocaust and genocide, Churchill forces her audience to confront the socio-economic basis of fear and prejudice.

The following song, "If Everybody Worked as Hard as Me," demonstrates the connection between sex-role chauvinism and national chauvinism (159–61). Running through this parody of the Protestant ethic is the line "Oh, the country's what it is because / the family's what it is because / the wife is what she is / to her man." By this definition, Alice and her mother, although parent and child, mother and grandmother, are not a "family." Without a man, they are perceived as a threat to society.

A parallel to contemporary lifestyles is reinforced later in the song "Lament for the Witches" (175–76), in which Churchill warns the audience, "Look in the mirror tonight / Would they have hanged you then? / Ask how they're stopping you now." This song, performed after Joan and Alice are hanged, again addresses the spectator directly as "you." In addition, the lyric posits the existence of an unidentified "they" who not only threaten the play's characters within the context of the production but also present a danger for the contemporary audience. The implication in Churchill's warning is that the insidious "they" control "our" actions in ways of which we are unaware. This "us" versus "them" division functions to connect Churchill's audience with her characters on one hand, but it also destroys the theatrical illusion by reminding the audience of their "real" existence.

Similar epic theatrical techniques occur throughout the play. One of the strongest occurs in the final scene, when the Inquisitors, Sprenger and Kramer, appear, portrayed by women dressed as Edwardian male vaudeville performers. By reducing the inquisition and torture of witches to a music hall popular entertainment, Churchill presents her audience with an analogue for the vicarious thrill potentially experienced by spectators at a public event, be it theater, vaudeville, or a public hanging. Sprenger and Kramer are clearly impostors, women playing men; in trying to "pass" they act against their own interests. Their stand-up question-and-answer patter, rather than being a comedy routine, is taken from the actual text of their handbook, *Malleus Maleficarum: The Hammer of Witches.* Spectators who are drawn into this entertainment, are, in fact, made complicitors. Hence, the music hall motif serves to comment upon the nature of theatrical form, as well as the insidious ways in which a representational construction may foster a regressive political position.

A number of critics and directors have taken issue with or misunderstood Churchill's intentional use of these Brechtian epic theater devices. For example, David Zane Mairowitz, in his essentially laudatory article on *Vinegar Tom* and *Light Shining in Buckinghamshire,* remarks that the impact of Churchill's songs in *Vinegar Tom* is "one of estrangement, especially when the lyrics become medically and physically graphic," and that "the play text is not strong enough to withstand the breaking of its rhythm and antagonism of the musical interludes"(25).

However, as with the work of Brecht, it is this very estrangement or alienation which Churchill intends. According to Brecht, epic-style acting, with a direct address to the spectator, and the use of songs which comment upon rather than support the action of a play, serve to awaken an audience from what Brecht regarded as a false emotional empathy with characters and theatrical illusion. Instead, these techniques encourage a critical and rational response to the conditions portrayed.

As Peter Demetz has written in his collection of critical essays on Brecht, "The Epic Theater, in which stage technique and Marxism finally correspond, strives to keep man [sic] sober, 'cool' and critical" (4). It is not surprising, therefore, that Churchill would increasingly choose to frame her abiding socialist convictions within a dramatic form which is founded upon those same principles. What is remarkable about Churchill is that she has adapted epic theater conventions, her own wry wit, and black humor into a style uniquely suited to her socialist-feminist vantage point.

Top Girls

Simone de Beauvoir wrote,

> In order to change the face of the world, it is first necessary to be firmly anchored in it, but the women who are firmly rooted in society are those who are in subjection to it; unless designated for action by divine authority . . . the ambitious woman and the heroine are strange monsters. (122)

In *Vinegar Tom,* women's autonomous desires are seen as punishable offenses because they are committed without official sanctions. However in *Top Girls,* written in 1982, as in *Owners,* we see how being firmly rooted in bourgeois society can dehumanize ambitious women. Marlene, the protagonist in *Top Girls,* is not monstrous like Marion, yet both women strive for material success and reduce motherhood to exclusively material concerns, rendering themselves emotionally vacuous. Although the two characters are in many ways similar, they differ in one important regard: whereas Marion always appears to be a monster (to use de Beauvoir's term), Marlene starts out appearing to be a heroine, thus calling into question the audience's concept of admirable female role models.

Act I of *Top Girls* opens with an elaborate fantasy in which Marlene, newly promoted managing director of the *Top Girls* Employment Agency, hosts a celebratory dinner. Her guests are five historical or fictional women from a variety of time periods and cultures. Each represents a woman who overcame a particular set of extraordinary obstacles in her historic period or social milieu.

Isabella Bird, a nineteenth-century Scottish woman, late in life became a solitary world traveller rather than live as a British lady. Lady Nijo, of thirteenth-century Japan, was the emperor's courtesan, who, when she fell out of favor with the court, became a Buddhist nun. Dull Gret is a stoic, peasant figure from a Brueghel painting. Although she says very little, her monosyllabic responses are indicative of her fortitude. Pope Joan was a ninth-century woman who, disguised as a man, eventually became Pope, until, her sex discovered, she was stoned to death. Patient Griselda is the obedient wife from Chaucer's "The Clerk's Tale," whose husband, a Marquis, cruelly separated her from her children for sixteen years to test her loyalty and forgiveness.

By attempting to equate Marlene's promotion at work with the extreme circumstances overcome by the other five guests, Churchill renders Marlene's achievement petty and ludicrous. As Marlene brags in almost a parody of self-aggrandizement, "Well, it's not Pope, but it is managing director" (13).

This note of irony is struck repeatedly throughout the first scene. In addition to the amusing juxtaposition of incongruous characters, the mundane restaurant setting, with its constant interruptions of ordering, serving, and consuming food and drink, renders all conversation trivial.

This triviality is underscored by a scripting technique which Churchill introduced in *Top Girls* and then continued in later work. Frequently characters' lines are written so as to interrupt or overlap with each other. Like an elaborately orchestrated score, the interplay between serious topics and mention of food, coupled with simultaneous speech by several character, leads to absurd resonances. For example, in the following exchange, while the women are ordering appetizers from the menu, Nijo exclaims, "The first half of my life was all sin and the second. . . ." Here Marlene interrupts with, "What about starters?" As Nijo finishes her sentence ". . . all repentence," Gret answers Marlene, saying "Soup." Joan follows up on Nijo's original comment by asking, "And which did you like best?" (5). These overlaps serve to relate the first "sinful" half of Nijo's life with "starters" or appetizers, "repentence" with "soup," and having a taste or preference for "sin" with an appetite for food.

Marlene diminishes the other women's experiences by conceiving of them only within the frame of her own limited situation. At one point in the luncheon, Marlene explains, "We were just talking about learning Latin and being clever girls" (4). Later, when Joan, Nijo, and Isabella speak about the "disguise" or form of dress which afforded them unmolested access into the world at large rather than keeping to the restricted women's sphere in their respective societies, Marlene responds with, "I don't wear trousers in the office / I could but I don't't" (8).

It is not only the historical conditions for women which Marlene misreads; the remainder of the first and second acts of *Top Girls* explores what it means to be "on top" and have power in the present day. Churchill highlights the economic rather than the psychological circumstances of her characters by having all but one of the performers play several different parts. This double casting, besides diffusing identification with an individual character's unique experience, functions to effect comparisons between the various conditions presented by the several characters portrayed by each performer. Only the performer playing Marlene takes on no other role, thereby focusing attention on her as a prototype.

Marlene's model of power is having power over others rather than being empowered to perform some social action. Marlene promises one of her clients at the *Top Girls* Employment Agency, "You'll be in at the top with new girls coming in underneath you" (31). This hierarchical model of success has a particularly male-identified dimension. Nell, one of Marlene's co-workers, describes Marlene as having "more balls than Howard" (46), her male competitor at work. The association of power and stereotypical masculinity is reinforced when Howard's wife, who describes herself as having been "behind" her husband all the way, refers to Marlene as a "ball breaker" for having gotten promoted "over" her husband. The linguistic positioning reflects gender-linked socio-economic positioning.

In *Top Girls,* as in *Owners,* Churchill engages her audience in questioning capitalist strivings. By presenting the moral and ethical deficiencies of women whose notion of success is "making it" by male terms in a male world rather than attempting to change the exploitative structure of that world, Churchill is advocating a socialist-feminist stance. In a 1983 interview, Churchill asserted that she wanted *Top Girls* "to 'seem' to be celebrating the extraordinary achievements of women, then it would cut another way and say that this sort of movement is useless if you don't have a socialist perspective in it" (Stone 81).

In presenting the dichotomy between a socialist feminist orientation and one which claims to be feminist without a class consciousness, Churchill is not alone. According to playwright Michelene Wandor, a self-defined socialist feminist, there are presently three tendencies in contemporary feminist thought. Wandor defines these as bourgeois feminism, radical (or cultural) feminism, and socialist feminism. Bourgeois feminism

> simply seeks a larger sphere of social power for a small number of 'token' women who aspire to current mainstream male values, thereby upholding the status quo. Radical or cultural feminism posits the existence of an alternate value system for men and women, and proclaims the female moral system superior. (131)

Whether women attempt to broaden their individual powerbase so as to be successful in bourgeois terms or attempt to set up an alternate hierarchy which regards certain female traits as laudatory, in neither case is there a socioeconomic theory which would encourage people to analyze "the way in which power relations based on class interact with power relations based on gender" (Wandor 136). This concept of socialist feminism advocates a complete restructuring (not a mere reversing) of the very existence of power inequities that Churchill presents in her plays, and with which many have taken issue. The two powerful female characters in *Owners* and *Top Girls,* Marion and Marlene, are clearly bourgeois in their orientation. They use and abuse others to get ahead.

In *Top Girls,* the audience learns that Marlene (herself the product of a working-class family) has bought her autonomy and social mobility through distancing herself geographically and emotionally from her sister Joyce and her somewhat slow, illegitimate daughter Angie, whom Joyce has raised since infancy as her own child. Marlene, in a position of privilege, chooses to ignore or discount the material conditions of others' lives. Unlike the bawdy and outspoken women in *Vinegar Tom,* Marlene states that she dislikes "messy talk about blood / and what a bad time we all had" (81). She hates the working class, "the way they talk," which she equates with "beer guts, football vomit and saucy tits" (85).

Rather than acknowledge the abuses of a system which renders most people powerless, Marlene (like Goody in *Vinegar Tom*) holds the working class responsible for their plight, attributing to them laziness, stupidity, or fear. Her sister Joyce, on the other hand, strongly identifies with their working-class origins and is ashamed of Marlene's selfishness. As Joyce points out, the conditions of most people's lives have not changed just because a few individual women or men have gotten more powerful.

Joyce embodies the socialist feminist response to Marlene's bourgeois feminist stance. Like Lisa, the working-class wife in *Owners,* Joyce experiences the extreme futility of her situation and her lack of options. As she expresses it, for the poor, the unexceptional, the marginally skilled, there is no avenue out of the present circumstances.

To those critics who look upon bourgeois successes like Marion and Marlene as models to which women should aspire, Churchill's refusal to place any character comfortably "on top" of others may be problematic. For example, Michelene Wandor claims that Marion in *Owners* appears to validate male fears of female sexual power and that in *Top Girls* no positively reinforcing relationships between the women appears (168). However, Churchill's goal, like Brecht's, is to present not a pleasing play, but a somewhat unsettling piece which will remind us of what we need in the real world. As Churchill answered in response to the question of why there is no "real" feminist in the play, "I quite deliberately left a hole in the play, rather than giving people a model of what they could be like. I meant the thing that is absent to have a presence in the play" (Stone 80).

The intentional creation of a feeling of absence, or incompleteness, is partially manifested through Churchill's innovative manipulation of the stage conventions of time. Chronologically, *Top Girls* ends with Act II, Scene 1, when sixteen-year-old Angie runs away from home to visit her "Aunt" Marlene at the employment agency. All of the action of the play has led up to this moment. In Act I, Angie has confessed both her intention to run away and her suspicion that she is really the child of her special aunt rather than her ordinary mother.

When Angie appears at the *Top Girls* agency, the inequities of a system that rewards the few exceptional women are made apparent. Angie, being intellectually limited and socially maladjusted, will never make it by Marlene's standards. With this condition as a given, the final scene of *Top Girls,* the confrontation between the two value systems represented by Joyce and Marlene, which occurred one year earlier, takes on an even more plaintive note, since Churchill has already shown her audience the dim prospects for Angie's future. This disruption of chronology is intentionally unsettling in that it refuses to allow the spectator to fantasize a sentimental ending for Angie and people like her. Instead, by manipulating theatrical convention, Churchill has dramatized Simone de Beauvoir's contention that "ontological aspiration—the projects for becoming— . . . take concrete form according to the material possibilities offered" (54).

In fact, comparable translating into concrete form may be found in all Churchill's work. In *Owners, Vinegar Tom,* and *Top Girls,* as well as in numerous other Churchill works not discussed, stage conventions about time and character portrayal are manipulated to highlight the social and economic conditions which govern and restrict human possibility. Sometimes the same character is written so as to be portrayed by multiple actors (as in *Light Shining in Buckinghamshire* and *Cloud Nine*), or the same actor is expected to play several different roles (as in *Top Girls* and *Cloud Nine*). Churchill has also written parts to be portrayed by performers of a gender different from that of their character, thus leading to the notion of gender identification as a socially constructed role as well as a theatrical one. Time in Churchill's work is frequently experiential rather than literal and linear. In *Cloud Nine,* for example, characters age only twenty five years although the second act is set one hundred years later. The restaurant scene which begins *Top Girls* is set in the present, but also exists outside of time as it is peopled by characters of multiple time periods. As we have seen, the play ends with a scene that occurs a year before its opening scene, circling in on itself.

In Churchill's work there are no easy, reformist solutions. The conditions she depicts, whether in a broad historical panorama, or in the domestic arena, or in the bourgeois work world, cannot be overcome either through individual will or personal relationships. In fact, the very conditions which frame the characters and their relationships limit them before the curtain is ever raised.

Top Girls ends with Angie's plaintive cry, "Frightening." It is not a dream which scares her and unsettles us, but the prospects for her waking reality. By raising these socio-economic issues for public view and leaving them unsettled, as they are in the real world, Churchill creates a space for dialogue and change outside the theater as well as in it.

Works Cited

Betsko, Kathleen, and Rachel Koenig. *Interviews with Contemporary Women Playwrights.* New York: Beech Tree Books, 1987.

Churchill, Caryl. *Owners.* In *Plays: One.* London: Methuen, 1985. 1– 67.

———. *Top Girls.* London: Methuen, 1984.

———. *Vinegar Tom.* In *Plays: One.* London: Methuen, 1985. 127–79.

de Beauvoir, Simone. *The Second Sex.* New York: Bantam, 1961.

Demetz, Peter, ed. *Brecht: A Collection of Critical Essays.* Englewood Cliffs: Prentice Hall, 1962.

Dworkin, Andrea. *Our Blood: Prophecies and Discourses on Sexual Politics.* New York: Perigee Books, 1981.

Mairowitz, David Zane. "God and the Devil." *Plays and Players* 24.5 (Feb. 1977): 24–25.

Marx, Karl, and Friedrich Engels. "The Communist Manifesto." *Essential Works of Marxism.* New York: Bantam, 1961.

Rowbotham, Sheila. *Women, Resistance and Revolution: A History of Women and Revolution in the Modern World.* New York: Vintage, 1974.

Solomon, Alisa. "Witches, Ranters and the Middle Class: The Plays of Caryl Churchill." *Theatre* 12.2 (Spring 1981): 49–55.

Stone, Laurie. "Caryl Churchill: Making Room at the Top." *Village Voice* 1 March 1983: 1, 80–81.

Wandor, Michelene. *Carry On, Understudies: Theatre and Sexual Politics.* London: Routledge & Kegan Paul, 1986.

More Real than Realism:
Horton Foote's Impressionism
Tim Wright

Many critics regard Horton Foote's plays and screenplays as expressions of dramatic "realism." And for good reason. His stories seem to reflect the reality experienced by most people. There are no artificial scenarios that strain plausibility—no "they-lived-happily-ever-after" twists to placate an audience or to fulfill preconceived expectations (Barr 40). His work seems very "real" to us. And yet there is another aspect of Foote's writing—something deeper, more intriguing—that extends beyond flat realism. Foote's work, despite its familiar surface, continually rejects realism's "corrected chronicle" of reality (Kirschke 140), offering instead Foote's distinctive brand of American impressionism. It is a dramatic wold in which the material world is at every moment interpreted, shaped, and hopefully redeemed by the consciousness of the writer, characters, and audience.

Impressionism, especially in drama, can often be mistaken for realism. As a matter of fact, it has been suggested that impressionism is actually more "true to life" than the "realistic" art that preceded it (Kirschke 206). In *Theatrical Style: A Visual Approach to the Theater,* for example, Douglas Russell points out that impressionism "will at times be accepted as reality" (20), and Albert Aurier considered impressionism "merely a kind of realism, a refined, spiritualized realism" (qtd. in Courthion 17). Such misinterpretation probably reflects the historical growth of impressionism out of realism: "The impressionist painters had begun as realists and then felt that they were deepening their realism through underlining nature's or people's moods" (Russell, *Stage* 392). However, as it developed its own style impressionism added to realism "a level of abstraction, with a strong element of subtle, intuitive emotionalism and a weak or vague compositional form"[1] (*Theatrical Style* 20). Impressionism stops short, however, of the radical subjectivity of symbolism and expressionism, remaining "nature-bound and reality-affirming" in its basic presentation (Shiff 44; Hauser 229).

Impressionism is distinguished from both realism and expressionism by insistence that objectivity be integrated with, but not replaced by, subjectivity. Believing that viewing an object dramatically shapes one's perception of that object, the impressionists allowed their focus to be determined by the conditions surrounding an object—rather than the actual physical traits of the object itself. Although impressionism is most commonly associated with the hazy application and mixture of colors of impressionist painters, it actually is a way of experiencing the world which varies according to the media and forms. In painting, for example, the central focus is almost exclusively the visual experience while in literature, film,[2] and drama traditional elements such as dialogue, plot, and character are implicated. But, while the styles are various, the impressionists—in whatever form—try to synthesize objective and subjective experience.

Impressionism is essentially an attempt to offer an artistic "objectification" of subjective phenomenon, as William Harms, in his dissertation *Impressionism as a Literary Style,* explains:

> Impressions are the fragmented parts of some presumed whole, not quite definitive, loosely arranged, sensually perceived and emotionally acknowledged—the very antithesis of scientific fact-mongering and mimetic rationality. The art of Impressionism, whether in painting or in literature, attests not only to an overwhelming belief that human existence is essentially made up of these myriads of impressions (instead of the linear accumulation of empirical facts and events), but it also attempts to establish a correspondingly appropriate medium which will itself become an objectification of the way it seems to feel inside oneself when one receives and forms these impressions. (133)

While many techniques of the impressionists vary with the media, the need for "objectification" creates identifiable traits across the disciplines, including literature and drama. These include: (1) a preference for atmosphere over subject or plot; (2) the deliberate use of ambiguity; (3) the appearance of being unfinished or fragmentary; (4) focus on the mundane and non-dramatic (in the traditional sense); (5) muted and subtle expression; (6) emphasis on the transient and impermanent; and (7) the presence of spiritual elements. Of course, these attributes do not operate in isolation; they are purposely integrated into a seemingly spontaneous gestalt.

EMPHASIS ON MOOD AND ATMOSPHERE

In most conventional works, the subject or plot is primary. Impressionism, however, shifts its focus to the ambiance generated by the creation of a specific work. As Georges Rivière points out, impressionist painting is distinguished by its "treatment of a subject for the sake of the tones, and not for the sake of the subject itself" (qtd. in Hauser 171). Similarly in dramatic impressionism the subjective experience of the "process" becomes the focal point, leaving the plot a means to an end rather than an end in itself. With this shift away from what happens, or might or should happen, impressionist drama is free to explore the subjective, subtextual concerns of the characters. Their conflicts, both physical and emotional ones, become more intriguing and meaningful than the action in the story.

This artistic emphasis is found repeatedly throughout Horton Foote's writing. As Samuel Freedman notes, the "major events [in Foote's stories] . . . do not propel the plot as much as they create a mood" (50). Like poetry, the concrete but resonant details in Foote's dramas dominate the story line; as one reviewer has noted, "I don't think it's the overall plot that grabs me, but the details—character's faces, their conversations, the discussion of a little lamb on the child's tombstone. Those are the things that haunt me" (Davis 300). In *The Trip to Bountiful,* for example, although the plot concerns whether Carrie Watts will return to her childhood home, Bountiful, Texas, the heart of the drama are her reflections during the journey. The completion of her physical journey is only peripheral; Mrs. Watts' quiet but determined recapturing of her dignity seizes the audience's attention. Little "happens" in the traditional sense of theatrical construction; the atmosphere of longing and the subtle revelation of character drive the work. "For Horton Foote, it's not only how the journey ends that matters, but what we perceive along the way" (Smith 27).

Mood and atmosphere similarly dominate *Convicts,* the second play in *The Orphans' Home Cycle.* Young Horace Robedaux is a clerk on a remote cane plantation worked by convicts. His employer and the overseer of the prisoner-workers, Soll Gautier, is an elderly alcoholic tyrant who ruthlessly governs his charge and evades paying him. Soll's frequent drunken rantings create an intense mood of potential danger and general chaos. Although violence surrounds the action of *Convicts,* the play focuses on the slow and sometimes comic sliding of Soll towards death. The real subject is Horace's vulnerability after the death of his father and his gradual development of a sense of distance, autonomy, and judgment about the injustice and disorder around him. Horton Foote's impressionism describes Horace's mood and predicament, showing little interest in what happens to him or what he can do in the physical world.

DELIBERATE AMBIGUITY

Impressionism also practices a "surrender to the uncertain, to the undefined" (Courthion 23, 26). Believing subjectivity makes universal interpretation impossible, impressionists create a style which embraces complexity and uncertainty:

> [The impressionists'] stylistic qualities emerged from the realization that
> since they lived in a prismatically impressionistic world, they must recreate

> that world of individualized sensory perception, epistemological indetermi-
> nacy, relativism, ambiguity, fragmentation, and surfaces. (Stowell 15–16)

Impressionism focuses on particulars in an atmosphere of relativism which dis-
courages any definitive interpretation. Impressionistic art does not construct a
solid representation of reality; it is filled with ambiguity and creative possibility. As Hurbert Muller summarizes, literary impressionists

> have . . . substituted the creation of atmosphere for inventory or set picture,
> subtle evocation for analysis or comment. They have discarded formal
> chronological narratives, with a definite beginning, middle and end, in favor
> of retrospective, discontinuous, or unfinished actions, streams of association
> canalized by emotion and the logic of the unconscious, of some kind of pro-
> liferous growth more nearly corresponding to the way in which we experi-
> ence life—life, as Conrad insisted, does not *narrate*. They have broken up
> the relatively simple, trim patterns of characterization, presenting figures
> who have no shape to speak of and who defy simple summary or category.
> In general they have destroyed the solidity and rigidity of life as tradition-
> ally represented, blurred the contours and, like the painters, have sacrificed
> symmetry and neatness to intensity and expressiveness. Hence the mysteri-
> ousness in much impressionistic fiction, the shadows deepened by the very
> brilliance of its illuminations. (qtd. in Stowell 20)

By inserting such "shadows" into a work of art, impressionism encourages the
integration of subjective participation in the creation of meaning. It invites the
onlooker to engage the work and to enter more deeply into the imaginary world
created by the impressionistic artist; "The comparative absence of articulation
forces the viewer to 'put the painting together' himself" (Kirschke 9).

This is one way in which Horton Foote's work is Chekhovian.[3] As Peter
Stowell notes, Chekhov crafted his plays toward a stimulating ambivalence:

> Chekhov has structured his plays so that every reaction is set against an
> obliquely conflicting reaction; we are meant to feel ambivalent toward
> every character, every line of dialogue, every human response, every scene
> and act, and finally, of course, toward everything in the play—even the play
> itself. (159)

Similarly, Foote engages his audience with a troubling but provocative sense
of mystery. For example, who is this young man from Atlanta who never
appears in Foote's Pulitzer Prize-winning play? What causes the transformation experienced by Carrie Watts at the end of *The Trip to Bountiful?* In *Tender Mercies,* why does Mac tell his daughter he can't remember "On the Wings
of a Snow White Dove" but then softly sing it to himself as she drives away?

Apparently there is more to this man, and to all men and women, than can be described by the play.

THE UNFINISHED AND FRAGMENTARY

Susanna de Vries-Evans notes that when the early impressionist painters first exhibited their work, "most collectors jeered at what they regarded as unfinished sketches" (9). Those collectors were responding to the sense of things happening beyond the boundaries of the work itself. It is impressionism's rejection of the artificial closure which dominates most realism, leaving "the way open for further possibilities" (Courthion 25). Seeking an art rigorously close to the reality of everyday experience, as Arnold Hauser notes, the "impressionistic vision transforms nature into a process of growth and decay. Everything stable and coherent is dissolved into metamorphosis and assumes the character of the unfinished and fragmentary" (169). Borrowing from the artistic methods of the Japanese, this technique creates the illusion of a moment in time, that which Norma Broude finds in Manet's "Boating" (1874):

> the natural movement of contemporary life is . . . here—the "slice-of-life" captured, monumentalized, and contrived to appear uncontrived, as the boat and its passengers, viewed up close and radically cropped by the frame in the manner of the Japanese print, threaten to drift away beyond our field of vision. (28)

In search of a realism that would include the fragmentary nature of much human experience, impressionism, in the words of Heinrich Wölfflin, employs incomplete "clarity of form and . . . depreciated component parts" (227).

Like other impressionists, Horton Foote is most comfortable with incompleteness. In an almost pointillistic fashion, Foote often constructs his plays and screenplays with truncated scenes and abbreviated dialogue; studying an implied world "beyond the picture-frame," Foote tells inconclusive stories which defy traditional closure. In *Tender Mercies,* for example, the courtship between Mac and Rosa Lee is executed in brief scenes of minimal dialogue:

> MAC and ROSA LEE in the garden; he is digging with a hoe and she is weeding.
> MAC: I haven't had a drink in two months. I think my drinking is behind me.
> ROSA LEE: Do you? I'm glad. I don't think it gets you anywhere.
> MAC: You ever thought about marrying again?
> ROSA LEE: Yes, I have. Have you?
> MAC: I thought about it, lately. I guess it's no secret how I feel about you. A blind man could see that. (Leaning on hoe.) Would you think about marrying me?

ROSA LEE: Yes, I will.
(MAC resumes his gardening, and so does ROSA LEE.)
(*Three Screenplays,* 96–97)

Later Mac's grief over his daughter's sudden death is expressed in a single
speech by Mac to Rosa Lee, again in their garden. There are no tears, no
heightened displays of anguish:

> I was almost killed once in a car accident. I was drunk and I ran off the side
> of the road and I turned over four times. They took me out of that car for
> dead, but I lived. And I prayed last night to know why I lived and she died,
> but I got no answer to my prayers. I still don't know why she died and I lived.
> I don't know the answer to nothing. Not a blessed thing. I don't know why I
> wandered out to this part of Texas drunk and you took me in and pitied me
> and helped me to straighten out and married me. Why, why did this happen?
> Is there a reason that happened? And Sonny's daddy died in the war. (Pause)
> My daughter killed in an automobile accident. Why? You see, I don't trust
> happiness. I never did, I never will. (*Three Screenplays* 144–45)

The film ends shortly afterwards with an inconclusive scene showing Mac and
Sonny passing a football as Rosa Lee watches from a distance with no comment. As Terry Barr notes:

> [Foote's] world is presented as is, for to understand how and why people
> make the crucial decisions that potentially decide the rest of their lives, the
> artist must allow his audience to see life in open-ended fashion, since rarely
> are our lives tied up in neat little packages. (*The Ordinary World* 4)

The open world of impressionism is integral to Foote's dramatic construction.

THE ORDINARY AND THE MUNDANE

Impressionistic art is typically centered on the ordinary; "The subject matter
of Impressionism is often casual, everyday life, captured with an immediacy
enhanced by transient effects of light and atmosphere" (Gerdts 29). It celebrates the quiet circumstances and events that comprise the majority of our
everyday experience.

> Often [Impressionists] simply painted people doing "nothing," enjoying
> themselves at concerts and dances in the park or picnicking or rowing on a
> holiday. In contrast to the most renowned painters who worked before them,
> the Impressionists treated mundane, everyday, non-dramatic, non-message
> subjects. (Kirschke 13)

Like the early impressionist artist Degas, who refused to "idealize or condemn" through his artistry, the tradition seeks to maintain a noncritical stance toward its subjects (de Vries-Evans 34). "The impressionist attempts to capture the feel, texture, and consciousness of the phenomenological *tabula rasa* or, as Muller notes in the impressionist lexicon, 'the innocence of the eye'" (Stowell 24). Resisting the temptation to be didactic or moralistic, the impressionistic artist strives to record the world as he or she perceives it, hiding no evil and exalting no virtue:

> In his essay on "Impressionistic Writing" [Walter] Symons more directly champions the cause of Impressionism when he states that of all of the qualities necessary to be an Impressionist writer, "the first thing is to see, and with an eye which sees all, and as if one's only business were to see; and then to write from a selecting memory." (Kirschke 116)

This radical acceptance of his characters and their world is fundamental to Foote's approach to writing. As the writer himself asserts, "I honestly do want to cast a cold eye, if you will. . . . An unsentimental eye. But no sense of superiority and no sense of condemnation" (qtd. in Davis 313). His work is filled with guileless observations of the quiet struggles of ordinary men and women. Foote does not moralize or pontificate; he merely looks on with an intensely focused interest. As Gerald Wood points out, Foote "writes to discover, not to preach. Rather than lecture his readers, he investigates with them the 'great mystery' about the sources of courage and personhood" (*Selected One-Acts* xix).

The fruit of this perspective is a subtle, understated drama about seemingly very ordinary people who live relatively quiet lives. By staying close to real, lived experience Foote endows his characters with a pervasive sense of authenticity; he "is a master craftsman at shaping parables from gentle folk tales. His characters talk like real people and act like real people. Nothing really happens to them; their lives just unfold" (Brown A1). As Terry Barr summarizes, Foote's characters are not "glamorous, sophisticated, and highly educated people"; they are "ordinary, middle-class men and women who struggle from day to day paying their bills, dealing with familial problems, and simply coping with the [*sic*] life's difficulties" (*Ordinary World* 3). In Al Reinert's words,

> They are no more clever or muscular or beautiful or villainous than the rest of us. Like us, they are only trying to cope with the indignities of the human experience, weary sinners yearning for a call to come home. (110)

Rebecca Briley asserts that Foote's commitment to presenting his characters in this manner is perhaps one of his most remarkable traits as a playwright.

> What does distinguish Foote from his contemporaries . . . is the demonstrated determination to concentrate on the development of character over

the other elements of play writing and his compassionate approach to characterization. Almost without exception, Foote depicts his characters as human beings, complete with flaws and virtues alike, providing insight into their misdirected lives to elicit the sympathy of his audience. (Briley 2)

But Horton Foote "is no Norman Rockwell" (Freedman 61); he uses neither saccharine-sweet characters nor nostalgia. His stories "seem gentle and full of decency; yet they have a dark side that drives them and that vibrates through all the action" (Anderson 26). Alcoholism, madness, stillbirth, parental abuse, and an assortment of other iniquities inhabit Foote's pages, stages and screens. He doesn't condemn those characters who manifest these weaknesses, however. As reviewer John Simon notes, "Everyone in [Foote's plays]—however ornery, meddlesome, mean-spirited, crazy, or just plain dull—somehow ends up likable" (115). This is a result of Foote's immense understanding and compassion for his characters. "I really do believe," states Foote, "that if you knew everything about the most evil person in the world, you would bring some understanding to him. But there are all kinds of antagonists; it needn't be just a character" (qtd. in "Dialogue on Film" 16). Even Jessie Mae, the churlish daughter-in-law in *The Trip to Bountiful,* has her strengths and virtues according to the author:

> I think that you have to be very careful that you don't caricature her. That's not my intention. Jessie Mae exists. I see her all the time. It's easy to feel superior to Jessie Mae, but they do endure, don't they? And in some ways they're very practical and pragmatic. (qtd. in Davis 308)

Foote's work is non-judgmental; rather than criticize or indoctrinate, he asks his audience to "see" theater and, ideally, their own lives, in new, more compassionate ways.

SUBTLE EXPRESSION

While impressionism stays close to clear and hard realities, it redesigns the distinct lines and shapes of naturalism into a more "painterly" technique of blended forms. This style, as described by Heinrich Wölfflin in *Principles of Art History: The Problem of the Development of Style in Later Art,* transforms the more "linear" techniques of earlier artistic methods into impressionism's diaphanous atmosphere in which objects often appear to "dissolve into the air" (Rapetti 9). Impressionism is, by definition, translucent:

> Impressionism meant also the suppression of line and of chiaroscuro, the objects no longer being separated from their setting, but enveloped by

atmosphere and heightened by reflections. No longer was the drawing fixed
or the outline sharp. Instead all was undefined, following the variation of
time, light, and taste. (Courthion 22)

Such diffusion, as in the case of ambiguity, makes subjectivity—for the artist
and audience—both possible and necessary.

The muteness of his literary impressionism liberates Horton Foote from the
excesses of melodrama. According to the writer, producers tend to "over-
theatricalize" (Foote, Interview 9 Nov. 1995) his work, often leaving them—like
many films—"visually conceived," "thinned out," without "substance" (Davis
314–15). What Foote prefers, and wise producers embrace, is a distinctive imaginary landscape in which everything "is suggested, little is demonstrated" (Kanfer 23). It is, as Rebecca Briley notes, an essentially understated drama:

> Foote's "taste" is one of understatement. A student of the "less is more" prin-
> ciple, Foote claims there is too much "real drama" for fiction, meaning that
> incidents from life do not need embellishment to create interesting theatre. (12)

Despite the muted expression, there is a rich sense of drama in Foote's
work. But the conflicts are emotional, not physical; "[a] great deal happens,
though much of it happens deep inside the characters" (Sarris 39). Foote
refuses to cater to modern theatrical appetites by inserting a false sense of "dramatic action" that violates his artistic conscience:

> Our loud and violent times are not particularly hospitable to retiring crea-
> tures like these [Foote's characters]. We like crackups on the stage, car
> crashes on the screen and brash characters who will at least go down swing-
> ing. Mr. Foote's gentleness will be viewed by some as torpor. Admittedly,
> his roads to home are little byways—not even paved, I suspect, and doubt-
> less no wider than a Model T. But they lead someplace humane and caring,
> where heartbreak doesn't have to be desperate and noisy to merit our con-
> cern. (Richards 5)

Since loss and change are constant and universal in Foote's imaginary world,
he studies "reaction," not just "the events themselves," as Gary Edgerton
explains:

> Each case exhibits his [Foote's] preference for portraying the reaction of lead
> characters to tragic happenings, rather than graphically showing the events
> themselves. This technique is important because it foregoes plot cliches for
> deeper resonances. Primary attention is forcefully shifted away from the
> more immediate, melodramatic potential of presenting a mother dying in
> childbirth; a newborn stricken with influenza; or a teenaged daughter being

killed in a drink-driving [*sic*] accident; to scenes of reflection and understatement which suggest meanings well beyond the simple actions and
words on-screen. (11)

As a literary impressionist, Horton Foote explores the subtle and complex reactions in which his characters reveal their true selves.

MUTABILITY

The early impressionist artists were obsessed with capturing the fleeting
impressions created by the shifting light and atmospheric conditions. In Diane
Kelder's words, they were "uniquely conscious of and responsive to the ever-
shifting physical reality of the moment" (13). Typically these artists returned
to the same subject again and again in an attempt to discover and record the
various effects generated by the changing conditions. Eventually impressionistic art became less interested in permanence and stability than in change and
uncertainty:

> The dominion of the moment over permanence and continuity, the feeling
> that every phenomenon is a fleeting and never-to-be-repeated constellation,
> a wave gliding away on the river of time, the river into which "one cannot
> step twice," is the simplest formula to which impressionism can be reduced.
> The whole method of impressionism, with all its artistic expedients and
> tricks, is bent, above all, on giving expression to this Heraclitean outlook
> and on stressing that reality is not a being but a becoming, not a condition
> but a process. (Hauser 169)

The result was a characteristic "apprehension of the world as a shifting semblance" (Wölfflin 27).

Once again Horton Foote is within the impressionist tradition, for change
is "at the center of [Foote's] literary world" (Barr 277). This is partly because
his subject is his native American South, "a community in transition" (Lawrence n.p.). His first full-length play, *Texas Town,* revolved around what critic
Brooks Atkinson called "a real and languid impression of a town changing in
its relation to the world" (Atkinson, Rev. of *Texas Town* n.p.). By keeping
Wharton/Richmond/Harrison as his primary subject, Foote has also maintained
that change is "the one dramatic certainty in Horton Foote's fictional world"
(Edgerton 6). More recently the nine plays of *The Orphans' Home Cycle* are
structured by what Foote himself named "change, unexpected, unasked for,
unwanted, but to be faced and dealt with" (Introduction, *Four Plays* xii).

But this theme transcends a particular place; "Foote is preoccupied with
change, with the erosion of tradition and identity" (Freedman 61) as a univer-

sal antagonist and opportunity. "I feel that finally there is something tragic about human life," states Foote, "as exciting as it is. It's finite. There's always that sense of loss, sense of change" (qtd. in Pacheco 5). And he asks his characters to grapple with this aspect of reality; for example, "When Elizabeth Robedaux says in *On Valentine's Day,* 'I want everything to stay the way it is,' she is uttering the one prayer Foote refuses to answer" (Freedman 61). Because change is unavoidable, flexibility becomes crucial: "In Horton Foote's world, compromise and change—being able to accept life on its own terms and to move forward—are the essential terms" (Barr 1). Those who are willing to accept the presence of loss and change survive; those who refuse are, more often than not, broken by them.

THE SPIRITUAL

Impressionistic art frequently implies and refers to a reality outside the material world; it is, in Pierre Courthion's words, a "spiritualized realism" (17) which studies the "incorporeal" (Wölfflin 27). Impressionism often generates moments of heightened awareness connected with a mysterious reality outside ourselves. Minor epiphanies, catching the outer edge of our attention, redirect our thinking, leaving us with new ways of seeing and relating to the world. Whatever we call them,

> these privileged moments, epiphanies, visionary instants, timeless moments,
> impressions, *instantanés,* or *moments bienheureux* do form a crucial basis for
> the impressionistic vision. These moments are not always transcendent, as
> they must be for the romantics. They are, however, the product of a change
> in perceptual perspective and occur at moments of heightened perceptual
> awareness. They may not "mean" anything beyond what they are, but they do
> result in a new grouping of fragmented experience. This often leads to a new
> way of seeing, a change in direction for the character, or an expanded con-
> sciousness. (Stowell 36–37)

Although these flashes of "expanded consciousness" do not necessarily have religious implications, the emotional content, the sense of something beyond the isolated self, is similar. As Paul Schrader notes, transcendence "in art is often equated with transcendence in religion because they both draw from a common ground of transcendental experience" (7). The obscure nature of this phenomenon makes it essentially mysterious:

> . . . the criticism of transcendental art is a self-destructive process. It con-
> tinually deals in contradictions—verbalizations of the ineffable. The concept

of transcendental expression in religion or in art necessarily implies a contradiction. . . . Like the artist, the critic knows that his task is futile, and that
his most eloquent statements can only lead to silence. (Schrader 8)

Inspired by Oriental, especially Japanese art (Roudebush 56), impressionism
explores the "numinous," often expressed in "silence" and "emptiness" (Otto 69).

Despite its understated surfaces, Horton Foote's work is filled with fleeting moments of transcendence, suggesting spiritual realities. Without dogma
or proselytizing, this "reference to the spiritual" becomes "one of the unique
contributions Foote's plays have made in American theatre" (Briley 247).
Christianity is, of course, inherent in the social climate of his fictional Harrison, Texas (based on his real-life hometown of Wharton, Texas); it is part
of the everyday life in the history Foote describes. However, in some
works—*The Trip to Bountiful* and *Tender Mercies,* for example—Christian
faith is integral to the characters' lives. While Foote's stories are not evan-
gelistic and they don't communicate a single moral message, religion is
indigenous and powerful. As David Neff notes, "Foote's God remains hidden. But he is there" (31).

This sense of the divine is revealed most tangibly in the "pure sounds" and
even "silence" of music, which is never "manipulative" (Davis 298). An
"organic" and thus unobtrusive presence in the plays, the music, as Samuel
Freedman notes, is both natural and "suggestive":

> Music plays an organic and highly suggestive role in Foote's work, from the
> hymns in "The Trip to Bountiful" to the norteño waltzes in "The Road to the
> Graveyard." These songs, rather than comprising a calculated sound-track,
> are the pastels on Foote's palette. (62)

By integrating Christian hymns, which "permeated the air when [he] was
growing up" (Davis 299), Foote creates the feel of religious experience without insisting on its validity: "I don't see how you can listen to those old hymns
and not fed something . . . even non-believers, you know, love those hymns.
I suppose they must get something from them" (qtd. in Neff 30). The hymns
are especially resonant when linked to the dominant theme of the story, as with
"Softly and Tenderly," which opens and closes the film *The Trip to Bountiful*[4]:

> Time is now fleeting, the moments are passing.
> Passing from you and from me.
> Shadows are gathering, death's night is coming.
> Coming for you and for me.
> Come home, come home. Ye who are weary come home.
> Earnestly, tenderly, Jesus is calling,
> Calling, oh, Sinner, come home.

While these opening lines describe Carrie's heartfelt longing to return home to Bountiful, they also suggest, in Rebecca Briley's words, Horton Foote's desire to connect "the physical homecoming with the spiritual" (191).

But Horton Foote's use of music is not isolated from the rest of his vision; it is one version of what Paul Schrader names a "transcendental style" (8–9). Basing his study on the films of Japan's Yasujiro Ozu, France's Robert Bresson, and Denmark's Carl Theodor Dreyer, Schrader divides this style into three major categories or stages of presentation: (1) "the everyday," which is "a meticulous representation of the commonplace"; (2) "disparity," or "an actual or potential disunity between man and his environment"; and (3) "stasis," "a frozen view of life which does not resolve the disparity but transcends it" (Schrader 39–49). Analogous to Thomas Weiskel's "sublime moments" (23–24), these dramatic events, according to David Desser, "strive for a genuine presentation of the spiritual," as in Foote's *Tender Mercies:*

> for the viewer trained in Hollywood's abundant means who needs guidance during every "significant" moment, it might perhaps be difficult to "see" Mac's love, just as it would have been difficult to see Mac's recovery from alcoholism or his religious conversion leading to his acceptance of baptism. What even a blind man could see, but which American viewers have trouble perceiving, is that Mac's presence, his words and his actions are his signs of love. His love is what he does, what he is, what Rosa Lee helped him to become. A declaration of love amounts to a declaration of faith. And faith cannot be shown, is not subject to rational discourse; it is accepted and possessed. In transcendental style, the things we do not see are equal to those we do. (26)

Thus silence, by Foote's own admission, is "very important" in his drama (Interview 9 Nov. 1995); it is part of the "shorthand" (Porter, Interview 12 Oct. 1994) of dialogue and scene that forms Horton Foote's version of Schrader's "transcendental style."

The poetic understatement, the intense longing of the characters, and the "sparse means" (Schrader 154) of expression in Horton Foote's work suggest a spiritual reality beyond everyday experience.

IMPLICATIONS FOR PERFORMANCE

Identifying the traits of impressionism in Foote's work provides a performance matrix as well as a critical framework for his artistry. For the director, actor or designer, understanding his literary impressionism helps fashion the distinctive mood, rhythm, and intensity of Foote's style. In his book *Period Style for the Theatre,* Douglas A. Russell points out that Chekhov's plays demand a uniquely "impressionistic" design. In presenting *The Cherry Orchard,* for example, only

> by understanding how an impressionistic painter would have perceived light filtered through cherry blossoms, the sunset hours of the day, and a chandelier-illuminated party can the director and the actor have an appropriate feeling for the settings, costumes, and atmosphere in this play. (361–62)

Similarly, directors who have successfully produced Foote's work have instinctively incorporated these principles of impressionism into their design. In *Tender Mercies,* for example, the sets help generate the quintessential mood and character of Foote's writing. The chipped and faded paint on the Mariposa Motel suggests the passing of time and an absence of concern about appearances; the newly-plowed fields surrounding the motel suggest the emptiness—and yet fertile possibility—in Mac's life; and the earth tones inside Rosa Lee's home reflect her warm and nurturing character.

The impressionistic quality of Foote's work is especially dependent on the skill of his actors. The unique rhythms and suggestive nuances of his dialogue, for example, are often contingent on the subtle pauses, inflections, and various intonations that the actors bring to their performances. Successful actors in Foote's work must incorporate a keen awareness of the near-excessive need for subtlety in their expressions and understanding of the subtext. In performing Foote's plays, actors must understand that their dialogue is often more dependent on what their characters *don't* say than on the actual words being spoken. The occasional pauses that Foote drafts into the text of his scripts are of vital importance in communicating the intention and intensity of his work.

NOTES

[1] Although the structural configuration of impressionism differs from traditional designs, I disagree with Russell in his labeling of impressionistic composition as "weak" or "vague." The arrangement of specific elements must frequently be quite intricate and precise in order to create the overall effect of the work.

[2] It should be mentioned that the concept of impressionism, as it will be used in this essay, is unrelated to the avant-garde "cinematic impressionism" practiced among a small group of French filmmakers in the 1930s. This "impressionist" school of filmmaking was led by Louis Delluc (1890–1924) "who founded the journal *Cinéma* and became, long before Eisenstein, the first aesthetic theorist of the film" (Cook 322). The unconventional filmic style developed by Delluc and his followers attempted to emulate the abstract visual experience of French impressionistic painting. Although Delluc's "cinematic impressionism" was based primarily on film's visual properties, most theatrical films are constructed with traditional dramatic elements in mind, taking into

considerations the conventional elements of plot, dialogue, character development, and so on.

[3] Foote has repeatedly been compared to Chekhov. Some have even hailed Foote as the "American Chekhov" (Berson F1).

[4] The song used in the film version of *The Trip to Bountiful,* "Softly and Tenderly," was changed from "There's Not a Friend Like the Lowly Jesus," which was used in the stage version (Briley 180).

Works Cited

Anderson, George. "Ambitious 'Dragons' Opens PPT Season." *Pittsburgh Post-Gazette* (PA) 29 Sept. 1988: 26. The Horton Foote Papers. Southern Methodist University.

Atkinson, Brooks. Rev. of *Texas Town* in *New York Times*. Horton Foote Papers. Southern Methodist University.

Barr, George Terry. *The Ordinary World of Horton Foote*. Diss. U of Tennessee, Knoxville, 1986.

Berson, Misha. "The Foote Factor: Oscar-Winning Dramatist Visits for Special Weekend at Belltown Theatre Center." *Seattle Times* 23 Aug. 1993, final ed.: F1.

Briley, Rebecca Luttrell. *You Can Go Home Again: The Focus on Family in the Works of Horton Foote*. Diss. U of Kentucky, 1990.

Broude, Norma, ed. *World Impressionism: The International Movement, 1860–1920*. New York: Abrams, 1990.

Brown, Tony. "Horton Foote Catches Us 'Dividing the Estate.'" Rev. of *Dividing the Estate* by Horton Foote. *The Charlotte Observer* 31 Dec. 1991: A-1. Horton Foote Papers. Southern Methodist University.

Cook, David. *A History of Narrative Film*. New York: Norton, 1981.

Courthion, Pierre. *Impressionism*. Trans. by John Shepley. New York: Abrams, 1972.

Davis, Ronald L. "Roots in Parched Ground: An Interview with Horton Foote." *Southwest Review* (Summer 1988): 298–318.

de Vries-Evans, Susanna. *Impressionist Masters: Paintings from Private Collections*. New York: Crescent, 1995.

Desser, David. "Transcendental Style in *Tender Mercies*." *Religious Communication Today* Sept. 1985: 21–27.

"Dialogue on Film: Horton Foote." *American Film* 12 Oct. 1986: 13–14, 16.

Edgerton, Gary. "A Visit to the Imaginary Landscape of Harrison, Texas: Sketching the Film Career of Horton Foote." *Literature/Film Quarterly* 17.1 (1989): 2–12.

Foote, Horton. *Roots in a Parched Ground, Convicts, Lily Dale, The Widow Claire: The First Four Plays in the Orphans' Home Cycle*. New York: Grove, 1988.

———. Interview. 9 Nov. 1995.

————. *To Kill a Mockingbird, Tender Mercies, and The Trip to Bountiful: Three Screenplays by Horton Foote.* New York: Grove, 1989.

Freedman, Samuel G. "From the Heart of Texas." *New York Times Magazine* 9 Feb. 1986, sec. 6: 30–31, 50, 61–63, 73.

Gerdts, William H. *American Impressionism.* New York: Abbeville, 1984.

Harms, William A. *Impressionism as a Literary Style.* Diss. Indiana University, 1971.

Hauser, Arnold. *The Social History of Art. Vol. 4: Naturalism, Impressionism, The Film Age.* New York: Vintage, 1951.

Kanfer, Stephan. Rev. of *The Roads to Home* by Horton Foote. *The New Leader* 5 Oct. 1992: 22–23.

Kelder, Diane. *The Great Book of French Impressionism.* New York: Artabras, 1980.

Kirschke, James J. *Henry James and Impressionism.* New York: Whitston, 1981.

Lawrence, Larry. "Plays Follow Replacement of Old Ways." *Abilene Reporter-News* (TX) 13 Aug. 1989. Horton Foote Papers. Southern Methodist University.

Muller, Hurbert J. "Impressionism in Fiction: Prism vs. Mirror." *American Scholar* 7 (1938). [Rpt. in *Literary Impressionism, James and Chekhov.* By Peter H. Stowell. Athens, GA: U of Georgia P, 1980]

Neff, David. "Going Home to the Hidden God." *Christianity Today* 4 Apr. 1986: 30–31.

Otto, Rudolf. *The Idea of the Holy: An Inquiry into the Non-Rational Factor in the Idea of the Divine and Its Relation to the Rational.* Trans. by John W. Harvey. London: Oxford UP, 1950.

Pacheco, Patrick. "Remember Me: In Their Searches For a Lost Time, Playwrights Neil Simon and Horton Foote Reveal Two Distinct Visions of America." *Daily News-City Lights* n.d.: 5. Horton Foote Papers. Southern Methodist University.

Porter, Laurin. Interview. 12 Oct. 1994.

Rapetti, Rodolphe. *Monet.* New York: Arch Cape, 1990.

Reinert, Al. "Tender Foote: Horton Foote Continues to Find Big Themes in Small-Town Life." *Texas Monthly* July 1991:110, 132–37. Horton Foote Papers. Southern Methodist University.

Richards, David. "The Secret Aches of Broken Families: 'The Roads to Home' Travls into the Heart of Loneliness." Rev. of *The Roads to Home* by Horton Foote. *New York Times* 4 Oct. 1992, sec. 2: 5.

Roudebush, Jay. *Mary Cassatt.* New York: Crown, 1979.

Russell, Douglas A. *Period Style for the Theatre.* Boston: Allyn and Bacon, 1980.

————. *Stage Costume Design.* NY: Appleton-Century-Crofts, 1973.

————. *Theatrical Style: A Visual Approach to the Theatre.* Palo Alto, CA: Mayfield, 1976.

Sarris, Andrew. "Do Audiences Want Mercy?" [Rev. of *Tender Mercies*] *The Village Voice* 8 Mar. 1983: 39.

Schrader, Paul. *Transcendental Style in Film: Ozu, Bresson, Dreyer.* Berkeley: U of California P, 1972.

Shiff, Richard. *Cézanne and the End of Impressionism: A Study of the Theory, Technique, and Critical Evaluation of Modern Art.* Chicago: U of Chicago P, 1984.

Simon, John. Rev. of *Lily Dale* by Horton Foote. *New York* 8 Dec. 1986: 115.

Smith, Amanda. "Horton Foote: A Writer's Journey." *Varia* July/Aug. 1987: 18–20, 23, 26–27.

Stowell, Peter H. *Literary Impressionism, James and Chekhov.* Athens, GA: U of Georgia P, 1980.

Symons, Arthur. *Studies in the Seven Arts.* NY: Dutton, 1910.

Weiskel, Thomas. *The Romantic Sublime: Studies in the Structure and Psychology of Transcendence.* Baltimore: Johns Hopkins UP, 1976.

Wölfflin, Heinrich. *Principles of Art History: The Problem of the Development of Style in Later Art.* Trans. by M.D. Hottinger. New York: Dover, 1950.

Wood, Gerald C., ed. *Selected One-Act Plays of Horton Foote.* By Horton Foote. Dallas: Southern Methodist UP, 1989.

Negotiating History, Negotiating Myth: Friel among His Contemporaries

Claire Gleitman

In recent years, a crop of playwrights has emerged in Ireland whose work is so fresh, so politically incisive and so theatrically rich as to prompt more than a few commentators to speak of a second Irish renaissance in dramatic literature.[1] Among these Irish playwrights, clearly it is Brian Friel who has achieved the widest international acclaim. Yet Friel is hardly a solitary star in an otherwise vacant sky. Rather, he writes amidst a constellation of innovative dramatists whose output owes something to the luminaries of the first Irish renaissance, but even more, perhaps, to a tradition of postmodernism marked with a distinctly Irish personality. Postmodern literature, according to Linda Hutcheon, "is a critical revisiting, an ironic dialogue with the past."[2] This is an apt description of not only the theatrical mood in Ireland, but of a theoretical and cultural climate in which it is widely felt that everything Irish, "including our politics and our literature, has to be rewritten—i.e., re-read."[3] Friel and his contemporaries are deeply invested in rereading and reassessing Ireland's history; hence, they escape the charges of regressive solipsism that have been levelled at other examples of postmodern art and criticism.[4] Indeed, Ireland's recent drama assiduously engages political and economic realities even as it participates in the more general postmodern reflection on representation.

The present article shall consider Brian Friel alongside two of his most prominent playwriting compatriots: Tom Murphy, whose career, like Friel's, is long and varied; and Frank McGuinness, a younger but increasingly visible and prolific dramatist. All three authors' involvement in the rereading project is manifested by their shared manipulation of (even reinvention of) the genre of the history play. Together, there authors have concentrated their attention upon charged events in Irish history and crafted from them a skeptical, ambivalent and affecting drama that dissects the mythologies that the culture holds most dear: mythologies that accrue around cataclysmic national events and around the very notion of Irishness itself. Their plays simultaneously restage history and question its reliability, thus acknowledging the contingency of any act of historiography.

For instance, in three important history plays—Friel's *The Freedom of the City* (1973); Murphy's *Famine* (1968); and McGuinness's *Observe the Sons of Ulster Marching Towards the Somme* (1985)—the dramatists revisit events that have taken on great emotional and political weight in sectarian mythologies, both Nationalist and Unionist. The subject of *Freedom of the City* is Bloody Sunday, 1972, when British paratroopers shot and killed thirteen unarmed citizens of Derry during a banned civil rights march. Friel's fictionalized enactment of Bloody Sunday concerns three civil rights marchers who stumble into Derry's Guildhall while striving to escape the British army's CS gas. In *Freedom,* as in the later play *Making History* (1988), Friel interrogates the process by which ideology transforms "brute fact" into myth. *Freedom* juxtaposes the actual events of the day as experienced by the marchers with the extravagant distortions of those events conjured by various "witnesses." Thus we see history being altered by its interpreters even at its inception, as the marchers metamorphose for their Irish admirers into messianic heroes of the stature of Patrick Pearse, and for their British revilers into a gang of fifty armed gunmen with sedition on their minds. Meanwhile, the actual story of three anonymous and bewildered citizens randomly caught in the crossfire (and eventually assassinated) is erased by the day's chroniclers, who are thoroughly engrossed by their own, spectacular revisions.

It is worth noting that *Freedom of the City,* which ostensibly is a history play, dispenses with historical fact almost entirely. In the drama, Friel shifts his dramatic moment from 1972 to 1970, and creates a scenario that—though based upon actual events and particularly upon the Widgery Tribunal—is in essence fiction.[5] Friel's casual rearrangement of historical phenomena, a characteristic of *Translations* also, suggest the impossibility of accessing "actual" history except as it is filtered through subjective and often self-serving interpreters. The real occurrences are of little importance to those interpreters: what matters is the way in which the actual can be manipulated for the sake of the mythic. In this regard Friel seems to intimate what Glover and Kaplan assert in another context:

> Though searching for an objective truth about this past against which to measure present deformations is no longer a viable political or theoretical project, thinking politically and historically about the many versions of it now in circulation certainly is.[6]

Tom Murphy's *Famine,* in its way, is also concerned to demystify the mystificatory impulses behind the making of history. But Murphy enacts the demystification through his analysis of a man who is himself a victim of an outmoded mythology. The central character in *Famine*—John Connor, an impoverished descendent of a long line of kings and chieftains—is as economically and politically marginalized as Friel's marchers, but he fails to realize it. Instead, Connor remains wedded to those concepts of noblesse oblige and ancient tribalism that were foundational for his ancestors. Such concepts drive him to play the patriarch in his village although he is as far removed from the ancient tribe of Connors as Jack Durbeyfield is from the knightly d'Urbervilles. Connor attempts to apply tribal ideals and an archaic, abstract value system to a situation that is implacably material: that is, the devastating potato blight of the 1840s. In the first scene of the play, John insists that the guests attending his daughter's wake must be fed generously: "We can't send them off mean . . . She *was* regal . . . And—we—won't—send—them—off mean."[7] The fact that John's daughter died of starvation and that his other children are starving as well is not sufficient to deter him from acting the part of the chieftain, whose honor depends upon his gracious gentility.

Thus, on the shaky foundation of abstractions that sum up the tribe's ethos, John formulates "a resolution" to guide the village's actions during the crisis: they must wait, he insists, and do what is "right." Out of touch with the realities of his historical moment, John believes that salvation is possible through a collective commitment to home, hearth and the all-knowing divine will. Conflating tribal laws with Christian ones, he insists that the village must endure with stoicism, denouncing all suggestions of active resistance: "Help will come, because it's right. And what's right has to be believed in if we're to hope" (40–41). But John's passivity results not in salvation but in his family's collapse: in the end, he is driven to the murder of his wife and a young son.

Murphy offers no assurance that a more active approach would have saved Connor. On the contrary, it is clear that the other options available to him also entailed risks and compromises. Nor does the play underestimate the repug-·nant amorality of the powers-that-be, who sit smugly pondering Irish dirtiness as crowds clamor for food outside their office doors. The image of fully laden corn carts laboring under police protection past the emaciated frames of Irish peasants; the abysmally cold and calculated "business" sense that propose either starvation or the "option" of emigration; the obtuseness of the House of Commons arguing in its London luxury while tens of thousands starve—all of this, so vividly portrayed within *Famine*'s expansive epic frame, conjures a picture of arrogance and indifference all the more horrifying given its basis in historical fact.

And yet there is something deeply vexing about the play's immobile "hero," whose ethical touchstones seem so woefully inadequate to the occasion. In fact, Murphy's history play interrogates one of modern Ireland's defining moments only to find failures all around. The British are what one expects, and the mythic Irish tribe proves unequipped to deal with the situation that confronts it. One conclusion invited by *Famine* is that disembodied notions of morality, no matter how heroic, are powerless to counteract the forces of economics and politics. But another, more troubling message is that Irish tribal culture may have abetted its own demise by virtue of its devotion to antiquated and, in the event, fatal concepts of tribal ideals. An abandonment of those ideals, for John, would necessitate a recognition of his family's devastating social and economic decline. Hence, he clings to them with ever more fervent desperation: "*All* that land was Connors' once! And I'll not go . . . I was born here, and I'll die here, and I'll rot here! . . . Cause I'm right" (81). In the end, John's unwavering view of "right" collapses beneath the weight of modern nation-state colonial politics.

Such a torturous passage is again staged in McGuinness's *Observe the Sons of Ulster Marching Towards the Somme*. Here, the audience witnesses the experiences of eight Protestant Irish soldiers, seven of whose lives ended at the Battle of the Somme. As is well known, many of the Irish Protestants in the 36th Ulster division chose to serve in the first World War in order to display their unwavering loyalty to the Crown at a time when threats of Home Rule loomed. When thousands of those enlisted men died at the Somme, they were extolled at home as martyrs to a sacred cause. As the *Belfast News-Letter* put it, "Ulster Protestants took their stand where their fathers stood . . . [in] costly self-sacrifice to our Empire."[8] Adding further sheen to the mythology, the Battle of the Somme began on July 1st, which is thought to be the anniversary of the Battle of the Boyne.[9] That battle, fought in 1690, ended in victory for the Protestant King William over the Catholic James; hence, it was viewed as a death-knell for Catholic Ireland and a great Protestant triumph. When the Battle of the Somme happened to fall on the same date, this seemed to add mystical confirmation to the Protestant wish to see the British war as a fight for home and country.

Observe the Sons of Ulster is cast in the form of a memory play in which one survivor, named Pyper, recalls events that preceded the battle. His memories revolve around the experiences of seven other soldiers, all working-class tradesmen, with whom he lived and fought. Although Pyper is an aristocrat, his homosexuality severed him from his family and class, and he feels an increasingly profound alliance with his disenfranchised fellow fighters. All right of the soldiers enlisted in the British Army, they assure each other, for Ulster and "For the glory of his majesty the king and all his people."[10] But the men's declared mission of keeping Ireland safe from "Fenian rats" turns out to be a slogan veiling a far more complex array of motives (26). These marginalized characters shield themselves from despair by means of vehement sectarian pride. The consequence is a huge contribution to Unionist mythology, which McGuinness shows in the making.

As the play begins, the Elder Pyper complains about recurrent visitations from ghosts of that July day in 1916. Yet his mutterings reveal that he has become a kind of Ian Paisley figure extolling the nearly theological mission of Irish Protestantism:

There would be, and there will be no surrender. The sons of Ulster will rise and lay their enemy low, as they did at the Boyne, as they did at the Somme, against any invader who will trespass on to their homeland. Fenians claim Cuchullian as their ancestor, but he is ours . . . Sinn Fein? . . . It is we, the Protestant people, who have always stood alone . . . and triumphed, for we are God's chosen. (10)

The hyperbole of the speech and its Unionist appropriation of Cuchullian, a central figure in Republican myth, display the nature of the mythic version of history which plagues Irish culture. Its dramatic irony is revealed through the remembered and reenacted scenes of July 1916. On the morning of the battle, the men turn to parody, performance and finally ritual in an effort to steel themselves for what awaits them. Their games are self-protective: they seek to avoid a recognition of their irrelevance in the theatre of war by showering contempt upon another group of marginalized people. First, a character named McIlwaine offers a burlesque version of the Easter Rising, which also took place in 1916. In McIlwaine's telling, the revolutionary figure of Patrick Pearse becomes a pathetic clown who "took over a post office because he was short of a few stamps"; he ends up being shot by his mother, who declares: "'That'll learn him, the cheeky pup. Going about robbing post offices" (64–65).

Thus the Easter Rising, which would find a central place in the opposing side's catalogue of mythic victories, is rewritten by the Unionist to rob it of valor. Later, the men decide to "play" the Battle of the Boyne—or, more accurately, to play the Battle of Scarva, which is the annual reenactment of the Battle of the Boyne held on its anniversary. By restaging not the actual battle but its annual commemoration, McGuinness (like Friel) suggests that actual history can be accessed only through representation—and in this case representation has been coopted by the ideological imperatives of Unionism. As the "director" of the piece remarks, "remember, . . . we know the result, you know the result, keep to the result" (70). While the battle is being performed, the director provides appropriate commentary, stressing the virtues of Protestant William versus the vices of the demonized Catholic James. His "script" loads the representation with the necessary ideological freight; thus he cloaks historical events under the propaganda of Unionist, Protestant myth.

But Pyper—who has acted as anarchic truth-teller throughout the memory-play—surprises the others by straying from the script. Though his role is to play the trusty steed for the victor, Pyper trips. His rider, King William, comes crashing to the ground, and James and his horse find themselves the startled victors. As one of the men declares woefully, this is "Not the but of signs" (71). Pyper's action is troubling became it destabilizes the ideologically cathected myth which had provided the thinnest veneer over the terrifying actuality they are facing. This deconstruction of the mythology might be considered a salutary act, except that it removes comforting delusions from men who are about to die. Pyper himself seems to regret depriving the men of their myths just when they most needed them, and he shows his contrition by quickly attempting to re-patch the mythology. After a ritualistic exchange of Orange sashes to confirm their confederacy, Pyper delivers an impassioned sermon in which he assures them that their fight has meaning; it is dedicated to Ulster: "Observe the sons of Ulster marching towards the Somme. I love my home. I love my Ulster" (80).

At the last moment, Pyper retreats from the abyss and clings to the mythology. Yet the play does not criticize him for doing so. Rather, McGuinnness suggests this paradoxical truth about mythologizing: it is arbitrary and artificial, yet it sustains as it deludes. The play provides no way out of the paradox; instead, it enacts the paradoxical formations and deformations of history-in-the-making. The process by which Pyper, the gadfly skeptic of 1916, becomes the righteous scourge of Unionism is a dramatic articulation of mytho-historiography; he participates in uncovering the hollow center of myth at the same moment that he helps to write another chapter of it.

McGuinness's play, then, reveals an insight into the ways that history is written: he recognizes that both sides of any historical impasse mythologize events, thereby distorting them into the shapes that their ideological imperatives require. In addition, his concentration on Unionist foot solders reflects his interest in history's silences, an interest that Friel and Murphy share. In all three plays that I have examined thus far, the dramatized episode is filtered through the perspective of figures typically relegated to the margins in historical narratives: that is, the weak, the powerless, the food for powder. In *Freedom,* in *Famine,* and in *Observe,* we see the event from a margin's-eye-view.

And Friel, Murphy and McGuinness manipulate other theatrical gestures in common within those margins. For instance, in the literal margin of no-man's-land, the forward trenches, McGuinness's soldiers await the order that will send them to their deaths, and endure the lull before zero-hour by enacting self-reflexive, performative gestures in an effort to persuade themselves that those deaths will have meaning. As I have discussed, the soldiers narrate burlesque versions of the Easter Rising; they "play" the Battle of Scarva; they cooperate in staging solemn and highly charged rituals.

This habit of performance is another tactic that the three playwrights share, and one to which I shall now turn. In a striking number of Ireland's recent dramas, performance serves as a strategy for coping with the experience of marginalization and loss.

To grasp the nature of the dispossession that prompts performance, it is necessary to consider the social and political backdrop against which these authors write. Friel and Murphy were born within six years of each other during the decade following Ireland's independence. Both grew up in a climate of deep economic malaise, when an Irish citizen's attachment to his or her homeland had to do battle with the knowledge that a decent life could not be had there by a large portion of its residents. McGuinness, born some two decades later, entered his young manhood during the painful resurrection of the "Troubles." These circumstances left their mark on the playwrights, whose works tend to be rooted in the economic and spiritual realities of mid- and late-twentieth century Ireland.[11] There are some generational differences to be noted, to be sure, and I shall have more to say about that later. Yet all three writers show a continuous interest in characters whose lives are circumscribed by material distress and social strife, and who respond by resorting to performance, ritual, story-telling or play.

In Friel's *Philadelphia, Here I Come!* (1964), for instance, the central character splits himself in two and performs endless duets with his alter ego. In the play's first episode alone Gar sings; he pantomimes conducting and then playing Mendelssohn's Violin Concerto; he dances; and he performs various scenes from his life with his alter ego as narrator, spectator, director, and co-star. In this manner, Gar seeks to distance himself from the miserable realities of his daily life and probable future, reconstructing them through energetic, nearly desperate play. Yet Gar is no Christy Mahon: imagination does not succeed in catapulting him toward mythic statute, nor does it allow him, as it allows Christy, to "talk [himself] into freedom."[12] Rather, Gar ends the play plagued by agonizing indecision, as the barrenness of *both* his options—that is, leaving Ireland or trying to make a life there—forces itself resoundingly to his attention.

Similarly, John Joe in Murphy's *A Crucial Week in the Life of a Grocer's Assistant* (1964) struggles to negotiate the conflicting promises of emigration and remaining at home. Incapable of acting decisively, he retreats into expressionistic fantasies or dream-plays that carry him away, briefly, from a sterile emotional and economic climate that seems intractable. Both Gar and John Joe mystify departure, imagining it in exotic terms akin to the escape fantasies so common in *Dubliners*. But, like Joyce, these playwrights are unflinching in their deflation of such fantasies: their characters are trapped not merely by economic distress but by an emotional poverty born out of the ravages of famine and colonization. Thus John Joe's mother clings to her son, assaults him with guilt, and ahistorically sings the praises of tribal loyalty, land and Mother Ireland: "We will stick to our own and the soot, as we did through the centuries."[13]

As these plays persistently indicate, it is this kind of self-defeating mythology that plagues the Irish consciousness. In a work evocatively titled *Carthaginians* (1988), McGuinness revisits Bloody Sunday to depict its aftermath in the lives of seven grieved survivors. While Friel concentrated upon a fictionalized version of the event itself, McGuinness suggestively sets his drama in 1988, sixteen years later. The choice is indicative of an attitude of impatience that abounds in McGuinness's drama, a sense that it is rather late in the day for rehearsing the same old pieties and grievances. In contrast to the focused analyses of Friel and Murphy, McGuinness's tendency to examine Ireland against the backdrop of an international canvas that works not to diminish the island's problems but to contextualize them within the framework of broader geopolitical realities. Thus, *Observe the Sons* places Protestant Ulster in the shadow of the first World War; *Someone Who'll Watch over Me* (1992) takes Ireland and Britain's squabbles and chains them to a wall in Beirut; and *Carthaginians'* title serves to inflect Bloody Sunday through the broader paradigm of imperialist confrontation and extermination.

Moreover, for McGuinness, performance often serves the purpose of exuberant debunking. *Carthaginians* is set in a graveyard, where the seven characters have withdrawn from the world and live in hope of the rising of the dead. Their hard-won success in putting Bloody Sunday behind them is accomplished at last with the aid of a play-within-the-play which they collaborate in staging. The play, entitled "The Burning Balaclava," is written by *Carthaginians'* central character and chief anarchist, a homosexual known as Dido, Queen of Derry. Dido's play appropriates the discourses of popular sentiment, popular culture, and canonized literature in a joyful send-up of a host of Irish sacred cows, ranging from the Troubles to *Juno and the Paycock.* Dido's success as play-maker and healer seems to stem from his transgressive posture, from his ability to slip the confines of either/or oppositions that so structure and debilitate Northern Irish lives. His play cheerfully deflates the cherished mythologies of sectarianism and literary sentiment, and as a consequence it seems to clear the air of the cant and morbid obsession that an event like Bloody Sunday can accrue. After participating in the play, which is followed by a ritualistic recital of the names of the Bloody Sunday dead, the graveyard dwellers at last are able to deep. Yet the playwright who scripted the burlesque concludes *Carthaginians* by announcing his intention to leave the troubled city, in a phrase that encapsulates not only Dido's own tortured ambivalence but also (mutatis mutandis) Gar's and John Joe's: "I believe it is time to leave Derry. Love it and leave it."[14] The actual, unpromising circumstances of life in Ireland assert themselves even on the heels of a triumphant act of play.

In this regard, the self-reflexive tendency in contemporary Irish drama is another reflection of the postmodernist spirit. Modernist self-reflexivity often assumes an ahistorical pose vis-à-vis its own production, focusing attention upon the work in an endless regress to an aesthetized consciousness. Postmodern self-reflexivity, however, installs historical horizons in the work's enunciatory moment.[15] Such gestures are part and parcel of the more general postmodern restaging of history. Characteristic of this restaging, as I have suggested, is a demystification of dominant mythologies—those associated both with particular historical events and with the notion of an essential Irish character as Yeats, for one, imagined it. It is with this latter brand of mythologizing that I shall conclude.

At first glance, two of Friel's most popular plays—*Translations* (1980) and *Dancing at Lughnasa* (1990)—seem prominently to feature the figure of the lovably drunken and eccentric Stage-Irishman (or woman).[16] In *Translations,* Hugh and Jimmy Jack Cassie bluster and strut and grow progressively drunker; and *Dancing at Lughnasa* contains an ensemble of comely maidens, each endowed with her own winning idiosyncrasies. Yet a corrosive undercurrent in both plays destabilizes the sentimentality, suggesting a rottenness at the heart of these apparent idylls of peasant harmony and good will. In *Translations,* as many readers have noted, Friel circumvents nostalgia by blending fondness with a trenchant critique. Rather than writing "a threnody on the death of the Irish language," which Friel early on maintained that he wished to avoid,[17] he provides in *Translations* a gradually emerging critique of what Leonard Pilkington calls the "quixoticism" in Gaelic culture "that contributes to economic decline."[18] The playwright implicitly attributes the act of imperial dispossession that *Translations* chronicles to an attitude of mind on the part of the peasantry that made the country ripe for colonizing. In addition, *Translations* establishes its context with reference to three general sources of instability operating concurrently with colonization: the economic hardships that pressured the young to abandon their country in increasing numbers; the incipient resistance movement that threatened community stability from within as did the imperialist presence from without; and the imminent blight of the potato, the staple of the community's diet.

Thus, in the Chekhovian spirit, Friel suggests that the struggle between old and new worlds is won by the new not only because of its efficient brutality, but because the old is exhausted and effete, and indulges in fantastic self-deception rather than finding practical methods to adapt to a changing world. The central characters in the play are defeated in part (like John Connor) by their dedication to an antique way of life. They are also a collection of cripples, mutes and drunks; they exhibit, Friel has remarked, "a physical maiming which is a public representation of their spiritual deprivation."[19] In short, the interplay between regret and irony in *Translations,* between its lament for a lost culture and its critique of that culture's malaise, allows the play to transcend simple nationalist sentiment in order to dissect a complex national condition.

Similarly, *Dancing at Lughnasa* invokes the Yeatsian mythology of a spiritually robust Ireland even as it deconstructs it. The god Lugh hovers over the play, whispering from the back hills of a vanishing culture in tune with its most lusty impulses. At centerstage is a family of women who have nearly lost touch with that ancient spirit and who seem to find their way back to it only through the magic of their sporadically reliable Marconi radio. As their sensibility and means of survival are under threat from religious, ideological and technological forces, the Mundy sisters are seduced despite themselves by the primal passions that the festival of Lughnasa once celebrated. These passions come to the fore halfway through *Lughnasa*'s first act, when the sisters suddenly give themselves over to a wild, passionate and almost frantic dance. One sister, whose fingers are covered with flour, "pulls her hands down her cheeks and patterns her face" with what looks like warpaint; another tosses a priest's sur- plice over her head in a gesture of religious burlesque, like a participant at a black Mass. Together, they dance as if they are possessed by alien spirits; their behavior, Friel writes, is both "out of character and at the same time ominous of some deep and true emotion."[20]

This scene, so quickly famous, is strikingly effective in its evocation of the repressed impulses that lie beneath the sisters' calm exteriors. "[T]here is a sense," the stage directions tell us, "of order being consciously subverted" (22), and this is as true formally as it is thematically and emotionally. For a brief moment, the play modulates from Friel's characteristic naturalism into an expressionistic interlude that reveals, with breathtaking compression, the sub- terranean lives of the characters. And what we see is only a hint of what there is to see. For the bulk of the play the sisters remain enigmas, who bury pas- sionate longings and ferocious regret beneath impassive and amiable facades.

The release that the women experience through dance is akin to what their Uncle Jack describes when he tells of the Ugandan native ceremonies that he witnessed during his twenty-five years as a missionary there. During such cer- emonies, he recalls, the entire village would light fires, drink palm wine and dance, "believe it or not, for days on end! It is the most wonderful sight you have ever seen" (48). By juxtaposing Jack's memories with the dying embers of the Lughnasa celebrations, the play suggests a link between the vitalism of Uganda's still-thriving customs and a lost Gaelic paganism—both of which are placed in opposition to the rigid decorum of Catholicism and a sterile, indus- trialized modernity. Yet, once again, a counterpointing irony subverts the apparent romanticism. In his innocent wonder at Ugandan rituals, Uncle Jack barely acknowledges the fact that the celebrants amongst whom he lived were the diseased inhabitants of a leper colony. Hence, his assumptions regarding their untarnished joy are questionable at best. Further, all of the action of the play excepting the narrator's monologues is the stuff of memory: everything that the audience witnesses has passed through a veil of years, of sentiment, of transfiguring wish. In his final monologue, the narrator confesses that the moment of the past which haunts him most evocatively is one that "owes noth- ing to fact": "In that memory atmosphere is more real than incident and every- thing is simultaneously actual and illusory" (71). The years that he recalls are tinged with disappointment, failure, and oppressive material demands. The Mundy sisters and their Uncle Jack find refuge from those demands through brief, ritualized forays into an age that they recreate and romanticize as surely as Michael romanticizes his childhood, wrapping it, as he says, in "a very soft, golden light" (70).

Like *Translations* and *Lughnasa,* Tom Murphy's play *Bailegangaire* (1985) considers the interplay between the past of Irish legend—the past of the rural Irish mythologized culture—and the present of economic and cultural deprivation. Though the drama is set in a "traditional three-roomed thatched house," this relic from the past is pierced by outside forces that are in marked contrast to the style of the cottage, and to the world that old Mommo summons in the story she tells her incessantly to her disaffected granddaughters.[21] A radio that broadcasts the news, the "putt-putt" of one granddaughter's motorcycle, the "rubber-backed lino" in the same woman's house, the computer plant bought out by the Japanese—all of these elements in the drama work to counterpoint Mommo's story of the past with the impoverished post-industrialism of the present. Meanwhile, there is little doubt that the past was any less limited than is the present. In *Bailegangaire,* the bucolic rural paradise of Irish legend is a fiction that has spawned an obsessive and crippling preoccupation with the past. Meanwhile, the present doles out destitution to a population that does not know how to make its way into the future except by limping along with the broken-down crutch of a partial mythology.

The centerpiece of *Bailegangaire* and the focal point of the interplay between past and present is Mommo's tale of a laughing contest, one that took place years ago in a town called Bochtán and renamed Bailegangaire, or "the town without laughter." Mommo's manner of telling her story is gleefully mock-epic: she makes use of stock epithets ("bold Costello"), grand foreshadowing gestures ("For there was to be many's the inquisition by c'roner, civic guard and civilian on all that transpired in John Mah'ny's that night" [55]), and boasting challenges ("'I'm a better laugher than your Costello'" (59). Mommo's tale summons the ancient Celtic and Norse traditions of flyting, of poetic contests, of Bardic rituals—while simultaneously and thunderously deflating them. This is, after all, no titanic battle between Conchubar and Cuchullian. It is a contest between peasants in a remote country pub to determine who is the finer laugher, and its combatants are a pair of peasants who are down on their luck. For all of its grand gestures, the laughing contest ends in a crescendo of pain, as the company speaks of the circumstances that engender frustrated lives: "the damnedable crop"; the rotted hay; and the children who refuse to stay alive:

> All of them present, their heads threwn back abandoned in festivities of guffaws: the wretched and neglected, dilapidated an' forlorn, the forgotten an' tormented, ragged an' dirty, impoverished, hungry, emaciated and unhealthy . . .—glintin' their defiance . . . an' rejection, inviting of what else might come or *care* to come!—driving bellows of refusal at the sky through the roof. Och hona ho gus hah-haa! . . . The nicest night ever. (75)

In vehement resistance to romantics who would have it otherwise, Murphy paints a portrait of a rural existence plagued by poverty, desperation and death, in which the only response available to the villagers is a defiant "bellow of refusal," a vehement challenge to an inscrutable God.

In fact, in its deflation of romantic mythologies and its depiction of a woman's paralysis within a fictionalized past, *Bailegangaire* can be read as a kind of political quasi-allegory. Mommo and her granddaughters are reflections of a people hobbled by a past that they cannot fully face, except through fragments of a mythologized narrative that sidesteps crucial elements. By the close of the play, the women at last succeed in bringing their gory to its conclusion. Once they do so, they are brought to terms with the past in all of its hideous facticity. The result is that they are able to see the present clearly and to imagine a richer future—both for themselves, and for a baby yet to be born. The difficulty that Mommo and her granddaughters have in finishing their narrative of the past is emblematic of the problem of accessing Irish history in all of its troubled complexity. But the very fact that the story does, at last, get told, indicates Murphy's sense of the importance of the attempt. The Irish history play, as manipulated by all three of these playwrights, can be viewed as a process of stripping away, of uncovering the sedimented deformations of successive layers of history. The process does not jettison the past; it does not destroy it. But neither does it enshrine it.

In short, I have been arguing, the contemporary Irish drama is characterized by a vigorous and complex reanalysis of Ireland's history and character, an exercise, I have maintained, that animates many intellectual and artistic endeavors in Ireland today. Conceivably, this activity is prompted by the "sense of fatalistic exhaustion" that Eamonn Hughes has diagnosed in contemporary Ireland, an exhaustion generated by a fear that the country's geographic, religious and political divisions have become an intractable part of life.[22] Motivated perhaps by an urge to pierce beyond and through that sense of intractability, these playwrights restage history in such a way as to resist the kinds of totalizing narratives that inevitably seem to result in stalemate. Their work critiques the construction of nationalist mythologies and imperialist dogma at the same time as it stages the material pressures that render Ireland's situation so seemingly intransigent. Like other postmodernist fictions, these dramas "structurally both install and subvert the teleology, closure and causality of narrative, both historical and fictive."[23] That these playwrights engage the concerns of the post-modern while at the same time creating a drama of astonishing emotional texture and richness suggests something of the wonder of this theatrical moment in Ireland—a moment eminently deserving of the international respect and mention that it has begun to receive.

NOTES

[1] Michael Conveney, for instance, in a review for *The Financial Times,* referred to Frank McGuinness's *Observe the Sons of Ulster Marching Towards the Somme* as "one of the finest in the extraordinary playwriting renascence in Ireland" (28 July 1986).

[2] Linda Hutcheon, *A Poetics of Postmodernism: History, Theory, Fiction* (New York: Routledge, 1988) 4. Further references are noted in the text.

[3] Seamus Deane, "Heroic styles: the tradition of an idea," *Ireland's Field Day* (London: Hutchinson, 1985) 58.

[4] See Steven Connor, "Postmodernism and Cultural Politics," *Postmodernist Culture: An Introduction to Theories of the Contemporary* (Oxford: Basil Blackwell, 1950) 224–248.

[5] See Richard Pine, *Brian Friel and Ireland's Drama* (London: Routledge, 1990), 110ff., for a useful discussion of the Widgery Report and Friel's dramatic response to it.

[6] David Glover and Cora Kaplan, "Guns in the House of Culture?: Crime Fiction and the Politics of the Popular," *Cultural Studies,* ed. Lawrence Grossberg, Cary Nelson and Paula A. Treichler (New York: Routledge, 1992) 216.

[7] Tom Murphy, *Famine* (Dublin: Gallery Books, 1984) 19–20. Further references are noted in the text.

[8] *Belfast News-Letter* (11 July 1916); quoted in Philip Orr, *The Road to the Somme: Men of the Ulster Division Tell Their Story* (Belfast: The Blackstaff Press, 1987) 197.

[9] As Orr notes, "The battle [of the Boyne] was generally celebrated on 12 July but on the Julian Calendar, in use up to 1752, it had been on the first day of the month" (161).

[10] Frank McGuinness, *Observe the Sons of Ulster Marching Towards the Somme* (London: Faber and Faber, 1986) 22. Further references are noted in the text.

[11] Even many of the plays that are ostensibly about earlier centuries (such as *Making History, Translations, Famine*) or other geographical locales (such as *Someone Who'll Watch Over Me*), can be read as analyses of contemporary Irish politics and personalities. John Andrews, for instance, has argued that *Translations* is "a play about late twentieth-century Ireland" (Brian Friel, John Andrews and Kevin Barry, "*Translations* and *A Paper Landscape:* Between Fiction and History," *The Crane Bag* 7 no. 2 (1983) 120; and Fintan O'Toole remarks that *Famine* is "a play about the twentieth century, about the spiritual and emotional famine of Murphy's own times." See *The Politics of Magic: The Work and Times of Tom Murphy* (Dublin: Raven Arts, 1987) 89.

[12] Seamus Deane, *Celtic Revivals* (London: Faber and Faber, 1985) 58.

[13] Tom Murphy, *A Whistle in the Dark and Other Plays* (London: Methuen, 1989) 104.

[14] Frank McGuinness, *Carthaginians and Baglady* (London: Faber and Faber, 1988) 70.

[15] See Hutcheon: "Modernism's 'nightmare of history' is precisely what postmodernism has chosen to face straight on" (88).

[16] One might argue cynically that it is this, in part, that accounts for the plays' international success. It is worth noting that Friel's later play, *Wonderful Tennessee,* which contains no comely dancing maidens and no winning clowns, survived for less than a week on Broadway. American audiences, one might venture, have certain expectations for Irish playwrights, which *Wonderful Tennessee* failed to meet.

[17] Brian Friel, "Extracts from a Sporadic Diary," Tim Pat Coogan, *Ireland and the Arts* (London: Quartet, n.d.) 58.

[18] Leonard Pilkington, "Language and Politics in Brian Friel's *Translations,*" *Irish University Review* 20 no. 2 (Autumn 1990) 291.

[19] In Paddy Agnew, "Talking to ourselves: Brian Friel talks to Paddy Agnew," *Magill* (Dec. 180) 60.

[20] Brian Friel, *Dancing at Lughnasa* (London: Faber and Faber, 1990) 22. Further references are noted in the text.

[21] Tom Murphy, *After Tragedy: Three Plays by Tom Murphy* (London: Methuen, 1988) 43. Further references are noted in the text.

[22] Eamonn Hughes, "To Define Your Dissent': The Plays and Polemics of the Field Day Theatre Company," *Theatre Research International* 15 no. 1 (Spring 1990) 70.

[23] Hutcheon, 63.

Hedda's Children: Simon Gray's Anti-heroes

Katherine H. Burkman

In Ibsen's *Hedda Gabler* Hedda denies her apparent pregnancy along with all other aspects of her life as the wife of George Tesman. She finds her pedantic husband, who is anxiously awaiting a university appointment, and his maiden aunts stifling, placing her hopes in a former admirer, Eilert Loevborg, who also disappoints her. A caged lioness, Hedda suppresses her fury and brings down not only Loevborg, but herself and her unborn child. Paradoxically, the fecundity of Hedda as a character, who aborts both her own life and that of her child, lies in the proliferation of characters created by other modern playwrights who have been deeply influenced in their drawing by Ibsen's heroine, by other characters in the play, and by Ibsen's point of view. Among Hedda's descendants are such characters as Regina in Lillian Hellman's *The Little Foxes,* Susan in David Hare's *Plenty,* and Jessie in Marsha Norman's *'night, Mother.* Simon Gray, who infuses many of his Ibsenite characters with a good dose of Shavian wit, seers to be particularly haunted by Hedda's ghost, although it is his male protagonists, rather than his bland heroines, who would seem to be her descendants, Hedda's children.

Critics have tended either to despise Hedda as a wicked woman, who temps Loevborg and contributes to his death by burning his manuscript,[1] to diagnose her behavior as hysterical and even psychotic,[2] or to admire her as a creative woman trapped in a mediocre environment, which she rightly despises, a feminist before her time.[3] It would be hard to dispute the cruelty of Hedda's behavior, whether it be directed at Aunt Julie, whose hat she purposely mistakes for the maid's, or at Loevborg, whose manuscript she destroys as the child of Loevborg and Thea Elvsted, who has helped Loevborg bring it to birth. Nor can one dispute the hysterical nature of Hedda's suicide, a seemingly frantic reaction to her final isolation as her deeds fail to produce the desired effect. Ibsen, however, seems to have put much of himself in his protagonist,[4] and his method of caricaturing those characters who surround her, from her blindly

pedantic husband to the basically secretarial Thea, to the smothering Auntie
Julie, and the morally corrupt Judge Brack, draws sympathy for his heroine.
Hedda may be too cowardly to defy those who surround her, but her sui-
cide becomes a desperate act of protest against the mediocrity of their lives.

Ben Butley, the protagonist of Gray's *Butley* (1971), is in many ways the
very incarnation of Hedda. An English university don, who despises his fellow
academics, his students, and his wife, he is filled with Hedda's kind of self-
hatred for remaining a cowardly part of a world for which he has such disdain.
He is unsaved by the Shavian wit with which he lacerates those who approach
him, partly because, like Hedda, he knows that he is tainted by that which he
despises.

Butley despises Edna, who after many years has had a book accepted for
publication: "She never did understand her role. Which is not to finish an
unpublishable book on Byron. Now the centre cannot hold. Mere Edna is
loosed upon the world" (30).[5] His protégé, Joey, who had once complained
about Edna's seminars, "can't afford to quarrel with Edna. Besides, I've got to
like her" (34), he explains to Ben. Like the frightened Hedda, Butley is too
cowardly to pull down his academic house and too lonely willingly to give up
his relationship with Joey, with whom he has been sharing apartment and
office, without a fight. But as Butley's behind-the-scenes machinations and
sniping confrontations catch up with him, he ends up as isolated and desperate
as Hedda, and almost as self-destructive.

While Butley denigrates Edna's manuscript for its mistaken success, he
despises Miss Heasman's manuscript on fertility in Shakespeare's *The Winter's Tale* for its clichés and for the determination of its writer to engage Butley in the academic endeavor of responding to a student's work. "'The imagery
changes from disease to flora, the tone from mad bitterness to joyfulness. As
we reach the play's climax we feel our own—spiritual—sap rising'" (44), Miss
Heasman notes as she reads the ending of her paper to the reluctant don. Butley's cruel treatment of Miss Heasman and her essay ("Sap. Sap. Yes, I think
sap's a better word than some others that spring rhymingly to mind" [45]) is
not quite as devastating as Hedda's burning of Loevberg's manuscript, but it
does convey a similar combination of protest and self-hatred. Butley longs, as
Hedda does, for the fertility that others embrace. But Hedda knows the weakness of Loevborg, who actually has created something of value in his manuscript, and Butley knows the superficiality of Miss Heasman, whose discourse
on fertility is as false as the symbolically named student, Gardner, whom Butley rejects as a relic of the 60s at play's end. "You're not what I mean at all,
not what I mean at all. I'm too old to play with the likes of you" (77), Butley
says when he dismisses Gardner, recognizing nevertheless in his Eliotic
rhythms his own Prufrockian role.

Sexually inhibited and impotent, whether in a heterosexual relationship
with his wife, or a homosexual one with Joey, Butley despises the easy fertil-

ity of those who surround him, but he continues to despise himself as a part of their world.[6] Although unwilling to teach in any conventional way, Butley's self-destructive behavior turns him into the kind of scapegoat figure that, like Hedda, becomes more deeply instructive than we as audience may find comfortable.[7]

The same combination of cowardly despair mixed with creative satire motivates Simon Hench, the publisher-protagonist of *Otherwise Engaged* (1975). Less aggressively caustic than Butley, Hench tries desperately to keep his distance from a life for which he harbors a similar contempt. Like Hedda, who turns to the piano for solace, a key to her more creative yearnings, Simon Hench turns to his new recording of Wagner's *Parsifal*. As the world intrudes on Simon, despite his efforts to keep it at bay, his wife Beth, whose affair with Ned her husband is making an effort to tolerate, asks the key question. She is responding to his statement that he would still rather live with her than with anyone else, but she wonders if he really wants to "live at all . . . since you hold such a deeply contemptuous view of human life" (56).[8] Like Ibsen's Hedda, whose unconscious desire for death seems to motivate her actions, Simon Hench unconsciously takes on the very scapegoat role he would avoid.[9]

"Your sanity is of the kind that causes people to go quietly mad around you" (56), Beth charges, although she has learned this from her lover. Simon's detachment, it scents, serves as a mirror in the play for the superficiality of the attachments of those he would avoid. He has apparently driven an old school chum to suicide (as Hedda tried to do with Loevborg), has driven his wife to another's bed (Hedda has lost first Loevborg, then Tesman to Thea), and at the end he is faced, as Hedda was with her own pregnancy, with the problem of fertility. Beth has been sleeping with both Simon (with whom she has agreed not to have children) and with Ned. If one does decide to "live at all," there is the danger (as so many Beckett characters are fond of noting) of propagation.

Unlike Hedda, whose envy prevents her from appreciating Loevborg's manuscript, Simon as publisher has a certain wistfulness about the manuscript that Davina, his friend Jeff's girlfriend, whom Hench has rejected, was "on to" (51). Manuscripts continue to be a focus of Gray's *The Common Pursuit* (1984), a drama that combines the academic and publishing worlds in its anatomy of the failed lives of several Cambridge students who have come together to start a literary magazine. Forgoing the unity of time of the two earlier dramas, Gray would seem to make of this play, spread over twenty years in the lives of his five anti-heroes and one anti-heroine, even more of a cautionary tale on the failure of creativity and the hollow victories of mediocrity.

Stuart, a character with integrity, who envisions a literary magazine of high quality, something to "give the world" (62),[10] loses all to an ostensibly inept but wealthy Martin, who "only thought of publishing because I can't think of anything else" (5). Martin, who reminds one of Hedda's husband, George Tesman, greatly admires the integrity of Stuart and the writing talent and intellect of their friend, Humphry, but he secretly envies their talents (as Tesman admits his envy of Loevborg's), and not only becomes the survivor in the publishing world, but the husband of Stuart's wife, Marigold.

Once again, fertility becomes the reward of the ineffectual and undistinguished. While Marigold aborts the child she has conceived with Stuart, whose own weakness has undermined the relationship and rendered him impotent, she manages twins with the entirely vapid Martin. Peter, whose initial role in the group was as "social officer," and who continues that role as he works his dubious charms on the Arts Council, can produce no manuscript of worth: his coffee-table book on religious leaders is mostly written by someone else. He, on the other hand, has fathered four children with Sonia and ends up with several more when his affair with Jane is discovered and he remarries, producing a new baby with the new marriage as well.

The not-so-unconscious death wish manifests itself in this play in Nick, who has sold out whatever literary talents he has to become a television celebrity and continues to smoke as he coughs his way to an early death. More significantly, the one real writing talent, the Loevborg of the group, Humphry, fondly referred to as Humpty by his friend who recognize him as a philosopher-poet, is never satisfied with his own work; he wishes to take back poems he has submitted to the Cambridge magazine and he refuses to give Martin his book on Wagner for the publishing house that Martin finally controls. "I appear to have an instinctive and ineradicable tendency to diminish what I most admire" (38), he explains as his reason for abandoning the manuscript. He has started the book after moving into a suicide's rooms, where he feels at home (21), and his own demise at the hands of a homosexual pick-up seems to be a disguised suicide as well: "Apparently he didn't put up much of a fight. Just let himself be beaten to death" (55), Nick reports. By the end Hubert Perkins's poems, much sought after by Stuart at the opening, have degenerated into shopping lists he has written on his death bed.

In an earlier drama, *The Rear Column* (1977), the manuscripts that in Hedda's mode have doubled for children are replaced with the drawings of one of the five Englishmen, whom Stanley has left behind in the Congo to guard his supplies and await porters who will help deliver them to him as he fights to relieve Emin Pasha. That the barbarities of civilized English life in the post-60s and 70s are what Gray exposes, ridicules, and broods upon becomes even clearer when he removes his English characters to the encampment of Yambuya on the banks of the Arruwimi River in 1887. Here Gray's characters are ostensibly Hedda's contemporaries (1890) as well as her children.

Like Hedda, Major Barttelot, who is in command of the rear column, fears for his reputation, carrying out the letter of Stanley's orders with all of the misguided cowardice that keeps Hedda trapped in her marriage. The nature of the trap is that Stanley has arranged for Tippu-Tib, an Arab slave trader, to deliver 600 porters to his rear column, but "Tippu is both totally indispensable and completely untrustworthy" (11).[11] Not one of the five men who await his arrival really believes he will come. Like Ibsen's anti-heroine, who despises the life she has elected to lead, the major sees the hollowness of Stanley's behavior and triumphs and has tried unsuccessfully to be sent home as an invalid. "I'd be out of his trap honourably and the rest of you'd be out of his trap too, d'you see? . . . All I wanted was the letter in my pocket, that meant I could if I wanted to, you see?" (23), he confides to his friend Jameson, a scientific observer, who has paid to accompany Stanley and whose sketches are pivotal to the drama's ironies.

Barttelot's contempt for the careless barbarity of the man whose orders he takes as absolute becomes evident as he describes Stanley's departure from the encampment.

> And when Stanley marched out—by God, what a business he makes of it, struts yards ahead of his officers—poor old Jephson in a terrible state of indecision, whether to keep him company or maintain a respectful ten yards behind . . . drums rolling, pipes blowing, and all file time Stanley not seeing the farce of it all, strutting along eyes focused on posterity by way of the London *Times*. . . . (24)

In the same speech, the Major talks about the careless way Stanley has left behind a broken-hearted slave boy, John Henry, who becomes one of Barttelot's victims as well Indeed, it is Barttelot's mindless interpretation of Stanley's orders, despite his awareness of Stanley's absurdities and barbarities, that leads him to his own barbarous cruelties and dooms not only him but most of the men under his control.

The Major's speech becomes central as well to a foreshadowing of the play's climax in Jameson's contributions to native cannibalism. Jameson, who seems to be the most civilized of the five and acts as general peacemaker, has apparently done "a marvelous sketch, one of the Soudanese he [Stanley] left for us to bury managed to die just as Stanley passed him, old Jameson got him in the sketch, eyes rolling, what was it you called it, A Faithful Zanzibari says his Farewell to H. M. Stanley, Esq. H. M. standing for His Majesty, hah, hah . . ."(24). Barttelot intuits his friend's dangerous detachment; Jameson here "captures" on paper the senseless death of the native, but later he will purchase a young native girl in order to deliver her to a cannibal so that he may "capture" the act of cannibalism in sketches that will overshadow Stanley's victories in all of the papers. Upon his return, Stanley, not as unaware of the absurdities of the colonial endeavor as Barttelot had thought, remarks: "God knows what form the story will finally take when it appears in *The Times,* but it will certainly take precedence with the public over my poor efforts, who will want to read of the successful relief of Emin Pasha when there are tales of Barttelot's lash and Jameson's experiments in slaughtering, cooking and consuming infant girls to wallow in, eh?" (73).

In *The Rear Column,* as in *The Common Pursuit,* the lack of a single anti-hero (Butley, Hench) to act as critic of the society for which he is ultimately a scapegoat somewhat diffuses the emotional power of the piece. Stanley sounds a bit like Judge Brack, whose comment at Hedda's death is that people just don't do such things, but whose unawareness of his own complicity in the tragic outcome is the object of Ibsen's satire, even as Stanley, with his limited awareness, is the object of Gray's. One of the other characters, Ward, who defines himself as a patriotic Englishman, is more aware than almost all of the others of the absurdities of the colonial effort and is recognized by Jameson as "a serious man who's not yet discovered what it is he came here to find out" (17). Rather than developing into a Butley or a Hench, however, Ward simply becomes as careless of human suffering as the others. He has arrived in a near state of despair, and rather than discovering why he came, he only "discovers" (as Stanley does not) his complicity in the cruelties that the colonial trap incurs. A kind of Beckettian lost soul, Ward makes his comments— "There are no noble causes in the Congo" (16), but as he loses count of numbers when he oversees a flogging, he seems to lose whatever humanity he had and simply disappears, Stoppard fashion,[12] at the end without the distinction of an actual death.

Major Barttelot, who has silenced a native woman's drumming by biting her neck, and whose taste of (and for?) blood complements Jameson's less direct contributions to cannibalism, is but one of the casualties of the colonial endeavor, which Gray both satirizes and uses as a symbol for the texture of English life at home. John Henry's death as one of the scapegoats for Barttelot's anguished wrath also complements the death of the native girl eaten by the cannibals. As in *Hedda Gabler,* the children are victims, the artist is corrupted, and the survivors are cynical or hopelessly obtuse. Hedda reenacts the Dionysian rites that are absent from the dried out intellectualism of her society and Barttelot succumbs to the beat of the drums that he would subdue.

When Jameson tries to explain to Ward why Barttelot is behaving so badly, he suggests that Stanley has insulted Barttelot by leaving him behind. "The Major was appointed Senior Officer to the Relief of Emin Pasha, and has been left behind to guard the supplies. He is a brave and active man, rendered temporarily inactive" (15). Is not Hedda a potentially creative and active woman, rendered not temporarily but permanently inactive by the situation of women in the time in which she lives? Not content to live vicariously through others as Thea is, nor to sell her favors as Loevborg's former mistress who runs a house of prostitution has done, those seem to be Hedda's only other options.

There is some discussion of options or choices in *The Rear Column.* Stanley apparently meant his orders to be flexible (74), but like the edicts of a religion they were open to interpretation, and Barttelot chose to be a fundamentalist in this respect. Barttelot does, however, wish to leave and offers the choice to Bonny, who refuses to take responsibility for sending him home. Barttelot's sense of honor prohibits him from making such a choice. Troup suggests that despite their trapped situation, the men have a choice about flogging disobedient natives, but the others don't really see this as a choice.

As in Ibsen, there is a curious Beckettian strain in Gray that seems to go beyond social criticism. Certainly one has a choice about how one behaves in the society Ibsen portrays, but even had Hedda been brave, she may be regarded as trapped by the human predicament as much as by the particular society that inhibits her. In such a Beckettian trap, the choice becomes the existential one between life and death. And even though the men of *The Rear Column* have partly chosen their service, since it so reminds one of the society they have left, its Beckettian strains may also be heard. Troup suggests that the situation of sickness and flogging can't go on, that "something must be done, and soon," but when Bonny asks what he proposes, Troup can only reply in *Godot* fashion: "Simply that we do something, anything, to get on the move" (34). But as the Beckett tramps so often observe, "Nothing to be done."

Perhaps the Beckett strain accounts for the frequent comparison of Gray with Chekhov, especially regarding *Quartermaine's Terms,* where the ineffectual anti-hero is pathetically caught up in inaction.[13] Withdrawal from action, however, is the undercurrent of most of Gray's serious characters: Ben Butley refuses to teach, Simon Hench to engage, Humphry to share his writing, and Jameson to be more than a bystander and indirect contributor to the horrors he observes.[14] Still, the major influence remains Ibsen, who was less tolerant than Chekhov of those who contributed to the texture of bourgeois life by drifting along with its standards. Gray identifies with his anti-heroes who make some form of protest, even if it is refusal or suicide, just as Ibsen identified with Hedda.

Hedda, who despises her pregnant state, envies Thea her abundant hair, a sign of fertility, and her courage in leaving her husband for Loevborg. It is Thea's belief in him that has helped Loevborg create his manuscript. When she offers to try to reconstruct that manuscript with Tesman, Thea again seems to Hedda to be the incarnation of fertility and promise. However, Ibsen made it clear in his notes for the play that the task of re-creation the two undertake is not going to be a productive one,[15] and a careful reading of the play suggests that Thea's and Tesman's kind of talent for fertility is a false one. Hedda's craving is for a deeper kind of fertility, a Dionysian renewal of her situation through Loevborg, whom she envisions with vine leaves in his hair. Her burning of Loevborg's manuscript, which he has carelessly lost, may on one level be an act of envy and despair, but on another level it reverberates with the Maenadic rite that is part of the Dionysian myth, in which the mother (Agave) sacrifices the child (Pentheus), whom in her possessed state she takes to be a lion. Pentheus, who plays the role of his enemy in the rite, Dionysus himself, must be sacrificed to ensure rebirth and the earth's fertility.

Hedda is indeed possessed by passions stronger than those who would seem to more easily fertile, and her frenzied acts place her on the edge of the tragic that the others are unable to perceive. In her insightful analysis of the mythic motifs in *Hedda Gabler,* Elinor Fuchs suggests that the play's sacrificial rite (the burning of the manuscript) involves what in Frazerien terms would be the sacrifice of Loevborg as old king, so that the new king, Tesman, may reign.[16] The ironies of such a transfer of power, however, are the source of much in modern drama that echoes the old myths in structure but finds little worth renewing in their enactment of bourgeois life. "Only Hedda," Fuchs concludes, "for all her misdirection, was fertile (220). So, too, in the plays of Simon Gray, the Theas and Tesmans may have numerous offspring (Martin and Marigold, Peter and Sonia, Simon's wife, Beth), but it is the impotent and deeply angry Butley, Hench, Stuart, and Humphry, who as Hedda's children are fertile. Like Hedda, they may despise pregnancy and fear their sexuality, they may withdraw from life or kill themselves, but they hunger for some of the Dionysian fire and vision that Ibsen has bequeathed through his deeply disturb heroine to their creator, Simon Gray. Singly and together, they provide a precise, cutting, and even a chilling tragicomic commentary on our times, as well as an oblique vision of what might be possible. At the end of *The Common Pursuit,* Gray takes us back in time to the play's opening scene, where we observe the literary group one last time in their youth, pondering what they can "give the world"(62).

NOTES

[1] See, for example, Caroline W. Mayerson, "Thematic Symbols in *Hedda Gabler," Ibsen: A Collection of Critical Essays,* ed. Rolf Fjelde (Englewood Cliffs, N.J.: Prentice-Hall, 1965), pp. 131–38.

[2] Maurice Valency, treating Hedda as Loevborg's twin, suggests "In them, the romantic impulse is a disease" (200). *The Flower and the Castle: An Introduction to Modern Drama* (New York: The Universal Library, Grosset & Dunlap, 1963).

[3] See Leo Lowenthal, "Henrik Ibsen: Motifs in the Realistic Plays," *Ibsen: A Collection of Critical Essays,* ed. Rolf Fjelde (Englewood Cliffs, N.J.: Prentice Hall, 1965), pp. 139–57.

[4] See Michael Meyer's Introduction to the play in *Henrik Ibsen: Plays: Two,* trans. Michael Meyer (London: Methuen, 1980, reprint, 1982, 1984), pp. 227–41, especially 232–34.

[5] Simon Gray, *Butley* (London: Methuen, 1971). All page references are to this edition.

[6] Peter Shaw notes that *Butley* catches the early seventies perfectly in its exploration of the disillusionment following the upheaval of the sixties. "Staging England's Decline," *Commentary,* 65 (1978): 88.

[7] For a discussion of Ben Butley and Simon Hench as scapegoat-fool characters, see my article, "The Fool as Hero: Simon Gray's *Butley and Otherwise Engaged, Theatre Journal,* 2 (1981):163–72.

[8] Simon Gray, *Otherwise Engaged, Otherwise Engaged and Other Plays* (New York: Penguin Books, 1976). All page references are to this edition.

[9] Thomas R. Whitaker has posited a suicidal movement or "quest for absence" in several of Ibsen's plays. *Fields of Play in Modern Drama* (Princeton: Princeton University Press, 1977), p. 37. He says of Hedda, "But it's clear that she tries to become both playwright and audience as she maneuvers others towards a 'beauty' that embodies her secret desire for death" (53–54).

[10] Simon Gray, *Quartermaine's Terms* (London: Methuen, 1983). All page references are to this edition.

[11] Simon Gray, *The Rear Column, The Rear Column and Other Plays* (London: Methuen, 1978). All page references are to this edition.

[12] In Tom Stoppard's *Rosencrantz and Guildenstern are Dead,* his two anti-heroes disappear rather than die, a final sign of their insignificance and lack of dignity.

[13] See the Introduction to *Quartermaine's Terms, Landmarks of Modern British Drama: The Plays of the Seventies,* eds. Roger Cornish and Violet Ketels (London: Methuen, 1986), pp. 445–50.

[14] In his depiction of Jameson, Gray captures "the ultimate horror of intellectual curiosity and emotional detachment" (206), Anthony Stephenson, "Simon Gray," *Dictionary of Literary Biography: British Dramatists Since World War II,* 13, ed. Stanley Weintraub (Detroit: Gale, 1982), pp. 199–208.

[15] "Then H. departs this world. And the two of them [Thea and Loevborg] are left sitting with the manuscript they cannot interpret" (334). "Notes for Hedda Gabler," *The Modern Theatre,* ed. Robert W. Corrigan, trans. Evert Springhom and A. G. Chater (New York: Macmillan, 1964), pp. 334–40.

[16] "What we witness at the end of Act II may be called a fertility rite. Lovberg's 'child' is sacrificed so that Tesman's child may be born" (217). Elinor Fuchs, "Mythic Structure in *Hedda Gabler:* The Mask Behind the Face," *Comparative Drama* 3 (1985): 209–22.

Romanticism and Reaction: Hampton's Transformation of *Les Liaisons Dangereuses*

Stephanie Barbé Hammer

A brief overview of critical reactions to Hampton's *Les Liaisons Dangereuses* reveals almost universal admiration for the dramatic adaptation of Laclos' 18th Century novel. When *Les Liaisons* opened at Ambassadors Theatre in October 1986 (after its highly successful run at the Other Place in Strafford [premise: Sept. 1985]), Frances King of the *Sunday Telegraph* praised the play in these glowing terms:

> An exact dramatic transcription of Choderlos de Laclos' 1782 *Les Liaisons Dangereuses* would consist merely of a man and a woman alternately reading the letters that make up the novel. Christopher Hampton's play is not such a transcription, but a transformation through the powerful lens of modern sensibility. The result is a remarkable play. . . . (10.19.86)[1]

The *Daily Mail* went even further and suggested that Hampton's adaptation actually enhanced and improved the original (10.17.86). Not surprisingly, other London critics responded in kind, hailing the play as "a feat in literary logistics" (Jim Hiley, *Listener*, 10.23.86), a brilliant work of "psychological acidity" (Kathy O'Shaughnessy, *Daily Telegraph*, 10.16.86), and a chilling erotic study an voyeurism (Joan Smith, *Sunday Today*, 10.19.86).

The play made an equally critical splash in the United States. When *Les Liaisons* came to New York, the Arts and Leisure section of the *New York Times* featured Hampton and his drama in a front page article, and when the play opened at the Music Box on April 30, 1987, Frank Rich expressed his admiration for the text which, "telescoped" and "preserved" the novel's "lubricious narrative" ("Carnal Abandon in *Liaisons Dangereuses*" *NY Times*, 5.1.87). Such influential magazines as *Time* also praised the adaptation, noting that:

> A novel of letters is not easily transmuted /into a cinematic montage of stage action. Yet, *Les Liaisons* has been adapted into an equally brilliant and witty tragedy of manners. (5.11.87)

Undoubtedly, Hampton's drama follows Laclos' novel with admirable skill. Stylistically, the play's major speeches are remarkably similar to the novel's epistolary discourses and the essential structure of the narrative has been respected; only a few incidental characters and one subplot (the Prevan episode) have been eliminated, to quicken the pace of the 379 page narrative. Like the novel, the play begins with the innocent Cécile's introduction to Parisian society, then shifts to outline the opposing projects of the two libertines. The scenes at Mme. de Rosemonde's chateau are the most accelerated portions of the play; in the novel Tourvel falls in love with Valmont very gradually and Laclos emphasizes that she has her own plan vis a vis the Vicomte, namely to reawaken his piety. Also Mme. de Merteuil does not intervene in person during this section. But the essential action remains the same.

However, we should note that *Les Liaisons'* fidelity to the novel halts abruptly near the end, for Hampton has considerably rewritten the duel scene between Valmont and Danceny. At first glance this new version seems to differ only superficially from the original scene, for while the drama necessarily presents the action in a more direct fashion than the novel, the outcome of the duel remains the same. But on close inspection Hampton's dramatization of the fateful confrontation between the Chevalier and the Vicomte causes the play as a whole to make an assessment of Valmont's character which differs substantially from that of the novel. Even more importantly, this reevaluation of Valmont leads Hampton to create a different ending for Laclos' story, and the new ending significantly alters our perception of Laclos' two heroines, Tourvel and Merteuil.

Hampton's adaptation thus presents a picture of the three main characters which is very different from that of the novel. This modern version of *Les Liaisons* proves to be, as we shall see, a curious marriage of sensibilities. On one hand the play expresses a more Romantic view of the relations between men and women than the novel does, while on the other hand Hampton's adaptation articulates a far less engaging (and far less engaged) political vision of 18th-century society than the one contained in Laclos' explosive original. The result yields an intriguing, if disturbing blend of sentimentality and rather simplistic political didacticism.

The considerable divergence between the two works becomes manifest when we scrutinize the ways in which Laclos and Hampton handle the closing scenes of *Les Liaisons*. In the novel, Bertrand, a member of Valmont's household, gives Mme. Rosemonde the following account of the deadly meeting between the Vicomte and Danceny:

Imagine my alarm at seeing Monsieur your nephew, carried in by two of his servants, bathed in his own blood. He received two sword thrusts in the body, and was already very weak. Monsieur Danceny was also there, and indeed was in tears. Ah, no doubt he had good cause to weep: but it is no time to shed tears when one has been the cause of an irreparable disaster.

As for me, I was beside myself. Of little account as I am, I nonetheless gave Monsieur Danceny a piece of my mind. It was then that Monsieur de Valmont rose to true greatness. He ordered me to be silent, and taking the hand of the very man who was his murderer, called him his friend, embraced him in front of us all and said to us: "I order you to treat Monsieur with all the regard that is due to a good and gallant gentleman." He moreover delivered to him/in my presence a great mass of papers . . . Then he asked that he and Monsieur Danceny should be left alone together for a moment. (370–1, Letter 163)

This scene is especially noteworthy because it typifies Laclos' ironic method of epistolary reportage throughout *Les Liaisons Dangereuses*. As Tsvetan Todorov has already remarked, although the characters of the novel consistently present allegedly trustworthy narratives of events, the reader soon concludes that these versions of the facts are either insufficient or even false, because Laclos has already provided him with information which the narrating character does not possess.[2] Thus, since we almost always know more than any of the characters in the novel do, we continually reinterpret the unfolding narrative in ways which either problematize or even contradict outright the interpretations offered by the narrating voices.

This is precisely the kind of interpretative reversal which occurs in this passage. Bertrand's tragic rendering of the duel and his admiration of Valmont's seemingly generous behavior towards his killer are both undercut by the reader's previous knowledge that Valmont is clearly the guilty party in the conflict and therefore merits the punishment which he has just received. In like manner Bertrand's lack of sympathy for the distraught Danceny is negated by our recognition that it is in fact the Chevalier who demonstrates true nobility of spirit here, in so far as he sincerely grieves for the man who has deeply wronged him. However, Danceny's reaction must also be seen in an ironized context. Although he does not know it, his grief is highly inappropriate, because Valmont's true feelings for the young man have always been extremely negative— a mixture of scorn and envy. Thus, like Bertrand, Danceny misinterprets the meaning of the reported events, because he lacks vital information which the reader already possesses.

But Laclos' ironic *coup de grace* occurs in Bertrand's passing comment that the Vicomte entrusted Danceny "with a mass of papers" and then conversed with him privately. This indifferent remark is, of course, the most vital information provided by Bertrand, although he fails to understand its importance. The reader however immediately recognizes that the mass of papers are probably letters from Valmont's correspondence with Merteuil and deduces that the ensuing private conversation must be about her role in the corruption of Cécile. In this manner, the reader formulates a provisional interpretation which threatens to completely undermine Bertrand's sentimental version of the events. The reader suspects that the gift of the letters and the ensuing discussion represent Valmont's last attempt to revenge himself on the recalcitrant Merteuil, who has just refused him her sexual favors and is now feuding with the Vicomte, as Letter 153 informs us.

> I might add that the slightest obstacle put forward by you will be taken by me as a genuine declaration of war. You see: the reply I ask for does not require long and beautiful sentences. A word will suffice.
>
> (The Marquise's reply, written at the foot of the same letter.)
>
> Very well: war. (358)

The novel's subsequent events validate the reader's provisional analysis of the duel scene, for immediately after Valmont's death Danceny takes a drastic and uncharacteristic action. He publicly distributes the most damning of Merteuil's letters to Valmont—letters which he could only have received from the Vicomte directly. Given the reader's appraisal of Danceny as a naive and idealistic young man and given the impression that he is at least somewhat enamored of the Marquise de Merteuil (not only is he having an affair with her, he also relies on her as a friend and advisor), it is logical to conclude that such a total reversal of the Chevalier's feelings could only have occurred during the mysterious death-bed conversation with the Vicomte. Danceny's letter to Mme. Rosemonde (Letter 169) reveals this to be the case:

> I have . . . extracted only two letters which I have taken the liberty of making public. One was necessary to the accomplishment of Monsieur Valmont's revenge and mine, to which we both had a right and with which he had expressly charged me. I thought, moreover, that it would be doing a service to society to unmask a woman as truly dangerous as Madame de Merteuil, who as you will see, is the only and the real cause of all that passed between Monsieur de Valmont and myself. (381)

Danceny's letter indicates that Valmont has successfully turned him against the Marquise by revealing Merteuil's part in Cécile's seduction and perhaps more importantly, by convincing the young man that his affair with the Marquise had meaning for her only in so far as it served a far grander scheme. Thus, thanks to Valmont's last desperate stroke of genius, the outraged Danceny once again serves as a pawn in the two libertines' stratagems; just as Menteuil arranged for him to fight and kill Valmont, so does Valmont now contrive Merteuil's ruin with the Chevalier as his instrument.

With these subsequent events in mind, we can now return to the duel scene with a greater appreciation of its significance. Seen from this perspective, Valmont's final moments testify not to his heroism, as Bertrand believes, but to his utter villainy. The Vicomte's "noble" behavior on his deathbed in fact reveals his chillingly absolute commitment to libertine principles in general and specifically to the desire to crush his one true opponent—the unseduceable Marquise.

Most importantly, the suggestion that the Vicomte's last energies are all directed towards the destruction of Merteuil implies in turn that Valmont's egotistical will to power is finally far more crucial to him that his desire for love, as the Marquise has already shrewdly observed:

> Yes, Vicomte, you were very much in love with Madame de Tourvel, as you are still in love with her: you love her to distraction. But because it amused me to make you ashamed of it, you have bravely sacrificed her. You would have sacrificed her a thousand times rather than take a joke. To what lengths will vanity lead us! (340–1, Letter 145)

Valmont's final manoeuvre, provides the reader with overwhelming evidence that it was not love but power gained through the manipulation of another's emotions which has been the Vicomte's goal from the very beginning. Thus, the Valmont of the novel is, as I have argued elsewhere, a malefactor who aims for perfection, and in his death he remains true to his ideal of sublime malfeasance (Hammer, 31–42). In this sense, the character of Valmont anticipates Sade's philosophically grounded and ethically resigned criminals, who break the law because transgression is the only logical and meaningful action possible to human beings of intelligence.[3] Seen from this point of view Valmont becomes the perversely perfect incarnation of 18th Century rationalism, and as such he represents a radical *mise en question* of the Enlightenment's faith in the power of the intellect.

We should also note that Danceny's actions during and immediately after the duel deeply problematize his apparently noble character. Having been all to quickly seduced by the Marquise, the Chevalier reveals in Letter 169 that he has been won over by the Vicomte just as rapidly. The degree to which Valmont has converted Danceny is illustrated by the fact that the latter places the entire blame for the duel on Merteuil and completely fails to recognize the Vicomte's equal role (and equal guilt) in the libertine's machinations. This failure is particularly disturbing because, since the Chevalier has in his possession the entire Valmont-Merteuil correspondence (see editor's note, 380), he should be able to come to a more accurate conclusion about the relationship of these two partners in crime. Seen in this light Danceny proves to have as little moral willpower and as little mental independence, as the pathetically malleable Cécile, who has consistently served the purposes of both libertines with a horrifyingly absolute obedience. Most disturbingly of all, Danceny refuses to admit any responsibility for the disastrous events of which he has been a pan although he tellingly observes that his desire to ruin Merteuil stems not only from his sense of justice, but also from a longing for personal revenge. This lust for vengeance clearly resembles that of the Vicomte, as the Chevalier himself implies in his letter to Mme. Rosemonde ("Valmont's revenge and mine, to which we both had a right"). Thus, in the last analysis, Danceny proves to be not a much better man than the man he has killed.[4]

When we compare the duel scene in the novel to that of the play it is plain that, although the end-result of the conflict is identical, the dramatic version tells a very different tale. The stage directions for the sword-play indicate that the world-weary Valmont actually wants to lose the fight, and more importantly, the vital information with which the dying Vicomte entrusts Danceny concerns, not Merteuil, but Tourvel:

> I want you to tell her I can't explain why I broke with her as I did, but that since then, my life has been worth nothing. I pushed the blade in deeper than you just have, my boy, and I want you to help me withdraw it. Tell her it's lucky for her that I've gone and I'm glad not to have to live without her. Tell her her love was the only real happiness I've ever known. (100)

Surprisingly, Valmont finally confesses his love for his victim (which he never does in the novel), and affirms the supreme value of this love in an otherwise meaningless existence. Moreover, he seeks to communicate this realization to Tourvel in a sincere—albeit vain—attempt to relieve her suffering, and hopefully save her life. But most significant is the fact that Valmont does not give Danceny Merteuil's letters, nor does he betray the Marquise in any way, even though such a betrayal would explain and might even partially excuse his behavior toward Tourvel. Instead Valmont gives only the most cryptic of warnings to his youthful opponent:

> . . . be careful of the Marquise de Merteuil . . . in this affair, both of us are her creatures. (99)

In this manner the death of Hampton's Valmont presents itself *not* as a cynical affirmation of libertine ideals but as a deeply felt moral metamorphosis. In an act of heroic resignation, the Vicomte accepts full responsibility for his action, which he now recognizes to be both detestable and vain; he simultaneously goes so far as to forgive his partner in evil—in so far as he does not expose her—and he thereby severs his ties to her. With this final gesture, Valmont demonstrates that he is ready at last to abandon the libertine game which has motivated his existence, and he actually welcomes death as a way to expiate his wrongs.

Thus, this Vicomte expires, not like Laclos' remorseless 18th century libertine, but in a manner which anticipates the deeply dissatisfied, proudly regretful villain-heroes of Romanticism—Chateaubriand's René, Byron's Don Juan, and certainly Goethe's. Faust, the quintessentially misguided desiring male who is also eventually redeemed by the love of his innocent victim. Moreover, Hampton's reworking of the scene suggests a variation of an important Romantic credo: depth of feeling in any human being, no matter how perverse, eventually ennobles and improves. Such a notion lies at the core of Romantic epistemology, as Lillian Furst has already argued.

> Instead of being a mere repository of tended sentiments aroused by sensibility, the human heart represented to the Romantics the very key to the universe. [. . .] On the whole, however, [The Romantics] envisaged the heart not only, or even primarily, as the fountainhead of happiness and sorrow, but particularly as an organ of knowledge. . . . (Furst, 219–220)

Valmont's conversion clearly reflects this worldview. His transformation proclaims the superior power of the emotions to enlighten in a way that the mind cannot. Correspondingly, this conversion casts a whole new light on Valmont's pursuit of Tourvel; it suggests that from the moment Valmont begins to pursue the Présidente, he embarks upon an odyssey toward self-understanding and moral self-reappraisal; this process is the necessary corollary to the growth of his love. Therefore, it is no coincidence that Valmont's amorous declaration accompanies the realization that his life has been an empty one; the two confessions stem from the same emotionally grounded *prise de conscience*.

In summary, while the novel provides a highly ironed indirect report of Valmont's duel with Danceny, the drama transforms the account into the emotional climax and moral core of the story. This scene obliges us to reevaluate Valmont's character and behavior much more positively, for if the awakening of his emotions eventually destroys the Vicomte, it is also that very destruction which gives his life significance, as he himself recognizes. Interestingly, Danceny's character is also enhanced by Hampton's reinterpretation. No longer the unwitting instrument of Merteuil's demise, he emerges as a nobler and kinder character than he is in the novel. Here he is an inexperienced but nonetheless sincere lover who is seduced in a moment of weakness. He quickly recognizes his fault, abandons his seductress, but takes no vengeful action against her. Moreover, he even goes so far as to befriend his mortal enemy and renders him a valuable service before retiring to monastic life. This service is a significant one; by bringing the Vicomte's message to the dying Tourvel Danceny affirms both the sincerity of the

Vicomte's feelings and the supreme value of love itself. The Chevalier's actions thus echo and reinforce the Romantic ideal suggested by the Vicomte's transfiguration.

Yet, we should note that, while his deathbed transformation elevates the Vicomte to heroic stature in the play (while also ennobling the character of Danceny), Hampton's reworking of the duel scene has a decidedly detrimental effect on our judgment of the two leading female characters—Tourvel and Merteuil.

The case of Tourvel may be illustrated briefly with a passage from her last letter in the novel:

> Where are the friends that loved me, where are they? My misfortune fright-
> ens them away . . . I am crushed, and they leave me helpless! I am dying and
> no one weeps for me. All consolation is denied me . . . And you that I have
> insulted . . . Return and punish an unfaithful wife . . . Pitiless in His
> vengeance, He has delivered me over to the very man who was my ruin . . .
> But Look! It is him . . Oh my beloved! Take me in your arms . . . God! Is it
> that monster again! (368–9, Letter 161)

This nightmare vision (in which a wrathful God, a wronged husband, outraged friends, demons and the still detestable Valmont are hopelessly intermeshed) gives the reader direct access to the mind of Tourvel in its last throes of agony. The Présidente's descent into delirium is particularly horrifying because we already know that her suffering serves no purpose, for as we have seen, her love for Valmont has in no ways redeemed him. In this manner, Laclos signals that Tourvel is a martyr of love who is denied the spiritual fulfillment and moral meaningfulness such a martyrdom should provide. Instead she deludedly con-demns herself to death and expires in a personal Inferno which repeatedly enacts the fragmented events leading to her fall from grace.

There is, therefore, no doubt whatsoever in the novel that Tourvel has made a fatal mistake in falling in love with the Vicomte, because her love has very literally been wasted on him. With this state of affairs the novel demon-strates that even the highest kind of love bestowed on an unworthy object utterly obliterates the lover without effecting any improvement on the beloved. Through Tourvel, Laclos reveals the futility of such misguided self-sacrifice, while he indirectly questions the value of the extreme Christian piety which has motivated Tourvel's actions.

In contrast, Hampton mitigates the degree of Tourvel's suffering at the hands of Valmont by suggesting that she may have died willingly, knowing that Valmont really loved her after all:

> I shall never forget those terrible sights. When she kept ripping away the band-
> ages after they bled her. The delirium and the convulsions. How she wasted

away. All the same, I think she might have recovered if that unfortunate young man hadn't somehow managed to let her know that Vicomte your nephew was dead . . . Apparently, as he was dying, the Vicomte managed to convince Danceny that Madame de Tourvel was the only woman he'd ever loved. (101)

The suggestion that the Présidente did not die in despair clearly diminishes the degree to which she has been victimized by Valmont, for it implies that the Présidente was not mistaken in her love for the Vicomte, and that he was, at least in the end, worthy of her.

The case of Merteuil is more subtle and thus more complicated. At first glance it might seem that the Marquise benefits as a character from the drama's reorganization of events, because Hampton not only allows her to survive unscathed, but he has her clearly win the libertine contest between herself and Valmont. To sum up this competitive image the drama shows us Merteuil playing cards at the end of the play in an ironic repetition of the opening scene.

In comparison to the play, the fate which Laclos arranges for Merteuil seems grim in the extreme. Although the novel makes the apparently just (if harsh) decision to have both evil characters mete out each others' retribution, Merteuil's punishment by society exceeds Valmont's in duration and animosity. While he dies honorably with his outward dignity still intact, Danceny's public circulation of Merteuil's letters results in a series of devastating humiliations for the libertine heroine, as Mme. Volanges reports:

Madame de Merteuil, returning from the country the day before yesterday, that is Thursday, had herself set down at the Comédie Italienne where she has a box. She was alone in it, and, what must have seemed extraordinary to her, not a single man presented himself to her during the entire performance. When it was over, she proceeded, as she usually does, into the small salon, which was already full of people. A murmur immediately went around, of which, however, she apparently did not suppose herself to be the object. She saw an empty place on one of the benches and sat down; whereupon the other women already sitting there rose immediately, as of one accord, and left her absolutely alone. This very marked display of indignation was applauded by all the men, and the hubbub increased to the extent, it is said, of hooting. (388–89, Letter 173)

Again, thanks to Laclos' narrative method we immediately realize that this public-embarrassment must be devastating to Merteuil because we have already learned from the Marquise herself how vital it is for her to conceal her true character from the society in which she lives. As she has explained in her famous letter of principles (81), Merteuil's claim to libertine greatness (and she does claim to be great in no uncertain terms) lies in her ability to both violate society's ethical regulations and win admiration from that very society as a paragon of the virtues against which she is rebelling:[5]

> I studied our manners in the novelists, our opinions in the philosophers; I went
> to the strictest moralists to find out what they demanded of us, so as to know
> for certain what it was possible to do, what it was best to think, and what it
> was necessary to seem to be. (184)

But Merteuil's fall from grace does not stop with her humiliation at the theatre, for eventually everyone deserts and ostracizes her. She loses her trial
against Prévan, the predatory Don Juan whom she had ensnared and ostensibly
ruined,[6] subsequently forfeits her wealth in payment of court costs and damages
and, most importantly, she is deprived of the very sexual attractiveness which
formed the necessary basis for her libertine success. Financially ruined and
grotesquely disfigured by smallpox, Merteuil becomes an expatriated vagabond
at the end of Laclos' novel. Her fate is apparently so horrible, that the fictional
editor of the *Liaisons Dangereuses* cannot even bring himself to recount it:

> We can, at the present moment, give the reader neither the subsequent adven-
> tures of Mademoiselle de Volanges, nor any account of the sinister occur-
> rences which crowned the misfortunes and accomplished the punishment of
> Madame de Merteuil. (editor's note, 393)

In this manner, Laclos endows [Merteuil's defeat with a radical com-
pleteness which ironically echoes that of Oedipus, for like the tragic hero this
libertine is also stripped of her figurative and literal possessions and cast out
of the community. And yet we should remember that the Marquise's ruin also
justifies her previous actions in so far as her destruction corroborates her vision
of the relationship between the sexes in society:

> In this unequal contest we are lucky not to lose, you unlucky when you do not
> win . . . we are lucky if upon an impulse you prefer secrecy to scandal, if,
> content with a humiliating submission, you stop short of making yesterday's
> idol the victim of tomorrow's sacrifice . . . At the mercy of her enemy, she
> is without resource if he is without generosity; and how can generosity be
> expected of him when, although men are sometimes commended for show-
> ing it, they are, notwithstanding, never thought the less of for lacking it.
> (179–80, Letter 81)

Ironically and tragically, Merteuil's own experience proves the accuracy of her
seemingly twisted socio-sexual theory, for it is after all she, not Valmont or for
that matter Prévan, who becomes the societal scapegoat.[7]

Thus, the fates of Laclos' two female protagonists provide a vital key to
our understanding of the novel. When placed beside the self-immolation of
Tourvel, the fall of Merteuil points an accusing finger at a profoundly unjust
society which condemns sexual promiscuity on principle but which in practice

indiscriminately punishes only the females, whether they be victims or practitioners of license. With this state of affairs, the novel suggests that if Merteuil is a greater villain than Valmont, she is also the greater victim, and she is therefore a kindred spirit of the woman she hates most—a state of affairs which horrifies Merteuil but which she is nonetheless perceptive enough to recognize:

> Were we to go on in this way, the Heavenly Devotee would continue to think herself the sole choice of your heart, while I should plume myself on being the preferred rival. Both of us will have been deceived, but you will be happy, and of what importance is anything else? (341, Letter 145)

In this manner the conclusion of Laclos' novel forces us to recognize the enormous similarities between these two diametrically opposed incarnations of femininity. Although they are enemies, Merteuil and Tourvel are both intelligent women who struggle to achieve and maintain independent selfhood by becoming paragons of male-established behaviors—the one by Christian virtue, the other by male principles of libertinage.[8] Their dual destruction is important; through their downfalls the novel makes the devastating suggestion that there is simply no viable alternative for a female to exist as a person—at least in the social world which Laclos is describing.[9] Woman's only hope is to persist as a sequestered icon—as a widow like Mme. Volanges and Mme. Rosemonde, as a nun like Cécile, or as a prostitute like Emilie.

In this manner Laclos presents the reader with two heroines who both reflect and explode the archetypal antinomy which our culture has assigned to its female members throughout history—the saint and the seductress, the martyr of love and the avenging fury.[10] Laclos demonstrates both how well Tourvel and Merteuil play these roles, but also painstakingly and painfully outlines what happens to women who dare to play their roles too well.

The novel's incisive and precociously feminist perceptions of the society which it portrays retreat to the background in Hampton's adaptation, for the changed circumstances of Valmont's death greatly diminish the tragic resonance of both female protagonists. In particular, the Marquise's survival subverts the validity of her socio-political views while destroying the kinship between herself and Tourvel. Deprived of this connection which makes her a much more sympathetic character, Hampton's Merteuil seems a little more than a calculating monster at the end of the drama. No longer a victim of gender, she is in the final scene the most repellent of the play's corrupt pre-revolutionary aristocrats.

Scene 18's triumphant villainess seems a whole other person than scene 4's *femme revoltée* who criticizes the sexual injustice of her social milieu with withering ironic understatement. This important speech now appears to be yet another example of an arch hypocrite's dramatic posturing.[11] Even the final stage directions conspire against Merteuil; Hampton reduces her to a stereotypical member of the decadent ruling class by indicating that a tricolore and the shadow of the guillotine should appear in the background at the end of the play.[12] Curiously and disturbingly, Hampton has arranged for Merteuil and not Valmont to meet the ultimate political punishment at the hands of the Revolutionary Tribunal.

In conclusion, Hampton's adaptation ruptures the novel's unified—albeit complex—presentation of the characters. The new duel scene radically alters our perception of every figure involved in it—the combatants, Valmont and Danceny, as well as the two female protagonists directly affected by the duel's outcome, and in so doing subtly shifts the play's sympathy toward the male characters. Admittedly, this alteration presents a certain artistic advantage. By upsetting the balance of power between Laclos' evil protagonists, Hampton arguably offers us a more poignant and a more optimistic vision than Laclos does of the possibilities for improvement of human society. Both novel and drama show us a cold rationalistic world which must die precisely because it cannot feel, but the drama suggests a way out of this deadly and deadening universe. The fact that love eventually triumphs even in this moral and emotional wasteland suggests that the noblest of human sentiments can never be utterly canceled out and that it will always prevail, just as surely and inevitably as democracy eventually triumphs over tyranny. Seen from this perspective, Valmont's conversion acquires microcosmic political significance; the Vicomte's painful private revolution foreshadows France's devastating but ultimately positive political renewal at the end of the 18th century.

However, for all its poignancy and Romantic conviction, Hampton presents us with a social portrait which is clearly less provocative than the one painted by the 18th century novelist. The play simplifies the corruption of pre-revolutionary France by reducing women's victimization within it, and more disturbingly, that drama does not explode the good woman/bad woman dichotomy, so much as reinforce it. In this manner Hampton's new ending for *Les Liaisons Dangereuses* causes the play as a whole to reaffirm the admittedly attractive emotional values of Romanticism while diminishing the continuing relevance of Laclos' shockingly hard-minded critique of sexual inequity.

And yet it is precisely this blend of Romanticism and reaction which marks Hampton's play as an artistic product of the 1980s. This *Liaisons* reflects our current ambivalence toward the complex realities of sexual desire and sexual politics as well as a deeply felt nostalgia for a world of absolute values. Hampton's adaptation betrays a familiar longing for a clear-cut moral universe where love (affirmed at no matter what cost) is always good and where democratic revolution (no mater how bloody) automatically rights all wrongs. It is no secret that both Reagan and Thatcher regimes owe their success to their ability to capitalize on such collective yearnings, and I suspect that in its own way, Hampton's play also both reflects and represses these concerns.

Perhaps the best argument for the play's strange contemporaneity lies in the reaction of Hampton's own children to the play's characters—whom they likened to the figures of *Dynasty (Newsweek)*. Certainly the world of *Liaisons* superficially resembles that of the television program. In both drama and soap-opera a powerful charismatic male is torn between the favors of one good woman and one relentlessly evil one against a background of opulence and corruption. But there is more to this analogy than meets the eye. For all its lurid glitz and promise of sexual licence, *Dynasty* tells a very moralistic tale.[13] Despite appearances, it consistently celebrates the most traditional of bourgeois values: money and social prominence obtained through industry, heterosexual monogamy, and an array of stereotypical behaviors connected to the family—maternal love, paternal discipline, and general filial loyalty. So it is with Hampton's play; for all its fascination with the lascivious, at the last possible moment it too rejects ethical ambiguity in favor of a fervently conservative moralism.

NOTES

[1] For this and all other references to reviews of Hampton's *Les Liaisons Dangereuses* see "Clippings—*Les Liaisons Dangereuses*," at the Lincoln Center Performing Arts Archive.

[2] In his helpful structuralist analysis of the novel Todorov emphasizes the importance of the "parole inadequate," i.e. the presence of signifiers which do not correctly refer to their signifieds. This inadequate language results in the characters' multiple, flawed visions of the same event (Todorov, 14, 38–39).

[3] Compare the vicomte's libertine philosophy with that of *Justine's* Coeur de Fer:

> Society is composed only of the weak and the strong; and if the [social] contract must displease both, then almost certainly it is not suitable to society. Therefore, the truly reasonable man is he, who . . . rages irrevocably against it and violates it as much as he can, certain that what he will gain from these infractions will always outweigh what he will lose if he proves the weaker. . . . (41)

[4] Such an interpretation of Danceny is corroborated by Bernard Bray who has already argued that the "good" characters in *Les Liaisons* are for the most part social conformists who are themselves guilty of the same hypocrisy exercised by the Valmont and Merteuil. See "L'hypocrasie du libertin" in *Colloque*, 97–109.

[5] The contents of this letter have been admirably condensed into two of the most powerful speeches of Hampton's play. See scene 4, 32–3.

[6] Prévan hopes to seduce and ruin Merteuil, but she skillfully turns the tables, seduces him, and then has him arrested as a rapist. With this adventure Merteuil puts her libertine principles to the actual test, and, I believe, prepares a similar fate for Valmont.

[7] Lester Crocker aptly notes that, "because she refuses to accept the rules of the game, her defiance is at once tragic and doomed to tragic failure. . . ." (89).

[8] In her controversial book *Beyond Power,* Marilyn French notes that that adoption of the image urged by patriarchy forces the individual to devote herself to creating an appearance of either power or submission. Merteuil and Tourvel clearly exercise these two responses to the male paradigm, and in so doing both act against their true desires and needs. See French's discussion of the power/pleasure antinomy, 539–40.

[9] In her ground-breaking article Anne-Marie Jaton argues that Laclos' novel shows women trapped between the utter refusal of love (Merteuil) and the sacrifice of love (Tourvel), that is to say, between a fatal rebellion against and an equally fatal submission to society's injustice. See "Libertinage féminin, libertinage dangereux," in *Laclos et le Libertinage,* 151–62.

[10] The revolutionary nature of Laclos' approach to his female characters has already been signaled by Simone de Beauvoir, who counts him as one of the few male authors in history who has recognized women as human beings. See Beauvoir, 393.

[11] This attitude is reflected in the critics' moral condemnation of the Merteuil character in the play. *Newsweek* dismisses her as "a dazzling genius of bitchery" (05.11.87), The *New York Times* also notes her "bitchiness" and observes that although Merteuil is a victim of her times, she "is chillingly indifferent to the fact that she is . . . as monstrous to women as to men" (*New York Times,* 05.01.87). Even the most feminist of reviewers, Joan Smith of *Sunday Today,* concludes that the marquise is "enslaved by her own evil" (10.19.86). Unlike Laclos' Merteuil, Hampton's marquise does not evoke much, if any, sympathy.

[12] Fortunately these extremely heavy-handed effects were not used in the productions in the West End or on Broadway.

[13] It is significant that the most negative review of the play specifically denounces Hampton's attempt "near the end, to shift gears into tragedy" and deplores the play's simplification of the novel's ambiguity. See John Simon's review "When 'Les' isn't more" in *New York Magazine* (10.18.87).

Works Cited

Colloque du Bicentenaire des *Liaisons Dangereuses Laclos et le Libertinage*. Paris: Presses Universitaires se France, 1983.

Crocker, Lester. "The Status of Evil in *Les Liaisons Dangereuses*." in *Critical Approaches to "Les Liaisons Dangereuses*." Lloyd R. Free, Ed. Madrid: Ediciones José Porrua Turazas, 1978.

Beauvoir, Simone de. *Le Deuxième Sexe*. Paris: Gallimard, 1949.

French, Marilyn. *Beyond Power: On Women, Men and Morals*. New York: Summit Books, 1985.

Furst, Lillian. *Romanticism in Perspective: A Comparative Study of the Romantic Movements in England, France and Germany*. New York: Humanities Press, 1970.

Hammer, Stephanie Barbé. "The Sublime Crime . . . Fascination and Failure in Schiller's *Die Räuber* and Laclos' *Les Liaisons Dangereuses*." *The Comparatist*, 11 (1987):31–42.

Hampton, Christopher. *Les Liaisons Dangereuses*, London: Faber, 1985.

Laclos, Choderlos de. *Les Liaisons Dangereuses*. Middlesex: Penguin, 1961. rpt. 1981.

Sade, Marquis de. *Justine*. Helene Weaver, trans. New York: G. P. Putnam, 1966.

Todorov, Tsvetan. *Literature et Signification*. Paris: Larousse, 1967.

Playing with Place: Some Filmic Techniques in the Plays of David Hare

John Russell Brown

Only a very few dramatists have made films. Many have written filmscripts and been involved with the cinema's revisionary processes; but they have not been in charge of that complex collaboration which leads to the finished film: from idea and story to development, casting, setting, shooting, editing—the manifold processes which collect and then order a film's fixed images of reality. David Hare is one dramatist who *has* done all this: only the camera itself has escaped his direct control.

Many English-speaking dramatists have written plays about theatre—*The Entertainer, Noises Off, A Chorus of Disapproval, A Life in the Theatre*—and still more have created plays in which the leading characters are performers before live audiences—*Burn This, The Real Thing, Amadeus, The Tooth of Crime, The Birthday Party,* and (to widen the idea of performance) *Waiting for Godot.* But David Hare, the dramatist, writes as a filmmaker about film-making. His play, *A Map of the World* (1983), begins with an international conference on poverty set in a luxury hotel in Bombay, but then everything that has been seen so far is revealed as having been a representation of reality, not reality itself. The whole opening scene had been created carefully by its characters, so that it could be recorded by camera, and subsequently edited, for the making of a movie. The dramatist is at home with all this business and has used his inside knowledge to awaken questions about the truth of what art can present about life, and about the efficacy of humanitarian goodwill. This is not unlike the way in which Shakespeare used his familiarity with theatre to juxtapose theatrical performance and the lunacies of authority, love, and sexual strife in *A Midsummer Night's Dream.*

This dramatist also understands those enthusiasts who feed greedily upon a film's plausible and engrossing illusion of reality. Whereas Hamlet had believed that a play was the thing to "catch the conscience of the king," Hare's characters turn to the cinema as a rather desperate escape from the intolerable

crises of conscience in their own actual lives. At the end of the first scene of
Act II of *The Secret Rapture* (1988), Irwin and Rhonda are discovered in an
intimate moment by Isobel, Irwin's lover. He is almost speechless, "*looking at*
ISOBEL*,*" while Isobel is "*standing thinking, taking no notice of* RHONDA";
so the initiative has to be Rhonda's:

> RHONDA: Well, anyway, I'm going to the flicks. Excuse me.
> ISOBEL: We'll come with you.
> RHONDA: I'm sorry?
> ISOBEL: I'd like to come.
> (IRWIN *looks across amazed,* RHONDA *puzzled.*)
> RHONDA: It's very violent. I saw the trailer. It's one of those Los Angeles crime
>   things. Rooms full of blood. Then the cop says, "Right, I want everyone here
>   to help look for his ear. . ."
> ISOBEL: Sounds fine. I'd like that. No really.
> (*She turns and looks at* IRWIN.)
>   That would be good. I mean it. Let's all go to the cinema. . . . Then we can
>   have a good time. (58)

The dramatist himself has not been carried away by the power of cinema;
Hare remains critical of these characters. Besides, he has turned back from film-
making, which at one time used all his creative energies, and is writing again
for the theatre. With *Racing Demon* (1990), he brought a theatre-person into his
play. This is Ewan Gilmour, an out-of-work stage actor, who is the lover of
clergyman Harry Henderson. But Ewan is not glamorized in conventionally
theatrical ways: he wears simple, unremarkable clothes, and speaks in a
Glaswegian accent; he is terse, not voluble, when he is angry, and seems to be
without very much guile; he is first seen reading a comic, with a pile more at his
side. Ewan is given a chance of earning easy money by selling his story to a
cheque-book journalist, but he does not incriminate Harry: this actor is loyal to
his friend. In a play about weakening faith and duplicity, in which the other
characters seek solutions to nothing more than their own difficulties, Hare has
introduced someone from the "unreal" world of theatre who stands true to the
intimate and scarcely-spoken feelings which bind two people together. The contrast with the successful and self-concerned film actors of *A Map* could hardly
be greater. So, in assessing Hare's work as a dramatist, it may be profitable to
notice both what his work as a film-maker has contributed to his stage plays and
how he has returned to the theatre to enjoy its own distinct opportunities.

I

The most fundamental difference between the film and the other arts is that,
in its world-picture, the boundaries of space and time are fluid. . . . In the

plastic arts, as also on the stage, space remains static, motionless, unchanging, without a goal and without a direction. . . .

Hauser 227

David Hare has, from his earliest plays, tried to buck this "static" limitation which others have seen as natural to the stage: he has constantly played with space. In *Knuckle* (1974), he took Curly successively from one location to another, in a quest for information about his sister who had disappeared; each new setting showed this central character in a new light. In *Teeth 'n' Smiles* (1975), he brought a loud and trendy pop group to a gig within the precincts of a Cambridge college, banishing time-honored proprieties and leaving the place itself barely recognizable. In *Pravda* (1985), written with Howard Brenton, the newspaper proprietors are not kept on their own turf; they are also shown in a garden, an Exhibition Hall, a London Club, a bungalow in Weybridge, a Greyhound Stadium, the Yorkshire moors, a TV studio.

In the shorter of two one-act plays of 1986, *Wrecked Eggs,* Hare brought two of its three characters from New York City to a cottage in Rhinebeck in upstate New York, displacing them from the habitat of their professional lives. This drama turns on a further change of context, for during its action the set is filled with preparations for a large party to celebrate the couple's divorce. Only one guest will come, however, and she and the hostess are left alone on the brink of this event; this very theatrical moment of quiet recognition is the heart of the play. A violent outburst then follows which alters what is about to happen, and revalues the entire action. It may seem that only the change which has been effected in the potential of the single set could have caused this detonation: the characters are confronted with a crisis by a visual transformation of the setting.

In many ways these manipulations of stage place operate very simply. Computerized switchboards have now brought a more filmic fluidity of scene to the theatre and endowed a dramatist with a much stricter control over an audience's attention. No longer are *dramatis personae* confined within the three walls of a constructed stage set, a limited and defined environment which has to be changed behind a curtain or during a meaningless darkness. Not does the play have to be enacted before some permanent background which serves for every scene by making minor changes—opening this door rather than that, thrusting out a bed or a table, carrying on flags or flowers, or changing the way the stage and its structure are lit. A more filmic illusion is now possible because stage lighting has become infinitely and finely variable, so susceptible to electronic control that onstage action has almost unlimited mobility from place to place. Hare uses these devices boldly and they become increasingly important in his plays, as if he were eager to bring theatre much closer to the "fluidity" of film.

Hare knows as much as almost anyone about the power of electronic switchboards; he has directed numerous plays at the National Theatre in London and at the Public Theatre in New York, where he has worked with the foremost lighting designers and the most sophisticated equipment. Already in *Plenty* of 1978, he called for an arbitrary change of place by using light and color; the scenery must change silently in full view of the audience, without apparent human aid. So Susan Traherne moves from England to France, and back in time, in a seamless continuation of performance. The penultimate scene is in a seedy hotel in Blackpool in 1962:

> (LAZAR *turns the nightlight off. Darkness.*)
> SUSAN: Tell me your name.
> (*Pause.*)
> LAZAR: Code name.
> (*Pause.*)
> Code name.
> (*Pause.*)
> Code name Lazar.
> (LAZAR *opens the door of the room. At once music plays. Where you would expect a corridor you see the fields of France shining brilliantly in a fierce green square. The room scatters.*)

SCENE TWELVE

> *St. Benoît, August 1944.*
>   *The darkened areas of the room disappear and we see a French hillside in high summer. The stage picture forms piece by piece. Green, yellow, brown. Trees. The fields stretch away. A high sun. A brilliant August day. Another* FRENCHMAN *stands looking down into the valley. He carries a spade, is in wellingtons and corduroys. He is about 40, fattish with an unnaturally gloomy air.*
>   *Then* SUSAN *appears climbing the hill. She is 19. She is dressed like a young French girl, her pullover over her shoulder. She looks radiantly well.*
>
> FRENCHMAN: Bonjour, ma'moiselle.
> SUSAN: Bonjour. (205–6)

This closing scene is rather like a walk into the sunset at the end of an old film: Susan smiles at the stranger, and they look at each other, about to go. But then Hare directs a pause, in which he pulls the focus back to Susan by giving her words to speak: "There will be days and days and days like this" (207). The effect is complicated because the audience knows what Susan at this moment does not: her prognostication is quite obviously untrue, having been denied by what has already been shown on this stage. In a film, the characters would now start walking into a real sunset, getting smaller and smaller in the distance; the camera might show them moving closer together or beginning to dance. But on stage, Susan is life-sized and close to the audience to the very end. Even though her whole self may shine with confidence and well-being on this brilliant summer's day, the darkness and waste of the days to come are summoned up in the audience's mind. Hare has used modern technology to control attention, plucking what he chooses from Susan's individual history and from the real history of a world at war and peace, as if he were a film-maker; but finally each spectator must make what he or she can of the contradiction between stage-present and stage-past. In its playing with place and time, *Plenty* was the most filmic of Hare's plays to date, but nevertheless it was still conceived for theatrical immediacy in performance.

In later plays, Hare refined this filmic device of a slow fade-out of one scene and fade-in to the next. For example, before Isobel, Irwin and Rhonda can leave to go to the flicks and have that "good time,"

> (. . . *we hear the sound of* MARION's *voice as she approaches from the back. The scenery changes as the others leave, and we are in Tom's office—an anonymously decorated room of glass and wood panel, dominated by a big, bare leather-topped desk. The glass runs unnaturally high, giving a feeling of airy emptiness.* TOM is *already at his desk to greet his wife, who approaches, putting down her coat as she comes.*)

SCENE SIX

Tom's office.
MARION: I can't see the problem. There really is no problem. People so love to talk problems up. Family things actually belong at the weekend. A drink on Sunday is lovely. Or lunch. Or walking after lunch. That's the right time for the family. 'It's crazy when it starts infecting your week. (58–59)

So dramatic images are juxtaposed, the new ones echoing those from the previous scene while marking contrasts with them. As one person moves on, three move off. The glass running "*unnaturally high*" establishes a new "*feeling*"— anonymous, airy and empty—like a cinema screen waiting to show some action drawn from the problems which "People so love to talk . . . up." The effect is fluent, imagistic, expressive, and unconfined by any one location. It is also contrived, and the play-maker is very much in charge, insisting that the drama is viewed in his way, as if he were showing only what the camera records. On one level of appreciation, the switch of setting, effected without any apparent difficulty, dominates attention; on another, the contrasting and yet echoing words offer stabs of superior insight.

Such transitions have become a hallmark of Hare's writing for the stage and he continually refines and extends their use. At the beginning of *The Secret*

Rapture, a few almost silent figures and a setting which is only partially revealed engage attention together, in the manner of a film thriller.

ACT ONE

SCENE ONE

Robert's bedroom. The curtain goes up on almost complete darkness. Then a door opens at the back and a dim and indirect light is thrown from the corridor. MARION, *in her late thirties, brisk, dark-haired, wearing a business suit, stands a moment, nervous, awed, in the doorway. She moves into the room which you can just detect is dominated by a large double bed, in which a man is lying, covered with a sheet reaching up over his face.* MARION *stops a moment by the bed, looking down. She then turns to go back towards the door.*

ISOBEL: Marion?
(MARION *lets out a scream, not having realized that* ISOBEL *was sitting in a chair at the end of the bed.*)
MARION: My God!
IISOBEL: I'm sorry.
MARION: You startled me.
ISOBEL: Don't turn the main light on. (1)

A door opens. A figure is seen in silhouette, and then a bed and a man in it. The standing and nameless person moves in one direction and then another; in the darkness, a voice calls out a name; then there is a scream. A second figure is now seen, seated; and the man is recognized clearly as a corpse. So the theatre audience is introduced to the situation and alerted to danger just as if the dramatist were in charge of a camera by which he can insist on his point of view and his choice and manipulation of successive images. But then, characteristically, having brought Marion and Isobel face to face, as in a film, Hare uses only words to impel the drama forward, and also to extend the audience's sense of where. the action is:

> ISOBEL: I needed some peace. . . . I decided this would be the only place. For some quiet. There's so much screaming downstairs. (1)

The filmic sequence of images had not supplied all the dramatist's needs: once the elaborate opening has provided the exposition, it has no further role to perform, and what follows is conventional onstage drama.

In *The Secret Rapture* and *Racing Demon* scenes flow together, changing place smoothly as in a film, and words illuminate the contrasts and similarities between the images. But in the later play the actual "built" stage set is kept to a strict minimum. The scenic contrasts are between two sets of human figures in disparate situations, rather than between their surroundings. The effect is to enhance the verbal connections between scenes and the effect of "montage"; here the device has something of the eloquence of strict and refined film editing. For example, at the end of the penultimate scene of Act I of *Racing Demon*:

> (*The doors throughout the hall are thrown open. Clergy and laity flock in to take their places. Men in legal wigs and gowns assemble at the central table, as the hall fills.*)
> KINGSTON: Well, here they come. A vigorous morning's debating. Rapier and bludgeon. Absolutely no holds barred. All opinions respected. And at the end, a view acceptable to everyone. Lord, guide our thoughts.
> (A MALAYSIAN WOMAN *rings a small handbell.*)
> WOMAN: The Synod is in session. Let us pray.
> (*At once there is silence. As the prayer in the hall continues, the lights go down until there is darkness.*)
> ALL: Our Father,
>   Which art in heaven,
>   Hallowed be thy name.
>   Thy kingdom come,
>   Thy will be done,
>   On Earth as it is in Heaven.
>   Give us this day our daily bread,
>   And forgive us our trespasses,
>   As we forgive them that trespass against us,
>   And lead us not into temptation,
>   But deliver us from evil,
>   For thine is the kingdom, the power and the glory,
>   For ever and ever.
>   Amen.
>
> ### SCENE TWELVE
>
> *The church. The lights have gone down through the prayers. At the end there is total darkness but for two candles in front of* TONY's *kneeling figure. Behind him,* LIONEL *stands, unnoticed. On* TONY's *face, a look of intense concentration. The organ plays, subliminally.* (44)

The whole theatre can be brought into the light to represent the assembling Synod and to encourage the audience to feel included in its business. Then as the voice of prayer makes its requests for "daily bread," forgiveness, and delivery from evil, and ultimately acknowledges an everlasting "power" and "glory," the focus in the gathering darkness must be increasingly on words alone, until two candles and then two contrasting figures are discovered, the dim light and new silence concentrating the audience's attention. When these figures speak, the words they use echo the earlier prayer and contrast with it: Lionel calls Tony's *name* and at first it is not heard; and he offers the suppliant a meal—a form of *daily bread*. The audience may sense that both the *power* and the *glory* are now almost totally absent, and that *temptation* is close at hand. *For ever and ever* is replaced by "some other time," words which seem set for endless repetition:

LIONEL: Tony.
(TONY *doesn't hear.*)
Tony.
(He hears but, transfixed, doesn't turn.)
TONY: It's you, Lionel.
LIONEL: You look like a ghost.
(TONY *turns and stares at him.*)
　　　I came in. I wanted . . . to ask you to dinner.
TONY: Dinner? That's very kind. But I can't. I've got . . . another invitation.
LIONEL: Really?
TONY: In town.
LIONEL: Oh yes?
TONY: I'm going to see . . .
(*He stops. There is a very long pause. LIONEL is quite still. Then*)
　　　. . . someone else.
(LIONEL *smiles.*)
LIONEL: Well, then, some other time.
TONY: Some other time, yes. (*Stares at him a moment.*) Well, I must be going, or
　　　else I'll be late. Good to see you, Lionel. (*Gets up from his knees.*) I'll see you
　　　soon.
(*He begins to walk from the church. Then, towards the door, he accelerates and runs out. . . .*) (45)

Silences and wordless confrontations are emphasized, so that the audience sees and hears as the dramatist has willed them to do: these Christians can scarcely summon each other's attention by calling their names; trespass and forgiveness are not talked about easily; neither character can be led out of temptation, or delivered from what has made him almost ghostly to the other.

For all the filmic devices in Hare's late plays, which free his characters from conventional stage settings, it is the living presence of actors on stage which continues to provide the essential dramatic experience. Here film can provide no alternative. In *The Bay at Nice,* the other one-act play of 1986, the-atrical and filmic devices work together to draw attention to a scarcely bear-able tension held silently within the mind and body of Valentina, the central character; and then, in the last moments, her experience is related to an imagined world established in wider dimensions and a stronger light than it could ever possess within a conventionally static stage set. Valentina had known Matisse in her youth and has been summoned to a Leningrad museum to authenticate an unsigned picture. By the end of the play the picture has been on stage since early in its action, with its back facing the audience; now, after Valentina's daughter has left,

> (. . . *There's a moment's silence. Then* VALENTINA *walks across to the chair and picks up the canvas. . . . She holds it out at arms' length for five seconds. Then, without any visible reaction, she puts it down. Then she walks across the room and stands alone. Then her eyes begin to fill with tears. Silently the* ASSISTANT CURATOR *returns, standing respectfully at the door.*)
> VALENTINA: You've come back.
> ASSISTANT: Yes.
> VALENTINA: I didn't hear you.
> ASSISTANT: Have you had time to look at it?
> VALENTINA: I've examined it.
> (*There's a pause.*)
> Yes. It's Matisse. (46)

Slowly the audience learns that Valentina has recognized the painting by the way in which light is represented as it shines through the shutters of a window. "The way the sun is diffused," she explains. "He controlled the sun in his painting. He said, with shutters he could summon the sun as surely as Joshua with his trumpet" (47).

It is for loss of that "power" and "glory" that Valentina has wept, and the truth of these feelings has been emphasized by the five-second examination, her silent crossing of the stage, and her tears. These are theatrical devices, but used with the confidence of someone used to film, where the camera can hold and fix attention on motion and silent performance. Valentina has little more to say, but the dramatist insists on a further vindication of what she has recognized by a filmic change of setting:

> VALENTINA: . . . he said the result was truer and more beautiful than anything that came as an effort of will.
> (*She stands a moment, then turns to go.*)
> ASSISTANT: I'll get you a car.
> VALENTINA: No. The tram is outside. It goes right by my door.
> (*She goes. He stands a moment, looking at the painting. The background fades and the stage is filled with the image of the bay at Nice: a pair of open French windows, a balcony, the sea and the sky. The* ASSISTANT *turns and looks to the open door.*) (48)

Neither of the persons on stage sees the brilliant image of Matisse's painting; that is the film director's and dramatist's message to the audience.

The close scrutiny brought to bear upon Valentina or Susan Traherne by the dramatist's control of focus is like that provided by a close-up on the face of a film actor, when the drama is sustained by the very being of the performer, with all its secret and manifest individuality. But here the actress is present on stage; the audience sees her completely and responds to her actual presence. Each performer will reveal something a little different from another and, for all the dramatist's cunning, the performer is finally in charge. Not surprisingly, Hare, as theatre director, has entrusted these stage roles to actresses—Irene Worth and Kate Nelligan—whom he can trust to hold attention in silence and to endow the roles with quiet, unforced, and unmistakable life.

In later plays such burdens are shared more widely among their casts, and their silences are sometimes superseded by the highly theatrical device of soliloquy—speeches on their own behalf, in the manner of plays from earlier theatres where asides and direct address to the audience were common. *Racing Demon* is a play about four parish priests, two bishops, and some churchgoers, so that here old-fashioned soliloquies blend easily with prayers addressed to the Almighty, as if to another person above the stage or present in the mind of the speaker. Thus, after encountering Tony in church following the Synod, Lionel is left alone to pray:

(LIONEL . . . *[s]teps forward and looks up to heaven.*)
What can you do, Lord? You tell me. You show me the way. Go on. You explain why all this hurt has to come. Tell me. You understand everything. (*Steps back.*) Why do the good always fight among themselves? (45)

Lionel's backward movement introduces a theatrical device which cuts off prayer for his last sentence: this makes a strong impact, one which closes the scene and the first act of the play. If the Synod has been an occasion for lighting the audience as well as the stage, thus involving its members more directly in the situation and dialogue, then, after the backwards step, the concluding sentence can be addressed to those listeners. Perhaps the auditorium lights have begun to come up for the intermission. Lionel has been speaking to the "Lord," almost as if to a distant, overhead camera, but now dramatic illusion shifts again. He steps out of character and out of his own place, to offer a question to any and every one who is attending the performance. Filmic mobility and passive attention yield to an essentially theatrical device as the author breaks the bounds of the stage world; the character steps out of a dramatic illusion and into a place from which he can communicate directly with an audience. This is not representation or filmic illusion; it is encounter.[1]

II

David Hare does not play according to a single set of rules, but mixes techniques from cinema and stage in order to focus attention where he decides it should be, and on occasion to break illusionistic reality and so challenge an audience's understanding. This can be seen again in his theatrical use of a device found variously at the end of his television and cinema filmscripts where he builds up a final statement by a series of cuts from one place, or one focus, to another. In the concluding minutes of *Licking Hitler* (1978), a blank screen is followed by five separate still shots, each accompanied with voice-over, and each set in a different place; then there are two more shots, the first moving inside a house and the second viewing its exterior, while the voice continues (126–28). At the end of *Wetherby* (1985), the audience is shown a school, the inside and outside of a house, and then a pub, each shot dominated by one or more of the film's leading characters; and then, in the last shot, the camera pulls away, so that Stanley and Jean are seen as *"two among many"* (130–32)—as customers in the pub who are looking around in silence. A similar multi-focused conclusion can be seen, to some extent, in the last moments of the stage play, *The Bay at Nice:* the viewing of the painting; the tears; the Assistant's entry; the vast projection of the subject of the painting; the open door.

The wide variety of viewpoints in the last moments of this short stage play may have suggested, in turn, the restless movement of the camera at the end of the filmscript *Paris by Night* (shot in 1987), which also focuses, at one point, on a representation of reality, not reality itself. After a fatal pistol shot, the audience is forced to look from place to place: first the view of a child asleep, then of a man in a car, then of a woman dead; then back to the car to show the woman's handbag and two drawings, which had been sketched on a napkin much earlier in the film; then, once more, back to the child who is now waking up (82–83). Using the precise focus of a camera shot, Hare has no need here for words in order to establish a wide context and differing modes of perception.[2]

Only a few years after these experiments, *Racing Demon* was given a multiple ending, but modified yet again. Its last scene begins with Lionel alone in his living room, *"speak[ing] into the empty air"* a soliloquy of loss and helplessness. Then "TONY . . . *appear[s] in the church, in another area of the stage,*" and he too soliloquizes. At this point, "FRANCES *appears at the other end of the area. All three are oblivious of each other.*" She speaks as if addressing the "Lord," in familiar talk rather than in prayer, as a means of settling her own mind:

A last look round, Lord. To close the subject. Like pulling down a blind. I am going, Lord. . . .

All three change their modes of address before the play is done—Tony to self-doubt, Lionel to urgent prayer, and Frances to contented daydream (like Valentina remembering the sunlight): "And then you turn and head towards the sun." Frances's words give the cue for *"(The stage darkens),"* and for the play to finish with each of the three characters in focus, simultaneously (87–88). In this experiment, which may have been suggested by the multiple focuses at the close of his films, the dramatist depends on the actors' performances and not on scenic images. In doing so Hare has drawn on theatrical devices which in recent years have been more common in opera or musicals than in spoken drama. The persons of the drama are the living images which conclude the play, separate and yet viewed simultaneously. The three stand together but they do not speak to each other; each is alone in a darkening world.

III

Hare's mingling of theatrical and filmic experiment distinguishes him from other dramatists who use their knowledge of film-making in writing stage plays. Trevor Griffiths's *Piano* (1990) is a play obviously indebted to Chekhov, whose characters, situations, action, and style it imitates and modifies assertively. But in the concluding scene a lighting change effects a shift of focus, as if the playwright had ordered a panning shot from one group of characters to another. The household is assembled:

> (YASHA *fusses up and down, with coats and capes and wraps. Greetings, hugs, kisses: another crisis over.*)
> ANNA: Nothing will change, my friends.
> (*The sun suddenly strengthens. They turn, like spectres, to watch it lift over the hill across the lake.*)

The light change seems to unsettle nothing: they continue to talk idly, remembering Chekhov's death, and they drink champagne. Anna repeats her comforting conclusion: "Nothing changes. Everything will be as it was." But the play is not over yet, for the focus changes. Out of darkness at first, but then in transforming light, the servant Radish makes a different comment (possibly it is a soliloquy; the text is ambiguous in this respect):

> RADISH: (*From above; unseen*) Grab dies. Iron rusts. Lies eat the soul. . . .
> (*The radiance spreads upwards; reveals* RADISH *and* ZAKHAR, PETYA *[a child] between them, holding their hands, on the plank bridge.*)
> (*Looking down on the spectres below*) . . .

Everything's possible.
(*Fade to black.*) (55)

And so, at the author's direction, the play ends with a firm counterstatement which is given force by technical means, as if the author were manipulating attention in a film.

Instead of playing one focus against another, Stephen Poliakoff, in *Coming in to Land* (1986), introduced filmic techniques by calling for television screens in banked array and, later, in large size, so that his characters see images of themselves, and the audience sees them too. He calls for these television images to be stopped in mid-action, so that they are held still for inspection and re-interpretation. More inventively, Poliakoff sought to increase the field of vision for his stage drama to filmic dimensions. He called for a vast mural to stretch across the back wall of the stage:

> *The mural shows people arriving on a shore with blue and white water behind them, shadowy travellers facing an idealized glowing city on a hill, across an expanse of green.*
>
> *Somebody has drawn one major piece of graffiti on the mural, a monster emerging out of the blue water with its teeth bared.* (54)

As Halina, the heroine, is interrogated about seeking entry to Britain from Poland, the mural, already double in its message because of the monster, is further modified by the presence of nameless supernumeraries in front of it, all clamoring for attention. In the following scene, as if altering the focal width of the camera, the official's office gets larger and more menacing. There is also an inset picture to be shown:

> PIERCE'*s office now fills the stage. The door is oddly large for the scale of the walls. Around and above the door is misted glass looking out on the passages beyond; we can glimpse the mural on the back wall, now looking smudged and diffused through the glass.*
>
> *There is a small picture on the wall of people on a golden beach mirroring the mural outside; it is the only ornament on the wall.* (60)

The dramatist has asked the scene designer to give multiple and changing form to the "world" in which he wishes his characters to be viewed, and in stage directions he has explained what he wants the audience to see. But there is little in the action or dialogue to impress these effects on the viewer's attention; he has played a filmic trick without integrating it with the presentation of his characters in speech and action.

Hare's way of switching from place to place between short scenes, while fading in and out with sound and image, is also found in the plays of other writers. Experience of working on filmscripts and a daily exposure to television seem to have encouraged many dramatists to think in terms of short episodes with changing locations, rather than of long scenes with a single setting which are sustained by talk, a series of cleverly motivated entries and exits, and a developing story or action. Short episodes are used to provide a sudden change of viewpoint, a quick turn of events, a new reaction, or an escalation in the passage of time. Harold Pinter's later plays, *Betrayal, Victoria Station,* and *Mountain Language,* offer many examples. In much earlier plays, such as *The Caretaker* (1960), episodes had stopped and others started with no change of location, and with only a change of lighting to indicated change of time. So, for example:

> DAVIES: You see, the name I go under now ain't my real one. It's assumed.
> *Silence.*
> THE LIGHTS FADE TO BLACKOUT.
> THEN UP TO DIM LIGHT THROUGH THE WINDOW.
> *A door bangs.*
> *Sound of a key in the door of the room.*
> DAVIES *enters.* . . . (44)

Little is changed by the device of a cut from episode to episode, beyond a new disposition of the characters. But in *Betrayal* (1978), time changes forwards or backwards; and the setting changes too, drawing attention to the change of fortune for the characters. In *Mountain Language* (1988), lights snap off and on again between episodes to effect a change of scene; and in the course of a single episode, lights go *"to half"* and the *"figures are still,"* while voices continue *"over,"* and then the reverse sequence follows (33–35). Here a change of light is part of the play's action and the means whereby the dramatist, like a filmmaker, can indicate a new pressure on the institution's inmates. The different "takes" in Pinter's plays operate to forward the action and reveal the varying potential of the *dramatis personae,* but filmic device does not alter radically the audience's mode of perception.

In contrast, Hare uses filmic devices in many and challenging ways, tightening and refining his hold over an audience's attention. In *Plenty, The Secret Rapture,* and *Racing Demon,* a sequence of episodes fade into each other and give an effect like that of montage in film: continuity as well as contrast is marked. An audience is given a sense of context beyond that expressed by a single stage set or by a single response of the *dramatis personae.* Hare's filmic effects can open up a view of the larger world in which the characters operate. Often the consequences of the characters' actions are thus expressed in a way which goes beyond their own understandings.

IV

By using a film-maker's techniques in the theatre and so controlling what an audience sees and senses, Hare might be accused of taking responsibility away from his actors and manipulating an audience's reaction to his drama. As viewers in a cinema have little chance of escape from what the camera has captured for them to see, in the form in which the editor has chosen to present it, so for these stage plays the audience's response is very carefully controlled from offstage, or out front, by manipulation of light, sound, and focus. How the action is perceived has been decided by the omniscient dramatist and has been specified in stage directions before the actors have started rehearsals.

But this is only half the truth. The audience's attention is being directed so that it will view the actors' performance with close attention and unusual subtlety, but the actors are not "fixed" by this process. In *Plenty,* how does Susan say "There will be days and days and days like this"? How does she vary those three "days," and by what sensations is "this" given definition? In *Racing Demon,* how do the various clerics and Frances hold the stage in close-up for soliloquy or prayer? The actors have to supply the necessary substance to these moments of special scrutiny which the dramatist has provided and forced the audience to observe. Speech and performance remain the mysterious heart of these plays, even when presented with artful and inescapable technique; and this centre is ultimately the responsibility of the actors.

The end of *The Secret Rapture* shows how Hare draws back from taking responsibility away from his actors. In the very last moments, after Isobel has been killed by Irwin and preparations are being made for her funeral, Marion and her husband come together in a house which she has just restored to its condition at the beginning of the play:

> Tom: Oh God, you feel wonderful.
> Marion: Yes, so do you.

There is scarcely any verbal or visual preparation for this, and nothing, at this moment, to lend credibility to these words. And for the actress, another and larger challenge is yet to come; the text continues:

> Marion: Yes, so do you.
> *(They kiss again. Then he takes a couple of steps back, smiling, slightly adjusting his tie.)*
> Tom. I love you.
> Tom: I'll be back soon.
> *(He pauses, and laughs a small laugh. Then turns and goes out.*
> Marion *is left alone. She sits on the sofa at the centre.)*

MARION: Isobel. We're just beginning. Isobel, where are you? *(She waits a moment.)* Isobel, why don't you come home? (81–82)

In these very last moments, Marion has to address her dead sister as if she were still alive and present before her. Then she senses that Isobel is not actually there, and so puts the possibility of her return into words, in the form of a question that she expects to be heard. Conviction, simplicity, lucidity, and a changing awareness of a non-physical presence: all these are required, and now the author does nothing more to help the actress, or to intervene. (Perhaps Tom's "*small laugh*" is intended, by its awkwardness, to help Marion's clear words to register more assuredly in contrast.) The printed text asks for neither fade-out, nor blackout, nor final curtain; decisions about all that will depend on what the actress has provided in her performance.[3]

In an introduction to the published filmscript of *Paris by Night,* Hare describes vividly what he looks for in performance. Having told how the film came to be made, he explains that the main difficulty had been in casting Clara, its central role, because she had to be "a notably strong woman, and what's more one who was, in the cant phrase of the trade, 'unsympathetic'" (vi). But all along he had maintained that Clara was "not that different from you or me" (vii). When Charlotte Rampling accepted the part, these difficulties vanished: "It was no longer important [that the film] should be made. It was absolutely vital" (viii). For Hare her performance clinched everything:

> In the fourth week, in the Halcyon Hotel in Notting Hill Gate, we found ourselves shooting the scene in which Clara lays out her philosophy of life to Wallace after they have made love. Clara is talking from her own experience, jumbled up with a certain amount of confused political prejudice, yet a mixture of things—the context in which she speaks, the tenderness with her lover, the play of the light, Charlotte's exquisite conviction in the role—combined to produce in those of us watching a feeling of total disorientation. We simply did not know what our response to Clara was. We were watching a woman whose head was apparently full of careless and half-thought scraps, yet in the image of her and her own self-awareness was something so moving that you could not tell if beauty was confounding truth, or if the two, as I suspect they are in life, were so mixed up that nothing could unlock them. We were all robbed of our usual reactions. This is something I have so long wanted to do as a writer that a profound and lasting contentment came upon me in that room, and it persisted through the remaining weeks of shooting. For as long as we worked, the process of art did what it has always promised: it comforted, it clarified, and set everything in order. (viii–ix)

Of course, the film was something else: images of that revelatory moment. The spell had lasted only for "as long as we worked."

Ironically, it is films and not stage plays that are said to have "the *appeal of a presence and of a proximity* that strikes the masses and fills the movie theaters. . . . The feeling of credibility, which is so direct, operates on us in films of the unusual and of the marvelous, as well as in those that are 'realistic'" (Metz 5). But such attraction is the contrivance of the film-maker: the chosen sequence of images, the sense of the inevitable which comes from the movement portrayed in those images. So the running of a film assures its audience that "there it *is;* it is happening." But *what* is there? Only very rarely and fleetingly is it an impression of truth from within the very being of hero or heroine:

> For a film heroine to exhibit, for even a fraction of a second, a gesture or an intonation that is true implies the success of a most difficult enterprise on the part of the film-maker; it is something that occurs once in a year, producing a shock in the viewer, and each time it occurs it renders forty films, retroactively devoted to the pure Plausible, obsolete in a single stroke. (Metz 246)

Hare's experience while working on *Paris by Night* was an experience of a different order; it depended on the entire presence of the actress and her closeness to the watchers, and their mutual suspension of disbelief.

When Hare returned from film-making to write for the theatre he knew how to manipulate the audience's viewpoint and focus. He is now able to encourage a perception of contrasts, connections and convergencies, and a sense of critical risk. But in the theatre he does not have to select a single and irrevocable image of any moment; nor does he have to edit, frame or manipulate that image. His task is limited to bringing the heart of the drama forward for attention and offering an unrestricted view of its performance, in all its subtle "confusion," "beauty," and "truth." For some of the audience and, perhaps, for himself, there may be a moment of disorientation and "a profound and lasting contentment," because the actor is there on stage, totally present, with an "exquisite conviction" which clarifies and places the whole play in some "order" which is beyond the contrivance of the dramatist.

Perhaps Hare returned to write for the theatre to escape from the omniscient role of film-maker and to discover a new sense of the world in which he lives. Each time the actors perform in his plays, they enjoy the freedom to create their roles afresh as they bring the action to a full conclusion; and so they may provide the author with a vindication which goes beyond what he had imagined. The end of *The Secret Rapture* depends on what the actress brings to her role; that of *Racing Demon* on the performances of two actors and an actress. The filmic elements in the plays of David Hare are at the service of his romantic quest for a halcyon truth which is essentially, and very simply, theatrical.

NOTES

[1] The distinction between prayer and soliloquy in this passage was even stronger in the first published version of *Racing Demon* (London: Faber, 1990), where Hare provided a *double* "shift." In that edition, Lionel begins by speaking to himself *before* launching into prayer: "I tried. Lord knows I tried. He [Tony] wouldn't listen. I did all I could. He just ran out the door like a madman. It was out of my hands. *(Steps forward and looks up to heaven.)* Where are you, Lord? You tell me . . ." (49). Lionel's movement forward and turning his eyes upwards helped to differentiate prayer from soliloquy, and thus helped to prepare us for his shift *away* from prayer in his concluding sentence.

[2] A further circumstance may provide another clue that this filmscript and this play are connected in their author's mind. As Clara and Wallace sketch each other's faces on the napkin, so, in the last moments of *The Bay at Nice,* Valentina tells a story about Matisse sketching his mother's head on a spare telegram form: "His hand did the work, not the brain. And he said the result was true and more beautiful than anything that came as an effort of will" (48).

[3] One difference between two productions of this play provides further demonstration of its author's reliance on his actors' performances. In London at the National Theatre, for its first production, the director, Howard Davies, added a new entry for Isobel at the end of the play; the scenery opened up (in the manner of the last scene in *Plenty*) to show the garden of the house bathed in sunshine where Isobel was entering slowly and calmly, to be present in sight of her sister for a final tableau, a tangible representation and reinforcement of Marion's state of mind. In the second production in New York, directed by Hare, the text was adhered to faithfully: the scenery did not open and the dead woman did not re-enter. Here the actress playing Marion carried the conclusion: the context in which she speaks, her new tenderness and, perhaps, the play of light, all prepared for the last moment. But then, finally, everything depended on an "exquisite conviction" in performance. In the event, the New York performances did not please the principal critics of the city. The production was withdrawn and the author became involved in a public dispute with Frank Rich of the *New York Times.* This outcome, very different from the play's reception in London, could be the result of an inadequate performance or an inadequate response. Perhaps the latter is the more likely, since the dramatist was making unusual demands on his audience's attention.

Works Cited

Griffiths, Trevor. *Piano*. London: Faber, 1990.

Hare, David. *The Bay at Nice* and *Wrecked Eggs*. London: Faber, 1986.

———. Introduction. *Paris by Night*. London: Faber, 1988. v–ix.

———. *Licking Hitler. The History Plays*. London: Faber, 1984.

———. *Paris by Night*. London: Faber, 1988.

———. *Plenty. The History Plays*. London: Faber, 1984.

———. *Racing Demon*. Rev. ed. London: Faber, 1991.

———. *The Secret Rapture*. Rev. ed. London: Faber, 1989.

———. *Wetherby. Heading Home, Wetherby and Dreams of Leaving*. London: Faber, 1991.

Hauser, Arnold. *The Social History of Art*. Trans. Stanley Godman and Arnold Hauser. Vol. 4. London: Routledge, 1962. 4 vols.

Metz, Christian. *Film Language: A Semiotics of the Cinema*. Trans. Michael Taylor. New York: Oxford University Press, 1974.

Pinter, Harold. *The Caretaker*. Rev. ed. London: Methuen, 1962.

———. *Mountain Language*. London: Faber, 1988.

Poliakoff, Stephen. *Coming in to Land*. London: Methuen, 1986.

Master Class and the Paradox of the Diva

Cary M. Mazer

Master Class begins with a double untruth. Maria Callas (or, more accurately, the actress playing Maria Callas) strides on stage, almost certainly to the accompaniment of the audience's applause, looks directly at the audience, and announces, "No applause. We're here to work. You're not in a theatre. This is a classroom" (1).

The first untruth is the statement that we are not in a theatre, since we in fact are in a theatre, both outside of and within the fictional world of the play.[1] In *Master Class,* the stage of the theatre represents the stage of a theatre—the recital hall at the Juilliard School, where Maria Callas gave a series of master classes in 1971 and 1972 before a full house of students and spectators. In the theatre, when *Master Class* is performed, it is, of course, not really 1971 but the present; it is not Juilliard but (for the play's Broadway run) the Golden Theatre; and the audience is comprised of paying theatregoers, not advanced voice students. But the audience is *there,* as an audience, in both the reality of the theatrical event and the fiction of the play. The actor may be (in the original production) Zoe Caldwell and not the "real" Maria Callas, but the response of the audience to Caldwell—applause—is the same response that the 1971 Juilliard audience (the fictional audience that the real audience pretends to be) has for Callas. For Caldwell/Callas to tell us that we are not in a theatre flies in the face of what we know to be true, both in life and in the fiction of the play.

The other untruth is that Maria Callas does not want applause. Maria Callas, we soon see, lives for applause, and thrives on having an audience, alternately revealing and concealing herself from it, pandering for its affection and sympathy and holding it in contempt. Later in the play (60) she will even deny that she had asked the audience not to applaud. Maria's attitude and her philosophical pronouncements are filled with such contradictions: that we cannot know what she suffered in Greece during the war and that we have to know it; that one can only create art if one has suffered and that one must not bring one's private suffering to one's art; that singers sing for the sheer joy of it and that singers must never give away their talent except for sufficient pay, etc., etc. The paradox of the audience's simultaneous presence and absence, of the fiction's theatricality and non-theatricality, is mirrored by Maria Callas's opinions—at best paradoxical and at worst contradictory and mutually exclusive—about life, art, performance, and their relationship. And at the heart of these paradoxes is the real subject of the play, what one might call "the Paradox of the Diva."

Terrence McNally has dramatized the phenomenology of the diva before, most notably in what might be considered the ultimate play about "opera queens," *The Lisbon Traviata.* But there the focus is not on the diva but on her fans, the homosexual protagonists who project onto the diva their own identity, desires, and suffering. In *The Lisbon Traviata* the opera queen's identification is both with the singer and with the operatic role she plays: both with Maria Callas, the self-consuming performer who makes her private suffering transcendently public through her performances, and with Violetta, the consumptive courtesan in *La Traviata,* who sacrifices her happiness and her health for love.

McNally is not interested in the phenomenon of the opera queen in *Master Class* (though in one of the flashback sequences, Maria ventriloquizes the voice of her lover Aristotle Onassis, who observes "The fags just want to be you" [26]). Instead he shifts his focus to the object of the opera queen's emulation, the diva herself. But the way he views the diva is clearly in line with the paradoxes and contradictions in the way opera queens admire and emulate the diva, a phenomenon most recently articulated in Wayne Koestenbaum's autobiographical polemic, *The Queen's Throat: Opera, Homosexuality, and the Mystery of Desire.* The opera queen, Koestenbaum argues, admires both the diva's persona—her arrogance, grandeur, and self-fashioned hauteur and sublime bitchiness—and the roles that the diva plays. Indeed, the opera queen's identification with the roles the diva plays magnifies the opera queen's emulation of the diva, for the diva, the opera queen believes, identifies with the character even more closely than the opera queen ever can and so becomes the opera queen's emotionally expressive, sacrificial surrogate. As Stephen, one of the two opera queens in *The Lisbon Traviata,* explains, "Opera is about us, our life-and-death passions—we all love, we're all going to die. Maria understood that. That's where the voice came from, the heart, the soul, I'm tempted to say from some even more intimate place" (61). At the end of the play, Stephen, having failed to enact Don Jose to his departing lover's Carmen, throws his head back in a silent scream of heartbreak while Callas's Violetta plays on the stereo, the diva's voice expressing a pain that is simultaneously the singer's, the character's, and the listener's.[2]

The diva, the subject of the opera queen's emulation, is simultaneously present and absent, playing a distilled and self-fashioned version of herself in every role she plays and dissolving herself into the music and the dramatic situation of the character she acts and sings, rendering herself transparent to the character and the composer (and librettist) behind the character. The difference between the actor and the character she is playing is erased in the eyes of the opera queen: the diva is both transcendently herself and transubstantially the character; indeed, that is to a great extent the source of her glory.

But the relation of an actor to the character he or she is playing is, in the theatre as well as in opera, much more complicated and more paradoxical than the opera queen imagines. And this complicated relationship of actor to role—the paradoxical complementarity of the consummately self-effacing actor and the transcendently-herself diva—is the real subject of *Master Class,* a play in which the opera-singer-as-lecturer is not "in character" ("You're not in a theatre. This is a classroom") and yet is never, strictly speaking, "out" of character, in which theatrical performances draw upon the performer's true "self" and yet the "self" is itself always performative.

The salient biographical facts about Maria Callas's life are all made reference to in *Master Class* her American and Greek upbringing, her training, the patronage of Battista Meneghini, her debut, her radical physical transformation and weight loss, her affair with Onassis, her conflicts with tenors, managers, directors, and rival sopranos, the hirings and firings, and the precipitate decay of her voice. But the play is less a biography of the artist than it is a play about the nature of artistry, the relation of a particular artist's life to her art. The paradoxes of this relationship are both the play's subject and dictate the play's form, and these paradoxes ultimately lead to a shift in the play's focus that muddies the play's focus and, as we shall see, finally undoes the play's otherwise pristine structure.

The play's action, such as it is, consists of three consecutive coaching sessions in real time: Sophie de Palma, a soprano, who sings Adina's "Ah, non credea mirarti" from Bellini's *La Somnambula;* Anthony Candolino, a tenor, who sings "Ricondita armonia" from Puccini's *Tosca;* and soprano Sharon Graham, who is driven from the stage by Callas's brow-beating but returns to be coached in Lady Macbeth's entrance aria, "Vieni! t'afretta" from Verdi's *Macbeth.* In each of these sessions, Callas is rude, condescending, dismissive, and egocentric. And in all three sessions she is a brilliant teacher. And there emerges from her teaching, however obnoxious, a coherent, if complex, philosophical position about the relationship of the singing actor to the operatic role.

Callas interrupts the first note that Sophie de Palma sings in the Bellini aria: "I want to talk to you about your 'Oh!'" The student answers, "I sang it, didn't I?" Callas explains:

> *That's just it. You sang it. You didn't feel it. It's not a note we're after here.*
> *It's a sob of pain. The pain of loss. Surely you understand loss. If not of another*
> *person, then maybe a pet. A puppy. A goldfish. (13)*

Mixed with Callas's patronizing examples ("a puppy. A goldfish") is a stereotypical "Stanislavski Method" acting exercise—Lee Strasberg's "emotional
memory"—in which the actor substitutes an experience from his or her own
life to generate an emotional response equivalent to the emotions of the character that are called for in the dramatic situation of the script. Callas repeatedly
rejects "just singing" ("You were *just* singing," she tells the tenor, "which
equals nothing" [40]). Instead she calls for acting, in the twentieth-century
Stanislavskian tradition: feeling "real" emotions based on the "given circumstances" of the script and embellished or translated in the imagination of the
actor (when the tenor complains that "It doesn't say anything about ten A.M. or
spring or Tosca's body in the score," Callas responds, "It should say it in your
imagination. Otherwise you have notes, nothing but notes"[43]).

The emotions that Callas calls for are not "realistic"; they are channeled
through the artifice of the operatic medium ("Anyone can walk in their sleep,"
she tells Sophie, singing a somnambulist's aria; "Very few people can weep
in song" [11]). Each successive level of expression in opera is more artificial:
speech is more active and demands more actively channeled emotional energy
and a more intense revelation of one's own more intense emotions than
silence; recitative calls for more energy and emotion than speech ("When you
can no longer bear to speak, when the words aren't enough, that's when he
[Bellini] asks you to sing" [18]); aria more than recitative; and a cabaletta
more than its preceding aria.

"This is not a film studio," she explains, "where anyone can get up there
and act. I hate that word. 'Act.' No! Feel. Be. That's what we're doing here"
(16). And she later tells Sharon, helping her "make an entrance" for her Lady
Macbeth entrance aria, "This is opera, not a voice recital. Anyone can stand
there and sing. An artist enters and *is*" (35). What Callas means by "be" and
"is" is clearly something more than passive existence or inexpressive emotion
and is rather a grand, artificial, projected distillation of one's identity and emotional truth: as she tells Sophie, "This is the theatre, darling. We wear our hearts
on our sleeves here" (11). When she tells Sophie "I'm not getting any juice
from you, Sophie. I want juice. I want passion. I want you" (16), she clearly
means that the "you" that an opera singer needs to "be," the being that breathes
and feels and sings on stage, is something grand, extreme, distilled, and
directed. Callas doubts whether Sophie has that magnitude of experience or the
magnitude of expressiveness: "He's broken her heart. Have you ever had your
heart broken?" she asks. When Sophie answers, "Yes," Callas adds, snidely,
"You could have fooled me" (11); and Sophie herself concludes, ruefully, "I'm
not that sort of singer. . . . I'm not that sort of person either" (16).

What "sort of person" does it take to be an opera singer? Here again there
are both paradoxes and contradictions in what Callas teaches. On the one hand,
she claims on her first entrance, the diva must practice complete self-effacement:
"If you want to have a career, as I did—and I'm not boasting now, I am not

one to boast—you must be willing to subjugate yourself—is that a word?—
subjugate yourself to music" (2). But, paradoxically, the singer both erases
herself and is completely herself. For subjugation involves sacrifice, and what
is being sacrificed is the singer's own self. The diva must be a supreme ego-
tist in order to make the supreme sacrifice of her ego to her audiences. And,
she argues, you must be well paid for your pains. "Never give anything away.
There's no more where it came from. We give the audience everything and
when it's gone, *c'est ca, c'est tout. Basta, finito.* We're the ones who end up
empty" (32). She invokes Medea's line to Jason in Cherubini's *Medea*—
"I gave everything for you. Everything"—to explain this: "That's what we
artists do for people. Where would you be without us? Eh? Think about that.
Just think about it while you're counting your millions or leading your boring
lives with your boring wives" (32). The sacrifice of the self is too great to be
wasted on psychotherapy: "Feelings like Sharon's"—who has run off stage to
vomit and has not yet returned—"We use them. We don't give them away on
some voodoo witch doctor's couch" (40). Instead, they should be saved for the
stage, where they are distilled and delivered, at great personal pain, to the
audience.

Callas's relation to her audience—both the audience of her operatic past
and the current audience in the classroom/recital hall—is fraught with contradictions. "The audience is the enemy," she says, quoting Medea's line to Jason;
"Dominate them. . . . Art is domination. It's making people think for that precise moment in time there is only one way, one voice. Yours. Eh?" (37). At
times (including the flashback sequences, in which Callas recalls singing only
for Meneghini or only for Onassis), the audience is worthy of the singer's self-
immolation and sacrifice. At other times the audience is passive, unapprecia-
tive, and unworthy: she talks scornfully of an acquaintance whose favorite part
of the operas are the intervals; and we see her hold in contempt the stagehand
in the recital hall, who neither knows nor cares about the art being created on
the stage within earshot.

McNally best dramatizes the capacity of an audience to be moved by the
artificially distilled expressive powers of the singer's voice and emotions
channeled through the composer's music when Callas herself listens to Tony
Candolino sing "Ricondita armonia." To the tenor's disappointment, after he
has finished singing, she says only "That was beautiful. I have nothing more
to say. That was beautiful" (44). Being an audience member, being the recip-
ient of the imagined emotions of Cavaradossi for Tosca as channeled through
the voice and soul of the tenor as she never was when she played Tosca herself
("I was always backstage preparing for my entrance" [45]), Callas is, for one
of the rare moments in the play, left speechless. And she stumbles awkwardly
from that moment—a moment that demonstrates why, from an audience's
point of view, the singer's art is worthwhile—to the unexpected admission that
"It's a terrible career, actually. I don't know why I bothered" (45).

Through her pedagogical encounters with Sophie and Tony, Callas teaches both the students and the audience what it takes to become an effective singing actor. One must have suffered sufficiently to provide the emotional raw material for embodying the character's emotion. One must be willing to re-experience the most difficult times of one's life over and over again, with all of the focused and distilled intensity of the first experience. One must be willing to display one's most private feelings and experiences in public, both to an uncaring and ungrateful audience (personified, in *Master Class,* by the stage-hand) and to an attentive and appreciative public that demands that each performance be yet another self-consuming and self-consumed display of re-experienced emotional agonies. And, finally, becoming a singing actor requires the singer to turn him- or herself into an artificial being, in part because the medium of musical and theatrical expression is so highly conventionalized and artificial and in part because of the cutthroat world of the operatic profession. One must, in short, play the part of the diva to be a diva; one must become a monster of egotism, selfishness, competitiveness, and vindictiveness, capable of cutting a swathe for oneself in the world of managers, conductors, directors, claques, and other divas, in order to get the opportunity to practice one's art. And, by practicing one's art, by dredging up every life experience and emotion in the service of the drama, and the dramatic character, and the music, one self-destructs, consuming irreversibly the raw material of the art in the very act of making the art. Becoming the diva leaves little more than dry tinder; singing sets the tinder alight, burning with a brilliant flame before the audience, until all that is left are ashes, thorns, and nails.

And so we see Maria Callas through the play: a brilliant actress still, still wearing her all-too-public life's pain on her sleeve, still grabbing the spotlight, indulging her ego, destroying with a glance or a quip everyone around her. And when she finally sings, the stage directions record, "What comes out is a cracked and broken thing" (47).[3]

By the middle of the second act, after Callas has coached two singers and driven a third from the stage, we have learned about the paradoxes of acting contained within the diva's craft, and we have come to some understanding of how this craft calls upon the singer to create a particular performative persona and to put that persona to the service of the self-consuming art of singing. Callas, in her roundabout and often contradictory way, explains these princi-ples to us as she coaches Sophie and Tony, and she demonstrates, in her abomi-nably egotistical behavior, what she has become in service of this art. But it not until the final third of the play, when she coaches Sharon Graham, that we see the means by which a younger singer can put these principles into practice, that we see a singer who can become, potentially at least, another Callas and, in this instance, chooses not to.

Sharon has returned to the recital stage after vomiting in fear and humili-ation, determined now to prove herself. Callas humiliates her and browbeats her into acting and not just singing the aria, as she did with Sophie and Tony. But here, as we watch, the Stanislavskian exercises and the Strasbergian emotional memory substitutions begin to work. Callas insists that everything be concrete, specific: the letter from Macbeth that Lady Macbeth reads, in unsung speech before the recitative, must be real, and not imagined ("I don't want pretending. You're not good enough. I want truth [46]); the news of Duncan's imminent arrival comes not from 'someone' but from 'a servant'" (51). When Sharon hesitates between the recitative and the aria, Callas, swept up in the flow of the drama and encouraging Sharon to be swept up too, insists "don't even think of stopping! You are Lady Macbeth!" (48). After the aria, with the news of Duncan's arrival, the emotional identification of Sharon with Lady Macbeth is, with Callas's coaching, nearly complete:

> MARIA: *How does that make her feel?*
> SOPRANO: *Happy?*
> MARIA: *Don't keep looking at me for answers, Sharon. Tell me, show me. Vite, vite!*
> SOPRANO: *Really happy.*
> MARIA: *Love happy? Christmas morning happy?*
> SOPRANO: *Murder happy!*
> MARIA: *Ah! And what is she going to do about it?*
> Soprano: *She's going to sing a cabaletta!*
> MARIA: *She's going to kill the king! Do you know what that means?*
> SOPRANO: *Yes, it's terrible.*
> MARIA: *Not to her! Do you believe women can have balls, Sharon?*
> SOPRANO: *Some women. Yes, I do!*
> MARIA: *Verdi is daring you to show us yours, Sharon. Will you do it?*
> SOPRANO: *Yes.* (51–52)

The stakes of the scene, the stakes of the act of performing itself, have become, for Sharon, nearly like those for Callas. "This isn't just an opera. This is your life," Callas insists (50). "Is there anything you would kill for, Sharon," she asks her, suggesting "A man, a career?" (53). "You have to listen to something in yourself to sing this difficult music," she insists, suggesting that the characters she has sung, and the characters of the classical tragedies of her native Greece—Medea, Electra, Klytemnestra—were real people, to whom she has a real connection:

> MARIA: *These people really existed. Medea, Lady Macbeth. Or don't you believe that? Eh? This is all make-believe to you?*
> SOPRANO: *I've never really thought about it.*
> MARIA: *That's because you're young. You will. In time. Know how much suffering there can be in store for a woman.* (53)

As Sharon sings, she feels in her soul, her body, and her voice the connection that Callas insists is the true art of the diva. And she is told, and undoubtedly understands, the life, emotions, and experience to which the singing actor's art must be connected: one in which she is capable of feeling that she *could* kill for a man or a career, where in time she will know how much suffering is in store for her, where she can not only believe in Medea or Lady Macbeth but can feel so strong a kinship with them that she can *become* them, emotionally and viscerally. Sharon, unlike Sophie and Tony, is capable of learning the lessons that Callas has to teach.

After Sharon finishes singing the complete aria and cabaletta, Callas, coming out of her reverie/flashback sequence, dismisses Sharon's professional prospects, damning her with the faint praise:

> *I think you should work on something more appropriate for your limitations. Mimi or Micaela maybe. But Lady Macbeth, Norma, I don't think so. These roles require something else. Something. How shall I say this? Something special. Something that can't be taught or passed on or copied or even talked about. Genius. Inspiration. A gift of god. Some recompense for everything else. (61)*

Sharon, in tears, responds:

> *I wish I'd never done this. I don't like you. You can't sing anymore and you're envious of anyone younger who can. You just want us to sing like you, recklessly, and lose our voices in ten years like you did. Well, I won't do it. I don't want to. I don't want to sing like you. I hate people like you. You want to make the world dangerous for everyone just because it was for you. (61)*

Sharon clearly wants to get back at Callas for her condescension. But there is more to her response than this. Sharon sees in Callas's cruelty the more important truth of the diva's art: that this type of art exacts too high a price, that one would not wish upon oneself the experiences and suffering that could generate such art, and that creating art from such personal and emotional raw materials is self-consuming, and ultimately destroys the medium of the art—the singer's voice. Sharon leaves the stage; Callas brushes off the confrontation, withdraws into the shell of her professional persona, utters a few platitudes about art and, saying "well, that's that" (62), brings both the master class and *Master Class* to a close.

Throughout the play, McNally has been putting forth as his hypothesis the myth of Callas the diva: she so channel, her own life and emotions into her singing and acting; she so fully becomes a conduit for her own sorrows and the object of projection for the fantasies and emotions of her audiences that she has ruined her voice and withered into a cruel and egotistical if magnificent monster, a *monstre sacre.* Sharon's defection at the end only confirms the hypothesis and elevates the diva to an even-greater level: a figure of sublime loneliness, shunned as a pariah, so monstrous that she can be watched in awe but is too horrifying to be emulated.

The dramaturgical mastery of *Master Class* lies in its twin strategies for representing Callas as a dramatic character. For, in watching her teach, we see the monster she has become; and in learning *what* she teaches—the practices of personal, emotional-based acting that she teaches unsuccessfully to Sophie and Tony and successfully if Pyrrhically to Sharon—we learn how she has become that person. We see less the genuine person and more the persona that Callas has created for herself and that has been created for her: the diva. From the moment that Callas singles out a member of the audience to demonstrate how "It's important to have a look" (3), we see the theatricality, the performativity of the diva's persona. "This isn't a freak show. I'm not a performing seal," she tells Sophie, explaining that her fabled fieriness is not a performance but an ingrained part of her identity: "My fire comes from here, Sophie. It's mine. It's not for sale. It's not for me to give away. Even if I could, I wouldn't It's who I am. Find out who you are. That's what this is all about. Eh?" (8). And yet Callas *is* a freak, a performing seal.[4] Within Callas's talents as a self-creator, within the persona that she has forged from her status as diva ("Never miss an opportunity to theatricalize," she tells Sharon [35]), everything is a performance. Acting, even when acting means surrendering to a character and effectively becoming that character, never entails the loss of self; indeed, it is where the performative self is created and articulated. As the stage director Visconti tells her (in the first-act flashback sequence), "You are not a village girl. You are Maria Callas playing a village girl" (24). Callas's "performance" as teacher of a master class *is* Callas. The diva uses herself to perform; consequently she only *is* when she performs.

And so it is—or should be—with McNally's drama: We see what she has become and we learn the process by which she became this way. But this is, of course, not the entire play, nor is the master class, despite the plays title, the only narrative and dramaturgical means by which the playwright shows us Callas's character. McNally has demonstrated for us what she has become and taught us the process of acting that has made her this way—one that demands that she wear her emotions on her sleeve and transmit her own life and suffering into her performances through her body and voice on stage. What we do not know—and what opera queens cannot know about a diva, except through gossip columns and the fanciful projections of their own imaginations—is the life lived, the nature of the actual sufferings that the singer transmutes into her performances.

The genius of *Master Class* is that, once we have seen what Callas has become and learned how she used (and used up) her life to get this way, we don't actually *need* to know the life that she lived. But this is precisely what

McNally gives us, in the most theatrically stunning sequences of the play: the flashback fantasy sequences, to the accompaniment of Callas's live recordings of the arias that the student singers are singing. These sequences—brilliant as they are in performance, affording an opportunity for the actor to jump back and forth between Callas's student years and her triumphant debuts and between her public and private lives—belong to two other genres of play entirely. One genre is the autobiographical one-hander (such as the Lillian Hellman vehicle that Zoe Caldwell played a few years before she created the role of Callas in *Master Class*), in which the historical figure, through some theatrical pretense (Emily Dickinson inviting us in as neighbors to share her recipes, Truman Capote speaking into a tape recorder for the benefit of a journalist) retells and relives formative events from his or her life.

The other genre to which the flashback sequences of *Master Class* belongs is, arguably, the largest segment of American twentieth-century dramatic writing, what might best be called the "psychotherapeutic whodunit." In such plays, a protagonist's tragic agony or a family's crippling dysfunction can be traced, as in the Freudian psychoanalytical model, to a single, traumatic event, real or imagined, that is concealed from several of the characters and the audience until late in the play: Biff sees Willy with a prostitute in a cheap hotel in Boston; Mary Tyrone regresses to a point in her life before she discovered her husband to be an alcoholic and, more significantly, before the infant Eugene died of the infection given to him by his older brother Jamie; George and Martha "kill off" the child which the audience and Nick discover to have been invented by them; Dodge and Bradley narrate the story of the child buried in the backyard.

The flashback sequences in *Master Class* satisfy the whodunit energies generated by the theories of acting taught and practiced by Callas in the real-time framework of the play. If Callas is indeed transforming her real-life suffering, to which she casually alludes repeatedly in her teaching, then the audience naturally desires to learn more about these traumatic experiences: Callas proving herself to her teacher, Callas's La Scala debut, her final performances at La Scala in defiance of the general manager who was firing her, the patronage of Battista Meneghini, and her abusive relationship with Onassis. Moreover, the flashback sequences confirm the ways that Callas's personal emotions—shame, desire, vindictiveness, revenge—are channeled into her singing. Just as Lady Macbeth invites the unholy spirit to enter her body, Callas invites the voices of her own life to enter her, through Verdi's "infernal music," to "Come, fill me with your malevolence" (55). As the house lights in La Scala come up as Callas finishes her *La Somnambula* aria on the stage of La Scala, she is able to reverse the audience's vampiric gaze, to see the eyes of the viewers devouring her performance, and can declare, "My revenge, my triumph are complete" (29).

The logic of the standard American dramaturgical master narrative demands that the audience know the biographical causes of characterological effects. For an audience, to understand the formative traumas is to know the character; for a character, to face the cause is to begin to heal; and, for character and audience alike, theatrically reliving these traumas is both a form of purgation and a fulfillment of the plays dramaturgical logic. In *Master Class,* the traumatic event to which the whodunit logic of the play points turns out to be a familiar one in American drama: Callas, having been told by Onassis that the greatest gift she can give him is a child, announces that she is pregnant and is now told by him that she must get rid of the child. As in *Long Day's Journey into Night, Desire Under the Elms, Who's Afraid of Virginia Woolf, The American Dream, Buried Child, Talley's Folly,* and countless lesser American plays, the central hidden trauma of the play turns out to be female fertility; the missing center of the play discover that Callas, the object of the opera queen's emulation and envy, is herself consumed with envy; and the object of her envy is something common both to American drama and to the mythology of male homosexuality: the womb.

In exploring the phenomenon of the diva, the play's own logic asks us to resist such easy answers. Callas was willing to create art from the material of her life at great cost. We learn how she did so, end we see the cost. If *Master Class* is indeed about art and its making out of life, then, ironically, we need to see the life *only* through the art. But in the flashback sequences and in their reversion to the traditional dead-baby trope, the playwright gives us too much. The sequences are arguably mote than just a violation of the playwright's own metatheatrical fiction and more than just a deviation from his chosen dramaturgical structure in favor of a return to the more traditional structural conventions of the psychotherapeutic whodunit: they are a violation of the theories of art explored in the play. The flashbacks effectively turn the playwright, and the audience, into opera queens: they not only allow us, like the opera queen, to imagine that the person's real pain can be heard in the diva's voice; they materially confirm that the pain and its origins is everything we imagine it to be. In narrating and reenacting her life to sounds of her own voice singing Adina or Lady Macbeth on a recording. Callas is effectively lip-synching her own life, just as Stephen lip-synchs to Callas's Violetta at the end of *The Lisbon Traviata.* Callas not only fulfills the opera queen's myth of the diva; in *Master Class* the queen of opera demonstrably becomes an opera queen herself.

NOTES

[1] Virtually every conventional twentieth-century play asks an audience to efface its existence, to pretend that it is not in a theatre: to pretend that the stage is not a stage but is an estate in Russia, a tenement in Brooklyn, or an apartment in New Orleans; and to pretend that the audience itself is invisible and incorporeal, voyeurs to the fiction of a life unfolding on the stage. Even in Pirandello's Six Characters in Search of an Author, which dispenses with one layer of fiction (the stage represents a stage and the

auditorium represents an auditorium), the audience present in that auditorium must pretend that they are not there, that the auditorium is empty, that the performance they are attending is actually a rehearsal before empty seats.

[2] The phenomenon of homosexual identification with the performer is dramatized in The Kiss of the Spider Woman, McNally's adaptation of Manuel Puig's novel for the musical stage. Molina, the homosexual pederast and movie buff, displaces his artistic expressiveness onto his fantasy film actress just as the opera queen displaces his own emotional expressiveness into the throat of the diva. While Aurora performs her song-and-dance numbers (in Molina's fantasy projections) downstage, Molina, seated upstage in his jail cell, moves his lips and silently gestures, mirroring Aurora's words and gestures.

[3] In this, McNally has cleverly found a way to compensate for the impossibility of casting an actress who can actually sing like Callas; the role was written for an actress—Zoe Caldwell—who is not a singer.

[4] And she demonstrates repeatedly (and demonstrated only a few seconds before) that fieriness and temperamentality are character traits only insofar as they put into action, and that a diva can put them into action at will. Sophie has boasted that her own Greek and Italian heritage has given her a fiery temperament Callas asks:

MARIA: Do something fiery.
SOPRANO: I can't Not just like that. No one can.
MARIA: WHERE IS MY FOOTSTOOL?
SOPRANO: Well, I guess some people can. (8)

[5] It is not unusual for male playwrights, of whatever sexual orientation, to turn to issues of fertility when they invent formative traumas for their female characters. A key example is the South African playwright Athol Fugard: in *The Road to Mecca,* his first (and to date only) play with two principal female characters and only a subsidiary male role, he needed to invent a biographical source for Elsa's dramatic crisis (the other principal female character, Helen, was drawn from life), and chose to have her reveal to Helen, in the play's final moments, that she had just had an abortion.

Works Cited

Koestenbaum, Wayne. *The Queen's Throat: Opera, Homosexuality, and the Mystery of Desire*. New York: Poseidon Press, 1993.

McNally, Terrence. *Master Class*. New York: Penguin Books, 1995.

Three Plays by Terrence McNally: The Lisbon Traviata, Frankie and Johnny in the Clair de Lune, It's Only a Play. New York: Penguin Books, 1990.

Phallus in Wonderland: Machismo and Business in David Mamet's *American Buffalo* and *Glengarry Glen Ross*

Hersh Zeifman

In an interview in 1984, David Mamet, deliberately echoing Calvin Coolidge, commented: " 'The business of America is business. . . . We're a nation of entrepreneurs.' "¹ Precisely what Mamet thinks of American business is the business of his two most celebrated plays—as he himself has made abundantly, and repeatedly, clear. *American Buffalo* (1975), he has stated, " 'is about the American ethic of business. About how we excuse all sorts of great and small betrayals and ethical compromises called business.' "² " 'It's a play about honor among thieves and the myths this country runs on. . . . The ethics of the business community is that you can be as predatory as you want within a structured environment.' "³ And of his Pulitzer-Prize-winning *Glengarry Glen Ross* (1983), written almost a decade later, Mamet noted: " 'To me the play is about a society with only one bottom line: How much money you make.' "⁴ "The play concerns how business corrupts," he told another interviewer, "how the hierarchical business system tends to corrupt. It becomes legitimate for those in power in the business world to act unethically. The effect on the little guy is that he turns to crime. And petty crime goes punished; major crimes go unpunished."⁵ And he added to still another interviewer: "American capitalism comes down to one thing. . . . The operative axiom is 'Hurrah for me and fuck you.' Anything else is a lie."⁶

Mamet's anatomization of the apparently oxymoronic term "American business ethics" is dramatized in a number of ways in the two plays: critics have variously focused on the plays' metaphoric central actions, for example, or on characterization, or, most prominently, on the telling dynamics of the language characters use to define themselves and their nefarious activities. I'd like to take a somewhat different approach in this essay, however, by examining a dramaturgical strategy that has received surprisingly insufficient attention from Mamet critics. " 'My job,' " Mamet once said to Mel Gussow during a discussion of his business plays, "'is to create a closed moral universe.'"[7] What's especially significant about this "closed moral universe" in both *American Buffalo* and *Glengarry Glen Ross* is that it is closed even more tightly by being portrayed as exclusively male. Mamet has written an astonishingly large number of such all-male plays; in addition to *Buffalo* and *Glengarry,* and ignoring for the moment his many monologues and short "sketches," the list includes *The Duck Variations* (1972), *A Life in the Theatre* (1977), *Prairie du Chien* (1979), and *Lakeboat* (1980). This insistent emphasis on an exclusively male world in so many of his plays clearly indicates Mamet's theatrical "fascination with the male tribe."[8] As Michelene Wandor has noted:

> The single-gendered play may be "unrealistic" in the sense that we all inhabit a world which consists of men and women, but it does provide an imaginative opportunity to explore the gendered perspective (male or female) without the complexities and displacements of the "mixed" play.[9]

In *Buffalo* and *Glengarry,* Mamet makes use of this exploration of "the gendered perspective" for specific thematic ends: a dramatic world in which women are marginalized to the point of literal exclusion provides *in itself* the most scathing indictment imaginable of the venality and corruption of American business.

The absence of women in *Buffalo* and *Glengarry* ironically underscores, as Christopher Bigsby has suggested, the pathetic impotence of Mamet's businessmen.[10] But it also has a much deeper significance: the exclusion of women from these plays implies that the values the male characters traditionally associate with the "feminine"—compassion, tenderness, empathy, spirituality—are seen as threatening to their business ethos; in the business world such values are characterized as weakness, "and weakness is despised as effeminate and dangerous."[11] By banishing women and the values they purportedly represent from these plays, Mamet thus shifts the focus to an examination of "the cocoon of the traditional American masculinity myths" inside which he himself was raised.[12] It is these values of machismo—toughness, strength, cunning—which have become appropriated and apotheosized by American business, alchemized into the fool's gold of power, greed, and competition. As Mamet has noted: ". . . the competition of business . . . is most times prosecuted for the benefit of oneself [i.e., the male] as breadwinner, as provider, as paterfamilias, as vestigial and outmoded as you may feel those roles to be."[13]

In an essay titled "In the Company of Men," Mamet wrote that men congregate under three circumstances:

> Men get together to do business. . . . Men also get together to bitch. We say, "What does she *want?*" . . . [And the] final way in which men get together is for That Fun Which Dare Not Speak Its Name, and which has been given the unhappy tag "male bonding."[14]

Buffalo and *Glengarry* mark the site where all three of the above circumstances conjoin: the bitchy business world in which men relate to other men, in which men *define* themselves as "men." The plays thus dramatize, to borrow Eve Sedgwick's term, a world of "homosocial desire":

> "Homosocial" is a word occasionally used in history and the social sciences, where it describes social bonds between persons of the same sex; it is a neologism, obviously formed by analogy with "homosexual," and just as obviously meant to be distinguished from "homosexual." In fact, it is applied to such activities as "male bonding," which may, in our society, be characterized by intense homophobia. . . .[15]

The homosocial world of American business so wickedly critiqued in *American Buffalo* and *Glengarry Glen Ross* becomes Mamet's theatrical "Phallus in Wonderland": a topsy-turvy world in which all values are inverted by characters who think with their crotch. Since machismo is the sole criterion of worth in the "closed moral universe" these plays depict, it therefore follows that the worst term of abuse in such a universe is one that questions masculinity. It's hardly surprising, then, that Mamet's businessmen are both deeply misogynistic and deeply homophobic. "[I]f you look around the United States of America," Mamet once noted in an interview, "you will see that we do have a certain amount of misogynistic men. For example, all of them."[16] A woman, by macho definition, is not a "man"; neither is a homosexual. In the values of a patriarchal culture which American business has internalized, misogyny and homophobia are inextricably linked; as Gayle Rubin suggests, "[t]he suppression of the homosexual component of human sexuality, and by corollary, the oppression of homosexuals, is . . . a product of the same system whose rules and relations oppress women."[17]

American Buffalo brilliantly exemplifies the debased values of an all-male business ethic in which the phallus reigns supreme. The epitome of macho business values in the play is Teach, whose total moral bankruptcy is deftly delineated in his succinct definition of free enterprise: "The freedom . . . Of the *Individual* . . . To Embark on Any Fucking Course that he sees fit. . . . In order to secure his honest chance to make a profit."[18] Indeed, like his counterparts in classical Greek comedy, this fumbling and incompetent petty crook might just as well be wearing his phallus strapped openly to his waist. But then the other characters could simply whip out a ruler and measure, which would bring the whole play to a crashing stop. Teach's self-preservation requires, instead, that the phallus be "covered," its presence less overtly—and less vulnerably—signalled in his physical and (especially) verbal swaggering. (Al Pacino, who played Teach in a series of revivals of *Buffalo* throughout the early 1980s, was constantly touching his crotch—as though talismanically touching base with the centre of his being, confirming that everything was still intact.)

Women constantly hover on the margins of *American Buffalo*—especially the "ghosts" of Ruth and Grace, ostensible friends of the three central male characters—but, though repeatedly invoked, their presence never literally materializes. There is no place for them on a stage where what they represent is debased and valueless, where women are routinely referred to as "cunts," "broads," "bitches," and "chicks." Value in *American Buffalo* is exclusively linked to testosterone: there are more reputed "balls" in this play than at Wimbledon. Since machismo is the coin of highest currency in the traffic of this business world, then its opposite—lack of "manhood"—signals utter worthlessness. Thus the off-stage Fletcher, having incurred the wrath of both Teach and Don, is repeatedly labelled a "cocksucker" (59, 72, 73); Teach calls Bob a "fruit" (94); and "(Fuckin' *fruits* . . .)" likewise becomes the dismissive term not only for the man whose coin collection the trio plans to rob but also for his sexy wife! (This same structure of abuse animates Mamet's *Speed-the-Plow* [1988], a further attack on American business—in this instance the film business. When Charlie Fox discovers he's been betrayed in a business deal by Bobby Gould, he explodes: ". . . you *fool*—your fucken' sissy film—you squat to pee. You old *woman*. . . .")[19] So ingrained in Mamet's businessmen is this specific vocabulary of abuse, and thus of the value system underlying it, that it extends, absurdly, even to women. When Don asserts that Ruth is a good card player, for example, Teach argues "She is *not* a good card player, Don. She is mooch and she is a locksmith and she plays like a woman" (14). This kind of polymorphous misogyny and homophobia reaches the true heights of absurdity in Teach's hilarious indictment of Ruth as a "dyke cocksucker" (54). Never mind that the phrase is oxymoronic; for the moronic Teach it makes perfect emotional sense. The patently illogical has been transformed into the patently tautological: in Teach's pantheon of abuse "dyke" and "cocksucker" are simple equivalencies.

Mamet's attack on corrupt business ethics in *American Buffalo* is deepened through an implicit equation with other violent male "homosocial" institutions—specifically the military and the police. In all such institutions, lack of substance is shrouded in a linguistic fog; citing the sociologist and economist Thorstein Veblen, Mamet has noted that "the more that jargon and technical language is involved in an endeavor, the more we may assume that the endeavor is essentially make-believe. As in Law, Commerce, Warfare. There we were in Vietnam. . . ."[20] Buttressed by these institutions, people find themselves committing "gross acts of cruelty and savagery"; as Mamet has stated:

We have it somehow in our nature, Tolstoy wrote, to perform horrendous acts which we would never dream of as individuals, and think if they are done in the name of some larger group, a *state,* a *company,* a *team,* that these vile acts are somehow magically transformed, and become praise-worthy.[21]

"A guy who isn't tense, I don't want him on my side . . ." (47), says Teach while plotting his business heist; later he echoes Don's "You want depth on the team" (51). This pathetic band of thieves huddling in Don's junkshop sees itself as a beleaguered paramilitary unit: Don's role in their incursion is to "mind the fort" (36); Fletch is brought in because, as Don notes, "We can use somebody watch our rear" (52); and Teach, having hocked his watch for the phallic extension and security of a gun, defends his bearing arms like any good cop or soldier: "Protection of me and my partner. Protection, deterrence" (85).

In the male homosocial institution of business depicted in *American Buffalo*, "alien" values like loyalty, friendship and tenderness have become inverted into obscenities. Thus Bob, having first been betrayed in a business deal by Don with the Judas equivalent of thirty pieces of silver ("I got to give you . . . thirty [dollars] . . ." [43]) and then viciously beaten by Teach, is finally forced to admit that the buffalo nickel he's been trying to sell Don throughout the second act ("I like 'em because of the art on it" [64], this innocent confesses) was not stolen from their mark but purchased from a coin store—not for profit (Bob wants fifty dollars for it [66], the exact price he paid [99]), but as a loving gesture toward his friend:

TEACH: You buy a coin for fifty dollars, you come back here.
    Pause.
    Why? . . .
    Why would you do a thing like that?
BOB: I don't know.
TEACH: Why would you do a thing like that?
BOB: For Donny. (99)

Teach's response to this, for him, utterly incomprehensible act of selflessness and kindness is perhaps the saddest line in the play: "You people make my flesh crawl" (100). "We all live like the cavemen" (103), Teach later acknowledges, and for once what Teach teaches is deadly accurate. In the brutally macho and materialistic dog-eat-dog world of American business, values like compassion and spirituality—implicitly inscribed as "feminine" and therefore, in the figures of Ruth and Grace, devalued and excluded—are totally lacking. The world of *American Buffalo*—the world of American business—is thus *literally* ruthless and graceless.

Glengarry Glen Ross has been called by Mamet "formally a gang comedy in the tradition of *The Front Page* or *Man in White*,"[22] but, as in *American Buffalo*, the "gang" is exclusively male. The only real difference between the businessmen-thieves in the two plays is one of scale; as Anne Dean has commented: "In *American Buffalo*, Mamet portrays a group of small-time crooks who thought themselves legitimate businessmen; in *Glengarry Glen Ross*, his subjects *are* businessmen but they all behave like crooks."[23] In *Glengarry*, then, the gang's all here—wearing better clothes, certainly, and working out of an office rather than a junkshop, but still manoeuvring sharklike within the homosocial sphere of business deals in which phallus is always intended. "A man's his job,"[24] states salesman Shelly "The Machine" Levene reductively—and tautologically, for in the all-male world of *Glengarry* the job of selling worthless property through guile and chicanery both defines and is defined by the salesmen's concept of "manhood."

The sole criterion of worth here, as in *Buffalo,* is machismo. "I'm the *man* to sell" (19), Levene boasts in the play's opening scene, and later, congratulating himself on having brought off a stupendous sale, notes "I got my *balls* back . . ." (102). Lamenting the "degeneration" of business into "a world of clock watchers, bureaucrats, officeholders . . .," Roma, the gang's star salesman, hilariously complains to Levene ". . . it's not a world of men, Machine . . ." (105). Roma's concept of manhood is precisely that of a "machine"— sleek, heartless, devoid of conscience, designed simply to make money. So morally benighted is this macho world that when Aaronow, another one of the gang, sighs "I'm no fucking good" and is then consoled by Roma's "Fuck that shit. . . . You're a good man, George. . . . You hit a bad streak" (57), "goodness" is defined solely within the terms of business sales. We have now re-entered the commercial world of Shakespeare's *The Merchant of Venice;* when Shylock comments that "Antonio is a good man,"[25] he means only that Antonio is a "good" financial risk. Human worth has been relegated to the demeaning context of a commodity exchange.

Again as in *Buffalo,* the only unforgivable failing in this macho world, and therefore the worst epithet one can hurl at another, involves failing the test of manhood. Customers, by definition, are there to be screwed and, thus, again by the salesmen's definition, not "men": Levene repeatedly refers to them as "cocksuckers" (16, 21, 63). Similarly the disgruntled salesman Moss, complaining of the sales competition which will result in the losers being fired, vents his spleen at his bosses' treatment of the salesmen as less than men: "Look look look look, when they *build* your business, then you can't fucking turn around, *enslave* them, treat them like *children,* fuck them up the ass . . ." (36). In Moss's lexicon—in Moss's value system which that lexicon reflects— slaves are equivalent to children are equivalent to homosexuals. (The mention of "slaves" in Moss's litany reminds us, of course, that within this homosocial world racism is merely another cognate of misogyny and homophobia. Thus when Teach attempts to defend his masculinity against Don's jibes in *Buffalo,* he does so by telling Don "I am not your nigger. I am not your wife" [100]. Similarly the eponymous hero of Mamet's *Edmond* [1982] strikes out at a black pimp by shrieking "You *coon,* you *cunt,* you *cock*sucker. . . ."[26] For Edmond, all three insults are not simply alliterative but, more important, interchangeable.)

The most sustained toner of abuse in *Glengarry,* however, is reserved for Williamson, the despised office manager who sits behind a desk and so, unlike the salesmen, never tests his manhood in the arena of "battle." Predictably, the terms of that abuse are misogynistic and homophobic. Levene's scorn for him is withering: "You don't know what it *is,* you don't have the *sense,* you don't have the *balls.* You ever been on a sit? *Ever?* Has this cocksucker ever been . . ." (76). (In the rehearsal typescript of the play, Levene further accused "You don't have the *blood,* John. You don't have the *blood* . . .,"[27] thus emphasizing the sheer animal savagery of the business world; as one of the characters in Mamet's *Reunion* [1976] comments: "It's a fucking jungle out there.")[28] But the strongest abuse of Williamson is unleashed by Roma, livid with rage that Williamson has blown one of his deals:

> You stupid fucking *cunt.* You *idiot.* Whoever told you could work with *men?* . . . I don't care . . . whose dick you're sucking on. You're going *out.* . . . What you're hired for is to *help* us—does that seem clear to you? To *help* us. *Not* to fuck us up . . . to help *men* who are going *out* there to try to earn a *living.* You *fairy.* . . . You fucking *child.* . . . (96–97)

For Roma, as for Moss and indeed *all* the characters of this exclusively male world in which machismo rules, "cunt," "fairy," and "child" are synonymous terms of abuse; each is equivalent to "non-man," and thus to nothing, to worse than nothing.

The arena of "battle" entered into by the salesmen of *Glengarry* reminds us that, once again, Mamet is linking business with other traditional male homosocial institutions. When Moss turns viciously on Roma, for example, the invective spewing out of him in great bursts of bile, Roma retorts: "What is this, your farewell speech? . . . Your farewell to the troops?" (71). Similarly, Levene's boasting of his incredible sale is interrupted by Moss's "Hey, I don't want to hear your fucking war stories . . ." (67). Levene's description of closing that sale is, indeed, very like that of a military engagement; the language he uses suggests both an epic battle and, in its compulsively orgasmic rhythm, a sexual conquest, casting his customers in the role of the enemy who must at all costs not simply be defeated but *annihilated.* "They signed, Ricky," he exults to Roma. "It was *great.* It was fucking great. It was like they *wilted* all at once. . . . They, I swear to God, they both kind of *imperceptibly slumped*" (74). A businessman, Levene implies, is constantly putting his life on the line—like a soldier, like a cop. "You can't learn [what it takes] in an office . . .," Levene instructs the deskbound Williamson. "You have to learn it on the streets. . . . 'Cause your partner *depends* on it. . . . Your partner . . . a man who's your 'partner' *depends* on you . . . you have to go *with* him and *for* him . . ." (97–98).

Levene's mock-heroic rhetoric, however, is belied by the play's action. There are, finally, no "partners" in *Glengarry Glen Ross,* nor—given the "values" of this world—could there be; each salesman is out strictly for himself. Don's definition of business in *Buffalo*—"People taking *care* of themselves" (7)—is dramatized with a vengeance in *Glengarry,* where the Practical Sales Maxim "ALWAYS BE CLOSING" (13), used by Mamet as the play's epigraph, applies to *all* relationships. Everyone in *Glengarry* exists potentially to be "sold": the customers, the salesmen, even the audience. Thus both acts end with a magisterial "selling" job by Ricky Roma, in which the audience too is "buffaloed": in act one when we ultimately realize that Roma's conversation with James Lingk is not simply a philosophical chat with a stranger over a drink but the cunning seduction of a sales pitch, and more lethally in act two, when "tricky Ricky" suddenly and viciously betrays his self-proclaimed "friend" and "partner" Levene.

"ALWAYS BE CLOSING" might also stand as *Mamet's* credo in *Glengarry.* For Mamet has once again "closed" this play about American business to women, excluding the "feminine" and its reputed values from the sphere of dramatic action; once again there is no place for such values in a world ruled by machismo. As in *Buffalo,* women haunt the margins of the text but never break through to the stage. Their presence is evoked only metonymically, as terms of abuse, or else in the form of "spirits" whose essence threatens male values. The most prominent of these off-stage women is the wife of James Lingk, who has ordered her husband to cancel the business deal into which Roma has "suckered" him. Roma tries desperately to change Lingk's mind, predictably lapsing into the language of commerce in characterizing Lingk's relationship with his wife—predictably, because Ricky can conceive of human intercourse only in commercial terms: "Come on, Jim. (*Pause.*) I want to tell you something. Your life is your own. You have a contract with your wife. You have certain things you do *jointly,* you have a *bond* there . . . and there are *other* things. Those things are yours" (93). Although Roma ridicules and attempts to dismiss her "prudence" as "something *women* have" (83)—akin to menstrual cramps, perhaps—Mrs. Lingk in fact implicitly challenges his macho code of behavior; she has a different agenda from his, a far less cutthroat one. Excluded from the stage, she is the "missing Lingk" whose values could destroy Roma's very existence.

Mamet once declared in an interview that he views his plays as "iconoclastic," "in the sense of tearing down the icons of American business, and some of the myths about this country."[29] In *American Buffalo* and *Glengarry Glen Ross,* one of the most powerful ways in which this iconoclasm is dramatized is through the exclusion from the stage of women and of the values traditionally associated with them. There are, of course, a number of potential problems here. First, to characterize women *as a gender* as compassionate, tender, empathetic, etc., is a remarkably sentimental notion; Mamet certainly doesn't sustain this view in his critical writings, say, or more significantly in those plays of his in which women actually appear.[30] Second, and far more serious, to use women metaphorically in this way, to inscribe them with certain values (however "positive" those values might be), may itself be a form of misogyny. Thus Michelene Wandor has noted that, even in plays by male dramatists in which women become "the conscience of humanity, . . . the perspective still remains male-determined . . .":

> What is interesting is that these plays simply represent variants on the "feminine." . . . Using woman as a metaphor may look like a compliment, but it is an unconscious way of denying her a real part of the stage action.[31]

Mamet has himself partially acknowledged this danger: "Men *generally* expect more of women than we do of ourselves," he has written. "We feel, based on constant evidence, that women are better, stronger, more truthful, than men. You can call this sexism, or reverse sexism, or whatever you wish, but it is my experience."[32] If there's a sense in which Mamet might be accused of misogyny in *Buffalo* and *Glengarry,* it's in this latter sense only—not that he shares the crudely misogynist views of those plays' male characters (which both plays clearly and explicitly condemn), but in this far more subtle essentialist reduction of women to a gender stereotype. Yet whether suspect in these ways or not, Mamet's insistence on all-male casts in *American Buffalo* and *Glengarry Glen Ross* makes his thematic point crystal clear. Both plays could thus have been titled *Sexual Perversity in Chicago,* for the perverse denial of an entire gender and its metaphorical import brilliantly exposes the moral wilderness of a business "ethic" ruled solely by the vile and violent values of a debased machismo.

NOTES

[1] Jennifer Allen, "David Mamet's Hard Sell," *New York,* 9 April 1984, p. 40.

[2] Richard Gottlieb, "The 'Engine' That Drives Playwright David Mamet," *The New York Times,* 15 January 1978, Sec. 2, p. 4.

[3] William A. Raidy, "Will Success Buffalo David Mamet? Are You Kidding?," *Chicago Daily News,* 2–3 April 1977, cited in Dennis Carroll, *David Mamet* (London: Macmillan, 1987), p. 32.

[4] Mel Gussow, "Real Estate World a Model for Mamet," *The New York Times,* 28 March 1984, Sec. C, p. 19.

[5] Matthew C. Roudané, "An Interview with David Mamet," *Studies in American Drama, 1945–Present,* 1 (1986): 74.

[6] John Lahr, programme notes for *Glengarry Glen Ross* (London: National Theatre, 1983), cited in Anne Dean, *David Mamet: Language as Dramatic Action* (Rutherford, NJ: Fairleigh Dickinson University Press, 1990), p. 190.

[7] Gussow, Sec. C, p.19.

[8] See Samuel G. Friedman, "The Gritty Eloquence of David Mamet," *The New York Times Magazine,* 21 April 1985, p. 40.

[9] Michelene Wandor, *Look Back in Gender: Sexuality and the Family in Post-war British Drama* (London and New York: Methuen, 1987), p. 140.

[10] C.W.E. Bigsby, *David Mamet* (London and New York: Methuen, 1985), p. 76.

[11] Ibid., p. 81.

[12] See C. Gerald Fraser, "Mamet's Plays Shed Masculinity Myth," *The New York Times,* 5 July 1976, Sec. L, p. 7.

[13] Mamet, "In the Company of Men," in *Some Freaks* (New York: Viking, 1989), p. 90.

[14] Ibid., p. 87.

[15] Eve Kosofsky Sedgwick, *Between Men: English Literature and Male Homosocial Desire* (New York: Columbia University Press, 1985), p. 1.

[16] Esther Harriott, "Interview with David Mamet," in *American Voices: Five Contemporary Playwrights in Essays and Interviews* (Jefferson, N.C. and London: McFarland, 1988), p. 84.

[17] Gayle Rubin, "The Traffic in Woman: Notes on the 'Political Economy' of Sex," in *Toward an Anthropology of Women,* ed. Rayna R. Reiter (New York and London: Monthly Review Press, 1975), p. 180.

[18] Mamet, *American Buffalo* (New York: Grove, 1977), pp. 72–73. All further page references will be cited in the text.

[19] Mamet, *Speed-the-Plow* (New York: Grove, 1988), p. 70.

[20] Mamet, "Capture-the-Flag, Monotheism, and the Techniques of Arbitration," in *Writing in Restaurants* (New York: Penguin, 1987), p. 5.

[21] Mamet, "Concerning *The Water Engine,*" in *Writing in Restaurants,* p. 109.

[22] Henry I. Schvey, "Celebrating the Capacity for Self-Knowledge" [an interview with Mamet], *New Theatre Quarterly,* 4, No. 13 (February 1988): 92.

[23] Dean, pp. 195–196.

[24] Mamet, *Glengarry Glen Ross* (New York: Grove, 1984), p. 75. All further page references will be cited in the text.

[25] Shakespeare, *The Merchant of Venice,* in *Shakespeare: The Complete Works,* ed. G. B. Harrison (New York: Harcourt, Brace & World, 1968), I.iii.12.

[26] Mamet, *Edmond* (New York: Grove, 1983), p. 64.

[27] See Bigsby, p. 120.

[28] Mamet, *Reunion,* in *Reunion and Dark Pony* (New York: Grove, 1979), p. 23.

[29] Schvey, p. 96.

[30] See, for example, such plays as *Sexual Perversity in Chicago* (1974), *The Woods* (1977), and *Speed-the-Plow* (1988). See also Mamet's description of women in the business world he knows best, that of theater and films: "The coldest, cruelest, most arrogant behavior I have ever seen in my professional life has been—and *consistently* been—on the part of women producers in the movies and the theater. I have seen women do things that the worst man would never entertain the thought of—I do not imply that he would he stopped by conscience, but he *would* be stopped by the fear of censure, which takes us back to [women's] inability to compromise." Mamet, "Women," in *Some Freaks,* p. 28.

[31] Michelene Wandor, *Carry On, Understudies: Theatre and Sexual Politics* (London and New York: Routledge & Kegan Paul, 1986), p. 157.

[32] Mamet, "Women," in *Some Freaks,* p. 24.

A Place at the Table: Hunger as Metaphor in Lillian Hellman's *Days to Come* and Marsha Norman's *'night, Mother*

Linda Ginter Brown

Food is my drug of choice.

—*Oprah Winfrey*

One does not have to search far to find examples showcasing contemporary society's love affair with food. Store shelves contain abundant supplies for those with the wherewithal to purchase. Restaurants cater to clientele all along the economic spectrum. Bookstores report continually increasing cookbook sales even in shaky financial times. Television shows featuring cooking segments garner large audiences.

At the same time, more than ever before, health problems related to diet demand attention. Rising numbers of anorexics, bulimics, and compulsive overeaters struggle to survive their twisted relationship with the food necessary to sustain their existence. Women comprise the majority of this struggling population. These battles belie the real issue—the need to find a true self in the midst of a false society. The hunger that haunts these women is not of physiological origin. It does not connote any quest to appease what Maslow calls the most basic human need[1], but rather a psychic one. Perched on the edge of the twenty-first century, women hunger to heal that "hole in the soul." They fight not to fix their Oedipal crisis, as Freud posited, but rather to find their true selves. Fragmented and confused, they search for the missing piece. Like Humpty Dumpty, they have fallen from the wall and cannot put themselves together. Psychically, they long for a cohesive self.

Food metaphors depicted in women's writing reflect that psychic search. Both Lillian Hellman and Marsha Norman use this "culinary approach" to foreground a number of their female characters' struggles with psychic issues. By examining their works, one can see how certain female characters use their relationships to food to symbolize the gnawing psychic hunger each experiences.

Reading Hellman's memoirs is tantamount to sitting at a banquet of culinary metaphors. Hellman's passion for food permeates many pages, starting with her childhood memories in New Orleans and ending with her last publication, *Eating Together: Recollections and Recipes,* a cookbook coauthored with Peter Feibleman and published after her death. In Unfinished Woman, she relates how she cleaned the crayfish for the delicious bisques her aunts would make and how she learned to kill a chicken without "any ladylike complaints" (13). Her reputation for hospitality is well known, along with marvelous parties at her home on Martha's Vineyard. Robert Brustein attributes her preoccupation with nourishment as "perhaps reflecting her blocked maternal instinct."[2] Even Marsha Norman, who interviewed Hellman shortly before she died, was invited to bring her husband and come back for dinner when Hellman was better able to cook. Her penchant for parties is well documented, for, unnurtured herself, Hellman sought to appease others' hunger. Her writings attest to that commitment.

Ironically, one of Hellman's weakest plays contains an abundance of food images. *Days to Come,* Hellman's second play, opened in December 1936 to generally negative reviews. Hellman's uneasy fears about the play turned to horror on opening night. Her inability to "stomach" the production manifested itself as she vomited in a side aisle near the back of the darkened theater. Audience response ranged from lackluster to outright disgust, with William Randolph Hearst leaving, with six friends, during the middle of the second act. *New York Times* critic Brooks Atkinson condemned the play[3], charging Hellman with laborious writing and confusing plots and counterplots. Robert Coleman, *New York Daily Mirror* critic,[4] contended that Hellman used "staccato and stuffy dialogue." Charles Dexter, writing in the *Daily Worker,*[5] noted that Hellman sympathized with the worker's plight, but was unable "to get under the skin of her characters."

This unsuccessful effort centers around the Rodman family, owners of a brush manufacturing company in Galion, Ohio, and foregrounds the inherent conflict between management and labor. Although company CEO Andrew Rodman abhors the thought, a team has been brought into break up a strike. Because Rodman has known the townspeople all his life, he believes reason will prevail. A weak and ineffectual man, he fails to see that his wife, Julie, is having an affair with family friend and lawyer Henry Ellicott. However, Ellicott "owns" more than just Rodman's wife. He has manipulated Rodman into borrowing funds to keep the company afloat, taking company shares as collateral.

Whalen, a union organizer, counsels company workers to refrain from fighting with Wilkie, the strike buster who arrives in town with two thugs, Mossie and Easter. Mossie kills Easter during a card game and plants the body at union headquarters to implicate Whalen. Julie, who hopes to initiate a "friendship" with Whalen, witnesses the plant, as she is at his office when it occurs. Whalen is jailed, and in the ensuing ruckus, a company worker's child is killed. Firth, the child's father, confronts Rodman at the family home. Wilkie is ordered to leave town.

During the entire episode, Cora Rodman, Andrew's maiden sister, worries about losing the company and how the strike will affect their family. Intensely jealous of Julie, she finally tells Andrew about his wife's lengthy affair with Henry Ellicott. After Ellicott leaves, Julie offers to leave or give Andrew a divorce, but he declines. As the curtain descends, he rather pitifully attests that they will live, "just as 'half-people' the rest of their lives—for days to come" (133).

While the political machinations of both management and labor obstensibly constitute the play's central action, the most interesting struggle, from a critical standpoint, focuses upon Cora Rodman, Andrew's spinster sister. While lamenting Hellman's ill-fated choice to include so many issues in one play, critics seldom mention Cora, whom Grenville Vernon called an "acidulous old maid."[6] Carl Rollyson, in his lengthy study *Lillian Hellman: Her Legend and Her Legacy,* terms Cora "a puzzle in the play" (95) and suggests that Cora is tormented by the same issues as the other characters—what the strike means and how management and labor can find a way to coexist (95). He rightly observes that "She does not know how to begin to live her own life" and "she exemplifies critic Joseph Wood Krutch's observation that Hellman is a 'specialist in hate and frustration, a student of helpless rage'" (95). However, Cora's torment goes much deeper than the family's trouble with the strikers, and her ceaseless preoccupation with food and its preparation signals the reader that Hellman, once again, is presenting a fragmented self in search of cohesion. Cora's continual focus upon food symbolizes her struggle for personal power, an identity, and the need to fill the "gnawing psychic hunger" she experiences as part of the Rodman family structure. Clearly, getting to eat what she wants when she wants it metaphorically symbolizes filling a psychic void. In her work *The Hungry Self,* Kim Chernin quotes a client who relates, "There is no I . . . There's just an immense hole at the center. An emptiness. A terror. Not all the food in the world could fill it. But, I try" (20). Cora also tries. From act 1, scene 1 where she berates Hannah, the housekeeper, for cutting her piece of cake too small, until the last scene of the last act, where she takes a bite of toast and chides everyone for "getting too excited," it is quite apparent that something is "eating" her.

That "something" is her response to the powerlessness she feels. More than anything, she desires a "place at the table," to be part of some satisfying relationship, to be acknowledged as a person. No one, either in or out of the household, supports her emotionally. Consequently, her manipulative behavior reveals a desperate woman posturing for attention, begging to be heard, but mostly being ignored. Like numerous other female characters of Hellman's, such as Martha in *The Children's Hour,* or Anna and Carrie in *Toys in the Attic,* or Regina in *The Little Foxes,* Cora struggles to find some measure of personal power denied her in the patriarchal culture within which she must exist. Her relationship to food illuminates that struggle.

A thin, nervous woman of forty-two, she has never married but lives with her brother Andrew and his wife, Julie, in the house left by their parents, the founders of the Rodman family business. She snipes. She carps. She criticizes. Her behavior belies an unhappy soul, whether she harangues Hannah, telling her, "You didn't bring me enough butter on my tray this morning and I had a roll left over . . . there always seems to be something wrong with the break-fast tray" (79), or whether she tells Henry Ellicott, the family lawyer, "I shall eat as much as I please. Just as much as I please" (130). Cora fears being short-changed. Like Beckett's Hamm in *Endgame,* she worries that supplies are run-ning out. She fears that nothing can satisfy, that there will never be enough. Her nervous stomach mirrors her inward turmoil. Outwardly, she attempts to soothe herself with chocolate pepsin drops prescribed by her doctor—even medica-tion meant to calm digestion needs a "sweet" coating. Cora cannot accept life "straight." She must seek solace in food for she cannot face the truth of a mea-ger existence. Even sleep escapes her, for, as she relates, "if a pin drops, it wakes me. I've always been like that" (81).

Interestingly, Cora has never married, nor has she "reproduced" herself through the birth of a child. Like her creator, she seeks nurturance from an Other who is missing from the picture. Although Hellman married Arthur Kober, the marriage was brief, and the child they conceived beforehand was aborted. Yet Hellman never stopped seeking nurturance, psychic food that would enable her to survive. Her relationship with Dashiell Hammett, her "ide-alized other," assuaged some of that hunger, but as Rollyson rightly suggests, "Always, something was missing for Hellman" (8), and "she was—even later in life—the type of person who liked to dress elegantly for dinner and then complain about the 'rat-fuck' food she was eating" (35).

Perhaps Hellman's attempts to find satisfying food belie a deeper fear— of losing herself *or* reproducing herself. In her ground-breaking book, *Bitter Milk,* Madeline Grumet describes this fear when she describes childbirth as "the wrenching expulsion of the infant" that "physically recapitulates the ter-rors of coming apart, of losing a part of oneself" (10). Perhaps Cora, as well as her creator, fears reproducing herself. If her search for a "replacement umbili-cal cord" has thus far been unsuccessful, she risks being unable to nurture any mirror image she may reproduce.

A useful construct to more fully illuminate Cora's struggle for a cohesive self is time—whether past, present, or future. In the past, Cora's family unit was intact. Her biological mother was present, and the interloper, Julie, who marries her weak, ineffectual brother, had not yet intruded. Papa, who "knew how to run the company," was alive and was certainly more effectual than his son, who has endangered the family fortune through his *laissez-faire* attitude. However, Andrew's climatic speeches at the play's end reveal the loathing and contempt he harbors toward Cora, as he tells his sister, "You hate me and I hated you from the day I was old enough to think about you." (132). His uncharacteristic venomous outburst certainly suggests that Cora's childhood was less than ideal.

What Cora needs more than anything is a supportive relationship with a nurturing mother figure. If she can obtain this necessary connection, she stands a chance to become psychically whole. Without it, she risks continued fragmentation. As Chodorow notes, "a girl cannot and does not completely reject her mother in favor of men but continues her relationship of dependence upon and attachment to her" (53).

Hellman is strangely silent concerning the biological mother. No mention of her is made during the entire play, but a surrogate mother is present in the character of Hannah, the housekeeper. Arguably the play's strongest female character, Hannah bows to no one, not even Cora. Perceptive as well as powerful, she usurps pantry supplies to support the striking workers. Unlike Andrew Rodman, the company CEO, Hannah has a much more realistic view of the situation, realizing that a confrontation is coming. She notes, "I haven't lived in this house twenty years for nothing" (78). When Wilkie arrives with his mafioso thugs, she refuses to answer the door. Even Andrew acknowledges her role in the family's structure in the last scene, as he relates, "Hannah shares the secrets of all of us. That's why Cora can't get rid of her, isn't it, Cora?" (132).

Cora and Hannah's relationship centers upon food. In Cora's first speech, she asks Hannah, "Did you make something sweet?" to which Hannah accedes, "Chocolate cake. All over" (79). Characteristic of an adult's desire to reestablish a childhood memory, Cora seeks something sweet, not a vegetable or salad, which might be better for one's arteries, but something like "mama used to make." Her food fixation leads her to inventory the food supply and her discovery that supplies are, indeed, low, sends her to Mossie and Easter for help in catching the responsible criminal. She concedes, "very funny things are happening here. Things are missing from the pantry. Or is that too unimportant work for you? . . . When I looked into the closet I was amazed to find at least eight or ten dollars worth of canned goods" (99).

As a surrogate mother figure, Hannah embodies what Melanie Klein referred to as a "good breast, bad breast" image[7]. Klein, in opposition to her mentor, Freud, focused upon an infant's preoedipal, rather than oedipal, development. Because the infant cannot distinguish between the mother and the breast during the earliest stages of development, the infant is inevitably frustrated and splits this "object" into a "good breast" and a "bad breast" in order to preserve it psychically. Hannah, as "keeper of the food supply," controls Cora's physical nourishment. Moreover, when confronted about the thefts, she shows not one iota of remorse. Instead she insists, "I wish I could have taken more. People need it. Do what you want about it, Mr. Andrew" (100). Cora's concern that there be enough food available does not impress Hannah in the least.

Hannah's position as a surrogate mother figure only enrages Cora. She finds no sustenance in their relationship, nor does she have anyone else who can meet her needs. As Chodorow posits, "women, therefore, need primary relationships to women as well as men" (53). In this motherless world (for Hannah refuses to fulfill her potential as a nurturing mother), Cora is bereft. If the past precluded any basis upon which to build the underpinnings of emotional stability, the present presents little hope either. The sad reality is that Cora is pushed aside. Andrew's tired answer that he will not do anything about the theft further humiliates Cora and serves as a stunning example that Cora deserves no place at the family table. Her opinions and actions are of no consequence. Just as she has no say in corporate decisions affecting family business, she has no say in the day-to-day management of the household budget. This "bread and butter" is off limits. Indeed, Cora has no say in anything that occurs in the Rodman household. Because she feels so powerless, she lashes out at each combatant and then seeks solace in food. As Cherin suggests, an association exists between a woman's eating habits and her struggle for identity (xi); she maintains that a woman must return to her roots to find what keeps her developmentally weak, "the hunger knot in which identity, the mother-separation struggle, love, rage, food, and the female body are all entangled" (xiv). Cora fits Chernin's definition of a woman with an eating disorder, one who is "trying to fill an ill-defined 'gnawing hunger' whose real nature she cannot admit to herself" (24).

Even the murder of Wilkie's thug, Mossie, right in the Rodman home, cannot keep Cora from her appointed snack. In Cora's view, nothing can be done for a dead man, but hunger can be appeased. Loudly ringing the bell to summon Hannah, she insists, "My milk and fruit aren't upstairs. We can't help it if he got killed. Whatever we do now isn't going to do him any good. . . . You forgot it, didn't you?" (117). Hannah's cryptic reply that, "I didn't think you'd starve. . . . Funny, how you drink it. Just like you need it" (117), reveals not only Hannah's hard-hearted approach, but also Cora's overriding need for nurturance. To borrow a line from Arthur Miller's Linda Loman, "Attention must be paid." In this case, Cora's starving self demands it. While the others gather to discuss the previous night's horrific events, she sends back the improperly made hot chocolate. Her curt reply to Ellicott's query as to whether she must have her breakfast in the library symbolizes her attempt to sustain structure in her powerless life, as she demands, "Mind your own business. I've had it here for thirty years. I shall continue" (130). Family and friends may manipulate her position, but Cora will not cave in so easily. If the hot chocolate will not soothe her psychic aches and pains, she will send it back to the kitchen until Hannah "gets it right." Just like Jessie in Marsha Norman's *'night, Mother,* Cora longs for the days when warm cocoa with Mama would take care of life's woes. The fact that those days are a fantasy is beside the point. One can try. One can demand one's place at the table as long as one's strength holds.

Cora's present sense of power is further diminished by her brother's wife, Julie. Before Julie married Andrew, Cora could function as the household's mistress. Her constant criticism of Julie's ability to coordinate household functions reveals her rage at being displaced. She loses no opportunity to illuminate Julie's incompetence, as evidenced by her remark to the man who comes to plant the trees. Cora notes, "I told him that you always did that. Forgetting about things" (82). She further establishes her fear at relinquishing her perceived place as mistress of the household when she deliberately snubs Julie's hoped-for paramour, Leo Whalen, the union organizer. Julie's immediate caustic attack as she demands, "Don't do that in my house again" (92), only enrages her more. Cora does not accept Julie's place in the Rodman household. She underscores the rage she feels as she shouts, "How dare you talk that way? So now it's your house? My father built it, but it's YOUR house now" (92). As long as Julie remains, Cora's place at the table remains in jeopardy.

Cora holds a losing hand in this game with her sister-in-law unless she plays her high card and reveals Julie's longstanding affair with the family lawyer, Henry Ellicott, as well as other clandestine liasons. However, her decision to reveal Julie's extramarital liaison with Ellicott, causing Julie's fall from grace, backfires. Metaphorically speaking, Cora feels that if she can pull the chair out from under Julie, she can regain a place at the family table. Unfortunately, for her, the plan fails. Whether Andrew knew or did not know of his wife's deception is of no consequence to him now. In view of the fact that he bears responsibility for two murders, he has neither the energy nor the inclination to demand an explanation from Julie, even though Julie insists, "Let her say it. She's wanted to for a long time" (130). Andrew's lackluster reply, coupled with Julie's taunt, causes an emotional explosion that serves as a catalyst to bring the missing ingredient to the table—truth.

When Cora acknowledges that she has known about Julie's extramarital behavior for years, she pinpoint, the powerlessness his marriage has supposedly placed upon her. What has eaten away at Cora's insides is that Andrew has, unashamedly, squandered family money (half of which belongs to Cora), upon European trips, fashionable clothes, and a year's study in Paris for his wife. Cora resents that Andrew has had to borrow thousands and thousands of dollars, resulting in deep debt, to make Julie happy.

However, Cora's bare-bones approach to truth elicits no appreciation from Andrew—or anyone else. Her strategy falters, and, as a result, her future as a Rodman family member appears dubious, at best. Each one harbors resentment about her revelation, but Andrew's response epitomizes the seething hostility present, as he insists, "It wasn't your business. It isn't your business now" (131). Instead, he discloses the denial in which each one, as well as Henry, participates, noting "It was all there before. It can be said now" (132).

Sadly, Cora's response to the debilitating diatribes indicates no success on her part at assuaging the ill-defined "gnawing hunger" that eats aways at her psyche. Her last speech, in which she mildly suggests, "Things went entirely too far. It comes from everybody getting too excited. Now you go to sleep and nothing will seem as bad when you wake up. People said a lot of things they didn't mean. A lot of things they didn't mean. I'm sure of that" (133), indicates her inability to accept the truth. Her final gesture, summarily chomping down on a bite of toast, signifies her continuing turn to food. Food denotes sustenance. It comforts. The hot chocolate like Mama used to make or the tea and toast she brought when you were ill conjure up a time—far removed—when needs were met, when hunger was fed. Cora's fixation on food represents an attempt to obtain the nurturing she never experiences in the Rodman family. Tragically, the food can never satisfy. It must be perfectly presented, and it must be in abundance. Supplies can never run out.

However, no abundance can ever appease the appetite within Cora. Hellman's characterization illustrates one way a woman may respond when confronted with the powerlessness of her life. As Chernin notes, these women are "filling the emptiness with food" (25). This preoccupation, for Cora, signifies the fear she feels when confronted with the obstacles before her—obstacles that leave her economically dependent as well as emotionally bereft. Cora wants what most women want—an identity that affords them some measure of power; a place at the table—but, just as other female characters in Hellman's works, she finds her chair missing. Like Lavinia in *Another Part of the Forest,* who escapes her confinement through fantasies that substitute for the reality she finds unbearable, or Regina, in *Little Foxes,* who responds to her powerlessness by, in effect, murder, so Cora escapes through food.

In this motherless world, Cora has no means of escape. She has no idealized other with whom she can bond. She will simply, as millions of her sisters throughout centuries, have to make the best of a brutal situation. In order to do so, she will continue to keep the food pantry, and the hostile Hannah, under surveillance. In this play, which William Wright terms "Hellman's most political play," Cora's character has no power base from which to muster a fight. Instead, she continues to struggle in a hostile and stifling environment. No other choices exist. Like her creator, Cora must remain "an unfinished woman," never finding the truth she needs to satisfy her appetite—the truth she needs to become psychically whole.

Like her literary progenitor, Marsha Norman also foregrounds food in her plays, particularly the two most successful, *Getting Out* and *'night, Mother.* Both female protagonists search for sustenance and nurturance. Arlene, in *Getting Out,* longs to be invited for her mother's Sunday pot toast dinner, and even though her mother ultimately rejects her, Arlene finds a friend, Ruby, an upstairs neighbor, with whom to break bread. Jessie, in *'night, Mother,* is not so fortunate. She can find no food that will satisfy, and even though her mother tries valiantly to stop her, she kills herself in order to gain control over her meager existence.

In this Pulitzer-Prize winning effort, Norman, true to her "calling" as a storyteller determined to give a voice to people not normally heard, presents the painful existence of Jessie Cates, a woman without hope—without a "self" for which she constantly hungers. Critics categorically raved about this ninety minutes of intermissionless, riveting theater. Brendan Gill, writing in the *New Yorker,* termed it "a very good play indeed," and *Louisville Times* critic Dudley Saunders saw its Broadway opening at the Golden Theatre as "refreshingly clean, honest and straightforward." Drama critic for the *New York Times* Mel Gussow, allowed that "the play stands out as one of the season's major dramatic events," and described Norman as a powerful dramatist. Robert Brustein, writing in *Who Needs Theatre,* likened Norman's technique and effect to that of Chekhov and O'Neill, while noting that Norman's scene depicting the attempt to make hot chocolate "the old way" is her version of "J.D. Salinger's consecrated chicken soup" (66, 67).

Mother and daughter, Thelma and Jessie Cates, live isolated existences in a nondescript house on a lonely country road. Jessie, an unhappy overweight woman, about forty, suffers from epilepsy, but the "disease" that drives her to take her own life is far more insidious than this lifelong affliction. Jessie starves for a cohesive self, a sense of personal autonomy, which has thus far escaped her. Because she has no "appetite" for life, she opts for death.

However, although suicide is certainly a factor, this play is *not* about suicide. Indeed, those who see it merely as a "death watch," instituted by a cruel daughter determined to "pay back" her mother for a lifetime of wrongs, err in their judgment. *'night, Mother* is a play about mother and daughter relationships, about psychic hunger, about tragedy, but also about triumph. With the final gunshot, Jessie assumes control over her life, and during the play's action she and Thelma connect in a way they never could before. At the same time, she separates from her mother—a task she has heretofore been unable to accomplish—and Thelma learns to let her daughter go.

Hunger, and the need to appease it, form the play's central metaphor. Both women experience psychic hunger brought about by the helplessness women have historically experienced as part of a patriarchal culture that offers little hope for personal power. However, Marsha Norman's female characters differ from Lillian Hellman's. Unlike Cora Rodman in *Days to Come,* Jessie Cates does not hopelessly vegetate in a powerless position at the play's end. Ultimately, she gets what she wants—death—which releases her from the incredibly boring existence she would have experienced if she had opted to live. And actually, Mama also gets what she wants, too. She finally communicates in a powerful way never before possible. Some mothers live and die without ever communicating with their daughters at such a deep level.

The kitchen becomes a metaphor for the play's action. Traditionally, we tend to view the kitchen as the heart of the house, symbolizing mother, warmth, and nurturance. We break bread, which mother prepares, in the bosom of our family. We experience connection and relationships that sustain our survival in the outside world. The kitchen, usually smaller than the other rooms in the house, functions as a womb—a warm and safe place. Memory conjures up images of mother fixing breakfast for us before we trudge off to school and taking cookies from the oven upon our return.

Norman begins the play's action in the kitchen, where Thelma searches for the sugary snowballs she loves so well. The kitchen serves as a base from which to launch the battle to save the mother/daughter relationship. Here they will attempt to recapture what never existed through the cocoa-making ritual. The living room, as Jenny Spencer points out in *Modern Drama,* "underscores our sense of physical entrapment and psychological impasse in the ensuing action" (365). Their separation and Jessie's eventual stand for autonomy, however, are symbolized by Jessie's departure to the locked bedroom, which Thelma cannot penetrate.

Thelma, too, starves for fulfillment. Norman's first stage directions tell us that "Mama stretches to reach the cupcakes in a cabinet in the kitchen. She can't see them, but she can feel around for them, and she's eager to have one, so she's working pretty hard at it" (5). Finding only a partial package with the coconut fallen off symbolizes Mama's life. Although she has never heard of Betty Friedan's *The Feminine Mystique,* she most assuredly knows something's amiss. The "coconut is always falling off" for Mama, and this confrontation with her only daughter who is determined to kill herself will only confuse Mama more. Thelma loves candy; its sweetness temporarily satisfies, and she must see that the supply continues. The play's first speech solidifies this position, as she tells Jessie while unwrapping a cupcake:

> *Jessie, it's the last snowball, sugar. Put it on the list, O.K.? And we're out of Hershey bars, and where's that peanut brittle? I think maybe Dawson's been in it again. I ought to put a big mirror on the refrigerator door. That'll keep him out of my treats, won't it? You hear me, honey?* (Then more to herself) *I hate it when the coconut falls off. Why does the coconut fall off?* (5)

Isolated upon a country road and burdened with an epileptic daughter who never communicates, Thelma lives a meager existence. Candy, her little "treats," become a crutch to help her survive. As Sally Browder notes in *Mother Puzzles,* Thelma, too, "has had her share of disappointments" (110). Rejected by a "silent" husband who refused to even talk to her upon his deathbed, Thelma endures her pyromaniac, okra-eating friend, Agnes, just to have someone who will talk to her. "Sweets . . . provide Mama with the sensual gratification, and the sense of fullness she failed to obtain from her marriage" (Morrow 24). Once again, Kim Chernin's patient probably focuses upon Thelma's pain best: "There is no I . . . There's just an immense hole at the center. An emptiness. A terror. Not all the food in the world could fill it. But, I try" (20).

Food functions as a complex metaphor here, and Thelma's psychic hunger begs for appeasement. Chernin's assessment crystallizes this "psychic gnawing" for all women, as she relates:

> *For food, after all, has defined female identity. . . . It has defined more even than the history of mother/daughter relations and that early sorrow and disorder that began, for many of us, at the mother's breast. Dating back to our earliest impressions of life, recorded in the symbolic code of food imagery, the vanquished story of female value and power returns to us again and again in our obsession with food. . . . (197)*

Rather than see Thelma as a "dodo" or a "caricature of a self-centered old baby" (Kauffman 48), we need to understand her position in the play as well as Jessie's. Because she views Jessie as an extension of herself, she finds herself upon the horns of a major maternal dilemma. Now that her "extension" has announced plans to blow her brains out with "Daddy's gun," Thelma faces losing a part of her self, her daughter. At the same time, she also risks repudiation of her entire existence as a mother. As Chodorow asserts, a mother, "tends to experience boundary confusion with her daughter, and does not provide experiences of differentiating ego development for her daughter or encourage the breaking of her daughter's dependence" (59). Thelma valiantly tries to forestall the inevitable, to find something that tastes good to Jessie, but Jessie rejects all offers. However, as they attempt to work through the psychological baggage that underlies every mother and daughter relationship, Jessie mounts an all-out effort to connect and make her mother understand this shattering decision. Ninety minutes of anger and accusations finally give way to acceptance and understanding.

Indeed, Jessie hungers for understanding, but more importantly, control. She loves her mother, but, ultimately, she leaves her. Unlike her mother, Jessie cannot subsist on the likes of sugary snowballs, peanut brittle, and Hershey bars. She now knows that this present life will never provide the nurturance she needs to be a truly autonomous self. Her only hope is to separate from her mother and reunite with her father—in death. But before she goes, she "mothers" Mama by preparing her sweet supply. She also lists Christmas presents for Mama to give and explains directions for disposal of her body and funeral etiquette.

While some may think Jessie incredibly selfish for subjecting Thelma to such agonizing torture, the fact is that Jessie cares deeply for Thelma. Her carefully planned evening reflects a desperate attempt to explain why no food, not even rice pudding, can make such an isolated existence bearable, as Jessie suggests, "How would you know if I didn't say it? You want it to be a surprise?" (13). Jessie's refusal to allow Thelma to call Dawson, Jessie's brother, underscores the fact that what occurs, this night, in this house, is for mother and daughter alone. As Jessie notes, "If Dawson comes over, it'll make me feel stupid for not doing it ten years ago. . . . I only told you so I could explain it, so you wouldn't blame yourself, so you wouldn't feel bad. There wasn't anything you could say to change my mind. I didn't want you to save me. I just wanted you to know" (17, 74).

Jessie wants Thelma to know that a place at her mother's table has not satisfied the psychic hunger she endures. No option Thelma offers appeals to Jessie. Supplies have run out. However, as Jessie methodically lines up the bags of sour balls, red hots, and licorice, she makes one last attempt to answer her questions and to recreate a sense of safety that never really existed. As she tells Thelma, "We could go on fussing all night. I mean, I could ask you things I always wanted to know and you could make me some hot chocolate the old way" (36). She adds a caramel apple to her request, and Thelma, who allows that she "makes the best caramel apples in the world" (37), willingly accedes to Jessie's wishes. No request is too difficult for Thelma, who desperately wants Jessie to stay as she asserts, "It's no trouble, what trouble? You put it in the pan, and stir it up. All right. Fine. Caramel apple. Cocoa. O.K. (37). Interestingly, this pan is the one Jessie instructs her to hold when she calls the police to report Jessie's death. Norman's stage directions tell us she grips the pan tightly "like her life depended on it" (89). As Lynda Hart notes, "Jessie's last request from her mother is for food. . . . This last bit of sustenance that mother and daughter share is highly charged with symbolic meaning as the pan Thelma uses to warm the milk becomes the object that will occupy her after Jessie's death" (76). However, Hart pinpoints the problems daughters have in separating from mothers when she suggests that Thelma's insistence that Jessie have three marshmallows in her cocoa reflects Thelma's attempt to retain maternal control over Jessie. As Hart asserts, "Even with the knowledge of her daughter's imminent suicide, Mama cannot acknowledge her daughter as a separate adult. . . . In this most basic of ways, Mama is asserting her power and denying her daughter's initiative" (76).

Mama wants to return to the "old way," in which she retained control over her daughter. Now, the table is turned as Jessie asserts her autonomy through her refusal to eat even though she starves psychically. In this battle over what and how much to eat the two wills clash:

> The child's efforts to impose her own will upon the world and to manipulate her environment are directed towards food very early in the development of a separate self. What will be eaten and how it will be prepared are questions that often form the basis of mother and daughter struggles. (Hart 76)

Unfortunately, however, their attempted ritual to recover their symbiotic relationship ultimately fails, as both mother and daughter realize the cocoa cannot satisfy the deeper longing. Significantly, the milk makes it taste bad. As both mother and daughter concede that it is, indeed, the milk, both women, together, confront their unfulfilled lives. Their mutual dislike of milk is one of the few traits mother and daughter share (Morrow 24).

Mama's avowal that "It's a real waste of chocolate. You don't have to finish it" (45) comprises one of the most important lines in the play. This statement suggests, at least on some level, Jessie's decision to halt her psychic "forage for food"; it also provides a connection to the play's last line, "Forgive me. *(Pause)* I thought you were mine" (89), where Thelma ultimately realizes that she and her daughter are not one, but two separate people.

While her dislike of milk reflects her rejection of the unadulterated and healthful, it also suggests "her dissatisfaction with motherhood which has proven no more rewarding than marriage" (Morrow 26). Now she faces coming to terms with a daughter's decision to reject the woman who bore her even though the men in her life, and not her mother, have abandoned her.

Thelma's rage at the realization that Jessie will never have an appetite for options her mother may offer erupts, as she complains, "I should've known not to make it. I knew you wouldn't like it. You never did like it" (45). Nothing Thelma can do will satisfy Jessie, and knowing that compels her to lash out in a tyrannical rage, threatening never to cook nor drink milk again. Her existence will be bolstered only by candy and tuna, and Jessie's maternal avowal that "You should drink milk" is met with a firm, "Not anymore, I'm not" (54). Moreover, she demands an accounting from the flesh and blood that has turned on her, as she insists, "Nothing I ever did was good enough for you and I want to know why" (55). Characteristically, Thelma assumes, as a mother, it must be her fault if her daughter refuses the food proffered. Thelma cannot accept that Jessie feels that "I cannot do anything either, about my life, to change it, make it better, make me feel better about it" (36).

No one has really taken time to know Jessie on any level except a surface one. All the men in her life, including her beloved father, have fled. Indeed, Jessie's identification with him, the "big, old faded blue man in the chair" (47), is so strong she uses his gun to complete her mission. Jessie could talk to him, even if it was only about why "black socks are warmer than blue socks" (48). Like her father, Jessie is both an epileptic as well as an introvert. Her desire to rejoin him in death is reflected by her wish to "hang a sign around her neck, 'Gone fishin,' like her daddy's" (29). Jessie does not wish to stay around and chat forever. "Unlike Mama, Jessie accepts her father's introversion and complexity because she recognizes the necessary (and desirable) limitation of our ability to communicate with others" (Morrow 29). Jessie wants out, and she wants out tonight.

Although her father leaves her through death, Cecil, Jessie's husband, leaves because, as Jessie tells it, he "made her choose between him and smoking" (56). Interestingly, although Jessie may refuse food, she enjoys smoking—an oral fixation. To Jessie this addictive but non-nourishing habit signifies "the only thing I know that's always just what you think it's going to be. Just like it was the last time, right there when you want it and real quiet" (56). Jessie associates smoking "with power and self-determination . . . smoking offers Jessie a sense of predictability and control—if only negative control—over her destiny" (Morrow 29). Even this failed relationship reflects back upon Thelma because she is the one who engineered it in the first place. Afraid that Jessie would have a hard time "catching" a man, Thelma contracted with Cecil for a porch and ended up with a son-in-law who left her daughter for another woman. Like Cecil, Jessie's juvenile delinquent son Ricky also leaves her.

An incorrigible youngster, he steals, does drugs, and may commit murder in a matter of time. Jessie has given up any hope for Ricky, much as she has for herself. Still, she recognizes his shortcomings are hers too, as she notes, "Ricky is as much like me as it's possible for any human being to be. We even wear the same size pants. These are his, I think" (59). Likewise, she realizes her maternal failure with Ricky, as she tells Thelma, "You know who laid that floor. I did" (60), much as Thelma failed in building a proper foundation for her. Even so, Jessie reaches out to nurture Ricky through her decision to leave him her watch. When Thelma complains that he will just sell it Jessie admits she hopes he gets a good meal, and if he buys dope as Thelma threatens, she hopes "he gets some good dope with it, Mama. . . ." (85).

The other man in her life, her brother Dawson, offers her no familial sense of community. In Jessie's view, Dawson calls her Jess "just like he knows who he's talking to" (23), and he and his wife, Loretta, invade Jessie's privacy by opening the package containing her mail-order bra, the one with the "little rosebuds." The grocery account bears Dawson's name even though Jessie orders the weekly food, and she is tired of dealing with her own brother, who gives her houseshoes every Christmas which never fit.

Aside from family relationships, Jessie has no standing in the community either. Isolated, out in the country, her life consists of day-to-day rituals such as changing shelf paper, washing floors, and coordinating grocery deliveries. She cannot hold a job, not the telephone sales job nor the one at the hospital gift shop where she made the people "real uncomfortable smiling at them the way I did" (35). The one satisfying job she liked, keeping her father's books, ended with his death. Jessie has had no real opportunity to practice socialization skills either, since she has never really been around people except in the hospital after a seizure. People avoid her. Even Thelma's okra-eating friend, Agnes, will not come to visit because she senses "Jessie's shook the hand of death and I can't take the chance it's catching. . . . I'll come up the driveway, but that's as far as I go" (43).

As Jessie sees it, her best bet is to leave this incredibly boring life. She has had enough of being subject to the convenience of other people's schedules and ideas of where her best interests lie. She has had enough of being at the mercy of possible epileptic seizures even though she has not had one in a year. On this particular night, she maintains perfect control. This control is reflected in her statement, "Whenever I feel like it, I can get off. As soon as I've had enough, it's my stop. I've had enough" (33). Her search for a cohesive self has ended in failure, and Jessie knows it. As she explains to Thelma, "That's what this is about. It's somebody I lost, all right, it's my own self. Who I never was. Or who I tried to be and never got there. Somebody I waited for who never came" (76). Jessie is a woman "in whom all desire is spent, not through satiation, but through the clear understanding of the world's false nourishment" (Hart 75). The only reason she remains is to make her mother understand why she had to make this radical decision. At the same time, she wishes to have her mother accept her as an autonomous adult and not the child she once was. "Through both her actions and her words, we sense Jessie's sincere desire to make some connections with her mother as a fully separate human being before she goes" (Spencer 366). Even though Thelma makes one last-ditch effort to assert her maternal power by proclaiming the inescapable eternal mother/daughter connection, as she insists, "Everything you have to do has to do with me, Jessie. You can't do *any-thing*, wash your face or cut your finger, without doing it to me" (72), Jessie retains the upper hand. In a poignant moment, Jessie reveals the enormity of her newly-found independence by insisting, "Then what if it does!. . . What if you are all I have and you're not enough?. . . What if the only way I can get away from you for good is to kill myself?. . . I can still do it" (72).

In this gripping speech, Jessie speaks for all daughters everywhere. Her outburst metaphorically reflects the anger we feel toward the woman who can never fufill our fantasy of the perfect mother. Jessie wants her mother to feed her, but Thelma is unable to provide the necessary nurturance. Her failure incurs Jessie's wrath:

> *Jessie expresses anger at her mother for not being able to fulfill her insatiable demands (you're not enough), anger at feeling powerless to change her situation any other way. . . anger for not providing her with an adequate sense of self, for controlling her life without giving it meaning. For women in the audience, it is anger that each of us has experienced. (Spencer 368)*

Jessie's carefully orchestrated suicide finally separates her from her mother. She will not opt for a life of desperation like Thelma. Unlike her mother, she will not seek succor in sugary sweets, and if she cannot control her life, she will certainly control her death. She has waited until the time was right, for as she sees the situation, "I'm feeling as good as I ever felt in my life" (66). "She is convinced that suicide is the only authentic act available to her" (Keysser 165). With this courageous rebellion, Jessie repudiates the false self assigned to her by others. She becomes the director in her own life's drama; she establishes the boundaries between mother and daughter as she responds to Thelma's poignant plea, "You are my child!" with the firm revelation, "I am what became of your child" (76). The infant self that drooled on the sheet and felt its mother's hand tucking in the crib quilt never progressed to any sense of psychic wholeness, never acquired a true sense of self. In Jessie's view, "I'm not going to show up, so there's no reason to stay, except to keep you company, and that's . . . not reason enough. . ." (76). No cupboard held the requisite food needed to nourish Jessie's self. Nothing, not even cornflakes for breakfast, can keep her here.

As the play's action moves closer and closer to the bedroom door with each ticking of the clock, Thelma faces the awful moment of truth. Desperate and scared, she has summoned every conceivable argument to place before Jessie's metaphorical plate, only to have them pushed aside. She realizes her loss as she tells Jessie, "Who am I talking to? You're gone already, aren't you? I'm looking right through you!" (78). This statement by Thelma establishes her realization that Jessie has now smashed the mirror that bonds them together. Thelma, in looking at her daughter, no longer sees her own reflection. She sees a separate person. In an interesting anecdote, Madeline Grumet focuses upon this shattering truth in *Bitter Milk,* wherein she speaks of being surprised after childbirth as she looked in a mirror and saw her own reflection and not her child's (10). This cohesion, the "you are mine and I am yours" feeling, is so prevalent in mother/daughter relationships because of the way mothers view their daughters as extensions of themselves. The connection is so powerful that when they look at their daughters, they see themselves. This continuity is not present, as Chodorow attests, in mother/ son relationships. Only by "smashing" that mirror can the daughter eventually own her reflection. As Sally Browder suggests, "Without some objective reference, some sense of oneself apart from others, one is totally at the mercy of others' experiences. One's sense of meaning is defined by others' choices. One's value is determined by how well one serves or provides for the needs of others" (111). In the end, Thelma realizes that she cannot possess Jessie, no matter how much she loves her. The action that began in the kitchen ends with Thelma screaming and pounding at Jessie's locked bedroom door. With her anguished confession, "Jessie, Jessie, child. . . . Forgive me. (*Pause*) I thought you were mine" (89), she faces the fact that she finally must relinquish control. Even so, the symbiotic bond remains. The bullet that pierces Jessie's brain symbolically rips through Thelma as well. As critic Leslie Kane points out in *Feminine Focus: The New Women Playwrights,* Thelma's physical reaction to Jessie's shot—her body crumples against the door—confirms Thelma's previous statement about mutually felt pain (267).

Interestingly, in the film version, for which Norman wrote the screenplay, the last crucial line is omitted. According to Stanley Kauffman, through this omission Norman avoids suggesting the dramatic work that it could have been, because:

> *If the play were true—to Norman's characters as she wants us to think of them—it wouldn't exist. Either Jessie would shoot herself before it begins, or*

> *as soon as she discloses her plans, Thelma would collapse . . . Thelma's one*
> *impeccable line comes right after the shot. Against the locked bedroom door*
> *she sobs: "Forgive me. I thought you were mine." The drama that really leads*
> *to that line—of a clawing Electra complex, of the mother's mirror-image*
> *hatreds, and of pity overarching both—has not yet been written. (26)*

Unfortunately, Kauffman misses the point here. Rather than improve the play, this omission weakens the important truth Thelma realizes while drinking the cocoa at the kitchen table—no mother can own her daughter. Ultimately, she must relinquish control no matter how much it hurts. That poignant realization constitutes the true drama of the play—not a "clawing Electra complex."

Norman, however, offers a more pragmatic reason for the omission. In personal correspondence with me (through her agent, Jack Tantleff), Norman concedes:

> *I chose to omit the last line because that kind of line is* only *permissable in*
> *the theatre, where the line between the real & the imagined, the said & the*
> *unsaid is more blurred. The line, as a piece of poetry, does not belong in the*
> *realism of the film. . . . It was always my feeling that the line was what*
> *Thelma* thought *or* felt *at the moment. The only reason we hear it in the the-*
> *atre, is because we* are *in the theatre.*

Even so, whether or not Thelma only thinks or feels that she can no longer "own" Jessie, she still confronts that realization.

With the curtains descent, Thelma grips the cocoa pan tightly as she calls Dawson for help. Jessie's journey, which began in the kitchen and ended in her bedroom, is now complete. Nevertheless, both mother and daughter have connected in a way never before possible. They work through their mutual anger, digging through layers of guilt and remorse in order to salvage nuggets of truth. Each forgives the other. Jessie shows love for her mother by the acts she performs during these last two hours of her life. She prepares Thelma for the inevitable truth—that Jessie must assume autonomy regardless of personal cost. Thelma, through overwhelming grief, finally does let go. Both communicate on a level many mothers and daughters never experience.

Neither is really to blame for the personal realities that bring them to this place on this particular night. Thelma, like many mothers, can only offer what she has. As a a participant in a patriarchal culture that places women in this no-win situation, she can hardly do more. Jessie, as a daughter, has to seek her true self—even if that quest ends in death. Both must seek their nurturance in the ways they know best. In this play, where hunger provides the controlling metaphor, Norman provides a tremendous sense of catharsis. However, she provides no answers to the contradictory lives mothers and daughters live as long as women remain the primary caretakers of children. She offers no solutions to unfulfilling lives due to societal constraints. She fails to challenge, as Jenny Spencer notes, "in any fundamental way the prevalent image of women in society—as those who reproduce, consume, and are consumed, who are powerless, inadequate, unworthy, and mutually destructive" (370).

Both Hellman and Norman, through these two plays, create representations of women working to fill that psychic hunger experienced when faced with the limited options for self-determination present in patriarchal society. Hellman's character, Cora Rodman, remains powerless, still striving at the plays end to control her psychic food supply through manipulation of family members. Norman's character, Jessie Cares, assumes control of her life and chooses death rather than face an unfulfilled life like her mother's. Even though Jessie chooses death, she triumphs because she, alone, decides what constitutes her proper nourishment.

NOTES

[1] I am referring here to Maslow's "Twelve Steps to Self-Actualization," where he gives the basic hierarchy of human needs; hunger is the most basic.

[2] See Robert Brustein's "Lillian Hellman: Epilogue to Anger," in *Who Needs Theatre: Dramatic Opinions,* Atlantic Monthly Press, New York, 1987.

[3] Brooks Atkinson, "The Play," *New York Times* (December 16, 1936), 35.

[4] Robert Coleman, Review of *Days to Come, New York Daily Mirror* (December 16, 1936), 19.

[5] Charles Dexter, "Strikes and Strikebreakers Viewed by Lillian Hellman," *Daily Worker* (December 18, 1936), 7.

[6] See Grenville Vernon's review, "The Play and Screen: *Days to Come,*" in *Commonweal,* 25 (January 1, 1937), 276. Vernon focuses on Hellman's unfortunate attempt to make the play more than just a "melodrama with a purpose."

[7] For a cogent discussion of Melanie Klein's work, I suggest the reader consult *Introduction to the Work of Melanie Klein* (New York: Basic Books, 1974) by Hannah Segal. This work is a compilation of several lectures given at the Institute of Psycho-Analysis in London by Segal illustrated by her clinical experiences. In Chapter 3, "The Paranoid-Schizoid Position." Segal more fully explains Klein's view of how the infant splits the mother's breast.

Works Cited

Atkinson, Brooks. "The Play," *New York Times* (December 2, 1934): 10:1.

Brustein, Robert. "Lillian Hellman: Epilogue to Anger." In *Who Needs Theatre.* New York: Atlantic Monthly Press, 1987.

Chernin, Kim. *The Hungry Self: Women, Eating, & Identity.* New York: Harper and Row, 1985.

———. *Reinventing Eve: Modern Woman in Search of Herself.* New York: Harper and Row, 1987.

Chodorow, Nancy. *Feminism and Psychoanalytic Theory.* New Haven, Conn.: Yale UP, 1989.

Coleman, Robert. "Review of *Days to Come.*" *New York Daily Mirror,* 4, 1936.

Dexter, Charles. "Strikes and Strikebreakers." *Daily Worker,* 7, 1936.

Grumet, Madeline. *Bitter Milk: Women and Teaching.* Amherst. U of Massachusetts P, 1988.

Hellman, Lillian. *The Collected Plays.* Boston and Toronto: Little, Brown, 1969.

———. *An Unfinished Woman: A Memoir.* Boston and Toronto: Little, Brown. 1969.

Murray, Edward J. *Motivation and Emotion.* Englewood Cliffs, N.J.: Prentice-Hall, 1964.

Norman, Marsha, *'night, Mother.* New York: Hill and Wang, 1983.

Rollyson, Carl. *Lillian Hellman: Her Legend and Her Legacy.* New York: St. Martin's, 1988.

Segeal, Hannah. *Introduction to the Work of Melanie Klein.* New York: Basic Books, 1974.

Vernon, Grenville. "The Play and the Screen: *Days to Come.*" *Commonweal,* 25 (January 1, 1937): 276.

The Personal, the Political, and the Postmodern in Osborne's *Look Back in Anger* and *Déjàvu*

Austin E. Quigley

Forty years after it made its historic appearance on the London stage, *Look Back in Anger* is widely regarded as a very important but not very good play. A generation of British playwrights, including Brenton, Stoppard, and Hare, have acknowledged its importance to their subsequent careers, but most, including Osborne, who later described it as a "rather old-fashioned play,"[1] now see its weaknesses as clearly as its strengths. Hare's recent praise of the play is characteristically qualified:

> I think that all of us, people who write, we all want to write a play after which things will be seen differently. . . . And most of us are very jealous of Osborne because he pulled it off. . . . Whether you think it's a good play or a bad play, it was a rallying point.[2]

This apparent disjunction between the quality of the play and the scope of its impact remains something of a puzzle, but one whose nature becomes clearer in the light of the sequel, *Déjàvu,* that Osborne wrote in 1991.

Structurally, of course, *Look Back in Anger* does indeed seem a rather old-fashioned play, tracing the separation and reconciliation of Jimmy Porter and his wife, Alison, through a stagey three-act format that hinges on Alison's pregnancy and Jimmy's wrath. To describe the pattern of events in that way, however, is to draw attention to the fact that Jimmy's wrath has little to do with Alison's pregnancy and that the old-fashioned plot line of separation and reconciliation contributes more to the scaffolding than to the substance of the play. The difficulties that emerge between Jimmy and Alison are symptomatic of much wider problems that are neither fully summarized in nor adequately exemplified by the strains and stresses of that particular relationship. Indeed, one of the oddities of a play that focuses upon a single major relationship is that so many other characters who never appear are, in one way or another, caught up in the action. Besides Cliff, Helena, and Colonel Redfern, who appear in minor roles, the following never appear at all: Jimmy's best friend Hugh and his mother, Mrs. Tanner; Jimmy's ex-girlfriend, Madeline; his dying father and his disapproving mother; Alison's brother, Nigel; their ferocious mother; their outraged family friends; a gay radical; a rabid bishop; and sundry other people who earn a name but not a place in the story. As the action of the play demonstrates, however, neither a name nor a place in the story suffice to gain characters an influential voice, for Jimmy's voice dominates everyone else's throughout, and this serves to make even more visible the disjunction between the scope of the issues raised and the restricted nature of the central relationship within which they are dramatically explored.

The evident imbalance between Jimmy's role and everyone else's is widely regarded as the major structural fault of a play to which many other faults are attributed. The ending, with Jimmy and Alison playing at squirrels and bears, seems to lack the weight of an achieved conclusion; the death of their baby seems conventionally contrived and a fortuitous rather than organic means of reconciling the estranged couple; the readiness of Helena to oscillate between love and hate for Jimmy to suit the movement of the plot seems likewise rather contrived; and the central character, Jimmy himself, exhibits an unappealing mixture of cloying self pity, deep-seated prejudice, radical insensitivity, and rampant inconsistency. So widespread are these faults that it becomes evident why so many find it difficult to reconcile the play's structural limitations with its remarkable historical impact. But if we are to come to terms with the play, it must be by understanding the peculiar power of its odd structure, not by explaining its problems away. Indeed, there are few more remarkable things about this remarkable play than the famous description that Osborne offers in his initial stage directions of the limitations of the character who is, in effect, to carry the action of the whole play:

> *[Jimmy] is a disconcerting mixture of sincerity and cheerful malice, of tenderness and freebooting cruelty; restless, importunate, full of pride, a combination which alienates the sensitive and insensitive alike. Blistering honesty, or apparent honesty, like his, makes few friends. To many he may seem sensitive to the point of vulgarity. To others, he is simply a loudmouth. To be as vehement as he is is to be almost non-committal.[3]*

The "disconcerting mixture" of traits exemplified by the play's central character is thus no accident, and Osborne anticipates the variety of responses Jimmy's behavior will provoke. His final sentence summarizes, in effect, a problem that seems central both to the character and to the play. Jimmy's aggressive rhetoric, which constitutes so much of the play's action, exhibits a savagery so widely deployed that it threatens to rob Jimmy of any clear point and the play of any clear goal.

To begin to make any sense of so peculiarly structured a play we need to come to terms not only with Jimmy's prominence and peculiarities but also with a further dimension of structural and tonal diversity: the one that generates Osborne's recurring insistence on the humor of a play that seems to have little to be humorous about. Jimmy's most famous remark, for example, that "There aren't any good, brave causes left" for his generation, is delivered not bitterly, as many might expect, but *"In [Jimmy's] familiar, semi-serious mood"* (104). Jimmy's humor and the *"cheerful malice"* that Osborne refers to at the outset are interwoven with his anger and aggressiveness throughout the action, baffling everyone at one time or another, but particularly Helena during their brief romance:

> JIMMY: Do I detect a growing, satanic glint in her eyes lately? Do you think it's living in sin with me that does it? *(To Helena.)*
>
> Do you feel very sinful my dear? Well? Do you?
>
> *She can hardly believe that this is an attack, and she can only look at him, uncertain of herself.*
>
> Do you feel sin crawling out of your ears, like stored up wax or something? Are you wondering whether I'm joking or not? Perhaps I ought to wear a red nose and a funny hat. I'm just curious, that's all.
>
> *She is shaken by the sudden coldness in his eyes, but before she has time to fully realise how hurt she is, he is smiling at her, and shouting cheerfully at Cliff.* (97)

These oscillations between humor and seriousness in Jimmy's behavior are exemplified most clearly in the newspaper rituals and music hall routines into which the characters are likely to lapse at any moment, but the humor has larger consequences than that of simply amusing the audience. The humor is characteristically an ironic humor that serves several purposes, not the least of which is that of saving the play from collapsing under the weight of Jimmy's self-pity and self-concern. Ironic humor provides distance, both for the audience from Jimmy and for Jimmy from his obsessive concerns. And this is of major importance in a play that is in many ways about the recurring problem the characters confront of relating their private lives to the urgent social issues Jimmy repeatedly raises. As Helena at one point exclaims in exasperation, "Jimmy, can we have one day, just one day, without tumbling over religion or politics?" (98). Jimmy's humor at his own, as well as everyone else's, expense prevents him from coming across as either an obsessive narcissist or an ideological fanatic. The humor serves, in effect, both to complicate his perspective and to establish a connection between the diverse issues that alternately command his attention. And this process of connecting

diversity rather than converting it to uniformity is of both structural and thematic significance to a play that exhibits an innovative approach to some
aggressively challenged conventions. But it is the nature of those conventions
and the room they leave for establishing alternatives that helps us recognize
what Osborne was trying to achieve by mixing rather than merging attitudes,
aims, and anxieties.

When Alison abandons Jimmy midway through the play, she leaves him
a note that concludes with "I shall always have a deep, loving need of you—
Alison" (90). The rhetoric of the letter, as much as the decision to leave, makes
Jimmy furious, and he denounces its civilized sentimentality as characteristic
of a homogenizing way of life and of writing plays for which he has complete
contempt. "Deep, loving need! I never thought she was capable of being as
phoney as that! [*To Helena.*] What is that—a line from one of those plays
you've been in?" (90). Jimmy would have much preferred, had Alison been
intent on leaving, that she emphasize, rather than diminish, their differences by
denouncing him as she feels he deserves: "Deep loving need! That makes me
'puke! . . . She couldn't say 'You rotten bastard! I hate your guts, I'm clearing out, and I hope you rot!' No, she has to make a polite, emotional mess out
of it!" (90).

It is, of course, the kind of play that presents "a polite, emotional mess"
that Osborne is trying very hard not to write. Both Jimmy's biting savagery and
his ironic humor give this play a tonal range, and with it a range of implication,
that lies beyond that characteristic of plays, particularly Rattigan's plays, that
immediately preceded Osborne's on the London stage. The genteel delicacy
and reserved nostalgia of the characters in Rattigan's *Separate Tables* (1954),
for example, provide an illuminating contrast with what Osborne was trying to
achieve with his oddly structured play. Whatever the virtues of Rattigan's plays
(and there were many that Osborne overlooked), they often depicted characters whose determination to cope in difficult circumstances exemplified the
civic virtues characteristic of a widely unified and steadily expanding country
in which everyone was expected to do his/her social duty for the greater good
of all. However, once English society, after World War II, began to lose both
its sense of external destiny and its sense of internal unity, well-mannered
acceptance of one's diminished lot seemed, to Jimmy, as to Osborne, a betrayal
of social responsibility rather than a salutary example of it. The cheerful malice and savage humor of Jimmy Porter are thus Osborne's ways of widening
the range of response of a country in increasing trouble and unable or unwilling to confront it. But this widening of the range of awareness of an increasingly divided society brings with it structural problems, not the least of which
are those of focus and direction, that have left their mark on the play in general
and upon Jimmy in particular.

One cannot, of course, deal with the structural imbalances of *Look Back
in Anger* without relating them to the widespread acknowledgment that

Osborne's plays are often "state of England" plays. While the thematic implications of that concern have been widely recognized, the structural implications have received much less attention. Yet Osborne's determination to
grapple with the difficulties of writing a play about England at a time of radical national change is precisely what has precipitated the odd disjunction
between the play's historical importance and its apparent structural infelicities. The key difficulty such a play confronts is that of preparing a canvas
large enough to deal with the diversity of national themes without thereby
losing the dramatic intensity generated by detailed attention to particular
characters. The difficulty of reconciling individual and social concerns is
thus an awkward issue both for characters seeking to impose some shape on
their lives and for the author trying to establish an appropriate shape for the
play. And it is only if we recognize the structural complexity of the situation
Osborne was exploring that we will be able to make sense of the mixed
moods, shifting contexts, and inconsistent arguments of a play that seeks to
deal with a national situation by focussing the action primarily upon an idiosyncratic character whose voice is clearly not meant to function as a representative one.

   To clarify the peculiar structural role of Jimmy in the play, we might consider again the structure of Rattigan's *Separate Tables*. In that double bill of
one-act plays, Rattigan locates his characters in a state of England context by
placing them in a residential hotel in the seaside resort of Bournemouth. The
hotel location provides a convenient site of intersection for the lives and experiences of a variety of English people whose current interaction reveals both
the diversity of their pasts and the common rules of social exchange that English society has taught them to observe. The key tensions in the two plays are
generated directly from the gaps that open between the competing claims of
the public and the private, the social and the individual, and the past and the
present in a postwar England no longer able to sustain a narrative of national
destiny that would serve to bridge its various social divisions.

   Within the framework provided by a community rhetoric of "deep, loving need" and a shared set of rules for public decorum, the plays are beauti-
fully structured, and they provide a painfully revealing exploration of the
necessity for and inadequacy of self-sacrifice in a world in imminent decline.
But, for Osborne, the plays lack the range and intensity of feeling that are
needed to deal with an England whose decline should not be sadly recognized
and nobly accepted but be angrily resisted with a range and intensity of
response commensurate with the impending loss. And the outraged voice of
protest is to be a means of registering not just a sense of personal deprivation,
but also a sense of what becomes central to the play: intergenerational responsibility and betrayal.

   When Jimmy looks back in anger, he is generationally situated as a voice
of contemporary youth even as he is personally agonizing over the deaths of

his father and his best friend's mother, struggling to come to terms with the hostility of his wife's father and mother, and grappling unsuccessfully with the implications of his and Alison's own imminent and aborted parenthood. To pursue the thematic implications of this generational approach to the state of England issue, we need to recognize how Osborne decided to deal with it structurally. Clearly it would have been possible for Osborne to follow Rattigan (and even Brecht) and widen the social canvas to give more time to opposing points of view and to include characters from a broader range of society. The danger would immediately be that the more characters and the more widely representative the characters the less room there would be for detailed presentation, in-depth exploration, and convincing dramatization of the complex authenticity of any individual character's response to England's changing world. What Osborne does instead, at great risk to the structure of his play, is to establish not one hotel room but one sensibility, that of Jimmy Porter, as the site upon which the generational crosscurrents of declining English society would be tracked. The gains would be the intensity of a detailed and lengthy personal response. The potential losses would be those of balance, representativeness, and persuasiveness. And it is precisely in terms of those apparent strengths and weaknesses that the play has widely been received. But if we are to do the play justice, we need to see clearly what Osborne managed to achieve by establishing a single idiosyncratic sensibility as his site of dramatic engagement with England's assorted and accumulating ills.

As we have noted, we will understand little of Jimmy's erratic and explosive behavior if we do not begin with a recognition that when critiquing the lives of other characters as well as himself, he is engaged as much with a national situation as with personal relationships. But he is no allegorical figure, and the play is not one of abstract analysis or general illustration. Osborne's effort throughout is to make Jimmy's response to the England invoked both idiosyncratically excessive and generally revealing. Jimmy functions in the play not by being balanced, authoritative, and right, but by raising in inflammatory ways questions that remain troubling even when the idiosyncracy of their formulation has been acknowledged. And this is, of course, the source of Jimmy's appeal even to those characters and members of the audience who are likely to find him the most objectionable.

Alison, Colonel Redfern, and Helena, in turn, acknowledge not that Jimmy is right but that some of his concerns should also be their concerns. In a manner doubtless calculated to outrage an audience, they all acknowledge, grudgingly or otherwise, that they have learnt something from him. Jimmy, however, is neither ideologue nor prophet. His generational claims to attention are that he is English and young, at a time when being young in England had acquired an historical and cultural resonance whose significance becomes clearer with each passing year. What was already evident in the '50s was that the naturally expanding contexts of youth were confronting the rapidly narrowing contexts of a country in decline.[4] The general tendency for the ambitions of youth to exceed its grasp was thus given particular historical resonance by recurring reminders that, for many members of an earlier generation, England provided a much more advantageous situation in which to grow up. And the odd mixture of sympathy and savagery that characterizes Jimmy's attitude to Alison's father captures an ambivalence about intergenerational perspectives that becomes central to the play:

> I hate to admit it, but I think I can understand how her Daddy must have felt when he came back from India, after all those years away. The old Edwardian brigade do make their brief little world look pretty tempting. All home-made cakes and croquet, bright ideas, bright uniforms. Always the same picture: high summer, the long days in the sun, slim volumes of verse, crisp linen, the smell of starch. What a romantic picture. Phoney too, of course. It must have rained sometimes. Still, even I regret it somehow, phoney or not. If you've no world of your own, it's rather pleasant to regret the passing of someone else's. I must be getting sentimental. But I must say it's pretty dreary living in the American Age—unless you're an American of course. Perhaps all our children will be Americans. That's a thought isn't it? (11)

It is only Jimmy's sustained irony that enables him to share the colonists' sense of loss without sharing their views on colonization, to sustain that sense of loss while suggesting that much of what was lost wasn't real in the first place, and to strike an international chord of disapproval of America's increasing prominence that continues to echo even as the envy generated by an England in decline is openly confessed. But the complex ironies that provide a degree of credibility to his vehement intergenerational judgments also serve to open a gap between Jimmy's passions and his actions that bears directly upon his odd role in the play.

    Though Jimmy establishes the note of generational responsibility and generational change by holding his parents' generation responsible for losing its grasp on national destiny, for bequeathing to the next generation no world of its own, he appears to have no clear plans for doing something constructive about it. He is certainly prepared to denounce his own generation for getting too used too readily to a diminished role in the world, and one of his recurring gripes is that "Nobody thinks, nobody cares. No beliefs, no convictions and no enthusiasm" (10). Indeed, Jimmy's attacks on Alison repeatedly focus on what he perceives as her lethargy, her timidity, and her readiness to accept whatever comes her way: "She's a great one for getting used to things. If she were to die, and wake up in paradise—after the first five minutes, she'd have got used to it" (10). This is a tendency widespread enough for Jimmy to recognize it in himself (33), but Jimmy's denunciations are usually strengthened rather than weakened by his recognition of dangers to which he too is subject. In his recurring bouts of condemnation, Jimmy exhibits more of an enthusiasm for thinking and caring about issues and people than for acting upon any beliefs and convictions that might significantly change people's lives or the historical direction of England. Though Jimmy is outraged when his friend Hugh decides to emigrate, he cannot produce for Hugh, any more than for himself, a promising English alternative. Jimmy's sense of national duty seems to require him to bear outraged witness to an unalterable national decline, but not necessarily to intervene. He has made no attempt to establish a career, join a political group, or become socially involved in any systematic way.

Jimmy's inability to do anything about the problems that concern him diminishes but does not destroy the credibility of his judgments and the persuasiveness of his enthusiasms, but more important is the light it sheds on the dramatic function of a character whose idiosyncratic sensibility provides the site of dramatization rather than the source of solution to the issues the play confronts. In effect, Jimmy serves more as a means of identifying and amplifying national problems than as a likely instrument of their solution. His role in the play is consequently not just that of a character with relationships to other characters on stage but also that of an historical voice seeking to relate events occurring here and now to those that occurred earlier or elsewhere. The large cast of characters who never appear thus serves as one of several means of broadening the implied context of a play whose implications become more extensive as the action progresses.

Across the stage of Jimmy's emotional outrage and rhetorical amplification run the assorted social ills of a difficult moment in English history that Jimmy, in effect, helps both to shape and define. It is a world in which disintegrating empire leaves the country with a sense of decline and guilt; one in which bewildered voters return to power (in 1951) the establishment party in place of the party of social reform; Christians trample upon each other to express their residual spiritual enthusiasms; bishops give speeches to support the manufacture of hydrogen bombs; literary critics squabble over historical trivia rather than cultural substance; and the young subside into resignation, alienation, or emigration. The picture presented is biased, distorted, and exaggerated, but sufficiently true to speak of a generation, though not necessarily for them. But this recognition returns us to one of the vexed problems presented by this putatively historical voice; while generationally engaged, it is not generationally well-situated, for it is neither internally consistent nor externally representative.

To criticize Osborne, however, for appointing the inconsistent Jimmy as the voice of a generation whose views he does not share is not yet to have come to terms with the precarious status of representative voices in a society that is increasingly divided. As a consequence of the discrediting of inherited narratives of national destiny, the world that Jimmy speaks in and for is one whose expectations of consensus foundered early on an increasing recognition of irreconcilable conflicts between people of different ages, classes, genders, education, wealth, religion, and politics. Jimmy himself both exhibits and amplifies some of those conflicts, alternately loving and despising women, attaching himself to Alison while rejecting her social origins, declaring affinity with gay rebels while anticipating that he will be a target of their wrath, trying to overcome the instant dislike Hugh and Alison have for each other, hoping to forge a bond between Alison and Mrs. Tanner, and sympathizing with Alison's father while savagely rejecting her brother:

> Have you ever seen her brother? Brother Nigel? The straight-backed, chinless wonder from Sandhurst? . . . you've never heard so many well-bred commonplaces come from beneath the same bowler hat. The Platitude from Outer Space—that's brother Nigel. He'll end up in the Cabinet one day, make no mistake. But somewhere at the back of that mind is the vague knowledge that he and his pals have been plundering and fooling everybody for generations. (14)

This is, of course, a very different view of England's military might and political establishment than that exhibited in his response to the career of Colonel Redfern. But Jimmy's inconsistencies are not mere inconsistencies. They are symptomatic of the divided perspectives that characterize both his function as an intergenerational historical voice and his function as a generationally situated character in the play.

The polyvalent Jimmy Porter voice that constantly threatens to drown out those of Alison, Cliff, and Helena is the voice of a larger than life character who functions for his own generation not as someone just like them or as someone completely remote from them, but as someone who seems something of a monster in their midst. They share his Englishness, his youth, and his concerns, but not the fury or the fatalism that give the country's problems for him such power, proportion, and preposterousness. But the odd dynamic of the interaction between Jimmy and the other characters, a dynamic described by Osborne as an "*uneasy polyphony*" (2), is characterized less by disagreements over substance than by disproportion of scale. Though Jimmy rails about politics and religion, he neither addresses nor offers arguments of political or religions scope. And a play that focusses extensively on issues related to empire and equity is also likely at any moment to deal with sweet stalls, tabloid gossip, and jazz bands. These oscillations between events of contrasting scale are partly the consequence of the ironic humor Jimmy adopts throughout the play, but they also prepare the way for a puzzlingly downbeat ending about stuffed squirrels and toy bears. Somewhere in this downbeat ending the concerns of Jimmy as divided historical voice and Jimmy as divided character merge, as personal, national, and cultural reasons for uncertainty and inaction lead inexorably toward issues of diminished scale.

From the outset, issues of historical change, social division, and diminished scale are given visual linkage in a stage setting that situates Jimmy and the other characters in a world of multiple transitions. The scene, we are told, is set in the present with Jimmy and Alison living in "*a fairly large attic room, at the top of a large Victorian house*" (1). The attic room is full of old furniture, some of it from the Victorian era, and its ceiling slopes down sharply to increase the sense of displacement, confinement, and constraint in an otherwise significant space. As Alison later on recalls the evenings she spent with Jimmy in this room, she describes them as "suspended and rather remote" (109). This constrained attic setting with its substantial Victorian foundations gives visual form to one of the unbridgeable and unacceptable historical divisions in Jimmy's life. Alison's and Helena's clothes, when the two are living with Jimmy, register similarly unbridgeable and unacceptable class divisions. Both wear an odd mixture of their own expensive clothes and Jimmy's more utilitarian ones. The Sunday ritual of reading the newspapers provides more examples of the social divisions that drive Jimmy to distraction, and his rhetorical question, "Why do I do this every Sunday?" (3),gives formal shape to a question generated by the whole set, by Jimmy's biting irony, and by much of the early action: why does Jimmy situate his personal life so insistently in the context of England's social history and social divisions?

It is central to the evolving relationship between Jimmy as intergenerational voice and Jimmy as generational character that we recognize that there are personal and not just historical reasons for Jimmy's insistence, in opposing Hugh's decision to emigrate and elsewhere, upon the importance of living nowhere else but England, even at a time when national issues generate more pain than pleasure. Jimmy has an evident personal need to maintain links with earlier generations of English people, whose strengths and weaknesses provide an inheritance with which he feels obliged to come to terms. And coming to terms with that inheritance involves the constant adjustments of scale that complicate Jimmy's life and the lives of everyone else who is haunted by issues of historical consequence and proportion.

The personal basis for Jimmy's intergenerational concerns can be traced back to the early death of his father, and to attend to that story is to encounter some of the reasons why Jimmy's anger is not matched by his actions, and to understand why the intensity of his concerns might captivate other members of his own generation who, though not sharing his anger, feel compelled to respect it. Jimmy had a father who believed there were still, even after the slaughter of the first World War, causes good enough to fight for and collective actions worthy of individual support. In the 1930s he joined in good faith the International Brigade that set out to rescue Spain from fascist domination. He returned, seriously wounded and defeated, to find that his idealistic efforts were greeted not with gratitude, but with doubt and suspicion.

Jimmy then felt the full force of his father's disillusionment and defeat at an age when both were likely to make a large and lasting impression:

> For twelve months, I watched my father dying—when I was ten years old. He'd come back from the war in Spain, you see. And certain god-fearing gentlemen there had made such a mess of him, he didn't have long left to live. Everyone knew it—even I knew it. . . . But . . . I was the only one who cared. (*Turns to the window.*) His family were embarrassed by the whole business. Embarrassed and irritated. . . . All that that feverish failure of a man had to listen to him was a small, frightened boy. I spent hour upon hour in that tiny bedroom. He would talk to me for hours, pouring out all that was left of his life to one, lonely, bewildered little boy, who could barely understand half of what he said. All he could feel was the despair and the bitterness; the sweet, sickly smell of a dying man. (*He moves around the chair.*) You see, I learnt at an early age what it was to be angry—angry and helpless. And I can never forget it. (Sits.) I knew more about—love . . . betrayal . . . and death, when I was ten years old than you will probably ever know all your life. (68–70)

Though Jimmy's recurring self-concern and self-pity are as evident here as elsewhere, they do not suffice to eradicate the impact of his experience on the dramatic situation emerging in the play. Jimmy as an individual character, as distinct from Jimmy as an amplifying voice, has personal as well as historical reasons for doubting the value of radical social intervention. His father's death provides the testimony of experience to oppose any testimony youth might offer that strenuous effort will produce its just reward or be its own reward. But worse than that, what the death of his father exemplifies is what the slaughter of world war had exemplified and would exemplify again: that the scale of the effort needed to produce significant change is not proportionate to the probability of success or to whatever might be conceived as constituting success. The death of Jimmy's father provided an early personal encounter with a widely resisted public recognition of the appalling individual costs involved in national responsibilities or national ambitions of imperial scale. And behind the issue of competing public and personal scales lurk questions both about the value of imperial victories so dearly bought and about the value of less visible achievements more locally situated and enjoyed. If no newly defined England could hope to match the scale of achievement that the efforts of earlier generations had, however ill advisedly, produced, what could or should serve, instead, to satisfy the youthful aspirations and ambitions of succeeding generations?

When Colonel Redfern left England in 1914 and returned in 1947, the dates mark key points in the national transition between counting gains and counting costs for large ambitions in the world. Colonel Redfern returns to an

England widely regarded as "going to the dogs" (83) but unable to sustain by moral argument or force of arms the scale of its earlier achievements. It is this problem of historical transition and historical scale that makes the English condition in this moment difficult for the generation growing old to accept, but even more difficult, as we have noted, for the young to deal with.

Jimmy as historically situated character is most fully in tune with his own generation when he addresses the issue of being young in England in the period after the second World War. His early comment that their "youth is slipping away" (8) captures a feeling that all the younger characters, in different ways, share. When Alison tries to explain to Helena why she married Jimmy, she describes the youthful fire that seemed to emanate from him and elevate him beyond his much less historically aware peers:

> It had been such a lovely day, and he'd been in the sun. Everything about him seemed to burn, his face, the edges of his hair glistened and seemed to spring off his head, and his eyes were so blue and full of the sun. He looked so young and frail, in spite of the tired line of his mouth. I knew I was taking on more than I was ever likely to be capable of bearing, but there never seemed to be any choice. (50–51)

Later, alone with Cliff, pregnant, and near despair, she responds to Cliff's argument that she is "too young to start giving up" (26) with a despairing acknowledgement that youth has little purchase in a world of inherited decline:

> I keep looking back, as far as I remember, and I can't think what it was to feel young, really young. Jimmy said the same thing to me the other day. I pretended not to be listening—because I knew that would hurt him, I suppose. And—of course—he got savage, like tonight. But I knew just what he meant. (26)

The larger implications of Alison's "I knew just what he meant" help her understand his savagery and help bind all the younger characters to each other whatever their differences. To be young in an aging country is to lose too early the possibilities that youth might otherwise supply and to encounter too early losses that age more regularly supplies. As Jimmy puts it, "I seem to spend my life saying goodbye" (104). But this is a process Jimmy can neither escape nor accept, and his ill-focussed rage is often an expression of the conflict between acceptance of the necessity for change and intolerance of its implications. Alison first regards Jimmy as someone whose youthful vigor can transcend the problem, and then as someone whose mercurial behavior can at least authentically exhibit it, but eventually she comes to see him, as the action of the play suggests we see him, as someone whose idiosyncratic way of dealing with the problem raises further possibilities. And it is in defining the nature of these further possibilities and their relationship to problems of scale that the action of the play clarifies the representative status of Jimmy's otherwise unrepresentative voice.

Alison admires the rigor but is exhausted by the consequences of Jimmy's determination to resist false narratives of national destiny without opposing them with some new one of his own. Jimmy's "blistering honesty" is the honesty, however intemperate, of someone who refuses either to disguise or dismiss temporal and social divisions but seeks to affirm them and try to live through them. Just as he insists upon Alison denouncing him if she feels justified in leaving him, he wants all his relationships to work through their local complexities, rather than work around them in the false name of historically characterized romance or nationally defined destiny. This determination to confront local differences is not for Jimmy a means of destroying larger patterns, but the only means by which he can sustain the possibility that larger patterns might eventually emerge.

Discussing with Helena the rather visible affection she shares with Cliff, Alison tries to describe the relationship in Jimmy's terms:

> It isn't easy to explain. It's what he would call a question of allegiances, and he expects you to be pretty literal about them. Not only about himself and all the things he believes in, his present and his future, but his past as well. All the people he admires and loves, and has loved. The friends he used to know, people I've never even known—and probably wouldn't have liked. His father, who died years ago. Even the other women he's loved. (46–47)

Though Jimmy's self-concern often borders on the insufferable, it is not without its social implications. Relationships survive for Jimmy not on the basis of traditional rights that disguise differences of opinion and value but on the basis of shared achievements that provide bridges across persisting differences. And here Jimmy's attitude strikes Alison as both timely and persuasive:

> Helena—even I gave up believing in the divine rights of marriage long ago. Even before I met Jimmy. They've got something different now—constitutional monarchy. You are where you are by consent. (109)

Such consent does not constitute a permanent commitment, but a repeatedly renewable one, and the implications of that renewal raise in another context the issue of scale that recurs throughout the action. Jimmy wants relationships to be contingent and contractual, but also to exceed their local origins and endure. As Alison points out, Jimmy wants to hold onto everyone he has ever loved, even as he wants love to be based upon freedom, contingency, and ever-revisable consent. He wants relationships to dictate their own terms but also to achieve a depth of intensity and breadth of scale if they are to be significant to him. And startlingly, this peculiar conjunction of convictions results in Jimmy's wife and Jimmy's lover both characterizing the play's most icono-clastic figure as something of an anachronism:

> HELENA: He was born out of his time.
> ALISON: Yes. I know.
> HELENA: There's no place for people like that any longer—in sex, or politics, or anything. That's why he's so futile. Sometimes, when I listen to him, I feel he thinks he's still in the middle of the French Revolution. And that's where he ought to be, of course. He doesn't know where he is, or where he's going. He'll never do anything, and he'll never amount to anything.
> ALISON: I suppose he's what you'd call an Eminent Victorian. Slightly comic— win a way. . . . (111)

Slightly comic, of course, not just became of his anachronistic status but also because his concern for historical scale impels him to live his personal life in impossibly public terms, because his uncompromising investment in genera-tional responsibility sustains the very sense of Englishness that he seems oth-erwise to despise, and because his impossible demands are uttered with the self-deprecating irony of someone who recognizes that his determination to define himself as a lost cause is both a contemporary indulgence and a histori-cal necessity.

Though Jimmy is, indeed, something of an anachronism, he manages not to be a mere anachronism. Somehow, his intergenerational concerns enable him to function simultaneously as a voice of outraged youth, a voice of semi-skeptical modern nostalgia, and a voice of imperious Victorian expectation. The divided voice is divided not just by differing values, but by differing senses of what suffices to constitute value. The differing value judgments of different eras, the differing expectations of what individual action can accom-plish, and the differing scales for judging what gives an individual life suffi-cient shape and sufficient point make Jimmy's attempts to amalgamate them impossible. Such incompatibilities of both substance and scale are amplified by Jimmy's rhetoric and given visual and aural exemplification in the contrast established between the church bells, whose chimes drive Jimmy to distraction every Sunday, and the jazz trumpet that he plays to drown them out. In the dif-fering balance they invoke between convention and innovation and in their sig-nificant differences of size and scale, the huge bells and the jazz trumpet offer very different possibilities for individual improvisation and control. And the comic contrast between these competing sounds returns us to the significance of the play's similarly comic ending in which toy squirrels and bears supply a complex context of diminished scale to earlier issues of much larger moment.

Helena is startled when she first encounters the stuffed teddy bear and squirrel in the Porter's flat, and even more startled when she learns that they have an established role in the Alison/Jimmy relationship. Alison explains it at first in terms of sheer escapism:

> ALISON: It started during those first months we had alone together—after Hugh went abroad. It was the one way of escaping from everything—a sort of unholy priest-hole of being animals to one another. We could become little furry creatures with little furry brains. Full of dumb, uncomplicated affection for each other. Playful, careless creatures in their own cosy zoo for two. (54)

And it is in just these terms that we see Jimmy and Alison playing this game with each other early in the play. The localizing of context and concern is indeed a temporary means of escape from the brawling over large scale issues of politics and religion. When Jimmy and Alison return to the game at the play's conclusion, however, it is in the generational context of their lost child and recent separation. No longer a means of escaping their problems, the game becomes a means of renewing a relationship whose complexities have become more apparent to them both. The game is no longer a mere escape from the past or an avoidance of the present but a means of engaging the future through a painful but pleasurable *"comic emphasis"* (119) on the value of the divided perspectives that they both now ruefully acknowledge. Their mutual sympathy and individual differences are exhibited in the remarks "Poor squirrels" and "Poor bears" (119). Their reconciliation is one that takes as its point of departure a *"mocking, tender irony"* (119) that is less negative than Jimmy's earlier savage irony and more authentic than the simplistic platitudes of Nigel and his like. In its tender acknowledgement of difference, the reconciliation offers a means of accommodating without equating differing scales of value, expectation, and duration, of coping with local situations saturated with larger generational concerns, of resisting false optimism and premature despair, of deciding to build, with whatever difficulty, from here.

Whether we think that this registers for Jimmy a significant defeat or a significant victory depends on how we evaluate the anger and aggressiveness he was earlier seeking to validate. To be young and English in the 1950s was for him to be trapped, as the Victorian attic setting suggests, in the debris of a dying civilization that not only restricted one's present but nurtured and contaminated one's roots. To live in any way, it was necessary, as Jimmy intermittently recognized, to die in some way. And the transition Jimmy and Alison undergo in the play is one of lowering the scale of imperial expectations in order to sustain any expectations at all. Their adjustment is indeed to one of reconciliation with the smaller world to which Jimmy is initially so opposed, but what is at issue is the nature of the reconciliation that Jimmy had so far steadfastly resisted. For it is the assumption that reduction in scale must imply a reduction in substance that has made Jimmy so frantically determined to affirm both local authenticity and larger significance, with or without an accompanying irony. The most famous lines of the play address directly the shift of national scale and its personal implications, but as we noted earlier, they are spoken in Jimmy's "*familiar, semi-serious mood*":

> There aren't any good, brave causes left. If the big bang does come, and we all get killed off, it won't be in aid of the old-fashioned, grand design. It'll just be for the Brave New-nothing-very-much-thank-you. About as pointless and inglorious as stepping in front of a bus. (104–5)

The challenge for the Jimmy/Alison generation as it succeeded that of its parents is to find some point to a world no longer glorious, to find a way beyond demanding or denouncing glory on an imperial scale, to find some means of measuring value that does not reduce to triviality, or worse, whatever is available in contexts of diminished scale.

Jimmy's "*semi-serious*" speech on good, brave causes is, in fact, precipitated by his acknowledgement that he would be prepared to sacrifice his friendship with Cliff to any woman whose romantic potential might provide in the personal realm a scale of experience that earlier generations enjoyed in the public realm. Jimmy, in characteristic fashion, both affirms and denies the possibility:

> It's a funny thing. You've been loyal, generous and a good friend. But I'm quite prepared to see you wander off, find a new home, and make out on your own. And all because of something I want from that girl downstairs, something I know in my heart she's incapable of giving. You're worth a half a dozen Helenas to me or to anyone. And, if you were in my place, you'd do the same thing. . . . Why, why, why, why do we let these women bleed us to death? . . . I suppose people of our generation aren't able to die for good causes any longer. We had all that done for us, in the thirties and the forties, when we were still kids. *(In his familiar, semi-serious mood.)* There aren't any good, brave causes left. . . . there's nothing left for it, me boy, but to let yourself be butchered by the women. (104–5)

Jimmy's characteristic irony both elevates and deflates what romance so conceived has to offer, and his actions are likewise inconsistent. Within minutes he is planning to make a new start to his life with Helena (107), later accepting her departure with resignation, then trying to reestablish his relationship with Alison through the squirrel and bear routine. But there is much to suggest that both Jimmy and Alison have learned something in the process. The reconciliation is, in effect, one that takes as given what the squirrel and bear game suggests: the smaller scale, more local context, and less grandiose expectations of a life in which personal relationships are not to be measured primarily on an imperial scale of public achievement. But this adjustment to the smaller scale is no longer treated as a matter of temporary escapism or long-term defeat. This context is treated more as a point of departure than as a necessary destination. The shared irony at the end neither precludes nor predicts significant depth, devotion, or duration, but it clearly suggests that matters of personal scale need be dominated neither by the national narratives of earlier generations nor by the diminished contexts of this. Furthermore, in establishing the issue of diminished scale as central to the play's conclusion, Osborne made the personal concerns of Jimmy and the national concerns of England resonate with larger cultural concerns whose implications have become clearer with the passing of time, but particularly with the performance and publication of his final play, *Déjàvu*.

Dealing with life in intergeneratinal terms gives the Jimmy of 1956 many problems, not the least of which is an uncertainty over the scale of the picture he needs to draw to make sense of his own life. His efforts to think intergenerationally put him at odds with his own generation and its inclination to narrow its concerns to what it can actually control. Jimmy's idiosyncratic voice achieves a larger resonance by resisting, initially, the retreat to smaller pictures and smaller values and, subsequently, the equation of smaller pictures with smaller values. *Look Back in Anger* achieved its initial impact in part because the depiction of historically situated and idiosyncratically articulated youthful alienation was able to speak beyond its historical moment by being so thoroughly situated in its historical moment. The role of Jimmy as amplifying voice increased the impact of Jimmy the historically situated character by relating it to and giving it implications for other youthful moments. But Osborne had his finger on the pulse of history in more ways than one. In recognizing that the issue of changing scale was as important to Jimmy as any issue of substance (Jimmy juxtaposes "pointless and inglorious"), he was tracing a larger cultural shift from the large ambitions of both Victorians and modernists toward those lower-scale ambitions of the postmodernists that were to come. Jimmy, a threshold character, was caught in a dilemma that we are only now beginning to be able to articulate, but which we can see much more clearly because of Osborne's 1991 sequel to the play, *Déjàvu*.

Much of the discussion of postmodernism as a cultural category or historical moment has hinged upon a disagreement over the implications of the term itself. As many have pointed out, the sense of a new era is conveyed by the term "post," but to describe the new era as "post" the one before is to anchor it to what it appears to transcend. This ambiguity in the term is further exacerbated by a famous argument from Jean-François Lyotard that postmodernism is not something that succeeds modernism but is, in fact, a recurring aspect of it.[5] Whether postmodernism precedes, accompanies, or succeeds a modernism itself very difficult to define has thus become a major bone of contention, one that puts at particular risk those who seek to discuss postmodernism primarily in terms of documents with some new kind of style that have appeared only in recent years.

To avoid that limiting presupposition and to consider postmodernism continually in its relationship to modernism is to adopt precisely the kind of inter-era/intergenerational perspective that makes Jimmy Porter's voice so powerful, so inconsistent, and so surprisingly authentic in *Look Back in Anger*. Indeed, one of the early theorists of postmodernism, Ihab Hassan, argued, in a famous essay, both that postmodernism marks a decisive break with modernism and that, in spite of the radical nature of period transitions, we are all something of Victorians, modernists, and postmodernists at once.[6]

To take such a view is to recognize that the divided perspective and intergenerational concerns of Jimmy Porter capture not just something of the youth of a particular character or of a moment in the decline of a particular nation but also something of a moment of cultural transition, one that has resonance for everyone concerned with what comes after modernism as a cultural movement and with what should happen to the modernist social values that accompanied it. Osborne's peculiarly structured play, with its insistent focus upon the divided sensibility of a central character, achieved and retains its historical importance because of the resonance it establishes between personal, political, and cultural issues at a moment of triple transition. In each of the three spheres, relationships between successive generations, competing values, and shifting scales are of central importance. Indeed, the issue of contrasting scales, so evident in the play's concluding images of squirrels and bears, marks a key difference between the Victorian/modernism transition, where it was a less important issue, and the modernism/postmodernism transition where it becomes an obsessive concern. Much of Lyotard's famous argument hinges upon the lost credibility of large unifying community narratives and upon their replacement by local group commitments of limited scope and durability. Cultural change, so conceived, intersects with the trajectory of post-imperial England's social change to generate Jimmy's persistent anger about the (often unwitting) betrayal by the previous generation and about his own generation's acquiescence, timidity, and general lack of aggression and enthusiasm. In *Déjàvu,* written thirty-five years later, Osborne voices his worst fears of where things might be headed, rather than the qualified hopes exemplified in the final pages of *Look Back in Anger*.

In *Déjàvu* (1991) Jimmy Porter is thirty years older and has found a way of surviving, even of thriving, but in a characteristically idiosyncratic fashion, rather than one he might recommend to anyone else. Still a determinedly unrepresentative figure, he is, he argues, "a spokesman for no one but myself."[7] Jimmy's marriage to Alison has ended in divorce, and much of the action of the play is devoted to Jimmy directing at the children of his second marriage the same scathing, but not always unsympathetic, irony that he once inflicted upon his parent's generation. The toy bear, which had once suggested the positive possibilities of life at a reduced scale, now exhibits only the negative possibilities of narrowness, conformity, political correctness, and stunted growth. Though seriously interested in such things as "meaningful relationships" (11), Teddy has been encouraged to avoid unusual "forms of self-expression" (86), to indulge only in "safe sex" (12), to consider himself a likely victim of oppression (74), to seek redress in a "European Court of Teddy Rights" (85), to degenerate into a "cuddly conformist" (63), to aspire no higher than "mediocrity" (101), and, in effect, to exemplify what J.P. regards as the worst of the post-Jimmy generation:

> CLIFF: Damn it, J.P., he's only human—
> J.P.: Damn *you,* that's just what he's not. It's what he's been told. (85)

The usual layers of irony confirm that from Jimmy's point of view, the possibility of building from the local something larger has collapsed into a collective myopia that diminishes both the scale and substance of the next generation's concerns. Oblivious to the potential virtues of the intergenerational perspective that has characterized, divided, and tormented his own life, the next generation deals with generational change, social diversity, and cultural transition by developing fashionable and fleeting means of unifying the otherwise un-unifiable. To Jimmy, the new generation seems determined to compromise its way into consensus, to become "unconnected to the past" (64) in general, and even to "erase the past" (83) whenever it suggests reasons for dissatisfaction with the current state of affairs.

The self-congratulatory disruption that Jimmy sought to impose upon his own quietly divided generation has little purchase on the next generation, which, to Jimmy's mind, has abandoned self-determination and individual responsibility for collective counselling, "sloppy fads" (57), mass opinion, "mob philanthropy" (75), and unearned European solidarity. The unifying imperial narrative of English destiny that pressured individuals to elevate their concerns to the rhetorical levels of the few born to lead have given way to random narratives that briefly unify otherwise disparate groups by appealing to the lowest common denominator, to the life of least disruption, to the path of least resistance. Jimmy's summarizing image is of mass attendance at a pop concert at which the audience members engage in a collective wave motion to exhibit the coherence and comfort of a "wave new world" (34). As church bells once more ring out in the background, Jimmy's critique of the succeeding generation echoes the one he had earlier made of the preceding generation: "against the noise and clamour of those who would impose their certainties upon us. God *rot* their certainties" (101).

Jimmy's daughter, Alison, spends much of the play at the ironing board once occupied by his first wife; she wears the ubiquitous earphones of a generation turned largely within rather than without, but attending within only to what has been collectively affirmed without. Jimmy's savage images of this generation, like his savage images of the preceding generation, are not without their justification, but, as the earphones suggest, his ability to attract attention has, like much else in the world, diminished sharply. To Alison, Jimmy is someone who has devoted himself to "a lifetime of useless snarling" (39), and it is evident in this play, as in *Look Back in Anger,* that Jimmy's function is to focus and amplify generational issues rather than to resolve them. And as in *Look Back in Anger,* Jimmy's idiosyncracy, inconsistency, and excess serve more to extend the play's range of awareness than to provide a model for others to follow.

Jimmy's mode of self-justification has, however, progressed one step further. The difficulty he encountered in the earlier play of affirming both the integrity of local events and the importance of imperial scale has been transformed from a baffling inconsistency into a paradoxical affirmation. In the face of a new generation's debilitating readiness to conform to fashionable narratives of many kinds, whether based upon nationality, class, gender, race, religion, or anything else, Jimmy preaches the virtues of the very inconsistency his intergenerational perspectives have repeatedly exhibited. Refusing to become anything so assimilable as "a member of the public" (9), the erstwhile jazz player argues in exasperation that "coherence isn't all," that "coherence . . . conceals as much as is revealed to the lost like me who contemplate the wreckage" (51). Jimmy revels in the "mess" of "muddled enthusiasm" (94), in the "rowdy passion" that once typified English life, and in that splendidly "English virtue" of "irony" (81), an irony that multiplies perspectives so rapidly and unceasingly that any affirmation of it is itself rendered irreducibly and comically ironic:

> *(Very crisply, like battle commands.)* Endow us with the courage of uncertainty. Accept an unruly but contrite heart. And in that frailty of disbelief we cannot overcome let us seek remedy from within ourselves and offer mercy that the world cannot give among the perils etcetera, etcetera. (101)

Jimmy's contingent affirmation of contingency parodies the style and conviction of the fashionable preacher, "the Rev. Ron" who has joined the successor to the former play's Bishop of Bromley in establishing a "liturgical leisure centre" and "liturgical café" at which various kinds of "pop chat" reassure the masses that the responsibility for aberrant behavior lies not with the individual but the state (98, 45, 76). Jimmy supplements his own characteristically modernist irony with a characteristically postmodern investment in parody to challenge both the "dumb pieties" (63) of the next generation (34–36) and whatever platitudes he feels himself inclined to offer as a substitute (49–51). To Cliff's plea for "No more questions," Jimmy retorts, "No more *answers*" (83), seeking always to situate himself intergenerationally between competing worlds. And to see Jimmy's divided sensibility as an exemplification of generational supplementation as opposed to generational supplantation is to recognize what Osborne was seeking to achieve by exploring cultural and national issues through the shifting sensibilities of an idiosyncratic and unrepresentative character. Strangely enough, it is Jimmy's very refusal to restrict his views to that of a single era, to unify his convictions into a single world view, or to align his actions with his assertions, that makes him serve as an unexpectedly successful site of dramatic engagement with the idiosyncratic shape of individual lives, the multilinear history of an evolving nation, and the contested development of a cultural process in a period of major transition.

Jimmy's inconsistency and excess mark him not as someone whose views we are expected to share, any more than the other characters share them, but as someone who provides, in spite of his many faults, a powerful and varied means of measuring those worlds that seek to exclude him. His excess, like Falstaff's in another era, prevents him from representing a world that any collectivity could occupy, but the vitality that accompanies it both measures and is measured by whatever seeks to oppose or ignore it. The "rowdy passion" that Jimmy both exemplifies and extols invokes a tradition of English irreverence that was already well established in the drama and poetry of medieval England and has persisted ever since.

Jimmy's divided sensibility provides a canvas wide enough to accommodate conflicting personal, national, and cultural issues. It shows how these issues can be mapped without being unified, can be related without being equated, can be measured without being standardized. Jimmy's determinedly intergenerational perspective exhibits inconsistencies whose virtues are clarified by an implied contrast with the costs—personal, social, and cultural—of any unified perspective, whether it be that of a generation, an era, a nation, a religion, a political philosophy, a cultural moment, or an aesthetic theory. What happens when a generation rejects too readily the voices of generations that have preceded or are succeeding it and settles for something currently fashionable is that the social divisions that generate future change are disguised rather than demolished, and a personal, national, and cultural resource is squandered. Jimmy, inconsistent and excessive, self-absorbed and generationally obsessed, seeks to be true to his own time by relating it continually and contentiously to the voices of other times. As inconsiderate of the pieties of one generation as of another, and of his own, Jimmy does, indeed, indulge in relentless "snarling," but its value depends upon its capacity to persuade us of the falseness of the hope that peace can be born of coherence, consistency, or consensus.

Osborne, by ruthlessly cataloging Jimmy Porter's faults before the action of *Look Back in Anger* begins, challenges himself to find the means of making a disagreeable voice theatrically viable and an idiosyncratic personal voice nationally and culturally functional. The revolutionary play he was soon to describe as "rather old fashioned" mixed old and new in ways that captured a pivotal moment in the history of England and a pivotal moment in the development of modernism. The theatrical function of the main character is not to provide the audience with an example for admiration or emulation but to supply an idiosyncratic site of exploration for the issues that bind and divide

citizens of a nation in flux. Like the jazz trumpet that selects from and recom-
bines a history of possibility, Jimmy Porter finds his way beyond the homogenizing imperatives and linear expectations of imperial or post-imperial scale.
His extravagant irony might indeed reduce his life to one of "useless snarling,"
but his persistent search is for a "snatch of harmony" (51) that might, like the
rhythms of the jazz trumpet and the games with squirrels and bears, resonate
both at some smaller scale and at some larger level of social and cultural development, thereby suggesting larger human bonds and more complex historical
patterns than any he can ever hope to summarize, circumscribe, or define:

> J.P.: *(Softly.)* . . . Anger is not hatred, which is what I see in all your faces. Anger
> is slow, gentle, not vindictive or full of spite. Also, it comes into the world in
> grief not grievance. . . . *(Still softly.)* "What's he angry *about*?" they used
> to ask. Anger is not *about* . . . It is mourning the unknown, the loss of what
> went before without you, it's the love another time but not this might have
> sprung on you, and greatest loss of all, the deprivation of what, even as a
> child, seemed to be irrevocably your own, your country, your birthplace, that,
> at least, is as tangible as death.
>
> *(Alison "waves" defiantly. Deliberately, J.P. removes her headphones, picks
> up the attached instrument, drops it to the floor and steps on it. It crackles
> and breaks.)*
>
> ALISON: *(Presently.)* Oh—well done, J.P.
>
> J.P.: I do try not to behave like the people I most despise. (36–37)

NOTES

[1] John Osborne, "That Awful Museum," *Twentieth Century* 169 (1961): 216.

[2] David Hare, cited in "Introduction," Hersh Zeifman and Cynthia Zimmerman,
eds., *Contemporary British Drama 1970–1990,* (London: Macmillan, 1993) 2–3. See
also Zeifman's accompanying discussion.

[3] John Osborne, *Look Back in Anger,* (New York: Bantam, 1971) 2. Subsequent
page references are to this edition.

[4] See, in particular, Jimmy's remark, "Our youth is slipping away" (8), and Alison's, "I can't think what it was to feel young, really young" (26).

[5] Jean-François Lyotard, *The Postmodern Condition: A Report on Knowledge,*
trans. Geoff Bennington and Brian Massumi, (Minneapolis, MN: U of Minnesota P,
1984) 79–82.

[6] Ihab Hassan, "Toward a Concept of Postmodernism" in *The Dismemberment of
Orpheus: Toward a Postmodern Literature,* (Madison, WI: U of Wisconsin P, 1982)
259–71.

[7] John Osborne, *Déjàvu,* (London: Faber and Faber, 1991) 97. Subsequent page
references are to this edition.

The Dumb Waiter, The Collection, The Lover, and The Homecoming: A Revisionist Approach

George E. Wellwarth

One of the few advantages of growing older is that one becomes wiser; and one of the few disadvantages of becoming wiser is that one is forced to look back in embarrassment and regret on the intellectual indiscretions of one's past. Especially if one has published them. The worst aspect of this mess, of course, is that one no more knows that one is right now than one did then. It is simply statistically more probable that the revision is more sensible than the original. It is in this spirit that I offer revised views of aspects of Pinter's *The Dumb Waiter, The Collection, The Lover,* and *The Homecoming* twenty-five years later.[1]

Among the most puzzling aspects of Pinter criticism is its extraordinary variety, ranging from disapproval through bafflement to a conviction that Pinter is one of the great modern playwrights. The last-mentioned is the most common view, leading scholars to see in Pinter's plays universal avatars of the human condition. Finding universal avatars in new writers is a little like panning for gold: all too often it turns out to be fool's gold. Unfortunately, scholars tend to be dazzled and blinded by the appearance, whereas prospectors soon have to face reality. Hence some of the extraordinary interpretations of Pinter's plays that have been foisted on us by scholars drunk on appearance instead of sobered by reality. To a certain extent this is understandable. Pinter has clearly been influenced by authors of intellectual stature, notably Beckett. It is no wonder, therefore, that he has been regarded as a playwright whose works seem to be more than meets the eye instead of the opposite and that he has become the victim of romanticizing critics who insist on seeing apocalyptic visions in his plays in much the same way that Beckett has been ludicrously misinterpreted by critics who see him as a Christian author.

I suggest that the time has come to recognize the fact that Pinter is the only critic who has made any sense of Pinter. In one of the interviews that he has given over the years Pinter, on having read to him a particularly convoluted example of *academese* and being asked to comment, replied, "I don't know what the hell he's talking about." In its way this is just as severe and just as deserved as Nigel Dennis's remarks in a review article on Martin Esslin's *The Peopled Wound* and James Hollis's *The Poetics of Silence:* ". . . writers like Mr. Esslin and Mr. Hollis . . . give no particular value to any word: when they talk of 'deep and organic connections between the multiple planes' [Esslin] or 'the world navel and vortex of all beginnings' [Hollis] they are using language with the same contempt and ignorance as the illiterate soldier who depends completely on four-letter obscenities."[2] One wonders what Pinter's comment on these two quotations would be.

However, none of this gets us any nearer to an understanding of Pinter's own view of his plays. This has, in fact, been clear from the very beginning of his career. As early as 1961 Pinter explained that his central image is a room which for him serves as an microcosm of the world. In the room people feel safe. Outside are only alien forces; inside there is warmth and light. The conflict in his plays occurs when one of the outside forces penetrates into the room and disrupts the security of its occupants. Pinter's role is that of dispassionate observer, and much of the apparent difficulty of his plays stems from the fact that he writes them as if he were eavesdropping on his characters and recording their often pointless stream of consciousness. At first glance this seems obscurantist, but, as Pinter put it elsewhere, "I only formulate conclusions after I've written the plays . . ."[3] and "I don't know what kind of characters my plays will have until they . . . well, until they are. Until they indicate to me what they are. I don't conceptualize in any way . . ."[4] This seems the exact opposite of the way a playwright of ideas works. The playwright of ideas supposedly begins with an idea or thesis and creates characters and situations to illustrate it. In other words, he works objectively. A perfect example of such a playwright would seem to have been George Bernard Shaw. Yet it was Shaw who said that it was his method to imagine characters together and then to take down their conversation. He saw himself as a stenographer recording the words of the characters he had imagined. In his mind they assumed an independent dimension and spoke of the ideas that were obsessing him at the time. Shaw even . found himself under the necessity of explaining the meaning of what he had recorded his characters as saying in lengthy prefaces to his plays afterwards. The difference in Pinter's method is that he imagines characters in a room and then asks himself what they would do; Shaw asked himself what they would say. The many different interpretations of Pinter's plays, not all of them invalid, might indicate that there *is* no "correct" interpretation, no precise meaning to his plays—only a vague allusiveness stretching tentative tentacles in obverse directions. In a letter he wrote to Peter Wood, director of the disastrous first production of *The Birthday Party,* Pinter clearly enunciated his theory of the play as a separate entity concerned only with itself. There is no connected philosophy running through his plays: each play, like each life, is an entity with no meaning beyond itself—and each play has a different meaning, just as each life has a different and self-sustaining meaning: "The play is itself. It is no other. It has its own life. . . . I take it you would like me to insert a clarification or moral judgment or author's angle on it, straight from the horse's mouth. I appreciate your desire for this but I can't do it. . . . I believe that what happens on this stage will possess a potent drainage image and a great deal of this will be visual. . . . The curtain goes up and down. Something has happened. Right? . . . Where is the comment, the slant, the explanatory note? In the play. Everything to do with the play is in the play."[5]

Pinter has often been praised for his realism, particularly for the realism of his speech patterns, and justly so. But realistic speech patterns are logically inextricably bound to realistic action; and in the light of Pinter's remarks to Wood it is worth considering what, exactly, realism in the theater is. Realism is an unfortunate term, implying, as it does, photographic reproduction, which is impossible on the stage and would be undesirable even if it were possible. Theatre is the selective exaggeration of reality. It is not reality. Only reality is. And perhaps a Warhol movie, which is consciously a precise reproduction of reality and thus supererogatory. Realism in art, as one writer has put it, "has, strictly speaking, nothing to do with life 'as it is'; it is, like expressionism or surrealism, a way of seeing things, a convention."[6] Its purpose, in other words, is to *explain.* When it attempts to explain the inexplicable it fails, of course. It cannot explain the surreal or irrational aspects of life; it cannot, in short, explain chance, the moving principle of all life. But by concentrating on the interpersonal minutiae of life it can impose the illusion of logic on it. Human beings are ultimately inscrutable in depth, even to themselves (on the surface, of course, they are perfectly clear: in life we deal in façades), but the theatre of realism gives us the comforting, if illusory assurance that human beings are explicable in depth. The spectator at a realistic play can understand the characters, what they do and what happens to them, because they are planned, squared away, and boxed-in by the God of the theatre, the playwright. Outside the theatre human beings are incomplete, mysterious even to themselves, and anything but logical. Most people feel they need relief from that—hence, theatre.

Pinter gives his audiences neither the illusion of control over life nor relief from its inscrutability. Worse: he assures them that there is neither a hidden meaning nor any superior force that might be hiding a putative meaning. Philosophically, he is, of course, following Beckett here with the sole difference that the surface reality that Beckett eschews makes Pinter's plays more ambiguous and has resulted in the strange and largely lamentable outpouring of interpretation of his works on the part of academic critics.

What is long overdue in Pinter criticism is the elimination of the philosophical façade erected to obscure the simplicity of his writing, which is to a very great extent random as far as the action is concerned and null as far as the ideas are concerned. Pinter's plays are situation pieces that encapsulate an atmosphere or mood, often vague in its specifics but emotionally pervasive, thus leaving his audiences puzzled after having been totally caught up in the action and emotion during the performance.[7] This is due to the fact that Pinter's plays are set within the context of contemporary reality, upon which they depend for their form and content and to which they refer; but they exist *in vacuo* as exemplary slices of reality but without the stresses and far-reaching interconnected motives of everyday reality as we know it. Nigel Dennis in his review essay[8] rather harshly describes Pinter's plays as acting exercises. They are much more than that, of course, but they are that too. Actors, Dennis points out, love Pinter's plays. Having played: Gus in *The Dumb Waiter,* Harry in *The Collection,* and Richard in *The Lover,* I can attest to that. The reason actors like playing Pinter gives us another clue to his dramaturgy. The plays exist by *themselves:* they are entirely self-contained entities. The actors find their characterizations in the lines. Everything is laid out for them. They do not have to worry about motivations because their motivations are obvious within the closed world of the play. To seek motivations through memory recall or through attempted connections with the external world would be ruinous to the production. There is no place in a Pinter play for the Method actor, in other words. And that is significant for an understanding of the plays since the Method actor is constantly trying to wrench the life of the play away from the author's imagination and sprinkle it with the dust of the streets, drape it with his own personal problems, and generally lower its meaning from the general to the specific.

In the light of the foregoing we can ask what, for example, *The Dumb Waiter* is about. Does the floating, motiveless situation of Ben and Gus have a meaning outside itself or is the play a mood piece contrasting deadly menace with quotidian ordinariness: a tacit commentary on "motiveless malignity" and "the banality of evil"? It is all too easy and tempting for critics seeking "profundity" and a spurious originality to interpret *The Dumb Waiter* as a variation on the theme of Godot, who, when he finally comes, turns out to be a sardonic joker sending whimsical and purposeless orders down on the dumb waiter and destroying—instead of saving—those who are bewildered by his demands for food-offerings. Or perhaps we might see the dumb waiter as being a parody of the Biblical altar from which burnt offerings are fragrantly floated up to placate an uncaring deity. Such interpretations are amusing but pointless. There is no justification in the text for this desperate lusting after symbols on the nonsensical premise that if it's good literature it *must* have symbols. The dumb waiter isn't God, and Ben and Gus are not mankind.[9] A more sensible view is that the play is about hierarchical domination, a universal aspect of the human condition as shown by the menacers menaced, the butcher butchered, and the potential rebel cut down. Gus becomes conscious of himself, he begins to wake up from the primal torpor in which he has passed his life so far, he wants to find out *what it all means;* and the search for meaning destroys him for it leaves him no belief to rely on, no explanation for anything. This has to be shown *dramatically*—hence the play. Gus is a modern Woyzeck, and the play in which he appears is a definition of life as a temporary state where domination—the exercise of power—is the supreme human motive. In a slightly higher stratum of the eternal domination hierarchy are the two mysterious intruders in *The Birthday Party* who might as well have been called Ben Goldberg and Gus McCann.[10] Like them, Ben and Gus are basically ordinary and rather amusing fellows, but, then, as we know from the newspapers, mass murderers are *always* people who were not only liked but well-liked by all who knew them.

The Collection is about the attempt to verify the story of one of the four characters to the effect that she had a one-night affair with one of the others while they were showing their collections at a dress designers' convention in the north of England. Nobody ever finds out, nobody here being the remaining two characters and the audience. *The Collection* has often been compared to Pirandello's *Così è se vi pare,* but the comparison is not entirely valid. Pirandello brings audience participation into the theatre by implying that the truth of the plot is no more the audience's business than it is the prying townspeople's, thus neatly eliminating dramatic irony. But Piradello's point is privacy, not the verifiability of truth. It is obvious that in the situation that Pirandello has set up either Ponza's wife is his first or his second (or she is someone else altogether) and either she is or she is not Sra. Frola's daughter.

Pirandello's other belief was that truth is subjective and that therefore there is no truth, only a myriad of truths. This is nonsense (if it isn't, everything else is). Pinter makes neither the point about privacy, nor does he believe that truth is subjective. He believes that truth is unverifiable: "The desire for verification is understandable but cannot always be satisfied. There are no hard distinctions between what is true and what is false. The thing is not necessarily either true or false; it can be both true and false. The assumption that to verify what has happened and what is happening presents few problems I take to be inaccurate."[11] This seems to me to make no sense whatsoever, either in general or in the context of the play. Stella and Bill in the play amuse themselves by making up constantly changing versions of what happened between them in Leeds but *they* know. One can forget details of what happened this morning, but if one has been unfaithful to one's lover less than a week ago—the case with both Bill and Stella—one does not forget. In his attempt to establish the general unverifiability of truth Pinter has taken absent-mindedness to ludicrous lengths. That at least is less despairing than Pirandello's taking subjectivism to virtually infinite lengths.

Twenty-five years ago I wrote that *The Lover* shows a typical modern couple illustrating the malaise of the age by being able to achieve physical communication only through an elaborate by-passing of emotional communication: "The sterility, both physical and emotional, of this typical modern couple is so great that they can come close to each other only in a fantasy world."[12] This seems to me now not only immature drivel but a complete misinterpretation of the play. Far from being either misanthropic or critical of the values attributed to Richard and Sarah, *The Lover* seems to me now to be Pinter's masterpiece. Unlike all of his other plays, *The Lover* is not a play of amorphous meanings and atmosphere, but rather a play of straightforward psychological observation and a celebration of life. Richard and Sarah are a prosperous upper-middle class suburban couple who, two or three times a week, play a fantasy game in the afternoons in which Richard, transformed from the staid and stuffy husband in whom decorum and deportment reach their full flowering into the sporty and devil-may-care Max, returns home and plays a series of interlocking and pre-sumably ever-varying sexual games with Sarah, also transformed, in her case from the mousey, dutiful housewife into a glamorous and desirable seductress. The games are mainly based on domination, which flows effortlessly from one to the other as seductress becomes timid victim and solicitous protector becomes seducer. The fantasy climaxes with sex under the tea table, a nicely ironic juxtaposition of that symbol of staid and stodgy English middle-class life with the freedom of asocial sex: the tea table sheltering with tablecloth as cur-tain the riotously free animalism underneath it.

In the course of the play Richard, the less adventurous partner, makes a concerted effort to stop the fantasies and the parallel life he leads as Max. The games have been going on almost since they were married some ten years ago, and although he is good at them and clearly enjoys them, Richard is a little too much the English public school boy, a little too much the well-to-do upper mid-dle class equivalent of whatever the English call Yuppies to feel entirely at ease with having a secret life. The scenes in which he tells his wife, as Richard, that he has no mistress, only a whore and in which, as Max, he invents a private life for that character involving a wife and children and says he can no longer bear to betray them are devastating in their duplicity and cruelty. The play is about the psychological conflict in Richard, who is torn between his quite genuine love for and infatuation with Sarah, who, for her part, returns both feelings completely sincerely. The fantasy life these two have constructed for them-selves does not regulate and encompass their whole lives; there is no reason to assume that their fantasy sex life necessarily excludes any other form of sex life. Fantasy is the variation on the basic theme of sexual love. Nor need we assume that Pinter sees lust as being incompatible with love. Richard and Sarah, as she perceives and he does not, live richer and fuller lives than other people. They are *more* alive than their compatriots in precisely the way the Actor as Absurd Man in Albert Camus. *The Myth of Sisyphus* is more alive than others because he lives parallel lives along with his own. The Absurdist meas-ures life quantitatively as well as qualitatively *because life is all that there is.* To live as many lives as possible, no matter how temporarily, how spuriously, how self-deludingly, is to enrich the basic life we live. Richard and Sarah live their real life, but they play variations on it and give these variations equal stature with their real, outward life while they are living them; furthermore, these variations are their own creations so that in their fantasies they are—momentarily—the gods of their own destiny. To fantasize in mutual confidence and abandonment is already to be liberated, for it creates an alternative world inhabited only by the fantasizers. Richard succumbs helplessly to his wife's spell in the last scene (a fiendishly difficult one for the actor):

> SARAH: . . . Take off your jacket. Mmmnn? Would you like to change?
> Would you like me to change my clothes? I'll change for you, darling.
> Shall I? Would you like that?
> *Silence. She is very close to him.*
> RICHARD: Yes.
> *Pause.*
> Change.
> *Pause.*
> Change.
> *Pause.*
> Change your clothes.
> *Pause.*
> You lovely whore.
> *They are still kneeling, she leaning over him.*
> CURTAIN

When Richard is vanquished here at the very end of the play, helplessly engulfed in the overwhelming sexual allure of his wife, he is saved because he remains far more fully alive than the respectable husband for whose state he had yearned.

The Homecoming has stimulated more speculation and criticism than any other Pinter play so far. Eighteen years ago, in writing about the play, I quoted Richard Schechner as saying that it was "a probe of the dark male attitudes toward the 'mother-whore' and the equally compelling female desire to play this double role."[13] I described this as "a provocative suggestion that is definitely on the right track."[14] I began this essay by remarking that one of the few advantages of growing older is that one becomes wiser, as an illustration of which I offer the information that if asked now what I think of this I would emulate Pinter himself by replying, "I don't know what the hell he's talking about."

The problem with most criticism of *The Homecoming,* once again, is the urge to seek a specific meaning. *The Homecoming* is not a semantically cohesive play. It does not have a "point," nor was it written in order to expound a particular idea or point of view. If considered as a play with a linear plot line—a plot impelled by logical cause-and-effect progression—it is seen to be riddled with inconsistencies. *The Homecoming* does not have a linear structure; it has a nuclear structure. In other words, it starts from a central node—or theme or atmosphere—and effloresces randomly from there. It is best described as a play of familial atmosphere, though this should not be taken to mean that it is a statement about the nature of the family as such. *The Homecoming* is a play about certain aspects of family life and relationships that are common to all families in greater or lesser degree—in some cases to a degree that makes the family relationship virtually unbearable to some of its members (to Teddy in *The Homecoming*) and in others to such a minimal degree that it makes that relationship a preponderantly happy one. *The Homecoming* is a play about the centripetal tentacular grasp of family relationships: the suffocating pressure of unwanted emotion and social expectation from the family and the conflict between the infantile and the independent as the adult seeks his own identity. As Pinter himself has noted, ". . . if ever there was a villain in the play, Teddy was it."[15] And it is indeed quite obviously Teddy who is the central character despite the fact that he plays a comparatively minor part: one could almost say that Teddy is the stage manager rather than the protagonist. Teddy approaches the meeting with his family with trepidation, half hoping for the friendly reception that he envisages in the words he speaks to Ruth with nervous reassurance as they enter the house like thieves in the night. When he sees that this was a delusive hope, he immediately erects impenetrable psychological palisades around himself and lets events take their course. Ruth's decision at the end of the play to remain with the family, implausible in realistic terms though it is, is a reversion to her original way of life—a resumption of the profession it is broadly hinted that she practiced before marriage. It is also her revenge on Teddy by treating him as he has treated her, with stony, unemotional indifference. Teddy returns to the comfortless yet comforting (because he is in control) sterility of academia in the American desert, cut off forever from his family and free to brood on whatever branch of philosophy *is* his province.

The problem, it has always seemed to me, with *The Homecoming* is not with what happens in it but with Pinter's description of Teddy. Teddy, we are told, is the oldest son of this family of brutish grotesques who straddle the working class and the underworld. Six years earlier, having picked up a local "nude model" and married her without informing any member of his family, Teddy disappeared and has been almost incommunicado ever since (he seems to have written from America that he has received a Ph.D., but has not mentioned either his marriage or his fatherhood). Pinter seems to know nothing of American academia or of philosophy, but he does seem to have a corrosive contempt for both—by no means an untenable or reprehensible point of view. Still, the idea of a scion of this family as the possessor of a Ph.D. in philosophy and as the occupant of a professorial post at an American university and as the author of "critical works" on philosophy is risible at best and totally incredible at worst. Were it not for the fact that when Teddy and Ruth are alone it is evident from their remarks that Pinter does indeed intend them to be married and parents living in America, where Teddy really is a professor, a Ph.D., and a published scholar, one would be tempted to suggest an alternative and more credible background for the pair. In this scenario the marriage, the children, the Ph.D., the professorship, and the publications would all be part of a cover story intended to aid Teddy's carefully planned revenge on his family. Six years earlier Teddy met Ruth and took her to a city in the industrial North. Brainier than his father or Lenny he has become, head of the underworld or chief pimp in, say, Blackpool or Scunthorpe with Ruth as his chief helper. The "homecoming" is a plot between him and Ruth, whom he has paid bounteously for her acquiescence, to destroy his family, all of them already impotent, as Teddy is also. When Ruth will have done her work, the octopus of the family will finally be torn apart, and Teddy, as he thinks, will be vindicated, revenged, and liberated.

Whatever interpretation one can give it and however one might think that Pinter was mistaken in his portrayal of the leading character, *The Homecoming* represents the quintessence of Pinter's dramaturgy. It is a play that does not *mean* anything: it simply *is*. And what it is is a baffling, unresolved and unresolvable human situation. Reality, not an escape from it.

NOTES

[1] Cf. my *The Theatre of Protest and Paradox* (New York: New York University Press, 1964), pp. 197–211, and (New York: New York University Press, 1971), pp. 224–242.

[2] *New York Review of Books,* XV, xi (1970), p. 22.

[3] *Ibid.,* p. 21.

[4] *Paris Review,* XXXIX (1966), p. 24.

[5] Harold Pinter, "A Letter to Peter Wood," in Michael Scott, ed., *Harold Pinter: The Birthday Party, The Caretaker, The Homecoming. A Casebook* (London: Macmillan, 1986), p. 80.

[6] L. A. C. Dobrez, *The Existential and its Exits* (London: The Athlone Press, 1986), p. 336.

[7] Leonard Powlick describes this situation very well in his essay "What the Hell is That All About?" in Steven H. Gale, ed., *Harold Pinter: Critical Approaches* (London and Toronto: Associated University Presses, 1986), pp. 30–37.

[8] Cf. *supra,* p. 2.

[9] The only thing in the play that borders on the supernatural, although I have been unable to find any commentary on it and must confess it drove me round the bend when I played the part, is Gus's entrance at the end through the door from the corridor, beaten up and stripped of his gun (not an easy thing to do soundlessly to a professional killer), although he left the room by the door that leads to the kitchen and toilet.

[10] "Goldberg and McCann? Dying, rotten, scabrous, the decayed spiders, the flower of our society." See Scott, p. 81.

[11] *The Theatre of Protest and Paradox,* 1st ed., p. 209.

[12] *Ibid.,* p. 211.

[13] Richard Schechner, "Puzzling Pinter," *Tulane Drama Review,* XI, ii (1966), p. 183, quoted in *The Theater of Protest and Paradox,* 2nd ed., p. 239.

[14] *Ibid.*

[15] Peter Hall, "A Director's Approach" in John Lahr, ed., *A Casebook on Harold Pinter's "The Homecoming"* (New York: Grove Press, 1971), p. 20.

What's Wrong with this Picture? David Rabe's Comic-Strip Plays

Toby Silverman Zinman

There is something oddly anachronistic in David Rabe's radically contemporary plays, but his use of anachronism is neither the conventional reference to something too modern for its context, nor the reverse, the nostalgic drift of so much contemporary art; it creates, rather, a puzzling and powerful distantiation.

Rabe's sort of anachronism is perfectly expressed by Phil in *Hurlyburly:*

> ARTIE: This is sex we're talking about now, Phil. Competitive sex.
> PHIL: That's what I'm saying. I need help.
> ARTIE: You're such a jerk-off, you're such a goof-off . . . . I don't believe for a
> second you were seriously desperate about trying to pick that bitch up.
> PHIL: That's exactly how out of touch I am, Artie—I have methods so out-dated
> they appear to you a goof. (81)

Here is a post-modernist critical dilemma: what is just outdated and what is a goof? And, even harder, what is just a goof and what is serious art? And harder still, can a goof be serious art? Rabe's use of anachronism creates these problems over and over, and it influences every aspect of his plays, generating that troubling sense of "What's Wrong With This Picture?" This question can be answered the way it always can, by concentrating on the visual field.

Consider how comic-strips have come to dominate the visual field of our popular culture; not only have POW! AARGH! BLAM! become ubiquitous in advertising, but they have crept into serious, literate communication as well as into the conversation of otherwise articulate people. Even more widespread is the influence of the visual style of comic-strips. And consider the bizarre sociological implications of the vivification of Superman, Popeye, Batman, Dick Tracy, and Little Orphan Annie through the agency of human actors playing comicstrip characters in recent films, an attempt—lavish and/or garish—to make the two-dimensional three-dimensional. This suggests a fairly desperate cultural need for simplified realism which would seem to belie our society's serious doubts about the realism of reality; it further indicates that our avenue to understanding and assessing character valorizes physical deeds rather than thoughts or feelings, thus the need for the outlandishly successful hero and the guaranteed happy ending; further still, it demonstrates our culture's total acceptance of film as a realistic medium. Disneyland, with its ambulatory Mickey Mice *et al* is one extreme of this vivifying impulse (ponder the phenomenon of adults waiting in line for 'his' autograph); the technically-acclaimed film, *Who Framed Roger Rabbit,* may be another, more sophisticated version of this impulse, and the movie *Teenage Mutant Ninja Turtles* is, surely, the most peculiar as well as shockingly lucrative mutation of it.

Given this prevalent torquing of the comic-strip, it is a remarkable confirmation of the avant-garde nature of David Rabe's plays that their force is exerted in the opposite direction: the flattening of "real" life, the framing of action, the ballooning of dialogue. Rather than moving from the comic strip to the actor, Rabe presses the actor and the dramatic arena into the disturbing illusion of two-dimensionality, creating cultural critique rather than wish-fulfillment.

Rabe creates characters who do not take their own humanity quite seriously. Pavlo Hummel's alter-ego, Mickey,[1] looks at Pavlo and says, "You're a goddam cartoon . . ." (69), and in a central speech in *Hurlyburly,* Eddie says, "You know, we're all just background in one another's life. Cardboard cutouts bumping around in this vague, you know, hurlyburly, this spin-off of what was once prime-time life . . ." (111). It seems to me that all Rabe's characters must be played as cardboard cutouts, cartoons gone wrong, gone big, and to read Rabe's plays in light of Roy Lichtenstein's big, wrong, comic-strip paintings is, perhaps, to get a handle on the answer to the question, "What's Wrong With This Picture?"

Neither Lichtenstein nor Rabe is dealing with anything so charming as "old-fashioned," but rather with images and characters weirdly passé; anachronism becomes a distorted lens through which love and war are viewed. Both Rabe and Lichtenstein "quote" in the art-historical sense of the word,[2] thereby creating temporal disjunction. Just as Rabe's characters in *Hurlyburly,* a play written in the 1980s, talk about sixties "karma," and his Vietnam soldiers want to be WWII heroes, so Lichtenstein paints pictures in the 1960s of comic-strip figures drawn from the forties, from bubblegum wrappers and Yellow Pages illustrations. And, by producing by hand that which was formerly reproduced by a mechanical process, that is, by handcrafting benday dots,[3] Lichtenstein reverses the usual chronology of artistic processes and progress.

Lichtenstein's comic-strip paintings, both the love group and the war group[4], contain narrative elements. The war stories are partial but obvious (as in, "I pressed the fire control . . . and ahead of me rockets blazed through the sky . . . WHAAM!"), whereas the ballooned dialogue in the love paintings suggests a caricature of a person to whom something has happened; passion is archly implied (as in "Oh, Jeff . . . I love you, too . . . but . . ."). But when Simon Wilson likens Lichtenstein to

> a Victorian narrative painter . . . who [in *M-Maybe*] invites the spectator to speculate: who is the girl? who is the man with the studio? film star, photographer, broadcaster, artist even? and what is the nature of the situation? has he stood her up for another woman? is he really ill? fatally injured perhaps? (12–13)

he misses the point as well as the joke ("artist even?"!); these soap-operatic questions are inappropriate. Everything Lichtenstein does is designed to create distance between the subject of the painting and the viewer: the gigantic disproportion of Lichtenstein's faces (often larger than $5' \times 6'$), the highly stylized, immediately recognizable use of the heavy black or blue outlines and the simple, primary colors, as well as the ridiculously large benday dots, suggest that this is not a painting one responds to in terms of the human drama of the content, but rather a painting about cultural clichés, and about surfaces that erase the record of the artist's hand. It is exactly this same soap-operatic impulse toward the narrative (which has realism at its heart) which audiences and critics often bring to a Rabe play, only to find themselves saying, What's Wrong With This Picture?

To create these distancing effects, Lichtenstein draws on a body of visual clichés, on the formulaic vocabulary which evolved in the history of cartoon making:

> A handsome man's face would have a cleft chin and strongly accented lower lip. . . . Discomfort was conveyed by droplets of sweat springing from out of, and down from, the hairline. . . . Transitions were jump cuts. . . . No one believed that this was how things really looked . . . but you believed that it was how *cartoons* looked and acted. (Kaprow, 7)

Although cartoons may look and act like this, paintings do not, and thus Lichtenstein's canvases create that same assault on genre expectations as Rabe's plays do.

This use of graphic clichés is much like Rabe's specifying cliché body language for his characters in their moments of ersatz emotional crises: for example, in *Hurlyburly*, when Eddie and Mickey feel shame at their treatment of Bonnie's six-year old daughter, Rabe's directions require them to moan and pound their heads on the kitchen counter, and then to straighten slowly with relief and encouragement; or when, in *In the Boom Boom Room*, Chrissy and her sexually abusive father blow kisses as they slowly back away from each other. Such gestures not only distance the spectator from the character, but the character from the emotion. Rabe's actors need to revive the whole catalogue of gestures they have learned to avoid. This is supported by Rabe's "Author's Note" to *Sticks and Bones* when he writes:

> Stylization, then, is the main production problem. . . . What is poetic in the writing must not be reinforced by deep feeling on the part of the actors, or the writing will hollow into pretension. In a more "realistic" play, where language is thinner, subtext must be supplied or there is no weight. Such deep support of *Sticks and Bones* will make the play ponderous. As a general rule I think it is true that when an actor's first impulse (the impulse of all his training) is to make a heavy or serious adjustment in a scene, he should reverse himself and head for a light-hearted adjustment. If his first impulse is toward lightheartedness, perhaps he should turn toward a serious tack. (226)

The cartoon elements are most obvious in Rabe's *Goose and Tomtom;* the two tough guys pull out their pistols and say:

> TOMTOM: Look at 'em. Look at 'em . . . guns.
> GOOSE: Bang, bang.
> TOMTOM: Bang, bang. (10)

Tomtom spray-paints graffiti images on the walls, creating pictures of events which have not occurred and then insists that the pictures authenticate his paranoiac fantasies. The entire action of the play is both replicated and interpreted on the stage walls, in a kind of simultaneous translation into visuals. Near the end of the play, the graffiti-covered walls fall down and:

> figures enter all in black: long black overcoats, black trousers, hats, gloves, and ski masks. One figure, perhaps, seems to emerge from the floor. They seem to be the target figures come to life. One carries a huge full-length scythe. Others have machine guns. One is huge—ten feet tall—another small, another humpbacked. (115)

Living cartoons replace the painted cartoons; Rabe seems to have parodied the comic-strip zeitgeist: a preemptive strike.

Rabe's war plays, *Pavlo Hummel* and *Streamers*[5], look much like Lichtenstein's war paintings. Consider these pictures of male violence fantasies: *Live Ammo, Whaam!, As I Opened Fire, Blam, Brattata, Takka Takka, Sweet Dreams, Baby,* and *O.K. Hot-.* Many of these are based on trite WWII images (the villains invariably speak German, as in "Torpedo, Los!") and on the noises which are standard sound effects on all playgrounds. This combination of datedness and childishness sums up Pavlo Hummel's trouble; he is a case of arrested development, a walking anachronism.

It is interesting to note that the basis of Pavlo's character is usually perceived quite differently. Most often critics (Werner, Hughes, and Homan, for
examples) talk about the play as demonstrating Pavlo's dehumanization by the
military machine and thus the play as an indictment of war. But in "The Basic
Training of American Playwrights: Theatre and the Vietnam War," Asahina
sees the play as failing in this political mission:

> All the stock characters and standard scenes were in evidence: the blustery
> drill sergeant, the squad bully, the uncaring family; the barracks-room ban-
> ter, the ritual brawls and other crude tests of manhood, and finally the sense-
> less death of the protagonist. . . . But instead of creating an agonized and
> extreme but nonetheless representative figure of humanity, Rabe deliberately
> designed Pavlo to be a cipher—a literal nobody instead of an Everyman. The
> net effect was to make his brutalization and anonymous death almost mean-
> ingless: The progressive dehumanization of someone scarcely human to
> begin with involved so little dramatic motion that the play was less revealing
> of the cruel irony of Pavlo's empty existence than of the barrenness of Rabe's
> imagination. (35)

This, it seems to me, mistakes the tone and the mode just as much as the war-
is-hell approach. To see Rabe's characters' lack of humanness as a flaw is to
assume that the play operates in a realistic mode. If we see the characters as
cartoons, the flaw ceases to be a flaw and becomes the point.[6]

The connection with Lichtenstein is again instructive; the same error in
apprehension often takes place in the critical assumptions about the paintings.
As Richard Mophet points out, there is the mistaken notion that a Lichtenstein
painting is identical to its source, that is, for example, "a canvas seven feet wide
can be regarded as an actual comic-strip . . . or a brushstroke as large as a man
as a single gesture of hand and brush" (17). Lichtenstein's paintings are not cartoons but cartoons of cartoons, that is, heavily stylized and self-conscious paintings rather than realistic renderings of the source. Further, to assume, as many
art critics have, that Lichtenstein's paintings, and by extension, the whole Pop
Art movement of the Sixties, including Warhol's and Rauchenberg's work, constitutes an indictment of crass, mechanical reproduction in our age of technological reproduction, is to politicize and sentimentalize the game being played.[7]

Reading Rabe's war plays as though they were realistic is tantamount to
making the same error in critical apprehension. Rabe denies that his war
plays are protest plays; they are, rather, a record of the "eternal human pageant" of which war is a permanent part (Introduction to *Two Plays,* xxv).
While he was stationed in Vietnam, he writes, he "kept no journal and even
my letters grew progressively more prosaic, fraudulent, dull, and fewer and
fewer. Cliches were welcomed, as they always are when there is no real wish
to see what they hide" (xvii).

Consider Rabe's comment on Michael Herr's now-famous Vietnam memoir *Dispatches,* a book that refuses to become The Great American War Novel:

> Michael Herr is the only writer I've read who has written in the mad-pop-poetic/bureaucratically camouflaged language in which Vietnam was lived. The trees take up attack postures, sanity defoliates before your eyes and the generals spin out theories like Macbeth's witches. He gets very close to taking you all the way over. (flyleaf)

This is not the language in which Rabe's "Vietnam trilogy" is written; the playwright knows the language, but writes his plays in another, retrograde language, the realistic speech of another generation. Like Lichtenstein, Rabe is creating images of images, not images of people. We have learned over and over since *Dispatches* just how witty and cynical the grunts could be; consider, for example, the advertising logo for Stanley Kubrick's film, *Full Metal Jacket,* a combat helmet with "Born to Kill" written next to a peace sign, a true-to-life detail, Herr tells us, not an adman's invention. But in *Pavlo Hummel, Sticks and Bones,* and *Streamers,* the characters are no more capable of that kind of linguistic/iconographic irony than they are of staying alive.

The explosion which kills Pavlo and which begins the play is perfectly visualizable in comic book terms. There is a shout of:

> "GRENA-A-ADE!" [And then, the stage directions tell us,] *(Pavlo drops to his knees, seizing the grenade, and has it in his hands in his lap when the explosion comes, loud, shattering, and the lights go black, go red or blue. The girl screams. Bodies are strewn about.)* (9)

We can imagine the bright red, flame-shaped exclamatory lines radiating from the grenade. And sure enough, Pavlo is not dead in naturalistic dramatic terms, since he bounces up on command and continues the play.

Pavlo's instincts for self-preservation have been short-circuited by his heritage. He was, after all, fathered by "the old lie" told Hollywood style. His mother tells him:

> you had many fathers, many men, movie men, filmdom's greatest—all of them, those grand old men of yesteryear, they were your father. The Fighting Seventy-sixth, do you remember, oh, I remember, little Jimmy, what a tough little mite he was, and how he leaped upon that grenade, did you see, my God what a glory, what a glorious thing with his little tin hat. (75)

Rabe can create high language out of his inarticulate characters' riffs and rants, just as Lichtenstein can make high art out of bubblegum wrappers. In each play there is at least one astonishing monologue, a mysterious and powerful story which contains a nondiscursive truth. These stories create odd visual images which seem inappropriately funny, and by so doing, convey Rabe's vision of the human condition. In the war plays, these are particularly harrowing; for example, the limbless Sgt. Brisbey's obsession with "ole Magellan, sailin' round the world":

> Ever hear of him Pavlo? So one day he wants to know how far under him to the bottom of the ocean. So he drops over all the rope he's got. Two hundred feet. It hangs down into the sea that must go down and down beyond its end of miles and tons of water. He's up there in the sun. He's got this little piece of rope danglin' from his fingers. He thinks because all the rope he's got can't touch bottom, he's over the deepest part of the ocean. He doesn't know the real question. How far beyond all the rope you got is the bottom? (89)

The visual image conjured up in the listener's mind by this story is essentially a comic-strip image of a tiny figure with question marks surrounding his head. That, Rabe would seem to be saying, is the way human beings deal with the incomprehensible: we invent answers which are pitifully inadequate.

Consider the similar cartoon image and similar pathos created by the story of O'Flannigan in *Streamers:*

> So O'Flannigan was this kinda joker who had the goddamn sense a humor of a clown and nerves, I tell you, of steel, and he says he's gonna release the lever mid- air, then reach up, grab the lines, and float on down, hanging. . . . So I seen him pull the lever at five hundred feet, and he reaches up to two fistfuls a air, the chute's twenty feet above him, and he went into the ground like a knife. . . . (40)

> [and] This [other] guy with his chute goin' straight up above him in a streamer, like a tulip, only white, you know. All twisted and never gonna open. . . . He went right by me. We met eyes sort of. He was lookin' real puzzled. (41)

Like Magellan, like this other guy, like all of us, O'Flannigan is deeply wrong.

In *Hurlyburly* Phil leaves a suicide note which reads: "The guy who dies in an accident understands the nature of destiny." Although Eddie finds this opaque and mystical, it is, for Rabe, as clear as things get. Phil has found, metaphorically, Rabe's empty Buick (which figures large in *Streamers* and small in *Sticks and Bones*), the car which causes meaningless havoc as it cartoonishly careens around. In the immortal words of heavyweight boxer Sonny Liston, whom Rabe is fond of quoting: "Life a funny thing" (epigraph to *Pavlo Hummel*); it is, as various characters in *Streamers* discover, "un-fuckin'-believable."

For Rabe, love is even more unbelievable than war, and Lichtenstein's female figures provide a perfect gloss, in every sense of that word, on Rabe's treatment of women. Consider this statement by Roy Lichtenstein when an interviewer asked him about his "highly-confectioned women," the red-lipped blondes:

> Women draw themselves this way—this is what make-up really is. . . . I've
> always wanted to make up someone as a cartoon. That's what led to my
> ceramic sculptures of girls. . . . I was interested in putting two-dimensional
> symbols on a three-dimensional object. (Coplans, 13)

Compare this to Chrissy in *In the Boom Boom Room* imagining herself as a
Playboy centerfold: "I'd be a good one. I'd be the best one, sittin' in fur, and
they'd polish me, make me smooth and glossy—all my marks away. Airbrush
me till I'd gleam" (69). Chrissy has confused herself with a two-dimensional
object, and as Rabe wrote her, she is right.

In the Boom Boom Room was greeted as a feminist play by critics who may
have rued their judgment once they saw *Hurlyburly,* about which Rabe said, "A
lot of people say the play is anti-woman. . . . I don't think that's true. It's about
the price some guys pay to be men" (Dudar, 5). And his own words indicate his
cartoon view of what it is to be a man: "There's this primal part of them, like
this creature from the black lagoon. It runs through all my plays" (Freedman,
13). Because these male characters' lives are in such horrific disarray, and
because they partially know that, the creature from the black lagoon finds a way
to keep self-loathing at bay: blame an enemy. The handiest enemy are the
"broads," the "bitches," the assorted ex-wives and girlfriends whose flaw lies in
gender rather than in personality. Once again, Phil's deranged voice is vatic:

> Football doesn't have a chance against it. It's like this invasion of tits and ass
> overwhelming my own measly individuality so I don't have a prayer to have
> my own thoughts about my own things except you and tits and ass and suck-
> ing and fucking and that's all I can think about. My privacy has been demol-
> ished. . . . You think a person likes that? (58–59)

Rabe's plays are predominantly male, but the female characters of *Goose
and Tomtom,* and *In the Boom Boom Room* and *Hurlyburly* out-Lichtenstein
Lichtenstein, each one more blonde, more red-lipped, more vacant than the one
before. Rabe has created his female characters as cartoon figures, quite likely to
sigh, "Oh, Brad. . . ." But this is not to suggest here that Rabe is anti-women
any more than he is anti-men; he does not grant full humanity to any of his dramatic creatures, and he writes plays which depend upon their two-dimensionality.

Perhaps the distinction between an object painting and a still life is useful
here: an object painting is a picture of a single thing, while a still life is a picture
of the relationship between things. Both Rabe and Lichtenstein treat their
characters/subjects as objects, and Lichtenstein's pictures *Aloha* and *Girl with
Ball* are no less object paintings than those he did of a golf ball or a hot dog or
an ice cream soda.

Rabe's characters exist on stage in emotional and psychological isolation,
and, in my imagined ideal production, in vivid visual isolation. We witness an

object painting in performance, in which each object/character stands in relation only to the ground rather than to the other characters. This is anachronism's counterpart—*anachorism,* that is, incongruity in space rather than time.
This visible isolation of the characters uses the stage space to reveal their lack
of capacity for relationship. Thus the characters and their vehicle are well
matched, repudiating, as do Lichtenstein's comic-strip paintings, everything
but surface.

This smooth, aggressive anonymity of surface reflects Rabe's view of contemporary American culture. Violent and vapid, our society seems capable of
only comic-strip responses to love and to war. Even our response to time has
been reduced to a cartoon; Rabe's plays seem to have slipped on a temporal
banana peel and WHOOPS!!! is about all we can say. This brilliantly disturbing drama leaves us just where it leaves his characters: dislocated in time and
deferred in space. He has reinvented stage space, not through special effects or
sets or lighting, but by forcing language to create new visuals, new concepts of
character and action which we then perceive visually, new ways of seeing ourselves. And that, I think, is what's wrong with the picture: it's a play.

NOTES

[1] Mickey is allegedly Pavlo's half-brother, but considering that Pavlo's name was
Michael before he changed it, it seems safe to assume, especially given all the mirror
imagery in this scene, that Mickey is Pavlo in mufti, speaking with the contempt Pavlo
believes his family feels for him.

[2] I am, for the sake of my argument, ignoring Lichtenstein's sculptures and brushstroke paintings, which are filled with quotations from Matisse and Picasso. These are
irrelevant to the discussion of Rabe's plays.

[3] According to the Columbia Encyclopedia, 3rd edition (New York: Columbia
University Press, 1963), p. 546, Benjamin Day (1838–1916) invented a process using
celluloid sheets for shading plates in order to print maps and illustrations in color. His
name has become a noun, a verb and an adjective: to give a map a Ben Day, to Ben Day
a map, and benday dots.

Benjamin Day was the son of Benjamin Henry Day, the American journalist who
started the *New York Sun;* he wrote the paper, and set the type all himself. The *Sun* was
the first paper to employ newsboys.

[4] Following are the titles of Lichtenstein paintings I included in the slide show
when I presented a shorter version this paper to the Drama Division meeting at the
convention of the Modern Language Association in New Orleans, December, 1988.

The "Love" Paintings:
    M-Maybe
    Nurse
    Two Swimmers

The Kiss
The Engagement Ring

The "War" Paintings:
Whaam!
As I Opened Fire
Torpedo-Los!
Tzing (Live Ammo Series, No. 4)
OK Hot Shot
Brattata
Takka Takka
Sweet Dreams Baby
Wall Explosion, No. 1

[5] I omit *Sticks and Bones* from the discussion of the Vietnam plays partly because its own dependence on television images confuses the visual issues here, and partly because it takes place on the domestic front and therefore lacks the visual images of war I am discussing here. It is worth noting, however, that anachronistic and cartoon images fill this play as well; consider the picture created by Ozzie's bragging about outrunning a bowling ball, and the solution to Harriet's crossword puzzle question, "a four-letter word that starts with "G" and ends with "B," to which Rick replies, "Glub. . . . It's a cartoon word. . . . cartoon people say it when they're drowning. G-L-U-B" (47).

[6] Compare this to the description of the Vietnam War as image-experience by veteran Philip D. Beidler.

Golden-age TV: cartoons, commercials, cowboys, comedians and caped crusaders, all coming across together at quantum-level intensity, in a single frantic continuum of noise, color and light—child-world dreams of aggression and escape mixed up with moralistic fantasies of heroism beleaguered yet ultimately regnant in a world of lurking, omnipresent dangers and deceits— in sum, a composite high-melodrama and low-comedy videotape of the American soul. (11)

[7] Carter Ratcliff discusses Lichtenstein in relation to Walter Benjamin's theories, particularly those in "The Work of Art in the Age of Mechanical Reproduction," and notes that although,

Lichtenstein's canvases mimic photo-mechanical processes, his prints employ them, and he delights in minimizing the difference between mimicry and the mimicked, . . . nowhere in the spacious labyrinth of his art is there a sign that his play with the mechanics of reproduction has deeply engaged him with history. (115)

Works Cited

Alloway, Lawrence. *Lichtenstein*. New York: Abbeville Press, 1983.

Asahina, Robert. "The Basic Training of American Playwrights," *Theatre* 9 (Spring, 1978), 30–37.

Beidler, Philip D. *American Literature and the Experience of Vietnam*. Athens, Georgia: University of Georgia Press, 1982.

Coplans, Johns. "Roy Lichtenstein: an interview" in *Roy Lichtenstein*. London: Tate Gallery, 1968.

Dudar, Helen. ". . . And as Rabe Sees Hollywood," *New York Times,* June 17, 1984: 12, 5.

Freedman, Samuel. "Rabe on the War at Home," *New York Times,* June 28, 1984: C, 13.

Homan, Richard. "American Playwrights in the 1970's: Rabe and Shepard, *Critical Quarterly,* 24 (Spring, 1982): 73–82.

Hughes, Catherine. *Plays, Politics and Polemic*. New York: Drama Book Specialists, 1973.

Kaprow, Allan. "Introduction" to *Roy Lichtenstein at CalArts*. Valencia, California: California Institute of the Arts, 1977.

Morphet, Richard. *Roy Lichtenstein*. London: Tate Gallery, 1968.

Rabe, David. *The Basic Training of Pavlo Hummel* in *Two Plays* by David Rabe. New York: Penguin, 1978.

———. *Goose and TomTom*. New York: Grove, 1986.

———. *Hurlyburly*. New York: Samuel French, 1989.

———. *In the Boom Boom Room*. New York: Grove, 1986.

———. *Sticks and Bones*. New York: Samuel French, 1987.

———. *Streamers*. New York: Knopf, 1987.

Ratcliff, Carter. "The Work of Roy Lichtenstein in the Age of Walter Benjamin's and Jean Baudrillard's Popularity," in *Art in America* (February, 1989): 112–121.

Werner, Craig. "Primal Scream and Nonsense Rhymes: David Rabe's Revolt," *Educational Theatre Journal,* vol. 30, 1978: 517–529.

Wilson, Simon. *Pop*. New York: Barron's, 1978.

The Artistic Trajectory of Peter Shaffer

C. J. Gianakaris

British playwright Peter Shaffer remains a puzzle today, particularly for critics and academic scholars. A "moving target" with respect to dramatic styles and thematic interests, he is difficult to categorize within tidy literary designations. Is he primarily a realist probing the psychological and social issues facing the modern age? Is he a somber metaphysician seeking answers to universal enigmas? Or is he a teasing farceur who targets mundane human follies? Regular theatergoers will recognize elements of all these types in Shaffer. Within the variety of styles evidenced in his many plays, however, stand key technical and conceptual loci which support his work as a whole, no matter what the veneer of the drama.

Those center points—essentially naturalistic in nature—will be taken up later in this discussion. But the puzzle of Peter Shaffer extends beyond mere technique or subject matter. In a larger frame of reference, there is difficulty in isolating the theoretical audience for whom he writes. Shaffer embodies that rare species of writer whose career straddles the worlds both of popular and "serious" drama. Impressive success on commercial stages has brought him enormous worldwide recognition, ready financial backing, and eagerness of top theater artists to work with him. *The Battle of Shrivings* (1970) alone of his dozen plays has failed to win an audience. *Yonadab* (1985), only a modest success, nonetheless ran for a year in repertory at the British National Theatre. All the rest of his works have received strong acclaim whenever they are performed. By most standards, Shaffer enjoys exceptional popularity on world stages and has earned his stature as one of our foremost writers.

Yet by no means does Shaffer pander to mass tastes to gain general audience following. Quite the contrary; his works involve intellectually demanding themes and innovative theatrical staging. Typically, at the center of his plays stands a questioning—or questing—protagonist, obsessed with discerning mankind's true metaphysical status. Shaffer's best known dramas—*The Royal Hunt of the Sun. Equus, Amadeus,* and *Yonadab*—feature heroes such as Pizarro, Dysart, Salieri, and Yonadab who probe their respective universes for answers to philosophical and theological puzzles. Eventually, each protagonist moves toward knowledge of God. At the same time, the hero seeks to discover how far man might assume the powers of God and *become* God—if indeed He exists. More than a hint of Promethian and Faustian hungers exist in his protagonists. Shaffer's underlying thrust in his major dramas resembles that found in ancient classical drama: to define the relationship of mortal man to immortal deity. Simultaneously, Shaffer's dramatic universe infers values mirroring today's God-is-dead intellectual system, thereby allying Shaffer with the existential world view as well. Small wonder that academics find it dicey to pigeonhole Shaffer as a proponent of a single vision. In his wide-ranging and eclectic thinking, he has few peers today, most of whom focus on psychological or social problems.

Nothing in Shaffer's family background mandated a career in the arts. Born in Liverpool on 15 May 1926, Peter Levin Shaffer and his identical twin brother Anthony grew up in a middle-class Jewish household. Jack Shaffer, a property company director, moved his wife Reka and the family to London in 1936. But with the start of the second world war, they moved frequently to evade the German bombers. Despite the ongoing war, Peter and Anthony attended prestigious St. Paul's School beginning in 1942. Both twins were accepted by Trinity College at Cambridge University; but satisfying their service obligations came first. In their case, they served as Bevin Boys, youths who dug coal in the mines of Kent.[1] In 1947 both Shaffers enrolled in Trinity College where they jointly edited the college paper.

Peter Shaffer came down from Cambridge in 1950 with a specialty in history but no definite career plans. Initially he tried his hand at various jobs until 1951 when he traveled to New York City. There, he worked for a book dealer, retail stores, and the New York Public Library. Shaffer later remarked that this period of his life was bleak and frustrating. But one positive outcome was his frequenting New York theaters. As a result of seeing so much theater, he felt encouraged to try writing plays, his first being "The Salt Land." Work in the business world provided him little satisfaction, and he returned to London in 1954 to work at a large music publishing house. While holding that position, Shaffer found his initial success in the realm of drama, when "The Salt Land" was telecast over ITV. Paradoxically, during this same period he also was establishing a reputation as a writer of fiction. He published three mystery novels in London and in the United States: *The Woman in the Wardrobe* (1951), *How Doth the Little Crocodile?* (1952), and *Withered Murder* (1955)—the latter two co-authored with his brother Anthony (the Tony-winning writer of *Sleuth*). In 1957, Shaffer had two more broadcast dramas aired—the unpublished radio play "The Prodigal Father" over BBC Radio and "Balance of Terror" (also unpublished) over BBC Television. Once his plays caught on, Shaffer never looked backward. Thereafter, he devoted his entire energies to the theater.

Shaffer's earliest full-length dramas, *Five Finger Exercise* (1958) and *The Royal Hunt of the Sun* (1964), immediately drew applause from critics who recognized a strong new voice in the theater. Awards came swiftly, initially in England and later in the United States, to confirm the importance of his writing to the modern stage. Later, *Equus* (1973) and *Amadeus* (1979) thoroughly won over audiences, earning both critical and popular applause. Both pieces became smash hits on Broadway, and each won a Tony Award as best drama. More recently, *Lettice & Lovage* (1987) received four Tony nominations, including one for best play. (Eventually the comedy won Tonys for Maggie Smith and Margaret Tyzack.) Thus, to this point Shaffer has established an enviable record of successes both commercially and critically.

Nor are Shaffer's plays solely popular on live stages. Movies have been made of nearly all his works to date. Here, the results are very mixed, however. Shaffer far prefers the stage medium to the screen, and readily admits the films of his works to be uneven. Interestingly, the factors that led to success or failure in transferring his plays to the screen—particularly the theatricality of his unique realism—also shed light on the nature of Shaffer's works themselves. Such a topic deserves separate consideration, and only a few points will be touched on here. But one unavoidable conclusion is that his plays, which are "exuberantly and unashamedly theatrical," have proven difficult to reconceive for the large screen.[2] Not surprisingly, the film director's task is easier with those works built on more conventional realism. One example may suffice. An interesting yet ultimately disappointing film of *Five Finger Exercise* was made in 1962. Despite an impressive cast (including Rosalind Russell, Maximilian Schell, and Jack Hawkins) the movie version never attains the psychological richness of the original stage production. However, because of the play's original naturalistic premises, the characterizations of the five principals, along with their fully delineated motivations, translate readily to a movie format.

Just how well *Five Finger Exercise* made the transformation to film—relatively speaking—becomes evident when considering Shaffer's dramas that move beyond realism in their original conception. A disastrous film adaptation of *Royal Hunt* (starring Christopher Plummer and Robert Shaw) followed in 1969, for instance. After viewing the hugely distorted movie made of his noble quest drama, Shaffer knew he no longer could entrust his plays to screen writers. Thereafter, he wrote the film scripts himself for *The Public Eye* (1972), *Equus* (1977), and *Amadeus* (1984). Considering how theater-oriented his pieces are in format and spirit, it is surprising that the movie versions fared as well as they did. There is proof that outstanding results are possible when the play transferences are achieved with imagination and flexibility. An example is Milos Forman's film of *Amadeus* which accumulated eight Academy Awards including Best Film of 1984 and Best Film Adaptation for Shaffer's movie script. Previously, Shaffer received an Oscar nomination for his film script of *Equus*—a movie whose graphic simulations during the horse-blinding scenes fatally compromised it at the box office.[3] As with *Royal Hunt,* the stage script for *Equus* prohibits its being reshaped for film in a literal fashion—a fact the director of the movie, Sidney Lumet, learned at a high price, according to Shaffer. On the more recent front, plans for a movie version of *Lettice & Lovage* are in the works, suggesting that the playwright remains open-minded about filmic versions of his works despite disappointments in the past. Additionally, unlike earlier statements denigrating movies, in a recent interview (see "A Conversation with Peter Shaffer [1990]" in this volume) Shaffer hinted that he might revise *Whom Do I Have the Honour of Addressing?* as a film. He even acknowledges that his most recent radio piece might also be an ideal candidate for a television play. The entire screen issue then remains open where Shaffer is concerned.

But to return to Shaffer's stage dramas, we need to delineate more closely the appeal of his ideas and techniques. Unlike the opaque conundrums underlying plays by certain other twentieth-century theater experimenters (Beckett and Pinter come to mind), Shaffer's dramas have remained accessible to the theater-going public. This fact tends to devalue his plays for politically oriented theorists who esteem a work according to its bewildering effect on audiences. For such detractors, to be "popular" with playgoers becomes an indictment of a play's worthiness. Only the puzzling, uncommercial, radical avant-garde retains merit for zealots like Brustein and Simon, accounting for their long and active distaste for Shaffer.[4]

Just as his success bridging artistic and popular values elicits mixed reactions, Shaffer evokes ambiguous response and controversy on dramaturgical grounds. If pressed to describe Shaffer's primary writing tools, however, most critics acknowledge the centrality of psychological naturalism. Conventional realism characterizes much of Shaffer's early work, including *Five Finger Exercise,* the one-act comedies, and the ill-fated *Battle of Shrivings* (1970, later rewritten as *Shrivings,* 1974). Although Shaffer temporarily returned to realism with *Lettice & Lovage* (1987) and the radio play *Whom Do I Have the Honour of Addressing?* (1989), naturalism never has been the playwright's favored dramatic approach. The initial draft for *The Royal Hunt of the Sun* already existed when the naturalistic *Five Finger Exercise* launched his career in 1958. His true inclinations lay in "big, sweeping theatre," as he explained to the interviewer D. Zerdin on BBC's "Profile" (11 September 1979). Shaffer elaborates in his Introduction to *The Collected Plays of Peter Shaffer* (New York: Harmony Books, 1982) that the times were not right for the unusual mannerisms of *Royal Hunt.* The tidal wave of realism during the 1950's, he declares, dictated that his early works follow standard conventions: "I became a playwright finally to be part of the grandiloquent and showy world of imaginative reality. It took me some time to acknowledge this to myself. The times, after all, scarcely favored such an ambition. The mid-1950s did not constitute a time when one could admit, with much chance of being sympathetically heard, a purpose to write about gods and grand aspirations, orators and ecstatics. It was a surging time for England, but the cry tended to be for social realism" (x).

Shaffer recognizes the value of representationalism, however. With this first success, he established his ability to write masterfully in the realistic mode. Shaffer states, "On balance, I feel I did crafted work in my first piece. It said what I wanted it to say, and it possessed a shape which made it play easily and finally accumulated its power" (viii). Shaffer's next plays—*Shrivings* and the one-act comedies *The Private Ear, The Public Eye, White Lies,* and *Black Comedy*—retained a realistic bias, thereby consolidating popularity with theater audiences. But careful observers of the stage understand that realism alone does not win audience support. His endeavors with realism permitted Shaffer to hone his talent for penetrating dialogue. The occasional intrusion of turgid prose and excessive sentimentality in *Five Finger Exercise* and in *Royal Hunt* largely was refined away in the crucible of this early period. Shaffer thus worked at and mastered dramatic realism with these works. Yet, good as these pieces played on stage, they did not satisfy what Peter Shaffer ultimately intended to achieve. *Five Finger Exercise* proved a valuable base from which he later could launch into more innovative theatrical enterprises.

Most crucial to Shaffer's dramatic style are the imaginative risks exhibited in his masterpieces. *The Royal Hunt of the Sun* (1964), *Equus* (1973), *Amadeus* (1979), and even the revised *Yonadab* (1985) all exhibit the daring theatrical techniques that make up the playwright's imprimatur. What makes the techniques fresh is his brilliant fusion of presentational narrative modes with traditional realism. The four dramas noted convey their respective stories through a system of narrative frameworks. At the outermost perimeter stand the plays' chorus-like narrators serving as moderators or masters of ceremony. Old Martin, Doctor Dysart, Salieri, and Yonadab address the audience from their posts, first as outside observers of the respective story lines; later, they will blend into the inner plot line as active participants. Though not entirely objective, each moderator as watcher enjoys a unique perspective that instantly engages the attention, interest, and curiosity of playgoers, drawing them into the action.[5]

Illustrations from the plays will help. Old Martin, Pizarro's young aide in *Royal Hunt,* quickly gains audience interest when addressing them directly with his opening lines to the play:

> Save you all. My name is Martin. I'm a soldier of Spain and that's it. Most of my life I've spent fighting for land, treasure, and the cross. I'm worth millions. Soon I'll be dead, and they'll bury me out here in Peru, the land I helped ruin as a boy. This story is about ruin. Ruin and gold. . . . I'm going to tell you how one hundred and sixty-seven men conquered an empire of twenty-four million. (From *Collected Plays of Peter Shaffer*, p. 247—all quotations of Shaffer's plays come from this edition unless noted otherwise.)

Following his tantalizing come-on, Martin conjures flashback scenes through which Pizarro and other characters are introduced.

Parallel opening scenes mark all of Shaffer's finest dramas, whereby a narrator entices the audience into the world of the play. Dr. Dysart in the opening lines from *Equus* speaks directly to the audience while gesturing behind him at a youth, Alan Strang, nuzzling a horse standing next to him. The puzzling tableau is further heightened by the psychiatrist's cryptic words:

> With one particular horse, called Nugget, he embraces. The animal digs its sweaty brow into his cheek, and they stand in the dark for an hour—like a necking couple. And of all the nonsensical things—I keep thinking about the *horse!* (401)

Amadeus opens similarly with a non-realistic invocation. Following an "overture" comprised of stichomythic exposition whispered by two chorus figures, Salieri turns directly to the audience. He then entices his playgoers with an irresistible summons:

> *Vi Saluto! Ombri del Futuro! Antonio Salieri—a vostro servizio!*. . . . I can almost see you in your ranks—waiting for your turn to live. Ghosts of the Future! Be visible. I beg you. Be visible. Come to this dusty old room—this time, the smallest hours of dark November, eighteen hundred and twenty-three—and be my Confessors! (486–487)

Shaffer seems satisfied with the general template laid out here, for he turns again to its use in his most recent serious work, *Yonadab* (1985, heavily revised in 1987). Once he greets the audience at the start of *Yonadab,* the title protagonist begins to spin his web of enticing intrigue:

> This is a singularly unpleasant story. The Rabbis of the Middle Ages omitted it entirely, when they read out the scriptures, to spare the ears of their congregations—and they didn't know the half of it. I alone know it all—and, let me assure you, I don't intend to spare yours.[6]

In the four major plays, once having introduced himself and the general subject of the play, the narrator moves into the play circuitry where he assumes an active role in the enacted scenes of the story. At irregular intervals, the narrator breaks the illusion to comment often to the spectators about the scenic actions.[7] Such "breaks" in the story line allow for clarifying commentary on the plot, just as the omniscient observer in fiction uses stop-action to offer all-knowing remarks on the proceedings. But beyond that useful advantage, the narrator's "interruption" of the tale privileges him to fast-forward to later episodes in the story at will. The narrators—Martin, Dysart, Salieri, and

Yonadab—become our guides as we traverse the actions of the plot, moving us faster or slower, directing our attention from one character to another, or from one detail to a second one.

Shaffer did not originate the narrator figure, of course. Witness Shakespeare's Richard the Second and Iago who also plot strategy for the audience before joining in the action. Similarly, tragic heroes in classical Greek drama often speak directly to the spectators. No one, however, develops the narrator character more effectively than Shaffer both as a story-telling device *and* as a fascinating figure unto himself. Use of the narrating "stage manager" also represents a hybrid version of presentational theater. For although the direct address to the audience cannot be considered realistic, the internal scenes introduced by the narrator are staged in what essentially is realism: characters communicate with each other through realistic dialogue, they move about the stage in conventional blocking, and the theatrical illusion is sustained for the duration of the scene being enacted. Shaffer thereby wrings important concessions from the realm of theatrical realism to gain flexibility in the narrative process.

Other non-representational modes emerge in the dramas of Peter Shaffer. Each of his four major works features striking iconographic sets and props to reinforce the substance of his themes. In *Royal Hunt,* the most stunning moments are evoked visually and through sound effects. Shaffer's stage directions to open scene 3 of the first act introduce the audience to the main visual emblem of the play:

> *The stage darkens and the huge medallion high on the back wall begins to glow. Great cries of "Inca!" are heard. Slowly the medallion opens outward to form a huge golden sun with twelve great inlaid rays. . . . In the center stands* ATAHUALLPA. (255)

Late in the play, that symbol of the sun is burned into the audience's memory during a scene called the Rape of the Sun; there, the greedy Spanish Conquistadors ravage the Incan emblem of gold to obtain its precious treasure. Again, the stage directions describe the non-verbal choreography involved:

> *Above, in the chamber, the treasure is piled up as before. DIEGO and the CHAVEZ brothers are seen supervising. They begin to explore the sun itself, leaning out of the chamber and prodding at the petals with their halberds. Suddenly DIEGO gives a cry of triumph, drives his halberd into a slot in one of the rays, and pulls out the gold inlay. The sun gives a deep groan, like the sound of a great animal being wounded. With greedy yelps, all the soldiers below rush at the sun and start pulling it to bits; they tear out the gold inlays and fling them on the ground, while terrible groans fill the air. In a moment only the great gold frame remains; a broken, blackened sun. (291)*

Other important moments in *Royal Hunt* form indelible imprints by innovatively combining sound with panoramic image. In The Mime of the Great Ascent (scene 8 of Act One), Shaffer conveys the sense of the Spaniards climbing the high, frigid Andes mountains on their way to meet Atahuallpa. Realistic depiction is abandoned for evocative symbols and strange sounds:

> As OLD MARTIN *describes their ordeal, the men climb the Andes. It is a terrible progress: a stumbling, torturous climb into the clouds, over the ledges and giant chasms, performed to an eerie, cold music made from the thin whine of huge metal saws.* (266)

Soon, the bloody conjunction of the European and Incan worlds is commemorated in The Mime of the Great Massacre that closes Act One. With no spoken dialogue, Shaffer portrays the horror of the Spaniards' betrayal of the Indians:

> *To a savage music, wave after wave of Indians are slaughtered and rise again to protect their lord, who stands bewildered in their midst. It is all in vain. Relentlessly the Spanish soldiers hew their way through the ranks of feathered attendants toward their quarry. They surround him . . . All the Indians cry out in horror. . . . [D]ragged from the middle of the sun by howling Indians, a vast bloodstained cloth bellies out over the stage. All rush off; their screams fill the theater. The lights fade out slowly on the rippling cloth of blood.* (277)

These illustrative passages only suggest the power of Shaffer's presentational techniques. *The Royal Hunt of the Sun* most fully embodies Shaffer's use of Epic and Total Theaters—modes advanced by Bertolt Brecht and Antonin Artaud.[8]

Analogous scenes of powerful non-verbal theater exist in the remaining serious dramas. Like its predecessor, *Royal Hunt, Equus* constructs its fable with a fusion of highly articulate dialogue in the mode of naturalism, embedded in mind-stretching visual scenes drawing on expressionism. Indeed, the central set utilized in the drama speaks metaphorically to the audience at all times. Shaffer's description of the set starts by calling it "A square of wood set on a circle of wood" ("The Setting," *Equus,* in *The Collected Plays,* p. 399). By requiring that the backdrop for the set consist of tiers of seats on risers with both audience members and cast seated there, Shaffer intends that those persons serve functions in the play as "Witnesses, assistants—and especially a Chorus" (399). Shaffer's set instructions further suggest the square set resembles "A railed boxing ring" and a "dissecting theater" in an operating room. Such images are entirely appropriate for a plot that entails savage battle between the powers of orderly society and the chaotic impulse of instinctual religious worship.[9]

Horses, of course, play a key part in *Equus,* and Shaffer's choice of how to represent them on stage fairly well determines his overall theatrical approach.

Shaffer is explicit in his stage directions that the horses only be portrayed abstractly. His descriptions of how actors are to play horses prohibit even the least element of realism. Brown-colored velvet tracksuits are to be worn by the actors, with matching gloves. On their feet are will be four-inch light-weight metal-braced lifts fastened to actual horseshoes. On their heads are large symbolic horse masks constructed of alternating strips of silver wire and leather, with no effort to hide the human head beneath.

Most telling of Shaffer's instructions about the horses is his mandate that "Any literalism which could suggest the cozy familiarity of a domestic animal—or worse, a pantomime horse—should be avoided. . . . Animal effect must be created entirely mimetically. . . . so that the masking has an exact and ceremonial effect" (400). The ritual base underlying *Equus* requires Alan Strang's orgiastic sessions of worship to be presentationally given. Only symbolic creatures and abstracted movements befit the play's theme. The result theatrically, however, is stunning. At the conclusion of the play's first act, Alan is hypnotized into reenacting his regular worship-rides on the horse Nugget. In Dysart's office, before the mesmerized psychiatrist, the boy activates the half dozen horse figures for his dream ride by calling out, "Equus—son of Fleckwus—son of Neckwus—*Walk*" (447). The rites which follow are described through stage directions:

> "*[A hum from the* CHORUS. *Very slowly the horses standing on the circle begin to turn the square by gently pushing the wooded rail.* ALAN *and his mount start to revolve. The effect, immediately, is of a statue being slowly turned round on a plinth. During the ride, however, the speed increases, and the light decreases until it is only a fierce spotlight on horse and rider, with the overspill glinting on the other masks leaning in toward them."]* (447).

All the while, Alan first croons, then shouts, instructions to the horse, projecting the lad's combined religious and sexual ecstacy that culminates in obvious spiritual and physical orgasm.

Equus contains an equally spectacular finale which relies on symbolic actions using presentationalism. Alan's attempt to make love with Jill at the stables is interrupted by what the boy believes to be Equus' warning from the adjacent stall. His sexual desire totally squelched by religious guilt, Alas brutally dismisses the girl and prepares to answer Equus' demands for obeisance. During this abreacted scene inspired by Dysart's promises for his total recovery, Alan exhibits through his actions why he stabbed out the eyes of six horses: Alan's hopes for a normal sexual life was blocked by hisself-designed religion making Equus his personal god. The lad knows of no other choice:

ALAN *[in terror]*:Eyes! . . . White eyes—never closed!
    Eyes like flames—coming—coming!

> . . .God seest! God seest! . . . NO!
> . . . . No more. No more, Equus
> . . . . Equus . . . Noble Equus . . .
> Faithful and True . . . God-slave . . .
> Thou—God—Seest—NOTHING!
>
> *[He stabs out NUGGET'S eyes. The horse stamps in agony. A great screaming begins
> to fill the theater, growing ever louder. ALAN dashes at the other two horses and
> blinds them too, stabbing over the rails. . . . The screams increase. The other
> horses follow into the square. The whole place is filled with cannoning, blinded
> horses. . . .] (474)*

As in *Royal Hunt,* Shaffer turns to traditional realism, with its highly
explicit and articulate dialogue, to promote plot and characterization for much
of *Equus.* But for the climactic moments in the plot, the playwright provides
emblematic scenes in which visual and aural effects move audience intellects—
and emotions—beyond what is possible through stage literalism. Those remarkable stage images epitomize the glory of Shaffer's playwriting.

Of all that Shaffer has written to date, *Amadeus* elicits the most praise for
its dramaturgical strengths. As in *Royal Hunt* and *Equus,* Shaffer punctuates
his major scenes in *Amadeus* with haunting theatrical effects to create an unforgettable picture. And as in all his dramas, he consciously designs symbolic
moments to conclude each act. Moreover, the epiphanous scenes represent far
more than riveting moments appealing to the audience's visual and aural
senses. Shaffer in those episodes succeeds brilliantly in embodying crucial
truths in a single image. He does so by the imaginative melding of realistic
speech with abstract image. The result is the coalescence of previous story
understanding into a new, revelatory whole.

The most dazzling scene of enlightenment in *Amadeus* occurs at the close
of Act One. By this point in the story, Antonio Salieri, principal musician in
Emperor Joseph II's court in Vienna, has come to fear the musical genius of his
younger rival Mozart. To measure the threat represented by the upstart new-
comer, Salieri coerces Mozart's wife into bringing him Mozart's manuscripts of
works-in-progress. Once Salieri begins to read the written musical scores, the
sounds of actual music are heard in the theater to designate what he was reading. Shaffer not only has solved the logistics of allowing his audience to share
the music Salieri hears in his head; the dramatist also mounts an electric experience on stage to suggest how transcendent the moment stands in musical history.

An analysis of this single scene reflects Shaffer's innovative mind at work.
He first needs to have Salieri become aware of the immensity of Mozart's
genius. Once that amazing fact has sunk in, Salieri must be made to revolt
against God's ordained design. Using a two-part schema, the dramatist first
stuns Salieri with Mozart's music itself. The stage directions interweave with
Salieri's monologue to forge the climactic moment in his life:

[. . . He contemplates the music lying there as if it were a great confection he is dying to eat, but dare not. Then suddenly he snatches at it—tears the ribbon—opens the case and stares greedily at the manuscripts within. Music sounds instantly, faintly, in the theater, as his eye falls on the first page. It is the opening of the Twenty-Ninth Symphony, *in A Major.* Over the music, reading it.]

SALIERI:She had said that these were his original scores. First and only drafts of the music. Yet they looked like fair copies. They showed no corrections of any kind. . . . Displace one note and there would be diminishment. Displace one phrase and the structure would fall. [*He resumes reading, and the music also resumes: a ravishing phrase from the slow movement of the* Concerto for Flute and Harp.] . . . The truth was clear. That serenade had been no accident. . . . I was staring through the cage of those meticulous ink strokes at an Absolute Beauty! (518–519)

To represent how devastating this new understanding is to Salieri, Shaffer instructs the composer to fall into a swoon. The question then arises, what will—or can—Salieri do about the situation with Mozart? With that unspoken query in the audience's collective mind, Shaffer shifts into the scene's second part: Salieri's new resolve. Upon regaining consciousness, lying amidst the fallen manuscripts of Mozart's compositions, Salieri *"addresses his God"*:

Capisco! I know my fate. Now for the first time I feel my emptiness as Adam felt his nakedness . . . *Grazie, Signore!* You gave me the desire to serve you—which most men do not have—then saw to it the service was shameful in the ears of the server. . . . *Why?* . . . *What is my fault?* . . . . I have worked and worked the talent you allowed me. . . . Solely that in the end, in practice of the art which alone makes the world comprehensible to me, I might hear Your Voice! And now I do hear it—and it says only one name: MOZART! . . . . Spiteful. sniggering, conceited, infantine Mozart! . . . . [*Savagely.*] *Grazie e grazie ancora!* [*Pause*] So be it! From this time we are enemies. You and I! I'll not accept it from You. (519–520)

And with Salieri's audacious challenge to God, Shaffer closes the first half of his drama. The overall design now is apparent, and the remainder of the play will chronicle Salieri's failed attempt to defeat his deity.

Nothing from the second act achieves quite the equivalent excitement, although the bizarre death scene of Mozart is highly charged as he discovers Salieri's machinations. Salieri's attempted suicide near the end also provides striking visual pictures that reenforce the final frustrated acts of the deranged court composer. Ironically, the emblematic scene which best counterbalances the close of Act One does not appear in Shaffer's play text but rather in his movie script for *Amadeus*. There, a new, important episode is added to depict Mozart—

on his deathbed—dictating to Salieri the unfinished score to his *Requiem Mass.* Though the added movie scene attains enormous dramatic power, the actions it proposes are wholly fictitious and incredible. In the stage script proper, the final graphic moment showing Salieri proves powerful enough: he stands before us—an aged, crazed, but still shrewd conniver—arms outspread to welcome us into his brotherhood of Mediocrities.

Shaffer's next drama was *Yonadab* (1985), his fable of human evil and aspirations drawn from Biblical accounts. Given the dark and foreboding tenor of the play, the initial emblematic scene seems entirely suitable. Again, the episode appears near the end of the opening act. Here, another complete scene (scene 8) follows before the act actually concludes. But for all practical purposes, little additional exposition or plot development can occur after the hair-raising events of scene 7.

The plot, in brief, concerns the devilry of King David's errant nephew Yonadab in Jerusalem long before the Christian era. Beginning with facts from Samuel 2 in the Old Testament, Shaffer fashions another god-seeking protagonist.[10] In the case of Yonadab, though he aspires to godhead, he hungers first for finite proof of God's existence. One of his tactics to "flush out God" is to challenge Him on every front. Yonadab gradually convinces his cousin Amnon, heir apparent to David's throne, that Amnon can take whatever he desires and thereby define his godhead. Yonadab, meanwhile, stands on the sideline to watch as those he dupes attempt to become earthly deities through arrogant actions usually reserved for gods alone.

When he confesses to Yonadab that he wants motre than anything to sexually possess his half-sister Tamar, Amnon is actively encouraged by Yonadab. Tamar is tricked into going to Amnon's palace and even to his bedroom, under the ruse of his being very ill. Once alone with her, Amnon reveals his true intentions to have her. She remains obdurate to his seduction, and Amnon quickly loses patience and rapes her. Yonadab is the voyeur *par excellence,* and he locates himself near the bed chamber to observe. Unexpectedly, Amnon drops the curtains surrounding the bed, leaving Yonadab the mere watcher of blurred shadows on the curtains. Shaffer ingeniously constructs a visual version of a momentous event in ancient history—all through a narrated account of shifting shadows. Yonadab is the audience's guide to a deed that ultimately leads to the demise of David's house and unrivalled empire:

> *(With increasing visibility the shadows of their bodies are thrown on to the curtain; immense black shapes enlarged and distorted by the lamps. During the following speech they make a series of abstract and strange shapes: a mysterious procession of glyphs.)*
>
> *(To audience)* All my life I remembered what I saw that night: the shadows!— more terrible than bodies. The limbs thrown up on the curtains like the letters of some grotesque language formed long, long before writing. There on the

fall of a Jerusalem drape I saw, writ enormous . . . the archaic alphabet of the Book of Lust. (127, from *Lettice and Lovage* and *Yonadab* [London: Penguin Books, 1989]. All quotations from *Yonadab* will be taken from this edition)

In *Yonadab* as in the other dramas considered here, the unique achievement of Shaffer's writing involves the surprising merger of realistic and presentational elements that usually remain antithetical to one another. Thus, even as Yonadab narrates the dreadful results of his plottings with Amnon, Tamar, and Absalom, Shaffer knows to insert a visual cameo to underscore the situation emblematically:

> *(Low music sounds. From high above descends the corpse of ABSALOM hanging by its long black hair.)*
>
> YONADAB: *(To audience)* Absalom died later—caught in a tree by his famous hair, fleeing the wrath of his father.
>
> *(KING DAVID) appears, his head under a prayer shawl. The HELPERS depart.)*
>
> The father mourned his eldest son, of course—but the mourning for Absalom far exceeded the mourning for Amnon. It was the hardest pain of his life. . . . I saw all their transports, this royal family, their lusts for transcendence—and I saw nothing. Always the curtain was between us. (181)

Parallel to Shaffer's other dramas, the passage just noted appears at the conclusion of *Yonadab,* serving as a neat sum-up of the entire play, thanks to articulate, realistic narrative joined to an unforgettable visual emblem.

Finally, lest we think Shaffer's patented curtain closers occur only with his serious plays, consider for a moment his comedy *Lettice & Lovage* (1987). Several features are found in *Lettice & Lovage* that resemble those of the more serious drama; but for now we shall focus on the crucial curtain scenes, particularly those ending the first two acts.[11] Act One closes with the tour guide Lettice Douffet fired by her superior at the Preservation Trust, Lotte Schoen. Their "exit interview" had been free-wheeling, and the contrasting views of the two women openly aired. Although she had tried to explain her infelicities with facts concerning the provincial estate of which she was tour guide, Lettice realized in advance that her attempts would be futile. Therefore, when Lotte indeed dismissed her, Lettice was ready. With great august bearing, Lettice likens herself to Queen Mary just before her execution by Elizabeth. Lettice asks her exeutioner Lotte if she recalled what Queen Mary had worn on that auspicious day:

> LETTICE: Queen Mary appeared in a dress of deepest black. But when her ladies removed this from her—what do you imagine was revealed?
>
> LOTTE: I really can't guess.
>
> LETTICE: . . . A full-length shift was seen. A garment the color of the whoring of which she had been accused! The color of martyrdom—and defiance! *Blood red!*

[She steps out of her cloak to reveal a brilliant red ankle-length nightdress, embossed all over with little golden crowns . . .]

Yes—all gasped with the shock of it! All watched with unwilling admiration—that good old word again—all watched with *wonder* as that frail captive, crippled from her long confinement, stepped out of the darkness of her nineteen years' humiliation and walked into eternity—a totally self-justified woman! (32, from *Lettice & Lovage* [New York: Harper & Row, 1990]. Quotations are taken from this edition.)

The graphic gesture of a doomed woman, metaphorically thumbing her nose at her captors, precisely matches Lettice's circumstances.

Lettice's black cloak figures in the emblem scene closing the play's second act, as well. By now in the plot, Lettice and Lotte are becoming good friends—with the help of "quaff," a strong brew Lettice alleges to be of Renaissance origin. Lotte even reveals that she wears a wig, showing how much a confidante, Lettice has become. The women decide to eat out, and Lettice urges her colleague to leave her wig off when they leave to dine. After a hesitation, Lotte agrees:

LOTTE: Very well . . . I will.
[They look at each other. Then LETTICE laugh, a clear bright laugh of perception, and walks away across the room. She laughs again.]
What is it? What are you thinking?
[But instead of replying, LETTICE takes off her black cloak and lays it ceremoniously at the base of the staircase, in the manner of Sir Walter Raleigh assisting Queen Elizabeth.]
LETTICE: Come,, madame. Your hedgehogs await! (61)

Again, a picture is worth the proverbial thousand words. In both emblem scenes, the logical and literal factors of the moment are fused with an apt pictorial rendition to effect striking theatrical results.

Nowhere among his plays does Peter Shaffer venture far from his personal version of "realism." That fact perhaps should not surprise playgoers, because Shaffer's dialogue stands with the finest written in our times. And articulate language, after all, is "literal" in all senses of that term. But Shaffer is not content with a single dramaturgical strength; his imagination reaches outward to encompass visual displays of literal thought. Nor are the graphic equivalents to realistic details limited to mere symbols on stage. Shaffer, with the help of equally innovative directors such as John Dexter and Peter Hall, stretches to embody spectacular but always intelligent theatrical techniques, as we have seen.

If we seek to isolate one specific attribute that defines Peter Shaffer's genius, then, we could do worse than to choose the methods chronicled here:

the masterful merging of the literalism of realism with the provocative of the abstract pictorial. Shaffer's power derives from a type of "trans-literalism" that invites the shorthand of stage emblems. No other playwright today can claim such an achievement.

NOTES

[1] Full details concerning Shaffer's youth may be found in Gene A. Plunka, *Peter Shaffer: Roles, Rites, and Rituals in the Theater* (Rutherford, N.J.: Fairleigh Dickinson Univ. Press, 1988). Also, see my forthcoming book *Peter Shaffer* from Macmillan (UK) in 1991.

[2] Clare Colvin, "Quest for Perfection," *Drama,* No. 159 (1986); 12.

[3] Useful comment on this entire issue is found in C. J. Gianakaris. "Drama into Film: The Shaffer Situation," *Modern Drama,* 28, No. 1 (1985): 83–98.

[4] See, for example, Mervyn Rothstein, "Passionate Beliefs Renew a Fight over Art and Profit," *New York Times,* 15 May 1990, Sec. B, pp. 1–2.

[5] Comparable narrator-protagonists occasionally have appeared on world stages, as in Brecht's *The Good Woman of Setzuan* and Robert Bolt's *A Man for All Seasons;* Shakespeare perhaps employed such a joint character most fully with the figure of Richard the Third.

[6] From *Lettice and Lovage* and *Yonadab* (London: Penguin Books, 1989), p. 87.

[7] Old Martin represents a slightly different case. Martin, as older man, appears at the play's beginning, at its end, and occasionally throughout. But because he tells of events in Peru when he was a boy, Martin in the story line proper is played by a youthful version of himself—another, younger actor altogether called Young Martin. In a shorter play, the presence of two Martins on stage would not be a drawback because spectators would encounter no problem in keeping the two characters straight; however, in *Royal Hunt* the large cast sometimes confuses audiences regarding the two Martin parts. In *Equus* there is no problem because the actions Dysart narrates seemingly occurred in the near past, a circumstance duplicated by Yonadab and his tale, as well. Shaffer solved the time shifts effectively for *Amadeus.* There, Salieri smoothly alters his appearance by disguises, from agedness to youth and back again, while continuing to address the audience.

[8] An informative and full discussion of the influence of Brecht and Antonin Artaud on Shaffer's plays is available in Gene A. Plunka's book cited above.

[9] I have discussed the ramifications of the set for *Equus* elsewhere in "Theatre of the Mind in Miller, Osborne and Shaffer," *Renascence,* 30, No. 1 (1977): 33–42.

[10] Shaffer freely acknowledges, however, an equally essential influence in his writing of *Yonadab.* The playwright had read with great interest the 1970 novel *The Rape of Tamar* by the South African writer Dan Jacobson (New York: Macmillan). Jacobson's book contains many of the features Shaffer was to use, including making Yonadab's the central perspective for the narration.

[11] The emblem scene closing the original version of *Lettice and Lovage* also matched the summary qualities of which we have spoken. But to make the overall story line more logical, Shaffer changed the ending and so dropped the marvelous visual affect of a petard being readied for battle against London's philistine establishment. Incidentally, the deleting in *Lettice and Lovage* of the conjunction "and" and its replacement with an ampersand (as in *Lettice & Lovage*) occurred when the revised play opened on Broadway in March of 1990.

Great Expectations: Language and the Problem of Presence in Sam Shepard's Writing

Ann Wilson

> Walt Whitman was a great man. He expected something from America. He had this great expectation.
>
> —Sam Shepard, *Action*

Sam Shepard is the pre-eminent playwright of the contemporary American theatre. His work has received numerous awards including the Pulitzer Prize in 1979 for *Buried Child.* Despite his success, Shepard has not always felt comfortable identifying himself as a writer. In the program note to *Cowboy Mouth,* the play which he co-wrote with Patti Smith, he announced, "I don't want to be a playwright, I want to be a rock and roll star" (Shewey 81). Later in the same note, he claims that "writing is neat because you do it on a physical level. Just like rock and roll" (Shewey 81). As glib as these two remarks may seem at first, they do suggest reasons for Shepard's ambivalence about writing.

The writer's medium is language which Shepard believes "has become so corrupt, laundered, stripped of meaning. We often don't know what we mean anymore" (Wren 90). In forging the link between writing and music, particularly jazz and rock-and-roll—two modes of music which often involve improvisation, Shepard expresses his yearning for a pure language which does not mediate experience but acts as a transparent medium which reveals fully the signified. He wants to discover a language in which the signifier does not *rep*-resent the signified but makes it present. It is this sense of language which allows Michael Earley to suggest that Shepard is heir to the transcendentalist tradition of American writing because he "brings to the drama a liberating interplay of word, theme and image that has always been the hallmark of romantic writing" (127). While I agree with Earley that there is a strain in Shepard's writing which relates his work to that of the transcendentalist poets (especially

Whitman), it is misleading to suggest that this is a strictly literary influence. The desire to discover a language or mode of representation which makes fully present the signifier is evident in a number of American cultural projects including the work of Shepard's friend and sometime collaborator, Joseph Chaikin and music (particularly jazz and rock and roll).

In an essay called "Language, Visualization and the Inner Library," he writes,

> From time to time I've practiced Jack Kerouac's discovery of jazz-sketching with words. Following the exact same principles as a musician does when he's jamming. After periods of this kind of practice, I begin to get the haunting sense that something in me writes but it's not necessarily me. At least it's not the "me" that takes credit for it. This identical experience happened to me once when I was playing drums with the Holy Modal Rounders, and it scared the shit out of me. Peter Stampfel, the fiddle player, explained it as being visited by the Holy Ghost, which sounded reasonable enough at the time. (205)

Shepard's remarks suggest that he constructs writing as a mysterious process which requires inspiration and which, when truly executed, has the power to reveal the unknown. He said, "I feel a lot of reluctance in attempting to describe any part of a process which, by its truest nature, holds unending mystery" (214). In answer to Amy Lippman's question about why he writes, Shepard responded, "I try to go into parts of myself that are unknown. And I think that those parts are related to everybody. They are not unique to me. They're not my personal domain" (21). From such a perspective the writer records his privileged vision; yet, necessarily, the rendering of the vision is always distorted and imperfect. "Words, at best, can only give a partial glimpse into the total world of sensate experience" (Shepard, 216). Despite his recognition of the limitations of language, Shepard still believes in the unrealized ideal of a language which can represent fully.

Although his remark about the inspiration of the Holy Ghost seems offhand, it indicates his sense of the essential mystery of writing. If we remember that "inspiration" is from the Latin words *in* and *spirare,* then the writer who has been inspired (or "visited") by the Holy Ghost is one into whom the Holy Ghost has breathed. The entry of the Holy Ghost into the body of the writer is a moment of unity when the spirit and body are one and utterance is pure because the signifier (spirit) and the signified (the sign) are one. Within a religious context, the unification of thought and expression which is said to create a pure, unmediated language, is called glossolalia. This is not to suggest that Shepard's theatre is evangelical but rather that his sense of language gives it a theological impulse. He admires Shakespeare because his language authentically represents the human condition. He "traveled very far in himself to find it. The language didn't come out of the air, it came from a tremendous search, a religious experience" (Wren 81).

Shepard seeks to discover within himself the language which will make the signified fully present by overcoming loss which attends the separation of the signifier and the signified. Jacques Derrida in his essay "Theater of Cruelty" calls this language "glossopoeia."

> Glossopoeia, which is neither an imitative language nor a creation of names, takes us back to the borderline of the moment when the word has not yet been born, when articulation is no longer a shout but not yet discourse, when repetition is *almost* impossible, and along with it language in general: the separation of concept and sound, of the signified from signifier, of the pneumatical and the grammatical, the freedom of translation and tradition, the movement of interpretation, the difference between the soul and the body, the master and the slave, God and man, author and actor. (240)

Derrida suggests that the failure of the project is inscribed at the moment of inception when he writes "repetition is *almost* impossible." As indicated, emphasis falls on "almost" because if glossopoeia is a language, albeit one which is liminal, then there must be the possibility of its repetition because this is the defining characteristic of language. Thus, the originary moment of language when the signified is made fully present by the signifier is always elusive, approached but never reached.

This sense of the failure of language to reveal fully that which it signifies marks the particularly American quality of Shepard's writing. Harold Bloom suggests, "Emerson wanted Freedom, reconciled himself to Fate, but loved only Power, from first to last and I believe this to be true also of the central line of American poets coming after him" (*Poems* 8). He explains that Emerson defines the terms "Freedom," "Fate," and "Power" as follows:

> Freedom or "the free spirit" makes form into *potentia,* into strength that Emerson defines as eloquence. . . . Fate, as a word, comes from a root meaning "speech," but by one of Emerson's characteristic dialectical reversals Power takes on meaning as eloquent speech while Fate is a script or writing opposed to speech. (*Poems* 7)

Bloom argues that the Emersonian triad of Fate-Freedom-Power appears in Whitman's work as *"my soul-myself-the real me or me myself"* (*Poems* 7). This triad is found in Shepard's work, too, although Freedom, the impulse or spirit which informs writing, is subsumed by Power: Freedom (eloquence) can be expressed only in Power (speech) thereby reducing the Emersonian triad to a pair, Fate and Power. This reduction is important because now the two elements are seen clearly as oppositional: Fate is the antithesis of Power. In this duality, speech is privileged over writing and so is attributed primacy. It is represented as an inchoate, less mediated mode of expression than writing, as having greater capacity to reveal the authentic self. Writing—merely a supplement to the privileged mode of expression, speech—is always secondary.[1]

This tension, although not addressed directly by Shepard, is implied by several remarks he has made. Speaking to the participants in a seminar on play-writing which he taught as part of the Bay Area Playwrights Festival III (1980), Shepard warned, "There is the tendency to trade experience itself for language which never really captures it and ultimately cheats experience" (Wren 81). He suggests that experience is pure but becomes sullied when expressed. Implied by his remark is the position that the plenitude of experience can never be spoken fully. This raises the question: how do we recognize experience except through language?

In "Language, Visualization and the Inner Library," Shepard writes,

> The picture is moving in the mind and being allowed to move more and more freely as you follow it. The following of it is the writing part. In other words, I'm taking notes in as much detail as possible on an event that's happening somewhere inside me. The extent to which I can actually follow the picture and intervene with my own two-cents worth is where inspiration and crafts-manship hold their meaning. If I find myself pushing a character in a certain direction, it's almost a sure sign that I've fallen back on technique and lost the real thread of the thing. (215)

That the writer records the action as it unfolds in his imagination without inter-vening and shaping it, implies that this action exists independent of and prior to language.

Shepard, while he is reluctant to admit that experience is inseparable from language, is not successful in suppressing the interpretative function of the writer. One of the participants in Shepard's seminar on playwriting, Scott Christopher Wren recalls, "Shepard comments that there is a real sense of fol-lowing the action from the inside . . ." (85). Again, he insists that experience and language are separate and that language is secondary to experience or, as he says, that it "follows." Subtly, almost imperceptibly, he amends his initial statement of the writer's role:

> . . . There is a real sense of following the action from the inside, such that the accidental gesture has purpose. It's no longer accidental because it's wit-nessed, followed very carefully moment to moment. (85)

The repetition of "follow" obscures the important shift of ideas in the remark. Initially the writer "follows" the action which implies that action occurs inde-pendently and he merely records. What interests me is the ascription of purpose to the gesture because it is the writer who assigns it. The writer no longer follows the scene but witnesses the action and, in so doing, actively enters the scene because in witnessing the action, he reads it. It is the writer who interprets the gesture as significant. Despite his professed belief that action is distinct from language, the ascription of purpose by the writer suggests that Shepard, to some degree, understands them as inseparable. Recognizing action is predicated on our ability to differentiate one action from another which can only be done through categories which are created within language. Shepard's suggestion that the imagination operates independent of language is a bit fanciful; yet, as fanciful as is this idealization of imagination, it is this which informs both Shepard's writing and Whitman's.

Both Whitman and Shepard yearn to discover a language which will make fully present the signified. Necessarily, this language is corporeal, the union of the body (signifier) and spirit (signified) celebrated by the sound of the voice. Wren recalls that Shepard taught "that developing characters is a process of coming in touch with *voice*" (81). He recalls Shepard saying "Voice is the nut of it. Character is an expression of voice, the emotional tone underneath. If a writer is totally connected with the voice, it will be in the words" (76). Shepard's remark implies a sense of character as an essence which is realized only through voice. The breath (spirit) translates this essence from its pure state of interiority to the exteriority of the sign (the actor's body or words).

For Shepard, the crux of the problem of identity is this process of translation. We can only constitute identity through language; but language is debased and so inevitably we lose sight of our "true" or "real" selves. In an interview with Michiko Kakutani, he explained the effect of debased language on identity:

> Personality is everything that is false in a human being. It is everything that's been added on to him and contrived. It seems to me that the struggle all the time is between this sense of falseness and the other haunting sense of what is true—an essential thing that we're born with and tend to lose track of. This naturally sets up a great contradiction in everybody between what they represent and what they know to be themselves. (26)

This nostalgic yearning for an authentic self is perhaps the single most striking feature common both to Shepard's writing and to Whitman's. We need only to think of the title of one of Whitman's poems, "Song of Myself," to recognize the importance of voice to his project of self-representation. The poem is a song which attempts to celebrate masturbation both as an image and inscription of *jouissance* of self-discovery. Here I use "*jouissance*" in Kristeva's sense:

> . . . "Jouissance" is total joy or ecstasy (without any mystical connotation; also, through the working of the signifier, this implies the presence of

meaning (jouissance = j'ouis sens = I heard meaning), requiring it by going
beyond it. (Roudiez, 16)

"Song of Myself" suggests that the ecstatic moment of orgasm is the moment
when the true or essential self is realized fully:

> I merely stir, press, feel with my fingers, and am happy,
> To touch my person to some else's is about as much as I can stand.
> Is then a touch? . . . quivering me to a new identity,
> Flames and ether making a rush for my veins, (616–20)

> I am given up by traitor:
> I talk wildly. . . . I have lost my wits. . . . I and nobody else am the
>   greatest traitor,
> I went myself first to the headland . . . my own hands carried me there.

> You villain touch! what are you doing? . . . . my breath is tight in its
>   throat;
> unclench your floodgates! you are too much for me. (636–41)

Two aspects of "Song of Myself" are relevant to a discussion of the relationship between Whitman's writing and Shepard's. First, although the poem
clearly celebrates masturbation, orgasm is marked by ellipses, by the absence
of words. We are given only a description—that the poet talks wildly—but no
transcription of what he says. If orgasm is indeed the moment when the true
self is realized, then the true self is beyond language. We are reminded of Derrida's contention that the originary moment is beyond knowledge, is always
already lost. Secondly, there is the sense of the poet's guilt suggested by the
words "traitor" and "villain touch." On the simplest level, it is the expression
of self-reproach for daring to acknowledge masturbation. It is the guilt of someone who feels that he is a traitor to himself because he engages in a practice
which has been taught, and to some degree believes, is wrong. The expression
of guilt divides the self into the traitor and betrayed which, ironically, replicates the onanistic gesture which divides the self into the toucher and the
touched thereby recognizing the binary opposition of interiority/exteriority.
". . . The outside, the exposed surface of the body signifies and marks forever
the division that shapes auto-affection" (*Grammatology* 165). That the touched
surface of the body is exterior insinuates the existence of the interior which
remains hidden by the surface. This structure, which recognizes the duality of
interior/exterior, is the structure of the sign which is divided into the signified
and signifier thus allowing Derrida to claim that "auto affection is a universal
structure of experience" (*Grammatology* 165).

For our purposes, what is important about this duality is that knowledge of
the interior is possible only through exteriority. The signified is known only

through the agency of signifier so that it is never itself present but is always represented. The signified is idealized as that which cannot itself be known. From such a perspective the "real-Me" is beyond knowledge because it cannot be made present. The poet is betrayed by onanism but not simply in the sense of sexual activity. The masturbatory gesture becomes a paradigm for signification because the poet is betrayed by his medium, language, which cannot realize the presence of the "real-Me" that it signifies. Yet, paradoxically, the "real-Me" is idealized only because of the structure of signification which admits the notion of the ideal. The project of making fully present the signified, which is common to Whitman and Shepard, is marked by failure from the outset because the structure of the sign protects the signified as the ideal beyond knowledge. Put simply, once the signified is known, it ceases to be the signified because it is now the signifier.

Chaikin's work never alludes to the influence of American literary figures;[2] however, accounts of his work (particularly in *The Presence of the Actor*) suggest the interest common to his work, Whitman's and Shepard's. The title of Chaikin's book points to his pre-occupation with the notion of "presence;" yet, despite its importance to his work, he never offers an exact definition of the term. Eileen Blumenthal interprets presence as "the quality of being here right now, with an awareness of the actual space and the actual moment of the vital meeting of lives in that space and moment" (113). In contrast, Chaikin's own description of "presence" is noteworthy for its refusal to define the term with any degree of precision. He writes:

> This "presence" on the stage is a quality given to some and absent from others. All of the history of the theater refers to actors who possess this presence.
>
> It's a quality that makes you feel as though you're sitting in the theatre. . . . There may be nothing of this quality off stage or in any other circumstance in the life of such an actor. It's a deep libidinal surrender which the performer reserves for his anonymous audience. (20)

Later in *The Presence of the Actor* Chaikin writes, "Just before a performance, the actor usually has additional energy like an electrical field" (21). The image of currents of energy recurs:

> . . . The actor must find an empty place where the living current moves through him uninformed. A clear place. Let's say the place from where the breath is drawn . . . not the breath . . . but from where the inhalation starts. . . .
>
> There are streams of human experience which are deep and constant moving through us on a level below sound. As we become occupied with our own noises, we're unable to be in the stream. The more an actor boasts of his feeling as he feels it, the farther he is from the current.

First, the actor must be present in his body, present in his voice . . .
The voice originates inside the body and comes to exist in the room. (66)

These passages illustrate Chaikin's insistence on a lexis of "presence," a lexis which is reminiscent of that developed by Whitman to write the "real Me." "Presence" is a kind of "deep libidinal surrender" which Chaikin renders metaphorically as "the living current." Like Chaikin, Whitman and Shepard use the image of energy to suggest the dynamic, ever-changing and mysterious nature of reality. Whitman, in *Leaves of Grass,* titles a poem "I Sing the Body Electric"; Shepard writes of "Words as tools of imagery in motion" (216) and of a work as having a "life-stream" (Wren 90). For Shepard, the sense of language in motion is particularly important because reality is inconstant. If it is to be made present, it must be done in a flash. "In these lightning-like eruptions words are not thought, they're felt. They cut through space and make perfect sense without having to hesitate for the 'meaning'" (Shepard 217).

In the writings of all three, the image of energy suggests the dynamic, ever-changing nature of reality, constituted as mysterious and unknowable, which relates this reality to identity: in Whitman's poetry, the "real Me" is the originary site of his identity; Shepard claims that through his writing he tries "to go into parts of myself that are unknown" (Lippman 21); Chaikin suggests that the actor attempts to reach an empty place where "the living current moves through him uninformed." Expressed in the work of all three is a nostalgic yearning for a moment of signification when the sign is inseparable from that which it signifies, the condition of language before it has fallen.

The romantic nature of this impulse is suggested by Shepard's remark "that the real quest of a writer is to penetrate into another world" (Shepard 217). Chaikin, too, uses the motif of the quest to describe his work:

Julian Beck said that an actor has to be like Columbus: he has to go out and discover something, and come back and report on what he discovers. Voyages have to be taken, but there has to be a place to come back to, and this place has to be different from the established theatre. It is not likely to be a business place. (34)

Indeed, in Chaikin's work the quixotic sentiment is so pronounced that it is manifest as a theme. In 1968, the Open Theater performed their collaborative piece, *The Serpent,* which is based on the account of creation in Genesis. "None of us," wrote Chaikin "believe there is or ever was a real Garden of Eden, but it lives in the mind as certain as memory" (67). For Chaikin, the Garden of Eden is not a geographic location now lost but a lost place within each person. Because of the post-lapsarian condition of language, this place cannot be recuperated in language; instead it can only be constituted through the allegoric resonances of myth.

Chaikin's desire to know the Edenic within man replicates Whitman's desire for the "real Me" which Bloom has suggested is a desire for the presexual:

> Whitman's "real Me" is what is best and oldest in him, and like the faculty Emerson called "Spontaneity" it is both nature's creation and Whitman's verbal cosmos. It is like a surviving fragment of the original Abyss preceding nature, not Adamic but pre-Adamic. The "real Me" is thus also presexual. ("The Real Me" 6)

The erotic in Whitman's poetry, the longing to express the "real Me" which is presexual, marks the failure of his poetic project. He can never satisfy his desire to retrieve his ideal, presexual self because of the relation between desire and language. Desire is the recognition of absence which is experienced as yearning. Because recognition is possible only through language, desire can only be recognized through language. But, language is itself an expression of desire because the signifier represents, and thus marks the absence of, the signified. That desire should be experienced only through that which is the product of desire is an unresolvable paradox which determines that Whitman can never retrieve his ideal presexual self because language cannot represent that which is presexual.

This problem, which faces Shepard as a writer, is reflected in the characters which he creates. Shepard comments, "Writing is born from a need. A deep burn. If there's no need, there is no desire" (218). He told Michiko Kakutani,

> People are starved for the truth and when something comes along that even looks like the truth, people will latch on to it because everything's so false. People are starved for a way of life—they're hunting for a way to be or act toward the world. (26)

Shepard's characters are often so hungry that they speak of themselves as starving. Think, for example, of Shooter in *Action* who says, "I'm starving. Did we eat already?" (139); or, in *Curse of the Starving Class,* of Ella's emphatic declaration to her daughter, "WE'RE HUNGRY, AND THAT'S STARVING ENOUGH FOR ME!" (142); or of the Speaker in *Tongues* who says, "This hunger knows no bounds. This hunger is eating me alive it's so hungry!" (311) and concludes, "Nothing left but the hunger eating itself. Nothing left but the hunger" (312).

The "Hunger Dialogue" is a paradigm for Shepard's use of hunger or appetite throughout his plays. In this piece, hunger is at first the physiological desire for food but, as the dialogue develops, it is clear that the food will not satisfy the speaker's hunger. Indeed, there is nothing which will sate his appetite because he is conscious only of his appetite and cannot identify what it is that he wants. Whether their appetites are for food, for the erotic (as in

Fool for Love or *A Lie of the Mind,* for example) or the simple desire to tell the true story (for example, in *Buried Child* or *Curse of the Starving Class*), many of Shepard's characters are desirous, their appetites impelling their actions. Yet their desires rarely are satisfied completely, as if the objects of their desire are impossible, which necessarily they are, because the structure of desire is such that desire can never be fully sated. As discussed, desire is recognized only through language which is itself the product of desire. This paradox marks the impossibility of desire being satisfied because the recognition of desire is predicated on language which marks the loss of the full presence of signified.

Invariably the impossible object of the characters' desire is themselves, whom they seek to realize through modes of performance which Florence Falk categorizes as role-playing, story-telling and music-making (188, 189). Shepard comments

> The stories my characters tell are stories that are always unfinished, always imagistic—having to do with recalling experiences through a certain kind of vision. They're always fractured and fragmented and broken. (Kakutani 26)

Given that identity is the story each of us tells about ourselves, the fact that Shepard's characters tell fractured, incomplete stories signals that none of them has a coherent sense of self. In a sense, each tries to call himself into being by performing himself.

As Richard Gilman notes, Shepard's sense of character as ever changing is influenced by Chaikin's work with actors in the Open Theater, particularly the transformation exercises (xv).

> Briefly, a transformation exercise was an improvised scene—a birthday party, survivors in a lifeboat, etc.—in which after a while, and suddenly, the actors were asked to switch immediately to a new scene and therefore wholly new characters. . . .
>
> Shepard carried the idea of transformations much farther than the group had by actually writing them into his texts, in plays like *Angel City, Back Bog Beast Bait* and *The Tooth of Crime* where the characters become wholly different in abrupt movements within the course of the work, or speak suddenly as someone else, while the scene may remain the same. (Gilman xv)

The purpose of the transformation exercise is to strip away the actors' contrived sense of how characters behave so that their performances do not rely on theatrical clichés. In theory, this sort of improvisational work encourages the actors to discover different aspects of themselves. As Shepard explains, "The voices of a lot of external-world characters are inside you. For example, when you write about a nun, it's not your 'idea' of a nun, it's the nun inside of you"

(Wren 80). Chaikin suggests that each of us has a myriad of characters inside us because within everyone is "a stream of human experiences which are deep and constant" (66). His remark echoes Shepard's answer to Amy Lippman, cited earlier, that the reason he writes is to go into parts of himself which are unknown but are related to everyone (21). In order to reach this place, Chaikin claims that the actor must first "be present in his body, in his own voice" (67); speaking about writing, Shepard corroborates Chaikin's remarks emphasizing "that writers have to begin with what they know and one of the best places is the body because the body is relating to everything and is grounded in experience rather than ideas" (Wren 86). Like Whitman who attempts to inscribe the "real Me" in "Song of Myself," Chaikin and Shepard use the analogy of music, in their case jazz, to explain how an actor will realize character. Chaikin suggests jamming a structure for improvisational work:

> The term comes from jazz, from the jam session. One actor comes in and moves in contemplation of a theme, traveling within rhythms, going through and out of the phrasing, sometimes using just the gesture, sometimes reducing the whole thing to pure sound. . . . During the jamming, if the performers let it, the theme moves into associations, a combination of free and structured form. (116)

In *Angel City,* jamming became Shepard's structural principle for the creation character. He instructs,

> The term "character" could be thought of in a different way when working on this play. Instead of the idea of a "whole character" with logical motives behind this behaviour which the actor submerges himself into, he should consider instead a fractured whole with bits and pieces of character flying off the central theme. In other words, more in terms of collage construction or jazz improvisation. (6)

As Florence Falk explains, "jazz in its very structure is improvisational—that is an alert, spontaneous, and dynamic creation" (190). It operates, as Shepard noted about rock music in the program note to *Cowboy Mouth,* on a physical level which allows (or at any rate gives the illusion of allowing) the union of impulse and expression: the signified is one with the signifier. Writing techniques based on jazz inhibit the mediation imposed by intellectualizing the process of writing. "When you're writing inside of a character like this, you aren't pausing every ten seconds to figure out what it all means," explains Shepard (217). We are returned to Shepard's sense of the writer following and recording the action.

Shepard's quest for an ideal language which will make fully present the signified clearly situates his project within the larger frame of American culture. "Presence" is not simply an attitude towards language but indicates no ideology which informs many aspects of this culture. It is manifest thematically as popular images of the frontier which is the borderline between civilization and wilderness. The frontier is a myth of eternal presence because when the frontier is encroached upon either by wilderness or civilization, it is not transformed but moves and is reconstituted in a new location. A frontier is always the same, is always the borderline. There may be a history of frontiers, but the frontier is itself a place without history because it is unchanging. In this sense the myth of the frontier enacts spatially the transcendentalist poetics to which Shepard is heir because the writer's desire is the discovery of a language which is pure, at the borderline when utterance is first made, "no longer a shout but not yet discourse."

Shepard's celebrated language is realized through his recurring interest in the West of popular culture (as, for example, in *Angel City, The Tooth of Crime, The Unseen Hand*). This thematic preoccupation exposes the ideological implications of presence in his work. First, the frontier is the domain of the cowboy who, as he is popularly represented, affirms the pre-adolescent values of a white, American boy. The sensibility is "usually anti-intellectual and anti-school" and so physical prowess is counted upon to resolve any conflict or problem (Davis 94–95). His strongest emotional tie (other than to his horse) is to

> a group of buddies, playing poker, chasing horse thieves, riding in masculine company. He is contemptuous of farmers, has no interest in children, and considers men who have lived among women as effete. Usually he left his own family at a tender age and rebelled against the restrictions of mothers and older sisters. (Davis 89)

Bonnie Marranca notes that the determination of the frontier myth is evident in Shepard's characterization of women:

> One of the most problematic aspects of the plays is Shepard's consistent refusal or inability, whichever the case may be, to create female characters whose imaginative range matches that of the males. . . . For a young man Shepard's portrayal of women is as outdated as the frontier ethic he celebrates: men have their showdowns or face the proverbial abyss while the women are absorbed in simple activities and simplistic thoughts. (30)

The pre-pubescent impulse of the myth casts women as dominating figures (mothers and sisters who are rebelled against) who want to rob men of their masculinity. In reaction to this fear of woman, the myth contains her by casting her as the complement to men. A woman, in westerns, is simply the site for a man to express tenderness. She "brings out qualities in him which we could not see otherwise. Without her, he would be too much the brute for a real folk hero, at least in the modern age" (Davis 89; Marranca 31).

In a broader political context, the myth of the frontier has important implications for Shepard's work. Although cowboys belong to gangs, these fraternal groups are devoid of any political (as distinct from moral) consciousness. The fact that the frontier is a borderline informs all aspects of life there. The social structures are informal, neither wilderness which has no social order nor civilization which is highly ordered but the liminality of emerging social organization. The structure of this paradigm replicates that of the transcendentalist's language which is seen as the threshold, "no longer a shout but not yet discourse." What is paradoxical is that the ideology of "present"—as it is articulated in the myth of the frontier and in the poetics of the transcendentalism—inscribes a politic which is both radical and conservative. It is radical because the individual is allowed to realize himself fully, unencumbered by social restraint; yet, the project is predicated on the existence of ideals which are accepted uncritically: the "true" self which can be realized; the triumph of good as the moral imperative of the frontier where the cowboy in the white hat always wins.

Shepard's romantic belief in the "true" self which is betrayed by language tends toward, if not conservatism, at least an apolitical perspective. The individual turns inward to discover himself rather than outward to the world in which he lives. Shepard's characters almost never indicate any sense of themselves as socially constructed beings. Perhaps by simple virtue of some concern for issues related to "class" as indicated by the title, *Curse of the Starving Class* comes closest to exploring the social determination of character. Yet even in that play, political concerns are transformed into concerns about performance. Faced with losing their land, the characters deny their situation by retreating into the world of fiction and memory as they tell the story of the eagle and the cat, even as the word around them literally and metaphorically blows up.

The concern with performance over politics characterizes all Shepard's work and is particularly important given his thematic preoccupation with the West. Shepard is critical of aspects of the West, for example, the new West represented by the film industry of Hollywood which manufactures images that delude people, thereby denying their realization of their identities. He does not examine, however, the relation of the new West to the old. The Old West, in which Shepard so delights, was generated by Hollywood and bears little relation to the historical reality.[3] This mythical West where men are men and women are their complements (and everybody is white) is surely not the place where the "true" self can be realized. Or perhaps this is the final paradox: the "true" self can be realized through fiction.

NOTES

[1] For a fuller discussion of the notion of the supplement see: Jacques Derrida, "The Supplement of Copula: Philosophy *before* Linguistics," *Textual Strategies,* ed. Josue Harari (Ithaca: Cornell University Press, 1979). 82–121.

[2] In *Presence of the Actor,* Chaikin cites theatre practitioners as having the greatest influence on his work. These include: Nola Chilton, Mira Roshiva, Judith Malina and Julian Beck, members of the Open Theater (45).

[3] Historically, the age of the cowboy is brief: from the period just after the American Civil War until just after 1874 when barbed wire was invented. With the invention of barbed wire, ranches were fenced in and the work of the cowboy became redundant. "The early cowboys were Texans—white, Negro, and Mexican, but outsiders of almost every nationality were also represented." Philip Durham, "The Cowboy and the Myth Makers," *Journal of Popular Culture* 1, No. 1 (Summer 1967): 58.

Works Cited

Bloom, Harold. *Poems of Our Climate*. Ithaca: Cornell University Press, 1976.

———. "The Real Me." Review of *Walt Whitman: The Making of the Poet* by Paul Zweig, *The New York Review of Books* 31, no. 7 (April 26, 1984).

Blumenthal, Eileen. "Joseph Chaikin: An Open Theory of Acting," *Yale/Theater* 8, nos. 2 and 3 (Spring 1977): 112–33.

Chaikin, Joseph. *The Presence of the Actor*. New York: Atheneum, 1972.

Davis, David Brion. "Ten Gallon Hero." *Myth and the American Experience*. Vol. 2. Ed. Nicholas Gage and Patrick Gerster. New York: Glencoe Press, 1973.

Derrida, Jacques. *Of Grammatology*. Trans. Gayatri Chakravorty Spivak. Baltimore: Johns Hopkins University, 1976.

———. "The Supplement to Copula: Philosophy *before* Linguistics." *Textual Strategies*. Ed. Josue Harari. Ithaca: Cornell University Press, 1979.

———. "The Theater of Cruelty." *Writing and Difference*. Trans. Alan Bass. Chicago: University of Chicago Press, 1980.

Durham, Philip. "The Cowboy and the Myth Makers," *Journal of Popular Culture* 1, no. 1 (Summer 1967): 58–62.

Earley, Michael. "Of Life Immense in Passion, Pulse and Power." *American Dreams: The Imagination of Sam Shepard*. Ed. Bonnie Marranca. New York: Performing Arts Journal Publications, 1981, pp. 126–33.

Falk, Florence. "The Role of Performance in Sam Shepard's Plays," *Theatre Journal* 33, no. 2 (May 1981): 182–98.

Gilman, Richard. Introduction. *Seven Plays* by Sam Shepard. New York: Bantam Books, 1981.

Kakutani, Michiko. "Myths, Dreams, Realities—Sam Shepard's America," *The New York Times,* 29 January 1984, Section 2.

Lippman, Amy. "A Conversation with Sam Shepard," *The Harvard Advocate* (March 1983). Reprinted *Gamut* 5 (January 1984): 10–28.

Marranca, Bonnie. "Alphabetical Shepard: The Play of Words." *American Dreams: The Imagination of Sam Shepard*. Ed. Bonnie Marranca. New York: Performing Arts Journal Publications, 1981, pp. 13–34.

Roudiez, Leon S. Introduction. *Desire in Language: A Semiotic Approach to Literature and Art.* Ed. Leon S. Roudiez. Trans. Thomas Gora, Alice Jardine and Leon S. Roudiez. New York: Columbia University Press, 1980.

Shewey, Don. *Sam Shepard.* New York: Dell, 1985.

———. *Curse of the Starving Class. Seven Plays* by Sam Shepard. New York: Bantam Books, 1981.

———. "Language, Visualization and the Inner Library." *The Drama Review* 21, no. 4 (December 1977): 49–58. Reprinted in *American Dreams: The Imagination of Sam Shepard.* Ed. Bonnie Marranca. New York: Performing Arts Journal Publications, 1981.

———, and Joseph Chaikin. *Tongues. Seven Plays.* By Sam Shepard. New York: Performing Arts Journal Publications, 1981.

Whitman, Walt. *Leaves of Grass.* Harmondsworth: Penguin Books, 1981. Fp. in Brooklyn, 1855.

Wren, Scott Christopher. "Camp Shepard: Exploring the Geography of Character." *West Coast Plays* 7 (1980): 71–106.

Funny Money in New York and London: Neil Simon and Alan Ayckbourn

Ruby Cohn

The American Neil Simon and the Englishman Alan Ayckbourn are magnets to the theatre in an age of mass media. Both playwrights are energetically productive, what with Simon's 30 plays and Ayckbourn's 40, although the numbers may be mounting as I write. Both men are devoted to comedy, but they have at times voiced a yearning for a Chekhovian blend of the comic and the tragic. Ayckbourn calls his plays "black farce" (Innes 317). Black or white, their plays have been translated into many languages, yet each playwright has had only limited appeal in the country of the other. Grounded in the middle-class mores of their respective countries—Simon urban and Ayckbourn suburban—the two playwrights are routinely paired, almost as though they were a comedy team, but no one has lingered over their likenesses as they craftily delineate family strains.[1]

Ayckbourn himself distinguished half-humorously between them: "If you dropped a play of [Simon's] in the street and the pages fell out in any old order, you'd still be laughing as you picked them up. If you dropped a play of mine, too bad. As a writer, he's highly verbal whereas I'm situational" (Kalson, *Laughter* 44). My quotation from Simon is more general, differentiating two cultures rather than two writers: "American humor is rooted in people's neuroses, while English humor is more slapstick" ("Make 'em Laugh" 14). There is some truth in both insights, each playwright surreptitiously defending his own practice. However, I am going to argue that the two dramatists create similar worlds, through quite different manipulation of the languages of the stage—verbal or situational, slapstick or neurotic.

I therefore disagree with the redoubtable British critic, Michael Billington, who has taken exception to coupling Simon and Ayckbourn: "The two dramatists have little in common other than that they write deceptively serious comedies, make a lot of money and get their work performed in their own theatres" (50–51). I suppose it is true that they both "make a lot of money," but Simon has never had a theatre to showcase his work regularly, even though one Broadway theatre has been named for him and he owns another. No theatre bears Ayckbourn's name, which does, however, grace a New York alley. More important, Ayckbourn has since 1976 been the artistic director of, and a very active director in, the Stephen Joseph Theatre at Scarborough, a resort town on England's northeast coast. Simon has opened some two dozen plays outside of New York before displaying them on Broadway, and this is comparable to Ayckbourn's Scarborough premieres before he ventures into London's West End, usually with a different cast. Since such "out-of-town" tryouts, and subsequent revision, account in part for their "lot of money," it is a salient similarity between the two writers, but it neglects the specifics of the plays themselves.

For that, we may begin with Billington's puzzling genre designation— "deceptively serious comedies." What the British critic probably means by his condensed phrase is drama with serious purpose beneath a deceptively comic surface. Since neither Simon nor Ayckbourn is monolithically farcical in the manner of English Ben Travers (to whom Ayckbourn dedicated his *Taking Steps*), or Americans Kaufman and Hart, some degree of seriousness may be discerned within the comic canon of each of these writers. By and very large, one might say that both dramatists have gradually groped their way through comic structures toward serious themes. In Ayckbourn's words: "Let's see how clever we can be at saying unpalatable things in a palatable manner" (Billington 165). What both playwrights *are* clever at is offering tasty lines to actors; those of Simon are snappy, whereas Ayckbourn's people tend to bumble.

After a quick tour through their respective careers, I will pair a few of their plays. Before molting into a dramatist, Neil Simon (b. 1927) wrote scripts for comic personalities on radio and television—Sid Caesar, Phil Foster, Jackie Gleason, Jerry Lester, Garry Moore, Phil Silvers. Alan Ayckbourn (b. 1939) came to drama by way of stage management and then acting in the theatre.[2] Their plays display the residue of this training. From *Come Blow Your Horn* (1961) to *London Suite* (1995) Simon is king of the one-line quip, which he dispenses prodigally among his characters. In Simon's first published play, for example, two brothers bicker, and their sallies bounce indiscriminately off either one; one brother complains, "I thought we were splitting everything fiftyfifty," and the other brother retorts: "We were until you got all the fifties."

In contrast, a *mute* protagonist energizes Ayckbourn's first published play (and the first of many that he himself directed). His eponymous *Mr. Whatnot* (1963) leaps, trips, falls, drives an automobile, climbs up a piano, treads on its keyboard, plays cricket with a tennis racket, bounces on a bed, and devours a banquet while concealed beneath a table. A frantic stage manager has to accompany these acrobatics with taped sounds. Ayckbourn's mentor Stephen Joseph summarizes the farcical mayhem: "Real properties, phoney properties and mime properties all enriched the scene, ranging from a genuine steering wheel to represent a car, to an entirely imagined piano that was played furiously" (57).

It is tempting to dive into Ayckbourn's various properties and Simon's several sallies, but that would contrast apples and oranges, whereas the two playwrights *are* comparable in their dramatic situations, stemming from Greek New Comedy (see also Arvid Sponberg's essay in this volume). In that genre the plot turns on the elimination of an obstacle that separates a nubile woman from her ardent young suitor. Simon and Ayckbourn may age the problematic couple, and by the end of their comedies the obstacle might still cast its shadow, but the two playwrights nevertheless address audiences who possess some residual nostalgia for the New Comedy form. Contemporary content often inflects that form in Simon's plays, but its residue may disappear in Ayckbourn's most serious plays.

As in sitcoms of the media, the plays of both Ayckbourn and Simon prowl around endemic predicaments—mismatched couples, disjointed generations, dissimilar siblings, bad neighbors, frail friends, and hilariously hostile modern environments. Both Simon and Ayckbourn skewer their characters so that they wriggle helplessly—and laughably—often within the family. Simon's unprepossessing characters yearn to be a little bigger than they are, or to reach a little further than they can, within low and limited horizons. Most of Ayckbourn's people are resigned to the traditional British suburban milieu, which repays them ungratefully. The plays of both writers tend to ignore wider issues; not only laws, wars, and poverty, but also racial and religious conflicts, drug abuse, energy depletion, global crises; in short, the world at large. Within their dramas, neither writer is irreparably addicted to the conventional happy ending, but Ayckbourn's finales are increasingly problematic, whereas Simon usually offers his characters an escape route, if only to another temporary clearing in the urban jungle—a quip on their parched lips.

Many Simon plays of the 1960s and 1970s string jokes on a thin thread of plot, but in his main work of the 1980s he filters jokes through time-bound plays that draw upon his own life—*Brighton Beach Memoirs* (1983), *Biloxi Blues* (1985), and *Broadway Bound* (1986). Simon's alter ego, a would-be writer named Eugene Morris Jerome, is 15 years old in 1937, when war clouds threaten Europe (and especially European Jews) while the Jewish-American Jerome family is mired in the economic Depression. *Biloxi Blues* departs from Simon's native New York to Biloxi, Mississippi, during World War II, where Gene undergoes military training, sexual initiation, and romantic yearning. *Broadway Bound* remains a promise in 1949, the year of the third play, when the senior Jeromes separate, but their two sons start a career as radio gag writers. Paradoxically named for the tragic O'Neill, Simon's comedic Eugene is at once the protagonist and the memorialist of his trilogy, in the manner of Tennessee Williams's Tom of *The Glass Menagerie.* Simon's more recent *Jake's Women* (1992) is even more ambitious in its model; like Arthur Miller in *Death of a Salesman,* Simon sets scenes in the mind of his protagonist.

Ayckbourn has been candid about his own debts—to Oscar Wilde for mis-prision, to Ben Travers for manic farce, to Noël Coward for an occasional scene, to Harold Pinter for a fine-tuned lexicon (Kalson, *Laughter* passim). He shrugged these mentors off by the 1970s, when he confounded audience expectation by a cunning blend of onstage neurosis, offstage action, and the most blatant manipulation of settings ever seen on the English (or any other) stage. His serious notes—especially in the whimper of his women characters—are sounded a decade earlier than those of Simon. Coincidentally, too, it is a trilogy, *The Norman Conquests* (1973), that established Ayckbourn as a dramatist of serious purpose, however he would mock that academic phrase. Unlike the plays of Simon's trilogy, which advance chronologically, those of Ayckbourn occur simultaneously, in a dizzying round of onstage and offstage action. Then, flaunting his control over plot mechanisms, Ayckbourn pro-duced alternative endings for *Sisterly Feelings* (1978) and sixteen variants for four scenes in *Intimate Exchanges* (1982), which was filmed by Alain Resnais as *Smoking and No Smoking*. A few years later *A Small Family Business* (1987) and *The Revengers' Comedies* (1989) virtually writhe through their convoluted plots.

Simon writes as though the subplot had not been invented, but he dis-plays concern for character. He told Edythe McGovern: "The playwright has obligations to fulfill, such as exposition and character building" (4). Sub-scribing to the worth of the traditional nuclear family, Simon's characters, particularly his married characters, are sometimes frustrated by their tradi-tion. As his policeman Murray remarks in *The Odd Couple*, "Twelve years doesn't mean you're a happy couple. It just means you're a long couple." Wittily complaining, Simon's families tend to endure, although the balance of power may shift.

Although Ayckbourn's ingenious plots have been admired more than Simon's conventional minitriumphs over miniobstacles, it is for their charac-ters that both playwrights have reaped praise—and particularly for their sym-pathy with women (see Michael Abbott's essay in this volume). Simon and Ayckbourn are similar in creating women whose ideal of happiness, or even of mental stability, rests upon a man. Simon's Jennie Malone of *Chapter Two* exults: "I'm wonderful! I'm nuts about me!" But in the next breath she nerv-ously asks her recalcitrant husband: "If you don't call me, can I call you?" Almost always Simon allows one or the other of his romantic leads to "call."

Both playwrights thrust farcically against women who are no longer eroti-cally viable. Simon peoples his sidelines with avatars of the Jewish mother of gagdom. Mrs. Baker of *Come Blow Your Horn* anticipates her husband's blame: "He'll say 'Because of you my sister Gussie has two grandchildren and all I've got is a *bum* and a *letter*.'" Ethel Banks of *Barefoot in the Park* inter-feres in her daughter's marriage: "I worry about you two." Mrs. Hubley of *Plaza Suite* cannot admit that her daughter cringes at resembling her. Although the Jewish mother of Simon's autobiographical trilogy loses her husband, the last line accommodates her to a running gag: "After all, she did once dance with George Raft."

For all their vaunted sympathy with women, both playwrights give more scope to men. Simon's protagonists are usually male, whether it be the romantic lead, who always *leads,* or the older frustrated comic. Simon's older men are either puritanical or philandering; Mr. Baker of *Come Blow Your Horn* imposes monogamy on his sons, but aging Barney Cashman of *Last of the Red Hot Lovers* grasps forlornly at illicit sex. No one in Simon's plays is evil, and his philanderers inevitably reform. Alan Baker of *Come Blow Your Horn* turns into a duplicate of his monogamous father. Victor Velasco of *Barefoot in the Park* finally accepts the sexual and digestive limits of his age. Barney Cashman, the last of the red hot lovers, makes his final assignation with his wife. Only Lou Tanner of *The Gingerbread Lady* remains unregenerately profligate, and even he is vulnerable and insecure: "Together, Evy, we don't add up to one strong person."

Not until Simon's fourth play did he hit upon the title *The Odd Couple* (1965), but it is apposite also to plays written earlier and later. This is hardly surprising, since the technique of a comically contrasting pair is at least as old as Plautus, with his Menachmus brothers, and that device was undoubtedly reinforced by the two-brother structure of Simon's own family. In Simon's first play, *Come Blow Your Horn* (1961), two brothers change and exchange their temperaments, and two dissimilar brothers recur in *The Prisoner of Second Avenue, Chapter Two,* the autobiographical trilogy, and *Lost in Yonkers.*

Traditional dramatic conflict is reduced by Simon to contrasting personalities. In *Barefoot in the Park* (1963) Paul, a conservative attorney, is newly married to Corie, who enjoys walking barefoot in the park, like a free-spirited Bohemian. *The Odd Couple* are middle-aged men who are rejected by their respective wives and who cannot dovetail in a common household.[3] *Last of the Red Hot Lovers* (1969) returns to compromise in marriage, after Barney Cashman has figured in odd couples with each of the three women he vainly tries to seduce. *The Sunshine Boys* (1972) pairs mutually loathing comedians. Although only one victim is designated by the title *The Prisoner of Second Avenue* (1971), a nagging married couple is trapped in its expensive cell, and they alternate in bemoaning its inconveniences. Even in the sunshine couples storm at one another through the four scenes of *California Suite* (1977). Throughout his work Simon infects his rival siblings, odd couples, or longtime friend/enemies with small or large neuroses, which he sees as the basis of American humor.

Given the box-office success of the two prolific playwrights, it is somewhat ironic that they are rarely sympathetic to successful males. Simon pokes fun at the wax-fruiterer Mr. Baker, the adulterous executive Sam Nash, the vain movie star Jesse Kiplinger, the self-pitying writer George Schneider.

Ayckbourn's successful men—philandering Phillip of *Relatively Speaking;* benighted Frank Foster of *How the Other Half Loves,* furtive Graham of *Time and Time Again,* and pompous Keith of *Way Upstream*—are merely foolish, but Sidney Hopcraft of *Absurd Person Singular* grows vicious as he slithers up the socioeconomic ladder. Gerry Stratton of *Time of My Life* is ruthless against business associates and competitors, but dictatorial Vince of *Way Upstream* and criminal Vic Parks of *Man of the Moment* are melodramatic villains. When smug Paul's distraught wife pours cream on his head in *Absent Friends,* Ayckbourn turns farce against his successful businessman. Rarely does Ayckbourn permit sympathy for this stereotype of the hard-driving male; the vulnerable solicitor husband of *Sisterly Feelings* is exceptional.

Unlike his successful males, Ayckbourn's bungling husbands drive their wives to madness, but still other ineffectual wimps are meant to be lovable. Len of *Time and Time Again* consoles his rival: "We just seem to have mislaid the trophy," where the trophy is the girl, who rejects both suitors. Len sets the pattern for Norman of the failed conquests and for the briefly approved Guy of *A Chorus of Disapproval.* Equally pleasant are a few Ayckbourn clodhoppers who do get their girls—Stafford of *Sisterly Feelings,* Tristram of *Taking Steps,* and Douglas of *The Revengers' Comedies.* Beneath cosmetic variants stumbles the stereotype of the clumsy male wooer. Despite Ayckbourn's designation of himself as situational and Simon as verbal, both playwrights exploit familiar situations, and both playwrights rely on gender and family stereotypes within those situations.

Even before we make the acquaintance of their comparable characters, we can distinguish Simon and Ayckbourn by their approaches to stage space and fictional time. Simon is a voluntary prisoner not of Second Avenue alone, but of many a Manhattan realistic living room (see also Peter Teitzman's essay in this volume). Granted that limitation, however, Simon furnishes his rooms with the inconveniences that elicit laughter from the bare attic of *Barefoot in the Park* to the messy poker room of *The Odd Couple;* from the neat pied-a-terre of *Last of the Red Hot Lovers* to the burglary residue of *The Prisoner of Second Avenue. The Sunshine Boys* presents a minuscule Broadway apartment that baffles its ancient occupant. *Chapter Two* (1978) is slightly more daring in its simultaneous staging of two dissimilar living rooms, on the East and West sides of Manhattan, a device repeated in the musical *They're Playing Our Song* (1979). East Side, West Side, all around the town, Simon's stage rooms are burdened with malfunctioning doorbells, telephones, and sundry appliances, which nevertheless function unerringly in farce.

Although Ayckbourn's props are equally familiar, his sets are far more various. His early *Mr. Whatnot* imposes cinematic scenes upon the theatre—games, chases, musicals, weddings, dinners, and a death-bed—all snuffed out by a flick of a light switch. Nearly a decade later, Ayckbourn in *How the Other Half Loves* stages "*two [living] rooms contained and overlapping in the same area,"* the one tasteful and orderly and the other trendy but sloppy. This is not mere contrast, as in Simon's *Chapter Two,* but actual overlap; the couch has cushions for each decor, and the characters are sometimes close enough to touch while being separated by invisible walls. At a dinner party a married couple are guests in two homes simultaneously; they swivel back and forth on the split set, at accelerating pace. Their dialogue resonates hilariously through the artifice of the stage.

Simon conveys the atmosphere of greater New York mainly through dialogue, and, comparably, Ayckbourn treats his faithful audiences to sporadic verbal references to an imaginary village, Pendon, that rhymes (roughly) with London, but puns on "penned on."[4] Pendon first emerges in *Relatively Speaking* (1965), since the heroine's lover and his wife live in Willows, Lower Pendon, Bucks. Ayckbourn's village acquires a cricket team, the East Pendon Occasionals, in *Time and Time Again.* In *Ten Times Table* a pageant honors the Pendon Twelve, agricultural laborers who were massacred two centuries ago. *Sisterly Feelings* bristle on Pendon Common in Berkshire, and the cabin cruiser of *Way Upstream* passes under Pendon Bridge. Pendon then skips to Wales, where Gay's *Beggar's Opera* is rehearsed by the Pendon Amateur Light Opera Society in *A Chorus of Disapproval.* (The National Theatre program for this last play also lists the Pendon Police Auxiliary Silver Band, the Pendon Magic Society, the Pendon Amateur Dramatic Society, and the Pendon Women's Institute—none receiving financial assistance from the Arts Council of Great Britain.) To Ayckbourn's surprise, he recently learned of the existence of an actual model village of Pendon (Dukore 7).

Like New York and Pendon, time is conveyed verbally by both playwrights. The fictional duration of the American's plays may vary from the actual playing time of his brief scenes in his three *Suites* to the twelve-year span of the three plays of his trilogy.[5] In contrast, Alan Ayckbourn plays a diapason of stage times as he inventories the foibles and follies of contemporary middle-class Britain. In the program note to his *Time of My Life* Ayckbourn registers his awareness of time as a dramatic tool: "I am hardly the first dramatist to be fascinated by time. Time, I mean, as an aid to dramatic story telling. . . . For I do suspect that the choice of time scale in a dramatic structure is often one of the most important basic decisions a dramatist needs to make about their [*sic*] play." Three Ayckbourn plays even contain the word "time" in the title. *Time and Time Again* (1971) unfolds a love story that opens in spring and closes in autumn (whereas Simon's love story in *Chapter Two* opens in February and closes more traditionally in spring). Ayckbourn's *Ten Times Table* (1977) digs at *repetitious* committee meetings but calls no attention to the passing of several weeks. *Time of My Life* (1992) deals more inventively with time. The first person possessive pronoun hints at a cliché of joy, as in: "I had the time of my life." No one utters this phrase in a play that moves backward and forward from a central event, a woman's birthday dinner in a restaurant.

Although both craftsmen are situational *and* verbal, as well as stereotypical of character, Ayckbourn alone deploys stage space and fictional time in new configurations that enhance the comic quality, and he is fascinated by the possibilities of taped sound and a spectrum of lights. Despite these differences, it is similarly with their humor that both playwrights draw audiences. Yet Ayckbourn in 1984 claimed: "I spend most of the time now taking out the jokes not putting them in" (91); similarly, Simon said in 1986, "I find I take more funny lines out of a play now than I ever have before" (interview Edwin Wilson). Nevertheless the old burlesque phrase—"Funny is money"—accounts for their continued audience appeal.

Into variants of New Comedy plots both playwrights usher stereotypical characters who utter funny phrases—Simon's consciously, Ayckbourn's unconsciously. These phrases bounce off that old comic staple—the running gag. Simon harps on the waxed fruit of *Come Blow Your Horn,* the five flights of stairs of *Barefoot in the Park,* Oscar's genial sloppiness and Felix's maniacal neatness of *The Odd Couple,* Barney's bungled lies of *Last of the Red Hot Lovers,* the Edisons' treacherous apartment of *The Prisoner of Second Avenue.* The alcoholic drinks of *The Gingerbread Lady* and the failing memories of *The Sunshine Boys* function thematically as well as comically.

Ayckbourn displays growing skill in enfolding running gags into his plots or characterizations: the lubricious telephone calls in proper households of *How the Other Half Loves,* the unappetizing food at the several meals of *The Norman Conquests,* John's onstage jiggling and Gordon's offstage illnesses in the mismatched marriages of *Absent Friends,* a soliloquizing wife and a split-phrased husband in *Bedroom Farce,* a temperamental garage door and an immobile automobile in *Just Between Ourselves,* Brian's interchangeable girls (played by the same actress) in *Joking Apart,* and a restaurant's interchangeable waiters (played by the same actor) in *Time of My Life*—all help accumulate funny money. In *A Small Family Business,* Ayckbourn's running gags are thematically significant—the senility of the founder of the furniture business, one son's penchant for new machines and the other's for exotic cuisine, the clothes and lovers of one son's wife and the fixation on her dog of the other son's wife; most sinister are the self-righteous claims to his honor by the gradually criminalized protagonist.

Running gags are security blankets for these two playwrights, with Simon the more verbal. Yet both playwrights also write funny dialogue for their individual character. Simon's one-liners, often couched in Yiddish rhythms, are wittily depreciative—of the climate, the environment, the actions and reactions of the characters, and the familiar inconveniences of life in greater New York. In contrast, Ayckbourn amuses by the innocent blunders of his imperceptive characters, especially in the confusion of festive occasions, into which Michael Billington reads an important social statement: "Look at Ayckbourn's work *in toto* and you see that it is about the way we preserve a whole set of rituals—

Christmas, family weekends, wedding anniversaries, birthdays, cocktail parties, monogamy even—which bear less and less relation to our actual needs" (51–52). Yet the celebrations misfire hilariously, while the needs remain vague. By and large, Ayckbourn's comedy differs from Simon's as the stage manager differs from the TV gag writer.

Like Billington, I have commented mainly on differences between Simon and Ayckbourn in their several stage techniques—plot but not situation, sets but not props, and the varied paces of their dialogue. I nevertheless argue for their basically similar worlds—of more or less comfortable Western abodes peopled by white middle-class characters who speak without eloquence, act without violence, and rarely rise above trivia or ephemera. In shifting now to a closer look at specific plays, I underline the very fact that certain of their plays *are* comparable, as to structure, subgenre, protagonist, or seriocomic tone.

In their early plays, Simon's *Barefoot in the Park* (1963) and Ayckbourn's *Relatively Speaking* (1965), both playwrights aim small—four-character, three-scene spinoffs of New Comedy, with climatic curtains and neat resolutions. Simon's comedy bubbles up primarily from petty crises of the temperamentally opposed newlyweds and, secondarily, from different life styles of an older couple. During the Act I exposition most of the humor arises from the small, unfurnished fifth-floor walkup apartment. In Act II the four characters on a double date pop exotic knichi into their mouths—with diverse degrees of dexterity and pleasure. When the foursome return from an Albanian restaurant on Staten Island, alcohol has fertilized their wits. Simon then interweaves the quarrel of the newlyweds with their anxiety about the bride's mother, before the comedy's final high note, when the once proper young husband drunkenly sings an Albanian folk song while precariously balanced on a skylight. He can be as Bohemian as his wife, who walks "barefoot in the park."

Ayckbourn's comparable family farce, *Relatively Speaking,* was originally entitled *Meet My Father.* It turns on a gullible young man's acceptance of his girlfriend's lying explanation that her middle-aged ex-lover is her father. Before the young swain meets the putative parents of his beloved, however, Ayckbourn swathes Greg in the accoutrements of farce. We see him in a sheet draped as a loincloth, slippers too large for him, festooned with dripping flowers. After struggling with a jammed drawer, he opens another drawer with such force that he scatters its contents. Finally, he gathers up a stranger's slippers and the cigarette packet with its telltale address of the action to follow. Through Greg's visible discomfort, Ayckbourn lightens his several reminders of the wellmade play—a woman with a past, incriminating letters, chance confrontations, suspenseful curtains. The Act I sight gags prepare for and dissolve into an Act II dialogue of mistaken identity. Although the plots of these early plays are pat, and the characters undeveloped, the profusion of comic detail is cornucopian, strategically paced by Simon and carefully sustained by Ayckbourn.

As both playwrights sharpened their skills, they learned to exploit their sets and to juggle several characters in *The Odd Couple* (1965) and *How the Other Half Loves* (1971). Coincidentally, the focus is on six characters in both plays. Each of Simon's three acts opens on a six-man poker game in Oscar's living room. The room is slovenly in Act I, but "spotless and sterile" in Acts II and III, after the divorced Oscar invites a suicidal Felix to share his eight-room apartment. Although Simon's "odd couple" substitutes contrasting characters for conflict, he does explore set and properties as background for the one-liners of his poker players. We had to take it on faith that the apartment of *Barefoot in the Park* was located on the fifth floor, whereas we actually *see* the transformation suffered by Oscar's living room. The frenzied housekeeping of Felix, along with his self-pity, provokes Oscar to rue his generosity. In Act III as in Act I the poker players worry about Felix's threats of suicide, but in Act III as in Act I Felix happily lands on his wellshod feet when neighborly sisters invite him to share their apartment. Oscar taunts his erstwhile roommate with one of the play's many quips: "Aren't you going to thank me? . . . for the two greatest things I ever did for you. Taking you in and throwing you out." One of the greatest things that was done for Simon in *The Odd Couple* was the casting as Oscar of Walter Matthau, the dourfaced actor who slouches impeccably into major Simon roles.

In contrast, the presence of Robert Morley in *How the Other Half Loves* almost scuttled Ayckbourn's West End career. The veteran actor told the neophyte author: "Look, nobody wants to come to the theatre and see people squabbling. . . . We don't want all these nasty cross people, and people shouting at each other" (Watson 77). He then edited Ayckbourn's lines accordingly. Little did Morley dream that these "nasty cross people" would delight audiences because the nastiness is funny. Inept Frank Foster, the Morley character, is the most affable of Ayckbourn's sextet, oblivious of his wife's adultery with his subordinate Bob Phillips, who thus escapes his disorganized wife and their offstage infant. Socially lowest are the Featherstones, the unwitting alibi of both members of the adulterous affair. The bravura dinner scene leads to fisticuffs between Bob and his putative rival, which leads in turn to a distraught Mary Featherstone fleeing the one household to fall in a faint on the threshold of the other—a stage footstep away.

As both playwrights edged toward serious themes, they enfolded jokes into the delineation of character, particularly that of women—Simon's *The Gingerbread Lady* (1970) and Ayckbourn's *Just Between Ourselves* (1976). Simon's plot turns on a single question: Will the ex-alcoholic Evy Meara be able to remain "dry"? Immediately after her return from a rehabilitation center, Evy Meara is deserted by her married friend Toby and her gay actor friend Jimmy. Just as Evy begins to panic at being alone, her 17-year-old daughter Polly arrives, and she nostalgically recalls her Christmas gift at age 9: "Don't you remember the gingerbread house with the little gingerbread lady in the window?. . . . I always kept it to remind me of you. Of course, today I have the biggest box of crumbs in the neighborhood." (Is it churlish to object that crumbs will not last eight years?)

Although Evy cites her inadequacies as a mother, Polly is adamant about moving in with her, and this fortifies Evy to reject her abusive lover: "What I need now is a relative, not a relationship. And I have one in there unpacking." Three weeks later Evy pours champagne for her friend Toby's birthday, but she herself drinks it at the news of catastrophe; Jimmy has been replaced in his stage role, and Toby's husband wants to divorce her. Disappointed at her mother's lapse, Polly locks herself into her bedroom, and a lonely Evy telephones her abusive lover: "Guess who wants to come over to your place?" The next morning Evy has a black eye and a hangover, but her daughter Polly, who has herself sought solace in alcohol, insists that she keep an appointment to discuss her future. The original version of *The Gingerbread Lady* ended with "Evy getting drunk in the dark . . . interrupted by a Puerto Rican grocery boy. Clearly, he would make a successful pass at her" (Meryman 60D). Originally, Evy was to send Polly out of her apartment and out of her life, while she herself was to sink to the level of a Puerto Rican lover (blatantly racist on Simon's part). However, negative reviews during Boston tryouts persuaded Simon to change the ending.[6] In the published version Polly cajoles Evy to attend the crucial meeting, and the uncrumbled Gingerbread Lady vows to her daughter: "When I grow up, I want to be just like you." The weak woman, using the weaknesses of her friends as an excuse to slip back into alcoholic oblivion, is not likely to grow up "just like" her purposeful daughter, but the wish ends Simon's play on a funny, reassuring line.

In Act I Evy's lover compliments her: "If nothing else, Evy, you have a way with a phrase . . . . whenever I needed a good honest laugh, I had to quote you, Ev." This is not mere self-praise on Simon's part. Since Evy is as bright as she is weak, her one-liners are in character, arousing "honest" laughter, mainly at her own expense. What is dishonest is the miraculous sitcom dissolution of Evy's critical self-appraisal, so that she is putty not only in her daughter's hands, but in those of Simon. Up to the revised ending, Evy Meara is the most fully formed woman in Simon's theatre, and if her horizon is limited to her immediate plight, that is not improbable for someone who has just emerged from ten weeks in a sanitarium. Evy's two insecure friends chant in running gags about Jimmy's acting and Toby's makeup—which spark Evy's witty deprecations. Occasionally, one of the friends steals Evy's wit, as when Jimmy replies to her joking proposal of marriage: ". . . you're a drunken nymphomaniac and I'm a homosexual. We'd have trouble getting our kids into a good school." At one juncture, too, Evy's friend Toby waxes tiresomely didactic: "We all hold each other up because none of us has the strength to do it alone. . . . The way I see it, you've got two choices. Either get a book on how to be a mature, responsible person . . . or get [Polly] out of here before you destroy her chance to become one." Toby underlines Evy's choice; as a mother, she must either relinquish Polly or contribute to her ruin. In the original version of *The Gingerbread Lady* Evy made the first choice, but in the revised version she undergoes an improbable conversion. In either case Simon grounds a play in a credible problem, alcoholism, spurring him to advance to the problem of unemployment in *The Prisoner of Second Avenue,* and that of aging in *The Sunshine Boys.* This is not to say that a contemporary play must focus on a problem, but unless Simon does so, his slender plot threads are overburdened by his jokes.

Although Ayckbourn has also devised alcoholic women, none of them is a protagonist. *Just Between Ourselves* resembles the original *Gingerbread Lady* in its tight plot, single setting, and, above all, in an action that traces the progressive deterioration of a woman. Ayckbourn himself called *Just Between Ourselves* "the first of my 'winter' plays," and although he amusingly explains that he wrote it in December for performance in January, winter also has the resonance of an unhappy ending—what Simon avoids in *The Gingerbread Lady.*

"Just between ourselves" is a colloquial cliché, and we hear it five times in Ayckbourn's play, always uttered by Dennis, three times *about* but never *to* his wife Vera. Dennis spends his weekends ineffectually tinkering in his garage, while his mother and wife vie for control of the offstage house. In *Just Between Ourselves* the running gags are indices of character: Over the course of a year Dennis keeps threatening to fix the garage door; over the course of a year Dennis, unable to sell his wife Vera's car, cannot even give it away. While the amiable Dennis laughs and lauds laughter, his wife's sanity crumbles away—an attrition that Ayckbourn traces through visible birthday "celebrations"—also the occasion of the breakdown of Simon's Gingerbread Lady.

In contrast to Simon's bright, boozy Evy, Vera is decorously submissive. Finally, Simon lacked the courage of his characterization, whereas Ayckbourn braves a woman's breakdown, and resists ending his play on a joke. One-set plays, *The Gingerbread Lady* and *Just Between Ourselves* are seriocomic as they trace the deterioration of a woman character. Except for drinks and doorbells, however, Simon ignores his set, whereas Ayckbourn anchors his dialogue in a garage door with a mind of its own, a stationary automobile that roars and rumbles, an ineffectual electric drill, crashing dishes, and "glorious technicolour." Even realistic plays challenge Ayckbourn to ingenuity.

For all Ayckbourn's inventive birthdays in *Just Between Ourselves,* the play is realistic in execution, like most of Simon's plays. Yet each playwright has launched into the baroque form of the play within the play—Simon's *The Sunshine Boys* (1972) and, over a decade later, Ayckbourn's *A Chorus of Disapproval* (1985). The latter is more thickly populated, for Simon focuses on a comedy act, Lewis and Clark, analogous to Laurel and Hardy, or Abbott and Costello, and based on Smith and Dale. Far from the intrepid explorers Lewis and Clark, the comedians have depended on well-rehearsed routines in their decades of vaudeville as the Sunshine Boys. Simon dramatizes them in a period long past their prime; both in their 70s, no longer on speaking terms, Lewis lives with his daughter in New Jersey, but Clark clings to his minuscule apartment on upper Broadway, where, health and memory failing, he deludes himself about a career. Less tightly plotted than *The Gingerbread Lady, The Sunshine Boys* also turns on a single question: Can the acerbic old men manage to reenact one of their successful sketches for big money on television?

Since Lewis and Clark are comedians, the play fittingly contains Simon's highest quantity of one-liners. Clark is the crustier member of the twosome, taking umbrage at any affront to his dignity, and lashing back in vituperative epithets. About his erstwhile partner Lewis, Clark snarls: "As an actor, no one could touch him. As a human being, no one *wanted* to touch him." Clark is sharp-tongued, too, about his loyal nephew, Ben the talent agent, who announces that CBS is doing a special program on the history of comedy, including the Sunshine Boys. Neither old man will admit to needing money, but Ben cajoles them into a rehearsal of their most celebrated skit, "The Doctor and the Tax Examination." The rehearsal bogs down at its opening line: Will it be the tried and true "Come in," or the freshening factor "Enter"? At the rehearsal studio, the two ancient comedians continue to bicker, and yet Simon adroitly slips an old-time burlesque skit into their repartee, before Clark suffers a heart attack. In the next scene tough old Clark is as sharp as ever, spurning his nephew's home for an actors' asylum as his last abode. Unapologetic though chastened, Lewis informs Clark that he will soon be leaving his daughter's home: "If you're not too busy, maybe you'll come over one day to the Actors' Home and visit me." Clark smirks: "You can count on it," but he does not reveal that he too will be living there. *The Sunshine Boys* closes as the two garrulous old men ramble on about the identity of familiar names in the Broadway weekly, *Variety*—a preview of twilight in the Actors' Home.

In this exceptionally unsentimental play Simon resists endowing his comedians either with warm hearts or new stage triumphs. He wisely limits the play within the play to the brief, rhythmic, visually dynamic skit performed by professionals. Out of the public eye, old age is dramatized as dirty, demeaning, confusing, and utterly lonely. Yet Simon also makes it funny, so that we laugh with a sympathy that the selfish old souls scarcely deserve.

Simon chooses an American burlesque sketch for his inner play, but Ayckbourn chooses an English classic, *The Beggar's Opera,* for his play-long inner play *A Chorus of Disapproval.* The solicitor director Dafydd cajoles his recalcitrant amateur cast toward performance, even though he is aware: "Here we are, playing around with pretty lights and costumes held together with safety pins. Out there it's all happening." The "all" that is happening is hardly cataclysmic, and Dafydd is unaware of most of it. Guy Jones, an English stranger in Welsh Pendon, is speedily involved in intrigues amatory, monetary, and intricately Ayckbournian, while he ascends the cast ladder to the lead role of Gay's Macheath.

Aside from the baroque subgenre, *A Chorus of Disapproval* is a familiar Ayckbourn farce interweaving adultery, inept deception, and general
mayhem. As in earlier Ayckbourn plays, the clumsy bumbler finally departs
without the girl, but Guy is nevertheless more fortunate than Norman of the
conquests, since he *has* shuttled between the beds of two wives, without the
annoyance of marriage to either one. Guy's victim Dafydd is as clumsy a husband as he is a director, and, as Dennis of *Just Between Ourselves* tinkers with
his tools, Dafydd tinkers with his cast. In this play about a play, Ayckbourn
the former stage manager relishes the trappings of theatre—curtain calls,
makeshift properties and costumes, graceless stagehands, missed cues and
unlearned lines, foreign-is-funny un-English accents, and the misplay of lights
at the technical rehearsal. Ayckbourn's reputed sympathy with women is
markedly absent from this play, where the women are sexually greedy—in
parallel with the financially greedy males. In a conversation with Ian Watson,
Ayckbourn comments: "I was chasing the theme of inner corruption inside a
society, and how an honest man in a dishonest society looks like the biggest
rogue of all" (111). Although Ayckbourn's society is dishonest, his Guy Jones
is not so much honest as naive. Perhaps Ayckbourn's mind was already on *A
Small Family Business.*

A *Chorus of Disapproval is* enjoyable as an adultery farce, but its parallels with *The Beggar's Opera* are somewhat forced, and they were elided in the
original production (even more so in the naturalistic movie, set in Scarborough). Simon, in contrast, chooses a diminutive inner play to enhance the
anachronism of his irascible protagonists, the erstwhile Sunshine Boys. An old
hand at radio and television, Simon is comfortable—as Ayckbourn is not—in
this metatheatrical venture.

In more recent plays, both playwrights reach for wider social commentary—Alan Ayckbourn's *A Small Family Business* (1987) and Neil Simon's
Lost in Yonkers (1991). The latter play might well be called "a small family
business," since the setting is an apartment in Yonkers, above "Kurnitz's Kandy
Store."[7] By means of that business and her rigid discipline, a German-Jewish
widow has raised her four living children, whom she continues to dominate in
adulthood. Unusually for Simon, the structure of the play has an Ayckbournian symmetry, with four scenes in each of its two acts. Even more unusually
for Simon, the play has a group protagonist, for all members of the Kurnitz
family are "lost in Yonkers"—most literally Bella, the 35-year-old child who
gets lost when she occasionally forgets where she lives: "She missed the first
year [of high school] because she couldn't find it." Metaphorically lost are
Bella's stern friendless mother, her lung-damaged sister Gert, her gangster
brother Louie, her widower brother Eddie, and his two sons, Jay and Arty.

The time is 1942, and the illness of Eddie's recently deceased wife has
plunged him into debt—"The doctors, the hospital, cost me everything I had
. . . And everything I didn't have." But since it is during World War II, jobs

are suddenly available, and Eddie can sell scrap iron in the Southern states. He has come to Yonkers to plead with his mother to shelter his adolescent sons while he is away working off his debt. Although she refuses, her childlike daughter Bella coerces the old woman into accepting the presence of the boys: "You and me and Jay and Arty. . . . Won't that be fun, Momma.?"

It is fun only for the audience, even though Simon reduces his one-liners while the strands of his plot unwind. Each scene opens with a voice-over—a new technique for Simon—usually a letter from absent Eddie to his sons. Grandma Kurnitz and her grandsons are at comic loggerheads. Her son, the gangster Louie, hides out in his old Yonkers home; her daughter, the brain-damaged Bella, falls in love with a mentally retarded movie usher. Unaware of these strains, Eddie writes to his sons: "The one thing that keeps me going is knowing you're with my family." When Bella enlists family support for money to marry, her mother dismisses the idea—"Dot's enough! . . . I don't vant to hear dis anymore!" Here foreign is *not* funny. Bella runs away, but she returns to her Yonkers home when her swain cannot bring himself to leave his parents. Eddie returns to Yonkers to reclaim his sons, while lawless Louie enlists in the Pacific War. A final victory belongs to Bella, who calmly informs her mother that she would like to invite a girlfriend to dinner, and the friend has a brother.

Simon's characters resemble other American prototypes—the harsh matriarch of Hellman's *Little Foxes,* the loving brain-damaged women of Shepard's *A Lie of the Mind,* the good-hearted gangster of Grade-B movies, the vivacious boys of *Tom Sawyer* and *Huck Finn*— but Simon's material is invested with a feeling of lived experience. In spite of a clumsy exposition, contrived exits and entrances, and misplaced one-liners—such as Louies "Sometimes bein' on the up and up just gets you down and down"—the characters bristle with independent energy. As in Simon's other plays, no one is evil; Grandma Kurnitz became tough to survive, and she undergoes no softening. An unreformed gangster Louie joins the army, and weak Eddie finds neither new strength nor a new wife. Although Bella triumphs twice, she remains a child mentally; even though her new friend has a brother, New Comedy seems far in the past. Grandma and Bella presumably carry on in the family business, but the boys have matured beyond the lure of its (invisible) ice cream sodas.

Loosely plotted, the play charms by its characters, whose jokes accord with their personalities. Eddie's subservience to Grandma is funny, as is that of criminal Louie. The latter calls himself a businessman, and adopts movie poses, but Jay cuts him down to size: "Well, you're no Humphrey Bogart." Sister Gert's wheezing is a minor running gag. Although Bella is often in a state of comic confusion, Simon displays rare delicacy in balancing the childlike mind and the woman's body—"*a mess at dressing.*" The plays humor arises mainly from the discomforts of life in the family, but unlike Ayckbourn's irrepressible physicalizations, Simon's family troubles are verbally stressed.

Ayckbourn's A SMALL Family Business (my emphasis) is several steps up the capitalist ladder from Kurnitz's Kandy Store; Ayres and Graces manufacture fitted furniture.[8] In Lost in Yonkers we had to take the downstairs candy store—and even its wares—on faith, but Ayckbourn never lets us forget the furniture business, since its products embellish the four visible stage households where the action takes place. Moreover, it may be a small business, but it is a large stage family, each of whose members dangles her or his subplot. Ken Ayres, who founded the firm, borders on senility—"the odd blank patch"—but not to the extent of designating his restaurant-craving son Desmond as his heir. Instead, he chooses his daughter Poppy's husband, honest Jack McCracken. Jack's brother Cliff already works for Ayres and Graces, as does Desmond's wife's sister and Jack's son-in-law Roy. The extended family is thus very much involved in the business—so involved, we soon learn, that they steal the firm's wares to be sold as Italian imports, with the connivance of the Rivetti brothers, whose own small business of a large family has connections with the Mafia. When honest Jack learns the extent of the chicanery, he furiously calls a family meeting: "We are going to sponge the shit off the family name, all right?. . . We are going to put the business together as it was. As a decent, honest, small family business."

Having already hired a private detective, however, Jack learns that this unsavory person will have to be paid off with a large sum, and the resident Rivetti brother assures him that the sum could "arrange something more permanent" to ensure the detective's silence. By the end of the play, that is exactly what happens. In Jack's absence his wife and elder daughter are threatened by the detective, who is then toppled into the bathtub by Jack's younger daughter, a drug addict. The Italian connection gets rid of the body, but the representative Rivetti demands payment: "I mean, their bill for the removal and disposal of our friend is costing an arm and a leg, if you'll pardon the expression" (and if you'll pardon the Simonized line). What it costs is distribution by the small family business of "urgent medical supplies," or drugs. Step by relentless step, Jack has yielded to corruption. Circling to another party—for the 75th birthday of senile Ken Ayres—the play closes with Jack McCracken's toast to the family business.

Although Ayckbourn's ending is predictable, the plot moves forward like a steamroller. Ayckbourn also enters Simon's terrain of generational conflict; Jack is out of touch with both his daughters, and old Ken confuses his son with his son-in-law. Private relationships are as crooked as the family business. The ubiquity of malefaction is implied by frequent generalities: "Everybody else works little fiddles. That's what the system's designed for." And yet the play seems confined by its social case history, without reaching out to indict a system—whether capitalism or Thatcherism.

In his mature plays Simon is still learning such basic dramaturgical techniques as exposition, relevance, climax, and the syllables of nonverbal languages of theatre. Ayckbourn is past master at intricate plot, economical exposition, acrid resolution, and the most ingenious scenescapes ever concocted. But clumsily as Simon draws them, Grandma Kurnitz and her daughter Bella evince a new level of complexity; whereas, deftly as Ayckbourn manipulates his large cast, the characters remain behavioral counters.

Over the course of their long careers, Neil Simon and Alan Ayckbourn have aroused laughter from many audiences in many theatres. In spite of the ethnic dissimilarity of their characters, however, they are white, middle-class, and Eurocentric. Notes of prejudice sound in Simon's plays. Do the anti-Hispanic remarks made in *The Gingerbread Lady* and *The Sunshine Boys* belong to Simon or his characters? Ayckbourn's characters are utterly unaware that Britain, like the United States, is a multicultural country. Is that the character's limitation or the playwright's?

Ayckbourn and Simon are amusing recorders of small experience, as displayed in small stage business. For all Simon's sentimetality and Ayckbourn's ingenuity, their stage countries are circumscribed in similar dimensions of irritating triviality, and I mean that in two senses:

1. Their characters worry about indecorous noises, incompetent cooking, overindulged pets, or sexual peccadilloes.
2. The playwrights themselves rarely situate such trivia on a large canvas.

Feydeau's farces, still spritely on stage, nevertheless indict *la belle époque;* the comedies of Simon and Ayckbourn indict the pace of contemporary life, or the characters bent on success, or the denseness of good intentions, but they rarely provide a context for the good or nasty humor on their stages. Their popularity is based on an appeal to social groups that account for a large percentage of dwindling theatre audiences on both sides of the Atlantic.

Reviewing Ayckbourn's *Way Upstream,* with its boating mishaps on the precarious River Orb, Sue Jameson noted: "Somehow my leaky roof at home didn't seem quite so bad" (549). If we extend her remark to the abrasive relations in the plays of Simon and Ayckbourn, we can appreciate much of their magnetism. Sight gags and verbal gags not only elicit our sympathy for the feckless and irritated; but the humor also confirms our own superiority to the mediocrities on stage. Both playwrights, in their different ways, amuse us with recalcitrant objects and situations so problematic that our own don't, "seem quite so bad" on either side of the Atlantic.

NOTES

[1] Simon and Ayckbourn also share the following details: (a) Homage to *The Importance of Being Earnest,* since English Cecily and Gwendolyn figure in Simon's

The Odd Couple, and a scribbled country address leads to mistaken relationships in Ayckbourn's *Relatively Speaking.* See Kalson, in *DNB* 13(1), p. 18, for an extended comparison of *Relatively Speaking* with *The Importance of Being Earnest.* (b) Un-Wildean is the treatment of suicide as farce by both Simon and Ayckbourn: In the former's *The Odd Couple* the friends of unhappy Felix walk him strenuously around to counteract the effect of deadly pills, and so do the acquaintances of Roland Crabbe in Ayckbourn's *Taking Steps.*

[2] The blurb about Ayckbourn in the program of *Time of My Life* cites "stage manager, sound technician, lighting technician, scene painter, prop-maker, actor, writer and director"—in short, an all-around theatre man.

[3] *The Odd Couple* became the basis for a television series starring Tony Randall and Jack Klugman, but Simon was not its author. In 1985 Simon reworked the play for a female odd couple.

[4] Rare in Ayckbourn's dialogue, puns often figure in his tides.

[5] Simon's *Jake's Women* experiments with the play of past against present, facts against fantasy. That play suffers from analogies with Arthur Miller's *After the Fall* (1964), as does Simon's *Chapter Two.* Similarly, *Brighton Beach Memoirs* (1983) echoes the Depression-era salesman father and two sons of Miller's *Death of a Salesman* (1949). Gerald M. Berkowitz hears the voice of Odets in Simon's *Brighton Beach Memoirs:* "Like [Odets's plays] it uses the native American dramatic form of domestic realism, here tempered with warm and unobtrusive humour, to depict a society in crisis and transition, through its reflection in the everyday lives of ordinary people" (174).

[6] Richard Meryman describes (in tedious adoration) the out-of-town adventures of Simon and *The Gingerbread Lady.*

[7] The 1993 movie of *Lost in Yonkers* (shot in Kentucky!) dwells in loving detail on the candy store. It also materializes Bella's beloved Johnny, and it introduces gratuitous wisecracks.

[8] It is piquant that Ayckbourn likens playwriting to furniture making: "I always compare [playwriting] with furniture making rather than with any other kind of writing" (Page 92).

Works Cited

Berkowitz, Gerald M, *American Drama of the Twentieth Century.* London: Longman, 1992.

Billington, Michael. *Alan Ayckbourn.* London: Macmillan, 1990.

Dukore, Bernard, ed. *Alan Ayckbourn: A Casebook.* New York: Garland, 1991.

Innes, Christopher. *Modern British Drama 1890–1990.* Cambridge: Cambridge UP, 1992.

Jameson, Sue. *London Theatre Record,* 1982.

Joseph, Stephen. *Theatre in the Round.* London: Barrie & Rockliff, 1967.

Kalson, Albert E. "Alan Ayckbourn." *Dictionary of Literary Biography: British Dramatists Since World War II,* vol. 13, pt. 1. Stanley Weintraub, ed. Detroit: Gale, 1982, 15–32.

———. *Laughter in the Dark: The Plays of Alan Ayckbourn.* London: Fairleigh Dickinson UP, 1993.

McGovern, Edythe M. *Neil Simon: A Critical Study.* New York: Frederick Ungar, 1979.

Meryman, Richard. "When America's Funniest Writer Turned Serious." *Life* 70.5 (May 7, 1971): 60B–83.

Page, Malcolm. *File on Ayckbourn.* London: Methuen, 1989.

Simon, Neil. "Make 'em Laugh." Interview with Clive Hirschhorn. *Plays and Players* 24.12 (September 1977): 12–15

———. Interview with Edwin Wilson on "Spotlight," CUNY TV, 8 Dec. 1986. Taped dialogue on file at the Theatre on Film and Tape Collection at the New York Public Library of the Performing Arts at Lincoln Center.

Watson, Ian. *Conversations with Ayckbourn.* London: Macdonald, 1981.

Broadway Babies: Images of Women in the Musicals of Stephen Sondheim

Laura Hanson

> First you're another
> Sloe-eyed vamp,
> Then someone's mother,
> Then you're camp.
> Then you career
> From career to career.
> I'm almost through my memoirs,
> And I'm here. (Sondheim, *Follies* 59–60)

The images of female characters in musical theatre have traditionally, as the Stephen Sondheim lyric suggests, been limited by certain categorizations. There is, of course, the virginal ingenue, the wise-cracking and slightly naughty secondary female lead, the wise older woman, or the suffering woman in love with the wrong kind of guy. From the early days of the musical theatre, young love was emphasized; physical beauty and a soprano singing voice were the staples of the heroine as she set out on the path to love, marriage, and family. Complications with members of the opposite sex usually resulted from simple misunderstandings or superficial differences in social or economic class.[1] "The ultimate reconciliation was usually achieved a few seconds before the final curtain . . . and the hero and heroine lived happily-ever-after" (Coward 8). As in straight romantic comedy, the act of marriage in musicals, with its promise of children, brings the characters in line with the civilizing morés of society and promises to perpetuate those values. Musical theatre, as an idealization of life in America and celebration of its abundance, tended to idealize women's roles as well. Hope and optimism for the future surged after the end of World War II, the beginning of the musical theatre's "Golden Age." The soldiers returned from war, women came home from the factories and took up their traditional duties of wife and homemaker. These values are reflected in the musical theatre of the post-war years, particularly in the musicals of Rodgers and

Hammerstein. In his article, "'I Enjoy Being a Girl': Women in the Plays of Rodgers and Hammerstein," Richard M. Goldstein discusses the traditional roles assigned to the heroines in some of America's best-known and best-loved musicals. In those works, the "heroine is an idealist, holding an extremely romantic view of male-female relationships." She is "not concerned with the dull, dark reality of the everyday world" (2).

By the time Stephen Sondheim's work emerged on Broadway, however, society and the role of women within that society were changing. A nation that had been through the Kennedy assassinations, the Vietnam War, and the women's movement no longer believed in love at first sight and the happily-ever-after endings of traditional musical theatre. In the words of critic John Lahr, "Sondheim's tough glibness echoed the mood of the unromantic era" (73). Musical heroines were no longer the young, sweet, virginal girls of earlier works from the twenties and beyond, but battle weary from the war between the sexes. In his musicals, Sondheim explores the increasingly complicated and ambiguous relationships between men and women, as well as the doubts and ambivalence that arise as his women try to sort out, through song, their conflicting feelings towards love, marriage, men, their own self-images, and the pursuit of their dreams. While the characters in a Rodgers and Hammerstein musical "kiss in the shadows" or fall in love suddenly "across a crowded room," a Sondheim lover is often dragged unwillingly, kicking and screaming into a relationship. This desire *not* to carry the torch of love is expressed eloquently by Sondheim's women in songs such as "Losing My Mind" and "Not a Day Goes By." These contrast sharply with the straightforward declaration of emotion in more traditional love songs or those in which the characters are so eager for love to come along that they express their longing for it before it has really had time to take root, as in "If I Loved You" from *Carousel* or "People Will Say We're in Love" from *Oklahoma!* As Lahr points out, "Instead of celebrating the ease and spontaneity of emotion that was the stock-in-trade of the traditional musical responding to a world it insisted was benign, Sondheim's songs report the difficulty of feeling in a world where, as his song says, there's 'so little to be sure of'" (74).

Sondheim's heroines no longer enjoy the self-assured ebullience of a Nellie Forbush proclaiming to all the world, "I'm in love with a wonderful guy!" (Hammerstein 194). For *Passion*'s Clara, her idea of love is not something to be celebrated, but hidden: "I thought where there was love/There was shame" (5). Nurse Fay in *Anyone Can Whistle* is so emotionally inhibited, she begs to be taught "How to let go,/ . . . Learn to be free" (109), and can only express herself emotionally by taking on another woman's persona. This "disguise" is kept under her bed as a constant reminder to the rational, self-controlled, professional woman that there was once a moment when spontaneous feeling prevailed. Perhaps there is hope that it could happen again; yet when Hapgood leads her to the bed, she freezes and cannot go through with consummating the relationship. The simplest human skills and emotion are beyond her ability.

In spite of Fay's logical and scientific mentality, she betrays a more emotional side of herself buried deep within by secretly wanting to believe in the town miracle. Ironically, when she is chased by the mayoress' henchmen, she sings her belief in the proverbial "knight in shining armor" who will rescue her: "There are heroes in the world,/Princes and heroes in the world,/And one of them will save me" (38). This is a belief that Cinderella, one of her later sisters in the Sondheim canon, will come to question. True to Fay's rationality, however, her hero won't arrive in the typical musical comedy manner, she may secretly believe in Prince Charming, but eschews the usual emotional trappings:

> There won't be trumpets or bolts of fire
> To say he's coming.
> No Roman candles, no angels' choir,
> No sound of distant drumming. (38)

Throughout the musical, Fay does develop a higher level of self-awareness and independence which can be traced through her songs. She progresses from the dichotomy of "There Won't Be Trumpets," in which she looks for a hero, but claims not to believe in the typical romantic accompaniments to his arrival, through her admission of emotional inhibition in "Anyone Can Whistle" to the realization that self-revelation has its price:

> Give yourself,
> If somebody lets you—
> See what it gets you,
> See what it gets you!
> Give yourself
> And somebody lets you
> Down. (161)

The hero she expected cannot save her, and Fay realizes, "And when you want things done, you have to do them yourself alone!" (161).

Toward the end of the play, Fay says good-bye to Hapgood, acknowledging that they would make an unlikely pair—her competent practicality juxtaposed against his crazy zest for life. In her song of farewell, in which she admits her need, but acknowledges the man's need to be his own person, Fay foreshadows a later Sondheim heroine, Dot, who (in *Sunday in the Park with George*) cannot allow her love for a man to overshadow her own need for self-respect. When Dot comes to the realization that her needs and desires will always take second place to George's work, she accepts what she cannot change: "It's because I understand that I left,/That I am leaving" (74). She is not content to live with a man who withholds himself emotionally, who relates more easily to the still images of her that he creates than to the real woman, and who tells her, "You know exactly how I feel./Why do you insist/You must hear the words,/When you know I cannot give you words?" (74). Refusing his explanation that she should be content because she is a part of his work, a silent image refracted through a man's gaze, Dot sings an assertion of her right to be her own person as well:

> No one is you, George,
> There we agree,
> But others will do, George.
> No one is you and
> No one can be,
> But no one is me, George,
> No one is me.
> We do not belong together.
>
>   . . .
> I have to move on. (76)

It is interesting to compare Dot to some of her musical ancestors, such as Eliza Doolittle, who rejects the man who has negated her feelings in the tirade of "Without You," walks out on him, but inevitably returns to fetch his slippers. As Goldstein points out, at various points in the Rodgers and Hammerstein canon, "Laurey *(Oklahoma!),* Nellie *(South Pacific),* Anna *(The King and I),* Mei Li *(Flower Drum Song),* and Maria *(The Sound of Music)* all contemplate leaving the men in their lives, but for one reason or another they all change their minds" (5).

In contrast, Dot takes the initiative, assuming responsibility for her own self-respect. Even as she prepares to leave the man she cares for, the beautiful torment of "We Do Not Belong Together" expresses more feeling and passion than most traditional love songs. Along with songs such as "Not a Day Goes By," "Losing My Mind," and "Loving You," Sondheim's female characters express the angst and agony of loving another person with chilling insight.

Before coming to her self-realization, Dot had put up with her distant lover, blaming herself for his emotional coldness: "George is very special. Maybe I'm just not special enough for him" (35). Compare her insecurity with the self-assurance of Linda Low in *Flower Drum Song* who enjoys being a girl in the traditional sense:

> I'm strictly a female female,
> And my future, I hope, will be
> In the home of a brave and free male

Who'll enjoy being a guy,
Having a girl like me! (Hammerstein 251)

The confident exaltation of femininity that she engages in as she gazes at herself in the mirror stands in marked contrast to Dot, who expresses self-doubt in her own mirror song:

If my legs were longer.
If my bust was smaller.
If my hands were graceful.
If my waist was thinner.
If my hips were flatter.
If my voice was warm.
If I could concentrate—[2] (35)

From Fay to Fosca, this idea of woman's self-image is explored in painful detail. In another "mirror song," the former chorines of *Follies* face their own aging selves and life's disappointments. The promises of beauty and youth, when love was fresh and all things seemed possible, have turned into the breathlessness and disillusion of middle age. Self-deception is one weapon which Sally wields against the brutal realities of life. In her haunting "In Buddy's Eyes," she presents the image of herself that she wants her former love to see—that she is content with her life and is in a happy marriage. The context of the play, the emotion of the actress, and the musical accompaniment belie her words, however. As she sings, Sally is trying as much to convince herself as she is trying to convince Ben that her life without him all these years has been a happy one. Having longed for this reunion for the past thirty years, Sally is so unsure of her own image that her first words to Ben are, "No, don't look at me—" (19), a phrase echoed later by the unattractive Fosca in *Passion.* In his book, *Sondheim's Broadway Musicals,* Stephen Banfield discusses the change in vocal register required for the song "In Buddy's Eyes" and the image of the woman that each evokes. When Sally sings the chorus, her idyll of a happy marital relationship, she sings in the sweet, innocent soprano of the traditional musical theatre heroine. Yet, the rest of the song is in the lower register, more akin to the blues with its "woman as sufferer" characteristic (183).

Ben, too, is guilty of self-delusion in the image he has created for himself of his love for Sally. He expresses his feelings for her in "Too Many Mornings," yet it is not the reality of Sally as she is now that he loves, but his memory of her as a young, beautiful woman. Ben ironically sings his heart-wrenching song of unfulfilled love to the image of Young Sally, not the middle-aged woman she has become. In a similar way, *A Little Night Music*'s Fredrik tries to recapture his own younger days by marrying his ideal of womanly youth and beauty. His dream marriage backfires on him, however, when his ideal woman cannot bring herself to sleep with her new husband. It is not that she is so chaste and pure, but that the relationship, as are most of the others in the play, is inappropriate. Anne is more like a daughter than a wife to Fredrik. He even admits this, obliquely, in references to her childish prattle and her habit of ruffling his ties, describing her as "So unlike a wife" (51). Anne, too, is hardly conscious of the imbalance at the beginning of the play, but her body tells her what her head refuses to admit: "When you're close and we touch,/And you're kissing my brow,/I don't mind it too much" (22). Anne's own insecurity manifests itself in her excuse for withholding from Fredrik for fear of losing his interest: "If I were perfect for you,/Wouldn't you tire of me . . ." (23).

Ironically, even though Anne cannot bring herself to sleep with her husband, she cannot bear the thought of his sleeping with another woman and schemes to get him back when it becomes apparent that he has fallen into the arms of his former love, Desirée. What she will do with him once she has him back, however, is doubtful. She and Charlotte commiserate with each other on the agonies of love in the poignant "Every Day a Little Death." Love is described as disgusting and insane, "A humiliating business!" for the woman in love with an unfaithful man (82). Again, themes of ambivalence and the agony of loving are evident. The irony is that Charlotte truly loves her louse of a husband, while Anne only thinks that she does because he is the type of man that young girls have been taught that they should fall in love with and marry—the prosperous, established kind who will provide them with dresses, maids, and spoil them shamelessly. In the end, Anne comes to her own moment of self-awareness, that she has never loved Fredrik and is in love with his son Henrik, a man closer to her own age. Desirée has her own moment of self-realization when she sings "Send in the Clowns." Coming up empty after a life of shoddy tours and casual lovers, she yearns for a second chance at happiness, ". . . a chance to turn back, to find some sort of coherent existence after so many years of muddle" (157). Her self-realization is not matched by the man in her life, however, who is still seduced by the image of Anne's youth and beauty. The inequity of the different effects of age on the image of men and women is reiterated later by Charlotte, who resents Fredrik's acquiring a young, pretty wife at an age ". . . when a woman is lucky if a drunken alderman pinches her derrière at a village fete!" (167). In the end, however, harmony is achieved, when all the women have found their proper partners, the ones most suited to them in age and temperament.

The emphasis on youth and beauty has traditionally been a staple of musical theatre heroines, but Sondheim and his collaborators have turned it into ironic comment in shows such as *Into the Woods, A Little Night Music, Passion,* and *Follies,* where the song "Beautiful Girls" introduces a line of middle-aged, former Follies Girls. Sally, Phyllis and Desirée have left their youth behind, but instead of growing wiser with the years as Aunt Eller in *Oklahoma!,* Nettie in *Carousel,* or Anna Leonowens in *The King and I* have, they are more confused than ever about life and love. The witch in *Into the Woods* must trade the one thing that makes her unique—her magical powers—in order to acquire the physical beauty that she thinks will make her more acceptable in the eyes of her child. The idea of a woman as a beautiful, but empty-headed, ornament is lampooned in *Forum*'s "I'm Lovely," where Philia, a recent graduate from courtesan school, proclaims, "All I am is lovely,/Lovely is the one thing I can do" (45). However, this paean to the most superficial of womanly virtues is satirized later in the play when the song is reprised by Hysterium dressed in women's clothing; it mocks the notion that all it takes are the external trappings to give one the sought-after loveliness.

Sondheim and James Lapine explored the issue of beauty and a woman's worth in the eyes of the world in their most recent collaboration, *Passion*. In this work, the musical theatre has come full-circle, from the lovely and lovable heroines who inevitably end up happily married to the man they love, to the "irredeemably ugly" Fosca, who, in the words of Sondheim, himself, "has not one redeeming quality. . . . If she had one ordinary, not passionate, moment, one moment that wasn't about herself, the character would not only be hateful, but unbelievable" (qtd. in Buck 278). Fosca's lack of the one thing that gives a woman her worth has denied her a normal life of domesticity and turned her into a bitter, self-pitying creature, seemingly incapable of taking other people's feelings into account. As a woman, her role in society has already been limited; her looks further constrict her choices in a way that is not felt by men:

> An unattractive man—. . .
> —Can still have opportunities . . .
> Whereas, if you're a woman,
> You either are a daughter or a wife . . .
> You marry—. . .
> —Or you're a daughter all your life. (76–77)

In a society where "Beauty is power . . ." and where "A woman's like a flower . . ./A flower's only purpose is to please . . ." (84), Fosca lacks the one quality that society values.

Ironically, it is not Fosca's appearance, but the sheer force of her passion that shakes Giorgio to his very core, shattering all his traditional notions of love as something pretty, tidy and self-controlled. In the same way, *Passion,* itself, shatters an audience's expectations of what a love story in a musical should be. There is no typical boy meets girl story here. The man is attractive; the woman is not only unattractive, but unpleasant as well. The traditional roles are reversed. The woman pursues the man and praises his beauty with the same phrase that Giorgio used to praise his ideal woman, the blonde and beautiful Clara: "God, you are so beautiful" (57). In a twist on the usual musical outcomes, the ugly woman triumphs over the beautiful one, thereby gaining through the sheer force of her emotion the power that was denied her by her looks. There is no happy ending, however, when the lovers are finally united at the end of the story.

Fosca is unusual in that she is able to admit the force of her own darker impulses. Her attraction to her husband, Count Ludovic, was based in part on an element of danger she sensed in him: "Deception,/Even violence./I must admit to some degree/That it excited me" (81). Traditional heroines of the musical theatre are nice girls, generally devoid of the darker impulses and conflicting passions that plague so many of Sondheim's women. In *Oklahoma!,* Laurey is only able to confront her darker desires in a dream. And there is never any real doubt in the audience's mind as to which way she is going to choose. Her predecessor, Liza Elliott, a *Lady in the Dark,* also explored her romantic desires through dream sequences. Yet, Sondheim's women confront their desires, passions, and conflicting emotions head on in the light of day.

Traditional musical heroines are usually virginal or, perhaps, chaste in their remembrance of a past love. Even those who do end up with a number of children manage to acquire them asexually either through marriage (Nellie Forbush, Maria Von Trapp), adoption (Mame), or simply by becoming a maternal figure for someone else's children (Anna in *The King and I*). But Sondheim's women deal openly, though perhaps somewhat confusedly, with the issue of their own sexuality. In *Company,* Amy expresses her fears about curtailing it with "fidelity forever" (64). From *Anyone Can Whistle* through *Passion,* Sondheim's women wrestle with their own needs and desires. For some like Fay, emotional inhibition and self-doubt prevent her from consummating a relationship, For Fosca, the compulsion to love is beyond her control and results in her own death and the destruction of the one she loves. The others in between struggle to choose between what they want, or think they want, and what they think is right. Infidelities sometimes occur as Sondheim's women explore, through song, their conflicting emotions and desires, or try to make up for a past choice they felt has gone awry.

For some, sexuality has a more practical application. It is used for business purposes by the elder Madame Armfeldt in *A Little Night Music:* "It's but a pleasurable means/To a measurable end" (60). She has elevated a Woman's sexual allure to a high art in the game of negotiation between men and women, using youth and beauty as weapons in order to achieve the wealth and social position a woman may have been born without. She abhors the lack of discretion younger women (her daughter included) display in their amorous adventures. This practical approach to male-female relationships is echoed by the maid Petra in her song, "The Miller's Son." She, too, knows that a woman has to take care of herself, think of her own future and vows to "Pin my hat on a nice piece of property" (162). In the meantime, however, ". . . a girl ought to celebrate what passes by" (163). Obviously, Petra feels that she, as a woman, will have to forego sexual fulfillment within marriage in favor of economic security. Before being locked into the role that society has dictated for her, Petra will make the most of her freedom and enjoy the sampling of life's pleasures: "It's a very short day/Till you're stuck with just one/ Or it has to be done on the sly" (164). Ironically, it is Petra, the lower-class servant girl, who has a healthier and more realistic view of her sexuality than the upper-class women, Desirée, Anne, and Charlotte, who manage to make a muddle of their relationships.

In "The Story of Lucy and Jessie," from *Follies,* Phyllis expresses the ambivalence and frustration of a woman who longs to combine the innocence, vitality, and sexual freedom she enjoyed in her youth with the maturity and financial security of her older self. Apparently, a woman cannot have it both ways. Anne, in *A Little Night Music,* has denied her own feelings for the security of marriage to an older, prosperous man; as a result, she is unable to express her sexuality at all. A similar sentiment is echoed by the Baker's Wife in *Into the Woods* after her brief extramarital affair with the Prince: "Have a child for warmth,/And a baker for bread,/And a Prince for whatever—" (112). She, too, takes it for granted that a woman's role as wife and mother is distinct from her own sexual fulfillment, and she must choose between the comfort and security of life with her Baker husband and a fling with the handsome Prince. Having had the brief moment enjoying that which every woman dreams of, her practical side pulls her back to reality and her duties. Yet, she relishes the moment for what it was and questions the limitations of life and society, where once one chooses one's path, there is no going back:

> Must it all be either less or more,
> Either plain or grand?
> Is it always "or"?
> Is it never "and"?[3] (112)

While marriage and the raising of children are the main purpose in the life of the traditional heroine, Sondheim's women do not seem to view this as their primary goal. While children abound in musicals such as *The King and I, The Sound of Music,* and *The Music Man,* they appear sparingly in the Sondheim canon. In *Company,* although it is known that Bobby is "Seven times a godfather" (81), the children are never seen and are only mentioned in passing, as in "Children you destroy together" (31). As can be seen in the case of the Baker's Wife in *Into the Woods,* motherhood—supposedly the goal of every heroine— does not cause her life to turn suddenly into that long-awaited happily-ever-after. With the child come problems which she never had to confront before, as well as the awesome responsibility for someone other than herself. And the perverse reward of motherhood is the eventual loss of one's child: "Children can only grow/From something you love/To something you lose . . ." (106). Jack, Cinderella, Little Red Ridinghood, and Rapunzel all grow up and come to maturity only by separating from their mothers and making their own decisions. Cinderella sings as much to herself as to the distraught Little Red Ridinghood:

> Mother cannot guide you.
> Now you're on your own . . . (128)
>
>   . . .
>
> Mother isn't here now . . .
> Who knows what she'd say? (130)

In contrast, the character of the witch represents "An archetypal possessive mother" (Holden 7), perhaps harking back to the similar character of Rose in one of Sondheim's earliest musicals as a lyricist, *Gypsy*. Instead of encouraging her child's independence, she keeps her locked up, fearful and dependent, smothering her ability to cope with life:

> Don't you know what's out there in the world?
> Someone has to shield you from the world.
> Stay with me . . .
> Who out there could love you more than I?
> What out there that I cannot supply?. . .
>
> Stay with me,
> The world is dark and wild.
> Stay a child while you can be a child.
> With me. (60)

Other glimpses of women in the maternal role are not particularly rosy either. Desirée does not seem to have much of the mothering instinct in *A Little Night Music*. She leaves her daughter with her own mother while she pursues her acting career. Her staccato letter to Fredrika is not especially communicative, focusing more on her own activities than those of her daughter. Apparently, Desirée's relationship with her own mother is not the best. There are hints of little barbs in the lyrics. When Desirée reports that she's performing in some little town, she says wearily, as though she has heard the question many times before, "And don't ask where is it, please." She then moves on to, "And are you corrupting the child?/ . . . I'll come for a visit/And argue" (29). The elder Madame Armfeldt seems to disapprove of the lifestyle her daughter leads. "Ordinary daughters ameliorate their lot," she sings, "Mine tours" (28). She disapproves especially of the mess Desirée makes of her love life, not using the art of love skillfully for financial security:

> Liaisons! What's happened to them?
> Liaisons today.
> Untidy—take my daughter, I

> Taught her, I
> Tried my best to point the way.
> I even named her Desirée. (61)

Ironically, while most mothers in the musical theatre would be trying to protect their daughters from the world of sex, Madame Armfeldt feels she has failed because she has not been able to teach her daughter how to turn sex into a financially rewarding career.

Even the evil Mrs. Lovett in *Sweeney Todd* cannot resist assuming the maternal role in her relationship with the slow-witted orphan Tobias. However, her good feelings soon give way to murderous thoughts when Tobias' suspicions of Todd are aroused. Reprising the boy's naive and heartfelt "Not While I'm Around," Mrs. Lovett sings her version of the song to an eerie and sinister accompaniment, which belies the sincerity of the words. Nothing may harm Tobias while Mrs. Lovett is around except, perhaps, Mrs. Lovett, herself.

In *Passion,* Clara has to choose between her own sexual fulfillment and her identity as a mother. The fear of losing her child is the reason she initially gives for refusing to run away with lover Giorgio, though in her responses to his pleas, it seems that she may simply be using that as an excuse to maintain a convenient, uncommitted relationship with him. She has second thoughts, however, and tells Giorgio this when the child is old enough to go off to school, then she will run away with him. The child is merely one of her "obligations at home" (114), but she loves Giorgio, though not in the unconditional way he has come to expect. It is interesting that this second chance for the lovers came about in a later revision of *Passion.* In early previews, Clara put a permanent end to the affair,[4] giving her lover no choice but to fall into the arms of Fosca. By having Clara dangle the possibility of future happiness in front of Giorgio, the show's creators have actually strengthened his character, allowing Giorgio to make the choice, rather than having it imposed on him.

Not all images of woman as mother are fraught with ambivalence and anxiety, however. While *Sunday in the Park with George* may offer one character's unflattering view in "The Day Off"—

> Still, Sunday with someone's dotty mother
> Is better than Sunday with your own.
> Mothers may drone, mothers may whine—
> Tending to his, though, is perfectly fine.
> It pays for the nurse that is tending to mine
> On Sunday,
> My day off. (52)

—it is only through the women, first Marie and then Dot, that George is able to trace his lineage and find the nurturing link with his artistic heritage.

Throughout Sondheim's body of work, it is obvious that marriage is not the blissful, "happily-ever-after" of traditional musicals, but a "ferocious pillow-fight battle of the sexes. . . . It simply is not the placid old heaven-ordained, till-death-do-us-part, for-better-for-worse institution it used to be" (Kalem 62). Contrast the upbeat dream world of love and marriage in "You're Gonna Love Tomorrow/Love Will See Us Through" from *Follies* with the reality of how those marriages turned out. While Young Sally claims she'll bolster Young Buddy's ego as a wife should (90), it comes out later in "Buddy's Blues" that the middle-aged Sally thinks her husband is a washout (98). Young Phyllis bids ". . . fare-thee-well, ennui" (89), yet later in life is so bored with her marriage to Ben that the couple resorts to hurting each other just to keep the relationship alive. The women, who traditionally are the ones who cannot wait to step down the aisle, are as suspicious of the old institution as the men.

The archetypal musical heroines wanted nothing more than to fall in love, get married and live happily ever after. Yet, this myth is exploded by Cinderella in *Into the Woods*. Pursued by the vision that is every girl's dream, as the Baker's wife tells her, Cinderella is not sure that a rich, handsome Prince is what she really wants. In fact, she is not at all sure what she should want. The standard choice does not look so appealing. "Like Robert (and more significantly from a feminist point of view), she sees commitment as limiting since any definite decision destroys all other possibilities" (McLaughlin 36). Decision is risky, and again the issue of self-image comes into play. Cinderella has put on a different persona, and that is what the Prince has come to love. She is afraid that once he discovers her true self, he will no longer be interested. Even Cinderella is not sure which of the two versions of herself is the one to choose:

And then what if you are

> What a Prince would envision?
> Although how can you know
> Who you are till you know
> What you want, which you don't?
> So then which do you pick:
> Where you're safe, out of sight,
> And yourself, but where everything's wrong?
> Or where everything's right
> And you know that you'll never belong? (63)

More pragmatic than her musical predecessors, Cinderella has, by the end of the play, come to doubt the dream and to realize that the reality of life is not painted in either black or white, but lies somewhere in the middle. Her father's house was a nightmare; the Prince's was a dream: "Now I want something in-between" (128).

As a counterpoint to Robert's desire, but inability to commit, in *Company,* Amy is afraid to get married to someone she has been living with for a number of years; there is hesitation and ambivalence as she senses that allying herself to another person for life somehow diminishes the self. The traditionally accepted attitudes are turned upside down when she says to Bobby, "I'm afraid to get married, and you're afraid not to" (73). As a group, the female characters in *Company* represent the various levels of commitment in a woman's relationship with a man, which Bobby is able to witness first-hand: living together and then newlywed, married with children, divorced, middle-aged and much-married.

Feelings of ambivalence and self-doubt are evident in many of Sondheim's songs concerning love and the uneasy relationship between men and women. In more traditional musical theatre, love's final goal was a happy marriage where the stereotypical roles for husband and wife were well defined. The choices for a woman were clearcut between the "nice" men (for example, a Curly) or the slightly roguish ones a woman hoped to redeem with her love (Billy Bigelow, or Gaylord Ravenal), but no matter what, a woman stood by her man. "What's the use of wond'rin'/If he's good or if he's bad," Julie asks in *Carousel,* "He's your feller and you love him—/That's all there is to that" (Hammerstein 156). Similar views are expressed by Lady Thiang in "Something Wonderful" from *The King and I* and in the song "A Fellow Needs a Girl" from *Allegro:*

> A fellow needs a girl
> To sit by his side
> At the end of a weary day,
> To sit by his side
> And listen to him talk
> And agree with the things he'll say. (Hammerstein 172)

But once in a relationship, the traditional male and female roles do not necessarily apply for Sondheim's characters. The Baker in *Into the Woods* discovers that he cannot achieve his goal without forming an equal partnership with his wife in "It Takes Two"; indeed, she is usually the impetus for his actions. Like the couples in *Company,* both the Baker and his wife come to realize that forging a bond with another person enables one to get through the terrors of life a little more easily, even if it means giving up a bit of one's independence. In other partnerships, Sweeney Todd's dream of revenge is only set in motion by the enterprising and amoral woman in his life, Mrs. Lovett. *Company*'s Sarah can best her husband at karate and takes great pleasure in doing so. She does not fed, like the heroine of *Annie Get Your Gun,* that she has to allow the man to win in order to gain his love,[5] or, like Julie in *Carousel,* endure his abuse for the sake of allowing him his self-respect. Sondheim's women hit back. No longer is the woman the submissive helpmate, and the confusion and ambivalence about her modern role is suggested in the following lyrics from *Anyone Can Whistle*. As Hapgood tries to separate the pilgrims from the inmates of the sanatorium for the socially pressured, a gender-bending couple sings of their own confusion:

> A woman's place is in the home,
> A woman's place is on the shelf.
> And home is where he hangs her hat,
> And that is where she hangs himself. (63)

The cynical Joanne in *Company* caustically comments on those women who have bought into the traditional female stereotypes and have been disillusioned by their false promises:

> Here's to the girls who play wife—
> Aren't they too much?
> Keeping house but clutching a copy of *Life*
> Just to keep in touch.
> The ones who follow the rules,
> And meet themselves at the schools,
> Too busy to know that they're fools—
> Aren't they a gem? (106–7)

She goes on to skewer the various types of upper-middle-class women who, not having any kind of career of their own, fill up their days with pastimes. She comes to the painful realization during the song that she, herself, can be counted among their number. To shield herself from this harsh view, she anesthetizes herself with alcohol and caustic wit.

In their often shaky relationships with men, Sondheim's women struggle with their own conflicting images of self. Their struggle is often made more difficult, however, by men's unrealistic image of them. Bobby is unable to commit himself to one *real* woman in *Company* because he is searching for the unattainable ideal woman, a composite of all the best qualities of his closest female friends:

> My blue-eyed Sarah
> Warm Joanne
> Sweet Jenny
> Loving Susan
> Crazy Amy,
> Wait for me. . . . (54)

He does achieve a certain kind of emotional closeness with his women friends, but it is a chaste one. To his girlfriends, he can only relate on a sexual level and nothing more. If only Bobby could combine these two types of relationships with women, perhaps he could commit. But instead, "He is seeking the ideal mate who exists only in the world of myth and fairy tale—or in the never-never land of traditional American musical theater" (Gordon 53).

Ironically, the image of Desirée as the "perfect woman" is the undoing of Carl-Magnus and Fredrik in *A Little Night Music.* "If she'd only been faded,/ If she'd only been fat," they lament (129). "If she'd cried or whatever/A woman would do in a pinch,/It would have been wonderful" (130). Rather than taking responsibility for their own foolishness, they blame this ideal woman for their predicament. Obviously, in the imperfect world of a Sondheim musical, a woman cannot win. She is blamed if she is perfect, and blamed if she is not. As he sings "In Praise of Women," the egotistical Carl-Magnus extols "Knowing their place" as one of the womanly virtues (72). In the traditional world where "There Is Nothin' Like A Dame," the women are always pretty and loyal, and they do know their place. Not so for Sondheim's women as they grope their way through life's choices. Although Carl-Magnus expects his wife calmly to accept his own infidelity, he cannot tolerate the same behavior in his mistress. But, to the egotistical count, the notion of Desirée being attracted to another man is unthinkable, and he finishes a song by proclaiming, "The woman's mine!" (73). The two Princes in *Into the Woods* also seem incapable of being true to their image of the ideal woman. For them, she is only ideal as long as she seems unattainable. But once they've conquered, they do not seem so adept at relating to the real flesh-and-blood woman behind the image they've created.

If the male-female relationship is sometimes strained in Sondheim's musicals, women's relationships with each other are not what one usually expects, either. The secondary female lead of traditional musical comedies acted as best friend and confidante, but Sondheim's women generally have only themselves to rely on, fumbling alone along life's path. Their insecurities and doubts about self-image are often manifested in their views of and relationships with other women. *Anyone Can Whistle* pits the rational Fay against the scheming mayoress, Cora. Their feelings toward each other are best summed up in a song that was cut from the original Broadway production, but recently restored to a concert version of the show at Carnegie Hall, "There's Always a Woman."[6] During the number, the two women bemoan the fact that there is always a woman to put a kink in the other one's plans; they then proceed to imagine ways in which to do each other in. *Sweeney Todd*'s Mrs. Lovett shows no mercy to the Beggar Woman and allows Sweeney to believe that his wife is dead so that she can establish the kind of relationship with him that she had always longed for. Old resentments between women also crop up at the *Follies* reunion, where Sally is reunited with an old love who married her former best friend. And *A*

Little Night Music's Charlotte and Anne team up to spoil their rival's conquest of Fredrik by emphasizing Anne's youth over the more mature Desirée.

This sense of female competition can also be seen in the song "Poor Baby" from *Company,* sung by all of Robert's married female friends. Although they tell Robert, "You know, no one/Wants you to be happy/More than I do" (93), they then criticize all of his girlfriends. Unable, and unwilling on a conscious level, to consummate their own relationships with Bobby, they nevertheless are jealous of his sexual relations with these other women. Under the guise of being concerned, they sweetly hurl insulting adjectives at the thought of them: dumb, tacky, neurotic, vulgar, immature, and ". . . tall enough to be your mother" (94).

From the early days of musical theatre, the majority of heroines sweetly sang their way to a fulfilling life as wife and mother. Even the spunkier ones, like Ado Annie in *Oklahoma!* or Carrie in *Carousel,* promised to mend their wandering ways once married and submit to their husbands. The choices were more clear-cut, between the nice men or the more risky ones. Those women who were unlucky enough to fall for the wrong kind of guy usually paid for it with a kind of romanticized martyrdom in which they even seemed to revel. For example, Julie in *Carousel* loves Billy so much that she does not even feel his abusive blows. And this is the message that she hands down to her own daughter—that loving your man hard enough makes everything all right. But in the past thirty years, the musical heroine has grown up, as exemplified by the women in the musicals of Stephen Sondheim and his collaborators. Sondheim's women tend to be more realistic and multi-dimensional than their more traditional counterparts. Their choices are not so clear-cut, their motivations not so predictable. They express doubts and fears about life and love and are not always so sure about what they want, as they proceed haltingly along the road to greater self-awareness. But fight or wrong, the choices have to be made, the consequences faced: "Where there's nothing to choose,/So there's nothing to lose" (*Woods* 64). Dot is all too familiar with the painful, yet necessary process of accepting and taking responsibility for one's own self. She expresses this eloquently and seems to speak for so many of Sondheim's women as she sings:

> I chose, and my world was shaken—
> So what?
> The choice may have been mistaken,
> The choosing was not.
> > You have to move on. (169)

NOTES

[1] In his foreword to *Musical Comedy* (by Raymond Mander and Joe Mitchenson), Noël Coward sums up the often silly and superfluous misunderstandings that created

the obstacles to true love in traditional musical comedy: "Either he would insult her publicly on discovering that she was a Princess in her own right rather than the simple commoner he had imagined her to be, or she would wrench his engagement ring from her finger, fling it at his feet and faint dead away on hearing that he was not the humble tutor she had loved for himself alone, but a multi-millionaire" (7–8).

[2] It is interesting to note that George later uses the same melody to describe a dog he is drawing in the park (48).

[3] Shortly after the Baker's Wife has her fling with the Prince, she is killed in the havoc wreaked by the giant. One critic, however, took this as commentary by the show's creators. In his article, "'No One is Alone': Society and Love in the Musicals of Stephen Sondheim," Robert L. McLaughlin makes note of that critic's reaction: "The implication of the Baker's Wife's death as punishment for her adultery caused Kramer in *The New Yorker* to accuse the authors of misogyny" (411).

[4] Preview of *Passion,* by Stephen Sondheim and James Lapine, dir. James Lapine, Plymouth Theatre, New York, 25 March 1994.

[5] This idea of a woman letting her man win in order to keep his love is a time-honored one and can even be seen in an early musical from the 1890s, *A Contented Woman,* in which a woman runs for mayor against her husband, but allows him to win.

[6] *Anyone Can Whistle,* by Stephen Sondheim and Arthur Laurents, perf. Scott Bakula, Madeline Kahn, and Bernadette Peters, Carnegie Hall, New York, 8 April 1995.

Works Cited

Banfield, Stephen. *Sondheim's Broadway Musicals*. Ann Arbor: U of Michigan P, 1993.

Buck, Joan Juliet. "Passion Play." *Vogue* May, 1994, 277–79.

Coward, Noel. Foreword. *Musical Comedy*. By Raymond Mander and Joe Mitchenson. New York: Taplinger, 1969.

Goldstein, Richard M. "'I Enjoy Being a Girl': Women in the Plays of Rodgers and Hammerstein." *Popular Music and Society* 13.1 (1989): 1–8.

Gordon, Joanne. *Art Isn't Easy: The Theater of Stephen Sondheim*. New York: Da Capo, 1992.

Hammerstein, Oscar, II. *Lyrics*. Milwaukee: Hal Leonard, 1985.

Holden, Stephen. "A Fairy-Tale Musical Grows Up." *New York Times* 1 November 1987.

Kalem, T.E. Rev. of *Company,* by Stephen Sondheim and George Furth. *Time* 95 (11 May 1970): 62.

Lahr, John. "Sondheim's Little Deaths." *Harper's* 258(Apr. 1979): 71–78.

McLaughlin, Robert L. "'No One is Alone': Society and Love in the Musicals of Stephen Sondheim." *Journal of American Drama and Theatre* 3(1991): 27–41.

Sondheim, Stephen, and George Furth. *Company* New York: Random, 1970.

———, Larry Gelbart, and Burr Shevelove. *A Funny Thing Happened on the Way to the Forum*. New York: Applause, 1991.

———, and James Goldman. *Follies*. New York: Random, 1971.

———, and James Lapine. *Into the Woods*. New York TCG, 1987.

———. *Passion*. New York: TCG, 1994.

———. *Sunday in the Park with George*. New York Applause, 1991.

———, and Arthur Laurents. *Anyone Can Whistle*. New York: Leon Amiel, 1965.

———, and Hugh Wheeler. *A Little Night Music*. New York: Dodd, 1973.

From Zurich to Brazil
with Tom Stoppard
Felicia Hardison Londré

In *The Real Thing*, the seventeen-year-old daughter of playwright Henry Boot humors her father by steering the conversation toward his lowbrow musical tastes. She asks: "How're the Everlys getting on? And the Searchers. How's old Elvis?"

"He's dead," her father replies.

"I did know that," she says. "I mean how's he holding up apart from that?"

Her father answers: "I never went for him much. 'All Shook Up' was the last good one. However, I suppose that's the fate of all us artists."

"Death?"

"People saying they preferred the early stuff."[1]

Of course, death is the fate of artists too, as well as taxes for the successful ones. But there is also some truth in what Stoppard's playwright-protagonist says about the public's tendency to prefer "the early stuff." Most people prefer Tennessee Williams's *The Glass Menagerie* to his *Clothes for a Summer Hotel*, or Arthur Miller's *Death of a Salesman* to his *Creation of the World* and *Other Business*, or Samuel Beckett's *Waiting for Godot* to his *Not I*. When it comes to Tom Stoppard himself, the axiom is not quite so clear-cut. In 1986, at forty-eight, he has been a professionally-produced stage and screen writer for twenty-three years, but he continues to delight audiences and win critical acclaim with his new points of departure: it's quite conceivable that everything he has written so far—including *The Real Thing* (1982), his 1984 television play *Squaring the Circle*, and his co-authored 1985 screenplay *Brazil*—may someday be lumped together as "the early stuff." But, without indulging in too many Stoppardian shifts in perspective, it can be conceded that "the early stuff" is the play that brought him international renown in 1967, *Rosencrantz & Guildenstern Are Dead*. Of all the plays in Stoppard's canon, this is the one that has been awarded the most prizes, has been translated into the most languages (over twenty), and is still the most frequently produced. There are reasons for these achievements that don't necessarily have to do with artistic merit. The clever audacity of *Rosencrantz & Guildenstern's* piggy-back ride on the greatest tragedy of the English language gained the play admittance to the classrooms and set it up nicely for festival productions in tandem with Hamlet. On a practical level, *Rosencrantz* is a lot cheaper to stage than Stoppard's *Jumpers* or *The Real Thing*, and less difficult to put across than the complex *Travesties*. Audiences enjoy the feeling that they have digested a play of ideas, which they get from Rosencrantz and Guildenstern's fairly simplistic philosophizing about death.

Considering how well Stoppard's artistry has matured over the years, one is tempted to dismiss *Rosencrantz & Guildenstern* as having been dead since the mid-1970s—that is, since Stoppard's *Jumpers* and *Travesties* appeared. The sparkling dialectical conceits and linguistic virtuosity of *Jumpers* and *Travesties*, I believe, showed up *Rosencrantz* for what it was: a good "first play," a hint of the talent that was to blossom so much more fully within the next few years, a brilliant idea that—unless it's more than brilliantly directed and performed—is only moderately entertaining.

Therefore, this essay will focus on Tom Stoppard's work from *Travesties* to the present. Although Stoppard has continued to reveal the same preoccupations throughout his entire career, he did not show nearly as much artistic development in the eleven years from *A Walk on the Water* (1963) to *Travesties* (1974) as he did in the eleven years from *Travesties* to *Brazil*. Metaphorically, the distance travelled in those latter eleven years is the distance from Zurich, the setting for *Travesties*, a real city in a real period of history, to "somewhere in the twentieth century" *Brazil*, a state of mind. In a certain sense, the Zurich of *Travesties* also exists only in a man's mind, that of Henry Carr, the character whose memory recreates the events that occurred there in 1917–18. But Zurich does have a reality external to the play, whereas the "Brazil" of the 1985 film has no intrinsic reality; it is merely a catchy tune that serves as a mental means of escape from reality. More literally, *Travesties*— like *Rosencrantz* and several others—employs a borrowed structure. Inspired by the historical fact that during the war years in Zurich James Joyce had worked with The English Players on a production of *The Importance of Being Earnest*, Stoppard constructed *Travesties* as a travesty of Oscar Wilde's play. Since then, Stoppard has relied more and more upon his own invention for the plots of his plays, and as a corollary of that growing trust in his own resources, he has become less and less reticent about dealing with emotions.

Before zeroing in on that progression from *Travesties* to *Brazil*, an overview of the totality of Stoppard's work is in order. Statistically, it comes to 9 full-length plays, 5 one-act plays, 7 radio plays, 10 or more television plays, 6 translation-adaptations of full-length plays originally written in other languages, 1 novel, 3 published short stories, 4 screenplays that have been made into movies, and a screenplay *Innocent Blood* based on a P. D. James novel by that title that Hollywood has not seen fit to make into a movie.[2] Another way of looking at the totality of Stoppard's writing is to organize it by categories; one night classify Stoppard's stage, radio, television, and motion picture plays to date into roughly six groups. First, there are the plays of his apprenticeship, the ones from *A Walk on the Water* to *Rosencrantz* plus the radio and television plays of the 1960s, all of which are to be airily dismissed from consideration here. Another group that can be merely mentioned in passing is the translation-adaptations. These tend to be increasingly free adaptations done from another translator's literal rendering of the plays into English. Stoppard adapted Slawomir Mrozek's Polish play *Tango*, Federico Garcia Lorca's Spanish play *The House of Bernarda Alba*, Arthur Schnitzler's German plays *Undiscovered Country* (*Das Weite Land*) and *Dalliance* (*Liebelei*), Johann Nestroy's play in a Viennese dialect *On the Razzle* (*Einen Jux will er sich machen*), and Ferenc Molnar's Hungarian play *Rough Crossing* (*Play at the Castle*). In the beginning, Stoppard probably took up adapting other writers' plays for the same reason that he borrowed the structures of Hamlet and *The Importance of Being Earnest* for Rosencrantz and *Travesties*: he knew he could come up with scintillating dialogue, but he lacked confidence in his ability to construct a plot. As he says in the introduction to *On the Razzle*, "All the main characters and most of the plot come from Nestroy, but almost none of the dialogue attempts to offer a translation of what Nestroy wrote. My method might be compared to cross-country hiking with map and compass, where one takes a bearing on the next landmark and picks one's way towards it."[3] Although Stoppard has now mastered plot construction, he continues—as he says—to "go around with a bag of tools doing jobs between personal plays."[4] Perhaps he does it as a sign of respect for those foreign authors. In making their plays newly accessible to contemporary theatergoers, he also refreshes his own creative drive.

To pursue that point, digressing briefly, one might note as another facet of Tom Stoppard's artistry the tremendous impact of Shakespeare's plays on his own. In fact, Stoppard seems to have acquired the habit of paying homage to Shakespeare, sometimes in barely perceptible ways, in every play he writes. If it were any other writer, one might be inclined to call it a gimmick, but Stoppard's sense of debt to Shakespeare appears to be deeply engrained. One of the librarians at the Folger in Washington, D. C., told me that when Tom Stoppard visited there he was like a kid in a candy store. Examples of this aspect of Stoppard's writing range from the obvious to the obscure. Among the hundreds of allusions that might he cited are his choice of *Undiscovered Country* as the title for his translation of Schnitzler's *Das Weite Land*, literally "distant domain;" it's a phrase from Hamlet's "to be or not to be" soliloquy: "the undiscovered country from whose bourne no traveller returns." A particularly delightful allusion is from *Jumpers*. It explains why the tortoise that George Moore uses as a visual aid is named Pat. This enabled Stoppard to take Hamlet's line "Now might I do it Pat," put a comma in it, and have George Moore speak the line to his tortoise: "Now might I do it, Pat." The much-discussed newspaper in *Night and Day* is named The Globe, presumably after Shakespeare's theater. Act I of *Travesties* contains a sustained exchange of dialogue that consists entirely of lines quoted from eight different Shakespeare plays.[5] In *Brazil* the acronym for Ministry of Information is stamped on every object, even the goldfish bowl, in Kurtzmann's office. Those letters, M.O.I., call to mind the teasing "M.O.A.I." in the letter that Malvolio receives in *Twelfth Night*.

A third category of Stoppard's plays is the frivolous comedies, plays written just for fun, almost like a busman's holiday from more serious playwriting. Some—like *Dogg's Our Pet* and *The (15-Minute) Dogg's Troupe Hamlet*—were dashed off as a favor for his friend Ed Berman, who uses the pseudonym Professor R. L. Dogg so that the children's verse he intends to write someday will go into library card catalogues under the heading "Dogg, R. L."[6] Stoppard thought that anyone who could wait that long for a bad pun to explode was someone with whom he could fruitfully collaborate, especially after Berman founded the British American Repertory Company: the acronym is BARC! Stoppard's longest exercise in frivolity, *Dirty Linen*, a play about sexual promiscuity in high places, was written to contain his short intermission sketch *New-Found-Land*, which commemorates the American-born Berman's naturalization as a British citizen. The citizenship papers are signed in the play, with the comment, "One more American can't make any difference."[7]

Stoppard's penchant for frivolity has been evident not only in the plays themselves, but in his spontaneous manner of working with actors in rehearsal. Davis Hall, an American actor who toured with BARC in 1979, recalled that "Tom Stoppard was great fun in rehearsal. Although Ed Berman had final directorial say, Tom took over at times. He would jump up to alter a line or improvise a new gag, sometimes spending fifteen minutes or more developing a bit of dialogue which he would then discard. There was a 'helmet . . . Himmler . . . Hamlet gag' in *Dogg's Hamlet* for a couple of rehearsals. Tom or Ed suggested it, Tom developed it, the actors rehearsed it, we all laughed a bit, and Tom cut it."[8]

The frivolous comedies also include some pastiches of other artists besides Shakespeare. *The Real Inspector Hound* is not only a spoof of Agatha Christie's plays, but it is also a send-up of various styles of literary criticism. *After Magritte* is a theatrical pastiche of the visual style of surrealist painter René Magritte. And this category would include a fairly recent radio play, *The Dog It Was That Died* (1982), about a British spy/counterspy; it's really a John LeCarrécature.

The frivolity of those comedies does not exclude idea-content, only overpowers it. Happily, the converse is also true: the plays in the fourth group—the ones that Stoppard himself has designated as his "intellectual plays"—do not exclude frivolity. In the category of "intellectual plays," Stoppard places

Rosencrantz, *Jumpers, Travesties, Artist Descending a Staircase, Professional Foul*, and *Night and Day*. There is no better illustration of the zany side of intellectualism than *Travesties*, which takes inspiration from Oscar Wilde's "trivial play for serious people"—or is it a "serious play for trivial people"? In addition, *Travesties* is what *Newsweek* reviewer Jack Kroll called "a dizzying collage of styles; joycean stream-of-consciousness, high comedy à la Oscar Wilde, an antic scene spoken entirely in limericks, another done to the tune of 'Mr Gallagher and Mr Shean,' still another that parodies the great 'catechism' chapter between Stephen and Bloom in *Ulysses*. Technically all this works because, as Stoppard says of himself, 'I fall into comedy like a man falling into bed.' But underneath the mattress is a hard board—Stoppard's lust for ideas."[9] In his book *The New British Drama*, Oleg Kerensky says that "*Travesties* is the richest and most thought-provoking of Stoppard's plays, though it is possible that the weight of argument is too much for the structure of the play. It is hard for any audience to take in all the arguments and enjoy the sheer humor and theatricality of the piece."[10] It is true that the play offers too much for the average theatergoer to take in at one sitting, but this is not necessarily a flaw. After all, what theatrical experience ever is the same as a literary-analytical approach to a play? Stoppard's plays may require a bit of mental effort from their audiences even as they revel in the certainty that ideas can be fun. The intellectual plays are merely the most obvious example of what his theater is really about: a celebration of the whole range of things that the mind can generate—from abstract concepts to a humorous coloration of ordinary data to, yes, even the emotions.

Plays that explore real people and genuine emotions make up Stoppard's newest category, and so far he has placed only two stage plays in it, *Night and Day* and *The Real Thing*, both of which also fit into other categories. Stoppard wrote *Night and Day* in 1978 to test whether or not he was capable of writing about love, but he hedged his bet by writing a play that also belongs with the intellectual plays as well as in the sixth category, political plays. Stoppard says that *Night and Day* was "a first go" at writing a love play; and of *The Real Thing*, he has said: "For better or worse, that's it—the love play? I've been aware of the process that's lasted 25 years, of shedding inhibition about self-revelation. I wouldn't have dreamed of writing about it ten years ago, but as you get older, you think, who cares?"[11] *The Real Thing* opened on Broadway in January 1984 to the most ecstatic reception by both the critics and the public that ever greeted a Stoppard play. In his earlier review of the 1983 London production, Frank Rich called it "not only Stoppard's most moving play, but also the most bracing play that anyone has written about love and marriage in years."[12] It is interesting that in the years since then, much of the critical writing on *The Real Thing* has compared it to *Travesties*. Although Stoppard didn't give any depth to the love interest in the intellectual play *Travesties*, he did work some fairly solid idea-content into the love play *The Real Thing*. A major thrust of both plays is concern with the difference between bogus art and "the real thing." According to Paul Delaney, "if it is sometimes difficult to tell the real from the ersatz, if the artificial can sometimes deceive us into believing it to be real, that in no way suggests that the real thing does not exist and cannot, upon discovery, be recognized."[13] "Like *Travesties*, *The Real Thing* celebrates a non-propagandistic art, praises art which 'works' aesthetically whether or not it 'works' in terms of social utility."[14]

Here we begin to overlap into the final category of plays, the "political plays." It is in this category that we see the clearest line of development from *Travesties* to *Brazil*. In 1967, when Stoppard's *Rosencrantz* gave him overnight celebrity, the other emerging British playwrights were David Storey, Edward Bond, Simon Gray, Peter Nichols, and Howard Brenton, to be followed shortly by David Edgar, David Hare, Trevor Griffiths, Howard Barker, Stephen Polia-koff, and others who were moving beyond the "kitchen sink" and "angry young man" plays of the late 1950s to the extremes of social revolution and demolition of traditional value systems. Stoppard pointedly stood apart from the fray, refusing to use the theater to promote any specific point of view. This is not to say that his comedies ever lacked for idea-content; he liked to think of them as "plays that make serious points by flinging a custard pie around the stage for a couple of hours."[15] Still, he was dogged by the insinuations of reporters, critics, and fellow playwrights that he should be writing socially-conscious or "political" plays. Gradually, irresistibly, he was drawn to the problem of the artist's responsibility to society. Should the artist uphold the ideal of "pure art" or should he become "socially committed" by espousing a particular political position through his work? Although *Travesties* is not classed as one of the political plays, it served—much as *Night and Day* did on the subject of love—as a "first go," a major impetus of which was Stoppard's need to resolve for himself the question of whether the artist has any obligation to justify himself in political terms. He did this by playing off against one another the four different attitudes toward art held by four actual historical figures who, by coincidence, all lived in Zurich during World War I. Henry Carr has a non-intellectual attitude toward art: he likes what he likes, and any relationship between what pleases him and what is socially useful is merely coincidental. Carr does offer in rough form some of the arguments for the integrity of art that are expressed in more polished images by Henry Boot in *The Real Thing*. James Joyce celebrates art for art's sake; he is able to remain quite disengaged from current events, secure in the knowledge that what he is doing has its own intrinsic merit. Tristan Tzara is a revolutionary in art, expressing his rejection of social conditions by smashing conventions in art and, when possible, demolishing established masterpieces as well. Lenin is a political revolutionary with traditional tastes in art; whatever the intrinsic value may or may not be, he wants an art that he can understand and thus keep in its place. This polemic may not be what the audience member remembers most about *Trav-*

esties, but it's important enough that Stoppard remarked facetiously: "I think that in the future I must stop compromising my plays with this whiff of social application. They must be entirely untouched by any suspicion of usefulness. I should have the courage of my lack of convictions."[16]

But, in fact, Stoppard did not lack convictions. As Paul Delaney has noted, "his ambiguities are intended neither to dazzle nor confuse but 'to be precise over a greater range of events.' "[17] Stoppard described his customary technique as "a series of conflicting statements made by conflicting characters, and they tend to play a sort of infinite leap-frog. You know, an argument, a refutation, then a rebuttal of the refutation, then a counter-rebuttal . . . "[18] Whereas in *Travesties*, "the characters, as debaters and antagonists, are equally matched,"[19] *The Real Thing* does not hold back from giving the weight of a better argument as well as the more sympathetic characterization to Henry Boot, the spokesman for Stoppard's own point of view, over Brodie, for whom "art" is nothing more than a blunt instrument of social change.

While Stoppard still likes to write arguments, "scenes where there are two people with bats, banging this ball across a net at each other," Stoppard admits: "I am more opinionated that I used to be."[20] When he got beyond the question of the function of the artist in life, and into issues with a political application on which he actually took sides, Stoppard turned out to be a conservative. However, his point of view has never been merely topical or "axe-grinding." Mel Gussow notes that "in contrast to such left-leaning British playwrights as David Hare, Howard Brenton, and David Edgar, he does not use the theatre as a platform."[21] David Hare has said, "I never find him politically narrow in any way. His friendship and encouragement and generosity to writers of all persuasion are legendary. We have far more in common than in conflict."[22] And, according to Mike Nichols, "he has no apparent animus toward anyone or anything. He's very funny at no one's expense. That's supposed not to be possible."[23]

The issue that has most engaged Stoppard and made a committed artist of him is that of human rights and the violation of those rights in totalitarian countries. Stoppard's political plays all deal with this issue. Although it is clear in all of them where his own sympathies lie, their ideological bias in no way diminishes their aesthetic value. These plays exhibit Stoppard's mature craftsmanship. There is an economy of means manifested in his increasingly tight construction, in scenic devices that metaphorically underscore content, and in a more sculptural sense of language that grows out of the paring away of some of his habitual trickery and superficial demonstrations of cleverness. By and large, the political plays constitute some of Stoppard's best work. These are the television plays *Professional Foul* (1977) and *Squaring the Circle* (1984), the short play *Cahoot's Macbeth* (1979), the experimental play-with-live-orchestra *Every Good Boy Deserves Favour* (1977), *Night and Day* (1978) and the movie *Brazil* (1985). The issue of political repression under a dictatorship is there in *Night and Day*, although it is subsidiary to an examination of the problems of moral responsibilities and practical failings of a free press. Every *Good Boy Deserves Favour* is set in a Soviet insane asylum where a political dissident shares a cell with a genuine mental patient who hears an orchestra in his head; the latter's delusion is represented on stage by an actual full-sized live symphony orchestra. Stoppard's metaphor for the logic of the dissident is geometry. Although the triangle as a geometrical figure is less tangible than the triangle as an instrument in the orchestra, there are absolute definitions of geometrical figures. The principles upheld by the dissident are as incontrovertible to a sane person as the rules of geometry, but the totalitarian state uses its power to distort even geometrical logic for its own self-interest. Stoppard again used geometry as a metaphor in his television play tracing the 1980–81 workers' Solidarity movement in Poland. The premise of *Squaring the Circle* is that the concept of a free trade union like Solidarity is as irreconcilable with the Communist bloc's definition of socialism as is the mathematical impossibility of turning a circle into a square with the same area. The earlier television play *Professional Foul* uses a soccer match as metaphor for examining questions of human rights in opposition to the "ethics" of the totalitarian state.

Cahoot's Macbeth, while based upon Shakespeare's tragedy, uses the metaphor of language as an arbitrary construction. Words, like the building blocks that are delivered in the course of the play (cubes, bricks, slabs, and planks), can be used to different purposes, either as an instrument of repression or as a vehicle of escape to freedom by the human spirit. *Cahoot's Macbeth* is dedicated to Czechoslovakian playwright Pavel Kohout who, before he was exiled from his country in 1980, wrote to Stoppard about the underground theatrical activities he was carrying on to help some politically oppressed actors. The totalitarian regime had prohibited some outstanding Czech actors from performing in public as a punishment for their having signed a human rights petition. Kohout's solution was to offer "Living Room Theatre" a 75-minute abridgement of *Macbeth* performed by five actors with a suitcase full of props for small groups in private homes.

Cahoot's Macbeth begins with a serious rendition of a shortened *Macbeth*, performed in pinpoints of light. When the Witches vanish, the lights go up to reveal that the performance is being given in an apartment living room. The action proceeds briskly to the murder of Duncan, but Macbeth's line, "I have done the dead. Didst thou not hear a noise?," is answered By a police siren approaching the house.[24] An Inspector, whose knock on the apartment door coincides with the knocking at the gate in *Macbeth*, interrupts the performance, interrogates the actors, addresses the "bug" in the ceiling, end tells the Hostess: "If you had any pride in your home, you wouldn't take standing-room-only in your sitting room lying down (53–54)." He warns the troupe that their performance is seen by the authorities as a provocation: "When you get a universal and timeless writer like Shakespeare, there's a strong feeling that he could be spitting in the eye of the beholder". . . (60). He orders the actors to resume their performance while he watches, but he leaves after the coronation of Macbeth, which he takes to be a happy ending. A truck driver named Easy arrives with a load of cubes, bricks, slabs, and planks. He pops in and out of view coincidentally with Macbeth's vision of Banquo's ghost. Easy speaks only Dogg's language, in which English-sounding words actually mean something else. Cahoot is able to translate and the actors quickly pick it up, so that when the Inspector returns, the actors foil him by switching into Dogg for the remainder of their performance of *Macbeth*. For example, Macbeth's "Tomorrow and tomorrow and tomorrow" speech begins:

> Dominoes, et dominoes, et dominoes,
> popsies historical axle-grease,
> exacts bubbly fins crock lavender. . . .
> (77)

In response to a telephone call from the "bug," the Inspector exclaims: "How the hell do I know? But if it's not free expression, I don't know what is!" (75). Easy's wooden blocks are unloaded from the truck and passed hand-to-hand through the window just when Birnam Wood comes to Dunsinane in the play-within-the-play. A step unit is built for the coronation of Malcolm, but the Inspector continues to call for blocks, with which he builds a wall of columns across the front of the stage. This brilliant visual metaphor that ends the play makes a clear statement: artists under a totalitarian regime are physically walled in, but their thoughts and creative imaginations will always find some form of expression—a whole new language if necessary.

That capacity for escape through thought and imagination is very much the point of the movie *Brazil*. The mild-mannered protagonist Sam Lowry works in a flunkey's job for the state; he escapes the drabness of that technology-encumbered, Orwellian 1984-like world through his dreams of flying about a clear blue sky, sometimes with a beautiful blond woman in a gauzy gown. A bureaucratic error that results in an innocent man's torture and execution jars Sam into action. His attempts to thwart the machinery of the state take him to the victim's chair in the torture chamber, but he is miraculously rescued by a so-called "terrorist." His escape from pursuers becomes more and more surrealistic, but he finally attains happiness with the woman he loves in a peaceful green valley under a blue sky. Only in the last moment of the film do we see that he is actually still strapped down in the torture chamber, and we realize that everything from the rescue on has occurred only in Sam's mind. "He's got away from us," says one of the torturers, while Sam wears a faint smile and hums the catchy 1930s tune "Brazil." There is a perverse kind of exhilaration about that final moment when the mind transports the man beyond pain, beyond confinement, beyond the reach of a monolithic state that has invaded every other aspect of life. The last freedom is that of individual thought. Thus we see again how far Stoppard has come from *Travesties*, in which Carr's mind merely recreates past events with adjustments to suit his own ego, to *Brazil*, in which Sam creates a separate reality from scratch.

Before proceeding further, Stoppard's part in the authorship of *Brazil* should be clarified. Three screenwriters are credited: the film's director Terry Gilliam, Charles McKeown, and Tom Stoppard. Asked about his contribution, Stoppard replied: "for a certain number of weeks I was working on it in my house. Then I gave the script to Terry Gillian, had a couple of meetings, and that was the last of it until the film came out."[25] *Brazil* is here referred to as a work by Stoppard because so much of it has his clear imprint upon it. For example, Stoppard has frequently spoofed the complexity of modern life as he does in *Brazil* with the many-plugged phones and ubiquitous ducts. Sam is an ineffectual "hero" trying to rise above those complexities in the tradition of George Moore in *Jumpers*, or the title characters of Albert's *Bridge* and *Lord Malquist & Mr Moon*. In the latter work, Mr Moon receives wounds in both hands; in *Brazil*, Sam's beloved Jill has a bandaged hand, Mr Kurtzmann hurts his hand so he can't sign a check, and Sam's hand is the focus of the torturer's work. There is also an amusingly angled shot when Sam returns to his apartment to find it in disarray after the Central Services repairman have pulled all the ducts out of the walls and ceiling; the shot in which Sam surveys the chaos is set up in such a way that his hand is hidden behind a pipe with wires protruding like veins from a severed wrist. Stoppard's fixation on boots (a constant throughout his work) is echoed in *Brazil* when Sam's mother wears a leopardskin boot as a hat, and similarly, Jill wears a black boot on her head at the surreal funeral.

The movie's initiating incident is a typically Stoppardian trivial event that unleashes a chain of consequences. Just as in Stoppard's early radio play *Artist Descending a Staircase* a swatted fly causes a man's death, so in *Brazil* a fly swatted on the ceiling drops into a typewriter which then mistakenly types "Buttle" instead of "Tuttle," and the very next scene shows the innocent Mr. Buttle arrested as he spends a quiet Christmas evening with his family. This sequence of events is soon mocked by a shot of the Socialist Realist-style sculpture in the lobby of the Ministry of Information, inscribed "The truth shall make you free," and we see that Jill cannot get anywhere with the truth.

Perhaps the most constant characteristic of Stoppard's writing from *Rosencrantz* to the present is the use of a shifting perspective on reality. Stoppard is like the Chinese philosopher who "dreamed he was a butterfly, and from that moment he was never quite sure that he was not a butterfly dreaming it was a Chinese philosopher."[26] Both in structure and in detail, his plays offer innumerable variations on the theme that there is no such thing as a single all-encompassing vision of reality. There are visual incongruities like those in *After Magritte*: what one person sees as a one-legged blind man with a white beard and carrying a tortoise under his arm is in reality (and with a perfectly logical explanation) a man with shaving foam on his face who, in his haste to run outdoors and move his car, put both feet into the same pajama leg and grabbed his wife's handbag and white parasol. There are aural incongruities like the tape that George Moore plays in *Jumpers* to illustrate points in his lecture—a romantic bit of Mozart, a braying animal mating call, and a trumpet falling down a flight of stone stairs—but since the audience does not know the source of these sounds, they are perceived in conjunction with the action in Dotty's bedroom: Dotty and Bones facing each other as in a dream of love, Bones raising his head during the animal mating call and dropping his vase of flowers when Dotty rushes toward him.

In several plays, Stoppard's penchant for shifting perspective is quite Pirandellian. *The Real Thing*, for example, begins with a husband-and-wife scene that we accept at face value, only to realize in the following scene that each of them is married to someone else and that the scene was from a play written by the woman's husband, in which they both perform. The entire context of *Travesties* is the skewed perspective of Henry Carr's self-serving memory, but it is not until the very end of the play that we learn to what a great extent his memory has falsified historical events. And the play offers a wryly clever comment on how one tends to perceive what one is already conditioned to perceive: the leftist-leaning Dadaist Tristan Tzara reads a tract by Lenin, but having been told it was a chapter by James Joyce, finds it inimical to his views. Similarly, Carr's pretensions to literary taste are short-circuited by Joyce's writing when he believes it to be by Lenin. *Squaring the Circle* begins with one possible image of Polish first Secretary Edward Gierek's summer 1980 meeting with Leonid Brezhnev by the Black Sea. Two men in dark suits, hats, and lace-up shoes walk along a deserted beach solemnly interchanging the standard Party platitudes. Then the Narrator interrupts to tell us that "everything is true except the words and the pictures."[27] Since we don't know for certain what that Black Sea meeting was really like, we are shown a second possibility: Brezhnev and Gierek wear bright Hawaiian shirts as they recline under beach umbrellas, drink pink cocktails, and shout at each other like gangsters.

The very structure of *Brazil*, as previously noted, is an alternation between one man's mental reality and the external reality that is constantly driving him to seek refuge in his own mind. But there are also in *Brazil* some delightful jokey perspective shifts, as when what appeared to be a pretty little cottage with a white picket fence is suddenly lifted out of its setting by a crane, and we realize that it was only an ugly boxcar. In his 1982 radio play *The Dog It Was That Died*, Stoppard takes the mental tempering of reality to mind-boggling extremes with his treatment of a British spy/counterspy who acted as "a genuine Russian spy in order to maintain his usefulness as a bogus Russian spy." Eventually he reaches a point of despair. As he explains it: "I've forgotten who is my primary employer and who my secondary. For years I've been feeding stuff in both directions, following my instructions from either side, having been instructed to do so by the other, and since each side wanted the other side to believe that I was working for it, both sides were often giving me genuine stuff to pass on to the other side . . . so the side I was actually working for became . . . well, a matter of opinion really . . . it got lost." Advised that he need only remember what he once believed, the poor man replies: "I remember I was very idealistic in those days, a real prig about Western decadence. On the other hand I was very patriotic and really didn't much care for foreigners. Obviously one scruple overcame the other, but. . . ."[28] Reduced to the same kind of intellectual frustration, George Moore in *Jumpers* cries out: "How the hell does one know what to believe?"[29]

These examples make it sound as though Stoppard's plays are illustrations of the maxim that "the truth depends upon where you're standing." But it's even more complex than that, because Stoppard has a conservative belief in absolute values. He calls himself "a moralist affronted by relativism." However, his latest stage play, *The Real Thing*, is on one level a coming to grips with the necessity in life of compromise. What will Henry Boot do when he learns that his own romantic ideals and artistic standards are not the same as those of the woman he loves? What does Henry Carr do in *Travesties* when historical truth conflicts with emotional truth? What does Lech Walesa do in *Squaring the Circle* when he faces the fact that Solidarity and Communism are intrinsically incompatible? What does Sam Lowry do in *Brazil* when external reality simply will not conform to his dream reality? In every case, there are two choices: one can stick to a principle or one can make a mental adjustment.

The triumph of Tom Stoppard's artistry is to affirm for us that we, as individuals, always have this choice. His plays are a cumulative celebration of the possible triumph of mind over reality. Like his characters, we have the power within ourselves, without ever leaving home, to travel from Zurich to Brazil.[30]

NOTES

[1] Tom Stoppard, *The Real Thing* (Boston: Faber and Faber, 1983), p. 62.

[2] The full-length plays are: *Rosencrantz & Guildenstern Are Dead, Enter a Free Man, Jumpers, Travesties, Dirty Linen/NewFound-Land, Every Good Boy Deserves Favour, Dogg's Hamlet/Cahoot's Macbeth, Night and Day, The Real Thing*. One-act plays are: *The Gamblers, After Magritte, The Real Inspector Hound, Dogg's Our Pet, The (15-Minute) Dogg's Troupe Hamlet*. Radio plays: *The Dissolution of Dominic Boot, "M" is for Moon Among Other Things, If You're Glad I'll Be Frank, Albert's Bridge, Where Are They Now?, Artist Descending a Staircase, The Dog It Was That Died*. Television plays: *The Engagement, A Separate Peace, Teeth, Another Moon Called Earth, Neutral Ground, One Pair of Eyes, The Boundary, Three Men in a Boat, Professional Foul, Squaring the Circle*. Translations/adaptations: *Tango, The House of Bernards Alba, Undiscovered Country, On the Razzle, Rough Crossing, Dalliance*, Novel: *Lord Malquist & Mr Moon*. Short stories: "Life, Times: Fragments," "Reunion,"

"The Story." Screenplays: *The Romantic Englishwoman, Despair, The Human Factor, Brazil*.

[3] Tom Stoppard, *On the Razzle* (London: Faber and Faber, 1982), p. 7.

[4] Mel Gussow, "Stoppard's Intellectual Cartwheels Now with Music," *The New York Times* (29 July 1979), p. 22.

[5] Tom Stoppard, *Travesties* (New York: Grove Press, 1975), p. 54. The lines following Gwen's recitation of the eighteenth sonnet are from *Julius Caesar, Hamlet, As You Like It, Hamlet, Much Ado About Nothing: Henry V, Henry IV, Part I, Othello, Hamlet*, and *Merry Wives of Windsor*.

[6] Tom Stoppard, "Yes, We Have No Bananas," *The Guardian* (10 December 1971), p. 10.

[7] Tom Stoppard, *Dirty Linen and New-Found-Land* (New York: Grove Press, 1976), p. 71.

[8] Response to a questionnaire mailed in June 1981 by Felicia Londré to members of the British American Repertory Company. Another American respondent, Stephen D. Newman, wrote: "As Stoppard so typically put his sharing of brainstorming sessions with the company, he was 'taking us into his lack of confidence' which is, of course, a very flattering place to be admitted. To watch ideas born in a brilliant man, perhaps even to root him on, lends a participatory pride to one's feeling about the play."

[9] Jack Kroll, "Stars over Zurich," *Newsweek* (10 November 1975), p. 66.

[10] Oleg Kerensky, *The New British Drama* (London: Hamish Hamilton, 1977), p. 164.

[11] Mel Gussow, "The Real Tom Stoppard," *The New York Times Magazine* (1 January 1984), p. 28.

[12] Frank Rich, "Stoppard's *Real Thing* in London," *The New York Times* (23 June 1983), p. C 15.

[13] Paul Delaney, "Cricket bats and commitment: the real thing in art and life," *Critical Quarterly*, 27 (1985), 47.

[14] Delaney, p. 49.

[15] Jon Bradshaw, "Tom Stoppard, Nonstop," *New York* (10 January 1977), p. 50.

[16] Ronald Hayman, *Tom Stoppard* (London: Heineman, 1978), p. 2.

[17] Delaney, p. 45.

[18] Tom Stoppard, "Ambushes for the Audience," *Theatre Quarterly*, 4 (May–July 1974), 6–7.

[19] Susan Rusinko, "The Last Romantic: Henry Boot, Alias Tom Stoppard," *World Literature Today*, 59 (Winter 1985), 21.

[20] Gussow, p. 28.

[21] Gussow, p. 21.

[22] Gussow, p. 22.

[23] Gussow, p. 23.

[24] Tom Stoppard, *Dogg's Hamlet, Cahoot's Macbeth* (London: Faber and Faber, 1980), p. 52. All subsequent quotations will be from this edition and will be cited in the text.

[25] Duncan Fallowell, "Theatrical incest and acquisitive lust," *The Times* (London) (23 August 1985), p. 8.

[26] Tom Stoppard, *Rosencrantz & Guildenstern Are Dead* (New York: Grove Press, 1967), p. 60.

[27] Tom Stoppard, *Squaring the Circle* (Boston: Faber and Faber, 1985), p. 21.

[28] Tom Stoppard, *The Dog It Was That Died* and Other Plays (Boston: Faber and Faber, 1983), pp. 33–34.

[29] Tom Stoppard, *Jumpers* (New York: Grove Press, 1972), p. 71

[30] This article is a version of a lecture given at the University of Toledo Humanities Institute in May 1986.

David Storey's Aesthetic of "Invisible Events"

William Hutchings

Although David Storey is among the most acclaimed and innovative play-wrights of his generation, and although his plays have on the whole received quite favorable reviews, a common reservation recurs in a number of them. It is typified by the comments of an American reviewer of *The Farm,* who remarked that

> although you discover certain things about these characters that you didn't know at the outset, you also discover that nothing has happened. . . . And in the theatre, something *ought* to happen. That . . . is what theatre *means.* But if [the play in question] isn't theatre exactly, it's an interesting something-or-other.[1]

Yet, however frequently such objections are voiced and however widely they are held, they are based on a conception of theatre that is not only restrictively narrow but also a century out-of-date—the equivalent of a belief that all con-temporary poetry should rhyme and contain regular metrics, that all novels should contain a cleverly constructed and intricate intrigue, or that all music should have a hummable tune. By focusing the audience's attention on unique and autonomous images rather than on traditional machinations of a plot, Storey's plays demand new standards that are comparable to those that seemed so revolutionary in the other arts nearly a century ago, when narrative verse, representational painting and sculpture, and intricately plotted fiction were the conventional order of the day—and the modernist movement was soon to be born. In each of Storey's best-known and most theatrically innovative plays (i.e., *The Changing Room, The Contractor,* and *Home*), the play's central action is what Storey calls an "invisible event," the formation and dissolution of a collective bond as his characters are united—though *only temporarily*—through a common purpose and a shared endeavor.

A proper critical assessment of such "plotless" plays, therefore, must be based on a judgment of the effectiveness and eloquence of the theatrical image rather than on traditional considerations of conflict, action, contrivance, and character development. Several of Storey's plays, for example, lack major incidents of a traditional plot: in *The Contractor,* the central action is the constructing and dismantling of a tent in which a wedding reception is held; in *The Changing Room,* members of a rugby team come together, prepare for the game, win their match, change from their uniforms back to their regular clothes, and leave. As they subordinate self-interest to the collective effort, the workmen and rugby players find a satisfaction and mutuality that their lives in the outside world do not afford. This, then, is the truly significant "change" in *The Changing Room:* as the players change their clothes, they cast aside their various differences and the preoccupations of the outside world and assume their responsibilities and interdependencies as members of a team. In effect, as the players put on their uniforms, they *become* uniform, putting aside individual differences as they remove the street clothes which reflect the personal tastes, individuality, class, income, and occupations that must be subordinated to the team effort during the game. Similarly, the workers in *The Contractor* must subordinate their personal differences to the collective enterprise, for which the constructed tent is not only the eventual product but the central theatrical image. Depicting seemingly ordinary events in a style that he terms "poetic naturalism," Storey's plays virtually abolish conventional plot in order to focus the audience's attention on the naturalistic depiction of the play's "invisible event."

Whereas the "invisible events" of *The Contractor* and *The Changing Room* are embodied in physical actions that take place on stage, no such activities occur in *Home;* instead, its central image is portrayed through a series of events that are almost as "uneventful" as those in *Waiting for Godot,* and the audience's *perception* of that image undergoes a radical change as the nature of the "home" in which the characters live is gradually revealed. As they pass their time idly in mundane but seemingly ordinary conversation, they are first perceived to be "ordinary people, really," as Storey himself has remarked, insisting that they are not "afflicted in any way more than anybody else is afflicted" (Lanouette, 1970, 20). Gradually, however, it becomes clear that they have been institutionalized—abandoned by their families, confined in an asylum, and forsaken, left to their own meager resources, passing their time idly as they await death, resisting only feebly a capitulation to despair. Having no "home" in which they can find the support and refuge that the family traditionally provides, they have been placed in an institutional "home," an impersonal agency of a bureaucratic society, the welfare state's *ultimate* "place where, when you go there, they have to take you in." Yet by disclosing the nature of the "home" in their reviews, critics tainted the audience's experience of the play as surely as if they had revealed the solution to a mystery, as Storey remarked in a conversation with Ronald Hayman:

The reviews did a disservice to the play in saying that it was about a nuthouse. In fact it's not the material of the play itself and to say it's a mental home . . . sets you away from the emotion, from the suffering. . . . To stress the metaphor of the mental home rather distorts the play. . . . Any of the characters . . . could quite as easily have been outside as inside, I feel. . . . There is a sort of disclaimer really when it becomes firmly a play about a mental home.[2]

Such objections reveal the need for new standards in the assessment of allegedly plotless plays: in the absence of an easily summarizable, conventional plot, an excessive critical disclosure of the play's complex and symbolic central image can reduce it to an unambiguous, literal fact—and can thereby diminish the audience's own experience of it in the theatre.

In an interview with Brendan Hennessy that was published in 1969, shortly before the works for which he would become most renowned were produced, Storey remarked that

I don't mind a play where there's nothing said at all, as long as it's right. I feel that progressive theatre is basically as didactic as Pre-Raphaelite painting. It is distorting reality in much the same way.[3]

The Contractor, The Changing Room, and *Home* could equally well be termed plays "where there's nothing said at all," since they are, as he remarked elsewhere, "plays of understatement in a way, and if you don't get what they're understating, then you've really had it, because there's nothing great going on on the surface."[4] It was not until *Life Class* was produced in 1975 that Storey offered a more overtly "didactic" play—set, appropriately, in a classroom where, before an onstage "audience" of students, the protagonist expounds his theories of life, art, and what be terms "invisible events." *Life Class* is not only Storey's most complex play but one of the most original and unusual works of metatheatre contemporary drama, offering his most detailed discussion (and justification) of his unique dramatic theory of "invisible events" that is best embodied in *The Changing Room* and *The Contractor.*

Surprisingly, however, Storey's exposition of these aesthetic principles occurs in the context of a play that is ostensibly "about" avant-garde art and makes no direct reference to the theatre at all. The central character is a beleaguered art instructor in a run-down provincial school, where he expounds his theory of "invisible events" to an uncomprehending "audience" of students in the shabby classroom, where they meet to draw the nude human form. The model's act of posing is inherently a *theatrical* event as well as an "artistic" one, however, for reasons that Peter Brook explained in *The Empty Space* (1969):

I can take any empty space and call it a bare stage. A man walks across the
empty space whilst someone else is watching him, and this is all that is needed
for an act of theatre to be engaged.[5]

In *Life Class,* however, each watcher's gaze is directed toward a nude woman
rather than Brook's hypothesized man, and she stands motionlessly in the
"empty space" for extended periods of time rather than walking across it; still,
her activity is no less inherently "theatrical" than the example that Brook proposes. Accordingly, an early stage direction specifies that the play's protagonist, who is identified only by his surname Allott, "circles the platform, chin in
hand, contemplating the empty space" before he "sets the pose" of the model
for the students.[6] In so doing, he is, in effect, the deviser, the director, and the
designer of the theatrical event occurring before the on-stage audience of students as well as the audience in the theatre.

The selection of the graphic arts as a metaphor for his activity in the theatre seems particularly appropriate for Storey, who, earlier in his career, studied
at the Slade School of Art in London and subsequently worked as both an artist
and a teacher in a particularly rough school in London's East End.[7] Allott is
said to have been "one of the leading exponents of representational art in his
youth" and was (according to his colleague Philips) comparable to Michelan-
gelo. More recently, however, he has become "an impresario . . . purveyor of
the invisible event . . . so far ahead of its time you never see it" (70). Explaining why he no longer paints or sculpts, Allott tells one of his students, Catherine, that he believes in a more "public" art (i.e., one more like the theatre),
which can nevertheless be understood within the artistic tradition:

> ALLOTT: It's my opinion that painting and sculpture, and all the traditional forms
>   of expression in the plastic arts, have had their day, Catherine . . . It's my
>   opinion that the artist has been driven back—or driven on, to look at it in a
>   positive way—to creating his works, as it were, in public.
> CATHERINE: In public, sir?
> ALLOTT: Just as Courbet or Modigliani, or the great Dutch Masters . . .
>   created their work out of everyday things, so the contemporary artist creates
>   his work out of the experience—the events as well as the objects—with which
>   he's surrounded in his day to day existence . . . for instance, our meeting here
>   today. (42)

These rituals—the class meetings and the posing—constitute the onstage
"invisible events" that are discussed at length throughout the play, though
Allott alone recognizes their value.

The "event" taking place in the classroom—and by extension in the
theatre—subsumes the "realities" of the mundane world outside, where, as
Allott remarks,

> We all sail, to some extent, under false colours. . . . I mean, you may not
> see yourself as an artist . . . I may not see myself as a teacher. . . . Stella
> [the model] earns her living; I earn my living . . . you earn your living . . .
> but between us, we convene . . . celebrate . . . initiate . . . an event, which,
> for me, is the very antithesis of what *you* term reality . . . namely, we
> embody, synthesize, evoke, a work, which, whether we are aware of it or not,
> is taking place around us . . . all the time. (46)

The essential function of this "invisible event" is, the teacher points out, "to
incorporate everything that is happening out there into a single homogenous
whole" (38), which is also, of course, a functional definition of the Aristotelian
"unity of action" in the theatre. Alllott's audience of students fails to grasp his
meaning, however—and one of them voices exactly the complaint that is often
lodged against Storey's plays:

> CATHERINE: (*gazing at* STELLA). There's nothing happening, sir.
> ALLOTT: There's a great deal happening . . . Not in any obvious way . . .
>   nevertheless several momentous events are actually taking place out there . . .
>   subtly, quietly, not overtly . . . but in the way artistic events *do* take place . . .
>   in the great reaches of the mind . . . (38–39)

Despite the shortcomings of his students, Allott reminds them of the importance of the purpose for which, in theory if not in fact, they have convened—
a purpose transcending the present moment and subsuming the cares of the
workaday world: "Art is above sex," Allott insists, finding there a refuge from
the failure of his marriage. ". . . and it's above politics, too. That's to say, it
absorbs sex, and it absorbs politics" (33). Like the event taking place in the theatre, the art class itself is in fact a ritual—a patterned (regularly scheduled)
event, the purpose of which Allott eloquently summarizes as "to pursue a beautiful and seemingly mysterious object, and to set it down—curiously—as
objectively as we can" (33).

     This wonder-filled "perusal"—an appreciation of the complexity and
beauty of the "life" before them—is more important than the actual lines that
the students commit haltingly and tentatively to paper. Accordingly, art has
become—for Allott, if not for his students—the surrogate religion of a
desacralized world, and the classroom is the "sanctified space" (exactly as the
earliest theatres were in the ancient world) in which the celebrants convene for
an exalted purpose that is inherently related to the concept of *performance:*
"The lesson that we've been convened, as it were, to celebrate . . . [is] that we
are life's musicians . . . its singers, and that what we sing is wholly without
meaning. . . it exists, merely, because it is" (30).

     The model herself is thus the central symbol of the play—occupying cen-
ter stage for much of the time, embodying the "impersonal" and idealized state

for which Allott yearns, but disrespected and defiled by those who fail to realize the symbolism, the transcendence, and the ritual that she represents. Thus,
in addition to his aforementioned roles as a director, deviser, and impresario
of inherently theatrical "invisible events," Allott, as the teacher, is also a virtual
priest of art, extolling its virtues and presiding over the novices' performance
of a ritual that surpasses the temporal reality. Unfortunately, however, Allott's
particular novices neither appreciate their teacher's beliefs, nor understand his
values, nor share his priorities; the students demonstrate neither particular apti-
tudes for art nor a serious interest in it, and they maintain a recurrent—almost
constant—chorus of crude remarks, sexual innuendos, double-entendres, and
coarse references to the model who poses before them and to each other as well.
Nevertheless, as Allott himself observes while consoling the model in her
remorse over being no longer "youthful young," the students are "myopic . . .
disingenuous . . . uninspired—. . . pubescent excrescences on the cheeks of
time" (15–16). Without particular concern, he points out that their priorities (in
obvious contrast to his own) place "mass before beauty, excrescence before
edification . . . [and] salaciousness before refinement" (40).

Such a view is not far removed from Storey's own view of the theatre-
going audience, as he remarked to me during an interview in his home in 1985:

> When we opened *The Contractor* in the West End, we were in competition
> with a play called *No Sex Please, We're British.* We were in competition
> because we both went to the same theatre [the Strand], and in the end our
> management panicked and went to a much smaller one around the corner, the
> Fortune. . . . We opened within a week [of each other], and that play got
> absolutely diabolical reviews. . . . They said it was absolute unmitigated
> rubbish and insulted the intelligence of the audience. It's been running ever
> since . . . a roaring success! We in *The Contractor* ran absolutely ecstatic
> reviews from all the critics, popular and highbrow, and it survived—but
> just—for about a year, and it came off.

The almost unrelievedly vulgar banter and crude antics of Allott's students suggest that their teacher's characterization of them is both accurate and insightful, but in some ways it exceedingly objectifies the problem and neglects both
the cruelty and the dehumanization that are implicit in their classroom behavior, which culminates when two of the students, Mathews and his friend Warren, enact an appallingly brutal rape of the nude model who poses defenselessly
before the class—an act which Allott, with characteristic detachment and indifference, does nothing to prevent.

Symbolically, the rape is the ultimate, destructive assertion of the most
crude physical and temporal reality over the transcendent, ethereal, and spiritual one—a vile and violent disruption of art by the most brutish form of life;
certainly, no one can possibly object that "nothing happened" in *this* Storey

play. Yet, virtually before the stunned audience on stage—or its counterpart in the theatre—has had time to recover from the shock of the event that has just been observed, an equally surprising fact is suddenly revealed: amid raucous laughter and gibes at their fellow students, the perpetrators of the rape reveal that it was in fact a *simulation*—a calculated hoax, a convincingly realistic deception, an "imitation" of "life," a work of artifice if not of art, and (the ultimate irony of the play) an "act of theatre" performed before the shocked onstage "classroom" audience; it is, in effect, Storey's play-within-the-play. The extent of Stella's complicity in the hoax remains unclear, though the fact that she does resume posing shortly after the incident implies that she too was aware of the students' ploy.

Simulated though it turns out to have been, the rape of the model remains, obviously, the ultimate assertion of unrestrained "natural impulses" as the most "ungovernable" and primal of urges "creates its own form" before the shocked members of the class (44). Allott's "spiritual" reality of transcendent art and invisible events is violated by the intrusion of its "antithesis" (46), the most base and sordid of worldly "realities." As Saunders (another of Allott's students) remarks while Mathews removes some of his clothing prior to the rape, "It's the dividing line, you see, between life and art . . . Stella represents it in its impersonal condition . . . Mathews represents its . . ." (77–78). Saunders's ethereal reflections are interrupted by Warren's shouts of the coarsest and crudest possible form of encouragement for Mathews: "Get your prick out. . .! Here . . . here, then! Go on. Grab her!" (77–78). As such, it is also the ultimate profanation of Allott's "temple," an outrage revealing the unworthiness of the priest as well as the novices—and causes the former to lose his job. Ironically, Allott is dismissed because of an event that never *actually* occurred. Yet, with typical cynicism and detachment, he accommodates even the act of violation itself within his theory, as he lamely tries to explain to Stella, the victim: "Violation, they tell me, is a prerequisite of art . . . disruption of prevailing values . . . re-integration in another form entirely. What you see and feel becomes eternal" (89). After this final (and unsuccessful attempt to account for the "ungovernable" in his theory, Allott's comments degenerate into nebulous (and rather trite) musings on the growth of flowers and the passage of time.

As Allott expounds the value of "the experience—the events as well as the objects—with which he's surrounded in his day to day existence . . . for instance, our meeting here today," his point is equally applicable to the theatre itself:

> ALLOTT: . . . the feelings and intuitions expressed by all of us inside this room. . . are in effect the creation—the re-creation—of the artist . . . to the extent that they are controlled, manipulated, postulated, processed, defined, sifted, *re*fined. . .
> CATHERINE: Who by, sir?
> ALLOTT: Well, for want of a better word—by me. (42)

Implicitly, this speech affirms the presence of the author's controlling consciousness in selecting and portraying the episodes of the play itself—although, ironically, the fact that Allott does *not* "control" the events taking place in the classroom is clearly demonstrated during the rape scene. The ultimate "purveyor of the invisible event" (70) is thus David Storey himself, and much of *Life Class* seems to offer a defense and explanation of his dramatic technique— particularly in his allegedly plotless plays.

The action of *Life Class*—and by extension the "invisible events" that constitute *The Contractor* and *The Changing Room*—are not merely random "slices of life" or the theatrical counterpart of *cinéma-vérité*. Their action—a detailed and naturalistic "imitation of life"—has been "controlled, manipulated, postulated, processed, defined, sifted, [and] refined" toward the expostulation of the Storey's recurrent thematic concerns. Clearly, too, the playwright wishes to differentiate himself from those whom Allott describes as "the *manufacturer* of events who . . . sees art as something accessible to all and therefore the prerogative not of the artist—but of anybody who cares to pick up a brush, a bag of cement, an acetylene welder . . . anyone, in fact, who can persuade other people that what he is doing is creative" (30). Unlike various types of undisciplined and free-form "happenings" (to which Allott's "invisible events" have sometimes mistakenly been compared), Storey's "plotless" plays are deceptively simple, enabling both theatregoers and critics to overlook the significance of the actions taking place on stage.

Allott's lecture to his snickering students on the appreciation of the complexity of the human form is equally applicable to the understanding of any work of art, whether on canvas or on the stage:

> It's merely a question . . . of seeing each detail in relation to all the rest . . . the proportion—the width as well as the height . . . the whole contained, as it were . . . within a single image. Unless you are constantly relating the specific to the whole . . . a work of art can never exist . . . It's not merely a conscious effort; it is, if one is an artist and not a technician—someone disguised, that is, as an artist, going through all the motions and creating all the effects— an instinctive process (29–30).

Accordingly, both *The Changing Room* and *The Contractor* present "a single image" (i.e., an "invisible event") within which "the whole" of the play is contained.

Surprisingly, many of the most abstract thematic statements in *Life Class* are given to Saunders—the student who reports the rape incident and causes Allott to lose his job—but one who, according to his classmates, talks, looks, and smells like Allott. "*He is Allott!,*" they exclaim (49), and, in terms of conveying many of Storey's principal themes, he clearly fulfills the same function as his teacher:

SAUNDERS: The human condition . . . is made up of many ambivalent conditions
. . . that's one thing I've discovered . . . love, hatred . . . despair, hope
. . . exhilaration, anguish . . . and it's not these conditions themselves that
are of any significance, but the fact that, as human beings, we oscillate
between them . . . It's the oscillation between hope and despair that's the
great feature of our existence, not the hope, or the despair, in themselves.
(*Pause.*)
STELLA: It's a wonderful observation . . .
(*Pause.* SAUNDERS *settles himself: gets out his equipment.*)
I like people who think about life.
SAUNDERS: I don't think about life. I'm merely interested in recording it.
STELLA: I see. (74)

Similarly, Storey has also maintained his own preference for "recording" rather
than "thinking about" life, claiming that "Intellectualism, it's the English disease . . . All these attitudes towards experience . . . it's the English Tradition,
isn't it? (laughter) . . . in the end, there's no experience *there*."[8] Nevertheless,
earlier in the play, Saunders offers another observation on dispassionate realism
(which is surely an "attitude towards experience" itself) as a technique in art:

There's something dispassionate in human nature . . . that's what I think . . .
something really dispassionate that nothing—no amount of pernicious and
cruel experience—can ever destroy. That's what I believe in . . . I think a
time will come when people will be interested in what was dispassionate at
a time like this . . . when everything was dictated to by so much fashion and
techniques. (49)

Yet despite the meticulous detail and realistic portrayal of the subject, as Allott
points out, "The essence of any event . . . is that it should be . . . indefinable.
Such is the nature . . . the ambivalence . . . of all human responses" (80–81).
Similarly, in discussing his own works, Storey maintains that "the best things
I do, I don't know what they're about when I've finished them. When I have
the ideas first, they're usually no good . . . At best, the illustration of a thesis,
at worst pretentious bullshit."[9]

Although the "thesis" is more explicit in *Life Class* than in *The Changing
Room, Home,* or *The Contractor,* the great majority of thematic statements in
Life Class concern *how* the play is to be understood (a technique that is also
applicable to his other plays) rather than specifically *what* the action of the play
means. "The artist sings his song," Allott remarks, "but doesn't contemplate
its beauty, doesn't analyze, doesn't lay it all out in all its separate parts . . .
that is the task of the critic" (30)—a position that Storey has also maintained
in his interviews. Nevertheless, with so much instruction being offered to the
audience, it is appropriate that the setting for *Life Class* is a classroom—and

the subtle irony of the title (that the play instructs the audience in understanding the author's other works) becomes clear.

Throughout its latter half, there are a number of indications that *Life Class* was intended to be a farewell to a certain *type* of theatre—if not, as was suspected by a number of reviewers at the time, a farewell to the theatre itself.[10] In a reference to his series of "invisible events" that seems equally appropriate to the author's series of naturalistic but allegedly plotless plays, Allott declares that his work to date has been "Ahead of its time . . . impossible to perceive . . . the pageant is at an end now. . . . The process, as you can see, is virtually complete" (88)—as if Storey felt a certain discouragement that his plays had been neither properly understood nor recognized for their innovativeness. Despite Allott's assertion that "I've achieved some of my best work, I think, in here" (90)—a statement that is equally true of Storey's relationship with the Royal Court, where *Life Class* and his other works had been produced—he (Allott) foresees no continuation of it in his career: "My next work may be something altogether less commendable . . . That's to say, more . . . substantial . . . if not altogether more extravagant than what I appeared to have achieved today . . . I shall have to see . . . sans means . . . sans wife . . . sans recognition who's to know what I . . . might rise to . . ." (88). There is also little hope that his works will be better understood in the future, as his conversation with his colleague Philips reveals:

> PHILIPS: Posterity, old son. If they don't see it now, they'll see it later. We're build-
> ing up an enormous credit . . . (*Gestures aimlessly overhead.*) somewhere
> . . . You with your. . . events . . . me with my designs . . . book-jackets,
> posters . . . Letraset . . . singular embodiments of the age we live in.
> ALLOTT: Sold anything lately?
> PHILIPS: (*shakes his head*) . . . You?
> ALLOTT: How do you sell an event that no one will admit is taking place? (55)

Whatever value might later be recognized in Philips's graphics, his remarks are irrelevant to Allott's "invisible events," which leave no artifacts for posterity to judge. Such is not entirely the case with Storey's plays, of course, since a number of them have been recorded on film and videotape, and the texts of all except *Phoenix* have been published. The apparent implication that he has been unable to "sell" his works could be easily refuted by citing the success of his productions at the Royal Court and the lengthy list of favorable reviews and awards that his plays have received (though relatively few have been revived since their initial productions). Nevertheless, the analogy between Allott's "invisible events" and the live performance of Storey's plays in the theatre (as opposed to their filmed or videotaped counterparts) remains clear.

Like John Osborne and Edward Bond, Storey has expressed a deep dissatisfaction with both critics and audiences who, he feels, have neither understood nor recognized (i.e., have not "bought") the ideas that his works embody. Even Katharine Worth's incisive *Revolutions in Modern English Drama* (1973) discusses Storey's work only briefly and in terms of the realism of the 1930s, noting that he "moves between novel and drama with Maugham-like ease" rather than attributing to him any innovations in form.[11] "How does one live as a revolutionary," Allott asks, "when no one admits there's a revolution there?" (56). Yet whereas Osborne and Bond have repeatedly and contentiously explained and defended their plays, proclaiming their social and political beliefs at the same time, Storey seems relatively resigned to the lack of comprehension that he detects. He has maintained a rather taciturn endurance of what he perceives to be the state of affairs in contemporary theatre, and he issues neither prefaces nor manifestoes to explicate his plays. Even so, as he recalled his anger "at the reception—or rather lack of reception—of [his] first two novels," he remarked (during the interview with Victor Sage in 1976) that in the early stage of his career he had not

> learnt that there's nobody out there . . . nobody knows what the hell you're doing. . . . It's no use telling everybody: "Look, this is what I'm doing." It's no use beating a fool about the head . . . you've got to find other, more subtle ways. . . . There's no audience, even at the Royal Court . . . every time you do a new play, you have to whip up an audience . . . they're all so bloody bourgeois . . .they sit there like this (laughter). . . . I can't go to the theatre myself, it's the audience, they put me off.[12]

Like Storey, Allott finds himself surrounded by those who do not comprehend the meaning of his works: his students maintain that "there's nothing happening" as he describes the "invisible events" that are taking place before them, and when he quotes a Latin epigram (which summarizes a major theme of both *The Changing Room* and *The Contractor*) to encourage their efforts, his audience—predictably—fails to understand:

> ALLOTT: Good . . .good. That's the spirit . . . Labor Ipse Voluptas Est.
> WARREN: Rest, sir?
> ALLOTT: No, no . . . Just carry on.
>   (*Fade.*) (57)

The students in Allott's classroom and the audiences for contemporary plays are apparently quite similar, in Storey's view, in both their lack of appreciation of art and their priorities, preferring "excrescence before edification . . . salaciousness before refinement" (40), as the record-breaking runs of such anodyne fare as *Oh! Calcutta!* and *No Sex Please, We're British* reveal. Arguably, the rape in *Life Class* may even provide a sole concession to those members of the audience who complained that 'nothing happened" in Storey's previous plays.

Yet whether or not such speculation is warranted—and Storey has given no indication that it is—a recognition of the analogy between the students in the classroom and the audience in the theatre (both of which are being instructed in the appreciation of "invisible events" at the same time) counters the seemingly valid criticism of the students that was noted by John Weightman in *Encounter:*

> There is never any indication that they are specifically art students, *i.e.* people who, in addition to their randiness and bowel-movements, are genuinely interested in the problems of art. They are all perfectly philistine. . . . In the most benighted educational institutions—and I have seen a few—there are always one or two teachers and pupils who save the honour of the place.[13]

Ironically, insofar as anyone "saves the honour of the place," it is Saunders, who reports the rape incident, "taking the part of public decency and order in this matter" as Allott himself remarks (84).[14] However, the most significant reason why the students "are all perfectly philistine" seems to be the suggestion that they are, in Storey's view, exactly like the audience for his own *theatrical* "invisible events": "there's nobody out there . . . [who] knows what the hell [he's] doing."

In fact, then, Storey has included within *Life Class* a summation of his views of life and art—a statement surpassing the discussion of impersonal methodologies and the technique of avant-garde "invisible events." The most poetic of these summary statements occurs near the end of the play, as Allott muses that art traditionally

> leaves objects—certain elements of its activity—behind . . . stone, paint, canvas . . . bronze . . . paper . . . carbon . . . a synthesis of natural elements convened by man . . . whereas we, elements as it were of a work ourselves, partake of existence . . . simply by being what we are . . . expressions of a certain time and place, and class . . . defying hope . . . defying anguish . . . defying, even, definition . . . more substantial than reality . . . stranger than a dream . . . figures in a landscape . . . scratching . . . scraping . . . rubbing . . . All around us . . . our rocky ball . . . hurtling through time . . . singing . . . to no one's tune at all. (82)

Allott recognizes the value of the traditional heritage, even as he seeks to explore beyond it and to open new frontiers. Accordingly, Storey's ostensibly "valedictory" play is best regarded as the culmination of a series of particularly innovative if seemingly "uneventful" plays, during the course of which a new dramatic form—the theatrical "invisible event"—was developed, refined, and ultimately defended in a uniquely provocative way.

NOTES

[1] Clifford A. Ridley, "Oops—the British are Coming." *The National Observer,* 2 November 1974, 23.

[2] Ronald Hayman, "Conversation with David Storey." *Drama* 99 (Winter 1970), 49, 52.

[3] "David Storey in Interview with Brendan Hennessy," *Transatlantic Review* 33–34 (1969), 10.

[4] Hayman, 49.

[5] Peter Brook, *The Empty Space* (1968; New York: Avon, 1969), 9.

[6] David Storey, *Life Class* (London: Jonathan Cape, 1975), 17, 19. All subsequent references cite this edition and have been inserted parenthetically into the text.

[7] For Storey's most detailed account of his career as a teacher, including his account of his involvement in a rooftop brawl with some of his more thuggish students, see Guy Flatley, "'I Never Saw a Pinter Play," *New York Times,* 29 November 1970, sec. 2: 1, 5.

[8] Victor Sage, "David Storey in Conversation with Victor Sage," *New Review,* October 1976, 64.

[9] Sage, 63.

[10] See, for example, W. Stephen Gilbert, "Life Class," *Plays and Players,* May 1974, 26.

[11] Katharine Worth, *Revolutions in Modern English Drama* (London: G. Bell and Sons, 1973), 26.

[12] Sage, 63, 65.

[13] John Weightman, "Art Versus Life," *Encounter,* September 1974: 57–58.

[14] Despite the obvious difference in gender, the relationship between Allott and Saunders is remarkably similar to that between Miss Jean Brodie and Sandy in Muriel Spark's *The Prime of Miss Jean Brodie* (1961), which was dramatized by Jay Presson Allen and later made into a much-acclaimed film (1969). Like Allott, Spark's central character is an eccentric and controversial but quite dedicated schoolteacher whose outspoken views and avant-garde attitudes are "out of place" in the conservative Marcia Blaine School for Girls in Edinburgh during the late 1930s; furthermore, she loses her job after being betrayed by her most promising student, who has been a model for (and later the mistress of) a married art teacher, Teddy Lloyd, a would-be lover of Miss Brodie's as well. (He, obviously, is the counterpart of Stella as the object of the "gaze" of both teacher and student, though there is no indication that Allott takes any sexual interest in her; his "gaze" is, in fact, wholly aesthetic and as "impersonal" as he contends art must be.) Beset with problems and frustrations in her personal life, Miss Brodie loses her job after an incident for which she bears at best only indirect responsibility (the death of one of her young charges, who, inspired by Brodie-instilled heroic visions, went to Spain to join her brother on the battlefront of the Spanish Civil War), just as Allott is made to bear indirect responsibility for the ostensible rape of the model. The future remains similarly uncertain for both protagonists when their respective works end.

Female Laughter and Comic Possibilities: *Uncommon Women and Others*

Miriam M. Chirico

> But when I grew weary or disgruntled—I too, like Emily Dickinson, tired of the world and sometimes found it lacking—the gentler joys of tea, sherry, and conversation with women friends—and I've made many good ones here— have always been for me a genuine pleasure.
>
> Mrs. Plumm

> It was all hypothetical.
>
> Kate

For Wendy Wasserstein, comedy is a way of concretizing hypothetical scenarios: "Sometimes funny things are almost like the fantasy, and then it comes real" (Interview 1988, 270). Her comedy *Uncommon Women and Others* puts this theory into practice by inviting the audience into the all-female world of Mount Holyoke College to witness a group of women create and define themselves in the wake of the feminist movement. Written originally as a one-act play for her Master's thesis at Yale School of Drama in 1975, *Uncommon Women* grew out of Wasserstein's desire to see an all-women's curtain call at the end of a performance. *Uncommon Women,* constructed as a series of vignettes, develops out of the collective flashback of a group of five college friends in a restaurant in 1978 to their senior year in college, six years earlier. While the vignettes connect loosely into a narrative, they are mainly episodic, exploring the different personalities of these women, their enjoyment of or irritation with each other, and their means of making (or evading) decisions at critical points in their lives. Wasserstein's play shows the confusion these women experience during a turbulent period of the early 1970s, when the feminist movement offered new opportunities and roles to women, oftentimes without the reassurance necessary to make these decisions (Interview 1987, 420).

Nothing changes in these characters' lives during the course of the play except that they graduate by the end, but it is the "emotional action"—a quality which is so much a part of Chekhov's dramatic design—that guides the play (Interview 1987, 430).

As social critique, the genre of comedy is often overlooked by women playwrights, either for its lack of authorial weight or inability to treat serious issues, a bias which originates with Aristotle's dismissal of comedy in the *Poetics*. Wasserstein's plays are often criticized for their lack of serious subject matter in comparison to other female playwrights such as Marsha Norman and Beth Henley. Benedict Nightingale, writing about *Isn't it Romantic,* criticizes Wasserstein's humor as "too strong, too infectious" (14), making it difficult to take her characters seriously and preventing Wasserstein from probing beneath the surface of the play to explore the pain more rigorously. John Simon also voices the concern that the playwright and the characters are too young to have had any meaningful experiences in their lives upon which they can reflect, although he seems to ignore the "coming-of-age" paradigm considered crucial in the developmental literature of young men. However, Wasserstein draws on a long tradition of comedy to reify her all-woman space, specifically comedy's emphasis on surmounting obstacles, creating community, and discovering alternative solutions.

Wasserstein's own theoretical reasoning of humor within her plays is that it permits women to disclose painful incidents while simultaneously deflecting that pain, and to discuss distressing events or feelings without naming them directly. "You are there [in the moment], and you are not there," she explains, adding, "You don't share equally about every topic" (Interview 1987, 425). The dialogue that results is a kind of layered conversation, where the humorous, spoken remarks at the surface belie the pain underneath, creating a subtext to almost every conversation that the audience senses on a nonverbal level (Interview 1987, 425). Holly's speech near the end of act 2 of *Uncommon Women,* for example, demonstrates this kind of subtext in which she expresses the fears she has for her future. Calling Dr. Mark Silverstein on the telephone, a man she has only met once at the Fogg Museum, she launches into a free-associative diatribe about her life and her friends at college. At one point in the rather one-sided conversation she admits that she giggles a lot and is too cynical: "I had my sarcastic summer when I was sixteen and somehow it exponentially progressed. Leilah—she's my nice friend who's merging with Margaret Mead—says sarcasm is a defense. Well, I couldn't very well call you up and tell you to move me to Minneapolis and let's have babies, could I?" she asks, hinting at the worries underlying her entire monologue. Through her jokes about being in a Salinger story and girls who "good-ga-davened" (prayed correctly) and thus married doctors, she exposes her fears that her life will not satisfy her mother's expectations for her, nor her own, although she is "having trouble remembering what [she] want[s]" (63). Through her use of humor, she reveals her desires and fears while simultaneously distancing herself from the present moment, as if to say, "this is me and not me"—a device which Wasserstein uses with all her characters.

While this example demonstrates how Wasserstein's humor works at the immediate, personal level, it does not illustrate how the genre of comedy supports and frames the play as a whole and permits a serious treatment of feminism. The fact that Wesserstein approaches a "woman-conscious drama" through a comic lens enables her to examine the feminist issues with hopefulness and vitality within a communal setting. While tragedy deals with change and development over time and usually focuses on the individual, comedy leans toward the episodic and the momentary with an emphasis on relationships between people. Through an examination of the play's traditional comic structure, comic characters, and comic spirit, I argue that Wasserstein's comedic form provides an ideal medium to examine feminist issues because it reinforces the female space and stems the patriarchal tides that constantly threaten to undermine the women's world.

STRUCTURE OF COMEDY

The play's temporal structure is a flashback from 1978 to 1972, when the women are seniors at college. This shift in time from the mature, present moment of their adult lives to the period of youthful irresponsibility which defined their college years reflects a pattern traditionally found in comedy. M. M. Bakhtin defines this as the period of "carnival" where normal behavior and rules are reversed. Northrop Frye and C. L. Barber both witness this structure in Shakespeare's comedies, Frye depicting it as the ternary movement from the everyday to holiday and back (171) and Barber comparing it to a "Saturnalian" pattern. This period of holiday is often marked by licentious behavior and subversive temperament. The medieval and Elizabethan customs of mocking religious practices permitted a type of release from a rulebound society, a release which was beneficial for the expulsion of "aberrant impulse and thought" (Barber 13). Within a designated frame of time, unruly, drunken, and ludic behavior was encouraged, as participants desecrated the sacred elements in the church and participated in sacrilegious acts, ruined holy statues, broke traditions, and deviated from everyday protocol. Nor was this behavior merely a release from the strictures of decorum and political life; the participants returned to the quotidian space with a better understanding of the status quo and hierarchical forces that held it in place. Just as Demetrius's experience of the world is altered when he returns from the forest in *A Midsummer Night's Dream* and says, "Methinks I see things with parted eye, / When everything seems double" (4.1 188–9), the dreamlike memories of their college days in an all-women's environment infiltrate the women's present view of the world and shape how they see reality.

This classic comedic shift into the holiday mode that the flashback initiates should not be overlooked; the transition into the fantastical "green world" of their college days permits Wasserstein to demonstrate exactly how the hypothetical space of the all-female world has shaped the characters' adult identities in the "present" moment of 1978. Even though their college experience was real to them at one point in time, the scenes unfolding before the audience are fantasy, and like fantasy, allow the characters to propose situations, to play, and to imagine. Wasserstein's comic frame in this play introduces this gesture of playful abandon not just for comic relief but as a means of exploring and understanding the patriarchal rules underlying society. This move back in time to college—to the "holiday world"—is what permits revelry and licenses nonsense, what allows the women to propose various possibilities and to revel in an "artificial" world away from the rules of patriarchal relationships. As the women in the play overturn gender stereotypes and poke fun at sexual limitation, they participate in a similar form of carnival, of mocking the status quo momentarily only to return to it with a better understanding of who they are as women and how they define their new roles.[1] For example, Rita's strong belief in reversing the power dynamics of sexual intimacy enables her to put feminism immediately into practice: she relates having left "Johnny Cabot lying there after [she'd] had an orgasm and he hadn't," or choosing to spend time with Clark who is a wonderful lover, even though he is a homosexual, explaining, "He's creative. I've had enough of those macho types" (34). Rita, always the "Lord [or Lady] of Misrule," also mischievously proposes that men should be forced to menstruate, that they "should be forced to answer phones on a white Naugahyde receptionist's chair with a cotton lollipop stuck up their crotch" (37).[2] While the image is farcical, what Rita deduces from this hypothetical suggestion succinctly reveals how men gain power over women's bodies through their construction of weakness as biologically linked. As she notes:

> The only problem with menstruation for men is that some sensitive schmuck would write about it for the *Village Voice* and he would become the new expert on women's inner life. Dr. David Ruben, taking time out to menstruate over the July Fourth weekend, has concluded that "women are so much closer to the universe because they menstruate, and therefore they seek out lemon-freshened borax, hair spray, and other womb-related items." (38)

What Rita stumbles upon in her hypothetical scenario is that men, if able to menstruate, would privilege the process as something valuable and natural, rather than unmentionable. She also demonstrates how men shape the ways in which women experience their bodies, as in believing that menstruation leads to an immediate desire for borax. Her hypothesis is skin to the kind of "truth-in-foolery" that the figure of the feel or clown offers in comedies, such as Lear's feel who constantly reminds Lear of his error through his puns and paradoxical riddles. Through her parodic proposal, she is able to comically point out truths which underlie patriarchal control, namely that a woman's ability to lead or to work is not affected by menstruating but rather by society's attitude towards menstruation—an attitude that would quickly change if men menstruated.

By placing her characters in a single-sex environment, Wasserstein situates the action in an alternate reality that both critiques the dominant society and offers diverse possibilities. A single-sex education provides women with the space and environment to develop intellectually and emotionally away from the oftentimes oppressive presence of men. Proponents of all-women's education argue that the presence of women in positions of leadership while at college provides models for their experience in the world after they graduate. They believe that altering young women's views of what women are capable of doing will lead them to expect and demand that women fulfill positions of leadership even after college—that the vision of an altered reality leads to the creation of a different world. Wasserstein uses the comic genre to explore this implicit directive behind an all-woman's college because comedy permits such self-fashioning and experimentation with identity by its speculative and hypothetical nature. Through its practice of inversion and its departure from the "everyday" into "holiday," comedy explores the sense of "what if?" as it probes the possibilities of an alternative world where women have as much power as men and allows the women to try on those roles. George Santayana discusses how this hypothetical mode occurs most readily in the realm of comedy in his essay "The Comic Mask." He praises the advantage of the comic form for providing the exploration of potential and possibilities:

> Perhaps the time has come to suspend those exhortations, and to encourage us to be sometimes a little lively, and see if we can invent something worth saying or doing. We should then be living in the spirit of comedy, and the world would grow young. Every occasion would don its comic mask, and make its bold grimace at the world for a moment. We should be constantly original without effort and without shame, somewhat as we are in dreams, and consistent only in sincerity; and we should gloriously emphasize all the poses we fell into, without seeking to prolong them. (137)

The all-women's environment that the women inhabit in the "dream mode" is equivalent to this space that Santayana proposes, permitting the women to try out specific roles through their spontaneous playacting and improvisational games. Their uninhibited poses and grimaces appear as the women test their own "uncommon potential" and their friends' wit. They playfully define a society without men as a positive one, as when Kate depicts her ideal society as an all-woman community, where everyone participates in child care and men visit only on the weekends. While this separatist community sounds remarkably similar to her experience at college, she insists that her plan is different because it "doesn't get boring," since each weekend the men are different and interesting people—"Arabian millionaires, poets, lumberjacks. Not corporate lawyers, or MBAs" (38). In her hypothetical scenario, Kate foresees a society that does not rely on men for economic, governmental, or parental reasons, but only for sexual needs, and in fact willingly excludes them. Holly similarly reveals her own idealistic scenario of being "divorced and living with two children on Central Park West" (38), highlighting the absence rather than presence of men in her life. At this point of the evening, Rita proposes the marriage game.

Reassured by Rita that this is "a nice game for nice girls," each woman chooses a friend who would make a good wife and gives reasons for her choice: Rita selects Samantha, for example, because she is "the perfect woman," while Kate picks Carter because she is more imaginative than she is. This scene of homosocial bonding allows the women to reverse society's dictates on marriage if only temporarily, a gesture reaffirming the women's desire to stay together. The game expands Kate's previous notion of an all-women's society and encourages the women to indicate the very qualities about one another that they admire and love. While Kate is quick to denounce the game as frivolous, protesting "It was all hypothetical" (42) when Carter discovers Kate's choice to marry her, this game goes beyond mere play by demonstrating the *possibility* at least of choosing a life partner of the same sex rather than unquestioningly following society's view of marriage as strictly a heterosexual union. Arguing precisely against this premise that women are innately heterosexual, Adrienne Rich demonstrates in her essay "Compulsory Heterosexuality and Lesbian Existence" how this belief ultimately undermines or harms any kind of female support of one another or any kind of female relationship as lesser value than marital union to a man. These women use their "game" to weaken the institution of heterosexual construction of marriage and to grant them a greater appreciation of their own intimacy; as Susan Carlson notes, "Its direct substitutions of female-female marriage for the traditional male-female kind must be read as a challenge to a world and comedy that expect otherwise" (570).

As Shakespeare completes his comic dramas with multiple marriages and a dance, Wasserstein uses the dance as a means of unifying this group of women. Rita, moving the women's game back to a "safe" heterosexual level by announcing that they should celebrate the fact "that none of our marriage proposals have been reciprocated" (41), suggests that they dance—the typical comic convention of a society righting itself. However, this dance subverts the usual convention. Dance, as an activity rooted in the body, has traditionally conveyed heterosexual union in performance, from ballets to ballroom dances, to Hollywood musicals, to folk dances. Wasserstein adopts this classical idiom and reverses it to show these women physically enjoying one another's presence and bodies; they compliment Kate on her dancing and encourage Samantha's grotesque imitation of her fiancé's dance moves. The marriage game, coming at a culminating moment at the end of act 1, represents a *lesbian continuum* in Rich's sense of the word, not necessarily sexual intimacy, but rather as a woman-identified experience—any form of intense and intimate relationships among women. The placement of this dance at the end of act 1 rather than at the end of the play as in traditional dramas can be read several ways. Susan Carlson sees this placement as indicative of Wasserstein's avoidance of comedy's easy endings; knowing that the play could not realistically end with a glib gesture of a dance, "she indulged her dreams and her characters' dreams of togetherness in this wish-fulfilling pseudo-ending" of act 1 (570). However, I read this dance as one of many signifying moments of union that occur throughout the play, such as the circular grouping in the restaurant or the group hug at the play's end. This dance permeates the drama's structure; rather than the traditional unifying gesture at the play's end as a goal to be reached, the placement of dance suggests that the group's sense of togetherness is a constant force. Just this one scene introduces three female spaces in three different representational modes: the narrated suggestion of Kate's all-women community, the dramatized proposals of marriage, and the communal dance which usurps a heterosexual ritual and challenges it. This dance represents feminism powerfully and immediately, more so than any theory would; Kate invokes Germaine Greer's name, in fact, asking, "Do you think Germaine Greet remembers the night she danced with her best friends in a women's dormitory at Cambridge?" to which Rita responds, "No. She was probably into dating and makeup" (41), dismissing theory in favor of female friendship.

Thus the holiday moment of the collective flashback allows the women to move back in time to a place where they played with possibilities of identity and of visions for their world, freeing them from the constrained attitudes of their adult lives. The audience, witnessing their lives at college, is privy to how this space of potentialities shaped their adult identities as independent and "uncommon" women. Wasserstein does not rely merely on comedy's structure, however, to explore feminist issues; she utilizes specific, comic character types that possess certain functions within the comic tradition, chiefly the Lord of Misrule, the scapegoat, and the benevolent grandfather.

COMIC CHARACTERS

Comedy, known primarily for its extravagant characters that are exaggerations of human idiosyncrasies and foibles, provokes our laughter as we perceive ourselves or others in the mimicry, as in the case of Molière's Tartuffe or Shakespeare's Falstaff. These caricatures appear in *Uncommon Women* in the guise of Susie Friend and Carter. "Susie Friend was a device," Wasserstein explains. "If you see *Uncommon Women* as a spectrum of women: on one end, there's Susie Friend, and on the other, there's Carter, the intellectual. . . . Lots of women I know have grown up with Susie Friends. Now that's a woman's story! There have always been these little organizers in women's colleges. Of course, now they're organizing banks!" (Interview 1987, 422–3). She uses these two women as shorthand devices for stock character types with whom women can readily identify from their own experiences, as figures who represent certain distinctive traits—the officious, ingratiating organizer, or the ethereal, eccentric intellectual—and who add a comic and realistic texture to the play. But in addition to these rapidly drawn Stereotypes, Wasserstein uses characters typical to comedy, characters not defined by their personalities but rather by their function in advancing the comic plot. Frye discusses "typical characters of comedy" in his essay "The Mythos of Spring: Comedy," but he is quick to stipulate that he does not intend "to reduce lifelike characters to stock types." Rather he explains that characterization depends on what function the character fulfills within the comic plot, either by acting as an obstacle to the protagonist's happiness or providing the solution to a problem. He therefore defines the scapegoat and the benevolent grandfather figures by their purpose within the comic structure. He mentions the scapegoat in his discussion of comedy's scenario: "Comedy often includes a scapegoat ritual of expulsion which gets rid of some irreconcilable character" (165), while the grandfather is a type of *eiron* figure, or self-deprecator.[3]

The Lord of Misrule is the person chosen in medieval carnival practice to lead the festivities and incite the rebellious behavior. Rita, described in the list of characters as having walked with the Yale Crew Team through the Yale Cross Campus Library wearing cowbells on her dress, serves as the *primum mobile* of mischief for this group of women. She stirs up unknown emotions and reveals the unexpected, ultimately forcing her friends to view their world differently. Paying more than lip service to feminist ideas, she applies the theories pragmatically. She informs Leilah and Holly that the "entire society is based on cocks," citing the *New York Times,* Walter Cronkite, and shopping malls as examples, concluding that the reason she feels alienated is "'cause I came into the world without a penis" (34). Not only has she has made Rorschach tests with her menstrual blood to summon back the ghost of Edvard Munch, but she also announces to her friends in one scene that she has tasted her own menstrual blood because Germaine Greer has designated this "the test of the truly liberated woman" (37). She derides authority and tells the new student Carter that their housemother, Mrs. Plumm, has syphilis. As the instigator of disobedience and the spirit of chaos incarnate, Rita alternatively shocks and delights her friends as she invites them to join her in her exuberant overthrow of sexual limitations. Thriving on smutty comments and bawdy topics, Rita leads the women into conversations that are sexual in nature, requesting they discuss such topics as masturbation. Smut is usually the domain of men, as Sigmund Freud notes in *Jokes and their Relation to the Unconscious.* He writes that "smut was originally directed towards women and may be equated with attempts at seduction" (97) because it forces the listener to imagine the particular body part mentioned and to become sexually aroused as a consequence. Thus Rita, reveling in a locker-room discourse usually identified with men, claims power by reversing the gender identification associated with bawdy humor. The joke is now on those members in the audience who believe women to be demure creatures hesitant to make ribald comments, let alone think about sex.

In one of the first scenes in which Rita appears, she stands up in front of the group to do a lewd impersonation of Susie Friend, the exasperating superachiever:

> Hi, I'm Susie Friend. I love finger sandwiches, Earl Grey, and Cambridge. I'm a psychology major, head of freshmen in North Stimson Hall, and I wax my legs. I'd let a Harvard man, especially from the business school or law school, violate my body for three hours; Princeton, for two hours and fifty minutes, because you have to take a bus and a train to get there; Yale, for two hours and forty-five minutes, because my dad went there and it makes me feel guilty; Dartmouth, for two hours and thirty minutes because it takes them time to warm up; Columbia, I just don't know, because of the radical politics and the neighborhood. I learned that in psychology. Now, if I could have a Wellesley girl, or Mrs. Plumm, that would be different. (20)

Through this preposterous litany, Rita not only mocks Susie Friend's time-management attitude towards sexual intercourse, but she also derides the Ivy League for its long history of excluding women.[4] Rita's list of Ivy League colleges with Susie Friend's supposed sexual responses reveals the hypocrisy of a system which deems only men educated at prestigious, Ivy League schools as worthy of marriage, a system which perpetuates a snobbery among the educated elite of this country and implicates the women, such as Susie Friend, in this attitude as well. More importantly, through this monologue *cum* stand-up routine, Rita creates an audience about her and brings the women together through the act of watching and listening to her. For as much as clowning figures disrupt the social order, they also unite disparate individuals. Remarking on their ability to create and guide an audience in *Hopi Clay, Hopi Ceremony*, Seymour Koenig attests to clowns' ability to "constantly work to include, interest, and amuse the spectators" (quoted in Babcock 120). Rita's impulse to draw attention to herself creates a focal point around which the group of women congregates and coalesces.

Rita's sense of jest enables her to retain her individuality and belief in her capabilities, and she provides a role model for her friends. She describes an interview with a publishing house in New York to edit beauty hints for women. At the end of a "delightful" interview, when asked by her "delighted" interviewer whether she had experience with a Xerox machine, Rita snappily responded, "Yes. And I've tasted my menstrual blood" (60), clearly ruining the interview but showing her remarkable spirit and rebellious attitude towards a regimented world. Taking her lead from Germaine Greer, albeit out of context, she voices a fundamental belief of feminism, not that a woman should not take a secretarial position, but that she should not live "down" to expectations—no matter whose. But more than a feminist stance, her laughter frees her from the oppressive forces working to quell her individuality. Nancy Wilson Ross, in *The World of Zen*, quotes a Zen student saying "When we laugh we are free of all the oppression of our personality, or that of others" (quoted in Babcock 116), justifying the gesture which underlies Rita's dalliance with authority.

On the other side from this iconoclastic "Lord of Misrule" stands the scapegoat figure, the character who prevents everyone's fun and who must be eliminated. Kate and Leilah's competition with one another demonstrates another way in which women relate, although not necessarily a positive one. Kate's best friend for the first three years of college, Leilah has recently grown distant from Kate, does not appear at tea, and spends all her time in her room. She avoids Kate because Kate's successes diminish her own sense of self-worth. Instead she hovers at the periphery of the circle of women as a dark, shadowy character who is unable to join in the festivities. Wasserstein touches on the forbidden topic of female competition since competition's emphasis on power and domination flies in the face of sisterhood and solidarity and is ultimately "a way of measuring accomplishment that is utterly patriarchal in its conception" (Rosenblum 175). Competition implies that one person's success means another's failure, which is a belief antithetical to feminism's tenets of collaboration and nurturance of one another's goals. Furthermore, because women have traditionally competed for men, one would suppose in an all-women's environment this competition would disappear, and yet the male judgmental eye is closer than would be expected; Muffet tries to reassure Leilah of her worth by quoting her boyfriend: "Pink Pants says you're prettier than Katie" (49). Leilah's father, too, congratulates Leilah on her choice of Kate as a friend, which encourages Leilah's desire to be like Kate in order to please her father. Likewise, an academic setting based on a patriarchal system of awards and acceptance to graduate schools instills in these women the competitive drive associated with male behavior, encouraging them to compare themselves to others in order to increase their own sense of worth; as Kate reassuringly tells Leilah: "Just think, you could be Muffet, or Samantha, or, God forbid, Rita. What are they going to do with their lives? At least you and I aren't limited" (31).

Wasserstein, with unflinching honesty, explores their friendship by examining how the patriarchal gaze disrupts and threatens same-sex relationships. Leilah's sense of inferiority begins on their trip to Greece when their two male companions fall in love with Kate, and continues as the philosophy department selects Kate for Phi Beta Kappa but not her. She candidly reveals to Muffet how she feels about Kate:

> Sometimes when I'm in the library studying, I look up and count me Katies and the Leilahs. They're always together. And they seem a very similar species. But if you observe a while longer, the Katies seem kind of magical, and the Leilahs are highly competent. And they're usually such good friends—really the best. But I find myself secretly hoping that when we leave here, Katie and I will just naturally stop speaking. There's just something . . . *Begins to cry.* It's not Katie's fault! Sometimes I wonder if it's normal for one twenty-year-old woman to be so constantly aware of another woman. (49)

The two have grown so close in their friendship that they are even viewed as a pair by others, like the other "Katies and Leilahs" she sees in the library, causing Leilah to view herself not as a separate entity but always in relation to Kate, because of the comparison that she believes occurs when others see the two of them; "I just want to get out of here so I'm not with people who know me in terms of her," she remarks (49). Her last line, "Sometimes I wonder if it's normal for one twenty-year-old woman to be so constantly aware of another woman" (49), hints at a homoerotic desire for Katie, suggesting a kind of prior intimacy between the two women that occurs in a lesbian-identified relationship. Leilah's description of her friendship with Katie as "always together" and "very similar species" indicates a union or a sense of oneness between people that is usually associated with a sexual relationship. In her essay "The Shattering of an Illusion: The Problem of Competition in Lesbian Relationships" (1985), Joyce P. Lindenbaun examines the particular nature of competitiveness within lesbian relationships, which can be applied to Kate and Leilah's friendship. Lindenbaum draws on Nancy Chodorow's premise that sexual relationships between women reproduce the primal intimacy between mother and daughter. Lindenbaum discovered in her psychiatric work that lesbian couples who are initially attracted to one another by the very qualities they would each like to exhibit actually imagine they possess these qualities during the illusionary phase of merging. However, Leilah's realization that Kate possesses talents she does not have—achieving Phi Beta Kappa, attracting the men in Greece—makes her experience a "felt difference" between the two of them which causes "a deep sense of abandonment and, depending on the pathological extent of the merger, a perceived loss of self" (Lindenbaun 200)—the very loss of self that Leilah experiences in relation to Kate.[5] Whether we read the relationship as repressed homoeroticism or not, the situation attests to the competitive force driving these women apart initiated by the patriarchal gaze, one that disturbs the same-sex community these women have formed.

As the malcontent figure who troubles the consciousness of this group of women, Leilah presents a dark tone to the festive atmosphere. Susie remarks to

Kate, "I notice your nice friend Leilah never comes to dinner anymore" (19). Wasserstein resolves the problem through the use of a character device typically associated with comedy: scapegoating. Comedy naturally inclines toward inclusion of as many people as possible in the final grouping: "[T]he blocking characters are more often reconciled or converted than simply repudiated. Comedy often includes a scapegoat ritual of expulsion which gets rid of some irreconcilable character, but exposure and disgrace make for pathos, or even tragedy" (Frye 165). Wasserstein does not reconcile Kate and Leilah; to reconcile them would only diminish the poignancy of Leilah's distress and undermine the original intensity of their friendship. Instead, Wasserstein makes Leilah the scapegoat figure, not through any group act of exclusion, but rather by having her ostracize herself from her group of friends and book a flight to Iraq the day after graduation. Not only does she not join the women at their reunion in the restaurant, but she has married an Iraqi journalist-archeologist, given up her citizenship, and converted to Islam (68). Leilah's act of removing herself from a liberated society full of opportunities for women to one of complete repression hints of self-immolation, as she struggles to escape from Kate and the competitive society by selecting a culture far removed from choices and opportunities and the inevitable judgmental system that results. Using Leilah as a dark, gloomy feature on the periphery of this close group of women allows Wasserstein to acknowledge the malevolence often underlying female friendships and also to retain a comic ending through the ritual of "scapegoating" a character.[6]

Lastly, Frye's figure of the benevolent grandfather "who overrules the action set up by the blocking humor and so links the first and third pans" (171) and "begins the action of the play by withdrawing from it, and ends the play by returning" (174) bears a resemblance to Mrs. Plumm, the loving and slightly eccentric college housemother of the women. Frye depicts a figure who is present at the initial stage of society before the status quo is disturbed, who observes the Saturnalian society that comes into being, and then aids the leading characters to solve their problems so that the stable, harmonious world moves back into place. Mrs. Plumm, though not physically present at the restaurant at the play's beginning, is called into being by the collective memory of the women and, as she recites a poem by Emily Dickinson (an early student at the college), provides a conduit for the characters to move back into their past lives. She resides quietly among them as a chaperone, giving advice, serving tea and sherry, and listening to their plans. Mrs. Plumm is also a contradictory figure for she represents a previous generation's values and reminds them of the traditional behavior for women even while she encourages their liberated career choices. For example, she admonishes Holly to take her feet off the furniture and to wear skirts to tea so their house does not develop a "reputation" (18) and she encourages Gracious Living, a regular event at which women elegantly dine by candlelight, in order to perpetuate good manners and hostess skills. But even while she affirms traditional proper behavior for women, she constantly talks about her dear friend Dr. Ada Grudder who organized a theater at the Christian Medical College in Nagpur, India. She speaks fondly of their friendship as bird-watching enthusiasts while at college together, and of how they bought rifles, set up a firing-range, and re-enacted the Franco-Prussian War. Mrs. Plumm exhibits the traits that the college was founded upon: she maintains traditions that foster community among women and exemplifies a pioneering spirit as she leaves the women to travel to Bolivia for its "ornithological variety" (67). Mrs. Plumm provides the balance between two periods, the figure who conveys the traditional wisdom of experience yet who still points out alternative directions. True to her role as benevolent grandmother, she serves the graduation tea at the end of the play, supporting each woman's choice of plans after graduation, and leading the women from the holiday moment back to the present, returning them to the everyday world. Not only is her function intrinsic to the comic plot, but her quirky spirit and kindliness permeate the comedy; we laugh at her because she reminds us of an antiquated grandmother, but we admire her pluck and her optimistic belief in the young women. This indefinable mixture of eccentricity and promise—the Life Force according to George Bernard Shaw—moves us the most in the world of comedy and consists of the belief that even against great odds the characters will triumph. Wasserstein, without resolving the feminist issues she raises, uses the spirit of comedy to reassure us of her characters' flexibility and tenacity in a changing world.

SPIRIT OF COMEDY

The action of comedy, as Frye notes, is one of surmounting obstacles placed in the hero's way, usually by a domineering father who sets certain laws, while the tone of comedy is subversive, propelled and conditioned by a desire to break them. The rules in this play are not set by the parents but rather by the patriarchy, Rita's entire "society based on cocks" (34), and the subversive force these women wield comes from their new-found wisdom in feminism, from role models such as Germaine Greer, Simone de Beauvoir, and Rosie the Riveter, as well as from their own wit and sense of humor for which they applaud one another.[7] But the women in this play face two central obstacles: first, the prominence of men, and second, the need to define new roles for themselves.

The influence of patriarchal rules and the prioritization of men in this environment seems a curious obstacle considering that the play occurs in an all-women's college, but Wasserstein presents female characters who have been made to view their lives with respect to male counterparts. Men, though physically absent from the play, infiltrate this world as the 'male long-distance callers' who periodically interrupt conversations, or in the guise of Professor Chip Knowles, whose book on female sexuality prescribes their knowledge of their own bodies, or during the Father-Daughter Weekend festivities that raise some innuendoes ("Hi, Daddy!" Samantha yells exuberantly to the "fathers" seated in the audience. "Hi, Mr. Stewart," Rita follows, with a wink [45]). Even though these women are in a private environment separated from the masculine world, the male gaze penetrates this space, and as much as an all-women's education prioritizes the experience of women in their private domain, it is ultimately defined by the *absence* of men. Holly voices this prioritization of men most specifically when she talks about her friends on the telephone to Dr. Mark Silverstein: "Sometimes I think I'm happiest walking with my best. Katie always says she's my best, . . . Often I think I want a date or a relationship to be over so I can talk about it to Kate or Rita. I guess women are just not as scary as men and therefore they don't count as much" (63). She instantly recants, but it remains an honest statement of how female relationships are valued. Because Holly has experienced such easy intimacy among her female friends, she assumes that intimacy between women cannot be worth as much as with men. Yet comedy provides a means for these characters to cleverly diminish the importance of men and to validate their own sex in turn.

The song these women sing at the Father-Daughter Tea offers a prime example of the kinds of mixed messages the women receive. This song, handed down by generation upon generation of Mount Holyoke women, reinforces certain beliefs of gender relations and expectations of women. The song "We're Saving Ourselves for Yale" amusingly relates tales of women who hold onto their virginity long enough to catch a Yale graduate to marry. That this song is performed in front of a crowd of fathers reinforces the economic system of marriage as the daughters "promise" their fathers not to let themselves be sold off "cheaply" but to "hold out" for the Ivy league man:

> For thirty years and then some
> We've been showing men some
> Tricks that make their motors fail.
>
> And though we've all had our squeezes
> From lots of Ph.D.ses
> We're saving ourselves for Yale. (45)

After the song ends, Mrs. Plumm gives her curiously mixed story about her strong friendship with Ada Grudder and her marriage to Hoyt Plumm, relating how she was the "dutiful daughter" and married at her father's wishes. As the benevolent grandmother figure, she relates her past predicament and decision to these women in her care, emphasizing the significance of her relationship with a woman as well as the importance of obeying her father. She implies that even though they continue the College's father-daughter traditions, their world offers them different choices than hers did. And these college seniors have certainly found ways of undercutting the song's meaning. Their subversive interventions, such as Rita's whispered "These women should have been in therapy," or Carter's ironic pronouncement at the end of the song, "I knew we had a purpose," both serve to illustrate their parodic treatment of the song's beliefs. As their individual spoken voices rise in counterpuntal opposition to the harmonious singing voices, they acknowledge the message society perpetuates and alter this message to their own liking.

As this scene clearly demonstrates, even while the women are urged to pursue "uncommon" careers after college, the traditional choice of marriage still resounds clearly within the halls of the college, especially when one of the women, Samantha, announces that she is getting married. Her friends, disappointed and jealous, do not know how to react; as Carlson mentions, "The others envy her not because she can so easily choose an established role, but because she can fit into it: they could not" (570). More importantly, her marriage is an outside threat to their community; it reminds them that they will no longer have the security and intimacy of their female world after graduation.

Rita attempts to dispel her anxiety over losing Samantha through a typical comic gesture of mimicry. She approaches Samantha in her room after the announcement, impersonating a man in a denim jacket and cap, and says, "Hey, man, wanna go out and cruise for pussy?" (52). Since language is the means by which we create a particular reality, especially in the theater, Rita's adoption of masculine-identified language modifies the reality of the situation; she interpolates Samantha as male and demands that Samantha acknowledge her as a man in turn—a man desirous of female bodies. Samantha catches on to the game but avoids the heavily sexual topics that Rita encourages; Samantha prefers being "the corporate type" she says, and suggests going out "to buy Lacoste shirts and the State of Maine," (52) but Rita brings the conversation back to aggressive sexual baiting. She picks up a bag of nuts and says, "Nice nuts you got there" and "I'll give you a vasectomy if you give me one" (53).

While the imitation of men introduces a comic convention into the play, it also indicates the cause of Rita's anxiety. On one level, mimicry provides a person with the means of mastering that which frightens her; behavioral theory argues that people tend to imitate and mock those forces that disturb them the most, and that deeply rooted fears are at the basis of such imitations. Thus Rita's play-acting a man and encouraging Samantha to do the same is ultimately an indication of Rita's anxiety over Samantha's choice to marry and be in an intimate relationship with a man. Rita, as noted earlier, is sexually involved with a gay man and constantly defines her "ideal husband" as Leonard Woolf because he allowed his wife the creative freedom to write. She fears being stifled by a man in a relationship and is distressed by Samantha's choice to marry. However, following this analogy, if Rita identifies with Virginia Woolf, she would also have the freedom to love other women—a desire which can be inferred from the aggressive nature of her behavior in this scene. When Samantha becomes anxious and threatens to leave the room, Rita drops her masculine role to tell

Samantha how much she admires her and that she wants to be her because she is the "ideal woman." In light of Rita's earlier choice to marry Samantha during the marriage game, this statement hints at Rita's desire of intimacy from Samantha and her fear of losing her. Thus Rita's wish to engage her in sexual dialogue, the slight punches on the arm, and the manner in which Rita grabs Samantha from behind and wrestles her momentarily all touch on the homoerotic undertones of this scene.[8] Only through her initial comic impersonation is Rita able to create a space where she can convey her affection towards Samantha ("I do want to be you" [54]) and express to Samantha her sense of loss. Samantha, responding to Rita's fears at some level, spontaneously creates a poem about Rita, in which she expresses her fondness and diffuses her anxiety over her own abandonment of their all-female world. With her poem, she moves Rita from the masculine role of aggressor, one who "talks of cocks and Aries blocks," back to the stereotypical notion of femininity as charming and kind, "I know secretly she's very sweeta" (55), diffusing her worries as well as her sexual aggression.

The spirit of comedy, as Susanne Langer points out, comes from the behavior of the individual facing obstacles and adopting to change in a tumultuous world (68–69). It is the energy to rise above malignant forces and the resiliency to accept change without losing a sense of identity. Rita, in the preceding example, adjusts to her friend's marriage by asking for reassurance of their intimacy. On a larger scale, however, all of these women must face the overwhelming vertigo of defining themselves within a society in flux as the roles for women shift from traditional homemaker to pioneer, where fulfilling expectations means not only being successful, wealthy, and married with children but being exceptional and "uncommon." These demanding ideals penetrate their consciousness through the male voice-over which initiates each vignette. This voice—supposedly the college bulletin being read aloud—intones the benefits of an all-women's education, setting the tone for each of these scenes and delineating the function of an all-women's college.[9] He mentions that the College contributes to society women "whose intellectual quality is high, and whose responsibility to others is exceptional." The hyperbolic adjectives he uses denote the pressures that these women face as professionals, wives, and mothers, but he still promises that they are prepared to meet any and all challenges "without loss of gaiety, charm, or femininity" (7). This disembodied voice seems superior and distant from the action, as he acknowledges that educated women sometimes fail to view themselves as successes because their talents are so diffuse, but he encouragingly and ingratiatingly concludes, "Just like the pot of honey that kept renewing itself, an educated woman's capacity for giving is not exhausted, but stimulated, by demands" (23). The convention of the voice-over suggests that the women do not hear the voice, but rather have absorbed its message through other means, as when Muffet reads the course catalogue out loud to herself in scene 4. However, these women challenge the voice through their actions as each scene grows more and more mocking and their very actions eschew his directives.

Carter provides one of the first examples of this defiance in scene 5, where she ironically mimes modern dance movements to the Man's Voice. He intones how Mary Lyon commanded her early students to "Go where no one else will go. Do what no one else will do" (27) and relates how these 25,000 alumnae blazed new trails for women in different professions, fields, and different parts of the world. While Carter originally begins by physically parodying the voice's directions, "marching" along with the "pioneers," the impressive litany of women's accomplishments ultimately frustrates her with its high expectations of the College's young women.[10] Carter, as a freshman, is new to this atmosphere of high achievement and tries to mock the demands that the "Voice" has decreed, but sits down at the end, exhausted. The older group of students, however, fares better.

These upper-class women have internalized the voice to some extent, but their communal activities show their ability to follow their internal voices and support one another's choices. At the beginning of act 2, scene 2, the Man's Voice boasts that "employers of graduates of the college seem to be looking for a readiness to work hard at learning unfamiliar techniques" (47), but the onstage action shows Muffet "putting on makeup" (47). The oxymoronic juxtaposition between women's ability to learn unfamiliar skills and the sight of Muffet performing a highly iconic gesture of femininity is comic. More than a slight at women's cosmetic predilection, however, this action serves as a direct refusal to acquiesce to the male authorial voice. Further, the private act of putting on makeup denotes a relaxed space in which Muffet and Leilah can interact intimately in a way that most women cannot in a public sphere. The scene immediately following again satirizes the Man's Voice; as he extols a liberal arts education for exposing students to "a wide range of opportunities—that is to say, uncertainties" (50), the lights reveal the group of women attacking large jars of peanut butter and spreading the Fluff on crackers with great gusto. Finally, in scene 6, the male voice insists that "The college places at its center the content of human learning and the spirit of systematic disinterested inquiry" (57). The scene focuses on the women's debate over whether or not they have experienced penis envy, which is admittedly a method of inquiry, but neither disinterested, when it becomes a personal question, nor systematic, when Holly's reply is "I remember having tonsillitis" (57). Again, the questions are of their own choosing, the topics of their own design, and their personal lives and values lie at the center of their conversations.

By the play's end the Man's Voice is superseded by a Woman's Voice who admits that women still have not attained all the goals and recognition they have hoped for because "society has trained women from childhood to accept a limited set of options and restricted levels of aspirations" (68). Her voice does not blithely depict the road for female pioneers as a surmountable and an exciting challenge, as he has, but demonstrates an awareness of the fears that women face. This reasonable voice leads the women back to the present moment in the restaurant, where they admit their worries of being judged by one another about their chosen career paths. Their insecurity and uncertainty comes across clearly, but what sustains them and blesses them at the end of the play is their ability to share this uncertainty through their laughter. Rita closes the play with a phrase she has been repeating throughout the play, "When we're thirty [or thirty-five, or forty] we're going to be amazing"—a comic device which Wasserstein borrows from Chekhov's *Three Sisters* (Interview 1996, 382)[11] in which the sisters always imagine they will return to Moscow some day. The phrase is funny in its unincremental repetition[12] but we also laugh *at* Rita and *with* her—at her ability to adjust the deadline to accommodate for their current circumstances and with her steadfast belief in their uncommon talents.

The spirit of comedy comes as much from the performance as from the script—the lewd faces, the accompanying ironic gestures to the songs, the communal dance ending act 1, and Rita's impersonation of Susie Friend. Wasserstein describes this sensation that occurred during the rehearsals for *Uncommon Women:* "There was something special between the actresses and me. I can remember being in the dressing room with Swoosie Kurtz and Jill Eikenberry and Alma Cuervo, and Anna Levine, Glenn Close, and Ellen Parker and there was the sense of embracing, a sense of all starting out together . . . again, that feeling of community. And I would say I feel it more at the laughter than at the applause" (Interview 1987, 429). She speaks here of the indefinable quality of renewal that comes not only from a successful opening performance but rather from the collaborative efforts of these women and the laughter that echoes this communal spirit. For comedy, as Langer reminds us, more than offering solutions to a predicament, heightens the vital feeling: "The conflict with the world whereby a living being maintains its own complex organic unity is a delightful encounter" (82). As spectators we have a secure emotional realization that the uncommon women before us will continue to strive and grow because of their laughter and wit. "Laughing at something is the first sign of a higher psychic life," Nietzsche says in *Beyond Good and Evil,* and Wasserstein fully relies on this sense of the comic spirit to draw the spectators into the triumphs of her characters in performance. "The comedy itself is a spirit," she remarks. "It's not an application form, a resumé, it's life. This life spirit creates a current, a buoyancy which, getting back to drama, is very important. It's important to reach the essence of that spirit in what you create" (Interview 1987, 421).

NOTES

[1] It seems Wasserstein wanted to create an unreal world by the play's complete lack of any references to contemporary politics. For instance, she remarks how originally the play had some pieces in it which were highly political, such as Susie Friend's

organizing a strike for Mark Rudd when he came to visit Mount Holyoke College, but she eliminated these scenes because she was concerned that this would open up discussions on the Vietnam War rather than permitting the women's voices to be heard (Interview 1987, 426).

[2] I am borrowing Wylie Sypher's term of the "Lord of Misrule" from his essay "The Meanings of Comedy."

[3] The other characters being the *alazon* (impostor), buffoon, and churl (172).

[4] Princeton and Yale admitted women in 1969, Amherst admitted them in 1976, and Columbia held out until 1983, partly due to Barnard College's association with the school.

[5] I thank Professor Gayle Austin of Georgia State University for pointing out the book *Competition: A Feminist Taboo?* as well as for suggesting that the relationship between Kate and Leilah could be read as repressed homoerotic desire.

[6] For the 1994 revival of *Uncommon Women and Others* at the Lucille Lortel Theater in New York, Wasserstein updated the ending, changing Leilah's outcome from a "subjugated Iraqi wife" to an Oxford don (Feingold 97), a choice that weakens the scapegoating device.

[7] Wasserstein prioritizes humor from the very start of the play. Her opening descriptions of each character illustrate this, from Kate who "always walks with direction . . . [so] it's fun to make her stop and laugh" (4), to Samantha, "a closet wit, or she wouldn't have made the friends she did in college" (5), to Holly Kaplan, the figure who most resembles Wasserstein and who uses her wit on those people who intimidate her (5).

[8] The staging of these gestures occurred in Theater Emory's production of *Uncommon Women and Others* in October 1996, directed by Rosemary Newcott. In the filmed version of the play televised for PBS Great Performances Series in May, 1978, this scene takes place in the women's locker room where Rita makes lewd gestures at women changing their clothes while Samantha joins her antics. The homoerotic tension is decidedly nonexistent; Rita appears more distressed about not being an "ideal" women like Samantha, who chooses to marry and fulfill her role as wife.

[9] While the identity of the voice is never specified, the copyright credits show that Wasserstein took these clips from the Mount Holyoke College Bulletin 1966/67, and from Richard Glenn Gettell's inaugural address as president of Mount Holyoke College in 1957.

[10] The backdrop for Theater Emory's 1996 production showed faces of famous women staring out at the audience and staring down on these young women, both inspiring them as their role models and beckoning them not to let down the cause of sisterhood.

[11] Wasserstein sees Chekhov as having influenced her work, in this line especially, but also in the ways she is fascinated by examining "moments in people's lives when they could turn to the right or turn to the left, or why they don't turn at all" (Interview 1996, 382).

[12] Northrop Frye discusses this "principle of unicremental repetition" in his essay, "The Mythos of Spring: Comedy."

Works Cited

Babcock, Barbara A. "Arrange Me into Disorder: Fragments and Reflections on Ritual Clowning." In John J. MacAloon. *Rite, Drama, Festival, Spectacle: Rehearsals Toward a Theory of Cultural Performance.* Philadelphia: Institute for the Study of Human Issues, 1984.

Bakhtin, Mikhail. *Rabelais and His World.* Trans. Helene Iswolsky. Cambridge, MA: MIT Press, 1968.

Barber, C. L. *Shakespeare's Festive Comedy.* Princeton, NJ: Princeton UP, 1959.

Carlson, Susan L. "Comic Textures and Female Communities 1937 and 1977: Clare Boothe and Wendy Wasserstein." *Modern Drama* 27.4 (1984): 564–573.

Feingold, Michael. "Gender is the Night." Review of *Uncommon Women,* Lucille Lortel Theater, New York. *Village Voice* 8 Nov. 1994: 97.

Freud, Sigmund. *Jokes and Their Relation to the Unconscious.* London: The Hogarth Press, 1960.

Frye, Northrop. "The Mythos of Spring: Comedy." *Anatomy of Criticism: Four Essays.* Princeton, NJ: Princeton UP, 1957. 163–186.

Koenig, Seymour. *Hopi Clay, Hopi Ceremony: An Exhibition of Hopi Art,* New York: Katonah, 1976.

Langer, Susanne K. *Feeling and Form.* New York: Scribner's, 1953.

Lindenbaun, Joyce P. "The Shattering of an Illusion: The Problem of Competition in Lesbian Relationships." *Competition: A Feminist Taboo?* Eds. Valerie Miner and Helen E. Longino. New York: Feminist Press at CUNY, 1987. 195–208.

Nietzsche, Friedrich Wilhelm. *Beyond Good and Evil: Prelude to a Philosophy of the Future.* Trans. Walter Kaufman. New York: Vintage, 1966.

Nightingale, Benedict. "There Really is a World beyond 'Diaper Drama.'" Review of *Isn't It Romantic,* Playwrights Horizons, New York. *The New York Times* 1 Jan 1984, sec. 2: 14.

Rich, Adrienne. "Compulsory Heterosexuality and Lesbian Existence." *Signs: Journal of Women in Culture and Society* 5.4 (1980): 631–660.

Rosenblum, Barbara and Sandra Butler. "Dialogue, Dialectic, and Dissent." *Competition: A Feminist Taboo?* Eds. Valerie Miner and Helen E. Longino. New York: The Feminist Press at CUNY, 1987. 171–176.

Santayana, George. *Soliloquies in England and Later Soliloquies.* New York: Scribner's, 1922.

Shakespeare, William. *A Midsummer Night's Dream. The Riverside Shakespeare.* 2nd Edition. Boston: Houghton Mifflin, 1997.

Simon, John. "The Group." Review of *Uncommon Women,* Phoenix Theater, New York. *New York* 12 Dec. 1977: 103–104.

Sypher, Wylie. "The Meanings of Comedy." In *Comedy.* Ed. Wylie Sypher. Garden City, NY: Doubleday, 1956.

Uncommon Women and Others. Theater Emory, Atlanta, Georgia. October 1996. Dir. Rosemary Newcott.

Wasserstein, Wendy. Interview with Jan Balakian. *Speaking on Stage: Interviews with Contemporary American Playwrights.* Eds. Philip C. Kolin and Colby H. Kullman. Tuscaloosa: U of Alabama P, 1996. 379–391.

———. Interview with Kathleen Betsko and Rachel Koenig. *Interviews with Contemporary Women Playwrights.* Eds. Betsko and Koenig. New York: Beech Tree Books, 1987. 418–431.

———. Interview with Esther Cohen. "Uncommon Woman: An Interview with Wendy Wasserstein." *Women's Studies* 15 (1988): 257–270.

———. *Uncommon Women and Others. The Heidi Chronicles and Other Plays.* New York: Vintage Books, 1991. 1–72.

Vision and Reality: *Their Very Own and Golden City* and Centre 42

Clive Barker

In my album I have some photographs taken early in 1963. The photographs give an odd feeling when I look at them since I do not appear in any of them. I took the photographs, and that fact makes it appear as I was not part of the activity that was captured on film. The settings for the photographs are the cloisters of Durham Cathedral and the North Yorkshire Moors. There is a heavy fall of snow visible in all of them. What the photographs show is a group of young people in their twenties and early thirties fooling around. They strike poses in the windows of the cloisters and throw snowballs as they roll around on the moor. The four people are Arnold Wesker, Beba Lavrin, Mike Kustow, and Geoffrey Reeves. The timing of the photographs was propitious and accounts for the presence of all four and myself as photographer. All of the people were connected with the project Centre 42, which underlies but is not directly depicted in Wesker's play, *Their Very Own and Golden City*. Wesker was Administrator, Beba Lavrin his assistant. I was Festivals Organiser, Mike Kustow my assistant, and Geoffrey Reeves was its Technical Director.

The time at which the photographs were taken represents the high point of Centre 42, riding on a wave of optimism, six major Trades Union Arts Festivals organized in 1962, 13 envisaged for 1963 and 20 for 1964. The 1963 and 1964 Festivals never took place, and the tone of *Their Very Own and Golden City* carries the frustration, bitterness, and pain of the failure to carry the project forward.

Centre 42 bore its curious name because of Resolution 42 of the Trades Union Congress of 1960, which called upon the Trades Union movement to support artistic activities, particularly those which were in keeping with the aims and objectives of the movement. The lead-up to the framing of this resolution had been a lecture tour by Arnold Wesker in which he presented a view of Trades Unionism moving beyond simply battling for better pay and working conditions for its members but taking into its sphere a concern with the whole range of living conditions, the total culture in which they lived. This view of Trades Unionism presents positively what William Morris issues as a warning of what will happen if the Trades Union movement does not adopt a radical political role in the long quotation with which Wesker prefaces the play in the published text.

These ideas arose in the late 1950s and early 60s out of a network of social processes. Wesker was born in 1932, which makes him a member of a generation with a specific history. He belongs to the last generation who would experience consciously the deprivation of working-class life in the Great Depression before the Second World War, who were the first generation, in the main, to be offered a much wider range of educational opportunities than previous generations of their class, who grew to awareness during the war-time period, in which a new society was being planned and the dream of socialism was presented as a social necessity and inevitability, who experienced in adolescence and early manhood the failure of the working-class movement, Labour Party and Trades Unions to establish the socialist utopia and who found themselves, after yet another war to end all wars, fighting in a range of colonial wars or in Korea.

It was this generation, fired by a belief in social progress and haunted by a sense of disillusionment, which was responsible for the breakthrough in the British theatre from 1956 onwards. Among others, John Arden, John Osborne, Harold Pinter, Dennis Potter, Trevor Griffiths, and John McGrath were responsible for breaking through the hermetical sealing off of the theatre from society, which Arthur Miller found so distressingly apparent in the mid-1950s British theatre, only to find yet more disillusionment, as Wesker records in his essay "Oh, Mother, Is It Worth It?" He accepts that his plays are well and frequently performed, no-one is censoring his works, but he complains that the audience he is writing for, the working class, are notably absent from the audience.

It was this frustration which moved Wesker into contact with the Trades Union movement, led to Resolution 42 being passed, against the advice and wishes of the ruling General Council, and was the inspiration behind a group of artists meeting at the end of 1960 to discuss their feelings of discontent about the commercial valuation of their work, and the absence from the audience of the formative communities for whom their work was conceived. This group discussed a range of other discontents, principal among them the ways in which the socialist dream had been sold out for material consumer benefits and the ways in which the rebuilding of Britain after the war had taken no account of the existence and continuation of the sense of shared community which characterized the old working-class neighborhoods. In *Their Very Own and Golden City,* Wesker projects backwards in time to look at the ways in which the dream of a new postwar world was lost through the sheer enormity of the task of reconstruction, a lack of vision and capital resources and the resulting necessity to compromise. All of which resulted in the patching up of the old and the preserving within the new much of the inequality, shoddiness, and spiritual poverty of the old.

The group meeting at the end of 1960 included writers, actors, and directors, principally, and their discussion focused on the above discontents and one how the artist could combat both the cultural poverty left over from the past and the materialist consumerism which had come in with the short, post-war economic boom. To this group Wesker introduced the idea of making a parallel gesture, comparative to the passing of Resolution 42, by means of which artists and Trades Unionists would join and work together to create new cultural structures. The first plans were to build a literal Centre, which would serve as a laboratory within which ideas could be discussed and tried out and which would serve as a display place for exhibitions and performances of all kinds. It was envisaged that participating artists would give their services for as little as they could afford and that wealthier writers and artists would contribute some portion of their royalties to help finance the running of the Centre. By projecting a possible multi-activity centre, drawing in a public directly through Trades Union memberships, Centre 42 drew on the experiences of some continental models but introduced to Britain the idea of the Arts Centre, which has become a standard feature of British cultural life.

However, the physical Centre 42 remained a dream and was never built. Early in 1961, a group of Trades Unionists from Wellingborough, a small town in the Midlands, approached the members of Centre 42, asking for a festival. Since this was the first positive demand made upon the proposed alliance, it was impossible to turn the request down and a Trades Union Festival was organized in November 1961. This admittedly small festival aroused such interest that invitations were received to mount six large-scale festivals in 1962, in Wellingborough again, the major cities of Leicester, Nottingham, Birmingham, Bristol, and the industrial conurbation of Hayes and Harlington on the western edge of Greater London.

The festivals were mounted during the autumn of 1962 in alternate weeks—one week of festival, one week of preparation. The content of the festivals was constant, the first compromise, since resources did not allow making each festival specific to the host town. The program included theatre, music theatre, poetry, jazz, and exhibitions of local artists and children's art. The first major concerts of the folksong revival movement were given in the program and a sixteen-piece band was formed, including most of the leading modern jazz soloists in Britain at a time when big band jazz desperately needed some encouragement. The production of *Hamlet,* by the National Youth Theatre, in which the title role was played by Simon Ward, included many young actors who in the 1990s are leading members of their profession. The festivals also included a documentary production *The Maker and the Tool* which was the first example of multi-media theatre in Britain and was certainly the most advanced experimental work seen in the two decades after 1945. The events were mounted in a variety of environments. In Leicester, a theatre was built in an ice rink. Folk singers and poets performed in public houses, schools, and factory canteens. In Birmingham the exhibition of children's art was estimated to have been seen by over a million people as it was sited in a wide corridor which linked two halves of a giant department store.

The organization of the festivals was split between committees of artists, responsible for the artistic content, and committees of Trades Unionists who were responsible for the local arrangements. The financial agreement was that the Trades Unionists would raise as much money as they were able and Centre 42 would raise the rest. In the event, the Trades Unions were unable to raise any money, although in Leicester they persuaded the local authority to contribute £1,000. Centre 42 enjoyed strong support at grass-roots level, where there was no money to spare, and failed to gain the support of the union leaders, who were passively sitting on massive sums of money as a precaution against having to support possible future strike action.

Money was slow to come in, and the organization was stretched simply by having to mount the festivals and had no time to spare for fund-raising. The Arts Council of Great Britain, whose function it is to subsidize the arts, gave a derisory £250 and that was paid directly to Wesker as a commission to write a music theatre piece, *The Nottingham Captain.* In a desperate attempt to raise money at a moment of crisis, Wesker offered to sell the television rights to the *Trilogy* of plays with which he first established his reputation, *Chicken Soup with Barley, Roots,* and *I'm Talking About Jerusalem.* One of the major independent television companies, which boasted a socialist as its chairman and major shareholder, made an offer of a derisory £250 for the full screening rights.

The six festivals, accordingly, had a loss of somewhere in the order of £38,000, which was below the cost of a small Bach Festival in Oxford. Of the many hundreds of artists taking part, only one, who had special skills, demanded the market price for his appearance. All accommodation was in the homes of Trades Unionists. This financial deficit was ultimately to dog the rest of Centre 42's career and to lead to its demise. A hope, which was understood to be a promise, was held out by Harold Wilson, who expected to be, and was, returned as leader of a Labour Party Government in 1964, that this deficit would be wiped out and future activities subsidized after the election. In the meantime, as part of a package deal, Wilson insisted on the appointment of an advisory board of financial experts and businessmen, to oversee the running of the project. Not only did this board fail to raise any capital; it effectively put a stop to any interim Centre 42 activities and, towards the end, succeeded in taking over the large premises in London, which had been donated to the project free of charge, for commercial exploitation. The support of Wilson's government failed to materialize, largely through Wilson's failure to establish direct subsidy, outside the control of the Arts Council of Great Britain, as a principle. Centre 42 was left without a home; its activities largely prohibited. The great optimism reflected in the games played in the photographs taken at Durham Cathedral led through a slow decline to the abandonment of the project and an end to the dreams. A challenge put down to tear the arts loose of commercial domination and bureaucratic control, to halt the drift towards a centralized metropolitan culture and to restore to people the means to create their own cultural environment was not taken up.

This was the major loss caused by the failure to sustain Centre 42. There were many gains arising out of the life of the project. The whole nature of the debate about the relationship between the arts and the community changed. Many other projects learned from the experience in constructing their own work. Most of these projects were grass-root organizations where artists moved out to live and work in communities. One, Inter-Action, started by the American Ed Berman, was large-scale and very ambitious, earning for itself the compliment of being called the most successful community arts venture within Europe. Although nothing would permit the bureaucrats to admit it, the policy underlying arts subsidy changed over the next years and a greater emphasis was placed upon provision for the regions outside London. In the new building program which resulted from this, many of the points raised by Centre 42, about freer access and a more positive policy towards building a socially, more broadly based audience, were incorporated. But for those who were closely involved in the running of the project, the great realization was that among the workers in any community there were enough skills and energy to change the nature of that society, if they could be harnessed. What the Trades Unionists brought was a range of practical skills and organizational capacities which made the running of major arts festivals a relatively simple matter. If a temporary theatre had to be built, the carpenters and builders would do it. If there were eight box-offices, running simultaneously, the bank workers union could handle that with no trouble. Transport problems, ring the transport workers union. With no vision this would be a way of exploiting cheap labor. What made it more than this was the engagement of the Trades Unionists in creating their own cultural event and the amount of control they were able to exert over it.

However, the ultimate astonishing achievement of Centre 42 lay in proving that any community has within it the capacity and power to create its own culture, which is a revolutionary concept. In *Their Very Own,* Wesker attaches to Centre 42 an affiliation to the overall dream of building a new world and appropriates for it the same level of importance as the play ascribes to the building of the Golden Cities, the design of which will be democratically determined by the choice of the future residents. The artist/architect will be given the opportunity to be truly creative in the service of the community. By extension, the artist can only be truly creative in the service of the community. At no point does Wesker present a utopian dream as a reality. Although he presents, through the character of Bill Matheson, a rampant philistine, a picture of small-mindedness, petty jealousy, and political reaction, Wesker elsewhere is concerned to be fair minded. The Trades Union leaders and politicians in the pla may be blinkered in their vision and timid in their actions, but they are constrained by pressures arising out of the real, external world they live in and not simply by limitations inherent in themselves. They are not fools, villains, nor bloody minded, and, in the course of the play, the visionary Andy Cobham has to learn to live with the same constraints and to make similar compromises. Wesker shows us the great efforts that have to be made to achieve no more than a token gesture towards progress and the effects that the necessary, if excessive, compromise has on the human mind, body, and spirit.

The play is written in episodic form, utilizing many short scenes, covering a period of almost sixty years. It concerns the plans and deeds of an architect, Andrew Cobham, and a group of friends, to build a network of new cities, which will constitute the ideal environment in which to live. In any event, only one of these cities is ever built; Cobham grows old, loaded with honors, bitterly frustrated that his grand dreams have only resulted in contributing one more piece to the patchwork, shoring up of the old society, which characterized the death of the war-time dreams of building a new society upon its conclusion. Along the way, Cobham has to learn many lessons. Through his friendship with the aristocratic Kate Ramsay, he learns that he who wants to create must learn to be assertive and elitist, if he wishes to bring in democracy. He has to learn to be a politician, a diplomat, and ultimately to accept compromise as the price of a minimal success. Politics, as we are told, is the art of the possible, but those who accept this without testing how far the possible can be pushed must bear the responsibility for stagnation. Cobham learns that those who give their lives to pursuing high ideals and progress can never enjoy the fruits of their labors themselves. One part of the price of Cobham's limited success is the slow destruction of his marriage and the enslaving of his wife.

In constructing this episodic play, Wesker cunningly uses the technique of flash-forward. The play opens with the friends playing games amid the glorious architecture of Durham Cathedral. At various points the play returns to this setting and the time of youthful dreams. The use of this time and place as a framework places a positive emphasis on what follows. To have used flashback would have been to create a play of despair and disillusionment as the aged Cobham looked back at his failures. In using flash-forward, Wesker asserts that, in spite of all the pain and compromise to come, there is value in the attempt. In every age people have to assert positive principles and to stand by their beliefs:

> I've no time for rebels, they hate the past for what it didn't give them. . . . Revolutionaries is what we want—they spend less time rebelling against what's past and give their energy to the vision ahead. (2:138)

> Defeat doesn't matter; in the long run all defeat is temporary. It doesn't matter about present generations but future ones always want to look back and know that someone was around acting on principle (2:141)

This positive intention is further borne out by the instruction Wesker gives in the text:

> N.B. If the cathedral scenes in either Act are heavily played this entire play
> will fail. Innocence, gaiety and a touch of lunacy is their atmosphere. (2:127)

The play becomes an assertion of the human spirit in the face of all opposing forces and adversity. The motto Wesker chose to embody the spirit of Centre 42 was a statement made by D.H. Lawrence, "If you are going to make a revolution, make it for fun." Those who are true revolutionaries, in Wesker's opinion, are those who aim to change people, not those who battle to bring down governments.

In beginning his play in 1926, the year of The General Strike, the high point of working-class militancy and the low-point of Trades Union leadership, Wesker tacitly acknowledges that Centre 42 was behind its time. 1945, not 1960, was the time when it should have been founded. But it would be foolish to write the project off in those terms. The value of Centre 42, and the Golden City of the play, is difficult to assess in concrete contemporary terms. I have tried to set out some of the positive influences the project was able to assert, but ultimately, the true and lasting value lies in the hearts and minds of those who were involved and touched by it. I have the photographs to remind me of the joy we experienced. My subsequent life and career have been molded by that experience. I recently met up with someone who had been involved. She asked me, "How did we manage to do so much?" Because we had a vision and we pursued it as far as it was allowed to go.

August Wilson's Folk Traditions

Trudier Harris

African American folkloric traditions have taken on many recognizable forms, ranging from the Brer Rabbit and John the Slave trickster tales to the blues, from legends and folktales to spirituals and gospels, from folk beliefs and ghostlore to preaching and folk expressions. Scholars studying such patterns have garnered their categorizations of the lore from a variety of collected sources, such as Zora Neale Hurston's *Mules and Men* and the seven-volume *Frank C. Brown Collection of North Carolina Folklore.* Patterns in the lore reflect patterns in African American history, including strategies for survival, ways of manipulating a hostile Anglo American environment, and a world view that posited the potential for goodness prevailing in spite of the harshness of American racism and the exclusion of blacks from American democracy and the American dream. African American folklore, as Ralph Ellison astutely pointed out, revealed the willingness of blacks to trust their own sense of reality instead of allowing the crucial parts of their existence to be defined by others.

In turning to examine August Wilson's plays and where they fit into this historical conception of African American folklore, it becomes clear that there is overlap as well as extension. Wilson's use of African American folk traditions approximates that of Henry Dumas and Toni Morrison. Certainly, he includes recognizable patterns of the lore in his dramas, but he is also about the business of expanding—within established patterns—what African American folklore means and what it does. Like Dumas and Morrison, he is as much a mythmaker as he is a reflector of the cultural strands of the lore he uses. His conception of "the shiny man" in *Joe Turner's Come and Gone* (1988) will serve to illustrate the point. "The shiny man" is an extranatural guide/seer who leads Bynum, one of the central characters, to discovery of the song that defines his being, his purpose in life, and his relationships with others. While there is no specific "shiny man" who can be documented in Hurston's work or any other collections of African American folklore, there are certainly references to unusual encounters with extra- or supernatural phenomena. Wilson adapts that pattern of human encountering otherworldly being from historical folklore; then, he riffs on the established pattern by naming the phenomenon "the shiny man." In imaginatively expanding traditional forms of the lore, Wilson shares kinship with Morrison, who also takes traditional forms, gives them new shapes, and bends them to her imaginative will throughout her novels.[1] Wilson's creation in *Joe Turner* of "the shiny man" and of powerful songs that define the essence of human significance and his creation in *The Piano Lesson* of a piano that evokes ghostly presences link him to the same creative folkloristic vein as Dumas and Morrison.

The references to "the shiny man" begin Wilson's transformation of traditional supernatural and religious phenomena into African American folkloristic phenomena. Jesus is obviously the supernatural being usually slotted into black folk religious encounters, yet Wilson argues that "the shiny man" serves the same purpose of rebirth or conversion. He will similarly reclaim rituals, such as baptism, for the African American folk tradition, for it is by resorting to rituals informed by their own culture and history that black people can save themselves. Songs, which play a large role in traditional conversion processes, become equally important for Wilson in relocating the power of conversion within Afrocentric forms. The process Wilson employs constantly encourages a rewriting of history and folklore as it relocates religious expectations and patterns firmly within folkloric traditions.

Wilson creates folklore, therefore, that is recognizable even in its surface unfamiliarity. It writes the history of a people tied to the South, to racism and repression, but simultaneously to a strength that transcends those limiting categories. Like Morrison, Wilson encourages a willing suspension of disbelief about the nature of the lore he presents. He does not establish the possibility of the existence of certain phenomena; he simply writes as if they are givens. We might say that his plays begin "in medias res." A world exists; Wilson invites viewers into it. Instead of going to meet the audience by trying to *prove* belief in supernatural phenomena, Wilson unapologetically invites the audience to come into his world, to rise to his level of belief. Wilson's willingness to receive black cultural phenomena into his creative imagination is reflected in his characters' willing immersion in those same traditions and in the power they have to influence audience participation in the worlds in which they live. *Joe Turner's Come and Gone* will make these points clearer.

Wilson begins the play with a striking reversal, the first signal that his treatment of folk traditions will have an individualistic signature. The play opens with the conjure man, Bynum, publicly conducting a voodoo ceremony in the backyard of the boarding house in which he rents a room. This public spellcasting (although it is offstage, it is clearly visible to the characters onstage) places Bynum in a category unlike that of most conjure men and women. Throughout their history, most of them have retained an element of secrecy about what they do, for their very reputations have depended upon an aura of mystery. Consider, for example, Aun' Peggy in Charles Chesnutt's *The Conjure Woman* (1899) or

M'Dear in Toni Morrison's *The Bluest Eye* (1970). Both women, like most conjure people historically, live *apart* from the communities upon which they exert their power. Rumors about them are an integral part of how they function within their communities, and such rumors are absolutely crucial to the power they wield. The fact that conjurers come from an area apart from the community into the realm of the belief in their power gives them a grander, more psychologically effective appearance; the spatial distance also serves to prepare recipients mentally for the power about to be exerted in their behalf. M'Dear's appearance at Aunt Jimmy's house, for example, is a little like the parting of waters; there is awesome respect, respectful distance from her person, and respectful adherence to what she says. If she were around Aunt Jimmy's house or the community every day, the familiarity would not only lessen her power but would reduce the fear and respect people hold for her.

Wilson's improvising on this tradition is twofold. First, it reveals the difference in spatial demands on Southern and Northern territory. Cities such as Philadelphia, New York, and Chicago, to which blacks migrated, even in 1911 had far less space for isolation than the South. A consequence of black migration to the North might have been the transformation of folk traditions to the extent that a formerly private conjure ritual can become public because the Northern public is more accustomed to advertisements about such activities.[2] This Northern/Southern clash, with its attendant attitudes toward belief in folk traditions, is also reflected in the characters of Bynum and Seth, the owner of the boarding house. Placing Bynum and Seth in the same space, with Seth constantly making disparaging comments about Bynum and his rituals, comments on the inability of those who attempt to escape their folk heritage to do so in reality. Secondly, *where* Bynum performs his ceremony might be a function of genre. Stage confinements on space might require that actions be in proximity to each other. That explanation does not really suffice, however, because we could simply just *hear* of Bynum's activities and thus assume the historical mystery surrounding conjure people.

Publicizing Bynum's actions is the beginning of Wilson's revision of the function of African American lore to the people it has served over the years. By making folk traditions central instead of peripheral, public instead of private, Wilson assigns them more power and potential to influence the life view of their practitioners as well as that of the supplicants. Seth and his wife Bertha might not approve of Bynum's actions, but they cannot ignore them. And his interactions with them are so normal that they cannot say definitively that he is some kind of crackpot. Though what he does might not have specific meaning initially, it has general value; that value will be realized later in the play.

Wilson alters, slightly but perceptively, our expectations of African American tradition by similarly redefining the audiences toward whom tellers direct their narratives. Storytelling occurs at significant points in the play, one of which is shortly after Bynum performs his initial ceremony with the pigeons. He relates the tale of "the shiny man," that spiritual, otherworldly being who has determined his path as a conjure man. Although we have been introduced to Seth and Bertha, they are not the primary audience to whom Bynum directs his story; indeed, Seth is offstage at that point. He selects Selig, the white peddler/"People Finder" instead; he has earlier sent Selig in search of "the shiny man."

This choice is an intriguing one, for if we were to adhere to stereotype, we might assume that the white Selig would be less inclined to respond favorably to Bynum's tale of having encountered a shiny man and that Seth, a black man, and Bertha, a black woman, would be more receptive. So the question immediately arises as to why Wilson would have made this choice. Obviously there is the functional reason of conveying information to the viewing audience. That information immerses them in a world view that equates knowing the self with the meaning of life and that equates the meaning of life with an individual song that in turn defines the self. This circular interrelatedness of one human being to another links Bynum to "the shiny man" for whom he has hired Selig to search, and it further links the audience to the action onstage. The story of Bynum's encounter with "the shiny man" therefore begins the process of "Africanizing the audience"[3] that is inherent in Wilson's presenting the lore as a given rather than arguing for its acceptance. I use the phrase "Africanizing the audience" to encompass the white viewers who undoubtedly made up the majority of the viewing audience for Wilson's play; of course African Americans in the audience would simply have their beliefs reinforced, or—in the case of those upwardly mobile (like Seth) who have forgotten their roots—reclaimed. The immediate audience (Selig) and the viewing audience are thus simultaneously encouraged to a different way of perceiving reality, to understanding that it is possible to see around corners, as the Invisible Man would say. Selig's skepticism might mirror that of those viewing the play, but neither can erase from memory Bynum's tale of "the shiny man." Wilson thereby gives whites no choice but to become immersed in a black reality.

The tale of "the shiny man" introduces the idea of journeying toward the full potential of self by recognizing the nascent value inherent within the self. The pattern is legendary and familiar in that a stranger assists the narrator to a new level of understanding; as a result, the narrator receives a mission that he in turn must pass on to another lost soul. With its overtones of religious conversion, Bynum's encounter with "the shiny man" places new emphasis on folkloristic material by suggesting that it indeed functions *as* religion. Bynum's travels with "the shiny man" are not unlike those of the penitent who meets Jesus, and the encounter results in a beatific transformation. When Bynum is told to rub his hands together and to wash himself with the blood that issues forth, echoes of being "washed in the blood of the Lamb" certainly come to the minds of those knowlegeable about the African American folk religious tradition. The image of the sparrow and the flash of light to which Bynum is exposed continue these parallels. When the stranger departs from him and

Bynum meets his long-dead father, other echoes of traditional and religious journeys are evoked. Bynum's father, in the role of helper, leads him to an ocean (in contrast to the River Jordan of religious tradition), shows him visions, and teaches him how to find the song that enables him to bind people to each other. The "Binding Song" (reflecting his name—"bind them") is the essence of who he is. Legend and myth, then, have practical purposes in the world in that they directly influence people's lives. With this entertwining of the secular and the sacred, Wilson suggests that the secular *is* the sacred. That equation is certainly a significant expansion from perceived ways of viewing African American folk traditions.

Wilson's use of "the shiny man" is the primary part of his rewriting of the savior motif in religious practices; another part is his use of the "bones people." Loomis' vision of the "bones people" similarly interweaves Christianity with mythology. That the bones people walk on water without sinking certainly evokes Jesus, but the phenomeonon more immediately evokes for Wilson's characters African American history and the enormity of the loss of lives and human potential during the middle passage. In the biblical tradition of Ezekiel 37:3 ("Son of man, can these bones live?") and the popular African American sermon where various bones are connected to each other to stand on their own as a result of "hearing the word of the Lord," the bones Loomis observes take on flesh and move forward from their dehumanized states; they stand on their own feet in ways that Herald Loomis is currently unable to effect. Thus Wilson uses the tale not only to "Africanize the audience," but to "Africanize" or signify on Judeo-Western Christian myths by adapting them to black history. The vision, which Bynum has apparently also seen because he can "respond" to Herald's "calling" forth of the story, is another representational level of the need to liberate the self, to find the best in the self and move forward with it. The story is a creation myth, reshaped to suggest that human beings can stand in in the role of god in shaping their own destinies; for black men to do so, they must also reshape the dehumanizing myth of the middle passage and move toward mental freedom. When Herald Loomis is able to stand on his own, that forward progress will be available to him.

Wilson further inverts Western mythology by denying that white men are altruistic or that they are the ultimate center of the universe around which everything else revolves. Joe Turner, the legendary white man who has shaped Herald Loomis's life, epitomizes this point; he enables Wilson to rewrite history even as he is in the process of redefining the meaning and function of folklore. Turner could rightfully be viewed as the devil, or even worse than that, for if he merely took people's souls, that would be an end to their misery.[4] By stealing their lives and their potential—without killing them—he consigns them to the fate of zombies. Men like Loomis become automatons, destined to live out the fate that others have prescribed for them, existing because they lack the imagination or the will to take their own lives. Loomis has committed the sin that Grange Copeland accused his son Brownfield of having committed; by blaming the white man for everything, he has made him into a god. Long after Loomis has been granted freedom several years ago—on Joe Turner's birthday—he still belongs to that man's definition of black male human beings. Lacking the will to extricate himself from his own history, or to change his life from the single-minded purpose of finding his wife, Loomis is so out of touch with the best in himself that he could not possibly have been a good father to the daughter he has paraded around for seven years in search of her mother. In order for Loomis to become a shiny man, he must lift himself from the pages of the ink that Turner has used to inscribe his life.

Turner looms over Loomis's past, his present, and his future. As an archetypal symbol of racism and repression, he is not simply a man, but a force. He represents the evil that takes away all the potential identified with black men, whether that evil historically took the form of slavery, sharecropping, or convict labor as a result of being jailed without any semblance of due process. He represents the collective failure of American democracy for all black people, the dismissal of the race from the American dream. It is not necessary for Turner to appear as a character in the play for the destructive history of his collective representation to be felt. As long as Herald Loomis lives, so will Joe Turner. As long as Bynum sings songs about this black male snatcher, he will live. Memory is stronger than experience, and as long as Joe Turner has captured the memories and imaginations of the men he jailed, he remains a part of their lives. His significance can obviously be diminished, however, in direct proportion to Loomis' ability to find the power and path to exorcise from the recesses of his being the negative effects of his encounter with Turner.

It is noteworthy that Loomis equates Martha and Joe Turner as the "stopping points" in his life, the time at which the fire of his potential was reduced to embers and when his mere existence began. He needs to find Martha in order to get "a starting place in the world" (72). It is almost as if he wishes to perform a rite of exorcism, one that can be accomplished when he hands over his daughter Zonia to Martha. Martha becomes a negative as well as a positive symbol in the text. By equating her with Turner as halting his life, Loomis evokes comparison to characters such as Bigger Thomas and Silas in Richard Wright's works; both blame black women for their plights and both link black women to a conspiring white oppressive system. Stereotypically, therefore, in answer to the question, "Who oppresses black men?", the response is "black women." This substitution of Turner with Martha and of the psychological effect of Turner with Martha's departure enables Loomis to make legends of both of them. In neither instance has he arrived at the state of being willing to take personal responsibility for his own future in the world. If we view Martha as more representative than human, however, her last name—Pentecost—and her ties to Christianity place her in the position of another unhealthy binding force from which Loomis must extricate himself.

The story that Loomis tells of having been caught in Turner's net reveals the extent of his continuing mental imprisonment. He relates the narrative almost in a trancelike state, as if he were re-experiencing the horrors of being under Turner's control. His narrative reveals the tranformative power Joe Turner has held over him, for his entrapment has forced him to wander "a long time in somebody else's world" (72). As Bynum recognizes, because Loomis has lived his life according to the directives of someone else's script, or their impact, he has forgotten his song. Exorcising Joe Turner from the essence of his being, the initial stage of which is turning his daughter Zonia over to her mother, will enable Loomis to move forward as a healthier, saner human being. Certainly Zonia is an innocent being, but she is tied to the Christian heritage that Martha represents; she thereby becomes more representational than individualistic. Giving her to her mother is another indication of Loomis' moving away from the confines of Western mythology—a painful process, but one that he and black people generally must nonetheless undertake.

Joe Turner, Bynum posits, captures black men because he wants their song, their souls. That song encompasses whatever black people can use to survive oppression. If Joe Turner takes it away, or represses black men so much that they become too stupefied to retain a will to survive, then he has won. What Loomis needs is comparable to what Hurston describes in her essay on High John the Conqueror; he needs the transcendant spirit of laughter and song, broadly interpreted, that will enable him to survive. Hurston identifies that spirit with a song and with the flying Africans who were able to lift up from their oppressive American burdens and fly back to Africa. If Joe Turner can suppress that alternative vision, that innate sense of trusting one's own reality, that singing spirit, then he can destroy a race of people without killing a single one of them.[5]

Singing and song in the play, then, have historical, folkloristic, religious/spiritual/metaphysical connotations. Not only do they represent the blues essence of the experience someone like Herald Loomis has undergone, but they also represent the voicing of the African American presence in the world—unchained physically and psychologically. Bynum's songs ("The Healing Song" and "The Binding Song") and the one that Loomis will shortly receive are pre-blues and post-gospel; they were there at the beginning of black presence in America and will transcend all the limitations of the early American experiences. In his presentation of African American folk forms, Wilson suggests that there is something almost preternatural about black people. When unburdened by societal repressions, they uncover or recover the sources of strength that guided their African and American forebears. Songs are literally and Figuratively a claim for unfettered being in the world, one for which each individual must bear the weight of his or her own physical and spiritual health. Communities of black people can offer assistance, but the ultimate responsibility belongs to the individual.

The redefining functions of history and folklore enter when Loomis can rewrite his personal history and move into the collective mythical possibilities of black manhood.[6] In finally giving voice to the fact that "Joe Turner's come and gone" (91), Loomis begins to understand that the past must be laid to rest;

the negative effects of his past life should be "gone" or certainly going. The future is available to him only when he can realize, like Sethe Suggs and Ralph Kabnis, that the pain of the past can finally have no claim on new lives. In rejecting traditional Christianity and bleeding for himself, Loomis achieves ultimate responsibility for his being in the world, which may be viewed as a state of godhead. Wilson uses our understanding of folk traditions to move Loomis to the level of myth and legend. As a designated shiny man, stories will surely develop about him as the stories have about the man Bynum encountered. And as a person with a newly discovered song of self-sufficiency, he will have the power to influence other people's lives.

Wilson's most conspicuous adaptation of African American history and folklore occurs in his bringing Joe Turner from the confines of song to the flesh of villainy. Wilson also collapses color consideration in the play. While Joe Turner might have been reputed in legend to have been a horrible *white* chain gang captain, the *documentable* history is that Joe Turner was a *black* blues singer as well as the title of a song. Eileen Southern, the African American musicologist, identifies Turner with Jimmy Rushing and others of the Kansas City ("Kaycee") school of blues singers and musicians.[7] The song, "Joe Turner," has been recorded in a single extended stanza:

> They tell me that Joe Turner's come and gone,
> Oh, Lord!
> They tell me that Joe Turner's come and gone,
> Got my man and gone.
> He come with forty links of chain,
> Oh, Lord!
> He come with forty links of chain,
> Got my man and gone.[8]

Wilson has managed some ingenious overlapping with the use of "Joe Turner." Since the original blues singer was male, and the original singer of the song itself was obviously female (lamenting in classic blues fashion the separation from her man), Wilson has incorporated both genders into the traditions that he presents just as effectively as he manages to work his themes across generations in the play.

Believed to be one of the—if not *the*—earliest blues songs, "Joe Turner" voices the susceptibility of black males to life on Southern chain gangs (a recurring theme in blues and work songs). Reduced in its published version to its essential elements, the song recounts how Joe Turner (obviously white by virtue of his full name and the action he effects) has removed a black man (obvious by the blues labeling, "my man," and the anonymity characteristic of white rule over generic black lives) through force ("forty links of chain") to a place that the plaintive tone suggests will be worse than hell. The word "gone" speaks volumes in its uncertainty in reference to condition and in its finality in reference to chronology.

By making Joe Turner a living white, legendary villain, Wilson gives flesh to the force that has historically separated black men from black women, that is, the white man—whether he did so through the sharecropping system or lynching black men or locking them away in jails with little possibility of escape. Joe Turner, as the characters in the play recall him, therefore personifies the *state* of the blues that has historically been imposed upon black people externally and the conditions that gave rise to the *singing* of blues songs. If the conditions that define some portions of the blues are white-derived, then black people have a conscious target at which they can direct actions for ending that blues state. It relocates power within them as they revitalize the forces within themselves that can destroy a Joe Turner. Simply singing about him in the blues form provides only temporary relief through the act of singing itself or through the cathartic function of the blues, as Langston Hughes so graphically presents that function in "The Weary Blues." The personification of Joe Turner as the state of the blues leads to a permanent way of exorcising that condition from black lives. This is not to eliminate blues *singing,* but the state that has led to the *need* for that singing. The songs can remain an art form without the attendant oppression, in this case, that has made them necessary. Joe Turner, in the last analysis, emblematizes the end of the state of the blues for Herald Loomis. By negating the potential that others have to capture his mind, body, and spirit, he can now turn to the best possibilities for creativity *within* himself, whether that creativity takes the form of singing (blues songs or otherwise) or something else.

This rewriting of the history and the song also places Wilson in league with other black writers. In writing about his experiences in Oklahoma City, ones that influenced his composition of *Invisible Man,* Ralph Ellison has commented on hearing Jimmy Rushing and other blues and jazz musicians perform (even at the Sunset Club in Kansas City).[9] In capturing the essence of the blues in the novel—not only in its compositional form, but in its ethos as well—Ellison included a blues song entitled "Peetie Wheet Straw." Some researchers claim that there was a historical figure of this name, and others identify the baggy pants black man with the wheelbarrow full of blueprints as "Peetie Wheet Straw." As a part of his bantering interaction with the Invisible Man, the little man says: "I'll verse you but I won't curse you—My name is Peter Wheatstraw, I'm the Devil's only son-in-law, so roll' em!"[10] The original song consists of these lines:

> I am Peetie Wheet Straw, the high sheriff of hell,
> I am Peetie Wheet Straw, the high sheriff of hell,
> And when I lock you up, baby, you're locked in a dungeon cell.

> I am Peetie Wheet Straw, the devil's son-in-law,
> I am Peelie Wheet Straw, the devil's son-in-law,
> The woman I married, old Satan was her paw.[11]

"Peetie Wheatstraw" was a blues signature; any bluesman could sign off with that name and therefore exhibit his ties to a history and a community of singers and songs, to a collectivity of experiences. The point is that transformation of blues, blues character, and form precedes Wilson and claims him for a tradition of such transformation in African American texts.

While Wilson's characterizations of Loomis and Bynum redefine the value of blues history and song, he debunks the romantic myth of the traveling blues man in the character of Jeremy. Black traveling blues men, so the mythology goes, strung their guitars and a small bundle of clothing over their shoulders and left the rural South for better territory in the urban centers of the South and the North. Langston Hughes offered an earlier version of the type in *Not Without Laughter* (1930), and Albert Murray immortalized the character in the person of Old Luze in *Train Whistle Guitar* (1974). Old Luze might hop a freight train and disappear for months on end, but he has high moral values, including encouraging his young would-be imitators to pursue their education. Jeremy, by contrast, has the country aura and a fast-talking desire for women, but he is lacking in values. He plays his guitar more out of a love for money than a love for music, and there is never any clear indication of how good a musician he really is. Jeremy, then, becomes local color for the migration north instead of a character who engages us because of some heartfelt tie to his music or to the history out of which the music evolved. Wilson strips the type of his romantic veneer and delivers him up as the superficial, unscrupulous womanizer that he is.

Such developments indicate again that Wilson is constantly revising the folklore, reinscribing it with features that enhance his own purposes. While Molly is on the scene ready to be the woman stealer of traditional blues, Mattie is there waiting for Loomis to get beyond his living blues and into a healthier male/female interaction; they thereby trade superficial romance for a deeper engagement with blues phenomenon, one that affirms cohesion rather than separation, and one that operates like Bynum's "Binding song." By transforming the blues from connotations of opression to connotations of liberation, Wilson can thus make the tradition elastic enough to achieve his goals without distorting it beyond a recognizable folk form.

Loomis' symbolic and literal transformation from the clutches of Joe Turner and Bynum's encounter with "the shiny man" are the major folkloristic occurrences in the play, but Wilson also saturates his drama with the richness of other African American folk traditions. In addition to the blues—and the history that spawned the blues—he textures the play with ghostlore and fetish animals, as well as with folk beliefs such as sprinkling salt to ward off bad luck and with the characters engaging in Juba, "a call and response dance" (52). We can certainly say that Bynum's encounter with "the shiny man" is a ghostly experience of sorts. And Loomis' relation of the story of the "bones people" similarly has its ghostly aura. Wilson cuts across generations, however, to suggest that the entire community is heir to these kinds of occurrences.

One of the children in the play, Reuben, sees the ghost of Miss Mabel, Seth's long dead mother. She instructs him to release the pigeons he had promised his dead friend Eugene that he would release. He relates the occurrence to Zonia, who, after an initial incredulousness, rather quickly believes in the ghost. The ease with which they accept this incident (they move from discussing Miss Mabel's appearance to sharing their first kiss) points again to the texturing of the culture with folkloristic forms. It is not unduly scary or unusual for these children to see something supernatural, just as it is not unusual for their adult counterparts—Bynum and Loomis—to have extranatural experiences.[12]

The major fetish animal in the play is really a bird: the pigeon. Bynum sacrifices pigeons in the binding ceremonies he performs in the back of the boarding house. While flight motifs are endemic to African American culture, ranging from tales of flying Africans to stories of pilots at Tuskegee's flight school during World War II to Morrison's *Song of Solomon*, pigeons are not omnipresent characters in the lore. African American folktales frequently include buzzards—as Hurston does in *Their Eyes Were Watching God*—but pigeons do not appear with any regularity. Wilson's inclusion of them, therefore, reflects another expansion in his use of folk materials.

So the question becomes, "What kinds of connotations do pigeons carry for spell-casting ceremonies?" As a "binder," Bynum ties the lives of his clients to the persons for whom they are searching. He has tied Zonia to Martha, thereby making it inevitable that Loomis and Zonia will eventually find their way to the boarding house. Even as he pays Selig to assist in this effort, he knows that his magic is stronger. By pouring pigeon blood into the ground, the power of flight inherent in the bird is reversed, grounded so to speak, in a way that will ensure the eventual gathering of the separated mother and daughter at the boarding house. Loomis is almost coincidental to the binding that Bynum has effected with Martha and Zonia, but Bynum nevertheless has him under a spell to the extent that he feels obligated to bring his daughter to her mother. Bynum repeats his ceremonies more frequently after Loomis and Zonia arrive and while Selig is looking for Martha.

Pigeons, devoid of the message-carrying function usually associated with them[13] (or that function has also been transformed), become themselves the message in the case of Miss Mabel's demanding that they be freed. Eugene, she says, is waiting for them. Releasing the pigeons would mean that Reuben is honoring the friendship he had with Eugene and recognizing—in a healthier fashion than keeping the pigeons locked up—the ties he has to his dead friend. The incident becomes a microcosmic expression of the influence of the past upon the present, the dead upon the living, that is being acted out with the grown-ups in the play. Releasing the pigeons will enable Eugene, a part of the past, to rest in peace, just as delivering his daughter will become part of the process of Loomis' settling of the past and claiming of peace. Releasing the pigeons becomes a transformative metaphor for the path away from stagnation, away from holding on to Eugene *as he was;* realizing that Eugene is not bound to the frozen point at which Reuben remembers him enables Reuben to move to a different psychological space. When Loomis realizes that he is not bound by Joe Turner's definitions, he in turn can move to a different mental territory. That the incident with the children precedes Loomis' transformation illustrates again the circularity of the drama that moves events and beliefs across younger and older generations.

The circularity is in itself indicative of African American folk traditions, for scholars long studying the culture have emphasized that blacks prefer circularity to linearity. Circularity in children's games, such as "Little Sally Walker," allows for more cooperation than competition and for greater inclusion in the telling of tales or with other activities among adults. The circular imagery also suggests a return to the best in the self as well as a return to the African cultural forms that underlie African American existence. Only by returning to the possibility he saw in himself *before* Joe Turner snatched him can Loomis move beyond his incarceration and the dead years that he has allowed to follow it.

It is of note, as well, that Wilson is not squeamish about the sacrifice of pigeons in his play. His willingness to have Seth describe Bynum's ceremonies so graphically indicates that he has not acquiesced to any contemporary societal mores about proper decorum. As a part of nature, as a part of a world where Joe Turner can claim men's souls, it is not a significant trespass that pigeons pay the price for the reuniting of a mother and daughter or for the reclaiming of one of those lost souls. Taking the culture as it is, not sanitizing it to placate the potentially hostile or antagonistic, is a conscious creative decision on Wilson's part.

In transforming history and reclaiming/revitalizing culture, Wilson outlines the process for Loomis to redefine himself as a man. African American folk belief, then, becomes the bridge over which Loomis walks to his manhood. It is also the road by which he finally travels to freedom. When Wilson uses secular mythology as the source of religious conversion and overwrites Christianity with African American folkways, he merges the secular and the sacred in ways that few African American authors have attempted. Centering Loomis' evolution into a shiny man upon his own blood as a cleansing agent, Wilson brings the hoodoo man into the pulpit, allowing him to become the sermon that those merely baptized in the blood of the Lamb can only imagine. His own blood enables Loomis to stand on his own two feet, like the bones people, and shape a future unfettered by traditional Christianity and its attendant themes of suffering and repression.[14]

NOTES

[1] For an extensive discussion of this phenomenon in Morrison's work, see my *Fiction and Folklore: The Novels of Toni Morrison* (Tennessee, 1991). In creating myths of sentient islands in *Tar Baby* (1981) and of the dead returned to life in *Beloved* (1987),

Morrison joined Dumas, who created myths of many otherworldly phenomena, including an "ark of bones," in his stories. Wilson's counterpart is a tale of the "bones people."

[2] Consider, for example, the Prophet David in Ann Petry's *The Street* (1946). David is a Northern version of a Southern phenomenon and reflects the segment of folk belief that would eventually lead to advertisement by business card and newspaper ads, the kinds of things that would eventually be manifested in faith healers.

[3] I coined the phrase "Africanizing the audience" to discuss authors I am treating in my latest book project, "In the African Southern Vein: Narrative Strategies in the Works of Zora Neale Hurston, Gloria Naylor, and Tina McElroy Ansa."

[4] Charles Johnson includes a character called the "Soulcatcher" in *Oxherding Tale* (Bloomington: Indiana University Press, 1982). That character and idea epitomize what Wilson intends in Joe Turner. I am grateful to Keith Clark and Valerie Matthews for pointing out this connection.

[5] What Joe Turner wants is also comparable to what Alice Walker describes in her short story, "1955," or "the Elvis story." A white male singer records a song from a black woman. Although it is successful and he makes a lot of money from it, he returns to her again and again looking for the indescribable something that he believes is missing from his rendition of the song. That something represents the core of her blackness, the innermost part of her will and spirit that he can never co-opt but that he continually tries to harness. If he can harness it, then he achieves not only the monetary success but the spiritual aura that stands behind that success. He is similar to Octavia Butler's Doro, sapping the energy of those upon whom he preys to the point that they are figuratively lifeless.

[6] Compare to Milkman Dead at the end of Morrison's *Song of Solomon* (1977) or Son Green at the end of *Tar Baby* (1981).

[7] See *The Music of Black Americans: A History* (New York: Norton, 1971), 390, 401.

[8] Included in Langston Hughes and Arna Bontemps, *The Book of Negro Folklore* (New York: Dodd, Mead & Company, 1958), 392.

[9] See Ellison's "The Golden Age, Time Past" in *Shadow and Act* (New York: Vintage, 1964), 206.

[10] Ralph Ellison, *Invisible Man* (1952; Rpt. New York: Vintage, 1972), 134.

[11] Muriel Davis Longini, "Folk Songs of Chicago Negroes," *Journal of American Folklore* 52, (1939): 108.

[12] Wilson continues to show his kinship to Dumas ("Ark of Bones" and other works), Toni Cade Bambara (*The Salt Eaters,* 1980), Morrison (*Beloved* and other works), and Tina McElroy Ansa (*Baby of the Family,* 1989) in the naturalness with which he treats interactions between the world of the living and the world of the dead.

[13] Keith Clark suggests that killing the pigeons may be another way for Wilson to signify on white culture. The whole idea of transmitting messages has been used to "bind" black people to a certain position and a certain role ("nigger") in the society. Killing these symbolic messengers negates the power of white American culture to shape black lives.

[14] I want to thank Keith Clark for reading this essay and providing several excellent suggestions for refinements, elaborations, and clarifications.

Works Cited

Bambara, Toni Cade. *The Salt Eaters.* New York: Random House, 1980.

Chesnutt, Charles. *The Conjure Woman.* 1899; Rpt. Ann Arbor: University of Michigan Press, 1969.

Ellison, Ralph. *Invisible Man.* 1952; New York: Vintage, 1972.

———. *Shadow and Act.* 1964; Rpt. New York: Signet, 1966.

Harris, Trudier. *Fiction and Folklore: The Novels of Toni Morrison.* Knoxville: University of Tennessee Press, 1991.

Hughes, Langston, and Arna Bontemps. *The Book of Negro Folklore.* New York: Dodd, Mead & Company, 1958.

Hughes, Langston. *Not Without Laughter.* 1930; Rpt. New York: Macmillan, 1969.

Johnson, Charles. *Oxherding Tale.* Bloomington: Indiana University Press, 1982.

Longini, Muriel Davis. "Folk Songs of Chicago Negroes." *Journal of American Folklore,* 52 (1939): 108.

Morrison, Toni. *Beloved.* New York: Knopf, 1987.

———. *The Bluest Eye.* New York: Holt, Rinehart, and Winston, 1970.

———. *Song of Solomon.* New York: Knopf, 1977.

———. *Tar Baby.* New York: Knopf, 1981.

Murray, Albert. *Train Whistle Guitar.* New York: McGraw-Hill, 1974.

Southern, Eileen. *The Music of Black Americans: A History.* New York: Norton, 1971.

Walker, Alice. "1955." In *You Can't Keep a Good Woman Down.* New York: Harcourt Brace Jovanovich, 1981.

Wilson, August. *Joe Turner's Come and Gone.* New York: Plume/New American Library, 1988.

The Artist in the Garden: Theatre Space and Place in Lanford Wilson

Thomas P. Adler

In his essay "Writing for Films," William Inge—whose plays share with several of Lanford Wilson's a distinctively midwestern setting—comments on the spatial limitations that would seem to restrict the dramatist's art: "In the theatre," Inge asserts, "one is always confined to the dimensions of the stage. . . . Writing for the theatre has its own satisfactions, but mobile geography is not one of them" (1). Such overstatement—some would argue inaccuracy—is understandable if one equates serious drama with a realistic set (the traditional room with an imaginary fourth wall separating audience from acting area) that allows for unity of place, at least within the acts. From Inge's perspective, the fluidity of moving from locale to locale and the possibility for simultaneity of action are properties associated with the freer medium of film rather than with theatrical realism.

And yet, from another perspective, just as the world in realistic film continues outside the boundary of the frame, the place in even a realistic play need not be contiguous with the stage space it inhabits but can be made to extend beyond it. As Bert O. States argues, "what the drama, of all the arts, requires is a way of allowing the stage to contain things outside of it and to make visible things that are invisible" (65), If it is true, as States says, "that the characters explicate the setting in their dialogue as one explicates a painting—at the same time, of course, [that] the setting is explicating character pictorially" (67), it is equally true that characters can create scenery rhetorically, out of nothing but words, that is unseen except in the mind's eye. Indeed, one of the characteristics—almost peculiarities—of Wilson's dozen full-length dramas is how frequently important places, rather than being visually represented, remain noticeably absent from the stage set.

In *Burn This* (1987), Wilson's most recent long play, the central character Anna, herself a dancer, defines choreographers by remarking: "They make the dance. You have bodies, space, sculptural mass, distance relationships; if they're lucky, they might even discover they have something to say" (36). Anna's comment could apply just as easily to the challenge facing the dramatist, who must take people and inanimate objects and position them in space, and move them through space, in such a way that the visual form will carry at least part of the play's meaning. The action of *Burn This* occurs in a *"huge"* white-walled Manhattan loft that features *"an exercise barre on one mirrored wall"* and *"a large framed dance poster"* (2) as the only decoration. The loft was home to Anna, to Larry, a gay advertising designer, and to Robbie, also a dancer like Anna who drowned in a boating accident with his homosexual lover before the play opens and whose sleeping loft is an element of the setting, making the absent present. During the play, Anna's lover Burton, a Hollywood filmwriter who has just returned from Canada where "land [that] looks like the moon, all gouged out," did not prevent his feeling a connection with "something" and inspiring a new story (10), will be displaced from Anna's life by the intruder Pale, Robbie's brother and a rather unlikely Jersey restaurateur.

In this work about dance, however, no dancing—not even practice or warm-up exercises—is ever seen. Though insinuated on the audience by the barre and mirror, dance in any traditional sense is relegated to unseen places (a rehearsal space, a recital hall stage) to indicate the divorce between art and life that Anna undergoes when she suffers the loss of her partner/mentor. When Anna turns choreographer, though, the connection reasserts itself as she draws upon the sexual maneuvering of her relationship with Pale for the subject of her dance, which can only be created once she, like any artist, has the essential "life experience to draw from" (59). As Larry who is present at the recital remarks to Burton, "The dance she's done is Pale and Anna"; his power to render that sculptured movement into words fails, however, since "you might as well try to describe a piece of music" (107). Pale, too, understands "That was me and [Anna] up there" on stage (112), and they seem powerless to stop in life an impulsive and intensely charged affair which may or may not end tragically but that has now been formalized through art.

The title of Wilson's play makes explicit the desired intersection of life and art: Burton advises Anna to "make [her dance] as personal as you can. . . . tell the truth, and then write 'Burn this' on it" (67)—words which Wilson himself etched on each page of his manuscript-in-progress. The playwright's injunction to himself, then, tacitly attests to the artist's frightening power, indeed necessity, to eradicate the line between life and art. Anna's dance is analogous to Wilson's play: both are representations that mysteriously transcend the thing being represented. Because the theatre audience never actually sees the dance performed, they, however, become aware that for them the disjunction between the life and the art remains. For the spectator there will always be an absence, a something unseen, at the very center of any work of art. It is the urge to fill this void which occasions the interpretive act.

No single visual element—unless it be the *"intense"* and blast-like "white-hot sunlight" (3) streaking into the interior of a mission in New Mexico—points to the unseen places in close proximity to this small church that dominate Wilson's *Angels Fall* (1982): a uranium mine where an accident has just occurred; the reactor at Los Alamos; the missile base at White Sands; an already polluted water supply; plus the prospect of a new dump for waste nearby. Turned back by the army from their westward journeys, several travelers arrive at this hallowed "sanctuary" seeking succor and protection, some of them finding renewed direction for their lives. The anomaly of a mission church surrounded by things nuclear and radioactive points to the worship of energy, the fascination with—even for some the attraction of—humankind's power to unleash apocalyptic destruction, as the new god in an age of unfaith.

As is true of one's response to art, faith requires a suspension of disbelief. So when Niles, a professor of art history (ironically hailing from Providence), undergoes a questioning of the increasingly "dogmatic" way in which he plied his vocation, sensing "a disturbance in [his] willful suspension of disbelief that allowed [him] to see what [he] had done for what it was" (35), Father Doherty deems Niles's "crisis of faith" as "right in [his] wheelhouse" (93). Doherty himself seems to be experiencing some disillusionment with his efficacy as priest: when the dozen or so Indians come to mass, he reports, "I mumble sincerely, they mumble sincerely, and they shuffle out. . . . Nothing on their faces, probably nothing on mine. In and out. Shuffle—shuffle" (63). He regards much more religiously his role as father-figure to Don Tabaha, a young Indian doctor ready to choose a lucrative and potentially noteworthy life as a medical researcher over ministering to his people.

Niles becomes the teacher of Doherty, counselling him that it might be his own vanity and selfishness that want Don to remain rather than answer the "call" of his "very special talent for research" (102). For everyone—teacher, artist, priest, doctor, athlete—"is called"; and, as Zappy the professional tennis player says, when one hears the call, "magic . . . happens and you know who you are" (96). This notion of calling or vocation is central to *Angels Fall,* which has to do finally with how we live, "what manner of persons ought [we] to be" when our daily existence is punctuated with "these rehearsals for the end of the world" (94–95). The disembodied voice from a helicopter announcing "'The road is clear'" (98) may recall the biblical injunction to make straight the path. The immediate threat may be ended, but the all-pervasive danger of annihilation in the blast of white light is still present. The pilgrims must leave their temporary sanctuary and go out into perilous places to live and work.

If the New York of *Burn This* and the New Mexico of *Angels Fall* were once places (east and west) of promise, they have now been blighted by urban unease and nuclear dust, and their "artist" inhabitants, that is, all those following their special callings, must now pursue those vocations outside the garden, so to speak. But in *5th of July* (1978), the garden, this time in the midwest and in the process of being restored—albeit offstage—is still an operative image. Several strains apparent in the two later plays appeared earlier in *5th of July.* Shirley, the youngest member of the Talley clan, has vowed to become a writer, even if this means the loneliness of never marrying; she stresses the link between one's life experiences and creativity, proclaiming: "I happen to, am going to be an artist, and an artist has no age and must force himself to see everything, no matter how disgusting and how low!" (27) Her uncle Ken, a double amputee who felt uneasy about coming home alive from the Vietnam War and who has sensed the invisibility imposed upon veterans when others refuse to "look" at them out of shame or guilt, overcomes the temptation to give up teaching and recommits himself to his calling, to his "mission" in life. And her great aunt Sally asserts the need for not succumbing to negativity and despair, opting for the continuation of life in the face of aloneness and death: "I've always had the feeling death wasn't all it was cracked up to be. . . . Matt [Friedman, her late husband] didn't believe in death and I don't either. . . . There's no such thing. It goes on and then it stops. You can't worry about the stopping, you have to worry about the going on" (114).

These characters resist the lure of other places (Shirley of Nashville, Ken of St. Louis, Sally of California) for the pull of the ancestral Talley home, *"a prosperous southern Missouri farmhouse built around 1860"* (5), whose family room and porch function as the setting for the play. Jed, Ken's lover, who has gradually been replanting the property in the manner of a traditional English garden that will take years and years to mature, recently rediscovered a lost rose which will "once, again be propagated and grown" at Sissinghurst Castle in England, "the greatest rose garden in the world" (82–83). If necessary, Sally herself will buy the Talley "place" so that it will not go out of the family and to save it from those who would build an air, strip on the property—especially now that she and Jed have spread Matt's ashes in the rose garden. So the remains of this man who thirty years ago had been rejected by Sally's father and brother for his Jewishness and liberal political views will now, as Gene A. Barnett suggests (112), fertilize the soil, just as the commitment of the younger generation to, in Shirley's words, "find your vocation and work like hell at it" (128) will renew the Talley clan. Jed, in his planting of the garden and his caring for and loving the disabled Ken, is the new Adam inspiring a sense of purpose and restoring a feeling of community after the fall. On all planes, the archetypal, the natural, the familial, the individual, the movement in *5th of July* is from death to resurrection and rebirth.

No similar sense of restoration from the diminution that has overtaken the past pervades—or is even the least bit apparent in—Wilson's *The Gingham Dog* (1969); this play about the desolation of an interracial marriage is among the darkest of the dramatist's works, precisely because it shows the breakdown in community without any subsequent rebuilding. The decline of Gloria and Vincent's young marriage into a battlefield of invective where both have lost the capacity for caring can be charted largely through imagery of unseen places described by the characters. Unlike the warm and lived-in Talley home in *5th of July,* the *"compulsively clean"* yet "sterile" apartment painted "refrigerator white" (4–5) in *Dog* is denuded, the emptiness signaling the breakdown of a marriage. Although not nearly as upscale, the flat in which they first lived was affectionately called "the Hutch," since it was the site of spontaneous parties after basketball games on the street outside; that sense of community and camaraderie has vanished, and among the props only "a *deflated basketball*" (33) remains from those days. Vincent describes the room at the "Y" into which he has moved as an insult to the Christians, "a renovated chicken coop" spraypainted "speckledy-spackledy" to look like "pigeon droppings" (50–51); and Gloria recalls that in Harlem where she "lived in misery . . . every apartment is wall-to-wall screaming and filth, every pore of the rotting building you live in is death" (27).

By far the major symbols undergirding Wilson's overt social commentary are the buildings that Vincent designs. Whether an "architect" (that is, an artist) as he claims, or simply a "draftsman" as Gloria insists, she describes his structures in terms that explicitly connect the urban ghettos with the genocide committed in the Nazi concentration camps: "a crematorium . . . uninhabitable brick ovens. Hi-rise slums" with "the physical dimensions of hell" that, rather than "elevate the spirit," only "elevate the floor" (28–29, 32). Although Vincent can try to rationalize away the result by claiming a good intention, Gloria judges that motive vitiated by a heartless system which feeds the rich at the expense of the poor. Not only is there no garden here, but no artist either.

This same contrast between the past and a somehow diminished present (and future) informs two of Wilson's plays that, rather than employ offstage or only talked about places, feature highly symbolic settings. The more straightforward of the two in its handling of theatrical space is *The Hot l Baltimore* (1973), set on Memorial Day in the lobby of a once *"elegant"* railroad hotel now *"scheduled for demolition"* (xi). Similar in atmosphere to the set of a theatre under the wrecking ball created by Boris Aronson for the Stephen Sondheim/Jerome Weidman musical *Follies* (1972), the scene design of *Hot l* calls not for an absolutely realistic rendering but for a somewhat impressionistic *"lobby. . . represented by three areas that rise as the remains of a building already largely demolished: the Front Desk, the lounge, and the stairway"* (xiii). Wilson's extra-dramatic comment that *"The theater, evanescent itself, and for all we do perhaps itself disappearing here, seems the ideal place for the representation of the impermanence of our architecture"* (xiii) clues the reader into change and decay as central motifs of his play.

The work builds not only on the dichotomy between past and present, but on those between country and city, permanence and progress, and, as in Chekhov, beauty and use. The young call girl listens ardently for the whistle of the train that could whisk her away into "the country. That's still beautiful;

some of it" (30). The trains, however, have declined, so that "you have to close your eyes on [one]," they never run on time anymore and "they've let the roadbeds go to hell" (30). If the machine in the garden was not at first a destructive intrusion, the symbiotic balance between technology and culture has long since been lost. Jackie, one of the hotel's temporary residents, decries processed foods and environmental pollution and, in her urge to rediscover some connection to rootedness with the earth, wants to go west, though the piece of land she is swindled into buying in Utah is worthless.

At one time, urban areas could be "beautiful," as were hotels such as the Hot l; now all that is changed, not only through neglect but through "the vultures" (129) who honor materialism and greed more than the cultural heritage of the past and the quality of life in the present. The play's symbolic network, then, hardly supports the note of affirmation that Wilson inserts at the end: although the prostitute April Green—whose "symbolic" name indicates a "life-loving and life-giving. . . . earth-mother/mistress" (Barnett 92)—enters into a ritual dance with Jamie, the brother Jackie has left behind, and although her gutsy, non-defeatist attitude that you must have "the convictions of your passions" and that "the important thing is to *move*" (142; 145) might echo other Wilson characters like Niles and Sally, this glorification of the down-but-never-outs of society as "repositories of its wisdom" (Kalem 96) here seems forced and hollow.

On the other hand, closure in *Serenading Louie* (1970; revised version, 1984) grows organically from all the dramaturgical elements, including Wilson's inventive handling of locale. *Louie* crosscuts between the disintegrating marriages of two suburban Chicago couples, for most of the play jumping back and forth from one living room to the other with blackouts in between the scenes. Wilson's ingenious use of theatre space by having "*one set, which should look like a home, not a unit set, . . . serve as the home of first one couple, then the other, with no alterations between*" (9) is by no means just a device or trick designed to save time or money. Rather, it indicates a flattening or sameness about comfortable, upwardly mobile, upper middle class Americans: the tired (the time is fall and autumnal imagery abounds) married lives of Carl and Mary and of Alex and Gabrielle are, except in the particulars, virtually identical. They are an in- between generation, not only in chronological age, but also in looking back to past values as they blunder into the future. Three of the four were students together at Northwestern, and they recall nostalgically a time and a place (the campus before the days of landfill) and relationships that were radically different; as Mary says of Carl in the play's most subtly poignant line, "I love him then now" (68). Diminishment is the leitmotif, expressed most forthrightly by the men: by Carl, who insists that his marriage, now scarred by his wife's affair, "WAS GOOD THEN" (49) and who pleads to "have it back the way it was" (107); and by Alex who, feeling emasculated by his wife's incessant sexual demands, yearns to be eighteen again when things were not all "falling apart" (27).

In the middle of Act Two, Wilson breaks the spatial convention that he established at the outset by jettisoning the blackouts that signaled a shift in locale between living rooms and then bringing the second couple onto the stage before the first has exited. The increased intricacy in the characters' movements and configurations that results from this new handling of spatial conventions emphasizes the interchangeability of these people. Carl, in desperation to preserve what he has already lost, literally kills his wife and daughter and then takes his own life. Yet any possibility for a sustained relationship between Alex and Gabrielle is equally dead, as the final "*sound of her leaving*" (63) underscores.

If the jumping between the two couples and the blackouts that separate the scenes in *Louie* might be seen as reminiscent of certain filmic devices, the handling of space in two other Wilson works depends even more heavily upon cinematic techniques adapted to theatrical use. Critics customarily classify the heavily populated ensemble plays, such as *Hot l* and *Balm in Gilead* (1965), as examples of documentary realism—*cinéma vérité* for the stage rather than the screen. As William Herman remarks in this connection, "The aesthetic reproduction of a milieu is redemptive and salvational" (201). And yet, Wilson is careful to indicate that the cafe in *Gilead,* for example, is only "represented, or suggested, in the center of a wide, high stage" (3), just the first of many ways in which he thwarts audience expectations of a naturalistic setting for this collection of prostitutes and addicts and dealers and hustlers who often talk in overlapping conversations.

Along with several Pirandellian or Brechtian or Wilderean distancing or illusion-breaking devices (such as the fictive play assuming a life of its own, out of control of the participants; direct address to the audience in the form of various songs, jokes, and moralizing or prophetic commentary; characters starting the play over, making metacritical comments about its plot deficiencies, or calling for the intermission; actors lining up across the stage to indicate the facade of a building), there are specific techniques more closely associated with the film medium. Spotlights picking out or highlighting individual characters replicate on the theatre stage the screen close-up. Having "*the people in the café silently lift every stick of furniture, the 'set,' about three feet off the ground and turn the set—as a turntable would—walk the set in a slow circle until it is facing the opposite direction*" (42) creates for the audience the effect of a camera doing a 360-degree pan, resulting in something akin to the shot/ reverse shot. Finally, the two repetitions of the scene of Joe's murder at the end create an instant replay of the senseless yet pervasive urban violence directed against someone who got in deeper than he should have. The traditional home away from home for society's misbegotten is no longer a sanctuary.

If the distancing techniques keep the audience at *Gilead* from sentimentalizing these "riffraff, the bums, the petty thieves, the scum, the lost, the desperate, the dispossessed, the cool" (3)—in a way that nothing prevents such romanticizing of the characters in *Hot l*—the devices approximating the cinematic pan and instant replay force the spectators to think about their role as perceivers, to become more aware of the emotional and ethical dynamics of the look and the gaze, to consider their responsibility to move from being onlookers to engagement, to act upon what they see. As Darlene, the all too brief love of Joe's life, says, "aren't we even moving?" (69)

The Rimers of Eldritch (1966), Wilson's tapestry or mural of the meanness, hypocrisy, petty flaws and larger sins of small town middle America, would adapt itself easily to readers' theatre, since it is essentially a play for voices. A stage production of *Rimers* demands absolute fluidity in time and space, as it moves back and forth through three seasons (spring to fall) and from one minimally suggested locale to another. Such shifts are effected largely through lighting, "the most important single scenic element" (4). Because "a scene continues—sometimes two or more in separate areas of the stage simultaneously—until the lights dim on the scene and focus attention elsewhere" (4), the transitions between segments would be similar to the fade outs/fade ins of the cinema. Furthermore, the sometimes simultaneous action with its overlapping dialogue would create a variation on the split screen technique. Finally, late in the play, the threnody of voices coming *"from all over the stage"* with its mournful refrain of loss, "Gone, gone, gone" (57–58), is like a montage sequence in film.

As in *Gilead,* the events leading up to the climactic violation and murder are repeated—a rerunning of the camera—so that the shock of the event in which another of God's harmless creatures is victimized and sacrificed to uphold the mask of respectability is indelibly etched. No one could ever mistake Wilson's Eldritch for Wilder's Grover's Corners: the rime, the hoarfrost, has blighted this garden where innocence has been either lost or corrupted.

Two of Lanford Wilson's short plays, the very early *Madness of Lady Bright* (1964) and the fairly recent *Thymus Vulgaris* (1982), exploit theatre *qua* theatre as an integral part of their meaning. *Lady Bright,* which occurs on a *"stage within a stage"* (75), traces the descent of a middle-aged queen into madness when memories summoned up from the past not only fail any longer to ward off loneliness but, more disastrously for the rememberer, point up the impossibility of the present reality ever measuring up to the past, as it existed either in fact or illusion. Place is handled flexibly (what is one moment an apartment window at the next *"become[s] the doorway to a symphony hall"* [78]); and the mirror before which Leslie applies his make-up and dons his costumes throws back at him the same image the viewers see: he becomes his own audience, watching himself. His mind serves as a theatre of sorts, where he (re)plays scenes from the past; his need, however, for something more than figments or memories, eventuating in his plaintive cry "TAKE ME HOME, SOMEONE!" (91), points to the inability of the imagination—of theatre, of art—to substitute adequately for a lived life and commitment to others.

In *Thymus,* withdrawal from contact with others into a solipsistic world is the characters' sought after end, and this equally entails a rejection of theatre, though for reasons other than illusion's failure to supply what reality cannot. This short work abounds in Pirandellian and Wilderean devices: from the *"raised platform . . . in the center of the stage"* (9) to suggest a house trailer; to the characters' awareness of the audience and their requests to the stagehands for adjustments in the lighting and background music; to the actor playing the Albeesque American Dream-like Cop who abandons fidelity to character to participate in exchanges about not "want[ing] to blow [his] big scene" (22). When the Cop brings the "good tidings of great joy" that the man wanting to marry Evelyn will be "waiting at Schwab's drugstore" (22–23) to take her and her mother Ruby off to a life of relative ease, they choose instead a private existence alone together. This decision was foretold by Ruby's earlier uneasiness over being up on stage "with the lights on me and everybody watchin'" (10)—an implicit desire to withdraw from the audience's gaze even if it means a movement towards death, since a dramatic character has no existence except through an audience. Although Evelyn shies away from closure, believing "all ends are bad. And we all come to a bad end" (26), she will accompany Ruby to the ocean (here archetype of death rather than birth, as is emphasized by the several repetitions of the word "time" in the last few pages), exiting to a "slow fade out." In choosing to reject the theatre space where audience and actor meet and where something other than "bad ends" can be made to happen, this mother and daughter reject the possibilities for community with others that theatre art as ritual can inspire, retreating instead into themselves.

The potentialities of the theatre are precisely what Wilson's Pulitzer Prize-winning *Talley's Folly* (1979) is all about. The play's setting is architect/builder Everett (Whistler) Talley's "folly," *"a Victorian boathouse constructed of louvers, lattice in decorative panels, and a good deal of Gothic Revival gingerbread"* (3), but it might just as well be the theatre itself, for here is a place where "magic" (31) happens. That the stage space *is* a theatre is emphasized for the audience by their first vision of the set: *"At opening: All this is seen in a blank white work light; the artificiality of the theatrical set quite apparent. The houselights are up"* (3). As Matt Friedman, liberal Jewish accountant from St. Louis, and Sally Talley, refugee from the anti-Semitic house up on the hill, meet in the boathouse on July 4, 1944, the folly becomes a place for storytelling since, as Matt implies, some tales like that of his own past are too painful to be told in anything except a story or a fable. The play opens with Matt as narrator à la Wilder and Williams, talking conspiratorially with the audience; filling out the scene by description of what lies beyond; justifying the chosen scenic conventions ("We could do it on a couple of folding chairs, but it isn't bare, it isn't bombed out, it's rundown, and the difference is all the difference" [4]); and establishing for the audience the type of play they are about to witness: a "valentine," "a waltz. . . . One-two-three, one-two-three" (6), a "once upon a time" romance (5) that will run exactly "ninety-seven minutes . . . without intermission" (3) and that could only happen in quite this way in the theatre.

Unacceptable to Sally's prejudiced father and brother as a beau or future husband for her, Matt is exiled to the boathouse where Sally furtively joins him; much like a Shakespearean couple loving in opposition to parental authority or prevailing social mores, they leave the established society for a garden/green world where their love will be tested, obstacles will be overcome, and goodwill prevail—though not without some prestidigitation by a providential artist-like force (Matt's refusal to bring another child into a world torn by nationalistic hatred dovetails perfectly with Sally's inability to conceive a baby). They cannot, however, effect an immediate rejuvenation of their society and so must go elsewhere rather than return to the house, though in time they will have a positive impact, as seen in the next generation whose story is told in *5th of July.* Their journey away from society to reside briefly in a realm of story or tale is analogous to the audience's temporary respite from reality, coming into the theatre for entertainment and enlightenment, and then going back out as a more generous community into the everyday world. So the boathouse/folly in the garden is the theatre, and what appears to be somewhat improbable romantic foolishness can elucidate the truth.

The confessedly autobiographical *Lemon Sky* (1970), generally considered Wilson's *Glass Menagerie,* assuredly is reminiscent of Williams's "portrait of the artist as a young man" in its memory structure and handling of theatre space; yet—as others like Barnett (152) have noticed—it is just as surely influenced, in its use of a skeletal house with "*no walls but indicated divisions of rooms*" (339) as well as in the dynamics of its father/son conflict, by Miller's *Death of a Salesman;* Douglas, the dad in *Lemon Sky,* even echoes the tone of Willy Loman's rhetoric when, blind to the reality of the relationship, he exclaims ecstatically of his son, "Hugged me, by God" (368). Wilson's alter ego Alan, twenty-nine years of age in the present when he finally succeeds in "get[ting] . . . down" the story of his seventeenth summer, at times employs his narrative passages metacritically, addressing the audience about his problems with recalcitrant characters, admitting the play's possibly confusing structure, apologizing for "the plot . . . such as it is" (345), or, rather like Sabina in Wilder's *Skin of Our Teeth,* commenting facetiously on the playwright's (that is, Wilson's) skills, as when he glosses "compromise purple" as "the funniest line in the play" (358). Like memory, the theatre is unbounded by time or space and can preserve the "continually young and alive and beautiful," which is part of its "magic" (356). From the beginning, the other characters are all "*on stage*" in this house of memory waiting for the light of recall to make them visible, and Alan shares the narration with them, which accomplishes a closer approach to omniscience than Miller's strategy of being locked much of the time inside the mind of Willy allows.

The emotional coloration of Alan's visit to his father and then his abrupt departure—after the macho Douglas murders any chance for love not only by rejecting the "effeminate" artist/son whose example threatens to make "sissies" of his younger boys but by his sexually abusive inclinations towards one of the foster daughters living with them as well—is underscored by the extensive imagery of place. In search of a father, Alan "left Nebraska to come to the promised land" at the far western "edge of the continent" (362, 364), yet California is no new Eden of infinite possibilities. Under the peculiar lemon sky, "the color green does not occur in California naturally"; rather than "that bright eye-breaking, bright-sun-shining-through-oak-and-maple-and-elm-unto-bright-green-ferns-and-grass-green," the dominant hues are "the colors of perpetually early autumn: umber, amber, olive, sienna, ocher, orange: acres and acres of mustard and sage" (356–57). Relationships that lack care and concern are as sterile as the fallen garden that Alan escapes, although his final cry for "LIGHTS!" (368) will not be able to erase from his mind what he flees from in space.

Virtually the last line in *Talley & Son* (1985; revised version of *A Tale Told* [1980]), which is set in the ancestral home on the same day (July 4, 1944) as the action in *Talley's Folly* occurs, reports that "The garden's pretty bad" (114). The speaker, Timmy, exemplifies yet another of Wilson's variations in the handling of his narrators, since Timmy has been killed in the Pacific just before the play opens. The presence of this "ghost" on stage, acknowledged only by his Aunt Lottie who has been engineering the relationship of her niece Sally and Matt Friedman behind the scenes, is in ironic contrast to the absolutely realistic stage setting, with no mitigating sense of the play as existing in the mind of Timmy or being filtered through his eyes. Without reducing war's horror ("splatted is more like" what happened when he was hit [85]), Timmy attempts to desentimentalize and de-heroicize it, claiming that "somebody has got to take this thing lightly" (86), since attitudes like his father Eldon's about the glory of getting the enemy before one dies are responsible for perpetuating war and killing off society's sons. Civic-minded and philanthropic Talleys like Everett who gave land to the city for a park have been replaced by those petty and materialistic ones who run off people of different backgrounds and gouge the government on war supplies. As Timmy exits, he remarks that those who won the war for America will not "recognize" her when they come home, since "the country's changed so much" (115). That such change is for the worse remains unsaid, but Timmy is yet another of Wilson's innocents to whom life in an earthly garden is denied in order to prove something for an increasingly cutthroat society.

Although presenting a dead narrator who converses with a sympathetic character, as Wilson does in *Talley & Son,* may be novel, the dramatist's most sophisticated handling of narrative technique and of theatrical space, as well as the most complex treatment of his recurrent themes, appears in *The Mound*

Builders (1975). The action essentially occurs in the *"mind's eye"* (4) of Professor August Howe as he recalls an archaeological dig of the preceding summer, and so Wilson's dramaturgy here approximates even more closely that of Williams in *Menagerie* than *Lemon Sky* had. Since *"the back wall serves as a screen onto which are back-projected slides from the previous summer"* (3), the playing area might be seen as August's mind, with the pictures as promptings to his memory; yet if Williams employed a similar device not only to replicate how the mind functions through association but in a Brechtian fashion to decrease mawkish sentimentalism, Wilson does not exploit the technique for emotional distancing.

The slides picture the artifacts of the Temple Mound People, remaining "evidence of. . . . craft, of a subtle skill and imagination, of. . . care and conscientiousness" (107) now threatened by developers bent on turning the area into a vacation resort. So the conflict is between preservation of a culture's heritage, on the one hand, and commercial progress and destruction on the other; between the past age of poetry—primitive art whose "truth is in dreams and nightmares" (54)—and the present age of facts—as represented in photography and the "compulsive compilers. . . . digging . . . evidence, piecing together shards, fragments, sherds" (102) as if these could provide some final answer. The scientists stand poised between commercial promoter and creative artist, capable of bending either way. When the young scientist Dan holds the death mask from the burial mound of the god-king *"up to his face, and almost inadvertently it stays in place"* (121), it is perhaps an act of hubris revealing his lack of appropriate awe for the primitive culture and leading to his death by the sexually jealous and money-crazed Chad.

The artist in this midwestern garden that is unearthed only to be forever destroyed by the encroaching waters is August's sister Delia. The author of one successful novel, she has been unable to summon up from "the cold depths of some uncharted secret currents" into "the light some undiscovered color" (104) that would have been a second book. The source of her creative block was the death of her father and separation from what might be seen as the garden of the paternal home, "the whole place filled with sunlight. Especially in the winter" (105). If the heritage of the past—the childhood home, the ancient burial mounds—serves as a creative spur to the artist, then once these garden places are lost or defiled, judged as worthless or anachronistic, the imagination atrophies, and all that remains are "syllables, not sense" (56).

In the history of drama, from the time of the Greek ampitheatre open to the heavenly abode of the gods to the closed, insular drawing room of the bourgeois well-grade play with its stratified manners and mores, there has been a link between theatre space and ideology. As an undergraduate, Wilson majored in art history, which taught him "what we have done, what our heritage was, and what we are doing to it" (quoted in Busby 20) and must undoubtedly have awakened him also to spatial dynamics and imagery of place. Throughout the history of art and literature, one of the central archetypal images has been that of the garden. Unfallen gardens are, however, difficult to come by in Wilson's world. In many of his plays—*The Gingham Dog, Serenading Louie, Balm in Gilead, The Rimers of Eldritch, The Mound Builders*—the garden has receded or is in process of disappearing, destroyed either by violence or by a materialistic progress that cares not for the culture of the past; in some—such as *The Hot 1 Baltimore*—it remains as only a fading memory or—as in *Lemon Sky*—as a now sterile place from which the writer/artist must flee. If fortuitously discovered, the garden can be a conducive space for the artist's creative energies, as Delia's paternal home in *Builders* was for her, or as those other gardens where imagination can grow—that is, theatres—prove to be for such characters as Anna in *Burn This* or Matt and Sally in *Talley's Folly*.

One of the most thematically charged spaces in Wilson's entire canon is the mission church setting in *Angels Fall,* a sanctuary or an oasis in the midst of a desert place whose inherent beauty has been threatened by contemporary man's idolization of technological progress at the expense of human values. The space around the mission is the nuclear garden of post-Hiroshima man in which everyone must become an artist, each by embracing his or her vocation or calling, to survive. If it is humankind's fate now to inhabit that "garden," Wilson neither forgets nor denies that another one—Jed's new Eden in *5th of July*—beckons those with the vision and courage to plant and nurture it. For Wilson, despite the dark realities that his plays chart, still clings, as Mark Busby notes, to "the pastoral ideal" that through a commitment to "work and art or artifice" (15) human beings in concert with one another, joined in a community, can have an ameliorative and restorative effect.

Works Cited

Barnett, Gene A. *Lanford Wilson*. Boston: G. K. Hall, 1987.

Busby, Mark. *Lanford Wilson* (Western Writers Series 81). Boise, ID: Boise State Univ., 1987.

Herman, William. *Understanding Contemporary American Drama*. Columbia: U of South Carolina P, 1987.

Inge, William. "Writing for Films." Manuscript Collection, Independence Community College, Kansas.

Kalem, T. E. "Transient Souls." *Time* 23 April 1973: 96.

States, Bert O. *Great Reckonings in Little Rooms: On the Phenomenology of Theatre*. Berkeley: U of California P, 1985.

Wilson, Lanford. *Angels Fall*. New York: Hill and Wang, 1983.

———. *Balm in Gilead and Other Plays*. New York: Hill and Wang, 1965.

———. *Burn This*. New York: Hill and Wang, 1987.

———. *5th of July*. New York: Hill and Wang, 1978.

———. *The Gingham Dog*. New York: Dramatists Play Service, 1969.

———. *The Hot l Baltimore*. New York: Hill and Wang, 1973.

———. *Lemon Sky,* in *Best American Plays*. 7th Series 1967–73. Ed. Clive Barnes. New York: Crown, 1975. 337–68.

———. "The Madness of Lady Bright," in *Rimers,* 73–91.

———. *The Mound Builders*. New York: Hill and Wang, 1976.

———. *The Rimers of Eldritch and Other Plays*. New York: Hill and Wang, 1967.

———. *Serenading Louie*. New York: Hill and Wang, 1984 (revised).

———. *Talley & Son*. New York: Hill and Wang, 1986.

———. *Talley's Folly*. New York: Hill and Wang, 1979.

———. "Thymus Vulgaris." *The Best Short Plays 1982–1983*. Ed. Ramon Delgado. Garden City, NY: Doubleday, 1983. 3–26.